A NEW APPROACH TO THE
(DOM/1) STANDARD FORM
OF BUILDING SUB-CONTRACT

A NEW APPROACH TO THE
(DOM/1) STANDARD FORM OF BUILDING SUB-CONTRACT

Glyn P. Jones MSc ARICS MCIOB

CONSTRUCTION PRESS
LONDON AND NEW YORK

Construction Press
an imprint of:
Longman Group Limited
Longman House, Burnt Mill, Harlow,
Essex CM20 2JE, England
Associated companies throughout the world

*Published in the United States of America
by Longman Inc., New York*

First published 1983

British Library Cataloguing in Publication Data
Jones, Glyn P.
    A new approach to the (DOM/1)
    standard form of building sub-contract
    1. Building contracts and specifications
    – Great Britain
    I. Title
    692'.8   TH425

    ISBN 0-86095-722-5

Set in IBM Press Roman and Univers
Printed in Great Britain by Pitman Press, Bath

CONTENTS

PREFACE

Much has been said since 1980 about the new JCT Standard Form of Building Contract upon which this Domestic Sub-Contract is based. Architects in particular have expressed dismay at the JCT's procedural sternness towards them, and Local Authorities, speaking like clients, have expressed a new-found desire for easier terms or alternatives that will relieve them of certain Speculative Risks.

Both have expostulated their views without conceding that the easier or alternative forms will raise the price the client pays unless we change our traditional ways to "design-and-build" or stereotype package deals. It may not be difficult *tomorrow* to induce the client to pay a price for peace of mind, an easier way, and a plainer product, but if the client *today* wishes to have his own way, choose his own independent designer, select his preferred suppliers or sub-contractors, freely change his mind over what he wants, *and* have a lump sum price for his incomplete design, which is as low as he can get – then the JCT/NFBTE trilogy of standard contracts (JCT/80, DOM/1, NSC/4) appear difficult to better.

If different forms of contract are chosen the Speculative Risks merely move around to rest on someone else's shoulders. No-one knowingly takes risk and gives a service for nothing. There is eventually a price to be paid, particularly where responsible Contractors and Sub-Contractors are concerned. One day we may have some construction risk/price ratios to show and convince clients the truth of bidding laws which surely will state:

(a) the higher the bidder's risk the higher his bid;

(b) the lower the number of bidders the higher the winning bid;

(c) the higher the number of bidders the lower *below cost* the winning bid;

(d) the responsible efficient non-gambling contractor knows about (a) and (c) and may in normal times decline to bid if risks and bidders are high;

(e) the irresponsible inefficient gambling contractor also knows about (a) and (c), and that his bid is below cost. He feels therefore quite justified in cutting corners and claiming extra sums from any client, or his sub-contractors, to secure a profit for himself.

The building industry now has, since the publication of JCT/80, NSC/4 and DOM/1, an integrated matching set of standard contracts created by consensus; a trio of forms enabling clients to choose an Architect to create buildings *their* way using Contractors to contract and work with any number of named, unnamed or nominated Sub-Contractors all under recurring standard terms requiring the whole 'team' to run certain risks, accept similar liabilities and follow identical principles designed to ensure everyone, including the client, carries (for a price) a consensus-allotted risk load; anyone not doing so being made to pay through unseen chains which tie them together into the triangle of project rules within and bounded by JCT/80, DOM/1, and NSC/4.

Being the third in a trio of standard flowcharted analyses, this book maps a way for parties to track these closely interwoven risks, rights, and remedies, in and out of both the sub- and main contracts. It also examines in detail other areas of importance in DOM/1 apart from the specific risk areas; amendments to the usual terms, claiming losses, setting-off, counterclaiming, and valuations etc. It does so in a style chosen to aid in particular the staffs of Sub-Contractors and Contractors reaching for solutions to their problems. It hopefully helps those who have only hours, not days or weeks, in which to arrive at the answer. Because this trio of contracts in places correspond and click together both the flowcharts and narrative have been laid out in a way designed to emphasise this where it occurs.

My sincere thanks go to those who have been involved with this book, in particular Margaret Smith who has with great grit and patience once again converted my scribblings into flowcharts.

Glyn P Jones

Saundersfoot
March 1983

1 INTRODUCTION TO THE DOMESTIC SUB-CONTRACT

Introduction

In our segmented construction industry we conventionally scrutinise the terms of our contracts in isolation, examining the detailed rights duties and remedies within each one, forgetting to some extent the crucial importance of integration between all the contracts necessarily entered into in connection with the one in hand; requiring terms and procedures to flow smoothly to and from several pairs of parties who are working together but not in contract with each other.

A Contractor contemplating a risk or burden in one contract needs to be certain he can securely hedge some of his bets, or use the resources of sub-contractors, under the same gap-free standard terms that clamp him to his client. On the other hand sub-contractors prefer to see the liabilities and benefits of the JCT/80 Main Contract mirrored in their own sub-contract rather than be engaged haphazardly under a multitude of gap-riddled one-sided sub-contracts stitched together by Contractors.

The old 'Blue' (and 'Green') forms of contract served us well but appeared to be designed more as general purpose forms for use with different types of main contract. They were therefore not tightly compatible with the JCT/63 Main Contract nor could they interlock with any other particular contract.

The logic and system of UK building contracts have now been pulled closer together into a triangle. We have recurring clauses, terms, and words, written into a trilogy of contracts. Contractors and Sub-Contractors can readily, from the JCT/80 Main Contract and DOM/1 (or NSC/4) Sub-Contract, track the risks, obligations, rights and remedies they are to take or receive from the Sub-Contracts in their link-up to the Main Contract. Furthermore, a Sub-Contractor who may be engaged on an unnamed, named, or nominated, basis, can with less difficulty comprehend, administer, and comply with the differences in risk, procedure and obligations when working (maybe simultaneously) on different projects under DOM/1 or NSC/4.

Nowadays multi-million pound team-designed mega-hazard projects cannot be built by a Contractor alone. He *must* sub-contract. It is also questionable whether such projects can be designed completely by the Architect's team. If the Main Contract is necessarily complicated and if compatibility between Main and Sub-Contracts is crucial it follows that the Sub-Contracts will also be complicated if they are to deal comprehensively with the necessary integration.

The smallest Sub-Contractor in the largest project (or vice versa) may throw everyone involved into the most severe disarray. The Contractor and affected Sub-Contractors will in turn disrupt each other and look around for both recompense and permission to take longer to complete. Integrated standard forms of contract come into their own in these complicated circumstances. All the affected parties will refer to identical terms and words requiring them to follow identical procedures of giving identical notices and applications with information and details of the differing amounts of time and money involved. These procedures will result in the defaulting Sub-Contractor knowing as rapidly as possible what he is in for, bringing pressure to bear on the contract-breaker to stem the flow of loss to everyone's door.

To Name, Not to Name, or to Nominate?

The system of ordinary sub-contracting by Contractors rises from their need for certain expertise they do not have, or a desire to shed risks, or for additional resources of manpower and machinery etc to supplement their own. The system of "nomination" stems from the Employer in the Main Contract (or his Architect) needing expertise and wishing to bargain direct with specialists, maybe before the Main Contract is let, without entering into a multiplicity of detailed contracts, merely becoming bound by a brief contract (NSC/2 or 2a) on limited but important matters once the bargain is made; the more detailed contract being one to be entered into later by the Contractor with the Sub-Contractor nominated.

If the Employer and Architect wish to avoid the administrative tasks and liabilities involved in NSC/2 or 2a in nomination the Architect must design virtually everything, and the Quantity Surveyor will measure all the work concerned, putting it into Bills of Quantities for the Contractor to price. The Contractor will then, however, be free to employ any competent Tom, Dick or Harry he wishes to carry out the work sub-let, and it is all this that "naming" seeks to avoid or at least restrict.

The Main Contract JCT clause 19.3.1 now enables the Employer, if he follows the rules of that clause, to restrict this comparatively free choice to a list of never less than three sub-contractors "named" by him to do certain work. Furthermore, the work concerned need not be measured and billed in the usual way. The work may be "otherwise described" in the Bills. These wide words allow the Quantity Surveyor (provided he observes JCT clause 2.2 in respect of the item) to simply itemise the work specified or to state a performance specification, with its attendant design responsibilities, against which the Contractor will design responsibilities, against which the Contractor will put a sum. Alternatively, the work could be described as being uncertain or undecided and therefore made the subject of a provisional sum, provided it was made clear the work would eventually have to be placed with one subcontractor from the list, of never less than three names, written into or annexed to the Bills.

In principle the Contractor would then take on his shoulders the risks the Employer takes when "nominating": that his chosen Sub-Contractor might cause delay, deliver work etc late, or fail in some other way, and, in serious cases, require replacing with another who might turn out to be more expensive and slower than the first.

On the other hand sub-contractors who are "named" rather than being "nominated" would not have the advantages contained in NSC/2 or 2a of early design payment, final payment and in certain circumstances direct payment if ever or whenever the Contractor failed to duly pay. Nor would the direct powers of the Architect be brought to bear upon the Contractor when decisions on delay and loss have to be made. The sub-contractor would be treated as an outsider, and be called a "Domestic Sub-Contractor".

More importantly the sometimes crucial facility afforded by nomination enabling the Employer and his Architect to enter into Forms NSC/1 and 2 or 2a for initial discussions and negotiations to make an early start on design work (without being bound into a full contract, other than the limited terms of NSC/2 or 2a) are not available unless the nomination system is employed.

Signing NSC/2 or 2a does not, however, assure Sub-Contractors of "nomination" even though they may have been instructed to carry out their early design work and to order or fabricate materials or goods. If no nomination takes place the Agreement in NSC/2 or 2a entitles the Employer to use their design but only for the particular

Sub-Contract Works and entitles the Sub-Contractors to the amount of any "expense" incurred by them in their design work together with payment for any materials or goods ordered. This appears to intend the Employer to be bound to make a reasonable payment to the Sub-Contractor for his design work, ie, cost plus a reasonable amount for his overheads and for profit. However, the word "expense" could be interpreted more narrowly to mean only the bare cost. The reimbursement for ordered materials or goods is likewise not clearly laid down to include overheads and profit. Sub-Contractors should therefore clarify these matters, and seek words to include, to remove all doubt. The question of *when* these payments, referred to in NSC/2, are to be made to the Sub-Contractor should also be clarified.

Sub-Contractors may wish to prohibit the use by others of their designs, in which case the words of NSC/2 clause 2.2.3 (NSC/2a 1.2.3) require changing but only to cover cases where a nomination did not occur, otherwise the Employer will have paid for nothing.

Under the naming or nomination procedure every proposed sub-contractor should clear the four hurdles referred to in column 3 adjacent and the Architect or Quantity Surveyor should ensure they do not negligently include in the list unreliable, incapable, incompetent, or financially unsound persons, simply to make up the number (to three).

Where a specialist's work is particular to *one* company but ancillary to the Main Contract, not substantial in scope, not involving design by the Sub-Contractor and not critical to the Contractor's own programme then the Contractor *alone* can under JCT/80 clause 35 be required to enter into contract (under NSC/4a) with a nominated person. If, however, any design work was to be undertaken by the specialist, or if early final payment or direct payment rights were required by the proposed specialist, then, as stated earlier, the Employer would himself be required to enter into the limited form of agreement (in this case NSC/2a) with the nominated person.

Where a specialist's work is significant in terms of cost, time, and design, and its early procurement is *crucial* to the Main Contract then the complete set of specially designed forms NSC/1, 2, 3 and 4 should be used. This is referred to in the JCT/80 Main Contract as the *Basic* method of nomination. The less comprehensive ways described in the

paragraph above are referred to as the *Alternative* method of nomination, whether NSC/2a is entered into by the Employer or not.

The term "Domestic Sub-Contractor" can be applied to a Sub-Contractor named in the Main Contract Bills in a list of at least three, or, as in the majority of cases, to a Sub-Contractor chosen with comparative freedom by the Contractor after gaining permission of the Architect under JCT clause 19.2. In either case the Main Contract makes no stipulation that such Sub-Contractors must be engaged under the DOM/1 form of Sub-Contract (see "Home-made Sub-Contracts", p 5).

There are therefore five categories of Sub-Contractor possible under the JCT Main Contract:

Domestic Sub-Contractors
1. Unnamed
2. Named

Nominated Sub-Contractors
3. Alternative (without NSC/2a)
(in these three cases there is no contractual relationship with the Employer (client) of the Main Contract)

4. Alternative (with NSC/2a)
5. Basic (with NSC/2)
(in these two cases there is direct contractual relationship between the Employer (client) and Sub-Contractor)

Choosing the Right Sub-Contractor

Having chosen correctly whether a Sub-Contractor should be unnamed, named or nominated there are four areas in which each Sub-Contractor should prove sound:

1. Resources
2. Experience and technical expertise
3. Finance
4. Management

Clearly the price at which a prospective Sub-Contractor is prepared to do work ought to be irrelevant until it can be seen he has the resources, experience, expertise and finance with which to carry out and complete his commitment; particularly so under DOM/1, NSC/4 or 4a, since these standard forms provide for prompt and virtually full payment to the Sub-Contractor as he goes along, not permitting nervous Contractors to build up any anti-bankruptcy fund against the day the risky Sub-Contractor runs out of resources.

A company efficiently and sufficiently *managed* usually ensures it has the resources, experience, expertise and finance necessary to fulfil all its obligations. A non-gambling efficient Sub-Contractor will endeavour to ensure he is bidding to a sound Contractor and will rarely bid a low price knowing he is short of resources or finance. He may do so when short of work in order to feed his fixed overheads, or to tide over a trough, keeping his resources together and ticking over until the tide turns. A gambling Sub-Contractor will on the other hand frequently bid low prices in the optimistic belief that a profit of some kind will be squeezed out of the contract; given dynamic managers this may well prove correct!

A well managed gambling low-bid Sub-Contractor might profitably be taken on by a well managed gambling Contractor but a mismanaged low-bid Sub-Contractor should be avoided by all.

Every Sub-Contractor wants to work for dependable Contractors at high prices but this rarely happens since all Contractors want dependable low-price Sub-Contractors, for they have themselves usually bid a low price in order to secure the Main Contract.

It follows that both parties will be eager to ensure their inevitably narrow margins, between profit and loss, are not eroded by each other's acts, omissions or defaults. Both sets of managers need to know the risks to be taken and the rules of the game, found written in their contracts. Risks may be high and play may become complicated.

Earlier, a simple situation was outlined in which only one Sub-Contractor disrupted others. It is more likely in practice to find a Sub-Contractor begins to disrupt others who, unknown to him, are already causing (in varying degrees) disruption to each other, partly due to their own acts, omissions or defaults, and partly due to Relevant Events outside their control. Loss may arise within chains of events initiated maybe by a breach of the Employer in the Main Contract further complicated by events at the Contractor's or Sub-Contractor's risk or by breaches committed concurrently by either or both of them.

It is in such complex situations that, to everyone's benefit, efficient Sub-Contractors will shine forth using standard forms of Sub-Contract with their detailed rights and rules of procedure to assist in bringing order to an otherwise confused state. Throw into such a mix a few home-made non-standard sub-contracts with differing rules, rights, risks and remedies then gaps may quickly appear leaving the wrong persons carrying risks they had not bargained for.

Choosing the Right Form of Sub-Contract

There was a time when a form of sub-contract was thought unimportant. A formal agreement was rarely signed and often not mentioned in the preliminary correspondence or negotiations. An order would eventually be sent to a Sub-Contractor in which words would appear which might incorporate some intended terms of sub-contract, eg, ". . . in full accordance with the appropriate form for Sub-Contractors".

The above words would readily be taken by both parties as meaning either the old "Blue" or "Green" form of sub-contract. They would not bother to sign it or even to eliminate inappropriate alternative clauses.

This practice, though loose and inherently likely to raise problems, was quite acceptable in many cases since the parties contemplated working together rather than running into serious disputes. Larger companies increasingly put forward their own forms of sub-contract where "Domestic" type sub-contracts were to be entered into. Others would put forward amended versions of the standard "Blue" or "Green" sub-contracts, wherein the rights and procedures or remedies (particularly in respect of payment provision) were changed to favour the Contractor. Sub-Contractors submitting a tender were (and still are!) in some cases required to signify their agreement to accept the particular terms and conditions proposed by the Main Contractor. The home-made or adapted form of contract has since grown to become a source of concern to Sub-Contractors.

Non-Standard Sub-Contracts

A non-standard sub-contract can range from a slightly altered form of DOM/1 to a completely home-made contract consisting of comprehensive clauses mostly favouring

the Contractor. In the case of the latter no Sub-Contractor can hope to completely understand, in the short bidding time, how to interpret the risks involved.

The words found within a set of non-standard terms may sound familiar yet prove to be vague. For instance, the Sub-Contractor may be required to include for a simple *"2½% cash discount"*. Now normally the Sub-Contractor knows such words mean the Contractor gains 2½% only if payment is made within a time specified or to be agreed. However, in the absence of words elsewhere within the non-standard terms, the Sub-Contractor will find the Contractor, by these words, is entitled to deduct the discount whenever a payment is made regardless of how long the Sub-Contractor is made to wait. Furthermore, payment would probably be made dependant entirely upon when the Contractor himself received from the Employer a sum which included the work in question.

Shrewd Sub-Contractors would, after working once under such terms, recognise it as an annoying ploy licensing the Contractor to take away 2½% of the Sub-Contractor's remuneration. They would counter this by merely adding 2½% to their bid. This might give the Sub-Contractor some inner satisfaction but would not in every case cover the extra interest involved in awaiting payment under a pay-when-paid clause. An additional month's delay reduces the Sub-Contractor's remuneration by a further 1¼% if he is paying his own bank a 15% interest charge on the money outstanding. If a Sub-Contractor's profit mark-up is 2½% of turnover (see Chapter 2, p 8) the innocent-looking term "2½% cash discount" can swallow all the expected profit on the sum concerned.

The more varied terms a Sub-Contractor has to consider the more difficult it is for him to determine the risks he is required to take and include for; even slight alterations to the standard form of DOM/1 may prove difficult to assess in terms of risk to be taken by the Sub-Contractor.

Slight Amendments to DOM/1

Amendments may be in the form of word deletions, additions or substitution, in various clauses. There follow some examples of the effects to be gained by tinkering with the standard words:

DOM clause 2

Any change in the words of clause 2.1.2 should be examined with great care since in its standard form it allays fear that there may be lurking in any supporting (non-contractual) subordinate descriptive schedule or other like document an unknown risk more onerous than the ones openly set out in the Sub-Contract Documents. The standard words prevent such subordinate documents having any contrary effect.

In clause 2.3 changes may be made requiring the Sub-Contractor to actually look for and find errors, and to notify the Contractor whether there are any or not and maybe within a stipulated period, (say) "within 28 days of receipt of any drawing, direction . . . etc" issued during the course of the Works. This kind of amendment places an onerous burden upon the Sub-Contractor and would raise considerable doubt on the questions of liability for errors where they are not discovered or notified within the 28 day period or so that might be expressed.

DOM clause 3

The words "or in part" (line 4) if deleted would bar the Sub-Contractor from part payments of additions until such time as the whole amount concerned had been ascertained and agreed. This would seriously diminish cash flow where substantial Variations were in hand and tend to cause the Sub-Contractor to have to accept unsatisfactory sums for the 'whole', otherwise face long delays in payment.

DOM clause 4

Deletion of the word "reasonable" (in 4.2 and 4.5) from the term "reasonable direction" together with the deletion of clause 4.3 would require the Sub-Contractor to obey virtually every written direction without question within 7 days and without clear rights to payment unless provided for elsewhere in the Sub-Contract. For instance, directions could be issued to do work completely different from the work taken on, or, to move temporary buildings from one place to another, or, to comply unnecessarily with over-cautious safety standards, or, to arrange and do work in a particular way. Failure to do so would give the Contractor the right to employ and pay others to carry out the direc-

tion and to deduct all the cost so incurred from any monies due to the Sub-Contractor.

DOM clause 11

The deletion of the words "insofar as the Sub-Contractor is able" would make the Sub-Contractor responsible for finding out the true cause of every delay immediately the delay became apparent.

The deletion of the word "properly" from 11.3 (line 2) or 11.7.1 (line 2) would relieve the Contractor of the important duty to consider the Sub-Contractor's notices of delay in an impartial way as swiftly as he can so as to let the Sub-Contractor know where he stands for time as soon as is possible in the circumstances.

Removal of the word "reasonably" from 11.8 (line 5) would create problems similar to those described under clause 4 above.

DOM clause 13

To reduce the Contractor's risk under the Sub-Contract of recovering loss and expense where caused by sub-contractors of the Sub-Contractor the words "or any sub-contractor . . . other than the Sub-Contractor" might be added into 13.4 (line 2). Alternatively, or as well, there may be a deletion of words in clause 26.2 "(which consent shall not be unreasonably withheld)" to prohibit the Sub-Contractor from sub-letting unless the Contractor agreed.

DOM clause 16

The provisions in 16.4 shouldnot be altered or deleted for they link up with clause 3 to grant interim payment of any amount agreed in part as the work goes along, aiding the Sub-Contractor's freedom to negotiate, or drive a hard bargain, without freezing the flow of cash to himself until the 'whole' is agreed.

Any changes in the Valuation Rules (16.3) should of course be scrutinised carefully. For instance, the words "significantly change the quantity" might be tampered with in 16.3.1.1 and .2 to read instead "change the quantity by a reduction or increase greater than 25%". The intention would be to give a clear-cut demarcation line but in practice might raise severe problems for a Sub-Contractor if quan-

tity changes reached only 24% of a major item set out in the Bills or other Document. The position would also need clarification if an error in the originally stated quantities was discovered.

DOM clause 17

The above-mentioned changes if made in this clause would prove crucial since the rules in clause 17 apply to *all* work executed not merely Variations and provisional sum work.

DOM clause 18

Changes in this clause should be viewed with concern for the clause in its unaltered form states any unintended departure in method of measurement or any error discovered in the Bills will be at the risk of the Contractor. If the risk is in any way thrown instead onto the Sub-Contractor see Chapter 4, p 41.

DOM clause 21

Alterations in the standard arrangements for interim payment may be against the Sub-Contractor's interests. The clause might be changed into a pay-when-paid arrangement where the Sub-Contractor would be reimbursed as and when the Contractor was paid.

The waiting period (in 21.2.3) of 17 days might be extended; the words "(if payment is made as provided in clause 21.2)" might be deleted enabling the Contractor to help himself to the cash discount regardless of when the Sub-Contractor was paid; the valuation might also be restricted by extending the "7 days" in 21.4 (line 3) to (say) "10 days"; the right to suspend work under 21.6 could be restricted by changing "7 days" (line 3) to (say) "14 days", and, if the words "clause 21.4.2" were added to clause 21.3.2 and 21.5.1, this would entitle the Contractor to take a discount and withhold a retention on sums otherwise to be paid fully.

DOM clauses 23 and 24

These clauses combined with clause 21 ensure cash flows to the Sub-Contractor. Any meddling at all with them should be scrutinised and questioned carefully before any acceptance is considered (if at all).

DOM clause 26

Changes may appear in 26.1 designed to prohibit the assignment of any benefit (eg, rights to payment) to a third party. Such changes may well be acceptable to Sub-Contractors unlikely to make any such assignment.

Deletion of the word "unreasonable" from 26.2 should not be accepted unless a Sub-Contractor has no intention whatsoever of sub-letting.

DOM clause 27

The Sub-Contractor is under clause 14.3 liable "to make good at his own cost" all defects, shrinkages and other faults. Rectification may, however, be required after all the welfare facilities, watching services, hoisting facilities and scaffolding for the use of the Sub-Contractor (see 27.4) have been removed from the Site. This clause may therefore be amended to clarify the Sub-Contractor's sole responsibility when normal attendance facilities have been given once and are no longer available, particularly under 27.1.2 where the Contractor would otherwise "provide and erect all necessary scaffolding . . .". The words "necessary scaffolding" may be added to, excluding the re-erection of scaffold solely due to any breach or non-compliance of the Sub-Contractor.

DOM clause 29

Further grounds for dismissing the Sub-Contractor might be drafted into this clause which is otherwise limited and reasonable in its scope. If under clause 4 the word "reasonable" has been deleted so as to require the Sub-Contractor to comply with *any* direction then this clause would probably include a new right of determination for failure of the Sub-Contractor to so comply (within 7 days); amounting in effect to an extensive right to summarily dismiss the Sub-Contractor.

DOM clause 30

The Sub-Contractor's rights under 30.1.1.3 and 30.1.2 to terminate his own employment if the Contractor "fails to make payment in accordance with the Sub-Contract" may be deleted. This would not prevent the Sub-Contractor determining under common law but combined with changes in clause 21 would involve the Sub-Contractor in higher risks and financing charges.

It should not be assumed this preceding narrative is stating the standard form of DOM/1 is sacrosanct. It is merely illustrating and reminding the Sub-Contractor's estimator that one or two words slipped in or out may present risks far greater than first thought. Bids must reflect risk. The greater the risk the higher should be the bid by all non-gambling Sub-Contractors.

Home-made Sub-Contracts

The largest Contractors, and Sub-Contractors, have 'in-house' formulated contracts prepared for themselves in which the terms are openly concerned with their own best interests.

There is nothing wrong with this. People can put what they like into their contracts as long as they observe particular rules of law concerning consideration and certainty; and are prepared to run the risk that their open bias might be judged unreasonable and rendered invalid by the Unfair Contract Terms Act. The core of a contract *must* contain an offer, acceptance and consideration. It *must* be wrapped in certainty and *may* be subjected to a test of reasonableness if a claim by one party arises (see Figure 1) under the Unfair Contract Terms Act.

Figure 1

The benefits and liabilities under terms of contract do not have to be legally regarded as roughly equal. The Sub-Contract Sum is not legally required to be reasonable and to reflect the risks involved. The Sub-Contractor is free to bid a silly sum for work but once the sum is agreed and accepted he *is* legally bound to carry out and complete his work whatever the cost. The law, including the Unfair Contract Terms Act, will (with a few exceptions) not automatically render unenforceable an unequal deal.

The Act will certainly strike down terms which endeavour to exclude or limit liability in cases of death or injury through negligence; such clauses are judged absolutely unfair and therefore invalid.

The Act will not invariably render invalid, nor does it in any way prohibit the use of, terms excluding or restricting rights or remedies, even in respect of economic loss or consequential loss or damages arising through negligence. Neither does it impose any penalty upon those who write unfair terms into contracts.

The Act will, if activated by one of the parties caught by a term, scrutinise the arrangement to see whether in the particular case concerned it was fair or not in the circumstances prevailing at the time when agreed upon. The fact that the party seeking the Act's protection had agreed with the terms earlier would not prevent the Act being operated. The term complained of may furthermore be held *partly* operable in so far as it is not unreasonable.

Unequal terms, disclaimers and raw deals are not therefore yet dead. The Act will, however, increasingly, by its presence, drive out obviously unfair terms, but the trouble is the Act has to be resorted to *after* damage has been done. The person claiming unfairness must *pursue* his rights. He cannot demand a contract be purged of unfairness before he enters into it.

This still leaves the parties scope to contract unfairly (ie, riskily) with each other. For instance, all the risks of bad ground can be ruinously but fairly and reasonably taken by a groundwork or piling Sub-Contractor. The Courts will not remedy a commercial and technical risk ruinously taken by a small weak Sub-Contractor in contract with a large powerful Contractor if the Contractor can prove (if needs be) the terms used were reasonable and not unusual having regard to all the circumstances which were or ought to have been known to or in the contemplation of the Sub-Contractor when the contract was made.

The Act, amongst other things, *will* consider the lack of bargaining strength of one party but will also ask whether the Sub-Contractor knew or ought to have known of the existence and extent of the terms used, bearing in mind the custom concerning these things in the construction industry, and previous deals that may have been similarly made between the parties.

The Act has an open mind on what is or is not reasonable. It does not give clear-cut guidelines on unfairness. Sub-Contractors should not readily rely on its powers. The Courts, despite our admiration for them, have a reputation for uncertainty when dealing with questions of fairness and unreasonableness. In any case the search for justice may prove more expensive than the sum lost. Only in the most obvious case of unreasonableness can the Sub-Contractor rely upon and rest easy in the knowledge that the Act will favour and protect him.

2 THE RISKS IN A DOMESTIC SUB-CONTRACT

Introduction

Some risks in contracts are worth taking and some are not. The risks worth taking in standard contracts do become quite well known whereas the ones in non-standard forms do not and cannot therefore be safely taken until they too become familiar to us.

There are of course risks of various kinds embedded in DOM/1, some of which carry with them a reasonable chance of financial gain or loss; others offer no-one any prospect of gain. Sub-Contractors should know them *all* and become so adept at handling them that their losses are lowered to comfortable levels.

The Classification of Risks

All the risks involved in working under the standard Sub-Contract DOM/1 can be divided into four categories:

1. Fundamental
2. Pure
3. Particular
4. Speculative

Incidentally, these same classifications of risk are all present in NSC/4 and 4a though the Speculative Risks (4.) do vary to some extent, mainly in relation to the collateral contracts NSC/2 and 2a (see p 2, bottom of column 1.)

1. *Fundamental Risks*

These risks arise in the form of events (eg, war, nuclear fallout etc) which one could call catastrophes or great misfortunes. They may affect society in general or the world at large as well as individual Sub-Contractors, or those involved in a particular project.

The Sub-Contractor is not required to worry or concern himself under DOM/1 with such risks. They are potentially of such magnitude that no one person or company could carry the worst cases of such events. Even insurers are relieved of the burden (and denied the premiums). Each nation's government normally and more economically takes these risks.

2. *Pure Risks*

These risks may affect individuals, small groups or particular projects. They offer no-one any prospect of gain whatever happens. If the event occurs, loss arises; if the event does not occur, no benefit accrues, no increased profit arises, the existing state of things remains as it is.

Examples of Pure Risk include fire, lightning, storm etc.

There is no reasonably practical means of completely avoiding Pure Risk. Fortunately the chance of its occurrence is slight, but the consequences, if the event does occur, are usually reckoned to be beyond the means of either the Contractor, the Sub-Contractor or the Employer. Therefore the JCT and NFBTE have in the Main and Sub-Contract respectively dealt with Pure Risks in the conventional way, requiring insurances to be arranged to cover these risks (under JCT clauses 21 and 22 and DOM/1 clause 7). The premiums will, no matter who insures, form part of the price to be paid by the Employer.

3. *Particular Risks*

These risks are events associated with particular construction techniques or activities not involving negligence, the consequences of which are comparatively restricted and, like Pure Risks, offer no prospect of gain for anyone.

Examples include the subsidence and damage caused to property other than the Works, by vibration or the lowering of the ground-water table etc carried out without negligence by Sub-Contractors.

The JCT deal with certain Particular Risks in an economical and efficient way, requiring the Contractor (not each Domestic or Nominated Sub-Contractor) to maintain insurances for these risks to any property other than the Works, at the Employer's expense in their joint names.

Sub-Contractors are therefore not required to carry the Particular Risks listed in JCT clause 21.2, although they are of course responsible if negligent and must (see JCT clause 21.1.1.1 and DOM/1 clause 7) for this eventuality have their own insurance cover.

All Sub-Contractors, whether Domestic or Nominated, take the same risks under the above three categories, whether working under DOM/1 or NSC/4 or 4a.

4. *Speculative Risks*

These risks, unlike the previous three categories, offer the chance of profit or of loss. These are the risks the Sub-Contractor is really interested in, for they are the only ones that carry with them the chance of gain; there is also a risk of loss in endeavouring to make the gain.

Speculative Risks offer Sub-Contractors the *certainty* of either profit or loss. Losses from this kind of trading risk cannot normally be formally insured against, although the insurance profession is increasingly prepared to take on certain Speculative Risks which in the past may have been uninsurable (eg, legal risks, ie, legal action costs; political risks, ie, the sudden imposition of taxes or business restrictions).

The risk of not getting paid can be dealt with by "factoring". "Loss of Profits" insurance is available to cover certain business interruptions (eg, by fire etc). However, the trouble with factoring or insurance is that the premium must of course be paid whether or not the risk materialises, making the Sub-Contractor's Tender less profitable or less competitive.

Finding the correct balance of Speculative Risks to carry without outside support is a continuing task for Sub-Contractor management. The moment a Speculative Risk is observed which if it arose could bring down the whole enterprise, then that is the time to run for cover; refusing the Risk, or entering a joint-venture, or consortium arrangement, or by insurance in one form or another.

Speculative Risks identifiable in construction work can be carried by those Sub-Contractors who have satisfactorily passed the four tests shown on page 2.

Efficient firms can comfortably carry the main elements of Speculative Risk, such as:

mistaken or uneconomic rates or prices
not getting paid or paid enough
bad ground conditions
variations
delay and disruption
defective work.

These elements rarely arise together to a severe degree. Efficient firms pay close attention to the matters below which give rise to the risks above:

weather
material shortages
political risks
inflationary trends
labour problems
management problems
technical problems (eg, negligence).

Making provisions against loss reduces the chance to, or margin of, gain. Obviously, the simplest and most direct provision takes the form of a loss buffer or "premium" added to the item or estimate for the project concerned. Risk analysis may be employed to ensure the greater the risks the bigger the mark-up. Most Sub-Contractors will,

however, simply add a mark-up for profit which contains within it their standard risk mark-up. The absolute minimum profit percentage to turnover, of about 1–2%, will be increased by about ½–3% to include for all Speculative Risks, thus setting an overall minimum of about 1½% and a maximum of about 5%. If an overall or composite Risk/profit mark-up of, say, 2% of turnover is expressed instead as a percentage of the working capital employed, this would become 22½–30%, dependant of course upon the terms of payment, cash discount, retentions and above all the liquidity ratio maintained by the company concerned.

Risk can be dealt with by devising improved methods, techniques and equipment, the cost of which forms part of the price to be paid for the item concerned if the bid is successful. Most Sub-Contractors also diversify their work, clients, Contractors, geographic locations, etc, spreading the possibility of too much Speculative Risk arising in the same way, place, or at the same time, to cause too much loss; relying on the unidentified extra mark-up of ½–3% referred to above in the form of a "premium" (representing their past losses) added to all their rates and prices in all their bids. This, when spread throughout all the company's bids, reduces the chance of a single occurrence proving too much. If they cannot spread the high risk in one project satisfactorily within it or over all their others they will qualify their tender or refuse to bid, if they are a non-gambling concern.

The Risk of Mistakes

Where Sub-Contractors have entered into a contract, they dread the discovery of serious arithmetical errors or errors of estimation or other mistakes they may have made within their tender, rates, calculations, extensions or additions.

Likewise, Architects, Quantity Surveyors and Contractors fear the discovery of mistakes or omissions in their design or in their measurements, descriptions and quantities.

The Sub-Contractor's Mistakes

Where a Sub-Contractor makes an error in his estimations or any calculation, which becomes incorporated into his tender accepted under DOM/1 Articles of Agreement 2 without either party being aware of such an error, a legal remedy of "rectification" will not commonly be granted.

The Sub-Contractor making such an error, where the Contractor wishes to adhere to the original tender, its rates and prices etc, is under a principle of common law bound by his original tender and its rates, prices etc. (This principle is to be found actually written into JCT clause 14.2 of the Main Contract.)

That is not to say there is no hope at all of obtaining legal rectification of any kind of error. Under certain special circumstances the Courts will listen to pleas for them to order rectification, especially where a contract fails to express the common and agreed intention of the parties, but the legal position on rectification is complex and previously decided cases do not provide clear guidelines. It can, however, be said that the mere discovery of an obviously uneconomic rate or price, an omitted rate or price, an unintentional error of estimation (including 'periods' of time) or calculation along the way is not sufficient to hope for "rectification" or to invalidate the DOM/1 agreement, nor does DOM/1 provide for the correction of any such error. (See principles, Gleeson Ltd v Sleaford UDC [1953].)

Neither is it possible, despite the reference to a "fair allowance" in clauses 16.3.1.2 and 17.3.1.2, to have the error put right for the purpose of valuing subsequent Variations (see the case Dudley Corp v Parsons & Morrison Ltd reported in *Engineering Law and the ICE Contracts*, 4th Ed, by Max W Abrahamson).

Thus, if after the signing of page 4 of the Articles a mistake is found to have been made by the Sub-Contractor in a rate or price or time or in his writing down of the Sub-Contract Sum (both numerically and in words being identical but wrong), then the mistake is binding unless an approach to the Contractor results in its correction by mutual agreement. Where in Article 2 of DOM/1 the Sub-Contract Sum written down in numbers varies from the words following, the words should govern.

If, however, a *Tender Sum* is involved rather than a Sub-Contract Sum, and the Tender Sum is found to have been based upon an error in bills of quantities in an extension, totalling, carrying forward or in a summary, then the error will have no effect (Jamieson v McInnes [1887], Wilkie v Hamilton Lodging House Co [1902]) because in such measure-and-value contracts the Ascertained Final Sub-Contract Sum is by virtue of clause 15.2 to be arrived at by remeasurement and recalculation simply using the rates or prices of the Sub-Contractor, ignoring any Tender Sum.

The Architect's or Quantity Surveyor's Mistakes under the Main Contract

Any mistakes by the Architect are expressly dealt with under JCT clauses 2.2, 2.3 and 6.1.2. These clauses combine with the Sub-Contract DOM/1 clauses 2.2 and 18 to state in effect the Employer does not warrant (guarantee) his Architect's design is right nor that the Quantity Surveyor's bills are right, but he does expressly promise, in those clauses of the Main Contract (which work through into the Sub-Contract), their correction to the extent that if there are mistakes in design, and its quantification, they will be dealt with appropriately by instructions from the Architect, the Employer paying for any resulting work as the Works progress. He will also pay for disruption in the regular progress of the Contractor and/or Sub-Contractor that may arise, and will furthermore grant, where appropriate, time extensions for any ensuing delay.

Sub-Contractors can therefore swiftly recover everything in the way of time, loss and/or expense where mistakes of the Architect, or Quantity Surveyor, occur. The provisions in DOM/1 clause 18 for correction of mistakes in bills of quantities do not allow any rectification by the Contractor of the Sub-Contractor's errors or omissions in pricing, nor, as stated earlier, in the case of a Sub-Contract Sum can there be any correction of errors in extending, adding or summarising in the bills. Furthermore, if the Sub-Contractor makes a mistake in transferring his BQ Sub-Contract Sum to the Articles of Agreement (undetected by either party before signatures are placed on p 4), the mistake is binding on the parties upon the Sum in the Form. The original Sub-Contract work is to be paid for at the actual lump sum total written into the Form. Any extra work subsequently ordered could justifiably be valued at whatever rate or price had been written into the bills for the work concerned regardless of the disparity between the bills and the Form total. Any omissions would, however, be subject to a percentage adjustment to match the disparity concerned. (See *Engineering Law and the ICE Contracts*, 4th Ed, Max W Abrahamson, p 12 and p 13 including note (j)).

There is usually of course considerable sympathy extended to any Sub-Contractor who makes a genuine and disadvantageous mistake. There is also a desire to be reasonable about it. However, the Contractor's view of the Sub-Contract should not be affected at all by the financial results flowing from the agreement originally made. He is in no position here under the Sub-Contract to be reasonable. He cannot act otherwise than strictly in accordance with the Sub-Contract and the law of contract. However, he may if he wishes make a special agreement over the mistake discovered. The parties are free in this way to rectify their mistake without reference to the Courts or anyone.

In the absence of a special agreement concerning mistakes it is not wrong for Contractors to use mistaken rates in making Valuations nor is it wrong to use mistaken rates as a basis in valuing (under clause 16.3.1.2 or 17.3.1.2).

The valuing of work using erroneous (exorbitant or uneconomic) rates is a risk the parties take, unless the parties sensibly agree to make an exception to the strict rules of their Contract.

It is not unusual (since it is mutually risk-reducing) to specially draft into the Sub-Contract a code to deal with unintentional mistakes of the Sub-Contractor detected before or after the Sub-Contract has been entered into. In the absence of such a code the position must, however, remain subject to the Sub-Contract as it is, and to common law principles, which will not in general allow the legal rectification of an oversight or error of judgement or arithmetic operating to the disadvantage of either party.

(See p 14 for further details on mistakes in bills and the risks involved.)

The Risk of Not Getting Paid

The JCT Main Contract and the DOM/1 Sub-Contract have both been assembled in such a way as to reduce the Speculative Risk of not getting paid properly. This does not mean the Sub-Contractor is certain of almost full payment, since set-off is not forbidden.

The Sub-Contractor may, however, rely on the Adjudicator preventing any Contractor attempting to set-off sums he has simply plucked out of the air, but rightful set-off will be allowed, provided the proper procedures concerning notices etc have been followed strictly as laid down in clauses 23 and 24.

There is a risk the provisions concerning set-off, rigorous as they are, may be vigorously (or even tactically) employed against a Sub-Contractor. Even if claims to set-off are not entirely valid there may inevitably be delay and possibly, in the short time available to the Adjudicator, a tendency to dispense a rough-and-ready splitting of the difference, particularly where poorly defended or badly presented written statements exist.

The Speculative Risk of not getting paid has not therefore been eliminated. The Sub-Contractor must still assess how much working capital is needed in reserve and how much its reservation will cost, based on the risks of strike, delay, weather, set-off and so forth, in the projects he contemplates.

Negative Cash Flow

In the initial stages prior to entering into an Agreement the Sub-Contractor will expend his own cash or working capital in the pre-contract preparation of his tender. He will have no 'positive' cash flow until about five or six weeks after he commences his work under the Sub-Contract.

The Sub-Contract basically provides for the Sub-Contractor being paid monthly in arrears. Mobilisation of new projects is an expensive time and much of the outlay will be repaid, not immediately but, over the whole period or periods of the Sub-Contract.

Until repayment equals direct cost the Sub-Contractor will not "break even" and will therefore have cash flowing out from his reserves. Some Sub-Contractors endeavour to stem this drain by, in the case where bills of quantities are used, enhancing the rates and prices for early work and reducing likewise the rates for late work. Where no bills exist, the same results are sought in different ways. This of course leads to an artificial financial state of affairs against which Contractors are rightly on their guard. If any pronounced imbalance is encountered they will require the Sub-Contractor to justify matters or will simply make their own reasonable valuation for interim payment purposes.

Figure 2

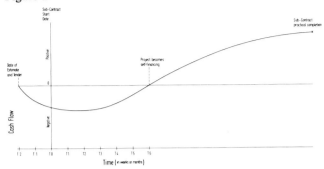

Figure 2 shows a classical cash flow curve. Present-day cut-price projects will show much flatter curves tending to hover below the 'break-even' line until the very last stages.

The Sub-Contractor will of course have several projects or parts of Sub-Contract Works in several places in progress, just starting or finishing. The cash position at any one time is illustrated in Figure 3. The company cash flow position in:

February $= (a_1 + b_1) - (d_1 + c_1)$

March $\quad = c_2 - (e_2 + d_2)$.

Sub-Contractors who have more than one period for carrying out their work (carcassing, finishing, commissioning/testing) will have an intermittent picture of cash flow peaks and troughs for each period. The observation and control of irregular flows of cash is difficult but neverthe-

Figure 3

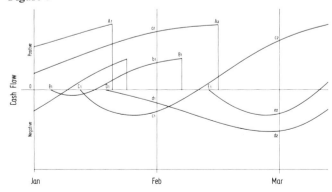

less crucial for it determines basically whether one is being properly paid and it shows the amount of working capital to be put into play, or put out in the short-term money market to earn interest, when a short-term surplus arises.

The amount of working capital always available should equal enough to pay all the company's creditors at once, if needed. Knowing the amount of working capital employed and the average working cycle time for that cash is invaluable when clause 12 or 13 claims for delay and disruption arise, since the money and time concerned are both resources in limited supply. Interim payment means the Sub-Contractor normally has a working capital cycle time of four to five weeks. This is excellent. However, when a claim arises, the cycle time is made indeterminate for the sum involved until the minds of the parties meet on a settlement figure. A claim cycle time can, however, be considerably shortened by an efficient claimant who successfully communicates his cause to the receiver concerned and picks off parts he can agree, for partial payment under clause 3.

Profitability (efficiency) can be measured by comparing gross profits earned with the working capital in use, and by comparing the working capital in use with the turnover. If gross profits or turnover increase and the working capital is reduced then it can be roughly assumed that proper payment is being received and there has been a general increase in the firm's efficiency. If gross profits or turnover increase but not in step with any increase in capital in use to obtain that profit then a clear warning is being given that for one reason or another the company is not being paid properly or is operating less efficiently, and risks are mounting.

Monthly interim payment valuations predict for a company its profits or losses and the working capital needed to finance its short-term trading. These valuations are a direct performance graph and a risk indicator which can also be used to predict longer-term trading needs in terms of finance.

When valuations show signs of falling, and progress is being delayed, losses loom on the horizon. When the planned progress begins to falter or the cost and income do not match that planned the Sub-Contractor must examine closely the valuations of Variations under clause 16 or 17, and if disruption is evident he must vigorously and promptly use the rights contained in clauses 11 and 13.

These are the clauses most likely to lower the risk of improper payment and bring about a change in the cash flow position. If the Contractor gives any notice of intention to decimate or to help himself to the Sub-Contractor's cash flow, then the rights in clause 24 must be employed to safeguard the cash concerned, unless the proposed deduction is agreed or is indisputable.

Finance charges, interest on the financial sums owed to a Sub-Contractor, for direct loss and/or expense under clause 13 now (since Minter v Welsh Health TSO 1979/80) form part of the loss and/or expenses recoverable. This will reduce the risks of long drawn out disagreements.

Although clause 21 lays down strict rules to ensure proper payment is made to the Sub-Contractor, and clause 13 deals with the ascertainment of loss and/or expense he may suffer, there are undoubtedly practical difficulties (see Chapter 3) in the recognition and quantifying of the sums concerned, even for the most zealous and experienced staff. For this reason the Sub-Contract does not lay down unchangeable deadlines for payment of such loss. The Sub-Contract is silent on the matter of a definite time-scale except to say in clause 3 that any such amount is to be "taken into account in the computation of the interim payment next following" on the moment "such amount is ascertained in whole or in part". The longer it takes to agree any part and to ascertain it, the longer it will be before payment is then made. Finance charges or the interest concerned may therefore be an important element of complex claims, where difficult questions of contract law and time-consuming measurement or rate negotiation or reduced productivity allegations arise. If the Sub-Contractor adds to this by taking a long time to recognise the claim exists and argues lengthily over minor elements or fails to submit promptly the clearest evidence of loss etc, then the dates of payment and his cash flow picture will reflect this.

Monthly Payments

Unless a special agreement is pre-arranged for stage payments, the Sub-Contractor promises to work for just over one month before being paid. Each calendar month he will be given back almost all the money his work is worth (properly carried out) during the previous month. If the valuation of this work is reasonable, the retention and discount low, the progress as good or better than planned, and the rates profitable, the Sub-Contractor may even have more cash given back to him than he has actually spent. He has a monthly working capital cycle. It is a very short cycle compared with many other businesses whose cycle may run into years. The shorter the recycling time of working capital, the lower the risk and cost of that capital (in terms of interest). This means the greater the profit from using that capital. Monthly payment terms are clearly a risk-reducing arrangement, particularly when linked, as they are, to the clause 21.6 right to suspend work if the flow of cash is blocked.

The Sub-Contractor should therefore take full advantage of these favourable recycling terms, ensuring:

1. Prompt measurement and agreement of quantities
2. Swift settlement of new or revised rates and prices
3. Advance face-to-face discussions on contentious matters
4. Regular transmission of supporting data, records, returns and invoices etc
5. 'Accuracy' of the valuation of the amount due (clause 21.4)

The question of 'accuracy' in monthly valuations is an open one, especially where bills of quantities do not exist and parts of the Works of the Sub-Contractor are to be separately completed. Preliminary items, particularly plant items, need clarification (such as under SMM 6th Edition Section B) to facilitate the monthly valuations and the valuing of Variations, particularly under clauses 16.3.3.3 and 17.3.2.3. The amount of many Preliminaries items will be directly related to the Sub-Contractor's methods or order for carrying out the work. There are two important elements of these prices to be identified:

1. *Fixed* costs (establishment/removal, setting up/taking down)
2. Time-related costs (operating/maintaining).

The costs of transportation, erection, dismantling, etc, are variable and need to be separately known. All-in running costs as opposed to standing costs should be separated, particularly where plant or machinery is involved in some parts of the work during some "periods" and is not involved in other "periods", but is standing by for later involvement elsewhere in the Works.

Sub-Contractors may confusingly show the whole purchase cost of a particular piece of new plant (for temporary work) as an initial establishment *Fixed* cost and the credit allowance expected upon selling the plant on completion shown set against the removal cost. This will probably not be accepted in bills by the Contractor. The difference between the buying and selling price is either *Time-related* or *Quantity-related* and should therefore be incorporated into the rate for the work concerned, so being recovered strictly as the work progresses.

Preliminaries items should be reserved for those numerous and diverse expenditures necessary at various times in connection with the permanent Works which are best shown separately rather than being spread over or integrated into unit rates for permanent Work items. They frequently form a substantial part of the Sub-Contract Sum or Tender and in general will be within the range of 5–25% of these totals. Knowing establishment and removal costs, operational and maintenance costs, running and standing-by costs, clarifies when such sums will be incurred and informs the Contractor of the Sub-Contractor's anticipated cash flow, so enabling budgets to be formulated to meet those flows.

Under clause 21.4 the Sub-Contractor is entitled to the inclusion in valuations of the "total value of the materials and goods" he has had delivered to or adjacent to the Works. These keywords initially look precise but will inevitably prove vague under closer scrutiny. Does the vital word "value" simply mean the purchase price without discounts, or does it mean (when joined as it is to the word "total") a compound sum to include:

(a) the purchase price after trade and cash discounts, duties, taxes, etc
and (b) the cost of carriage, unloading, site transporting, storing and returning packing cases etc
and (c) the wastage factor for in-store or offloading breakage, spillage, rejects, consolidation, shrinkage, etc?

The Architect or Quantity Surveyor may not under the Main Contract agree to the wider meaning, in which case the Sub-Contractor will receive from the Contractor the net cost, which may be 10–20% less than the "total value". The Sub-Contractor is unlikely to quarrel over this (though he would be justified in so doing) since he may not have

paid for any of the materials or goods, even though proof of payment and ownership is not expressly required prior to payment.

Clarification in advance should be sought on this point so that the tender submitted can, if desired, reflect the slight diminution in cash flow that would otherwise occur.

There is also the difficult question of rights of ownership which will rightly worry Architects and Quantity Surveyors, which will in turn concern Contractors, where very important or expensive Sub-Contract materials or goods are concerned. There are no rights under clause 21.4 entitling the Contractor to pick and choose which materials or goods, reasonably and properly delivered, he will or will not include for payment; nevertheless, he may simply and unexpectedly (after discussion with the Architect) refuse to include certain materials or goods where he considers ownership has in some way been reserved by the supplier or maker. It is difficult for the Sub-Contractor to deal with such a deliberate tactic, since there are complex questions of law arising from the whole field of "ownership". These are referred to in the annotation to JCT clause 16 "Materials and Goods Unfixed or Off-Site", p 134, *A New Approach to the 1980 Standard Form of Building Contract*. (See also Dauber Williamson Roofing Ltd v Humberside CC [1979] 14 BLR.)

Clarification should, on any reservation of title proposed on important or expensive materials or goods, be sought in advance of bidding and the Architect's intentions on payment should be obtained. This will enable the Sub-Contractor to choose whether or not to increase his tender figure to include for the additional working capital he might need in the event of non-payment pending transfer of ownership.

For further details on the risks of not getting paid see Chapter 4, p 43, under "Clause 21".

The Risks of Bad Ground Conditions

Specialists are increasingly involved in making 'poor' sites suitable for multi-storey buildings; drilling for grouting, ground anchoring, diaphram walling, sand draining and of course piling. All this raises the crucial and complicated question of responsibility for the state of the site of the

Works and its surroundings. The actual site of the Works and the precise extent of its surroundings under the ownership or control of the Employer should always be clearly defined and shown on drawings with great accuracy, especially of course where other structures bound the site or where the sea, a river or lake adjoins or forms part of the site.

The Sub-Contractor concerned with the site must under DOM/1 satisfy himself on all matters, including unforeseeable difficulties, in connection with hydrological and sub-surface conditions. However, it is impractical and uneconomic to have any number of tenderers boring and digging up a site to investigate its sub-strata. The Sub-Contractor will therefore have been asked to base his Tender upon Employer (or even Contractor) commissioned data and maybe a Consultant Engineer's interpretation and presentation of that information. Whether or not the data are sufficient and representative of the site between boreholes must still be decided by the Sub-Contractor before submitting his Tender.

If no bills of quantities are employed, questions concerning the measurement of rock, or artificial hard materials or obstructions encountered, should be clarified; so too should work affected by bodies of water (rivers, seas, lakes) and ground-water. If ground-water is to be dealt with in a particular way the Architect or Contractor must specify this, otherwise the Sub-Contractor will himself decide. In any case, the Architect should ensure a provisional sum is provided in the Main Contract Bills for JCT clause 21.2 special joint name insurance.

Site subsoil investigations can never claim to be representative of the subsoil *between* boreholes. Experience, local enquiry, the study of geological records (and even extra boreholes by the Tenderer) will combine to tell the specialist Sub-Contractor the extent to which he can rely upon the results being representative. Employers will not guarantee (therefore Contractors will not guarantee) the ground's conditions nor will they warrant its suitability. Where the Employer provides the subsoil survey information he and the Architect or Consultant will write a disclaimer stating the information is not guaranteed to match the conditions encountered, nor is it a guarantee of the ground's suitability.

Such disclaimers are of course designed to prevent the Main Contractor from claiming there had been a misrepresentation of the ground, if in the event he runs into ground he had not, or his Sub-Contractor had not, expected to encounter. The Architect should, despite the written disclaimer, ensure he has the Employer's authority in negotiations to give any assurances written or oral inside or outside the Documents in respect of the subsoil's condition or the feasibility of his design in relation to the ground conditions assumed to exist; otherwise the Main Contractor may claim a special direct relationship exists between the Contractor and the Architect wherein he could rely upon the assurances, which subsequently might be shown to have been negligent misstatements. Sub-Contractors who lose heavily through their gamble on the ground's condition may also join in the action and seek to reduce their losses by claiming compensation under an implied agreement based upon the parties' intentions and behaviour (despite a disclaimer) that the ground *would* accord with the information given.

The facts in a subsoil survey are not usually wrong. It is the interpretation of the facts that is sometimes wrong. The Sub-Contractor, where factually correct bore data are provided by the Contractor, therefore carries a heavy responsibility, priced for in his Tender, for the interpretation of the unforeseeable ground condition between boreholes, apart from any relevant SMM rules concerning the measurement of any rock, water, etc, that may be encountered. The more risk the Employer and the Contractor place on the Sub-Contractor, by skimping on boreholes, or by withholding any unpleasant results of subsoil tests, expecting the Sub-Contractor to carry the risks, the more expensive will the Tender be and the more likely a loss-making Sub-Contractor is to claim a misrepresentation or to seek compensation under an implied understanding arising from the parties' intentions and behaviour. Bidding theory warns Contractors that if they require tenderers to foresee the technically unforeseeable they will generally pay for it.

The more detailed, expert and extensive the soil survey for tenderers, the less likelihood of unexpected ground, and the less likelihood of higher risk-carrying Tenders with later claims of misrepresentation or negligence. If the Contractor (or his Employer) obtains comprehensive soil information from competent ground investigators and furnishes *all* that

information to Contractors (who in turn pass it to sub-contractors), disclaiming the results given are an accurate representation of the ground between boreholes or in the area in general, then the representation should prove both reasonable and free from negligence, provided no unintentional assurances are otherwise given or made in discussions or negotiations with the Sub-Contractor.

The site does after all usually belong to the Employer, the price he paid or its value reflecting how good or bad the location and ground are, so he should expect to pay some (if not all) the saving in the land's price or value to bring the ground's condition up to par. The Employer can, however, profit on this part of his venture by placing the risk of unforeseeable ground difficulties out to Tender. Gambling ground-contractors will make greater losses or smaller profits than non-gambling ground-contractors whose tenders will generally produce lower losses or higher profits.

The Risk of Variations

Are Variations a risk or not? They are not like ordinary work; they cannot be seen in advance and planned for; it is acknowledged that Variations and provisional sum instructions tend to disrupt the regular progress of the Sub-Contractor's work. They also upset the arrangements made by the Sub-Contractor to carry out his other work, not part of the change order, and may affect his liabilities associated with the instructions. Variations generally increase one's turnover and should therefore nearly always result in more profit, but somehow they often create or exacerbate loss; though it is difficult to know or show where the loss occurs and its extent, because of the usually entwined activities concurrently in progress when an instruction to vary is issued (see Chapter 3 on "Intertwined and Overlapping Causes . . .").

The very wide words used in the definition of the term "Variation" (clause 13) enable the Contractor to issue a considerable number of change orders at any stage during the execution of the Sub-Contract Works until the Sub-Contractor has achieved practical completion. (Any order issued after practical completion should be made subject to a separate agreement.) The Sub-Contract recognises that change orders may come at an inopportune time and also prove disruptive and loss-making. The Sub-Contractor is under its terms entitled to have his rates and prices reviewed, his disturbance costs reimbursed, his loss and/or expense paid and his time for completion pushed onward. Furthermore, the financial adjustments concerned (under clauses 16/17 and 13) are, under clause 3, to be paid as soon as any divisible part of the sums concerned has been ascertained. What more could the Sub-Contractor wish for? Sub-Contractors who, despite these arrangements, still suffer in some way a loss, must conclude it is probably their own fault or possibly the fault of the Contractor who wrongly or unfairly wishes to undervalue the work concerned.

However, any disruption, waste or delay in the carrying out of the Variations or provisional sum work which materially affects the Sub-Contractor's basic resources of:

1. Manpower
2. Materials
3. Machinery

will give rise to consequential loss of:

4. Management (overheads)
5. Money (interest on working capital employed)
6. Time
7. Profit.

It is important to note here that the recovery of the loss and/or expense caused by the disturbance of the Sub-Contractor's regular progress, by Variation or provisional sum instructions, is to be distinguished from rate or price review or new rates, fair valuation, etc, in respect of the work so instructed, and is to be made by claim under clause 13. If such a claim cannot be quite made to fit for one reason or another into the detailed procedures laid down in clause 13 then the loss may possibly be pursued as damages under common law for a breach of contract, which laws always overlay or underpin any standard contract. However, a claim which cannot be made to fit under clause 13 will inevitably prove difficult to pursue outside the four walls of the Sub-Contract. DOM/1 clause 13 has, despite its initial appearance of exactitude, words of surprising flexibility in all its key areas, viz:

"materially affected"
"as soon as it has become . . . apparent"

"within a reasonable time of such material effect becoming apparent"

and the crucial but flexible words "direct loss and/or expense" mean and encompass the same in the Sub-Contract as they do in common law.

Fitting claims into their proper place under the Sub-Contract is important. For instance, an Architect may inform a Contractor that there will be a delay in the issue of an instruction specifically applied for in writing by the Sub-Contractor through the Contractor to the Architect, in good time. When the delayed instruction is finally received it requires additional work to be done which is not of similar character to work set out in the Sub-Contract bills. Furthermore, it will materially affect the regular progress of the Sub-Contract Works.

Firstly, the delay awaiting the instruction, notified promptly under clause 11 by the Sub-Contractor to the Contractor, will fit into clause 13.3.1 because all the required notices were given properly, otherwise this *part* of the claim would at least under DOM/1 and its terms fall by the wayside. Secondly, the uncharacteristic nature of the work will be fitted under clause 16.3.1.3 or 17.3.1.3 when the "Valuation" of the work is carried out. Thirdly, the disturbance caused by the work ordered, to the regular progress of the Sub-Contractor in his other work, will, provided the Sub-Contractor makes the written notice and follows the procedures in clause 13.1, be fitted into clause 13.3.7.

However, when a multitude of instructions for relatively minor change orders is issued it may be misleading to view them singly and to endeavour to slavishly segregate and process each one into a particular precise spot under the Sub-Contract. The combined effect of many minor concurrent orders may be far greater than the apparent effect of each one. It is necessary sometimes to stand back in order to see more clearly this combined effect. By grouping change orders, into appropriate "chunks" of change, a much clearer picture may emerge, resulting in more accurate and realistic claims, ascertainments, and Valuations, arrived at swiftly and settled more promptly.

Although Variations are worryingly widely defined in clause 1.3, it is not permitted to introduce *new* obligations

or restrictions into the Sub-Contract that were not originally set out in the Documents. It is, however, permitted to change obligations or restrictions, already set out in the Appendix, part 1, Section C, on access or use of parts of the site, limitations on working space and working hours, or the order of carrying out or completing the Sub-Contractor's work, provided the change is contained in an instruction of the Architect. In such cases clause 4.3 gives the Sub-Contractor the right to object to any proposed or ordered change, and to have "immediate" arbitration to settle the reasonableness of the change before proceeding with the order. Thus the risk is minimised of having to do work in an unacceptable way.

Rate and Price Reviews

The Sub-Contract made initially lays down in clause 15 the basic terms of reimbursement, ie, the Sum to be paid, using certain rates or prices. This was a bargain struck by the parties, that, given the work set out and shown in the original Documents, that Sum, or those rates and prices, originally quoted would apply. However, the Sub-Contract agreement goes on to say in clauses 16/17 that if the original work to be done is varied by instruction then the original basic terms of the bargain may no longer apply.

Where a Variation or provisional sum instruction orders work not *similar* in character to, or *significantly* changes the quantity of, or must be executed under dissimilar conditions to, the work originally laid down, then a review of the rates and prices to be paid for that additional or substituted work is called for. All such instructions must be valued strictly in accordance with the rules laid out in 16.3 or 17.3 unless the Contractor and Sub-Contractor otherwise agree (under clause 16.1 or 17.1).

The keywords "similar" and "significantly" are therefore, to the Sub-Contractor, crucial, since they unlock the Sub-Contract's door to new and "better" rates and prices which will reflect the affect such changes have on the economic use of the resources involved. (The Contractor will incidentally also look equally objectively for any savings accruing, as for instance in clause 16.3.3.3.) Another keyword, "substantially", appears in clauses 16.3.5 and 17.3.4 requiring a rate and price review to take place where work other than the directed work is affected, compliance with the direction substantially changing the conditions under which it is to be executed.

None of these crucial keywords has been defined in clause 1.3. The draftsman (or any Practitioner) would find the compiling of a suitable definition, for every conceivable case, extremely difficult. The words have been left in their flexible state. They have no *unalterable* meaning, though obviously there are limits to be applied by the parties in their understanding and application of these words. If the Contractor attributes too little flexibility the Sub-Contractor will refuse to agree with him; leaving arbitration as the last resort unless agreement by negotiation is reached.

To find the meaning of "similar", it is not enough to simply look up the word in the dictionary, nor is the Contractor or Sub-Contractor entitled to dogmatically say he *knows* what it means. They cannot possibly know in advance. They must set each problem up on its unique base of facts and context before delivering judgement. They must also always keep one eye on relevant Law Reports whenever the Courts have considered words we seek meaning for; if they have, what were the facts of the case in question and in what context was it considered? The rules of Courts on contract law (which are in principle followed by all who use Contracts) require us always to look at words, in contracts, in their 'plain and literal' sense. However, if a suitable Court case has already considered a word, based on like facts and in the same context, then that ready-made meaning would carry a great deal of weight. Where the judge had stopped the pendulum there lies the meaning of the word in that particular case and any others not differing appreciably from it. That is how certainty and positive meaning are achieved; when the minds of the parties meet, or, alternatively, when an arbitrator or judge makes up their minds for them following his consideration of all the forces that were at work on that word they disagreed upon.

Drawing the line between "similar" and "dissimilar", or "significant" and "insignificant" may therefore prove difficult. Practitioners should not expect each other to agree readily in every project, but should generally achieve agreement. Even where the parties concerned have actively pursued agreement there may nevertheless, pending settlement, be a worrying diminution of cash flow to a Sub-Contractor (who may at the time have a temporary reduction in his working capital ratio) forcing him to more readily capitulate on points of principle or percentages he had earlier claimed to be not negotiable. The Sub-Contractor should in his working capital, Tender rates, and prices, allow for the time inevitably needed to negotiate acceptable settlements. If he cannot afford to wait for the Contractor to see it his way, that is no fault of the Contractor unless there has been dilatoriness or a patently wrong understanding of the rules of Valuation. The Sub-Contractor must realise he accepted the risk and arrangement that the parties would have to mutually agree Valuations and questions concerning similar or dissimilar work etc, unless, in disagreement, they called for arbitration. The Sub-Contractor can of course reduce the risk here by taking the most he can get at the earliest moment under clause 3 for any *part* he is prepared to agree to.

Methods of Working

The question of methods of working will frequently arise in rate reviews or when the execution of other work is alleged to have been substantially changed due to compliance with directions (under clause 16.3.5 or 17.3.4) involving an appraisal of the analysis for the original rates concerned.

For various reasons methods of working may not have been thought of in any great detail by the Sub-Contractor at the pre-Tender stage. There may have been insufficient time or information available for him to seriously consider the best methods to employ. On the other hand, he may have had any number of methods open to him or in mind when he assembled his rates and prices.

However, when in the course of rate negotiation or review the Sub-Contractor brings forward his analysis of original rates or prices in order to establish an increase (or reduction) or to calculate a new rate on the basis of the original rate, it is inevitable that a method of working has to be shown or assumed by him. In such cases the Sub-Contractor must ensure the breakdown of a rate or price shown to the Contractor is either the original detailed analysis of the estimator, confirming the method he had in mind, or, in the absence of any such details, the Sub-Contractor may openly break down the rate or price to show the conditions that prevailed and the method of working that would have been obvious or open to him and chosen by him if he had been specifically asked to do so when his original rate or price was first assembled, or written into the bills or schedule of rates.

The Sub-Contractor is entitled to adopt whichever method or material supplier he wishes, or to change his methods and suppliers as he wishes, provided there are no express stipulations on a particular method or supplier or source written into (or to be implied from) the Documents. Having submitted a rate or price analysis based upon certain methods of working, material costs, etc, he is not then bound to stick to that method or material source, although he will of course be bound by the rate itself and thereonafter in subsequent negotiations where its displayed elements (manpower, materials costs, waste factors, overheads percentage, profit percentage, etc) recur, the Sub-Contractor will be bound to his original basis of costs, factors, percentages, etc, in negotiations for amendments to rates or in building up new rates or in establishing fair values.

If the Sub-Contractor insists he has in his Tender consciously adopted various costs or factors or percentages (eg, for overheads in one period of his work as opposed to another) for virtually the same work to be found in different parts of his Tender or in elemental bills, then clearly he must have good logical reasons and must identify and explain them to the Contractor, preferably before the Tender is accepted. If the logic for the disparity is explained and accepted the difference must be strictly maintained, but if no logical reason really existed for the difference it must be assumed and agreed it was an error.

In displaying the breakdown of rates or prices all sorts of inconsistencies or mistakes may be brought to light. As stated earlier (see p 8, "The Risk of Mistakes") no error or inconsistency in the Sub-Contractor's rates or prices can be corrected at all under the terms of DOM/1. This strict rule will of course produce incongruous results and much head scratching when wrong rates are used in making valuations for interim payments or when new rates have to be assembled from the original wrong ones, especially if perchance there is a wrong rate in one section of a bill and a right one for the same work in another and additional or omitted work is required in both the sections concerned. (A Tender-time check of bills *never* seems to eliminate this risk!) However, the rate, right or wrong, must be applied in the valuing of Variations in each of the relevant sections, even though this may seem odd, but there is nothing to prevent the parties mutually agreeing not to slavishly adhere to their Sub-Contract strict rules if they can find a satisfactory solution.

The valuation of Variations using erroneous or uneconomic (or exorbitant) rates or prices is a risk the Sub-Contractor takes; so too he takes the risk an erroneous rate may crop up as a basis to be used for a new rate, thus spawning another wrong rate. To arrive at any other result would require the parties to run against the strict understanding and agreement reached originally, that, regardless of whether a rate was profitable or not, it would be used in the ways laid down in clause 16 or 17. These ways do not provide for or allow them to make any fair allowance for errors. The Sub-Contract does in clause 16.3.1.2 or 17.3.1.2 enable them to make a fair allowance where the work *itself* justifies it but definitely not when a wrong rate justifies it. (See, however, p 9, where a Code for dealing with errors may be incorporated into the Agreement.)

The Risks of Delay and Disruption

Isolating the issues of time and cost, recognising the grounds for rightful claims, and deciding accurately how much money should be reimbursed in the case of delay under clause 12 and disruption under clause 13, by a contract-breaker, to the loss sufferer, is never easy. The JCT has in its Main Contract and the NFBTE have in the Sub-Contract laid down rules enabling the parties concerned to get together under their contracts (see JCT clauses 25 and 26, also DOM/1 clauses 11, 12 and 13), to themselves agree and settle most of these disputes likely to arise between them without going to Law or the legal profession, unless they prefer to do so, or their case requires Law not found written in their Contracts.

Obviously any system designed to enable practitioners alone to bring about swift, private, and accurate reimbursement of loss, alleged by one party to flow from one of several intertwined events, is bound to be both strict and complicated. However, these predetermined ways of the JCT, and NFBTE, despite their rigorous and intricate nature, are probably better, and undoubtedly involve less risk, than simply trusting each other to pay up when things go wrong; and are definitely preferable to any pursuit of a settlement under nebulous common law principles, at the Law's timeless pace and unpredictable expense.

The Employer and Contractor know from the Contract and Sub-Contract exactly what they must do, and roughly what they are in for financially, if they default, are in delay, or issue a Variation order or instruction which by direction of the Contractor throws the Sub-Contractor's regular progress into disarray. Likewise the Sub-Contractor and Contractor know from clauses 12 and 13 exactly what they must do and their liability to each other for any act, omission or default of theirs or other sub-contractors of the Contractor.

When financial claims are being made the question of cash flow becomes increasingly uncertain as the claim develops unless its validity, quantum and evidence are indisputable. Indisputableness is a rare state. Legal, technical, and financial advice or in-house expertise will usually be required and the facts should meanwhile, in every case, be recorded in detail and if possible mutually agreed (without prejudice) as rapidly as possible by the parties concerned. Where sub-contractors of the Sub-Contractor are involved the Sub-Contractor should ensure their approach, validity, quantum and evidence, too, are consistent with and as sound as that within his own claim details.

A claim will usually be a mixture of indisputable, marginal, and disputable matters. To aid cash flow it may be prudent to segregate these matters so that swifter or some agreement at least can take place, particularly on issues under clause 13.1 enabling parts of claims to be paid (under clause 3) whilst other divisible parts remain to be argued over.

If undue difficulty is encountered arbitration is of course available in the Sub-Contract. Arbitration should, however, not be sought on every justified claim rejected or not sufficiently reimbursed (see Ref 3, p 69, Chapter 4 'In Search of Justice').

The Time to Build

The Sub-Contractor and Contractor are vitally interested in the time they have in which to do their work. The Employer is on the other hand vitally interested in the time he has to wait for their work to be done. Both interests are served in the Main Contract (see JCT clauses 24 and 25) and likewise in the Sub-Contract under clauses 11 and 12.

On the one hand the Contractor and Sub-Contractor are entitled to apply for or be given a new completion date if certain events, called Relevant Events (clause 11.10), cause completion to be delayed. On the other hand, the Employer can, despite having to extend their time, still enforce a claim against the Contractor for liquidated damages due to any delayed completion not classed as a Relevant Event. The Contractor can similarly enforce against the Sub-Contractor a claim to loss or damage including damages payable to others, due to delayed completion of the Sub-Contractor's Works.

Not every cause of delay will justify a new completion date, if necessary, being fixed (eg, ordinary bad weather), and not every cause of delay will entitle the sufferer to reimbursement of the loss and/or expense arising (eg, exceptionally adverse weather). However, many, but not all, of the causes called Relevant Events, which do justify a new completion date being fixed, are also causes listed as "Matters" entitling the sufferer to reimbursement of the direct loss and/or expense arising, under JCT clause 26 and clause 13.3.

It is therefore necessary to separate *Employer Given Time* for "Relevant Events" from *Employer Given Money* for "Relevant Matters". It is further necessary to separate out those causes of delay which are not "Relevant Events" but are an "act, omission or default" of the Contractor (or his sub-contractors) entitling the Sub-Contractor to *Contractor Given Time*, and to separate out those causes of direct loss and/or expense which are not "Relevant Matters" but are an "act, omission or default" of either the Contractor or the Sub-Contractor entitling them to money from each other as the case may be.

The settlement of time claims, also, where appropriate, the sums recoverable as "loss or damage" (clause 12.2) or "direct loss and/or expense" (clause 13), as between the Employer, Contractor and Sub-Contractor, is never going to be easy. It may involve disentangling differing causes of concurrent delays. Clause 11.2 requires these interactive occurrences to be clearly laid out *by the Sub-Contractor* so far as they affect *him*.

In the past, applications for an extension of time for completion were frequently put off until the original date for completion (or any previously extended date) had been passed and the Works actually handed over to the client. It could then be seen just how much time had been taken and how much of that time was deserved by the applicant for completion, which was then granted to him retrospectively.

The trouble was that the Contractor or Sub-Contractor did not know, since they had no *new* completion date, exactly where they stood for time until it was too late to do anything about it. If the extension granted retrospectively did not relieve them of their full liability for liquidated or other damages they would say that their original completion date had ceased to apply, and since no new date had been set for them to aim for time was therefore at large and the Employer's right to apply his liquidated damages clause was inoperable.

The new Main Contract and Sub-Contract recognise these enjoined difficulties of prospectively setting new completion dates. It is not always possible or desirable when certain events occur to fix straightaway a new date. The full effects are not always measurable when the cause first arises. It may prove, or be seen, to be an intermittent problem or one that causes delay until and including the very last day of the work. When there are multiple entangled causes of delay the Contractor, led by the Sub-Contractor's information, is the one entrusted to establish a new completion date. However, there may be no alternative but to leave the final decision on the fixing of a completion date or periods for completion until just before but not later than "the expiry of 16 weeks from the date of practical completion of the Sub-Contract Works, or from the date of Practical Completion of the Works, whichever first occurs . . ." (clause 11.7).

The Contractor, if it is at all possible, must therefore endeavour under clause 11.3 or .4 to set a new completion date in advance, giving the delayed or 'late' Sub-Contractor

a new target to aim for, but if he cannot the Sub-Contractor must soldier on in the hope of a retrospective extended date given under clause 11.7. The Contractor must meanwhile continue to pay the delayed or 'late' Sub-Contractor in full the interim valued sums, until the right to set-off damages for delay arises under clause 13 or clause 12 upon any failure to complete by the last agreed date. All this is pending a final and retrospective decision, to be taken not later than 16 weeks from the date of practical completion under clause 11.7, to fix a final date when completion ought to have occurred.

If the Contractor, with the benefit of hindsight, does fix a later completion date than the one last worked to, there are no express words to deal with reimbursements. The Sub-Contractor may, with the liability for "loss or damage" hovering over him, have spent extra money in accelerating in case he would not be retrospectively granted a later completion date. This is a clear risk the Sub-Contractor must carefully consider. He has no right written into the Sub-Contract to be recompensed the monies so spent when later the Contractor retrospectively finds a later completion date should be set. If that later date could have been prospectively fixed but through maladministration of his duties the Contractor failed to be decisive earlier on, then the Sub-Contractor may have a claim for damages equal to his acceleration costs for a breach of contract in failing to administer time decisions at the right (most reasonable) time.

If ever the Sub-Contractor fails to complete his Works or any part of his Works within the period or periods designated and agreed in the Appendix, part 4, without justified right to an extension, then the Contractor's damages suffered or incurred (not predetermined in one sum per day/week/month) will be set-off or payable from the date the Sub-Contractor ought to have finished to the date he does finish.

Acceleration Costs

Both the Contractor and Sub-Contractor when faced with a prospect of no certainty that their completion dates will be extended may separately or jointly consider using different and more costly methods and resources to accelerate their pace, to reduce delay and so reduce the risk of paying out financial damages to others.

The Architect cannot order such accelerations, although (see statement DOM the Sub-Contractor has an obligation 174/5) to keep reasonably in step with the Contractor. The Sub-Contractor must also use his best endeavours to prevent delay and must "do all that may reasonably be required", to the satisfaction of the Architect and Contractor, to proceed with the Sub-Contract Works under DOM clause 11.8. But nowhere other than in clause 13.1 is the Sub-Contractor entitled to reimbursement when his regular progress has been materially affected. This clause expressly refers to "direct loss and/or expense", which is flexible enough to cover extra expenditure brought about by disruption but may not be wide enough to include much costlier ways chosen unilaterally as a means of achieving accelerated progress. It may be possible to recover acceleration costs under an implied contract or alternatively under clause 11.8 where a Contractor clearly requires a Sub-Contractor to perform differently and beyond the original terms.

To remove such doubts and make the risk less the Sub-Contractor should obtain a clear undertaking in advance by the Contractor concerning acceleration costs, including some clear method of establishing the sums involved.

Arbitration over Time

There is in clause 11.3 no special provision for instant arbitration over grievances about time and failures of the Contractor to be decisive prospectively or promptly about new completion dates. It has been mentioned earlier that there are often considerable difficulties, and even disadvantages to the time-claimant, in making an early declaration of time extensions when the effects of all interactive causes may not be clearly divisible or may not have shown themselves completely. This same difficulty would face an 'instant' arbitrator. Nevertheless, awaiting a decision or receiving a 'bad' decision is bound to be a worrying time for the claimant, who may be under threat of huge loss or damage claims for alleged delay. The Sub-Contractor can, under the provisions of clause 24, hope to convince the Adjudicator, when any set-off is proposed, that the set-off is unjustified in view of the lack of a time decision. However, this remedy is only temporary pending either arbitration or agreement.

The Sub-Contractor has of course agreed the Contractor should be the decision-maker in the Sub-Contract. Once the risk in so doing was accepted the die is cast. The remedy of arbitration is long-winded and uncertain (for both parties). It should be reserved for insoluble and expensive problems and not entered into whilst there is any possibility of a negotiated settlement.

The Risks Arising from Defective Work

This is a risk where there is no chance of gain; only financial loss can arise if defects manifest themselves. The losses are not limited under DOM/1 merely to the Sub-Contractor's own remedial costs. The Contractor is entitled to his damages that may flow through to him due to the defects, so too the Employer, under the Main Contract, may claim his losses, from the Contractor who will in turn look to the Sub-Contractor for satisfaction.

This is clearly an unwanted risk but one that must be taken. The unlimited liability stretches on for years after the Sub-Contractor completes his work.

The Sub-Contractor has therefore a vested interest in finding early enough, or eliminating, the chance of, defects. This risk is one capable of bringing down the Sub-Contractor's whole enterprise. Therefore enough should be spent (in supervision and expertise) to reduce the risk to one that cannot be ruinous. The cost of this forms part of the price to be paid to the Sub-Contractor for the risk taken. There are, however, many Sub-Contractors who irrationally do not include enough in their rates or prices to justify the risks they are in this respect carrying.

For further details on defect liability see Chapter 3, p 37, under "Clause 14".

The Risk of Inflation

In the immediate post-war years costs of labour, materials, and plant, were generally steady and predictable. Sub-Contractors could, without risk, make allowances for slight cost trends by fine adjustments in their rates and prices. They would, during this period, enter readily into contracts which contained no provision for the contract sum to be adjusted in respect of variations in cost.

Gradually, the swell of variation in cost grew and during the 1950's it became distended between labour rates which increased and materials prices which decreased. As an alternative to quoting a firm price for projects Sub-Contractors would, if required, tender a sum exclusive of any allowance for possible increases and rely instead upon a 'VOP Clause' (Variation of Price Clause) in the contract to recover or adjust any movement in costs by recording the actual change in wage rates and certain important materials costs.

These 'VOP Clauses' were developed in the form now to be seen in clauses 35 and 36.

From 1970 onwards costs rose swiftly and unpredictably. Contractors found Sub-Contractors reluctant to bid for firm price projects. Contractors who averaged the customary 2–4% net profit on turnover could not risk cost fluctuations of the order of 10–20%. Governments adopted ostrich-like attitudes to the problem of spiralling costs by continuing to call for firm price bids for major projects during the inflationary years 1970–1973. The British Minister of Housing, for example, authoritatively decreed on 28 September 1973 that a firm price policy was 'deflationary in effect'. But by 20 December of the same year the same Minister had to announce that UK Government projects which exceeded one year's duration would, because of inflation, from April 1974 onwards, contain an agreement concerning fluctuations in costs. However, a 'VOP Clause' would no longer be used at all for Government projects. Instead, the Government would use movements in price represented by indices of certain materials, and the cost of labour. There were already being recorded in great detail for statistical purposes by the Department of Trade and Industry. These indices were to be published and up-dated each month, and, by incorporating these indices into a formula, the average changes in costs of construction would be calculated. This would in effect provide the industry with an index-linked 'vending machine' approach to the problems of increased costs which could be swiftly dispensed by the formula chosen, thus ensuring cash flow to Contractors in times of spiralling trends, to be passed on down the line to Sub-Contractors.

This Formula system now appears in DOM/1 in the form of clause 37.

If any formula is to produce an answer rapidly it must simplify the factors employed in the formula. In so doing it arrives at a comparatively insensitive result. Sub-Contractors employed under DOM/1 clause 37 take the risk that the result arrived at by the Formula does not coincide with the fluctuations in costs they actually experience.

The more traditional 'VOP' clauses (35 and 36) are far more sensitive than the Formula clause 37. However, there are problems of interpretation and much tedious paperwork involved with clauses 35 and 36 resulting in delays and sometimes dispute over the reimbursement of increases.

In either case, 'VOP' clause of Formula, the Sub-Contractor runs a risk of not recovering *entirely* the cost increases he incurs. The unrecovered sum is termed 'shortfall'. Allowance for shortfall can of course be included within the Sub-Contractor's bid but assessing the sum involved is fraught with difficulty unless records of shortfall experienced in projects previously carried out are available to the estimator. However, the bid ought to contain some consideration in respect of the inevitable difference (increase or decrease) between raw costs and the clause 35, 36 or 37 reimbursements (or deduction), particularly in times of anticipated cost instability.

This buffer, included at bid stage, may, however, be thrown askew by a breach of contract or significant changes affecting the planned progress of the Sub-Contractor. The project's centre of gravity (cost-wise) may therefore be shifted into a later and more expensive period, in times of inflation, eroding or swallowing the buffer's protection. This is an item of "loss" recoverable by the Sub-Contractor under the Sub-Contract (see Chapter 3, p 18).

The risks of raw cost instability rest largely with the Sub-Contractor if clause 35 is in operation. If clause 36 is applicable the risks are largely in the hands of the Contractor although the Sub-Contractor may suffer some shortfall (which could run to about one third of the cost increase) and some delay in reimbursement together with the necessary administrative and clerical costs of recovering the fluctuations. Clause 37 will dispense (or deduct!) sums swiftly, but in an arbitrary way based upon the 'swings and roundabouts' principle inherent in the Formula method's use of national (and notional) indices.

3 THE QUESTION OF LOSSES

Introduction

Chapter 2 has examined generally the DOM/1 risks, with their certainty of either profit or loss. This chapter is concerned more specifically with the losses that may arise from the significant risk of delay and disruption. It describes and explains the system adopted by the Sub-Contract (which integrates with the system in the Main Contract) in which the loser is required to speedily identify and then to segregate and calculate his losses, within a reasonable time, for the other party to see.

This crucial task of identification, segregation and calculation (laid down in clause 13) is never easy. For one thing, a contract-breaker or person liable to pay compensation is never at his best when confronted with matters which to him may mean paying something for nothing. The Sender and Receiver see the same *facts* differently initially but must eventually see them the same if the claimant is to be justifiably reimbursed a 'correct' claim.

The Contractor, as a Sender, holding the purse strings, is not allowed by clause 23 to secure any advantage over the Sub-Contractor where losses are concerned. Both parties are in effect required to set down in writing their case well enough for a third person, the Adjudicator, to quickly (within 7 days) decide who is right and what to do about the money if they are in disagreement.

This chapter is therefore an overview of this method. Chapter 4 gives a more detailed commentary upon the actual words used in the interrelated clauses 11, 12 and 13 which contain the rules and rights where lost time and money are concerned.

What Losses are Claimable?

The Sub-Contract generally contains promises by both parties to either perform or pay compensation. The compensation for not performing must never be punitive and the aggrieved party must not hound the contract-breaker for too much nor must he be put in a more favourable financial position than in an otherwise unbroken contract.

On the other hand, the aggrieved party must not be under-compensated.

The contract-breaker must therefore pay the sum needed to put the victim in the same position as if the breach ("act, omission or default") or certain events ("Relevant Matters") had not occurred. This sum payable has, in the Sub-Contract, where the parties disrupt each others' progress, been labelled "direct loss and/or expense", or, where the Sub-Contractor fails to complete on time the *whole* of his work, the sum is called "loss or damage".

Instead of or as well as the parties settling their claims and differences under the rules of the Sub-Contract, they are free to go to Law. If they did so, under common law rules the damages awarded would generally amount to no more nor no less than the sums payable to the aggrieved party under the rules of the Sub-Contract.

It is therefore obviously going to be swifter, cheaper and more convenient for parties to settle their grievances under the rules of the Sub-Contract, giving the formal notices strictly as required, carefully measuring the "loss or damage" or the "loss and/or expense", and promptly reimbursing it to each other in the predetermined ways of clauses 12 and 13. That is the theory of it; in practice, for one reason or another it does not work too well.

Perhaps it is that the people (generally Quantity Surveyors) who deal with these matters are creatures in constant pursuit of total exactitude and cannot easily switch from the exactness undoubtedly needed initially in correctly formulating or recognising rightful claims, to the flexibility essential later in the negotiations needed to bring about agreement. This does not mean they should be more easily persuaded to accept doubtful grounds or vague and dubious evidence. It simply means that, when they have established *with exactitude* that grounds for a claim do exist and do fit within the terms for accepting and settling claims under the Sub-Contract, and that undoubtedly some loss and/or expense is flowing, has flowed, or will flow one way or another from the event, a degree of flexibility is required in agreeing the *basis* for establishing, assessing, or measuring that loss, and flexibility is essential in agreeing the *factors* involved.

As Lord Upjohn said in the renowned case The Heron [1969], "the *assessment* of damages is not an exact science" (author's italics). The words for damages used in the Sub-Contract ("direct loss and/or expense", "loss or damage") were deliberately chosen. They match the Law's flexible approach to damages, expressed above. Total exactitude cannot be achieved. Clearly no-one can ever say *exactly* how much diminution in productivity results, say, from delayed directions or drawings nor can anyone therefore say *exactly* how much that ill-defined diminution is worth in financial terms. This is where the pendulum of meaning for the words "direct loss and/or expense" will inevitably swing about until the minds of the parties meet. This is the intention of the NFBTE; they hope practitioners will go about this part of their DOM/1 contract vigorously, without dilatoriness, and with no unfairness towards one another.

There is, however, a practical difficulty where one party, the Contractor, in negotiation holds the purse strings and gently forces the Sub-Contractor to give way more than he wants to before their minds can meet. It is this that the exaggerated claim predicts. Its presenter expects to have his sums automatically diminished, therefore he multiplies his figures by a factor arrived at after years of experience in having his sums reduced by a reflex action of the purse-holder's representative. This entrenched ritual or bargaining rite cannot be ignored. For some it symbolises that they have not easily or slothfully agreed. It is difficult to fault a claim presenter who correctly perceives and includes reasonable buffers to use when forced to enter this ancient ritual; he is after all only making sure he finishes up rightfully reimbursed.

Obviously, the proof offered of loss will vary in its quantity and certainty. Courts and arbitrators fear both under- and over-compensating a victim, but they do also recognise the very real difficulty loss sufferers may have in showing precisely the financial effects of certain events. This difficulty will not bar them from making an award, though the less certain the evidence of loss the more modest would be their award.

Separating the Cause of Loss

A claimed loss may in its simplest form arise directly and clearly from a single breach. A loss may, however, be the result of a direct chain of events initiated by an Employer's breach but complicated by the occurrence of events at the Contractor's or Sub-Contractor's risk or by breaches committed concurrently by either of them.

There can therefore be multiple causes and effects of overlapping or concurrent events raising intertwined liabilities between the Employer and Contractor and Sub-Contractor.

There is no contract between the Employer and Domestic Sub-Contractors so the Contractor, who has contracts with them both, carries liabilities in both directions for loss. If the Employer causes or is liable for certain losses (which causes loss to the Sub-Contractor) (these are in clause 13.3 called "Relevant Matters") the Contractor is liable, knowing though he can in turn recover that loss, payable to the Sub-Contractor, from the Employer. Similarly losses caused by the Sub-Contractor by any "act, omission or default" which causes loss to the Employer is paid over by the Contractor but recovered from the Sub-Contractor.

Where "Relevant Matters" arise to cause loss to the Sub-Contractor, although strictly speaking the Contractor is liable, it is the Architect who is charged with operating JCT clause 26 of the Main Contract to ascertain the amount of direct loss and/or expense involved (the liability of the Employer) payable by, and the liability of, the Contractor to the Sub-Contractor under the Sub-Contract clause 13.1. The Architect is not involved in any claim solely between the Contractor and Sub-Contractor (under clause 13.1 or 13.4), he is only concerned where "Relevant Matters" arise, under 13.3.

The word "ascertain" used to denote the Architect's (or QS's) task has under the Main Contract the plain meaning:

to make oneself certain
to establish as a certainty
to find out or learn for a certainty
to make sure of, get to know
to make certain, or definite; to decide, fix, limit.

However, the word "ascertain" is, in DOM/1 clause 13.1, not used. It has been replaced by the words "agreed amount". This indicates there may be an intended difference between the sums that might be agreed between the Contractor and Sub-Contractor, and the sums ascertained under the Main Contract.

Certainty is however the keynote of the Architect's duty under the JCT Main Contract when charged with ascertaining, in the case of "Relevant Matters", the quantum of loss. But as a prelude, and before any loss can be quantified with certainty, the cause of the alleged loss must be laid out clearly for the Contractor by the Sub-Contractor, under DOM/1 clause 13.1. This will then form the basis for the Contractor's JCT clause 26.1 application, under the Main Contract, through to the Employer via the Architect.

In the most complex cases, where there are intertwined multiple causes, the Architect may have to face up to the task of seeking out the dominant and direct cause of DOM/1 clause 13.3 claimed loss due to "Relevant Matters" but not loss etc under DOM/1 clause 12.2 or 13.1 or .4 where "acts, omissions or defaults" are the causes of major or minor importance in a chain of events, wherein the liabilities of the Employer under 13.3 and the Contractor under 13.1 are interwoven with those of the Sub-Contractor under 12.2 or 13.1. Clearly skilled communication is required in such cases if the parties are to rapidly and fairly apportion and establish the compensation involved.

For instance, assume a Sub-Contractor was by exceptionally bad weather completely prevented from carrying out his Sub-Contract work for a continuous period which lasted four weeks, but during the second of those weeks was given under DOM/1 clause 4.2.2 an Architect's instruction via the Contractor to postpone (ie, not to restart) a major part of his work for one week, due to impending change orders. It is clear that the most direct cause of all the Sub-Contractor's loss is all his own liability; none is attributable to the postponement order. This order was a more remote event or cause which did not materially affect the state of suspension the Sub-Contractor was already in because of the weather.

A Sub-Contractor may in such circumstances suggest a compromise to the Contractor here; that there should be charged one week's loss through the Contractor to the Employer and the Sub-Contractor should stand the rest. But common sense and hindsight tell us the Sub-Contractor could not have proceeded anyway during the second week even if the Architect's instruction to postpone had not been issued. The dominant, effective, and direct cause of loss was therefore bad weather, and it would be wrong of the Contractor to accede to the Sub-Contractor's compromise suggested earlier.

From this it follows that if on the other hand an Architect's instruction to postpone had started off the suspension of a major definable part of the work for a period of four weeks but during the second week there had been recorded exceptionally adverse weather, which would prevent all work progressing, the financial loss from the full four weeks recorded on the major part of the work would fall entirely upon the Contractor (and therefore upon the Employer) and a suitable time extension should be granted; whereas the financial loss on the remaining *minor* part, during the one week of bad weather, would fall upon the Sub-Contractor, although he would of course during that one week be entitled to a time extension, from the Contractor.

Losses of both time and money from a chain of events will undoubtedly generate practical difficulties in the task of ascertainment (ie, in making absolutely certain) and therefore may cause delays in agreement whilst firstly the dominant cause is being identified and from thereon the loss quantified. Under the Main Contract the Architect, aided by the QS, is given an unwritten reasonable time in which to make his ascertainment. It will therefore assist the Contractor and thereby the Sub-Contractor's cash flow if the Sub-Contractor communicates clearly to the Contractor his analysis of the dominant cause and its effects, showing the financial sums involved, segregated where the liabilities fall under different parties and differing clause provisions.

Figure 4

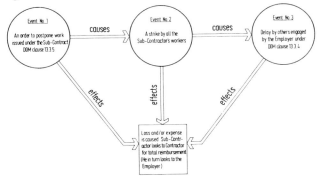

Figure 4 illustrates each event, after the first, causing other events. The Employer's initial act of postponement has directly caused all the loss arising. If, however, other independent causes (in this case, the Sub-Contractor's workers' strike) were discovered but were trifling, they should be disregarded if they leave the dominant cause (Event no. 1) still clearly distinguishable as the *real* culprit.

Figure 5

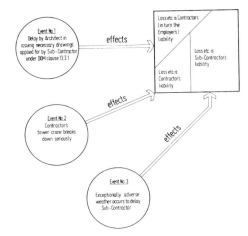

Figure 5 shows Events nos 2 and 3 arising after Event no. 1 but *not* caused by that Event. Events nos 2 and 3 run concurrently for a time with Event no. 1 and therefore would require the Architect to trace the effects to ensure the Contractor was reimbursed by the Employer (for the losses of his Sub-Contractor) but only for the loss arising directly from the Event no. 1. Where the effects cannot be clearly separated but loss is obviously evident then the dominant cause will establish where and with whom the losses will *mainly* lie, enabling the lines of division, shown in Figure 5 as neatly but notionally dividing the total loss into divisible parts, to be pulled around in negotiations once the dominant and effective cause has been agreed.

The Sub-Contract deals in clause 13 with loss the Sub-Contractor is *likely* to incur (see DOM clause 13.1.1 and 13.1.2), thus enabling the Contractor (and in turn the Employer) to be forewarned of his likely liabilities to financially reimburse the Sub-Contractor under that clause. If such liabilities are seen to be high, the Employer may wish to vary the Works to mitigate the effects. Architects (and the QS) may therefore be called upon by the Employer not only to retrospectively deal with claims but also to predict prospective losses. Sub-Contractors may be required by the Contractor (acting under instructions in the Main Contract) to reorganise their arrangements in order to mitigate the losses flowing from certain events. The Sub-Contractor is through the Sub-Contract under a duty to take all reasonable and prudent steps to thriftily mitigate the financial damage resulting from a breach.

Thus if the Architect's drawings are found to be wrong, the Sub-Contractor is expected to put himself out, but this does not impose a liability to take any steps that a reasonable and prudent Sub-Contractor would not ordinarily take in the course of his Sub-Contracting business. If the Sub-Contractor's own fault had been the cause, the steps he would then ordinarily take to mitigate his own loss (eg, moving his workers around to places where work could continue) would be the kind of step expected from him to alleviate the Employer's loss in the same situation.

The drawing of 'ascertainment trees' (see Ref 3, pp 61–64, Chapter 3 'Tracing Cause and Effect') may be helpful in communicating cause and effect where interrelated events are concerned, enabling the parties to openly examine an honest display of the certainty and uncertainty in intertwined matters and graphically assisting to establish a rational way to resolve the problem.

The Admissibility of Sums Claimed under the DOM/1 Sub-Contract

To foresee and agree what normal financial loss a Sub-Contractor or Contractor may have suffered and require reimbursement for, under clauses 12.2, 13.1, .3, or .4, it is necessary to consider what resources the Sub-Contractor or Contractor has in use, at risk, committed, or in reserve for the project.

Every DOM/1 Sub-Contract and JCT Main Contract requires the expenditure or investment by both the Contractor and Sub-Contractor, of:

1. Manpower (men and their supervisors)
2. Materials (goods, etc)
3. Machinery (plant, sheds, equipment, tools)
(some of these resources, 1–3, may be sub-sub-contracted)
4. Management (on-site and off-site administration)
5. Money (capital, interest)
6. Time.

In addition to the five real resources listed above there arises the normal profit-earning capacity of those five real resources concerned coupled to the time (6.) involved normally in earning that profit. From this we can foresee seven loss factors in all, which may arise in the event of a breach, or if a "Matter" listed in clause 13.3 arises, or if an act, omission or default of the Contractor or Sub-Contractor (and any of the Contractor's sub-contractors) occurs.

The parties are, in such circumstances, entitled to recover their direct loss and/or expense, or loss or damage actually resulting which was reasonably foreseeable, when the Sub-Contractor and Contractor made their Sub-Contract, as likely to result from a breach or "Relevant Matter" or "act, omission or default".

Let us apply this rule to an example. A Sub-Contractor makes a bid for Project "x" of £49 920, having reckoned it up as follows:—

	£	
1. Manpower costs	14 000	6. Profit required = 4% of turnover
2. Materials	18 000	ie, $\frac{4}{100} \times 48\ 000 =$
3. Machinery	10 000	= £1 920
4. Management	4 500	7. Time required = 50 weeks
5. Money	1 500	
	48 000	

Note carefully resource 5. This £1 500 is the interest involved in financing the venture. It pays for (or represents the value of) the money or capital needed to make the resources 1 to 4 for the time, 6, for the Sub-Contractor, so earning him profits, 7.

We can *foresee* from Project "x" that the Sub-Contractor intended to profit at an average rate of £1 920/50 weeks = £38 per week. If the Contractor (or any "Relevant Matter") delays the Sub-Contractor one week (without affecting resources 1, 2 and 3) they effectively prevent the Sub-Contractor from moving on his same resources elsewhere to earn yet another £38 or thereabouts. Similarly, we can foresee that the Sub-Contractor intended to expend £4 500 (resource 4) in administrating the project, at an average rate of £4 500/50 weeks = £90 per week. In the event of a one

week delay those resources will have to largely and wastefully be spent on this Project "x" instead of Project "y" or elsewhere, to earn profit. Finally we can see the Sub-Contractor intended to expend £1 500 in borrowing money to finance the project, at an average rate of £1 500/50 weeks = £30 per week. This extra borrowing expense similarly will arise in the event of delays.

The Sub-Contractor's losses above arising from an extended contract period would in common law be held to be real losses 'actually resulting', because we can all reasonably foresee and contemplate them arising naturally according to the usual course of things from any breach of contract or "Relevant Matter" or "act, omission or default". There is nothing exceptional, abnormal or unusual about them, nor are they remote, they are "direct" and there is nothing we should have been specially warned about, or given warning of, when entering the Sub-Contract. They are normal business losses both parties would have agreed would arise if they had prior to signing the Sub-Contract listed the losses likely or 'on the cards' if such a breach occurred in the future course of Project "x".

It matters not if the Sub-Contractor is unable to factually show profits of £38 actually flowing into his bank account, or pocket, each and every week from Project "x". He will obviously in some weeks be earning more than 4% of turnover, or less. So long as the profit claimed is a normal one and the Sub-Contractor normally earns that kind of profit and there is evidence to show that, overall, the Sub-Contractor could reasonably expect to earn that or to move on to other work within his normal sphere and earn about the same level of profit — then the Sub-Contractor is entitled to recover that same percentage loss of profit (6). If at the time of the breach the Sub-Contractor's Project "x" was actually making a loss, then the Sub-Contractor would be entitled to recover the increase in his loss brought about by the breach.

These principles apply also to Management (4) expenditure, and to Money (5) costs. In business, money costs money. Capital, if borrowed, will cost interest and if owned will earn interest — the rates either way being roughly similar. If, however, any *abnormal* or special money interest costs are claimed there is cause to query whether the Sub-Contractor is entitled to it unless he had given written

warning at the making of the Sub-Contract, and the term had been agreed by the parties.

Where a Sub-Contractor or Contractor who has been delayed cannot show satisfactorily that he was denied the opportunity to earn profit elsewhere (eg, due to a severe market slump), a claim to interest on the capital value of the assets involved could be substituted and amount to much the same as loss of anticipated profit.

The principles stated above can be converted into a simple formula for the reimbursement of profit, overheads and capital to a Sub-Contractor (or Contractor) who has been delayed by a breach, a "Relevant Matter", or an "act, omission or default".

Project "x" referred to earlier was anticipated to cost:—

	£
1. Manpower	14 000
2. Materials	18 000
3. Machinery	10 000
4. Management (overheads)	4 500
5. Money (interest on capital in use at 20% p.a.)	1 500
	48 000
Profit	1 920
Sub-Contract Sum or Tender Sum	49 920

From the above summary of costs we can say:

1. Loss of profit (P) =

$$\frac{\text{Profit Percentage}}{100} \times \frac{\text{Total Project Cost}}{\text{Total Project Period}} \times \text{Project delay}$$

The loss of profit recoverable by the Sub-Contractor in the event of a one week delay caused by a breach, "Relevant Matter", or an "act, omission or default", will equal:

$$(P)\ \text{lost} = \frac{4\%}{100} \times \frac{£48\ 000}{50\ \text{weeks}} \times 1\ \text{week}$$

$$(P)\ \text{lost} = £38$$

2. Similarly, the excess expenditure of overheads recoverable by the Sub-Contractor in the event of a one week delay caused by a breach, "Relevant Matter", or an "act, omission or default", will equal:

(O) overheads (or Management) =

$$\frac{\text{Overheads Percentage}}{100} \times \frac{\text{Total Project Cost}}{\text{Total Project Period}} \times \text{Project delay}$$

$$\text{excess (O)} = \frac{9.37\%}{100} \times \frac{£48\,000}{50\text{ weeks}} \times 1\text{ week}$$

$$\text{excess (O)} = £90$$

3. Similarly, the excess expenditure of interest monies on borrowed (or owned capital) recoverable by the Sub-Contractor in the event of a one week delay caused by a breach, "Relevant Matter", or an "act, omission or default", will equal:

$$\text{excess (C)} = \frac{3.12\%}{100} \times \frac{£48\,000}{50\text{ weeks}} \times 1\text{ week}$$

excess (C) = £30

Many practitioners will recognise the formula shown above as being familiar but not exactly the same as the one advocated in Hudson's 10th Edition (at p 599). A warning should, however, by given in regard to the quantum dispensed by this type of formula for it produces unreal results due to its tendency (an inherent fault of every formula) to over-simplify the factors involved. In this case profit, overheads and interest are, during the course of a project, assumed perfectly constant but in reality they are not. The commitment of overheads, the profit earned and the interest on capital employed all move roughly in line with turnover, which conventionally starts slowly, accelerates to a peak or plateau, then falls away, as demonstrated in Figure 6. Where a Sub-Contractor is engaged upon the

Works during several periods, each period will start slowly and accelerate to its peak and fall away.

The profit expectation, management commitment and the interest on the capital employed in the single period of Project x will be at its highest in Week 12 and its lowest during Week 50. Management costs may also actually increase due to the disruption caused, and records should be kept of increased off-site overheads incurred because of the disruption, under item 2 above, as proof of this will be required.

A breach or "Relevant Matter", or an "act, omission or default" causing a complete stoppage of one week during these two particular weeks may give rise to the following differing claims for direct loss and/or expense in Project x:

				Claim "A" (using flat rate "Formula")	Claim "B" (using cummulative turnover	Claim "C" (using expected or denied turnover
Week 12 Direct cost of idle resources 1 and 3 (manpower and machinery),			say =	2 000	2 000	2 000
Loss of profit	Claim "A" $\frac{4\%}{100} \times \frac{£48\,000}{50\text{ weeks}} \times 1\text{ week}$	Claim "B" $\frac{4\%}{100} \times \frac{£18\,000}{12\text{ weeks}} \times 1\text{ week}$	Claim "C" $\frac{4\%}{100} \times \frac{£2\,500}{1\text{ week}}$	38	60	100
Loss of (or excess) Management	$\frac{9.37}{100} \times \frac{£48\,000}{50} \times 1$	$\frac{9.37}{100} \times \frac{£18\,000}{12} \times 1$	$\frac{9.37}{100} \times \frac{£2\,500}{1}$	90	140	234
				£2 128	£2 200	£2 334
Week 50 Direct cost of idle resources 1 and 3,			say =	40	40	40
Loss of Profit	Claim "A" $\frac{4\%}{100} \times \frac{£48\,000}{50\text{ weeks}} \times 1\text{ week}$	Claim "B" $\frac{4\%}{100} \times \frac{£48\,000}{50} \times 1$	Claim "C" $\frac{4\%}{100} \times \frac{£50}{1}$	38	38	2
Loss of (or excess) Management	$\frac{9.37}{100} \times \frac{£48\,000}{50} \times 1$	$\frac{9.37}{100} \times \frac{£48\,000}{50} \times 1$	$\frac{9.37}{100} \times \frac{£50}{1}$	90	90	4
				£ 168	£ 168	£ 46

Figure 6

Sub-Contractor's turnover (at cost) anticipated for Project 'x'

Week	Valuation Month	£	Week	Valuation Month	£
1			26		
2			27		
3			28		
4	1	4 000	29		
5			30	7	4 000
6			31		
7			32		
8	2	5 000	33		
9	2 000		34	8	3 500
10	2 250		35		
11	2 250		36		
12	2 500 3	9 000	37		
13			38		
14			39	9	3 250
15			40		
16			41		
17	4	5 500	42		
18			43	10	2 250
19			44	75	
20			45	75	
21	5	6 000	46	75	
22			47	75	
23			48	100 11	400
24			49	50	
25	6	5 000	50	50	
				Turnover Total	48 000

The simplistic flat rate "Formula" dispenses in Claim "A" less profit and overheads reimbursement than is needed in the peak Week 12 but grants more than the Sub-Contractor would expect in Week 50. There is a strong correlation between profit and turnover, which ought to be recognised. This same relationship is not as readily accepted in the case of off-site overheads though it is logical to argue that the greater the turnover *in hand* at the time of a breach then the greater the call on (or waste of) management resources, and vice versa. However, clear proof of loss and/or extra expense in "Head Office" expenditure should dispel doubts upon this particular item.

Where Sub-Contractors are employed during more than one period in the Works they will have peaks of turnover during each period and differing turnover during each period.

The timing of a breach must be recorded and will usually coincide with the centre of gravity of the consequent loss. In times of raging inflation and unstable interest rates this shifting centre needs to be closely observed and evaluated to reflect the real losses arising at the time. But this search for accuracy must not be so slavishly followed as to put the claimant in a better financial position *overall* than he would have obtained if the Sub-Contract had not been broken, or a "Relevant Matter", or an "act, omission or default" had not occurred.

There may be times or Sub-Contract periods when the Project is profitable and periods or times when it is not. The most important point though is that overall the Project is profitable. Should claims reflect these ever-changing fortunes? The answer is basically "yes"; damages or direct loss and/or expense should reflect the loss arising at the time of the breach or event giving rise to the claim. However, the governing purpose of clause 13 is to put the party (whose rights to progress in an uninterrupted way have been violated) in the same position, so far as money can do so, as if his rights had been observed. If the loss is or ought to have been within contemplation then the measure of reimbursement is the loss to be seen at the time of breach and the Sub-Contractor or Contractor cannot escape it because the quantum at the time of the breach is unusually large, eg, because of a sudden rise in normal interest rates; neither can there be any escape if the Sub-Contractor can be shown to be then engaged in a loss-making project, for the Sub-Contractor will then rightly argue that the breach or "Relevant Matter", or "act, omission or default" is *increasing* his losses, which sum would probably amount to much the same as lost profit.

Summarising, direct loss and/or expense incurred by either the Sub-Contractor or Contractor and claimed against each other or, in the case of a "Relevant Matter", is to be assessed as at the time a breach or "Relevant Matter" or "act, etc" occurred. Retrospective and prospective loss suffered at the time are to be reimbursed. The amount compensated is to remunerate the Sub-Contractor or Contractor their actual loss and this is to include those sums (profit) they had in prospect, within their grasp, but for the breach or "Relevant Matter", or "act, etc". Care must be taken not to under- or (eg, in the case of "Head Office" overheads) over-compensate. The amount allowed for profit must not have within it any element of expense saved by the breach or event. The words "gross profit" are troublesome. The parties must, when asserting their rights against each other under clause 13.1 or .4, not elect sums which are neither clear nor specific. The word "gross" may simply refer to profit before tax, but if it also includes any element of overhead expense then this would confuse matters if elsewhere in the claim they also seek lost overheads (see Tate & Lyle v GLC [1981] 3 AER).

Claimed sums for lost or extra amounts of interest are more readily validated from diagrams (as shown in Ref 3, pp 47/8).

But if either of the parties seeks reimbursement for any extravagant or unusual interest rate he will run into an allegation that the abnormal excessive amount concerned was not foreseeable, there should have been warning of it, and (rightly) will not reimburse sums that could not have been foreseen as likely.

Diminution of Productivity Due to Delays and Disruption

Knowing that productivity has gone down due to a breach, "Relevant Matter" or an "act, omission or default" is one thing; proving that diminution is quite another.

Unit rates found in bills or schedules are generally the rates payable for repetitive tasks the Sub-Contractor and

Contractor are required and entitled to carry out in an uninterrupted way unless special restrictions have been written into the Sub-Contract or Contract.

Once their regular progress is disrupted and "materially affected" then clauses 12 and 13 come into play, entitling them to their losses ensuing.

It is an acknowledged 'work-study' fact that output will improve exponentially, without any greater physical effort on the part of workers, or any greater commitment of other helpful machinery or plant, when work is being carried out which requires a high degree of repetition.

It follows from this that when the rhythm of repetition is "materially affected" then the Sub-Contractor or Contractor will rightly lay claim to diminution of output. This diminution is the difference between the expected output *at the time of disruption*, plus the improving output he could inevitably go on to, or expect to achieve, and the actual output obtained (whilst working as efficiently as possible in the circumstances), during the period of the disruption.

If, however, a Sub-Contractor or Contractor, upon having his regular progress disrupted, abandons normally efficient ways then he is not to be reimbursed any loss attributable to his own sloth or choice of inefficient ways. For all that, wherever a loss-sufferer is put in a difficult position due to a breach, "Relevant Matter", or "act, omission or default" his conduct should not be criticised too severely if he does not immediately come up with the cheapest possible way of coping with the disruption caused him.

The rates displayed in a bill of quantities or schedule are a declaration of the rate at the centre of gravity of output. When compiling rates for repetitive tasks estimators take into account this exponential improvement in productivity referred to above and set their rate accordingly. Disruption may, however, occur either side of that centre of gravity and this will therefore result in widely different figures for diminution in productivity dependent upon whether it occurs early or late in the task concerned. Furthermore, if recurring, rather than once-and-for-all, disruption occurs this will prevent workers progressing steadily up the 'learn-ing curve' of their repetitive tasks. This may put the peaks of production, possible from all repetitive tasks, comple-tely out of their reach, so increasing the diminution in output. If, therefore, a factor of, say, 10% reduction in output is agreed for the effects of a particular disruptive event upon a particular activity, that factor should later be renegotiated if subsequently the same disruptive event recurs.

Table 1 shows a Domestic Sub-Contractor's estimate papers for his proposed bid for a water-storage tank. He is of course free to choose whatever method of working, or solution, out of the six he originally contemplated, or to adopt any other solution he may think of, provided there are no restrictions or requirements written into or specified in the Sub-Contract. Having started his work he may, if he wishes, change his methods and in any case is entitled to progress in an uninterrupted way.

The falsework/formwork erection targets shown are the centre of gravity figures for output when averaged out. Dis-ruption could occur at the very start of the 'learning-curve', when output is low, or at the peak of production, when his workers are earning larger bonuses with no greater effort than in the early days. His output returns immediately prior to a disruption may therefore differ considerably from the targets shown in his original estimate papers. The output he actually obtained at the time of disruption, and would have continued to obtain, or even improve upon, but for the breach, "Relevant Matter", or "act, etc" of the Contractor, is the measure of loss he is suffering.

Incentive Payments

Continuity is crucial to productivity, and further financial encouragement to workers will generally act as an incentive to increase their efforts. Any diminution in opportunity to earn such rewards may lower moral, cause unrest, and lower productivity even on tasks unaffected by the disruptive events.

In times of delay and disruption Sub-Contractors and Contractors may 'carry' their workers in terms of bonus, by lowering their targets and/or increasing a guaranteed ele-ment; otherwise their workers would drift away to more profitable pastures.

Extra cash spent in this way is really being paid out to mitigate the effect of the breach, "Relevant Matter", or "act, omission or default", in which case it is reimburseable as a loss — it is "direct loss and/or expense".

Inflation Shortfall

Clauses in the Main and Sub-Contract provide for the rise or fall in construction costs. The protection afforded is, however, never absolute. Sub-Contractors are of course not concerned if cost indices dispense more money to them than they have actually incurred, but do worry about any shortfall they may actually suffer. They therefore often include a buffer sum based upon their estimation of the *actual* increase in cost they may suffer as compared with the notional increase they reckon will be dispensed by the formula written into the Sub-Contract.

If a breach, "Matter" or "act", etc occurs the claimant may then be forced to use his resources or purchase mate-rials and services at widely different and more expensive times than originally planned and programmed, resulting in the shortfall provision, or buffer in their bid, being thrown askew to cause a "direct loss and/or expense", which is reimburseable to the sufferer.

The Agreed Period or Periods for the Sub-Contract Works

The Appendix part 4 requires details and dates to be agreed before the Sub-Contract is entered into. These details are contractual and binding upon the Sub-Contractor to work to. If he fails to achieve completion of his Sub-Contract Works in the stated period he must pay "loss or damage" suffered or incurred by the Contractor. The procedure in default by the Sub-Contractor is written in clause 12 and clause 13 deals with delay even if completion *is* achieved within the period stated but not without disrupting the Contractor.

To establish the amount of time lost in the event of delay, and subsequently to argue the justification of losses claimed, the Sub-Contractor's estimator should produce two, if not three, statements:

1. Method Statement
2. Programme
3. Special Statement.

Table 1 Comparative costs of formwork for slab thickness 250 mm (including repropping at 14 days)

Dense concrete 24 kN/m^3, soffit height 4.7 m; superimposed construction load and self-weight of equipment = 2 kN/m^2

Summary of falsework and formwork costs (for fair finish: plane horizontal) excluding overheads and profit

	Description	Plant false/fwrk				No uses	Net m²	Cost m²	Erection target	Rate	Net cost m²	Unit rate for formwork	Estimator's comments
		Cost new	Cost new	Per m²	Per m²								
Solution 1	Blogg's Patent system on 25 kN/leg with special ply panels for 3.1 m²	58	75	18.71	24.19	50/50	0.37	0.48	2hr/m²	1.90	3.80	4.65 per m²	Fast and easy to erect. Could be hired. High re-use potential
Solution 2	Blogg's Patent system on 25 kN/leg with ordinary plywood for 3.1 m²	58	50	18.71	16.13	50/20	0.37	0.80	2.25/m²	1.90	4.28	5.45 per m²	Fast to erect. Plywood to be purchased. Re-use related to ply usage
Solution 3	Blogg's Patent system on 40 kN/leg with ordinary plywood for 4.5 m²	88	78	19.55	17.33	50/20	0.39	0.86	2.50/m²	1.90	4.75	6.00 per m²	Not as easy to erect as solution 2 as heavier beams to be fixed on a larger grid. Plywood to be purchased. Re-use related to ply usage
Solution 4	Falsework on 25 kN/leg with timber and ordinary plywood for 2.3 m²	54	14	23.47	6.08	40/10	0.59	0.61	2.60/m²	1.90	4.94	6.14 per m²	Skilled workers required to fix timbers, wedges, plywood etc. No quick strip available. Timber and plywood to be purchased. Re-use related to ply usage
Solution 5	Falsework on 40 kN/leg with timber and ordinary plywood for 3.3 m²	86	45	26.06	13.60	40/10	0.65	1.36	2.60/m²	1.90	4.94	6.95 per m²	Comments as for solution 4. Heavier timbers to place on a larger grid. Access and hoisting may be difficult
Solution 6	Falsework of 'Superman', individual heavy towers with steel girders and ordinary plywood for 22.1 m²	619	383	28.00	17.33	35/17	0.10	1.02	2.75/m²	1.90	5.23	7.05 per m²	Erection costs higher than all other solutions due to larger spans and bracing to be added. Re-use dependent on ply usage and overall deflections

25

These are bench-marks ensuring the Sub-Contractor has satisfied himself and calculated he can achieve completion of the whole Sub-Contract Works. These statements are invaluable in the establishment of the validity and quantum of loss if the Contractor delays or disrupts the Sub-Contractor (see Harrison v Leeds [1980] 14 BLR 118).

1. *A Method Statement*

This is a concise general description of the arrangement for and methods of construction the Sub-Contractor proposes to adopt in carrying out the Sub-Contract Works and parts of the Works. It will not normally be a Numbered Document and need not be amongst the papers referred to by the parties. It is a document that may, however, prove invaluable to a Sub-Contractor particularly if he suspects the risk of disruption is high.

2. *Programme*

This will show the order of procedure of the main events in each part and in the overall project. It may stem from a more detailed Method Statement than above, taking into account the resources, the order of working, and the quantities involved, thus expressing the time involved.

3. *A Special Statement*

This is concerned with any unusual technical, contractual or managerial problem that has arisen for deliberation upon by the estimator. The Statement briefly describes how the estimator has approached and allowed for the matters concerned.

Bona-fide papers should be available for claims purposes that declare:

(a) what the Sub-Contractor intended to do; and
(b) when he intended to do it; and
(c) how he proposed tackling it; and what Management (especially Head Office) resources would be commited; and
(d) low long he reckoned it would take.

These are invaluable when claims require negotiating. They form the basis or start point for establishing 'lost' time and money. They are also acceptable proof to arbitrators and Courts where evidence of intention is required and evidence of "Head Office" losses is claimed, for this particular area of loss is perhaps the one most difficult to ascertain.

4 A COMMENTARY ON THE CLAUSES

Introduction

This chapter discusses the important points within each of the clauses reviewed. Its purpose is to clothe the skeletal analysis of the flowcharts and to emphasise the function, or workings, of a clause. This, together with some detailed commentary on difficult parts within important clauses, is designed to assist the reader in tracing his problem to a conclusion.

Clause 2 Sub-Contract Documents

Clauses 1 and 2 could easily and perhaps more logically have been put down as last clauses instead of first. They are both important in their way for they tell us what documents the Sub-Contract has been made upon and (by clause 1) what the draftsman means by certain key words he uses in his draft (eg, the word "Works" means the main contract works including the Sub-Contract Works). All this is very illuminating but initially seems secondary in importance. However, the later clause 4.1 does look far more interesting for it *states* fundamentally what the Sub-Contractor must do; it connects with clause 2, which identifies the Documents that collectively *show* what he has to do. Clause 2 also usefully states what is to be done about discrepancies in or divergencies between the Documents and which ones are the most important when it comes to sorting out mistakes. Thus if the Appendix says one thing and the Conditions say another then the Appendix will prevail; if a letter written before the Sub-Contract was made contains remarks which contradict or appear to impose terms different from those in the

Documents then clause 2 renders the letter's contents invalid against the Documents.

Because of the fundamental importance of the statements made in clause 4.1 the flowcharts to appear first (p 56) have logically merged clauses 2 and 4.1 analysing the Sub-Contractor's basic obligation to carry out and complete the Sub-Contract Works in accordance with certain identified (Numbered) Documents. The first chart therefore shows the Documents that delineate the Sub-Contract Works and what may happen if the basic obligations are not complied with.

The parties look to the Numbered Documents to see what the Sub-Contractor must do. In certain places (eg, the Specification) there will usually be stated a particular way in which the work is to be done (eg, falsework striking times and methods etc) and the standards to be achieved (eg, concrete strengths). Where no such standards are expressed the Sub-Contractor has the right to carry out the work and achieve completion in whatever way he chooses without interference from the Contractor (or Architect) provided his methods are timely, safe, sound, and fit in with the other work of the Contractor, and his sub-contractors.

All contracts can contain unwritten unseen terms affecting both parties. These are called implied terms. They emanate from the general Law of Contract and Statute Law. Whenever the Documents of a contract are silent on matters, such as on quality or fitness for purpose, and a dispute arises in relation to the unexpressed intention of the parties, then there is usually (in construction contracts)

an implied duty to carry out work in a sound and workmanlike way using materials of proper standards or quality to create something fit for its purpose.

But no term requiring work to be fit for its purpose will be implied where a Contractor (or his Employer) puts forward drawings and/or a specification for the work in question. The drawings and specification have in effect *ousted* the implication that the skill and judgement of the Sub-Contractor was being relied upon and that the Sub-Contractor would be responsible for the work's fitness for its purpose.

On the other hand where the Sub-Contractor has (as in statements DOM 2 and 7) agreed to carry out the work and to complete it he cannot by the same token rely on an implied term that work shown on the drawings and specification (by others) is possible to complete. The expressed term he has signified his agreement to has in effect ousted any implication there might otherwise be concerning its feasibility. The Sub-Contractor will therefore have to pay damages to the Contractor if he fails to complete work which proves an impossible task unless there is elsewhere in the Sub-Contract (such as in DOM/1 clause 30) expressed a term which in some way will relieve him of his burden. If otherwise a Sub-Contractor has contracted to do something technically or physically impossible he will generally be required to pay damages if he cannot carry out the bargain.

It is therefore in view of the principle of implied terms a mistake to think that where one has a detailed set of Conditions, such as DOM/1, together with comprehensive Documents, that absolutely everything we need to know will be found between the covers of those papers. The Law of Contract and Statute Law set out the context in which Contract and Sub-Contract operates. Implied (unseen) terms are as binding as those written. However, *most* important and as binding on a day-to-day basis is to be of what we need to know expressed in the Conditions DOM/1 and Documents. These expressed terms fill the spaces into which the Law of Contract might otherwise imply certain terms. Such implied terms are usually only read into a contract where disputes arise and the contract without them would be commercially unworkable. Terms cannot conveniently be implied here and there simply to make a contract more reasonable, or fairer, for either party in its consequences.

Statement 2 obliges the Sub-Contractor to comply with the standards expressed in the Documents. Thus it is only in the absence of specified standards or where approval of standards is a matter for the opinion of the Architect (see DOM 4/5/6) that an implied duty, to use materials of a reasonable standard and do work in a workmanlike way, would arise.

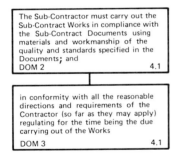

Statement 3 places an additional obligation upon the Sub-Contractor whilst carrying out the work in compliance with the Documents to conform with all reasonable directions of the Contractor. This does not grant the Contractor the power to govern or instruct the Sub-Contractor on working methods, sequence, speed or technique but does enable the Contractor to direct the Sub-Contractor and to regulate his ways so as to ensure the final work resulting complies with the Documents and the standards specified, or meets the Architect's approval where the Documents have reserved for the Architect the right to be the judge of certain standards (DOM 4/5/6).

As stated earlier, the Sub-Contractor must achieve completion (practical completion) whatever difficulties he encounters unless circumstances arise which can be fitted exactly into the relieving clauses 30 or 31.

The Sub-Contractor cannot decide, as he goes along, to complete earlier than first agreed. In clause 11 he promises to carry out and complete his work reasonably in accord with the progress of the Works as a whole. The Sub-Contractor should obtain the Contractor's agreement to any proposed changes in his pace, furthermore progress must be kept reasonably in step with other interdependent activities of the Works. If changes in the otherwise regular pace of the Sub-Contractor stem from an "act, omission or default" of the Contractor, or another of his sub-contractors, then the Sub-Contractor may under clause 13.1 qualify for reimbursement of his direct loss and/or expense arising. On the other hand under clause 13.4 the Contractor may likewise qualify for the reimbursement of his direct loss etc if the Sub-Contractor disrupts the regular pace of the Works.

Documents of the Sub-Contract

During preliminary communications between the parties, prior to any signing of the Sub-Contract, many utterances, letters, proposals, sketches, outline drawings etc may have changed hands. If these papers were put together there might emerge an agreement which was more, or less, onerous than, or contradicted, the one (DOM/1) actually entered into. It is crucial therefore to declare (and number) on page 12 of the Articles of Agreement the Documents which definitely constitute the agreement intended by the parties.

> Nothing contained in any descriptive schedule or other like document issued in connection with and for use in carrying out the Sub-Contract Works must impose any obligation beyond those imposed by the Sub-Contract Documents
> DOM 9   2.1.2

If is comforting to know that statement DOM 9 outlaws terms to be found in any other document not numbered and listed on page 12, debarring their contents from having any effect beyond those terms to be found in the Numbered Documents and Sub-Contract.

However, there may still remain to be discovered irregularities between the provisions of the Numbered Documents and the terms of the Sub-Contract; or conflict between the terms of the Sub-Contract and those of the Main Contract. There may also appear conflict between what has been handwritten into the Appendix and the printed terms of the Sub-Contract. Clause 2.2 sets out which term will prevail where such irregularities are discovered and clause 2.3 requires the Sub-Contractor to give written notice if he finds any discrepancy in or divergence between the contents of the Documents, and documents issued by the Contractor, or between documents (not necessarily Sub-Contract Documents) of the same description.

If a mistake is discovered promptly all is well but in cases where much abortive work has been carried out and in cases where money wasted due to an undetected error then dispute over payment may arise. The difficult questions surrounding mistakes are discussed in more detail in Chapter 2, p 8.

Clauses 3 and 15

It is difficult to see why the draftsman kept separate the contents of clauses 3 and 15. The former deals with the "Sub-Contract Sum" and additions, deductions or adjustments of the Sum that may be made. The latter simply confirms there are differing methods of establishing the price payable depending upon whether a lump sum or measure-and-value agreement was originally entered into.

Logically the contents not only of clauses 3 and 15, but also 16, 17 and 21, could all have been put together for they are collectively concerned with payment. They total about one sixth of the Conditions, which is a rough indicator of their importance. They are all designed to ensure the Sub-Contractor gets paid regularly as he progresses.

This policy of prompt, almost full, regular payments to the Sub-Contractor of absolutely everything he is entitled to on the dot every month is easier agreed to than complied with. Variations take time and skill to measure and value. Cost fluctuations under clause 35 or 36 involve much clerical work. Claims under clause 13 may generate much paperwork and time-consuming negotiations.

Clause 3 is a new provision intended to recognise the

above difficulties. It ensures that, despite practical difficulties, as soon as any parts are agreed, if not in whole, they are to be paid and the remainder taken into account in the next interim payment following upon the ascertainment and agreement. Clearly a Sub-Contractor should agree as many parts as he can as rapidly as possible to whittle down his negative cash to a minimum. It is also important for him to note that clause 3 is not to be used by the Contractor as a bargaining clause whereby he may offer the Sub-Contractor a substantial part payment on condition it is accepted in full and final settlement of a whole claim made, for instance, under clause 13.1. Neither is a small part payment under clause 3 to be made simply to keep the Sub-Contractor quiet. Dilatoriness in ascertaining, and tardiness in agreeing, is in breach of the promise (made in clause 21.1) to pay the amounts (no more – no less) listed in clause 21.4 which list includes Variations, sums due under clauses 13 and 35 or 36; not to mention sundry other sums that may arise under the Main Contract.

If the Sub-Contractor fails to receive sums he considers due he must ensure he has (under clause 21.4.4) provided any details "reasonably necessary to substantiate any statement submitted by him as to the amount of any valuation". So, the Sub-Contractor must be prepared to back his contentions (which are not required specifically in writing or any particular form) with details *reasonably necessary* to substantiate his assertions.

If this fails to produce any further payment Article 3.3.1 provides for arbitration straightaway. Alternatively, or as well, clause 21.6 permits the Sub-Contractor to suspend his work until he gets a payment that accords with the rules of clause 21. However, the Sub-Contractor must be certain he has been improperly paid before he goes as far as to suspend work, otherwise he risks being denied any extension of time, any loss caused, and will become liable to pay a cross claim made against him by the Contractor under clause 13.4.

Clause 4 (excluding 4.1)

It is only reasonable directions of the Contractor permissible under clause 4 (see statements 42/3/4) that can be issued to the authorised representative of the Sub-Contractor. Any other communications (eg, notices under clauses 13, 23.2.2, 29.1, 20A(or B).3 etc) should not be addressed to anyone other than the Sub-Contractor himself.

The Sub-Contractor is not entitled to be paid any extra expense, or extra sum for extra work done, without proper prior directions made out in writing. However, this clause 4 recognises the long tradition in the construction industry of doing work before the paperwork and proper written orders are ready. It also endeavours to cope with the difficult questions of unnoticeable or unintended Variations that may have emerged from issued drawings or letters etc. It does so by requiring the Sub-Contractor himself to confirm in writing any "directions" not already written out. A drawing or a sketch may constitute a direction "in writing" if it clearly shows what is to be done.

The Contractor is permitted to exercise his discretion under clause 4.4.2 to confirm an otherwise unwritten direction at any time prior to the Final Payment.

If a Contractor has already made payment for unconfirmed work, properly carried out to the Contractor's unwritten directions, it may be possible to say from the form and manner in which the payment has been written by the Contractor into a valuation that the form of its inclusion was itself a confirmation in writing.

Not every direction involves payment. A direction may simply require the Sub-Contractor to comply with certain safety requirements.

Failure to respond immediately to a *reasonable* (see below) direction correctly given entitles the Contractor to employ and pay others to carry out the direction remaining undone. This right does not extend to allowing others to take over the whole execution of all the Sub-Contractor's work. If the Sub-Contractor more seriously defaults in any one (or more) of the ways described in clause 29.1 or .2 then the right in that clause rather than the clause 4 machinery becomes operable. In any case, loss and/or expense caused by disruption can be recouped by the Contractor under clause 13.4 and if and when determination occurs any loss and/or expense caused by the determination must under clause 29.4 be allowed or paid to the Contractor.

Not every direction of the Contractor needs be complied with. The Sub-Contractor may refuse a direction which is not *reasonable*. The word "reasonable" is a key one, in its plain and literal sense meaning the direction has to be one:

> having sound judgement
> not asking for too much
> not irrational or absurd
> not extravagant or excessive
> moderate
> sensible.

One could also say that any direction not permitted under the Sub-Contract would of course be an unreasonable one. For instance, a direction requiring the Sub-Contractor to change his own sound methods of working to sound ways preferred by the Contractor would be unreasonable unless the Documents laid down the ways, as called for by the Contractor, to be followed.

Clauses 5 and 6 Sub-Contractor's liability under the Main Contract

The Appendix, part 1, sections A B and C, gives details of the Main Contract Conditions alternative clauses; it states any amendments to the terms, together with any obligations or restrictions imposed by the Employer; it may also stipulate the order of the Works and give details on the location etc of access given. Giving all this information formally is purposeful since the terms of the Main Contract are generally interwoven into the Sub-Contract so far as they apply to the Sub-Contract. Furthermore, certain clauses of the Main Contract apply particularly to the Sub-Contract. These are JCT clauses:

  6 — compliance with Statutory requirements
  7 — provision of setting out details
  9* — treatment of royalties etc and infringement indemnity
  16 — unfixed goods on site (not to be removed without consent etc)
      unfixed goods off site (ownership, removal, safekeeping etc)
  32 — outbreak of hostilities
  33 — war damage provisions
  34* — effect of finding antiquities

(*neither interim nor final reimbursement is referred to in DOM/1 clause 21 – see statements DOM 67/8, 734 and 741).

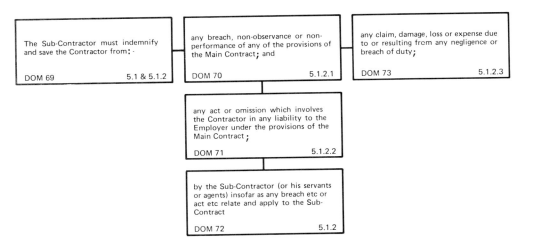

The Sub-Contractor must indemnify and save the Contractor from: -
DOM 69   5.1 & 5.1.2

any breach, non-observance or non-performance of any of the provisions of the Main Contract; and
DOM 70   5.1.2.1

any claim, damage, loss or expense due to or resulting from any negligence or breach of duty;
DOM 73   5.1.2.3

any act or omission which involves the Contractor in any liability to the Employer under the provisions of the Main Contract ;
DOM 71   5.1.2.2

by the Sub-Contractor (or his servants or agents) insofar as any breach etc or act etc relate and apply to the Sub-Contract
DOM 72   5.1.2

These statements place a long-term burden upon the Sub-Contractor to carry for a period of many years the liability for any breach which runs through to the Main Contract and for any claim arising due to negligence or breach of duty.

It is obviously in the Sub-Contractor's own best interests to spot his own misdoings and rectify them as his work progresses to minimise the consequences and repercussions.

Having in clause 5 made the Sub-Contractor responsible for breaches of duty or negligence under provisions of the Main Contract in so far as they are incorporated into and relate and apply to the Sub-Contract, clause 6 then deals with the Sub-Contractor's liability for injuries etc, and for damage to or loss of property arising out of the Sub-Contract itself.

Clauses 7 and 9   Insurance

Clauses 7 and 9 belong together. Clause 7 calls for policies which will (by and large but never absolutely) cover the responsibilities placed upon the Sub-Contractor's shoulders by clauses 5 and 6. These responsibilities do not, however, include the "clause 22 Perils" listed under DOM clause 1.3. Clause 9 details rights to see evidence that insurance has been properly effected and is being maintained. It also grants the Contractor to himself insure, should the Sub-Contractor fail to do so, and to take away the cost of the premium from monies due to the Sub-Contractor.

Clause 8   Loss or damage by the "Clause 22 Perils"

This clause deals with the so-called "clause 22 Perils" whether they affect *any* work executed or *any* unfixed materials or goods on site. Clause 8.4 obliges the Sub-Contractor to observe and comply with the conditions of the Contractor's (or Employer's) insurance but the Sub-Contractor is nevertheless *not* responsible for any loss or damage in respect of the listed "Perils" howsoever caused. However, see the annotation on this under DOM 120, 133 or 144) in respect of this matter.

Clauses 8.3 and 10

Clause 8.3 deals with loss or damage to the Sub-Contract materials and goods during the progress of the Sub-Contract Works and clause 10 deals with questions of liability for loss or damage caused to or by the Sub-Contractor's plant, tools and equipment.

Briefly, the Sub-Contractor is responsible for loss of or damage to all materials or goods on site for the Sub-Contract Works until they are fully incorporated into the Works, *unless:*

(1) the loss etc is due to negligence of the Contractor or his other sub-contractors, or of the Employer
or (2) the loss etc is due to a "clause 22 Peril".

The liability for loss or damage caused to or by plant etc of the Sub-Contractor on site temporarily, or for materials or goods on site prematurely or improperly, is solely the Sub-Contractor's unless the loss or damage is due to the reasons stated in (1) above.

Clause 11   Sub-Contractor's obligation . . . extension of Sub-Contract time

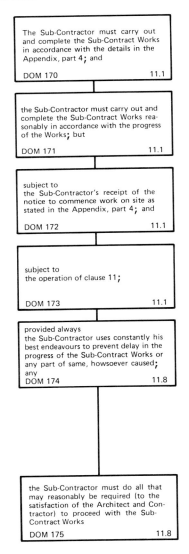

The Sub-Contractor must carry out and complete the Sub-Contract Works in accordance with the details in the Appendix, part 4; and
DOM 170   11.1

the Sub-Contractor must carry out and complete the Sub-Contract Works reasonably in accordance with the progress of the Works; but
DOM 171   11.1

subject to the Sub-Contractor's receipt of the notice to commence work on site as stated in the Appendix, part 4; and
DOM 172   11.1

subject to the operation of clause 11;
DOM 173   11.1

provided always the Sub-Contractor uses constantly his best endeavours to prevent delay in the progress of the Sub-Contract Works or any part of same, howsoever caused; any
DOM 174   11.8

the Sub-Contractor must do all that may reasonably be required (to the satisfaction of the Architect and Contractor) to proceed with the Sub-Contract Works
DOM 175   11.8

The person entrusted by the parties to decide upon any new date for completion is the *Contractor*, behaving in a contractually appointed way in that he is duty bound to "properly consider" matters put to him by the Sub-Contractor on questions of delay; having done so he may then emerge from that role and revert to his normal role of being the Contractor!

Just as clause 4 lays down the Sub-Contractor's obligations, in respect of *standards*, so statements DOM 170–175 lay down his obligations in respect of *time*.

Firstly, DOM 170 stipulates that the time available for the Sub-Contractor to carry out and complete is detailed in the Appendix, part 4.

Secondly, DOM 171 stipulates the Sub-Contractor must also work reasonably in accord with the Work's progress.

Thirdly, DOM 174 requires the Sub-Contractor to do his utmost to prevent delay on his part no matter what may cause delay.

Fourthly, DOM 175 obliges the Sub-Contractor to do all that may be required of him to keep the job (his work) moving and to make progress with the Sub-Contract Works.

The *second* and *fourth* obligations above appear on the face of it to run against each other and may prove troublesome if the Sub-Contractor is, in accordance with the progress of the Works, required to slow down to a time-scale outside those detailed in the Appendix or to speed up his progress to shorten the Appendix time-scale in ways involving substantial deceleration or acceleration costs. If either occurs, clause 13.1 entitles the Sub-Contractor to claim its reimbursement because his regular progress has been materially affected. The loss and/or expense caused in decelerating is clearly recoverable. Whether costlier ways, chosen unilaterally by the Sub-Contractor to achieve acceleration, are recoverable, is not so clear (see Ref 2, p 351). Clauses 11.2.1 and 13.1.2 and .3 require the Sub-Contractor (see DOM 180–182 and DOM 299–301) to inform the Contractor of the cause and give details of direct loss and/or expense so that it may be agreed. At this stage the choice of acceleration methods should be agreed as the direct loss and/or expense, to remove any doubt.

The Sub-Contractor could obviously not be allowed to jog along at his originally agreed time-scale if all around him others were having to speed up and/or slow down. For this reason the Sub-Contract simply *had* to provide for:

1. The regular progress being maintained to accord with the Appendix time-scale

and 2. The Sub-Contractor fitting in with the changing pace of the Works, if necessary.

Thus statements DOM 171, 174 and 175 are clear in intent although perhaps vague in their application. The "operation" of clause 11 in favour of the Sub-Contractor may be denied unless the Sub-Contractor works in accord with the others around him, constantly doing his best to prevent delay to himself "however caused" resulting in him going beyond his Appendixed period/s, or Contractor extended period/s.

It is essential therefore for the Sub-Contractor to *constantly* (see 11.8) show willing. The words "use constantly his best endeavours" are the keys with which to start up the clause. If the Contractor can show the lack of constancy he would be entitled not to operate the clause.

> provided always
> the Sub-Contractor uses constantly his best endeavours to prevent delay in the progress of the Sub-Contract Works or any part of same, howsoever caused;
> any
>
> DOM 174   11.8

The word "constantly" means (OED, p 874):

in a constant manner	in every case
steadfastly	always
steadily	continually
resolutely	perpetually
uniformly	continuously
regularly	pemanently

and the words "best endeavours" mean (OED, p 158) to do all one can (to prevent delay).

A question often arises as to whether a Sub-Contractor is entitled to have clause 11 operated to grant an extension for a just cause occuring after the Appendixed period or previously extended period has expired where the Sub-Contractor is through his own fault in the overrun period.

Being in the overrun period through *not* having constantly used his best endeavours would appear from 11.8 to entitle the Contractor not to operate the clause in the overrun period, thereby denying the Sub-Contractor an extension of time.

> the Sub-Contractor must do all that may reasonably be required (to the satisfaction of the Architect and Contractor) to proceed with the Sub-Contract Works
>
> DOM 175   11.8

Statement DOM 175 obliges the Sub-Contractor to do whatever is reasonably required to proceed with the Sub-Contract Works. Whatever he does he is obliged to achieve the satisfaction of the Architect and Contractor. If the Sub-Contractor is under-achieving then the Contractor can freely expect an increase in pace with, if necessary, an increase in expenditure on the part of the Sub-Contractor. If the Sub-Contractor is achieving his own targets satisfactorily but, due to the changing pace of progress of the main Works, is required to materially change his own regular pace so losing or spending more money, then clause 13.1 will come into play to reimburse the Sub-Contractor.

Clause 11 extensions of time and clause 13 claims for disruption of progress are not always unified and inseparable matters. If a Sub-Contractor vigorously tackles his work and is well on the way to an early completion without his accelerated pace causing problems to the Contractor's own or his other sub-contractors' work then any "act, etc of the Contractor (or his sub-contractors) or any "Relevant Event" which disrupts the Sub-Contractor's own reasonably early completion will bring into play clause 13.1 without clause 11 being operated.

The Operation of Clause 11

There are two distinct stages in the clause's operation:

Stage 1. The Sub-Contractor must initially swiftly give in writing:

> the Sub-Contractor must give the material circumstances including the cause or causes of the delay, insofar as he is able; and
>
> DOM 180   11.2.1

(1) the cause of delay

(2) identify any of the causes given under (1) which are in his opinion an "act, omission or default" of the Contractor (or his sub-contractors etc)

> the Sub-Contractor must identify in the notice any event which, in the Sub-Contractor's opinion, is a Relevant Event;
>
> DOM 182   11.2.1

(3) identify any of the causes given in (1) which are in his opinion a "Relevant Event"

(4) if practicable, give particulars and estimates in respect of (2) and (3) with the notice but in any case as soon afterwards as is possible.

Having 'switched on' the clause by giving written notice to the Contractor in the required form it is then to be "operated" by the Contractor in a dutiful way. He *must* "properly consider" (11.3) the matters notified "on receipt" of the notice, particulars and estimate, provided (11.8) the Sub-Contractor has constantly used his best endeavours to prevent any kind of delay to himself howsoever caused.

Further notices and details of changes in the particulars and estimates given in (4) above must thereonafter be given where necessary.

Stage 2. On receipt of a notice the Contractor must dutifully decide if:

(1) the cause/s notified amounts to an "act" etc or a "Relevant Event"

and (2) the completion of the Sub-Contract Works will be delayed.

If the answer to (1) and (2) is "Yes", the Contractor must "then" (11.3) give a reasonable extension of time in writing to the Sub-Contractor.

If the answer to (1) is "Yes" but to (2) is "No", or to either is "unlikely", the Contractor is "then" under no duty to do anything or to write anything but is to reconsider the whole matter again during the ensuing $15^6/_7$ weeks or upon reaching the completion date of the Sub-Contract Works if that occurs before the $15^6/_7$ weeks are up.

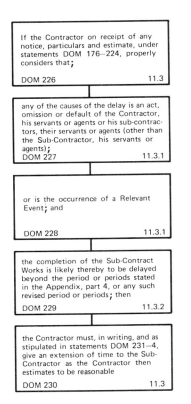

> If the Contractor on receipt of any notice, particulars and estimate, under statements DOM 176—224, properly considers that;
>
> DOM 226   11.3

> any of the causes of the delay is an act, omission or default of the Contractor, his servants or agents or his sub-contractors, their servants or agents (other than the Sub-Contractor, his servants or agents);
>
> DOM 227   11.3.1

> or is the occurrence of a Relevant Event; and
>
> DOM 228   11.3.1

> the completion of the Sub-Contract Works is likely thereby to be delayed beyond the period or periods stated in the Appendix, part 4, or any such revised period or periods; then
>
> DOM 229   11.3.2

> the Contractor must, in writing, and as stipulated in statements DOM 231—4, give an extension of time to the Sub-Contractor as the Contractor then estimates to be reasonable
>
> DOM 230   11.3

This later reconsideration may be more fruitful for the Sub-Contractor if the original particulars or estimates were unclear, inadequate or indefinite. Further and better particulars and estimates of the Sub-Contractor given under clause 11.2.2.3 may change the Contractor's mind. In any case a review of the completion period is called for under clause 11.7 not later than $15^6/_7$ weeks from the date of practical completion of the Sub-Contract Works or of the Works as a whole, dependant upon whichever occurs first.

There is a right for the Contractor, on his own initiative, to fix shorter periods for completion than had previously been fixed by way of extensions under this clause. If no extension has ever been made under clause 11 then no shorter period can ever be fixed but once an extension has been granted the right arises thereafter to take into account time saved by having work omitted thus enabling

an earlier date for finishing to be fixed than previously thought reasonable.

This does not mean the Sub-Contractor can have time which was previously properly awarded because it was needed taken away arbitrarily. It simply means that an omission of work ordered *after* any extension has been made can be taken into account in reviewing that period previously fixed and may result in a shorter period being set without taking away time the Sub-Contractor really needs. In other words the Contractor can only take away time not needed by the Sub-Contractor, ie, because the work concerned has been taken away from him (see Figures 8 and 9).

"Act, Omission or Default"?

The Contractor's first duty under stage 2 (above) is to decide *for himself*, independently in the dutiful way expected of him under his appointment as the trusted decision-maker, whether or not the cause notified is an "act, omission or default"; not allowing any views expressed by others, notably the Architect, to overrule his own judgement.

The words "act, omission or default" are wide in scope. They could include an act of bankruptcy of any sub-contractor of the Contractor. The two latter words "omission" and "default" appear jointly to confine matters to any breach of the Sub-Contract, since the word "omission" when joined to "default" would generally be taken to mean not doing something that ought to have been done. However, when the word "act" is added in, the *combined* effect of the three words when taken together makes the term much more difficult to grasp. As a whole it appears to mean that something more than a straight breach of contract can be the just cause of a claim for an extension of time (or loss and/or expense under clause 13.1 or .4).

For example, the Contractor uneasy about standards may decide to examine/test/dismantle work of his own (without prompting or instruction by the Architect) only to find his original work had been in order after all, and without causing delay or disruption to the Employer under the Main Contract he had merely spent his own (float) time ensuring he had complied with the standards expressed in the Main Contract. If at the time a Sub-Contractor was delayed whilst this sort of examination etc went on he would rightly make a clause 11 notification alleging an "act" of the Contractor was the cause. It could not be classed a "Relevant Event" under clause 11.10.5, nor would it be in breach, since nothing was found wrong and the Employer had no cause to claim any breach. It is therefore an "act" of the Contractor.

These words "act, omission or default" are not new. They were present in clause 10 of the FASS Non-Nominated Sub-Contract. It seems they have been chosen or reselected because collectively they are wider in scope than the simpler alternative term — "any breach of the Sub-Contract", which could have been chosen. Contractors, when making their consideration under clause 11.3, should therefore respect the apparent intentions of the draftsman that the term's meaning should be more flexible and not as unalterable as one might think. Clearly there must be limits to the term's meaning but those limits appear to go beyond the confined one of any act in clear breach of the Sub-Contract.

The Completion of the Sub-Contract Works will be Delayed?

The Contractor's second duty under stage 2 (above) is to decide *for himself* the likelihood of delay in completion of the Sub-Contract Works. The whole procedure is designed to ensure the Contractor knows as soon as possible of any likelihood of delay and for the Sub-Contractor to be told as soon as possible where he stands for time. If it is not reasonably practicable to decide matters *prospectively* then there remains a duty to reconsider the claim to time *retrospectively*.

The principles to be considered concerning prospective and retrospective extensions of time were summarised succinctly by Judge Roper in the New Zealand case, Fernbrook v Taggart [1979]. These principles can be seen (below) to fit in almost exactly with the system of granting extensions of time written into the Main and Sub-Contracts:

"I think it must be implicit in the normal extension clause that the [Sub-Contractor] is to be informed of his new completion date as soon as is reasonably practicable[a]. If the sole cause is the ordering of extra work then in the normal course the extension should be given at the time of ordering so that the [Sub-Contractor] has a target to which to aim. Where the cause of delay lies beyond the [Contractor] and particularly where its duration is uncertain then the extension order may be delayed, although even there it would be a reasonable inference to draw from the ordinary extension clause that the extension should be given a reasonable time after the factors which will govern the [Contractor's] discretion have been established[b]. Where there are multiple causes of delay there may be no alternative but to leave the final decisions until just before the [expiry of 16 weeks from the date of practical completion as 11.7] [c]".

(a) The JCT clause 25.3.1 and DOM/1 clause 11.2.2 both expressly require the Contractor and Sub-Contractor to be informed of their new completion date "upon receipt of any notice, particulars and estimate". If the Architect or (under the Sub-Contract) the Contractor can form an opinion on a new completion date as soon as they get a notice, particulars and estimate of the time involved, then they are duty bound to do so at that time, if it is "reasonably practicable". (Note the obligation on both the Contractor and Sub-Contractor to clearly apply, inform and assess the time loss when applying for a new completion date.)

The Architect's decision under the Main Contract may of course influence the Contractor's decision to be made under the Sub-Contract but, as stated earlier, it is crucial for the Contractor to make his own ascertainment, which must be both "proper" and "reasonable". If this matches the estimate first put to him then so much the better, if not an arbitrator may, by an aggrieved party, be asked to review it.

To facilitate Contractors and Sub-Contractors reaching a decision on whether a granted time extension is both "proper" and "reasonable" the Contractor, under clause 11.5, must state which of the Relevant Events has been taken into account and the extent if any to which there has been a reduction made in extra time needed by taking into account, in the same estimate, omissions of work that may have been ordered *since* fixing a previous new completion date.

(b) JCT clause 25.3.1 and DOM/1 clause 11.4 both *expressly* permit, where an extension cannot be given straightaway, up to 12 and 16 weeks respectively to be taken in considering matters of delay and decision on a new completion date where, as (see earlier) Judge Roper said, the "duration is uncertain". Note, if the duration of the effects of delay can be claimed to be certain, Contractors and Sub-Contractors may expect a prospective extension, and new target date to aim at, *then*, without waiting the expiry of the 12 or 16 weeks referred to here.

(c) JCT clause 25.3.3 and DOM/1 clause 11.7 both *expressly* permit retrospective decisions wherever neither (a) nor (b) above applies. Where the disentanglement of multiple causes, or delayed or intermittent effects apply, these would be suitable cases for retrospective treatment; although they must not be allowed to gather dust and pile up for consideration all together just before 12 or 16 weeks respectively after practical completion. Wherever it is reasonably practicable for a decision to be taken as the Works or Sub-Contract Works progress as to a new completion date then a decision should be made *before* the deadline for the Contractor (or Architect) to decide.

Summarising, it can be seen that Contractors and Sub-Contractors are themselves largely responsible for leading their respective decision-makers by the hand swiftly and surely to an award of extended time. They may bring about their own downfall if they apply for more time than they deserve, asking for it later than they should, in ways which confuse or fail to communicate with the decision-maker. This will extend the period in which it would be "reasonably practicable" for the Architect or "proper" and "reasonable" for the Contractor to decide and consent, thus delaying the granting of a new target. Only in the most intertwined, intermittent and continuous cause of delay need the Contractor or Sub-Contractor, in the Main or Sub-Contract respectively, go without "a new target to which to aim".

Intertwined and Overlapping Causes of Delay in the Regular Progress of the Sub-Contractor

Assuming the Sub-Contractor in his notice of delay, if practicable, has given full and clear particulars of the causes, effects and the extent of delay, the acid test of time claims

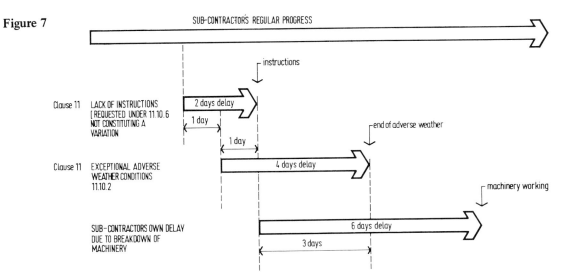

Figure 7

is whether the Contractor "properly considers" he can give an extension which is "reasonable" or "fair and reasonable". Those keywords, appearing in 11.3 and 11.7, enable and require the Contractor to be both impartial and realistic within the confines of the clause, when viewing the many grey areas (eg, as shown in Figure 7) of overlapping and intertwining that will inevitably appear before him from the numerous Sub-Contractors employed by him in the Works. The words want him to be strictly fair "and reasonable". Being strict yet reasonable is a delicate task involving honesty, openness, and sensible flexibility.

Having dealt strictly but fairly and reasonably with the questions of time, he must then go on to answer the separate questions that may arise from allegations of "loss or damage" under clause 13, in respect of "loss and/or expense" claimed from some if not all of the events concerned.

In the case of Figure 7 we can see the first day of delay clearly justifies an extension of time and would if claimed under clause 13 justify the reimbursement of loss and expense arising. The second day of delay would in any case justify an extension of time but carries no clearly divisible right to reimbursement under clause 13, because any loss claimed would not have arisen *solely* from the "listed matter" (clause 13.3.1). The causes cannot be distinguished,

they have become intertwined. When the awaited Architect's instructions are issued, three further days of delay arise and are also attributable to concurrent causes, namely, exceptionally adverse weather justifying an extension of time, and a breakdown of a machine of the Sub-Contractor, not justifying an extension. This poses a difficult dilemma similar to that arising on the second day. The answers may be found by identifying, in each overlapping or intertwined case, the *dominant and most effective cause*. This is a "fair and reasonable" approach to the problem.

In the first overlap of one day the dominant and effective cause of delay was lack of instructions. This justifies an extension of time under clause 11.10.6 and the reimbursement of direct loss and/or expense under clause 13.3.1.

In the second overlap of three days the dominant and effective cause was exceptionally adverse weather. This justifies an extension of time under clause 11.10.2 but no reimbursement of course of any direct loss and/or expense.

Figure 8 illustrates a case where the Sub-Contractor was unable to start activity 'y', although the Architect's inability to issue the required details resulted in only one week of delay *actually* being suffered. Although the Architect has a clear duty under JCT clause 5.4 to issue details as may be necessary, the separate tests under clause 11.10.6 and clause 13.3.1 require separate questions to be asked, namely:

Under clause 11.10.6: Is the completion of the Sub-Contract Works, or any part, likely to be delayed by the Relevant Event of delayed details?

Under clause 13.3.1: Has the Sub-Contractor suffered loss because his progress has been materially affected by the delayed details?

The answer to both questions is "yes", but only in respect of the one week following the termination of the dominant and most effective cause of delay, ie, the Sub-Contractor's *own* delay.

Figure 9 shows the situation where the resources required for extra work, ordered as a Variation, are similar

Figure 8

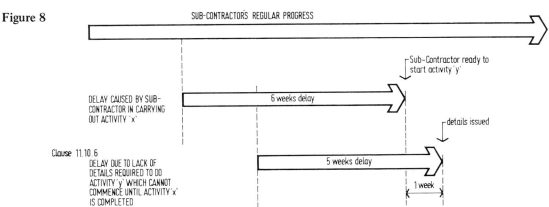

Figure 9

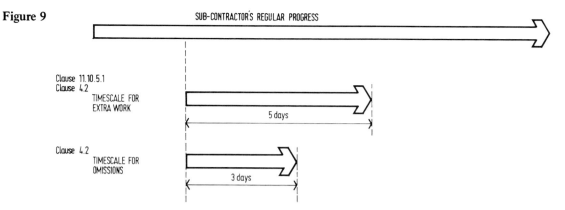

to those involved in work omitted. The Contractor, after having first extended the Sub-Contractor's period for completion, can subsequently under clause 11.6 fairly grant an extension of time equal only to the (net) difference (two days) between arrowheads. If the extra work had involved the importation of new and different resources (skilled workers, as opposed to semi-skilled, etc) the the Sub-Contractor would be entitled to the five days shown in Figure 9, since there cannot fairly and reasonably be a set-off of omissions against additions in such a case.

Figure 10 illustrates an example where the right to unilaterally make a net reduction can be justifiably exercised, after the first extension of time has been made. Where there are clear savings in time due to the ordering of omissions then a shortened date may be set. There cannot,

however, be any "storing up" of insignificant decreases to later set-off in one fell swoop against a subsequent application for an extension. The consideration of savings in time due to omissions must be dealt with as they arise, not retrospectively.

Summary

The granting of an extension of time, or reductions in time due to omissions in the work required, carries with it no recognition at all that any loss and/or expense flows from the events concerned. Clauses 11 and 13 serve different purposes; though they may both deal with time, they do not (and are not meant to) speak in unison on any correlation there might be between time and money, between Sub-Contractor and Contractor.

Clearly, if omissions are significant enough to reduce the time needed to complete, then questions concerning the financial effect of such instructions may require answering under clauses 16 and 17, which require the parties to value all omissions by the rates or prices originally included for the work concerned, but if their valuation "does not relate to . . . the omission of work" then a fair valuation must be made. (See clause 16.3.6 and clause 17.3.4.)

Clause 12 Failure of Sub-Contractor to complete on time

This clause deals with failure to complete, the whole of the Sub-Contract Works, on time. To be "complete" the Sub-Contract Works need only be practically complete; that is to say virtually but not absolutely finished. Questions on completion are dealt with under clause 14.

There is required a formal notice in writing of a failure to complete. Without this the Contractor's right in the clause to recover loss or damage caused by the failure, and suffered as a result, cannot become due. Once served with the required notice the Sub-Contractor must pay over or allow the Contractor to deduct his loss etc from money due. If the Sub-Contractor does not pay or agree to the deduction the Contractor must commence the process of set-off laid down in clause 23.2.

The formal notice of failure to complete must not be given prematurely. It cannot be properly served before the date for completion. It must await the expiry of the period Appendixed or as extended under clause 11. Before this formal notice is served the Contractor should ensure he has "properly considered" (see clause 11.3 and.4) and promptly administered his duties under the Sub-Contract to make any justifiable extension of time. Unless this has been done the Sub-Contractor will inevitably and rightly refuse to any deduction of the loss that may be alleged; the Adjudicator will eventually be informed under clause 24 by the Sub-Contractor of the Contractor's failure to properly consider matters of time thus resulting in the Adjudicator deciding against the Contractor's intended set-off.

There is due later a final review of time under clause 11.7 but meanwhile the right to recoup loss or damage, referred to in paragraph 2 above, begins. If the later review

Figure 10

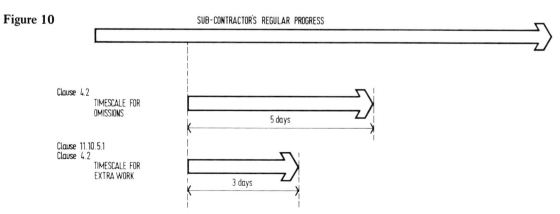

results in a longer period for completion being fixed a financial adjustment or settlement of the over-compensated loss will be necessary and the lost interest should be reimbursed (see DOE for Northern Ireland v Farrahs, BLR Vol 19).

Clause 13 Matters affecting regular progress – direct loss and/or expense

This is the boiler-house clause. The one that generates heated argument and much hot air. However, without this clause both parties would be equally disadvantaged in not having a convenient and economical way of settling their differences over each other's disruptive acts, omissions or defaults. As an added benefit (designed to lower risk and thereby lower bids) the Contractor promises to safeguard the Sub-Contractor against loss etc he may incur from the disruptive effects of events outside each other's control – called "Relevant Matters". The bill for losses due to these particular "Matters" finally drops onto the Employer's desk under the Main Contract.

There are key words in clause 13 which are crucial to the correct operation of the clause's terms:

(a) "regular progress . . . materially affected" (13.1 and 13.4)
(b) "act, omission or default" (13.1 and 13.4)
(c) "information . . . reasonably necessary" (13.1.2 and 13.4.2)
(d) "details . . . in order reasonably to enable" (13.1.3 and 13.4.3)
(e) "direct loss and/or expense" (13.1 and 13.4).

(a) "regular progress . . . materially affected"

The words "regular progress" obviously refer either to the progress originally dictated by the Contractor or planned by the Sub-Contractor and summarily declared in the Appendix, part 4. However, the Sub-Contractor's progress must also (see statement DOM 171) reasonably accord with the progress of the Works. Therefore the words "regular progress" mean one of two possible paces:

1. that pace which would enable the Sub-Contractor to fulfil the primary promise given in clause 11.1 (statement DOM 170) to complete within the period for

completion expressed in the Appendix, part 4, or any revised period granted under clause 11

or 2. that pace adopted under clause 11.1 (statement DOM 171) to fulfil the secondary promise given to carry out and complete not at his own pace but reasonably in accordance with the progress of the Works.

The words "materially affected" mean substantially affected. They were chosen to eliminate piffling effects from the clause's provisions. Unless a material change in the regular pace is evident the clause is inoperable. If it is evident that advancement is being disrupted then we are part way to establishing the claim has validity under this clause.

As soon as it should reasonably have become apparent that the regular pace is, or has been, affected, then the application to have the clause's provisions brought into play must be made. Note it is simply the initial application that needs to be swiftly delivered. This mirrors the legal principle that a person in contract witnessing loss or damage should mitigate the loss by informing the party responsible, as soon as possible, what is happening so putting them in a position to stem the flow of loss.

The parties' rights against each other in this clause (and under common law) might therefore be prejudiced if there is an unreasonable time-lapse between the clear and obvious likelihood of disruption happening and the actual disruption occurring. The parties must whenever possible give their application notices prospectively rather than retrospectively, otherwise their rights to *full* recovery might be denied. They must therefore be on their toes, looking ahead at the likelihood of loss rather than waiting for it to happen.

It is occasionally difficult to identify an "act, omission or default" or a "Relevant Matter". It may also be difficult to be certain the affect upon progress is material. In such cases, until the "act" etc or "Relevant Matter" and its effect become *apparent* (OED p 49, evident, plain, clear, obvious or likely so far as appearances go) the duty to deliver an early enough application does not arise.

(b) "act, omission or default"

For an explanation of these words see p 32.

(c) "information . . . reasonably necessary"

"Information" can take the form of a concise complaint against the other party or (especially in the case of a "Relevant Matter") may simply be a short statement of facts. In any case the form must be such as is reasonably necessary and adequate to enable the other party to see and understand the charge being made.

Totally unacceptable information (ie, an unagreeable charge based upon a wrong opinion) will bar the clause from being validly operated. Partly inadequate information (ie, a partly correct charge) will partly but not totally bar the rights to begin recovery (see statement DOM 293 coupled to 29/30 or 39/40).

Claims can be presented in many ways. The Sub-Contract does not lay down a standard format but clarity will generally be achieved more readily if a consistent or standard format (along the lines indicated in the box on p 37) is adopted.

(d) "details . . . in order reasonably to enable"

The "details" the parties should submit to each other must deal with matters item by item and should include:

(1) a *detailed* narrative or description of the cause (ie, the full grounds for the claim)

(2) details of the sums actually, or likely to be, involved, stating:
 (i) the reasons why the sums arose, or will arise, from the grounds or causes stated in (1)
 (ii) the basis used in the calculations (fuller details of which should follow, or, if available, should be appended
 (iii) details of the evidence:
 letters
 drawings
 programmes
 schedules
 reports
 photographs
 measurements
 calculations
 rate and price analysis
 models

laboratory results
etc etc.

(e) "direct loss and/or expense"

This expression means the sum of money that would be awarded (in a Court action) as financial damages to put the party claiming in the same position (financially) as he would have been in if the cause of loss had not arisen.

For a Court to award damages a claim must be right in law and right in fact. For the parties to recover damages under clause 13 their claim must be right under clause 13 and correct in fact, ie:

   (i)   an "act etc" or "Relevant Matter" must have occurred
   (ii) regular progress must have been materially affected
   (iii) direct loss and/or expense must have been suffered.

The application, information and details to be given under clause 13 are obviously designed to ensure the claimant gets what he deserves, the great advantage being that both claimant and respondent are able to get and give the money concerned privately and at minimum cost to each other.

Clause 14 Practical Completion . . . liability for defects

This clause deals with two things:

   1. The establishing that completion has occurred
   2. The liability of the Sub-Contractor for defects in his Works

> The Sub-Contractor must notify the Contractor in writing of the date when in his opinion the Sub-Contract Works are practically completed
>
> DOM 328   14.1

The Establishing that Completion has Occurred

The procedure requires the Sub-Contractor to serve a formal notice upon the Contractor that the Sub-Contract Works are complete. Unless the Contractor then dissents within 14 days the Sub-Contract Works are taken to be complete. This procedure applies to the Sub-Contract Works as a whole; sections are not to undergo the procedure. There is no sanction or provision for liquidated damages for failure to complete any part of the Sub-Contract Works by a particular time. There is of course clause 13.4.1 with its right to loss and/or expense if the Contractor's regular progress is materially affected by any "act" etc of the Sub-Contractor causing delay (see statements DOM 324–326). If the Main Contract is subject to a sectional completion agreement this must be reflected in and referred to in the Appendix, part 1, section A, thus making clear to the Sub-Contractor the Contractor's liability to pay the Employer liquidated damages for failure to complete *sections*.

The Sub-Contractor is not restricted in the number or frequency of notices claiming completion. But the words "in his (honestly held) opinion" would entitle the Contractor to simply ignore patently premature notices of completion, on the grounds such claims were not bona fide ones. There is no duty upon the Contractor to respond to any notice of completion but failure to do so will deem the Sub-Contract Works complete unless the notice unresponded to can be shown to have been not bona fide.

> Practical completion will be deemed to have taken place on the date of Practical Completion of the Works as certified by the Architect under JCT clause 17.1 of the Main Contract
>
> DOM 333   14.2

If the parties fail to agree on whether or not completion of the Sub-Contract Works has been achieved there is a (DOM 333) long-stop provision (14.2) that states the date of completion of the Works as a whole as certified by the Architect under the Main Contract must be taken as the date concerned.

Defects

If defects in the Sub-Contract Works arise which are not due to any fault of the Sub-Contractor the Contractor may employ others or rectify the defects himself. If the Sub-Contractor is responsible for any defect due to a breach of the Sub-Contract or bad workmanship, faulty materials etc, not only must the Sub-Contractor for years carry the liability to pay any damages arising, he must also put himself at the "direction" of the Contractor to make good at the Sub-Contractor's expense any such defects, shrinkages, or other faults. However, the Sub-Contractor is not liable for design faults of the Architect or Contractor.

> without prejudice to the obligation of the Sub-Contractor to accept a similar liability of the Contractor under the Main Contract to remedy defects in the Sub-Contract Works
>
> DOM 339   14.3

There is no specific right (as there is for the Contractor in the Main Contract — see JCT statements 289/90) for the Sub-Contractor, for a stipulated period, to be able to remedy his own defects rather than pay damages for the breach. However, the Sub-Contractor (in clause 14.3) is required to accept "a similar liability" (DOM 339) to that taken by the Contractor under the Main Contract to remedy defects. It may also be implied that the directions of the Contractor to remedy defects should be given within a reasonable time in all the circumstances (ie, within the Main Contract Defects Liability Period).

If the Sub-Contractor fails to carry out within 7 days a direction of the Contractor in respect of defects then others may (statements DOM 54—56) be employed and paid to do the work, resulting in the Sub-Contractor not only paying damages for the breach of the Sub-Contract's standards but also paying for non-compliance with a "direction".

To place liability for defects in the Sub-Contract Works fairly upon the shoulders of the Sub-Contractor the Contractor must have evidence to justify his opinions. The evidence of the Architect will of course assist enormously but it cannot be conclusive simply because it is the Architect's opinion. The burden is upon the Contractor to prove that a defect was caused by a breach of the Sub-Contract with its standards. Where it is impossible to prove on the balance of probability the cause of a defect was due to a Sub-Contractor's breach then the benefit of such doubt should in arbitration go to the Sub-Contractor, since in Law the burden of proof lays with the Contractor.

If remedial work is required of the Sub-Contractor, due to his breach of the Sub-Contract and its standards, there is no limit to the Sub-Contractor's liability for direct loss etc caused to others such as the Contractor (and his sub-contractors) or the Employer (through the Contractor) where the remedial work causes them interference etc.

Clause 16 Valuation of Variations and provisional sum work

Clause 16 deals with the financial changes in a *lump sum* agreement whereas clause 17 deals with the valuation of all work comprising the Sub-Contract Works where a *measure-and-value* agreement has been entered into.

Generally a lump sum agreement is made where most of the proposed work is certain and foreseeable. A measure-and-value agreement is made where the proposed work, or its extent, is uncertain and unforeseeable; the intention then being that the whole of the work done will be measured and payment made for that work.

In practice the differences between a lump sum and measure-and-value agreement are difficult to detect since a sum is tendered in both cases and measurement may take place in a lump sum case (Variations etc). Furthermore, identical documents may be proffered to both kinds of

bidders (drawings, specification and bills of quantities), and the interim payment procedures are no different.

However, there are some legal differences in the two kinds of agreement which lawyers like to see recognised by a clear statement — as in the Articles 2.1 and 2.2, linked to clause 15.1 and 15.2 in the Conditions, cross referred to clause 16.1 and 16.2 — to complete the circle which delineates clearly between these two basic kinds of construction contract price agreement made between the parties, namely:

(a) (under Article 2.1) a "Sub-Contract Sum"
or (b) (under Article 2.2) a "Tender Sum"

(a) A "Sub-Contract Sum"

This expression and agreement means the Sub-Contractor has given a basically unchangeable binding lump sum price for the Sub-Contract Works, though any Variations ordered or provisional sum work carried out or certain cost fluctuations (clauses 35—37) will entitle the so-called lump sum to be varied somewhat, up or down.

A lump sum Sub-Contract may be based upon drawings, specifications and bills of the quantities; or a schedule of rates may be drawn up by the Contractor or proffered by the bidding Sub-Contractor in conjuction with a lump sum bid where the use of bills of quantities is inappropriate. The bills or schedule would be used for settling the value of any Variations or provisional sum work. The monthly amounts due to a Sub-Contractor out of the lump sum concerned for interim payment would be established either by agreeing in advance certain stage payments or usually by using the priced bill of quantities or schedule of rates, whichever of the two had been incorporated into the Agreement. Where stage payments are agreed in advance the sums involved make up only the lump sum of course, leaving Variations etc to be dealt with as and when they arise.

(b) A "Tender Sum"

This expression in the Standard Sub-Contract means the accepted Sum is not an unchangeable one. On the contrary it is definitely intended to be a changeable sum ascertained by completely measuring and valuing the work as it progresses.

A measure-and-value sum Sub-Contract may be based upon drawings, specifications and bills of quantities, or a comprehensive schedule of rates.

When bills of quantities are proffered by the Contractor and are intended to be made a Numbered Document, Sub-Contractors may usefully and safely rely on such bills in view of the obligation accepted by the Contractor under clause 18 to correct any errors etc that may be found within the bills. The Contractor will usually enter into this arrangement, whenever he proffers parts of the Main Contract Bills to bidders, because he is himself granted a similar safeguard by the Employer to have remedied any such errors.

It is important therefore for Sub-Contractors to observe whether or not bills of quantities are contractual or not:

Lump Sum (Quantities Sub-Contract)

Where the bill of quantities is made a Sub-Contract Document (see clause 2.1.1 and clause 18.1), under a lump sum agreement, the Sub-Contractor is entitled to rely upon the bill of quantities to establish his lump sum. He is therefore entitled to extra payment due to any shortcomings (numerically or by method of measurement) discovered in the bills of quantities; on the other hand the Contractor is entitled to make a deduction where the quantities (or method of measurement) prove to be less than expected.

However, any error of the Sub-Contractor in extension, totalling, carrying forward or in the Sub-Contract Sum, whether unfavourable or advantageous to the Sub-Contractor, cannot normally be rectified. Only in cases where a special code for dealing with unintended mistakes has been drafted into the Agreement, can rectification occur.

Lump Sum (Quantities Non-Contractual)

Where a proffered loose bill of quantities is *not* to be made a Sub-Contract Document (see Chapter 4, clause 18), and its accuracy is disclaimed, the Sub-Contractor may generally be considered to have accepted the document as a Schedule of Rates and Prices with Quantities for him to complete in respect of the rates etc. Thus the risk of its

errors, adverse or advantageous, will be carried by the Sub-Contractor bound by the lump sum he tenders excepting where under clause 4.2.1 a Variation or provisional sum work is called for, or cost fluctuations occur under clauses 35–37, and change the sum otherwise fixed.

In such Agreements rates and prices should be entered into the Appendix at part 5, or listed separately in the schedule as proffered to the bidder and made a Numbered Document, for the purpose of valuing Variations and provisional sum work.

Measure-and-Value Sum (Quantities Sub-Contract)

Where the bill of quantities is made a Sub-Contract Document (see clause 2.1.1 and clause 18.1), under a measure-and-value agreement the Sub-Contractor is entitled to rely upon the quantities and method of measurement in the bill of quantities to establish his individual rates and prices tendered in the bill of quantities but is not entitled to a Variation direction if the actual quantities differ from those billed since none is needed (see statement DOM 442).

However, by clause 17.1 (line 1) and 17.3.1.2 an increase in or decrease of a rate or price may result where a difference significantly changes the quantity in the work required. The correction would therefore *not* be "treated as if it were a Variation" (clause 18.1.2).

The Sub-Contractor will not be entitled nor forced to have his own errors (unfavourable or advantageous) of extension, carrying forward, totalling, or in the Tender Sum, rectified under clause 18 since these errors are not:

(a) a "departure from the Method" of measurement

or (b) an "error in description . . . quantity or omission of items".

Therefore the resulting wrong Tender Sum will have no effect since the Ascertained Final Sub-Contract Sum is to be arrived at in any case by remeasurement and recalculation simply using the rates or prices, ignoring the original (wrong) Tender Sum in the contractual bill of quantities.

Measure-and-Value Sum (Quantities Non-Contractual)

Where a bill of quantities is proffered but is not to be made a Sub-Contract Document and its accuracy is disclaimed

the Sub-Contractor will generally be considered to have accepted the risk of its errors, adverse or advantageous, but the position with regard to significant changes in quantity will be as stated above (where quantities are contractual) in that clause 17.1 (line 1) and 17.3.1.2 require such changes to be revalued and of course in any case all the work actually done is to be measured and valued.

The Sub-Contractor's own errors (unfavourable or advantageous) of extension, totalling etc, as stated above (where quantities are contractual), are not to be rectified since the bill of quantities is not (see clause 18.1) a Sub-Contract Document. Therefore the resulting wrong Tender Sum will likewise have no effect.

Variations and Provisional Sum Work

> The term "Variation" means any of the following changes which are required by a direction of the Contractor issued under the Sub-Contract: -
>
> DOM 343   1.3

Without clause 4.2.1 there would be no need for clause 16 because the Sub-Contractor would be required only to carry out and complete the Documented work — no extra work, omissions or changes or provisional sum work would be permitted, neither therefore could the (lump) Sub-Contract Sum be changed.

This clause 16 is therefore concerned with change. It is not concerned with valuations for first or interim payment unless there are Variations or provisional sums to be dealt with therein.

The clause envisages (see clause 1.3) quite considerable changes in the work and has in statement DOM 343 etc defined change. Provisional sums may also be included in the Documents which sums are not defined but are apparently to be expended under the directions of the Contractor. Unlike the Main Contract (JCT clause 13.3.2) which stipulates the Architect not only has the power but also the *duty* to instruct the Contractor in regard to provisional sum expenditure, clause 16 merely infers (see 16.1, lines 1 and 2) that directions must have come from the Contractor for the expending of such sums.

The clause lays down very detailed rules for arriving at the binding sum for Variation and provisional sum work which has been properly carried out. These sums are to be added to or (in the case of omissions) deducted from the (lump) Sub-Contract Sum. The clause also permits (16.1) the parties to mutually agree their own methods of valuing, rather than slavishly follow the very detailed rules of the clause. The Contractor cannot otherwise unilaterally impose short-cuts to, or different ways of, making Valuations.

The clause prohibits the incorporation of sums for loss and/or expense into the values where such loss should be established under clauses elsewhere within the Sub-Contract. This clarifies and obviates argument over cash discount and retention as well as the question of VAT, on damages — which is another word for loss and/or expense.

The valuation rules specify that all valuations must be determined using the rates, prices and allowances to be found within the following Documents:

(a)   (i) Appendixed schedule of rates or prices (for measurable work)
      (ii) Appendixed daywork rates or prices (for unmeasurable work)
(b) (iii) bills of quantities (for measurable work)
    (iv) daywork definitions with Appendixed percentages
(c)   (v) other documents comprised in the Sub-Contract Documents.

The rules require (a) to prevail over (b), and (c) may be used in conjunction with (a) or (b); (a) prevails because of the general rule in the interpretation of contracts that if any terms have been specially written into (the Appendix of) an otherwise standard form, these should be taken in preference to the terms expressed by the standard printed words.

The Contractor is entitled to direct that Variations be carried out including the omission of work but he cannot order the omission of work to give it to another sub-contractor (see Simplex Floor Co v Durancean [1941] 4 DLR 260). Under general law governing contract the omission of work would entitle the Sub-Contractor to the loss of profit to be expected on the value of the work omitted. However, the general law has here in clause 16 been ousted by the detailed rules which in the case of omissions (see 16.3.2) state in effect the Sub-Contractor loses his expected profit on work omitted. Furthermore, reductions in allowances put in as preliminary items may well be made if they are connected with the omissions concerned.

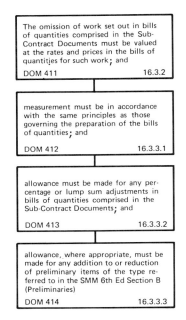

On the other hand, compliance with a Variation direction or provisional sum direction may change the conditions under which any other work is executed, in which case the work affected is itself to be valued as if it had been varied by direction of the Contractor, using the rules for Valuation in the clause.

The definition of Variation (clause 1.3) does not include the right to direct the Sub-Contractor to accelerate any part, nor the whole, of the Sub-Contract Works; nor can the Contractor (or Architect) dictate the methods or sequence of working. However, if the Sub-Contractor's methods or sequence do not comply with any which were stipulated in the Documents then there is of course a breach. The Contractor should in such cases merely state non-compliance had occurred and the Sub-Contractor should comply. If the speed of working was not reasonably in accord with the progress of the Main Contract Works clause 11.1 (statement DOM 175) would apply, so too would clause 13.4.

The Contractor or Sub-Contractor may, for various reasons, suggest informally (and later confirm) a change in materials or goods and even a minor change in the design of the Sub-Contract Works with or without reference to any reduction in or extra charge to be made to the Sub-Contract Sum; and with no clear agreement on the responsibility assumed for the design change. This can raise numerous difficulties if an increase or decrease is later claimed or a defect in the changed design occurs involving other changes to be made to other work, and time to be extended due to resulting delays.

It is essential to agree, before such changes are implemented, whether the change is:

(a) a *concession*, without increased or decreased payment
(b) a *Variation*, in which case whether the full rules of clause 16 apply, or if any other agreement on value is made under 16.1
(c) a combination of (a) and (b), in which case the agreed terms for payment should be detailed
(d) approved by the Architect as a design change for which he assumes responsibility and whether the financial effect is to be dealt with under (a), (b) or (c) above.

Where work in Variations or the expenditure of provisional sums is quite different in character or conditions from the character or conditions included for in the bills' or schedules' rates or prices, so that those cannot provide for the basis for determining the valuation, then the work concerned is to be valued at fair rates or prices. A fair rate would obviously be the cost (if efficiently executed) together with a fair addition for the overheads needed to service the work and for a profit element reasonable in the circumstances. A fair rate could also be an acknowledged 'market' rate for the same work.

Allowances are also be be made to lump sums or percentages to be found in the bills or in other Documents. Where appropriate allowances are to be made in priced preliminary items, these can be additional or reducing in nature. This does not mean priced preliminary items should be slavishly adjusted pro-rata the financial value of Variations, or pro-rata any extra time taken. Each case for an allowance should be judged on its merits. For instance, a priced item for supervision would rightly be related to and adjusted initially according to the time involved in extra (or reduced) work; but if the amount of work was increased or decreased to such an extent that the supervisory staff concerned had to be doubled or halved then time only would not be the sole factor involved in arriving at the allowance to be made.

Problems may arise where a preliminary item is left unpriced or marked "included", meaning it did not justify a sum or that other rates or prices for the work included for it, ie, a small element in the rates for units quantified in the bill of quantities covered the cost concerned. Subsequent Variations may, however, justify a sum being put to an item that otherwise would not have justified such a sum. For example, security initially may have been an item so low in risk the Sub-Contractor considered it did not justify a sum in return for the risk. A Variation may subsequently introduce extremely high risk materials, goods or work into his Works, thus justifying a payment for the new high risk concerned. (See further on this under clause 18 in column 3.)

Clause 17 Valuation of all work comprising the Sub-Contract Works

For an explanation of the differences between a measure-and-value agreement and a lump sum agreement see clause 16, p 38.

Under a measure-and-value agreement, entered into where work or its extent is uncertain and unforeseeable, an increase or decrease in the quantity of work may very well result not from a Variation but simply due to the quantities exceeding or being less than those stated in the Sub-Contract bill of quantities or shown in the Sub-Contract Documents.

The important difference between unintended and intended (ie, Variation) changes in quantity may be observed in clause 1.3 wherein it *omits* to state that a change in

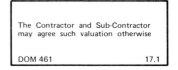

quantity is a Variation. Only in cases where a change in quantity is the result of an alteration or modification of the design or quality of the Sub-Contract Works . . ., including the addition, omission or substitution of any work, can such changes require the "ordering of any Variation" (see clause 4.2.1).

The provisions in 17.3.4 only apply in cases of changed quantities emanating from Variations or provisional sum directions or from directions as a result of which work is not executed, ie, it is to be omitted.

The provisions in 17.3.5 only apply to Valuations in cases of Variations or provisional sum directions.

From the foregoing it can be seen that straightforward increases in quantities over and above the quantity stated in the Sub-Contract bill of quantities or shown in the Documents (drawings, specification, etc) are not classed as Variations and although the provisions of 17.3.1 to .3 (excepting 17.3.2.3) do apply to those increased quantities, enabling amongst other things a renegotiated valuation to be made (17.3.1.2), these principles do not extend to or apply if such changed quantities substantially alter the economics of any priced preliminary item; or any conditions under which other work is executed under 17.3.4; nor do they apply to the 17.3.5 provision.

Problems of demarcation and valuation will, because of the above differences, arise where for instance the actual quantity of an item is increased over and above the quantity billed or shown in the Documents and at the same time a Variation direction involves the same item in an increase of quantity — the combined effect of which substantially

changes the conditions under which some other work is executed.

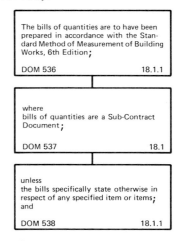

Statement 461 does enable the parties to agree to value otherwise than in strict accordance with the written rules and the above case might be a suitable one in which to depart from the rules.

For further details on the application of the rules of Valuation see the preceding clause 16 notes.

Clause 18 Bills of quantities — SMM

The bills of quantities, if made a Sub-Contract Document, must have been prepared in accordance with the SMM 6th Edition unless the bills themselves state this is not the case in respect of any specified item or items in the bills (see statement DOM 538).

Bills not conforming or found to have numerical errors, or omissions or wrong descriptions, are to have their wrongs put right by treating the correction needed as if it were a Variation required by a direction of the Contractor. This will bring into play all the rules of valuation in either clause 16 or 17.

If the Sub-Contract bills are the Contractor's creation, or are merely a photocopy of parts of the Main Contract bills, the risks arising from errors are carried by the Contractor. In most cases the Contractor will be safeguarded against the risk of errors in his Sub-Contract bills by only using or handing down replicas of the Main Contract bills whose errors are the liability of the Employer. If, however, the Contractor in stitching together a replica bill for use in the Sub-Contract creates an error, or makes an omission, he alone may be liable under DOM/1 clause 18.1.2.

The Contractor is not prohibited from proffering his own peculiar brand of bills provided they state there is a departure in method. The Contractor may use a mixed bag of accurate quantities using the SMM 6th Ed, together with relatively approximate quantities employing his own method of measurement as long as his way is made clear and his numerical results using his way are in fact right. To depart from the SMM is not wrong as long as the departure in the item(s) specified is stated. It is not right to depart either in an unclear, or clear way giving wrong results.

Obviously it is easier to determine and agree an error has arisen, where SMM 6th Ed rules were used in the bills' preparation, than where a home-made method of measurement has been utilised. In attempting to resolve disputes where non-standard methods of bill preparation have been used one must take the words expressed in the item(s) concerned in their plain and literal sense in conjunction with any other Document relevant, or referred to, and from there ask -- "Is there any mistake here?" If the words in the suspect item adequately inform the reader the extent of the work covered by the item and to be priced, given the other Documents, drawings, specification and DOM/1 and information the Sub-Contractor could have obtained for himself, eg, by a site visit, then there can be said to be no mistake. If, however, there is work to be done for which there is no item or inadequate coverage in the items given, then there is an "omission" or an "error in description" which under clause 18 is to be put right at the Contractor's expense if his bills were a Sub-Contract Document. This applies even if the work concerned was obviously essential to the proper carrying out and completion of the Sub-Contract Works for there is no duty on the Sub-Contractor to look for and find errors of the Contractor in his bills.

Work, temporary work, processes and risks which are ancillary to, incidental to, and indispensably necessary for an item are always reckoned to be reasonably inferred and therefore included for, with an item (unless specific items are separately provided) and therefore no "error in description" can be claimed for such matters. For example, an item for flooring of sheet or boards need not describe or even mention nails or the means of securing the flooring to the joists. If the specification does not detail the nails, screws, etc, the Sub-Contractor will be under an implied obligation to include for a method of securing the flooring, adequate for the intended purpose, using materials of a reasonable standard in the circumstances concerned.

If on the other hand the Contractor in his bills failed to itemise floor boarding or sheeting but does itemise floor joists he cannot say it is obvious the boarding should have been included in the item for joists. It might be obvious to the *Contractor* that you cannot have floor joists without floor boards or sheets but it may not have been obvious to the *Sub-Contractor* that he was the one being asked to do both. If the words used in the item for joists did not make it clear beyond any reasonable doubt that both joists *and* boards or sheets were being asked to be included for together in one item, then the benefit of the doubt would go to the Sub-Contractor (especially where the price entered by the Sub-Contractor can be shown to be too low anyway to include for boards or sheets).

Drawing the line between clarity and ambiguity, or between work indispensably necessary or not, may prove extremely difficult whenever non-standard methods have been utilised; that is why the SMM (which calls for *certain* levels of detail in item descriptions) has over the decades been developed.

A genuine ambiguity may be capable of being read in two ways one of which adversely affects the Sub-Contractor, the other the Contractor. Under a general rule in law the benefit of the doubt should go to the Sub-Contractor since he did not write the bills containing the ambiguity.

If a Contractor does not have a proper bill of quantities (from the Employer) and does not wish to carry the risk of preparation errors in his own proffered 'bills' he should call the Document a "Schedule of Rates and Prices with Quan-

tities". He should also make it clear the quantities given are estimated ones not claiming to be comprehensive or correct but that nevertheless the Document will be used to select the successful tenderer and his rates and prices therein will be used as described in DOM/1 clause 16.2 or 17.2. The Contractor's quantities should not be guessed. They should be "estimated" as warranted. No notional quantity should be included merely to obtain a rate.

Preliminaries items and percentages, or lump sums, in bills

Preliminaries items are as important as work items with their measured quantities. The adjustment of these items when work is varied becomes as necessary as the recalculation of varied quantities. The measurement of measurable work poses far fewer problems than the making of "allowances", under clause 16.3.3.2 and .3 or 17.3.2.2 and .3, to preliminaries items.

Preliminaries items may be time-related, method-related or cost-related. For instance, a clause 7 insurance item has a cost ratio based upon the Sub-Contract Sum (or Tender Sum). Any changes in the Sum will bring into play clause 16.3.3.3 (or 17.3.2.3) to provide for an "allowance" in the priced item since the premium payable is usually strictly proportional to the Sub-Contract Sum (or Tender Sum).

Other items may be a mixture of a time- and cost-related sums. If a Sub-Contractor has included a sum for an "authorised representative" to supervise his Works the sum concerned is mainly time-related. However, if the Sub-Contract Sum was substantially increased due to extra work *not* involving extra time but requiring his representative to be joined by another then the allowance to be made would have to be related to the actual cost and not strictly pro-rata the increased amount of the Sub-Contract Sum.

Thus each priced preliminaries item should be considered on its merits as to whether or not an allowance should be made (by increase or decrease). Where changed work brings into play a preliminaries item originally unpriced, or marked "included", problems may arise. For instance, in the example quoted in the last paragraph, originally an item for a Site Office may not have been necessary and therefore not priced but if due to changes a supervisor is augmented by another who will have to be desk-bound and need an office where previously none was needed then a justifiable claim to an allowance will clearly arise.

In the above case, under clause 16.3.3.3 due allowance can be made but under clause 17.3.2.3 there appears a bar by the restricting words allowing only "any amounts *priced*" to be adjusted. However, the provisions of clause 17.3.5 might be invoked (see statement DOM 533). If the Sub-Contractor had marked the Site Office item "included" it will usually be argued that in the valuation of the increased work using rates or prices containing an element (say 1%) for the Site Office, the Sub-Contractor's extra expense would thereby be met. However, this argument would not hold up if 1% of the increased work clearly would not pay for the office now needed. To prove this point the Sub-Contractor would have to show the Contractor his rate or price analysis and the preliminaries item cost.

Clause 21   Payment of Sub-Contractor

The intentions of clause 21 are quite clear. The Sub-Contractor is meant to have in his hand each month virtually all of the value of all the work up till then he has properly done, and of the materials etc properly delivered to the Works and stored away, together with any amounts allowable or to be ascertained under the terms of the Sub-Contract.

The Contractor is only allowed to hold back from this a small ("Retention") percentage otherwise everything up until then unpaid for must go to the Sub-Contractor out of which the Contractor can take a small (usually 2½%) discount provided he has made a gross valuation of the monthly amount when due and more importantly has handed over the actual payment concerned no later than 17 days after the monthly due date.

So, the first payment will involve working for about six weeks before having virtually all of the money involved in the valuation paid over. Thereonafter, as regular as clockwork, every month similar payments must be put into the Sub-Contractor's hand. This arrangement results in a very short capital cycle for the Sub-Contractor. He is returned virtually all of his outlay and more if he takes all the credit

The amount of the first and each interim payment to the Sub-Contractor must be the gross valuation of the following amounts: -

DOM 686   21.3

the total value of the sub-contract work on site properly executed by the Sub-Contractor, including any work properly executed to which DOM clause 16.1 refers;

DOM 687   21.4.1.1

the total value of the materials and goods delivered to or adjacent to the Works for incorporation in the Works by the Sub-Contractor but not so incorporated;

DOM 690   21.4.1.2

provided that
the value of such materials and goods must only be included as and when they are reasonably, properly and not prematurely delivered and are adequately protected against weather and other casualties

DOM 691   21.4.1.2

the total value of any materials or goods where the Architect in his exercise of his discretion under JCT clause 30.3 of the Main Contract has decided that such total value shall be included in the amount stated as due to the Contractor in an Interim Certificate;

DOM 693   21.4.1.3

provided always
the Sub-Contractor observes any relevant conditions set out in the Main Contract to be fulfilled before the Architect is empowered so to include the value

DOM 694   21.4.1.3

any amount ascertained in whole or in part in respect of payments made or costs incurred by the Sub-Contractor for;

DOM 696   21.4.2.1—.3

fees or charges
setting out Works
defects or faults etc
direct loss and/or expense
fluctuations in costs
under clauses 6 or 7 of the Main Contract and under DOM clauses 14.4, 13.1, 35 or 36;

DOM 697   21.4.2.1—.3

any amount allowable by the Sub-Contractor to the Contractor under DOM clause 35 or 36, whichever is applicable

DOM 699   21.4.2.3

he can conventionally get from his suppliers, who will usually be paid well after the Sub-Contractor has banked the money concerned.

This process continues until the Sub-Contractor reaches a stage of practical completion of the Sub-Contract Works. Once this stage is reached the Contractor's right to hold back the small sum in "Retention" is cut by half. The next payment due will release half to the Sub-Contractor of the sum the Contractor would otherwise be entitled to have in his hold as "Retention". This small balance withheld from the Sub-Contractor remains with the Contractor until the Sub-Contract Works have been made the subject (under the Main Contract) of a Certificate of Completion of Making Good Defects. At this point the remaining "Retention" is released by way of what will probably be the last *interim* payment before the Final Payment.

At this stage virtually everything owed to the Sub-Contractor should have been paid to him. There remains only a Final Payment to be made when the Final Certificate to be issued by the Architect under the Main Contract has been made to the Contractor. This Sub-Contract Final Payment, unlike the valuations to be made for the purpose of interim payment, is the absolutely correct financial balance and binding sum the parties have finally settled upon for the Sub-Contract Works; quite different from interim payment valuations which are the best estimated value one can make at the time.

Interim gross valuations are not necessarily absolutely representative of everything done and due according to the Sub-Contract and its Documents, ie, the bill of quantities or schedule of rates or prices. For instance, Variations may only have been given an estimated value.

The favourable payment terms referred to above are a reflection of those granted the Contractor under the Main Contract. The JCT/80 and DOM/1 terms enable the Contractor to be paid 3 days before he is due to pay the Sub-Contractor. If, however, the Contractor's rights under the Main Contract are not met he has no right to make the Sub-Contractor suffer similarly. Of course the Contractor may decide to ignore the Sub-Contractor's rights and *make* him wait or *make* him receive less than he should under the Sub-Contract. The remedies then for the Sub-Contractor are:

(i) clause 21.6 — suspend the further execution of the Sub-Contract Works

(ii) clause 21.6 — use common law remedies (eg, seek an Order 14 Summary Judgement, where a sum is indisputably due)

(iii) clause 30.1.1.3 — end his own employment under the Sub-Contract

(iv) clause 30.1 — use common law remedies.

If the Sub-Contractor suspends his work he can (in theory at least) under the Sub-Contract recoup the time (by clause 11) lost. More importantly, he can recoup his direct loss and/or expense either conveniently under clause 13.1 or under common law procedures. If the Sub-Contractor decides he has had enough, that he stands no hope of adequate recompense under the Sub-Contract, and he has justifiable grounds for ending (under clause 30.1.1.3) his own employment, then the rights under the Sub-Contract still operate — including the clause 13 right to recover disruption losses.

The Sub-Contractor should not regard the right to suspend work as a panacea for every financial misdemeanour of the Contractor. If the wronged Sub-Contractor does suspend, the Contractor may simply refuse to admit a payment he has made is not in accordance with clause 21; he may coldly ignore the Sub-Contractor's suspension and proceed to cross claim under clause 13.4 for disruption, at the same time indicating no extension of time will be given to any application under clause 11.10.13, on the grounds that the Sub-Contractor's exercise of his right to suspend is not "valid" (see line 1, clause 11.10.13).

If the Sub-Contractor is not prepared *if necessary* to go all the way, ie, to terminate his own employment under clause 30.1.1.3 (or common law), being certain the payments in question were wrong (and that he would not under any other provision get adequate recompense) then he should perhaps endeavour to make the best of a bad job — not hastily suspending, or, alternatively, uncomfortably sweating out a suspension trusting the Contractor will not have the nerve to determine the Sub-Contractor's employment under clause 29.1.1; furthermore, trusting the Contractor will eventually capitulate, pay up, and square up favourably to the inevitable clause 11 and 13.1 claims from the Sub-Contractor.

It should be noted that unless an interim payment proposed by a Contractor is seriously adrift it is not easy (see p 9, Chapter 2) to be absolutely correct about such payments. Although statements DOM 686 and 687 etc in effect clearly say 'pay the Sub-Contractor the "gross valuation" of the "total value" of his work etc', the term "total value" is debatable. Clause 17 differs from clause 16 in that it stipulates *all* work (ie, at any stage) comprising the Sub-Contract Works is to be valued using the clause 17 Rules whereas clause 16 Rules are applicable only to the Valuation of Variations and provisional sum work. Thus, clause 16 is not applicable to the valuation of unvaried or non-provisional work to be included in an interim payment. It appears therefore to be in order for the "total value" to be arrived at in any reasonable way *provided* it produces a reasonably accurate and bona fide "total value". For instance, if a Sub-Contractor has entered a rate for walling work from ground level to roof it is obvious the rate entered is an average one being marginally too high for walling work at ground level

and too low for work at high roof level. The Contractor in a lump sum Agreement would not be bound to multiply the area of work done by the rate entered by the Sub-Contractor. He would be justified in setting a "total value" on ground level work which was somewhat less than the product of the area of work done multiplied by the *entered* rate. However, in subsequent valuations the "value" of the work would increase as it rose towards the roof to finally compensate the "total value". In the case of a measure-and-value Sub-Contract the entered rate would have to be applied to "all work executed" (see clause 17.1, line 1), thus compensating the Sub-Contractor strictly in accordance with his entered rate whether or not the work done was at low level or high level.

The need under clause 21 to arrive at a "total value" for interim payment may also prove difficult where errors have come to light in the Sub-Contractor's bill of quantities rates or prices under a lump sum clause 15.1 Agreement. Is the "total value", for interim payment, to be decided upon regardless of its cost to the Sub-Contractor and without reference to the obviously wrong rates or prices in the bill of quantities? It could be argued the "total value" should be the proportion the work bears to the original lump sum regardless of any rates or prices in the bill of quantities which are only there in order to put a value on Variations (if called for) or provisional sum work.

A further problem would arise in the above example in respect of associated preliminaries items linked to items with wrong rates or prices. Should these be paid out or "adjusted" (see 16.3.3.2 and .3) upon a financial ratio known to be wrong or upon a more sensible time-for-completion ratio?

There are no written answers to be found to these questions in the Sub-Contract. The uncertainty will only prevail during the interim period of course since the Final Payment *must* consist of the original unaltered lump sum together with any Variations and provisional sum work valued using the entered rates or prices even though they are obviously wrong unless a code for dealing with such errors had been incorporated into the Agreement.

If the Sub-Contractor wrongs the Contractor in some way, and a financial sum can be put upon that wrong to compensate the Contractor, the Sub-Contract enables the parties to deal administratively with the matter by the Contractor making a deduction of an agreed sum or a sum fixed by an arbitrator or Court. In most cases of wrong-doing there is no agreement or award of an arbitrator or Court. There is usually considerable disagreement all round.

The Sub-Contract, in clause 23, recognises the Sub-Contractor is likely to disagree any sum the Contractor proposes to set-off against monies due; it also recognises the Contractor is likely to exaggerate the sum owed and if pushed for time may just pluck a figure out of the air. Furthermore, he may seek to set-off sums owed by the Sub-Contractor to the Contractor, elsewhere incurred, from monies due under this particular Sub-Contract. All of this is brought strictly under control by a detailed set of rules to ensure the Sub-Contractor is not unduly denied pay-ments, neither is the Contractor denied a rightful set-off.

These rules of clause 23.2 apply to all interim payments and the Final Payment. The Contractor cannot therefore craftily cut down the Final Payment by any amount he reckons is owed to him by the Sub-Contractor. Statement DOM 744 requires the Final Payment to be put together in a particular way. Having done so the Contractor can then go about a rightful set-off from that Payment sum and the Sub-Contractor can under clause 24 properly go about re-sisting the set-off or introducing any rightful counterclaim.

> The Final Payment must be made to the Sub-Contractor in accordance with the provisions of DOM clause 21
>
> DOM 744   21.1

Any timely move commenced towards arbitration or other proceedings (see DOM 754–757) would prevent the Final Payment becoming a binding and conclusive act. Otherwise, the Payment signifies:

(i) standards specially identified under the Main Con-tract as being subject to the Architect's scrutiny and satisfaction have been met,

(ii) the Final Payment is (except for error or omissions in computations that may later be discovered) cor-rect and closes questions as to whether or not the Sub-Contractor is entitled *under the Sub-Contract* to any more.

Clause 23   Contractor's right to set-off

The most crucial statement to be found in this clause is made at the very end (DOM 786). In effect the statement

> The rights of the parties to the Sub-Contract in respect of set-off are fully set out in Sub-Contract DOM/1 and no other rights whatsoever must be implied as terms of the Sub-Contract relating to set-off
>
> DOM 786   23.4

forbids the Contractor from *freely* setting-off any sum he feels he is owed (from this or any other contract with the Sub-Contractor) from any sum due to the Sub-Contractor under the Sub-Contract.

The clause does, however, permit the Contractor to deduct any amounts mutually agreed between the parties or awarded in arbitration or litigation. It also permits the Contractor to claim a right to set-off unagreed amounts. To qualify for this right and to later withhold the sum claimed the Contractor must have actually incurred the amount in question (it cannot be for an *anticipated* loss) and must have calculated his amount, for the Sub-Con-tractor to see, with reasonable accuracy. Furthermore, his intentions to, and grounds for, set-off must have been previously notified to the Sub-Contractor in writing not la-ter than 20 days before the Sub-Contractor could otherwise have expected the money (see format for Notice, p 46).

This 20-day minimum period runs back from the "due" date (for it is then technically payable) and not the actual date when the money, from which the set-off is intended, is normally paid over, ie, usually 17 days later (at the most) than the "due" date; or in the case of the Final Payment, 14 days (at the most).

It is important to note the right to set-off only applies to amounts incurred. For instance, the Sub-Contractor may carry out work wrongly or badly and fail to rectify it. The Contractor cannot apply to set-off a sum to cover the work concerned. He must actually incur the cost before becoming entitled to set-off the cost.

It is interesting to note the Main Contract contains no similar total prohibition (as found in statement DOM 786) upon the Employer exercising his common law right to set-off sums owed him by the Contractor, from sums certified as due under an Interim Certificate of the Archi-tect. There are express rights (JCT clause 30.1.1.2) for the Employer to make certain deductions, without prior notice and without details of the calculations etc.

Clause 24   Contractor's claims not agreed by the Sub-Contractor – appointment of Adjudicator

This clause only comes into play if clause 23 is correctly operated by the Contractor and the Sub-Contractor wishes to resist an intention to set-off. If the Contractor simply withholds money and does not conform at all with the strictures of clause 23 then the Sub-Contractor should swiftly apply to the Courts for judgement in his favour for the amount indisputably "due" under the Sub-Contract. In the meantime the right to suspend the further execution of the Sub-Contract Works could be exercised. If then the Contractor began to comply with the procedures of clause 23, and gave belated notice of intention to set-off, the 20-day minimum period would preclude the right to set-off so far as the current "due" date was concerned, meaning full payment (of the sum arrived at under clause 21) would have to be made to the Sub-Contractor (not to the Trustee) even if there was seen to be complete justification for the intended set-off.

If both parties follow the strict procedures of clauses 23 and 24, communicating their case to the Adjudicator who, in turn, does what he should within the 7 days (see state-ment DOM 821) allowed, then rough justice will be done. The problem will not be solved but merely temporarily decided in a binding way, so far as the money is concerned, leaving the parties, if they wish, to come to grips and settle or go to arbitration; indeed, the Sub-Contractor must, whether he likes it or not, give formal notice (DOM 790) of arbitration, at the onset, even though he may have no firm intention of going that far.

Success once, on the issue, by either party is no licence to subsequently freely set-off (or prevent it) on the same matter. Once having gained the right to set-off, or in the Sub-Contractor's case to full payment or to monies being lodged with the Trustee, the whole process has to be re-peated if another notice is subsequently served of intended set-off. Obviously a Contractor is unlikely to intend to set-off another "amount" on exactly the same grounds as previously refused but if he has new or better evidence

CLAUSE 23.2
NOTICE OF INTENTION TO SET-OFF

Project Name . . . . Date of Notice . . . .

Reference . . . .

Sub-Contract Details . . . .

. . . .

. . . .

Contractor's Name . . . .

Sub-Contractor's Name . . . .

Breach of the Sub-Contract   *(Brief details of the act,*
. . . .

omission or default concerned)
. . . .

. . . .

Incurred amount of loss and/or expense to be set-off
£ . . . .†

†Quantified in detail as shown on sheeets . . . . . . attached
*Attached details

The Grounds on which the rights to set-off is relied upon*
. . . .

(Identify the grounds relied upon stating:
. . . .

  (i) the clause(s) involved, and
. . . .

  (ii) any implied terms, with the reasons for arriving at
. . . .

      the implication, and
. . . .

  (iii) the alleged actions constituting the breach
. . . .

Letters, drawings, programmes (indicating delay/disrup-
. . . .

tion), reports, photographs, measurements, rate and price

analyses, etc, should be attached where relevant, as an

Appendix.)

. . . .

. . . .

. . . .

. . . .

. . . .

. . . .

. . . .

to justify his previously unaccepted claim then he will (and must) start up clause 23 again.

Communicating with the Adjudicator

It is absolutely crucial that both parties communicate clearly the justification of their case to the Adjudicator in such a way that he is able to swiftly make his decision, about the money, given the facts and the quantum in the parties' statements.

At worst, the Contractor's clause 23 notification may amount to several pages of disputable matters written in verbose or vague terms mixed up with some justifiable and indisputable items; his grounds, his evidence and calculations of loss may be thrown together in disorder. This will be of no help to his case nor will it assist the Sub-Contractor for he *has* to set out *his* reasons for disagreement with the amount of or any part of the sum specified in the clause 23 notice. Furthermore, a rambling notice will be difficult to respond to logically and point-for-point, especially if the Sub-Contractor has a counterclaim of his own to make and the Contractor responds to it with a further rambling defence.

A confusing set of notices and written statements may increase the chances of the Adjudicator naturally reaching for a rough compromise. What else can he do? He *is* entitled to seek clarification or an explanation of any ambiguity but if the persons who wrote to him initially could not make themselves clear in the first place what hope would he have in seeking clarification?

> save only
> further written statements as may appear to the Adjudicator to be necessary to clarify or explain any ambiguity in the written statements of either the Contractor or the Sub-Contractor
> DOM 825   24.3.1

It seems vital to get it right first time, for both parties' sake not to mention the Adjudicator. A suggested format for a Notice of Set-off and a Statement of Disagreement is given on p 47.

Incurred Amount

The amount should be detailed and broken down into parts where various headings of claim are concerned. The reasons

PART A

CLAUSE 24.1.1
STATEMENT OF DISAGREEMENT

Project Name . . . . Date of Statement . . . .
Reference . . . .

Sub-Contract Details . . . .
. . . .

. . . .

Sub-Contractor's Name . . . .

Contractor's Name . . . .

Reasons for Disagreement with the Amount (or part) specified in the Notice of Intended Set-Off dated . . . .
ref . . . .

(Reasons should here be set out in full attaching relevant

evidence for disagreement with the amount (or any part)

shown by letters, drawings, programmes, reports, photo-

graphs, measurements, rate or price analyses, etc)

We hereby request action by the Adjudicator . . . .   *(Name as*
in Appendix

to decide the matters referred to in the attached Notice of
Intention to Set-off dated . . . .   Ref . . . .
and hereby give notice of arbitration, as required under
clause 24.1.1 to

. . . .   *(Contractor's name)*

We also set out (in Part B) particulars of a counterclaim to
which we are entitled (to be deleted if inapplicable).

- -

PART B (detach if inapplicable)

CLAUSE 24.1.1
PARTICULARS OF COUNTERCLAIM

Project Name . . . . Date of Counterclaim . . . .
Reference . . . .

Sub-Contract Details . . . .
. . . .

Sub-Contractor's Name . . . .

Contractor's Name . . . .

Amount of Counterclaim £ . . . . †

Particulars of Counterclaim arising out of the Sub-Contract
(detailed above)

(Brief details of the act, omission or default concerned)

. . . .

. . . .

. . . .

The grounds on which the counterclaim is made*

(Identify the grounds relied upon stating:

(i) the clause(s) involved, and
. . . .

(ii) any implied terms, with the reasons for arriving at

the implication, and
. . . .

(iii) the alleged actions constituting the breach
. . . .

Letters, drawings, programmes (indicating delay/disrup-

tion), reports, photographs, measurements, rate and price

analyses, etc, should be attached, where relevant, as an

Appendix.)

. . . .

. . . .

. . . .

†Quantified in detail as shown on sheets . . . . . attached
*Attached details

why the sums incurred arise from the grounds stated should be detailed and the *basis* for any calculations should be given, with measurements, quantities, etc.

Continuation of Payments to the Sub-Contractor

It is important always to read clauses 21, 23 and 24 together. Payments under clause 21 are intended to continue at all times until such time as an Adjudicator decides otherwise and dictates what is to happen in the case of the particular amount notified by the Contractor as intended for set-off. Clause 21 is not to be put into any state of suspension whilst the clause 23 and 24 routines are followed. It continues to operate fully, whilst the Sub-Contractor is at work, churning out money for the Sub-Contractor (if he is owed it under the clause) unless the Sub-Contractor voluntarily agrees to a deduction or the Adjudicator by a clause 24 decision entitles the Contractor to wholly or partly retain a *particular* amount properly notified for set-off.

Following one resort to set-off, whether successful or not, if the Contractor wishes to exercise his right to set-off further sums or other sums in respect of other breaches then he must start up the whole machinery of clause 23 again (and again) as further sums become due to the Sub-Contractor from which the Contractor intends to set-off. Likewise, the Sub-Contractor must, if he wishes to resist, respond separately again and again to each and every notice of intention to set-off of a particular amount, as stated in **DOM 861—863** unless he wishes to waive his right to disagree.

Clause 29 Determination of the employment of the Sub-Contractor by the Contractor

The first part of clause 29 gives the Contractor the right to terminate the Sub-Contractor's employment under the Sub-Contract if he commits certain specified breaches. The second half of the clause deals with termination if certain events connected with and including insolvency occur.

It is important to note that any breach unspecified in this clause cannot be swept in and dealt with using these procedures. It would have to be dealt with under common law rules which are open and not denied to the Contractor by the presence of this clause with its narrower confines.

In any case the Contractor may choose not to use the provisions of this clause to deal with a breach covered by the clause, using instead common law to deal with the matter.

> if the Sub-Contractor without reasonable cause, fails to proceed with the Sub-Contract Works in the manner provided in DOM clause 11.1
>
> DOM 905   29.1.2

If the Sub-Contractor does breach the Sub-Contract under DOM 905—909, provided there are no signs of insolvency or any shortages of capital, termination of employment should not be jumped at too readily but resorted to only in hopeless cases, or where the Contractor's reputation with the Employer may suffer. Otherwise the Contractor should vigorously use his rights to set-off any loss and/or expense incurred by the breach. Such actions should soon stir the Sub-Contractor to operate efficiently, in the end proving a cheaper and quicker solution than firing the defaulter and finding a replacement who may be more expensive and no less inclined to commit breaches.

If the Sub-Contractor fails to proceed with a particular part of his work the Contractor may issue reasonable directions to him to get on with it. The defaulter must then immediately react doing all that may be reasonably required to proceed with the Sub-Contract Works. Failure to do so entitles the Contractor to employ others to carry out the given direction and to deduct the costs incurred from money due to the Sub-Contractor under the Sub-Contract.

Likewise the above remedy is available in cases of breach under DOM 906 and 907/8. It is difficult to foresee a Sub-Contractor choosing to have his employment terminated under clause 26.2 or 32 rather than remedy the situation by ceasing the breach.

Only in the case of an irremediable assignment would termination be the first course to take rather than seeking an alternative solution.

If the Sub-Contractor wholly suspends the carrying out of the Sub-Contract Works without reasonable cause, and by his actions or inaction shows no intention of resuming his work, then termination as rapidly as the clause permits

> if the Sub-Contractor refuses or persistently neglects, after notice in writing from the Contractor to remove defective work or improper materials or goods and such refusal or neglect materially affects the Works
>
> DOM 906   29.1.3

> if the Sub-Contractor wrongfully fails to rectify defects, shrinkages or other faults in the Sub-Contract Works;
>
> DOM 907   29.1.3

> which rectification is in accordance with the Sub-Contractor's obligations under the Sub-Contract
>
> DOM 908   29.1.3

will reduce the loss and/or expense that may be incurred. If insolvency or insurmountable financial difficulty is at the root of the problem the Contractor should find it simpler to invoke his rights to terminate under DOM 904 rather than under DOM 920—928. If bankruptcy etc occurs the problem is clouded by statutory rights under bankruptcy law and the Companies Act which can override the terms of this clause whenever they may diminish the interests of any creditors.

> if the Sub-Contractor without reasonable cause, wholly suspends the carrying out of the Sub-Contract Works before its completion
>
> DOM 904   29.1.1

If the Contractor terminates the Sub-Contractor's employment under this clause without sufficient grounds or by not recognising, or going beyond, the reasonable meaning of the clause's key words then the Sub-Contractor may claim his employment was terminated unreasonably or vexatiously, eg:

(a) in DOM 904 and 905 the words *"without reasonable cause"* give the Sub-Contractor grounds to allege unreasonable termination if there was a reasonable cause for his breach. In the construction industry it is never difficult to find a cause exists for a breach many of which could be claimed as "reasonable causes".

(b) In DOM 906 the Sub-Contractor's default must *"materially"* affect the Works. If the Sub-Contractor can show his breach had less than a significant effect and that the Works in general were not substantially affected then the right to termination is doubtful.

(c) In DOM 907/8 the word *"wrongfully"* may have be been judged solely in the eyes of the Contractor whereas it means wrongfully in the eyes of an independent objective person.

A Sub-Contractor running into financial trouble may commit breaches serious enough to justify termination. If bankruptcy and serious breaches occur simultaneously the grounds for termination should be for the breaches rather than the bankruptcy. This does not avoid entanglement with a trustee, liquidator or receiver, or with the law concerning insolvency, but at least a clean break can be achieved without having to await a possible claim to re-instatement by the trustee etc.

The Contractor should keep the trustee etc informed and send to him any requisite notices under the Sub-Contract. He should not seek assignment from, nor make payments to, any supplier or sub-sub-contractor of the original Sub-Contractor otherwise the trustee etc will claim the payment or benefit should go into their bankrupt's account.

Whilst the Contractor continues to carry out the Sub-Contract Works he has the right to refuse to make any further payment to the Sub-Contractor, his trustee, liquidator etc, after the last payment prior to the termination. But once the Sub-Contract Works are complete (probably meaning practically complete) any amounts previously

the Sub-Contractor must allow or pay to the Contractor in the manner shown in DOM 954 the amount of any direct loss and/or damage caused to the Contractor by the determination
DOM 950   29.4

deduct the amount of any direct loss and/or damage caused to the Contractor by the determination
DOM 954   29.4

unpaid to the Sub-Contractor become due. However, this is not likely to amount to much by the time the Contractor has under DOM 950 and 954 taken away his direct loss and/or damage caused to the Contractor by the termination.

Clause 30 Determination of employment under the Sub-Contract by the Sub-Contractor

if without reasonable cause the Contractor wholly suspends the Works before completion;
DOM 957   30.1.1.1

if without reasonable cause the Contractor fails to proceed with the Works so that the reasonable progress of the Sub-Contract Works is seriously affected;
DOM 959   30.1.1.2

if he fails to make payment in accordance with this Sub-Contract;
DOM 961   30.1.1.3

There are three risks the Sub-Contractor takes which this clause identifies and relieves him of the risk by enabling him to terminate his employment as soon as the risk arises. These are that the Contractor may:

1. Fail to make payment
2. Fail to proceed
3. Wholly suspend the Works before completion.

If risk no. 1 arises it is likely the Sub-Contractor may already have suspended the execution of the Sub-Contract Works, under clause 21.6. Before deciding whether to suspend or terminate the Sub-Contractor should always endeavour to ascertain whether the failure is likely to be temporary or not. Where a permanent failure or a persistent and serious underpayment is envisaged a joint suspension and notice of default with a view to termination may extend the necessary qualifying period for termination. The words in DOM 967/8 appear intended when joined to DOM 962 to prevent the Sub-Contractor using the threat of

termination to harass the Contractor when a mere technicality has caused a temporary failure to pay properly. Clauses 21.6 and 30.1.1.3 serve two distinct purposes. The former is a right to be used when a temporary breach is envisaged; the latter when a permanent or serious and irremediable breach has occurred. The joint remedies of clauses 21.6, 13.1 and 11 could hardly be held to adequately recompense the Sub-Contractor if no short-term settlement was envisaged so as to provide enough cash flow to the Sub-Contractor. The term "adequately recompense" should not be scrutinised too harshly as a general rule against an offended Sub-Contractor.

Risk no. 2, failing to proceed, is quite different to wholly suspending the Works, although it may not look any different to the Sub-Contractor concerned. Usually risk no. 2 shows some sign of arising before risk no. 3 occurs. In either case, but especially where only risk no. 2 is evident, the Sub-Contractor should ensure before terminating under DOM 957 or 959 he can show he is "seriously affected" and that no extension of time coupled to a clause 13.1 remedy would "adequately recompense" him.

If the Sub-Contractor was affected but not seriously, or if the Contractor gave or promised a full extension of time and adequate financial recompense then the Sub-Contractor would under DOM 964 be in danger of terminating unreasonably if he proceeded under this clause. He does of

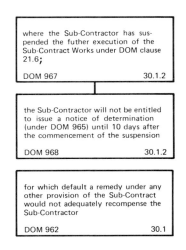

where the Sub-Contractor has suspended the futher execution of the Sub-Contract Works under DOM clause 21.6;
DOM 967   30.1.2

the Sub-Contractor will not be entitled to issue a notice of determination (under DOM 965) until 10 days after the commencement of the suspension
DOM 968   30.1.2

for which default a remedy under any other provision of the Sub-Contract would not adequately recompense the Sub-Contractor
DOM 962   30.1

course have common law rights but expert advice should be sought on these courses available.

However, if termination takes place, the Sub-Contractor should continue to treat *all* the terms of the Sub-Contract as if everything was normal. The rights of both parties are by and large unaffected by a clause 30 termination. In fact, the further rights of clause 30.2 come into play once termination occurs.

For instance, the Sub-Contractor's normal liabilities to indemnify the Contractor against any claim for damage to property under clause 6 remain exactly as they were prior to termination but a further right and duty brought about by the termination arises under clause 30.2 for the Sub-Contractor to take away all his temporary buildings, plant etc, with all reasonable dispatch being still liable under clause 6 as if termination had not occurred and using every precaution he would have used anyway.

If the Sub-Contractor did not remove his possessions with "all reasonable dispatch" the Contractor's rights under clause 4 (see DOM 42) to issue reasonable directions remain alive, so too does his remedy of employing others if the Sub-Contractor does not respond immediately to his direction.

Clause 21 remains to govern payments but further rights arise in clause 30.2 wherein the value of work *completed* is to be dealt with under clause 21 but not using its rules to

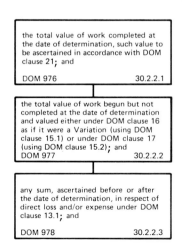

the total value of work completed at the date of determination, such value to be ascertained in accordance with DOM clause 21; and

DOM 976   30.2.2.1

the total value of work begun but not completed at the date of determination and valued either under DOM clause 16 as if it were a Variation (using DOM clause 15.1) or under DOM clause 17 (using DOM clause 15.2); and

DOM 977   30.2.2.2

any sum, ascertained before or after the date of determination, in respect of direct loss and/or expense under DOM clause 13.1; and

DOM 978   30.2.2.3

also value *uncompleted* work — this is to be dealt with by using the rules of either clause 16 or 17 depending on whether the Agreement made originally was a lump sum one or a measure-and-value arrangement. Furthermore, "direct loss and/or expense", whether ascertained before or after termination, is to be paid but only in respect of the loss etc caused by the regular progress of the Sub-Contract Works having been materially affected up to the act of termination.

The right to recover the cost of materials etc ordered and the cost of removal of plant etc is also written into the clause but the right to loss of profit on work incomplete at the time of termination is not written into the Sub-Contract. However, the Sub-Contractor's right to pursue a claim to loss of profit remains open to him under common law. This denial of an express right to recover under the Sub-Contract the direct loss and/or expense caused by the determination (as contrasted with that caused by disruption to progress up to the act of termination) is one distinct difference to be noted between JCT/80, NSC/4 and DOM/1.

Clause 33   Strikes — loss or expense

This clause makes the parties bear their own losses and/or expenses caused by:

(a) a work to rule or go-slow affecting the Works } "local combination of workmen"

(b) strikes official or unofficial affecting the trades employed on the Works or engaged in preparing, making or transporting materials or goods for the Works } "a strike"

(c) a refusal to give work to operatives except on certain conditions, which refusal affects the Works } "a lockout"

Furthermore, the parties owe each other a duty to take all reasonably practicable steps to carry on in the face of the above circumstances. A breach of *this* duty owed will enable the party suffering to claim damages amounting to the direct loss and/or expense arising from the breach. This would be an entitlement under either clause 13.1 or 13.4.

Nothing in this clause must affect any other right of the Contractor or Sub-Contractor

DOM 1009   33.2

The presence of this clause does not prejudice or deny either party their other rights. For instance, the Sub-Contractor is entitled to the right to claim an extension of time due to the above reasons. He is also entitled to total relief from responsibility for any loss or damage caused by the above reasons (clause 22 Perils) to the Works.

On the other hand, DOM 1009 does not deny the Contractor the right to have the Sub-Contractor to "do all that may be reasonably required . . . to proceed with the Sub-Contract Works" under clause 11.8 (statement DOM 175). Furthermore, the clause 12 right to recover any loss or damage caused by the Sub-Contractor's failure to complete on time remains fully operational.

5 THE REASON FOR FLOWCHARTS

There is no simpler question than that which can be answered by a direct "Yes" or "No". However, only if the question is right can the answer be right. Using right "Yes/No", or two-way questions correctly positioned in a graphic diagram we find that we have the basis for an algorithm.

An algorithm is the word used to describe a logical procedure for the solution of any problem in a given class. An algorithmic approach to a problem uses a step-by-step procedure in a reasoned logical way. Flowcharts are a logical network providing a pictorial step-by-step representation of a process (algorithm), indicating the arrangement and action of its parts by which it produces a given result. Flowcharting simplifies any plan, process or procedure, no matter how complex the problem.

Low-level communications theory can be applied to the Domestic Form of Sub-Contract to create some degree of simplicity out of its complexity. People have throughout the ages always endeavoured to improve their method of conveying information and reducing the ambiguity that is present in every method of communication. Improvements are always worthwhile and here can be made by developing methods of deduction, by organising facts into units, by reducing the load on memory, by arranging the task in such a way that we make a sequence of several absolute judgements rather than strain our low capacity immediate memory. This approach enables us to dump the devilishly intricate legal sentence, separating exceptions and provisos into branch lines to await questioning only if they are relevant.

Figure 11 sets out six basic symbols required to enable legal language to be decoded, organised into manageable units, and arranged for sequential questioning, so that we arrive in a logical step-by-step way at the only correct conclusion. These basic symbols are taken from BS 4058 which sets out signals *internationally* agreed for use in data processing, problem definition, and problem analysis.

Figure 11

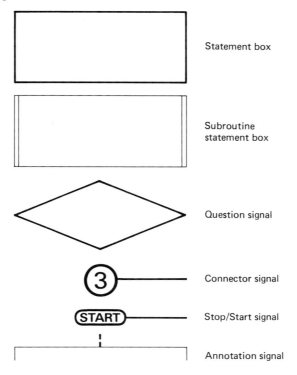

Statement box

Subroutine statement box

Question signal

Connector signal

Stop/Start signal

Annotation signal

Standard methods of measurement, standard phraseology and standard ways of programming have already transformed the technical documents that order the activities of the construction industry. There seems no reason why we should not also standardise ways of communicating the contents of our standard forms of contract, by the use of such flowcharts.

Simple English sentences on average contain about twenty words and only one idea. Legal sentences conventionally contain a host of ideas all requiring questioning in a mechanistic way to arrive at the information next needed to predict the next step to be taken correctly from a set of steps available to eventually arrive at the only correct conclusion.

A legal sentence containing only six ideas is in effect presenting the practitioner with 64 alternatives. This is one way of quantifying the information content of a statement. There is, alas, no way of likewise measuring its *meaning*.

Method Rules

To create consistent flowcharts certain rules emerged (from work previously carried out by the author[1]) for the production of these charts:

1. *A New Approach to the Standard Form of Building Contract* (1972);
A New Approach to the ICE Conditions of Contract (1975);
A New Approach to the International Civil Engineering Contract (1979);
A New Approach to the 1980 Standard Form of Building Contract (1980);
A New Approach to the (JCT) 1980 Standard Form of Nominated Sub-Contract (1982).

1. Simplify (or decode) the problem to form statements.
2. Reorganise the facts into statements which are 'manageable', (ie, within the capacity of our immediate memory).
3. Arrange the statements into a logical sequence.
4. Question each statement.
5. If any predefined process or routine has to be followed at any particular point in the sequence, a subroutine 'obey' signal is required.
6. If any additional information is essential, to aid the reader in his understanding, this can be tagged onto any statement or subroutine by the use of an annotation signal.

This same signal can be used to confirm a logical conclusion.

Using the Flowcharts

The flowcharts in Chapter 6 follow the principles outlined above. The reader is required to read the charts from top to bottom and left to right, in that order. Arrowheads to indicate the direction of flow have not been necessary except in isolated situations where the reader is required either to move directly to a certain position in the charts or to move against the normal flow of top to bottom and left to right.

The legal source of a statement is indicated in the bottom right-hand corner of each box. The numerical code in the bottom left-hand corner is a reference aid for simplifying the use of subroutines, enabling readers to readily find the exact point at which to enter an 'obey' routine, whether that point is within the Sub-Contract itself or in the Main Contract. In the former case the letters DOM precede the code number; in the latter case the letters JCT precede the code number and those readers who possess the author's work on the Main Contract[2] may thereby follow or pursue their problem through to its conclusion if declared there, or otherwise return to the Sub-Contract to continue their step-by-step analysis.

The flowcharts should be self-explanatory although certain signals require explanation. The sign :- is used to break information up into manageable units or signifies there are *variable* endings to be fitted to such a statement. The sign ;

is also used to break information up into manageable chunks and indicates that *additional* text follows.

Obviously every question demands an objective answer. When disputes arise the parties should proceed step by step to the question point at which one states "Yes" and the other "No". This then would pinpoint where their disagreement lies, and the flowchart will indicate to the parties their remedies or the contractual consequences.

Draftsmen may recoil at the suggestion that their statements can be arranged in flowchart form to upset their original syntax. However, statements *can* be reorganised without impairing meaning if great care is taken to preserve the traditional syntactical chunk.

One word spells trouble for everyone. The word "shall" (used lavishly by all draftsmen) frequently causes confusion by disguising its meaning behind the words which surround it, not revealing on first reading whether it represents a promise, intention or command. Indeed, it sometimes is used merely to express futurity. The word has therefore been dumped by the author whenever a promise, intention or command is involved. The reader will find instead either the word "must" or "may" is used to denote more positively the appropriate obligation to act, as conveyed by the words surrounding "shall" in the original draft.

Reference numbers 1 and 2 are used occasionally in the annotation where legal tomes are to be referred to, and where the author's flowchart annotations concerning the Main Contract may provide further clarification or information the Reference number 3 is used.

Reference 1 = *Hudson's Building and Civil Engineering Contracts*, 10th Edition, by I N Duncan Wallace.

Reference 2 = *Building Contracts*, by D Keating.

Reference 3 = *A New Approach to the 1980 Standard Form of Building Contract*, by G P Jones.

---

2. *A New Approach to the 1980 Standard Form of Building Contract.*

6 FLOWCHARTS

55

Sub-Contract Documents — Obligation to carry out the Sub-Contract Works

START

Sub-Contract DOM/1 and the Numbered Documents constitute the Sub-Contract Documents

DOM 1   2.1.1

The Sub-Contract Works must carry out the Sub-Contract Works in compliance with the Sub-Contract Documents using materials and workmanship of the quality and standards specified in the Documents; and

DOM 2   4.1

The Sub-Contractor must carry out and complete the Sub-Contract Works in accordance with the details in the Appendix, part 4; and

DOM 170   11.1

Sub-Contractor does carry out the Sub-Contract Works as stipulated ?   YES / NO

The Contractor must not without the written consent of the Architect sub-let any portion of the Works;

JCT 304   19.2

The words in DOM 3 grant the Contractor the right to reasonably direct ("instructing how to proceed or act, authoritative guidance" OED p 391) the Sub-Contractor (not necessarily in writing) to secure his compliance with the requirements of the original Sub-Contract Documents so far as they may apply to the carrying out of the main and Sub-Contract Works. The words in DOM 42 go further and wider, enabling the Contractor to (in writing) reasonably direct the Sub-Contractor on any matters "in regard to the Sub-Contract Works". This right extends to ordering Variations (as defined in DOM clause 1.3) in the Sub-Contract Works

---

in conformity with all the reasonable directions and requirements of the Contractor (so far as they may apply) regulating for the time being the due carrying out of the Works

DOM 3   4.1

The parties' agreed period/s for carrying out and completion of the Sub-Contract Works as detailed in the Appendix Part 4 is contractual. Remedies for default are expressed in DOM clauses 12 and 13.4 for the Contractor, and in DOM clause 13.1 for the Sub-Contractor

---

The Contractor may issue any reasonable direction in writing to the Sub-Contractor (or his authorised representative) in regard to the Sub-Contract Works;

DOM 42   4.2.1 & 4.4

---

the Sub-Contractor must carry out and complete the Sub-Contract Works reasonably in accordance with the progress of the Works; but

DOM 171   11.1

The Contractor may issue any reasonable direction in writing to the Sub-Contractor (or his authorised representative) in regard to the Sub-Contract Works;

DOM 42   4.2.1 & 4.4

The Numbered Documents are crucially important for they will, in detail (eg, bills, drawings, schedules of rates etc), describe the Sub-Contract Works. They are required to be identified simply by numbering and listed on page 12 of the Articles of Agreement. They combine with the Sub-Contract DOM/1 to denote the agreement concluded between the two parties. If any discrepancy or conflict appears between the Numbered Documents and the Sub-Contract DOM/1, go to statement DOM 12. If any standard clauses or sub-clauses of DOM/1 are struck out, or if optional clauses or sub-clauses are inadvertently not struck out, see Ref 2 p 348

Where bills of quantities are a Numbered Document they will be deemed to set out matters of quality and quantity. Otherwise such matters must be gleaned from whatever may be found referring to standards and scope in any other Numbered Documents eg. in drawings, specifications etc. Wherever standards are not expressly described there is an implied duty to do the work in a good and workmanlike manner

---

The quality and quantity of the work included in the Sub-Contract Sum or Tender Sum must be deemed to be that which is set out in the bills of quantities;

DOM 546   18.1.3

Nothing contained in any descriptive schedule or other like document issued in connection with and for use in carrying out the Sub-Contract Works must impose any obligation beyond those imposed by the Sub-Contract Documents

DOM 9   2.1.2

The Sub-Contractor must immediately give written notice to the Contractor if and whenever it becomes reasonably apparent that: -

DOM 176   11.2.1

The Contractor may issue a notice to the Sub-Contractor (by registered post or recorded delivery, specifying the default) if the Sub-Contractor defaults in any one or more of the following respects: -

DOM 903   29.1

The Sub-Contractor must: -

DOM 62   5.1

---

observe, perform and comply with clauses 6, 7, 9, 16, 32, 33 and 34 of the Main Contract;

DOM 67   5.1.1

This subroutine includes an obligation to carry out certain emergency compliance with statutory requirements without formal instructions or directions via the Contractor

This subroutine details the Sub-Contractor's duties and rights if commencement or progress is delayed

---

The Sub-Contractor must: -

DOM 62   5.1

---

observe, perform and comply with all the provisions of the Main Contract as referred to in the Appendix, part 1;

DOM 63   5.1.1

Nothing contained in the Sub-Contract Documents must be construed so as to impose any liability on the Sub-Contractor in respect of: -

DOM 77   5.2

---

any act, omission or default on the part of the Employer (or his servants or agents)

DOM 78   5.2

---

any act, omission or default on the part of the Contractor (or his servants or agents)

DOM 79   5.2

The DOM clause 2.1.1 identifies the Documents which make up the Sub-Contract and when joined with DOM clause 4.1 sets out the full scope of the Sub-Contractor's overall obligation to carry out all the work to complete the Sub-Contract Works in strict accordance with the standards declared in those Sub-Contract Documents.

However, statements DOM 62/3 additionally incorporate, in the Appendix Part 1, certain crucial main contract terms into the Sub-Contract but only so far as they relate and apply to the Sub-Contract.

There may also be implied terms concerning quality, fitness for purpose, etc, to be read into the Sub-Contract (as there are in any construction contract) although implied terms are generally considered to be excluded wherever particular provisions on such matters exist in writing in the Numbered Documents.

The Sub-Contractor has the right to achieve completion in ways he thinks fit without interference from the Contractor (or Architect) provided the agreed commencement date and work period/s, or any accepted revision of same, is being complied with, also, the methods of working are not causing injury damage or unacceptable permanent work.

The Contractor's task is therefore to ensure that all work done by the Sub-Contractor on his behalf accords strictly with the terms of the Documents and with certain main contract terms where they are relevant and applicable to the Sub-Contract, or, that the Sub-Contractor's work achieves the Architect's satisfaction referred to in DOM 4/5/6 wherever approval has been specifically stated to be a matter for the opinion of the Architect.

The basis of Domestic Sub-Contracting is that the Contractor always remains fully liable to the Employer in the Main Contract for all sub-let work and JCT clause 19.2 requires prior consent to proposed sub-letting. Failure to obtain prior consent is a serious breach entitling the Employer to terminate the Contractor's employment; he would not be entitled to payment for work done by way of unauthorised sub-letting even if such work was satisfactory (see 'Engineering Law and the ICE Contracts', Max W Abrahamson 4th Ed p 40)

The Contract Drawings, Contract Bills, Articles of Agreement, Conditions and Appendix are in this Contract referred to collectively as 'the Contract Documents'

JCT 1   2.1

The Sub-Contractor must carry out the Sub-Contract Works in compliance with the Sub-Contract Documents to the reasonable satisfaction of the Architect: -

DOM 4   4.1

---

where approval of the quality of materials or of the standards of workmanship is a matter for the opinion of the Architect

DOM 5   4.1

---

to the extent that approval of the quality of materials or of the standards of workmanship is a matter for the opinion of the Architect

DOM 6   4.1

Sub-Contractor does carry out the Sub-Contract Works to the reasonable satisfaction of the Architect where and to the extent stipulated ?   YES / NO

The Contractor must carry out the Works shown described and referred to in the Contract Documents, to the reasonable satisfaction of the Architect: -

JCT 4   2.1

---

where approval of the quality of materials or of the standards of workmanship is a matter for the opinion of the Architect

JCT 5   2.1

---

to the extent that approval of the quality of materials or of the standards of workmanship is a matter for the opinion of the Architect

JCT 6   2.1

The Contractor may issue any reasonable direction in writing to the Sub-Contractor (or his authorised representative) in regard to the Sub-Contract Works;

DOM 42   4.2.1 & 4.4

Omnibus phrases that state "all workmanship and materials shall be to the approval of the Contractor and the Architect" should not be used in the Numbered Documents because such generalised statements would conflict with the specific statements DOM 2 to 6 which together express two things:

1. work or materials must meet the standards pre-stated or shown in the Sub-Contract Documents, or
2. work or materials must meet the specific approval of the Architect where this "approval" right is expressly reserved in the Documents.

Thus the example omnibus phrase quoted above, if used in the Numbered Documents, would be in conflict with the terms DOM 2 to 6 and, as stated in DOM 12, the terms of DOM 2 to 6 would prevail.

It is important to note that statements DOM 4/5/6 have a special relationship through statements JCT 4/5/6 to the Main Contract Final Certificate. Furthermore, the Contractor must ensure he has the Architect's approval (wherever the Architect has reserved the right to judge the standards of particular materials or of particular work) under DOM 4/5/6, before making Final Payment to the Sub-Contractor otherwise the Contractor assumes all the responsibility if disapproval subsequently occurs in respect of the materials or work so reserved

---

The Final Payment, where made in accordance with DOM clause 21.9, must be conclusive evidence that: -

DOM 751   21.10.1

---

the standard of workmanship or the quality of materials are to the reasonable satisfaction of the Architect where the same are required to be to his satisfaction

DOM 752   21.10.1.1

The Sub-Contractor must forthwith comply with any direction referred to in statements DOM 42/3/4

DOM 54   4.3

The Contractor may issue a notice to the Sub-Contractor (by registered post or recorded delivery, specifying the default) if the Sub-Contractor defaults in any one or more of the following respects: -

DOM 903   29.1

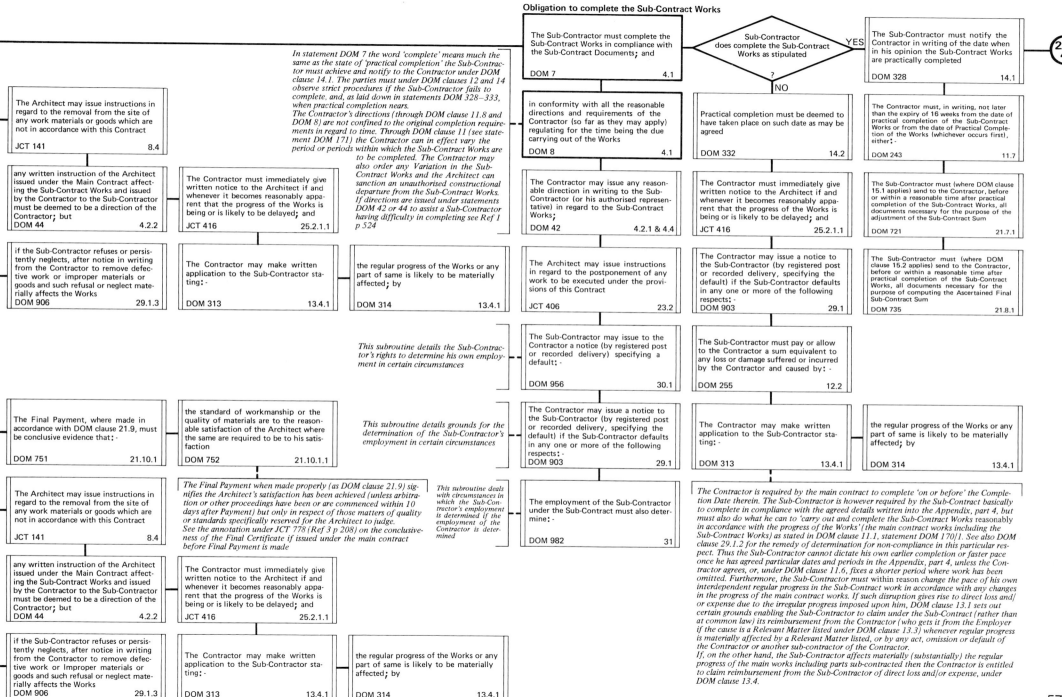

Obligation to complete the Sub-Contract Works

The Sub-Contractor must complete the Sub-Contract Works in compliance with the Sub-Contract Documents; and

DOM 7   4.1

in conformity with all the reasonable directions and requirements of the Contractor (so far as they may apply) regulating for the time being the due carrying out of the Works

DOM 8   4.1

Sub-Contractor does complete the Sub-Contract Works as stipulated ? — **YES**

NO

The Sub-Contractor must notify the Contractor in writing of the date when in his opinion the Sub-Contract Works are practically completed

DOM 328   14.1

2 & 4.1

In statement DOM 7 the word 'complete' means much the same as the state of 'practical completion' the Sub-Contractor must achieve and notify to the Contractor under DOM clause 14.1. The parties must under DOM clauses 12 and 14 observe strict procedures if the Sub-Contractor fails to complete, and, as laid down in statements DOM 328–333, when practical completion nears.
The Contractor's directions (through DOM clause 11.8 and DOM 8) are not confined to the original completion requirements in regard to time. Through DOM clause 11 (see statement DOM 171) the Contractor can in effect vary the period or periods within which the Sub-Contract Works are to be completed. The Contractor may also order any Variation in the Sub-Contract Works and the Architect can sanction an unauthorised constructional departure from the Sub-Contract Works. If directions are issued under statements DOM 42 or 44 to assist a Sub-Contractor having difficulty in completing see Ref 1 p 524

The Architect may issue instructions in regard to the removal from the site of any work materials or goods which are not in accordance with this Contract

JCT 141   8.4

any written instruction of the Architect issued under the Main Contract affecting the Sub-Contract Works and issued by the Contractor to the Sub-Contractor must be deemed to be a direction of the Contractor; but

DOM 44   4.2.2

if the Sub-Contractor refuses or persistently neglects, after notice in writing from the Contractor to remove defective work or improper materials or goods and such refusal or neglect materially affects the Works

DOM 906   29.1.3

The Contractor must immediately give written notice to the Architect if and whenever it becomes reasonably apparent that the progress of the Works is being or is likely to be delayed; and

JCT 416   25.2.1.1

The Contractor may make written application to the Sub-Contractor stating: -

DOM 313   13.4.1

the regular progress of the Works or any part of same is likely to be materially affected; by

DOM 314   13.4.1

This subroutine details the Sub-Contractor's rights to determine his own employment in certain circumstances

---

The Contractor may issue any reasonable direction in writing to the Sub-Contractor (or his authorised representative) in regard to the Sub-Contract Works;

DOM 42   4.2.1 & 4.4

The Architect may issue instructions in regard to the postponement of any work to be executed under the provisions of this Contract

JCT 406   23.2

The Sub-Contractor may issue to the Contractor a notice (by registered post or recorded delivery) specifying a default: -

DOM 956   30.1

The Contractor may issue a notice to the Sub-Contractor (by registered post or recorded delivery, specifying the default) if the Sub-Contractor defaults in any one or more of the following respects: -

DOM 903   29.1

The employment of the Sub-Contractor under the Sub-Contract must also determine: -

DOM 982   31

Practical completion must be deemed to have taken place on such date as may be agreed

DOM 332   14.2

The Contractor must immediately give written notice to the Architect if and whenever it becomes reasonably apparent that the progress of the Works is being or is likely to be delayed; and

JCT 416   25.2.1.1

The Contractor may issue a notice to the Sub-Contractor (by registered post or recorded delivery, specifying the default) if the Sub-Contractor defaults in any one or more of the following respects: -

DOM 903   29.1

The Sub-Contractor must pay or allow to the Contractor a sum equivalent to any loss or damage suffered or incurred by the Contractor and caused by: -

DOM 255   12.2

The Contractor may make written application to the Sub-Contractor stating: -

DOM 313   13.4.1

The Contractor must, in writing, not later than the expiry of 16 weeks from the date of practical completion of the Sub-Contract Works or from the date of Practical Completion of the Works (whichever occurs first), either: -

DOM 243   11.7

The Sub-Contractor must (where DOM clause 15.1 applies) send to the Contractor, before or within a reasonable time after practical completion of the Sub-Contract Works, all documents necessary for the purpose of the adjustment of the Sub-Contract Sum

DOM 721   21.7.1

The Sub-Contractor must (where DOM clause 15.2 applies) send to the Contractor, before or within a reasonable time after practical completion of the Sub-Contract Works, all documents necessary for the purpose of computing the Ascertained Final Sub-Contract Sum

DOM 735   21.8.1

the regular progress of the Works or any part of same is likely to be materially affected; by

DOM 314   13.4.1

The Final Payment, where made in accordance with DOM clause 21.9, must be conclusive evidence that: -

DOM 751   21.10.1

The Architect may issue instructions in regard to the removal from the site of any work materials or goods which are not in accordance with this Contract

JCT 141   8.4

any written instruction of the Architect issued under the Main Contract affecting the Sub-Contract Works and issued by the Contractor to the Sub-Contractor must be deemed to be a direction of the Contractor; but

DOM 44   4.2.2

if the Sub-Contractor refuses or persistently neglects, after notice in writing from the Contractor to remove defective work or Improper materials or goods and such refusal or neglect materially affects the Works

DOM 906   29.1.3

---

the standard of workmanship or the quality of materials are to the reasonable satisfaction of the Architect where the same are required to be to his satisfaction

DOM 752   21.10.1.1

The Final Payment when made properly (as DOM clause 21.9) signifies the Architect's satisfaction has been achieved (unless arbitration or other proceedings have been or are commenced within 10 days after Payment) but only in respect of those matters of quality or standards specifically reserved for the Architect to judge.
See the annotation under JCT 778 (Ref 3 p 208) on the conclusiveness of the Final Certificate if issued under the main contract before Final Payment is made

The Contractor must immediately give written notice to the Architect if and whenever it becomes reasonably apparent that the progress of the Works is being or is likely to be delayed; and

JCT 416   25.2.1.1

The Contractor may make written application to the Sub-Contractor stating: -

DOM 313   13.4.1

This subroutine details grounds for the determination of the Sub-Contractor's employment in certain circumstances

This subroutine deals with circumstances in which the Sub-Contractor's employment is determined if the employment of the Contractor is determined

the regular progress of the Works or any part of same is likely to be materially affected; by

DOM 314   13.4.1

The Contractor is required by the main contract to complete 'on or before' the Completion Date therein. The Sub-Contractor is however required by the Sub-Contract basically to complete in compliance with the agreed details written into the Appendix, part 4, but must also do what he can to 'carry out and complete the Sub-Contract Works reasonably in accordance with the progress of the Works' (the main contract works including the Sub-Contract Works) as stated in DOM clause 11.1, statement DOM 170/1. See also DOM clause 29.1.2 for the remedy of determination for non-compliance in this particular respect. Thus the Sub-Contractor cannot dictate his own earlier completion or faster pace once he has agreed particular dates and periods in the Appendix, part 4, unless the Contractor agrees, or, under DOM clause 11.6, fixes a shorter period where work has been omitted. Furthermore, the Sub-Contractor must within reason change the pace of his own interdependent regular progress in the Sub-Contract work in accordance with any changes in the progress of the main contract works. If such disruption gives rise to direct loss and/or expense due to the irregular progress imposed upon him, DOM clause 13.1 sets out certain grounds enabling the Sub-Contractor to claim under the Sub-Contract (rather than at common law) its reimbursement from the Contractor (who gets it from the Employer if the cause is a Relevant Matter listed under DOM clause 13.3) whenever regular progress is materially affected by a Relevant Matter listed, or by any act, omission or default of the Contractor or another sub-contractor of the Contractor.
If, on the other hand, the Sub-Contractor affects materially (substantially) the regular progress of the main works including parts sub-contracted then the Contractor is entitled to claim reimbursement from the Sub-Contractor of direct loss and/or expense, under DOM clause 13.4.

57

Clauses 2 & 4.1 (contd) SUB-CONTRACT DOCUMENTS

2 & 4.1

Documents other than Sub-Contract Documents

Nothing contained in any descriptive schedule or other like document issued in connection with and for use in carrying out the Sub-Contract Works must impose any obligation beyond those imposed by the Sub-Contract Documents

DOM 9   2.1.2

Sub-Contract DOM/1 and the Numbered Documents constitute the Sub-Contract Documents

DOM 1   2.1.1

These provisions deal with irregularities in or between the various Sub-Contract Documents (ie, between Sub-Contract DOM/1 and the Numbered Documents). Firstly, statement DOM 9 deals with documents not ranking at all as Sub-Contract Documents. The words in DOM 9 debar any such further subordinate or supplementary documents from being effectively used as repositories for contradictory or more onerous terms than those contained in the "Documents" identified in statement DOM 1.
Secondly, statements DOM 10–15 deal with any discrepancies in or divergences between the Main Contract, Sub-Contract DOM/1 and the Numbered Documents; granting all the Sub-Contract Documents' terms priority over the provisions of the Main Contract and granting the Sub-Contract DOM/1 terms priority over terms in the Numbered Documents; finally, granting the Appendix priority over the printed Conditions (ie, clauses 1 to 37 of DOM/1)

the quality and quantity of the work included in the Sub-Contract Sum or Tender Sum must be deemed to be that which is set out in the bills of quantities;

DOM 546   18.1.3

where bills of quantities are a Sub-Contract Document;

DOM 537   18.1

Where bills of quantities are not a ("Numbered") Sub-Contract Document their contents (preliminaries, preambles etc) cannot impose any obligation beyond those contained in the declared Sub-Contract Documents, such as in Numbered drawings and specifications. Non-contractual bills of quantities should be clearly shown to be subordinate and the quantities to be provisional or approximate. The rules for remeasurement, if that is the parties' intention, should also be made clear

Discrepancies in or divergencies between documents

The Sub-Contractor must immediately give to the Contractor a written notice, if he finds any: -

DOM 16   2.3

discrepancy in the Sub-Contract Documents and any directions issued by the Contractor;

DOM 17   2.3

except insofar as any such direction requires a Variation

DOM 18   2.3

The intention of this provision is to oblige the Sub-Contractor to tell the Contractor if he finds any technical or quantity discrepancy or differences existing in or between the Sub-Contract Documents, also, if he finds any divergence between other documents or parts of them.
However, this does not make the Sub-Contractor responsible for seeking out hidden errors. But if the Sub-Contractor happens to find any unintended variance then he must give to the Contractor the stipulated notice referred to in statement DOM 23. Furthermore, there is in DOM clause 5.1.1 an obligation to notify divergence between Statutory Requirements and Contract Drawings, Bills etc.
Any errors therefore which could be classed as obvious to an experienced sub-contractor must not go unnoticed by the Sub-Contractor under this clause for he has an obligation to report the matter. Any error not obvious to any experienced sub-contractor must be reported if discovered; if it is not discovered the Contractor cannot hold the Sub-Contractor responsible under this clause for abortive work etc in connection with such an error.
A Variation will usually involve an intentional change or difference to whatever was previously documented therefore statements DOM 18 and 20 obviously exclude from these procedures the reporting of intended differences resulting when Variations are required

Direction does require a Variation

? YES

Relationship of Sub-Contract Documents

The terms of the Sub-Contract Documents must prevail if any conflict appears between: -

DOM 10   2.2

the terms of the Sub-Contract Documents and the provisions of the Main Contract

DOM 11   2.2

Are the provisions of the Main Contract in conflict with the terms of the Sub-Contract Documents

? NO / YES

The Contractor is responsible for any unintended mistakes or for gaps in liability or obligations arising for him from the application of the terms of the Sub-Contract Documents where they do not correspond with the provisions of the Main Contract

The terms of the Sub-Contract DOM/1 must prevail if any conflict appears between: -

DOM 12   2.2

the terms of Sub-Contract DOM/1 and the Numbered Documents

DOM 13   2.2

Are the terms of Sub-Contract DOM/1 in conflict with the Numbered Documents

? NO / YES

For example, where bills of quantities are a Numbered Document the terms of clause 18 in the Sub-Contract DOM/1 will prevail requiring the Contractor to carry quantity errors etc and to carry the risk of any departure from the SMM of Building Works unless the departure etc was by the Contractor otherwise specifically dealt with as strictly laid down in DOM clause 18.1.1 (statement DOM 538)

The Appendix must prevail if any conflict appears between: -

DOM14   2.2

the Appendix and the Sub-Contract Conditions

DOM 15   2.2

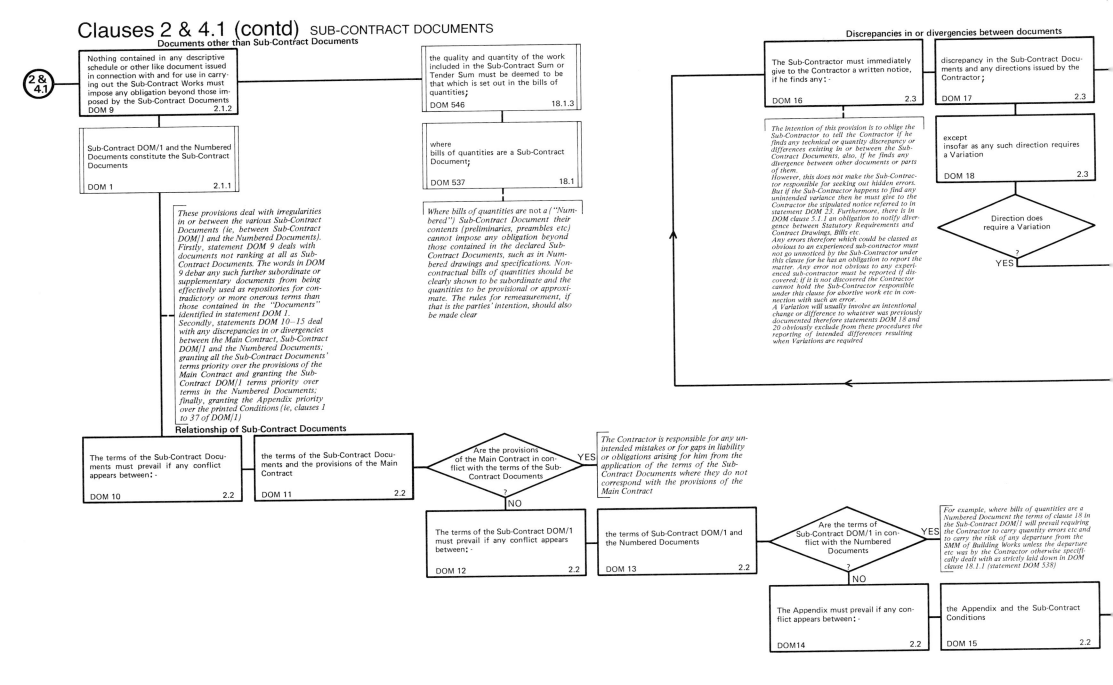

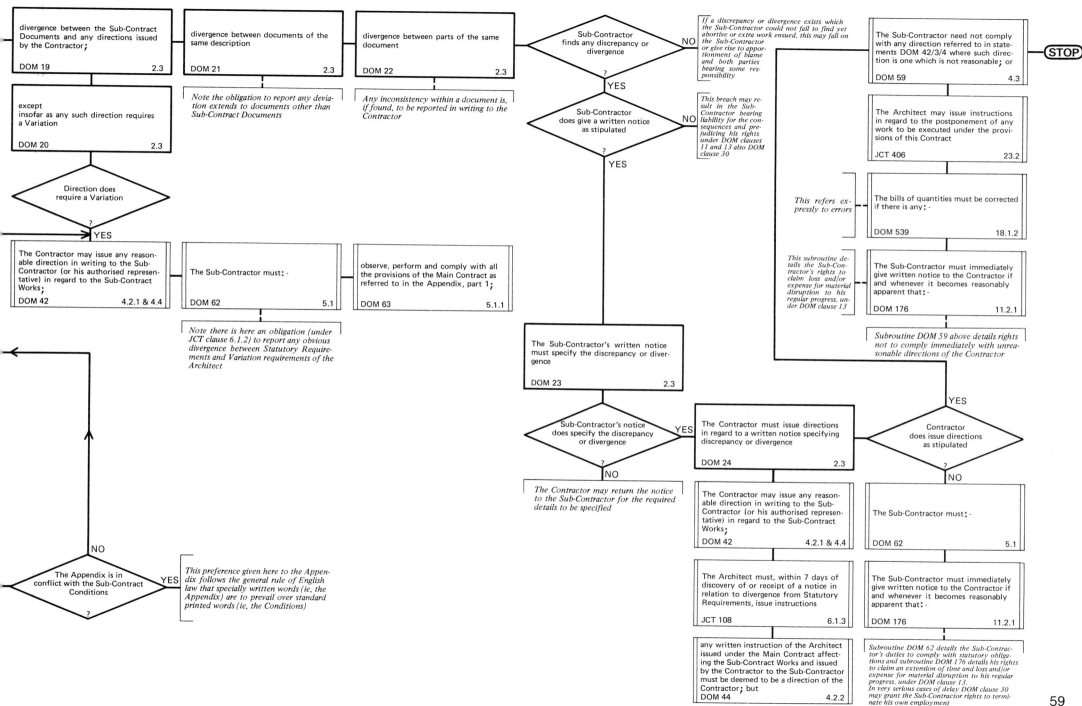

divergence between the Sub-Contract Documents and any directions issued by the Contractor;

DOM 19   2.3

---

except insofar as any such direction requires a Variation

DOM 20   2.3

---

divergence between documents of the same description

DOM 21   2.3

Note the obligation to report any deviation extends to documents other than Sub-Contract Documents

---

divergence between parts of the same document

DOM 22   2.3

Any inconsistency within a document is, if found, to be reported in writing to the Contractor

---

Sub-Contractor finds any discrepancy or divergence
?   NO
YES

If a discrepancy or divergence exists which the Sub-Contractor could not fail to find yet abortive or extra work ensued, this may fall on the Sub-Contractor or give rise to apportionment of blame and both parties bearing some responsibility

---

The Sub-Contractor need not comply with any direction referred to in statements DOM 42/3/4 where such direction is one which is not reasonable; or

DOM 59   4.3

(STOP)

Sub-Contractor does give a written notice as stipulated
?   NO
YES

This breach may result in the Sub-Contractor bearing liability for the consequences and prejudicing his rights under DOM clauses 11 and 13 also DOM clause 30

The Architect may issue instructions in regard to the postponement of any work to be executed under the provisions of this Contract

JCT 406   23.2

Direction does require a Variation
?
YES

This refers expressly to errors

The bills of quantities must be corrected if there is any: -

DOM 539   18.1.2

The Contractor may issue any reasonable direction in writing to the Sub-Contractor (or his authorised representative) in regard to the Sub-Contract Works;

DOM 42   4.2.1 & 4.4

The Sub-Contractor must: -

DOM 62   5.1

Note there is here an obligation (under JCT clause 6.1.2) to report any obvious divergence between Statutory Requirements and Variation requirements of the Architect

---

observe, perform and comply with all the provisions of the Main Contract as referred to in the Appendix, part 1;

DOM 63   5.1.1

This subroutine details the Sub-Contractor's rights to claim loss and/or expense for material disruption to his regular progress, under DOM clause 13

The Sub-Contractor must immediately give written notice to the Contractor if and whenever it becomes reasonably apparent that: -

DOM 176   11.2.1

Subroutine DOM 59 above details rights not to comply immediately with unreasonable directions of the Contractor

---

The Sub-Contractor's written notice must specify the discrepancy or divergence

DOM 23   2.3

The Appendix is in conflict with the Sub-Contract Conditions
?   YES
NO

This preference given here to the Appendix follows the general rule of English law that specially written words (ie, the Appendix) are to prevail over standard printed words (ie, the Conditions)

Sub-Contractor's notice does specify the discrepancy or divergence
?   YES
NO

The Contractor may return the notice to the Sub-Contractor for the required details to be specified

---

The Contractor must issue directions in regard to a written notice specifying discrepancy or divergence

DOM 24   2.3

Contractor does issue directions as stipulated
?   YES
NO

The Contractor may issue any reasonable direction in writing to the Sub-Contractor (or his authorised representative) in regard to the Sub-Contract Works;

DOM 42   4.2.1 & 4.4

The Sub-Contractor must: -

DOM 62   5.1

The Architect must, within 7 days of discovery of or receipt of a notice in relation to divergence from Statutory Requirements, issue instructions

JCT 108   6.1.3

The Sub-Contractor must immediately give written notice to the Contractor if and whenever it becomes reasonably apparent that: -

DOM 176   11.2.1

---

any written instruction of the Architect issued under the Main Contract affecting the Sub-Contract Works and issued by the Contractor to the Sub-Contractor must be deemed to be a direction of the Contractor; but

DOM 44   4.2.2

---

*Subroutine DOM 62 details the Sub-Contractor's duties to comply with statutory obligations and subroutine DOM 176 details his rights to claim an extension of time and loss and/or expense for material disruption to his regular progress, under DOM clause 13.
In very serious cases of delay DOM clause 30 may grant the Sub-Contractor rights to terminate his own employment*

Clauses 3 & 15 PRICE FOR SUB-CONTRACT WORKS

Sub-Contract Sum

START

The price for the Sub-Contract Works must be:-

DOM 25   15.1

the Sub-Contract Sum; or

DOM 26   15.1

The provisions of clause 16.3 must be applied in the valuation of:-

DOM 354   16.1

There is an obligation (DOM 683 and 721) to submit all necessary documents and any details necessary, before practical completion if prompt and correct interim or final ascertainment and agreement is to be reached for payment purposes under DOM 29/30/31 and DOM 745/6

This DOM clause 15 deals with the situation where either:
*   a Sub-Contract Sum (lump sum) has been accepted under Article 2.1*
or a Tender Sum (measure-and-value) has been accepted under Article 2.2.
In either case DOM clause 3 combines with this clause 15 to provide for the Sub-Contractor receiving, in the next interim payment, all the sums to be ascertained as stated in DOM clause 21.3 (DOM 686 to 700) as soon as such amounts are agreed in whole or in part. Note DOM clause 3 does not refer to either the first or Final Payment.
The quality and quantity of work to be carried out by the Sub-Contractor in return for the Sub-Contract Sum is that set out in the Sub-Contract bills of quantities. If bills are not used as a Sub-Contract Document, the Documents referred to in statement DOM 1 (ie, the Numbered Documents) will set out the scope and standard of the work included for in the tendered Sum. Where alternatively a measure-and-value Sum is tendered (under DOM clause 15.2 and Article 2.2) the price to become payable is established by measurement and valuation of "all work executed by the Sub-Contractor", as stated in DOM clause 17.1; the documents referred to in statement DOM 1 (ie, the Numbered Documents) showing the scope and standard of the work to be executed.
Since the Sub-Contract also contains provisions in DOM clause 13 for settling claims for direct loss etc due to disruption to regular progress, and for Variations (under DOM clause 16 or 17) in the quality and quantity of work to be carried out, the financial sums involved may vary and the (lump) Sum will therefore require adding to or deducting from; or, in the case of a measure-and-value agreement, the Sum will require ascertaining, as the Works progress. Furthermore, in either case the conditions of working etc may require rates and prices to be varied and other financial adjustments of preliminaries etc to be made. Agreement upon everything to both parties' financial satisfaction may therefore not be readily reached, in which case any partial ascertainment and agreement is to be paid pending establishing and agreeing the whole or final sum (see JCT Guide p 19 re clause 3). Dilatoriness in ascertaining and tardiness in reaching any sort of agreement, by the Contractor, is a breach if it results in the Sub-Contractor not being paid the proper amounts as laid down in DOM clause 21.4 (no more – no less) as he goes along as soon as they can reasonably in the particular circumstances be ascertained and agreed upon. Any properly disputed amounts may remain unpaid therefore until agreement is eventually reached. However, under Article 3.3.1 it is possible to call for an immediate hearing where it is alleged payments are being improperly withheld or are not in strict accordance with the Sub-Contract (for further annotation on this see Ref 3 p 91).
It is not the intention of clause 3 to enable the Contractor to offer the Sub-Contractor a part payment in full and final settlement of a whole claim made for instance under DOM clause 13.1. Such actions would be in breach of the Sub-Contractor's rights here to prompt payment of any ascertained (substantiated) part of a claim etc, without prejudicing his rights to the unagreed remainder

such other sum as shall become payable in accordance with the Sub-Contract;

DOM 27   15.1

The Sub-Contract Sum, where DOM clause 15.1 applies, must be adjusted as follows:-

DOM 722   21.7.2

where Article 2.1 applies

DOM 28   15.1

◇ **Article 2.1 does apply** → NO

YES ▸ ## Sub-Contract Sum — additions or deductions

Where in Sub-Contract DOM/1 it is provided that an amount is to be added to or subtracted from the Sub-Contract Sum, then:-

DOM 29   3

as soon as such amount is ascertained and agreed in part the amount must be taken into account in the computation of the next interim payment following partial ascertainment

DOM 30   3

as soon as such amount is ascertained and agreed in whole the amount must be taken into account in the computation of the next interim payment following whole ascertainment

DOM 31   3

◇ **Amounts are added to or subtracted from the Sub-Contract Sum and included in the next interim payment** → YES / NO

Interim payments must be due at intervals not exceeding one month;

DOM 681   21.2.2

Subroutines DOM 681 and 686 detail when and what payments are due, stating exactly what amounts are to be added together (or deducted) to arrive at the interim correct total amount due. The total is to include the valuation of Variations, unfixed materials and goods, direct loss and/or expense under DOM clause 13.1, fluctuations, and certain other sundry sums that might have arisen under the Main Contract. It is then to be partly subject to certain Retentions until the making good of defective work (if any) has been certified as completed.
The Contractor does have limited rights to set-off amounts owed to him by the Sub-Contractor but only where such amounts are mutually agreed. Any disputed amounts may be successfully set-off if the Contractor satisfies all the strict requirements of DOM clause 23 and obtains the Adjudicator's agreement in cases where he is called upon by the Sub-Contractor to decide the matter, under DOM clause 24

The Sub-Contractor is here entitled to payment for sums ascertained and agreed in whole. The whole amount may eventually prove less than the sum of the parts ascertained and agreed earlier under DOM 30 (or 33). In such cases the correction may favour either party and the previous part sums paid seem clearly not intended to be conclusive and finally settled until the amount as a whole is here established. Interim payments are, when made, not normally binding in respect of standards of workmanship, quality of materials or financial sums or measured quantities. They are intended to be temporary sums subject to final adjustment (see DOM clause 21 statements DOM 722 and DOM 736)

The Sub-Contractor may suspend the further execution of the Sub-Contract Works:-

DOM 707   21.6

Arbitration before completion is available here (see Article 3.3.1)

The amount of the first and each interim payment to the Sub-Contractor must be the gross valuation of the following amounts:-

DOM 686   21.3

The Sub-Contract Sum, where DOM clause 15.1 applies, must be adjusted as follows:-

DOM 722   21.7.2

This details all the additions and deductions to be made to adjust the Sub-Contract Sum as the Works proceed

Certain adjustable sums exist already within the Sub-Contract Sum and here are required to be adjusted as soon as any part of same can be ascertained

Where in Sub-Contract DOM/1 it is provided that an amount is to be dealt with by adjustment of the Sub-Contract Sum, then:-

DOM 32   3

as soon as such amount is ascertained and agreed in part the amount must be taken into account in the computation of the next interim payment following partial ascertainment

DOM 33   3

as soon as such amount is ascertained and agreed in whole the amount must be taken into account in the computation of the next interim payment following whole ascertainment

DOM 34   3

◇ **Amounts are dealt with by adjustment and included in the next interim payment** → YES / NO

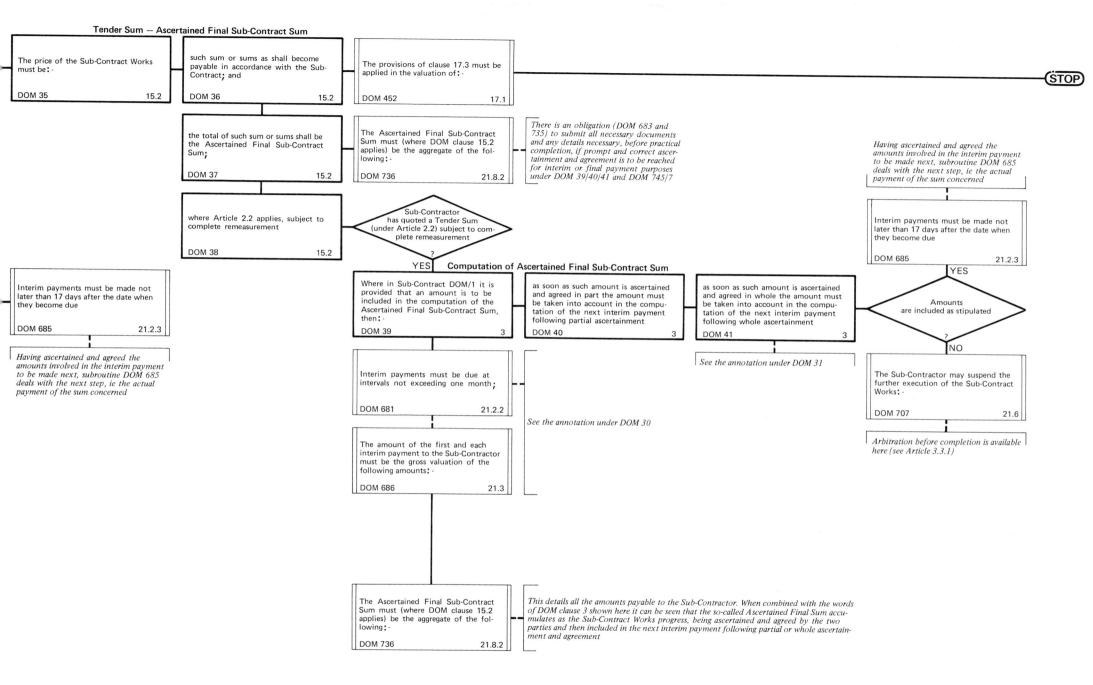

Tender Sum — Ascertained Final Sub-Contract Sum

The price of the Sub-Contract Works must be: -

DOM 35   15.2

such sum or sums as shall become payable in accordance with the Sub-Contract; and

DOM 36   15.2

The provisions of clause 17.3 must be applied in the valuation of: -

DOM 452   17.1

STOP

the total of such sum or sums shall be the Ascertained Final Sub-Contract Sum;

DOM 37   15.2

The Ascertained Final Sub-Contract Sum must (where DOM clause 15.2 applies) be the aggregate of the following: -

DOM 736   21.8.2

There is an obligation (DOM 683 and 735) to submit all necessary documents and any details necessary, before practical completion, if prompt and correct ascertainment and agreement is to be reached for interim or final payment purposes under DOM 39/40/41 and DOM 745/7

Having ascertained and agreed the amounts involved in the interim payment to be made next, subroutine DOM 685 deals with the next step, ie the actual payment of the sum concerned

where Article 2.2 applies, subject to complete remeasurement

DOM 38   15.2

Sub-Contractor has quoted a Tender Sum (under Article 2.2) subject to complete remeasurement ?

Interim payments must be made not later than 17 days after the date when they become due

DOM 685   21.2.3

YES   **Computation of Ascertained Final Sub-Contract Sum**

Interim payments must be made not later than 17 days after the date when they become due

DOM 685   21.2.3

Having ascertained and agreed the amounts involved in the interim payment to be made next, subroutine DOM 685 deals with the next step, ie the actual payment of the sum concerned

Where in Sub-Contract DOM/1 it is provided that an amount is to be included in the computation of the Ascertained Final Sub-Contract Sum, then: -

DOM 39   3

as soon as such amount is ascertained and agreed in part the amount must be taken into account in the computation of the next interim payment following partial ascertainment

DOM 40   3

as soon as such amount is ascertained and agreed in whole the amount must be taken into account in the computation of the next interim payment following whole ascertainment

DOM 41   3

YES

Amounts are included as stipulated ?

NO

See the annotation under DOM 31

The Sub-Contractor may suspend the further execution of the Sub-Contract Works: -

DOM 707   21.6

Interim payments must be due at intervals not exceeding one month;

DOM 681   21.2.2

See the annotation under DOM 30

The amount of the first and each interim payment to the Sub-Contractor must be the gross valuation of the following amounts: -

DOM 686   21.3

Arbitration before completion is available here (see Article 3.3.1)

The Ascertained Final Sub-Contract Sum must (where DOM clause 15.2 applies) be the aggregate of the following: -

DOM 736   21.8.2

This details all the amounts payable to the Sub-Contractor. When combined with the words of DOM clause 3 shown here it can be seen that the so-called Ascertained Final Sum accumulates as the Sub-Contract Works progress, being ascertained and agreed by the two parties and then included in the next interim payment following partial or whole ascertainment and agreement

61

Directions of Contractor

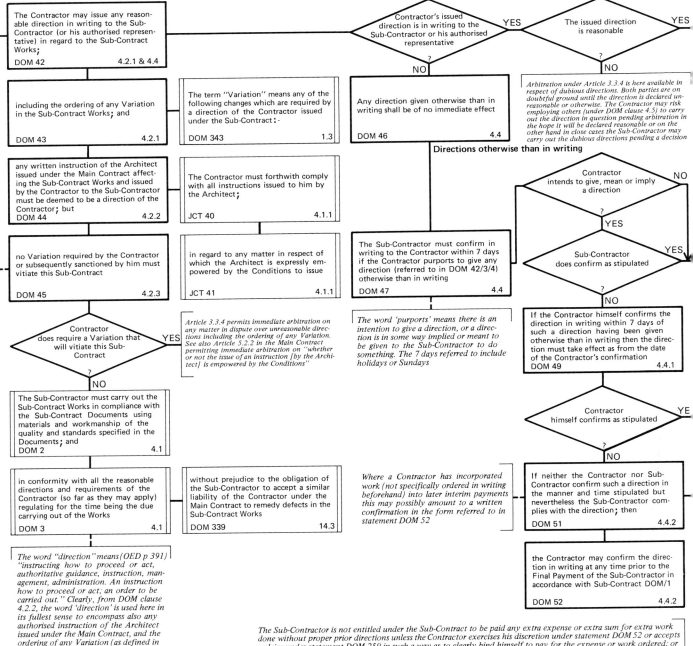

START

DOM clause 4.4 refers to an "authorised representative" of the Sub-Contractor, indicating (as is usual in the industry) a person may be delegated to have the power to receive directions. However, other much wider duties and authority may be granted by the Sub-Contractor to his representative, subject of course to Head Office supervision and control. The Sub-Contractor should define for the Contractor any authority, additional to simply receiving DOM clause 4.2 directions but short of full and complete authority, delegated to his representative (eg, not to agree rates or prices nor settle the Final account), otherwise the Contractor might be entitled to assume a representative has full authority to act for the Sub-Contractor, and make binding agreements, if it appears the representative has complete authority. In any case the Sub-Contractor is liable to the Contractor (and third parties) for the acts of his authorised representatives (or any other employee) but would not be bound if a representative exceeded either his apparent, or his actual, authority. Although DOM clause 4.2 states directions must be given to the "Sub-Contractor" as stated above, from DOM clause 4.4, they may instead be given to his "authorised representative". This facility is however confined to "any direction referred to in clause 4.2". Therefore, in the case of any default (eg, DOM clause 29.1) or other application (eg, under DOM clause 13.4) notice should be sent to the Sub-Contractor himself, strictly in accordance with the particular Conditions.

Drawings or sketches will constitute a direction "in writing", provided they clearly show in an instructive manner whatever the Contractor requires the Sub-Contractor to do. The power to issue directions does not entitle the Contractor to govern or dictate the speed methods or sequence of working of the Sub-Contractor unless his methods etc do not comply with or follow the methods etc already laid down in the Numbered Documents (eg, in the specification), or his speed of working is not reasonably in accordance with the progress of the Main Contract Works (see DOM clause 11.1), in which case the Contractor would be entitled to direct the Sub-Contractor under statement DOM 175.

Statement DOM 54 requires the Sub-Contractor to "forthwith comply" with any direction of the Contractor but only if they are reasonable. The word "forthwith" means "immediately, at once, without delay (SOED p 740). Failure to respond immediately to a reasonable direction is therefore a breach entitling the Contractor, in this clause, to employ others to put into effect the direction and charge the cost to the Sub-Contractor.

This clause recognises the difficulties arising from unnoticeable variations and the inherent reluctance of some Contractors to promptly commit to writing their Variation orders. There are therefore provisions in this clause enabling the Sub-Contractor in effect to write out the "direction" for the Contractor. The clause also recognises both parties may overlook this Sub-Contract's (DOM 42) need for all directions to be written down before the additional or varied works should be done (see Ref 1 p 536), so, statement DOM 52 enables works done without prior written confirmation to be sanctioned afterwards but not if the Contractor refuses to exercise his discretion, in DOM 52

These words endeavour to prevent the Sub-Contractor claiming that a substantial addition, alteration or omission has resulted in something he had not bargained for thus entitling him to refuse the Variation concerned or to seek to renegotiate the Sub-Contract on new financial terms. The Contractor cannot however fundamentally alter the character of the Sub-Contract by a Variation, without the Sub-Contractor being allowed to claim the right to rescind the Sub-Contract

The word "direction" means (OED p 391) "instructing how to proceed or act, authoritative guidance, instruction, management, administration. An instruction how to proceed or act; an order to be carried out." Clearly, from DOM clause 4.2.2, the word 'direction' is used here in its fullest sense to encompass also any authorised instruction of the Architect issued under the Main Contract, and the ordering of any Variation (as defined in DOM clause 1.3)

The Contractor may issue any reasonable direction in writing to the Sub-Contractor (or his authorised representative) in regard to the Sub-Contract Works;
DOM 42   4.2.1 & 4.4

including the ordering of any Variation in the Sub-Contract Works; and
DOM 43   4.2.1

any written instruction of the Architect issued under the Main Contract affecting the Sub-Contract Works and issued by the Contractor to the Sub-Contractor must be deemed to be a direction of the Contractor; but
DOM 44   4.2.2

no Variation required by the Contractor or subsequently sanctioned by him must vitiate this Sub-Contract
DOM 45   4.2.3

Contractor does require a Variation that will vitiate this Sub-Contract — YES / NO

The Sub-Contractor must carry out the Sub-Contract Works in compliance with the Sub-Contract Documents using materials and workmanship of the quality and standards specified in the Documents; and
DOM 2   4.1

in conformity with all the reasonable directions and requirements of the Contractor (so far as they may apply) regulating for the time being the due carrying out of the Works
DOM 3   4.1

The term "Variation" means any of the following changes which are required by a direction of the Contractor issued under the Sub-Contract:-
DOM 343   1.3

The Contractor must forthwith comply with all instructions issued to him by the Architect;
JCT 40   4.1.1

in regard to any matter in respect of which the Architect is expressly empowered by the Conditions to issue
JCT 41   4.1.1

Article 3.3.4 permits immediate arbitration on any matter in dispute over unreasonable directions including the ordering of any Variation. See also Article 5.2.2 in the Main Contract permitting immediate arbitration on "whether or not the issue of an instruction [by the Architect] is empowered by the Conditions"

without prejudice to the obligation of the Sub-Contractor to accept a similar liability of the Contractor under the Main Contract to remedy defects in the Sub-Contract Works
DOM 339   14.3

Contractor's issued direction is in writing to the Sub-Contractor or his authorised representative ? — YES / NO

Any direction given otherwise than in writing shall be of no immediate effect
DOM 46   4.4

Directions otherwise than in writing

The Sub-Contractor must confirm in writing to the Contractor within 7 days if the Contractor purports to give any direction (referred to in DOM 42/3/4) otherwise than in writing
DOM 47   4.4

The word 'purports' means there is an intention to give a direction, or a direction is in some way implied or meant to be given to the Sub-Contractor to do something. The 7 days referred to include holidays or Sundays

Where a Contractor has incorporated work (not specifically ordered in writing beforehand) into later interim payments this may possibly amount to a written confirmation in the form referred to in statement DOM 52

The issued direction is reasonable ? — YES / NO

Arbitration under Article 3.3.4 is here available in respect of doubtful directions. Both parties are on doubtful ground until the direction is declared unreasonable or otherwise. The Contractor may risk employing others (under DOM clause 4.5) to carry out the direction in question pending arbitration in the hope it will be declared reasonable or on the other hand in close cases the Sub-Contractor may carry out the dubious directions pending a decision

Contractor intends to give, mean or imply a direction ? — YES / NO

Sub-Contractor does confirm as stipulated ? — YES / NO

If the Contractor himself confirms the direction in writing within 7 days of such a direction having been given otherwise than in writing then the direction must take effect as from the date of the Contractor's confirmation
DOM 49   4.4.1

Contractor himself confirms as stipulated ? — YES / NO

If neither the Contractor nor Sub-Contractor confirm such a direction in the manner and time stipulated but nevertheless the Sub-Contractor complies with the direction; then
DOM 51   4.4.2

the Contractor may confirm the direction in writing at any time prior to the Final Payment of the Sub-Contractor in accordance with Sub-Contract DOM/1
DOM 52   4.4.2

The Sub-Contractor is not entitled under the Sub-Contract to be paid any extra expense or extra sum for extra work done without proper prior directions unless the Contractor exercises his discretion under statement DOM 52 or accepts a claim under statement DOM 259 in such a way as to clearly bind himself to pay for the expense or work ordered; or unless the extra work done is in the form of quantities to be remeasured in any case; or includes quantities (necessary to achieve the Works documented) exceeding the amounts originally contained in any Numbered bills. See however the principles in Evans Ltd v Andrea Merzario Ltd [1976] 1 WLR 1078, 1081 (CA) in which oral agreements were held to be binding even though express terms stated differently

Sub-Contractor to comply with directions

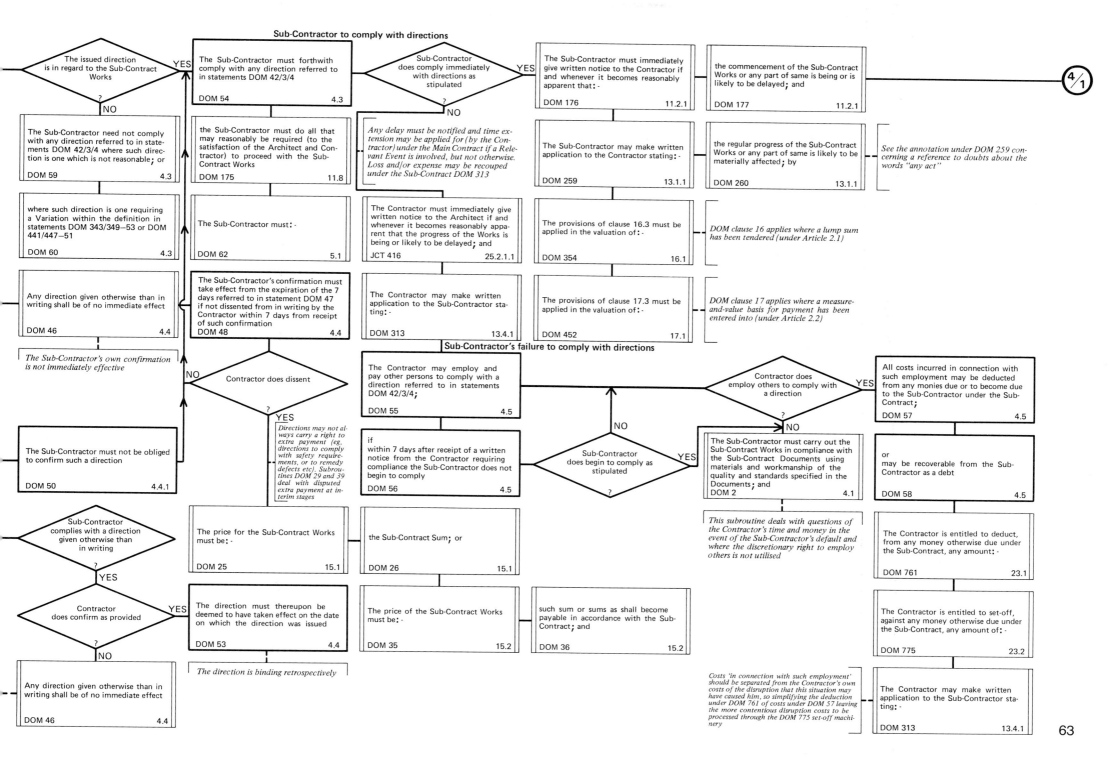

The issued direction is in regard to the Sub-Contract Works ? **YES**

The Sub-Contractor must forthwith comply with any direction referred to in statements DOM 42/3/4

DOM 54   4.3

Sub-Contractor does comply immediately with directions as stipulated ? **YES**   **NO**

The Sub-Contractor must immediately give written notice to the Contractor if and whenever it becomes reasonably apparent that: -

DOM 176   11.2.1

the commencement of the Sub-Contract Works or any part of same is being or is likely to be delayed; and

DOM 177   11.2.1

NO

The Sub-Contractor need not comply with any direction referred to in statements DOM 42/3/4 where such direction is one which is not reasonable; or

DOM 59   4.3

the Sub-Contractor must do all that may reasonably be required (to the satisfaction of the Architect and Contractor) to proceed with the Sub-Contract Works

DOM 175   11.8

Any delay must be notified and time extension may be applied for (by the Contractor) under the Main Contract if a Relevant Event is involved, but not otherwise. Loss and/or expense may be recouped under the Sub-Contract DOM 313

The Sub-Contractor may make written application to the Contractor stating: -

DOM 259   13.1.1

the regular progress of the Sub-Contract Works or any part of same is likely to be materially affected; by

DOM 260   13.1.1

See the annotation under DOM 259 concerning a reference to doubts about the words "any act"

where such direction is one requiring a Variation within the definition in statements DOM 343/349–53 or DOM 441/447–51

DOM 60   4.3

The Sub-Contractor must: -

DOM 62   5.1

The Contractor must immediately give written notice to the Architect if and whenever it becomes reasonably apparent that the progress of the Works is being or likely to be delayed; and

JCT 416   25.2.1.1

The provisions of clause 16.3 must be applied in the valuation of: -

DOM 354   16.1

DOM clause 16 applies where a lump sum has been tendered (under Article 2.1)

Any direction given otherwise than in writing shall be of no immediate effect

DOM 46   4.4

The Sub-Contractor's confirmation must take effect from the expiration of the 7 days referred to in statement DOM 47 if not dissented from in writing by the Contractor within 7 days from receipt of such confirmation

DOM 48   4.4

The Contractor may make written application to the Sub-Contractor stating: -

DOM 313   13.4.1

The provisions of clause 17.3 must be applied in the valuation of: -

DOM 452   17.1

DOM clause 17 applies where a measure-and-value basis for payment has been entered into (under Article 2.2)

The Sub-Contractor's own confirmation is not immediately effective

Contractor does dissent ? **NO**   **YES**

Sub-Contractor's failure to comply with directions

The Contractor may employ and pay other persons to comply with a direction referred to in statements DOM 42/3/4;

DOM 55   4.5

Contractor does employ others to comply with a direction ? **NO**   **YES**

All costs incurred in connection with such employment may be deducted from any monies due or to become due to the Sub-Contractor under the Sub-Contract;

DOM 57   4.5

Directions may not always carry a right to extra payment (eg, directions to comply with safety requirements, or to remedy defects etc). Subroutines DOM 29 and 39 deal with disputed extra payment at interim stages

The Sub-Contractor must not be obliged to confirm such a direction

DOM 50   4.4.1

if within 7 days after receipt of a written notice from the Contractor requiring compliance the Sub-Contractor does not begin to comply

DOM 56   4.5

Sub-Contractor does begin to comply as stipulated ? **NO**   **YES**

The Sub-Contractor must carry out the Sub-Contract Works in compliance with the Sub-Contract Documents using materials and workmanship of the quality and standards specified in the Documents; and

DOM 2   4.1

or may be recoverable from the Sub-Contractor as a debt

DOM 58   4.5

Sub-Contractor complies with a direction given otherwise than in writing ? **YES**

The price for the Sub-Contract Works must be: -

DOM 25   15.1

the Sub-Contract Sum; or

DOM 26   15.1

This subroutine deals with questions of the Contractor's time and money in the event of the Sub-Contractor's default and where the discretionary right to employ others is not utilised

The Contractor is entitled to deduct, from any money otherwise due under the Sub-Contract, any amount: -

DOM 761   23.1

Contractor does confirm as provided ? **YES**   **NO**

The direction must thereupon be deemed to have taken effect on the date on which the direction was issued

DOM 53   4.4

The price of the Sub-Contract Works must be: -

DOM 35   15.2

such sum or sums as shall become payable in accordance with the Sub-Contract; and

DOM 36   15.2

The Contractor is entitled to set-off, against any money otherwise due under the Sub-Contract, any amount of: -

DOM 775   23.2

Any direction given otherwise than in writing shall be of no immediate effect

DOM 46   4.4

The direction is binding retrospectively

Costs 'in connection with such employment' should be separated from the Contractor's own costs of the disruption that this situation may have caused him, so simplifying the deduction under DOM 761 of costs under DOM 57 leaving the more contentious disruption costs to be processed through the DOM 775 set-off machinery

The Contractor may make written application to the Sub-Contractor stating: -

DOM 313   13.4.1

4/1

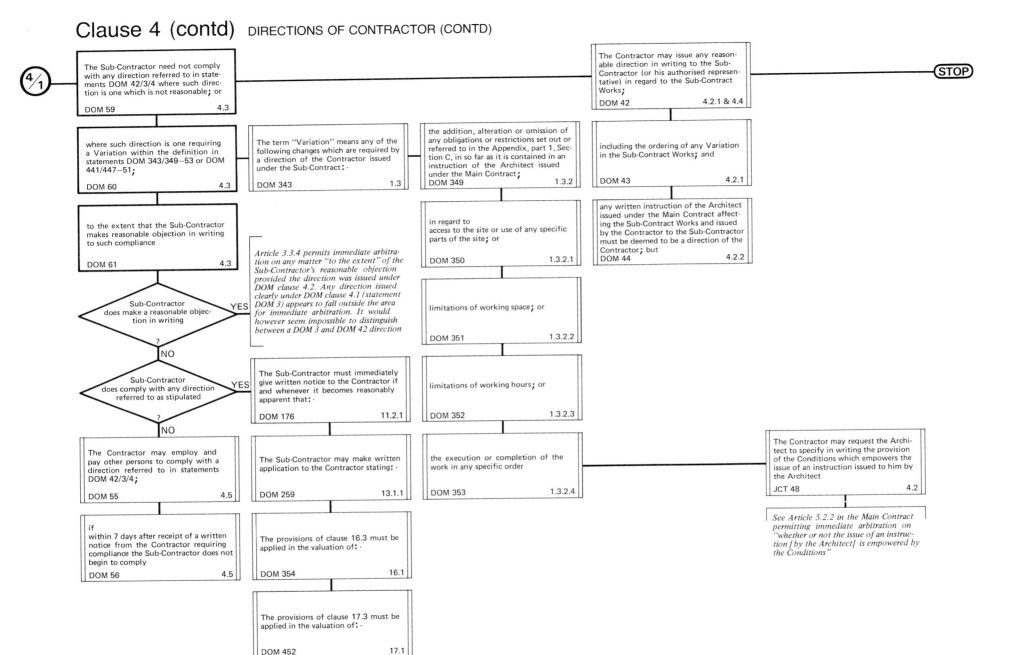

4/1

The Sub-Contractor need not comply with any direction referred to in statements DOM 42/3/4 where such direction is one which is not reasonable; or

DOM 59   4.3

where such direction is one requiring a Variation within the definition in statements DOM 343/349—53 or DOM 441/447—51;

DOM 60   4.3

to the extent that the Sub-Contractor makes reasonable objection in writing to such compliance

DOM 61   4.3

Sub-Contractor does make a reasonable objection in writing ? — YES / NO

Sub-Contractor does comply with any direction referred to as stipulated ? — YES / NO

The Contractor may employ and pay other persons to comply with a direction referred to in statements DOM 42/3/4;

DOM 55   4.5

if within 7 days after receipt of a written notice from the Contractor requiring compliance the Sub-Contractor does not begin to comply

DOM 56   4.5

Article 3.3.4 permits immediate arbitration on any matter "to the extent" of the Sub-Contractor's reasonable objection provided the direction was issued under DOM clause 4.2. Any direction issued clearly under DOM clause 4.1 (statement DOM 3) appears to fall outside the area for immediate arbitration. It would however seem impossible to distinguish between a DOM 3 and DOM 42 direction

The term "Variation" means any of the following changes which are required by a direction of the Contractor issued under the Sub-Contract:-

DOM 343   1.3

The Sub-Contractor must immediately give written notice to the Contractor if and whenever it becomes reasonably apparent that:-

DOM 176   11.2.1

The Sub-Contractor may make written application to the Contractor stating:-

DOM 259   13.1.1

The provisions of clause 16.3 must be applied in the valuation of:-

DOM 354   16.1

The provisions of clause 17.3 must be applied in the valuation of:-

DOM 452   17.1

the addition, alteration or omission of any obligations or restrictions set out or referred to in the Appendix, part 1, Section C, in so far as it is contained in an instruction of the Architect issued under the Main Contract;

DOM 349   1.3.2

in regard to access to the site or use of any specific parts of the site; or

DOM 350   1.3.2.1

limitations of working space; or

DOM 351   1.3.2.2

limitations of working hours; or

DOM 352   1.3.2.3

the execution or completion of the work in any specific order

DOM 353   1.3.2.4

The Contractor may issue any reasonable direction in writing to the Sub-Contractor (or his authorised representative) in regard to the Sub-Contract Works;

DOM 42   4.2.1 & 4.4

including the ordering of any Variation in the Sub-Contract Works; and

DOM 43   4.2.1

any written instruction of the Architect issued under the Main Contract affecting the Sub-Contract Works and issued by the Contractor to the Sub-Contractor must be deemed to be a direction of the Contractor; but

DOM 44   4.2.2

The Contractor may request the Architect to specify in writing the provision of the Conditions which empowers the issue of an instruction issued to him by the Architect

JCT 48   4.2

See Article 5.2.2 in the Main Contract permitting immediate arbitration on "whether or not the issue of an instruction [by the Architect] is empowered by the Conditions"

STOP

Sub-Contractor to observe etc all provisions of Main Contract

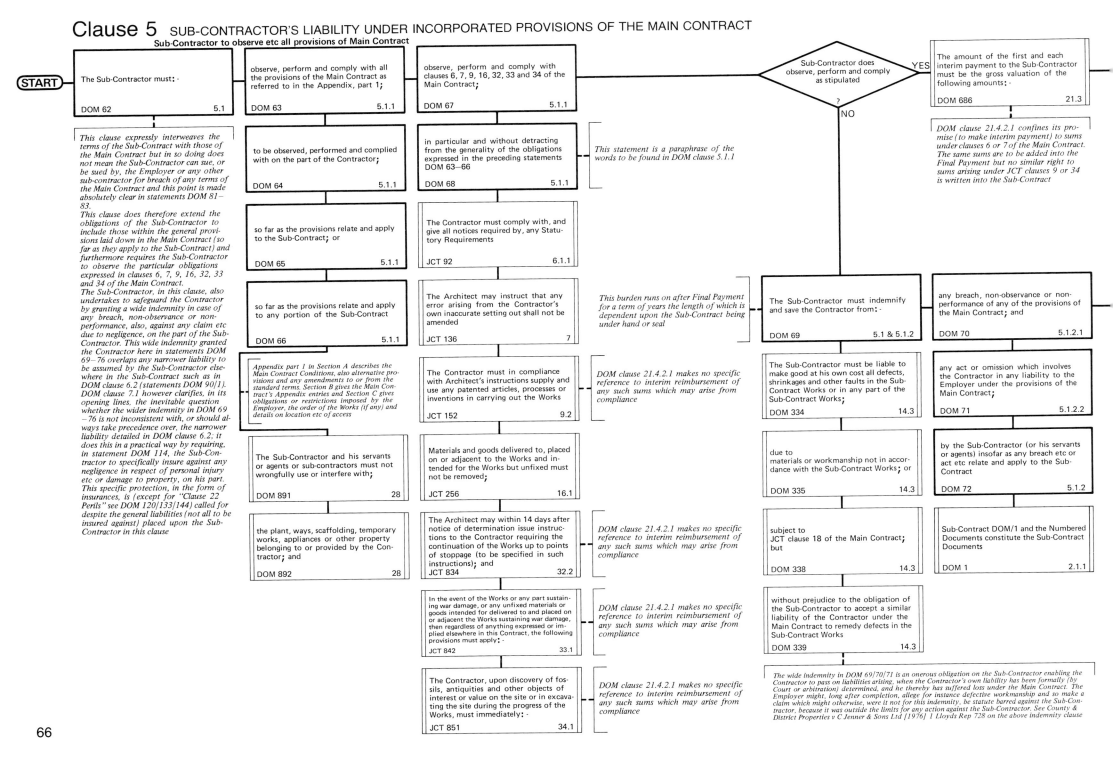

START

The Sub-Contractor must: -	observe, perform and comply with all the provisions of the Main Contract as referred to in the Appendix, part 1;	observe, perform and comply with clauses 6, 7, 9, 16, 32, 33 and 34 of the Main Contract;	Sub-Contractor does observe, perform and comply as stipulated ?	The amount of the first and each interim payment to the Sub-Contractor must be the gross valuation of the following amounts: -
DOM 62 5.1	DOM 63 5.1.1	DOM 67 5.1.1	YES / NO	DOM 686 21.3

This clause expressly interweaves the terms of the Sub-Contract with those of the Main Contract but in so doing does not mean the Sub-Contractor can sue, or be sued by, the Employer or any other sub-contractor for breach of any terms of the Main Contract and this point is made absolutely clear in statements DOM 81–83.

This clause does therefore extend the obligations of the Sub-Contractor to include those within the general provisions laid down in the Main Contract (so far as they apply to the Sub-Contract) and furthermore requires the Sub-Contractor to observe the particular obligations expressed in clauses 6, 7, 9, 16, 32, 33 and 34 of the Main Contract.

The Sub-Contractor, in this clause, also undertakes to safeguard the Contractor by granting a wide indemnity in case of any breach, non-observance or non-performance, also, against any claim etc due to negligence, on the part of the Sub-Contractor. This wide indemnity granted the Contractor here in statements DOM 69–76 overlaps any narrower liability to be assumed by the Sub-Contractor elsewhere in the Sub-Contract such as in DOM clause 6.2 (statements DOM 90/1). DOM clause 7.1 however clarifies, in its opening lines, the inevitable question whether the wider indemnity in DOM 69–76 is not inconsistent with, or should always take precedence over, the narrower liability detailed in DOM clause 6.2; it does this in a practical way by requiring, in statement DOM 114, the Sub-Contractor to specifically insure against any negligence in respect of personal injury etc or damage to property, on his part. This specific protection, in the form of insurances, is (except for "Clause 22 Perils" see DOM 120/133/144) called for despite the general liabilities (not all to be insured against) placed upon the Sub-Contractor in this clause

to be observed, performed and complied with on the part of the Contractor;	in particular and without detracting from the generality of the obligations expressed in the preceding statements DOM 63–66	*This statement is a paraphrase of the words to be found in DOM clause 5.1.1*
DOM 64 5.1.1	DOM 68 5.1.1	

so far as the provisions relate and apply to the Sub-Contract; or	The Contractor must comply with, and give all notices required by, any Statutory Requirements	
DOM 65 5.1.1	JCT 92 6.1.1	

so far as the provisions relate and apply to any portion of the Sub-Contract	The Architect may instruct that any error arising from the Contractor's own inaccurate setting out shall not be amended	*This burden runs on after Final Payment for a term of years the length of which is dependent upon the Sub-Contract being under hand or seal*	The Sub-Contractor must indemnify and save the Contractor from: -	any breach, non-observance or non-performance of any of the provisions of the Main Contract; and
DOM 66 5.1.1	JCT 136 7		DOM 69 5.1 & 5.1.2	DOM 70 5.1.2.1

Appendix part 1 in Section A describes the Main Contract Conditions, also alternative provisions and any amendments to or from the standard terms. Section B gives the Main Contract's Appendix entries and Section C gives obligations or restrictions imposed by the Employer, the order of the Works (if any) and details on location etc of access	The Contractor must in compliance with Architect's instructions supply and use any patented articles, processes or inventions in carrying out the Works	*DOM clause 21.4.2.1 makes no specific reference to interim reimbursement of any such sums which may arise from compliance*	The Sub-Contractor must be liable to make good at his own cost all defects, shrinkages and other faults in the Sub-Contract Works or in any part of the Sub-Contract Works;	any act or omission which involves the Contractor in any liability to the Employer under the provisions of the Main Contract;
	JCT 152 9.2		DOM 334 14.3	DOM 71 5.1.2.2

The Sub-Contractor and his servants or agents or sub-contractors must not wrongfully use or interfere with;	Materials and goods delivered to, placed on or adjacent to the Works and intended for the Works but unfixed must not be removed;		due to materials or workmanship not in accordance with the Sub-Contract Works; or	by the Sub-Contractor (or his servants or agents) insofar as any breach etc or act etc relate and apply to the Sub-Contract
DOM 891 28	JCT 256 16.1		DOM 335 14.3	DOM 72 5.1.2

the plant, ways, scaffolding, temporary works, appliances or other property belonging to or provided by the Contractor; and	The Architect may within 14 days after notice of determination issue instructions to the Contractor requiring the continuation of the Works up to points of stoppage (to be specified in such instructions); and	*DOM clause 21.4.2.1 makes no specific reference to interim reimbursement of any such sums which may arise from compliance*	subject to JCT clause 18 of the Main Contract; but	Sub-Contract DOM/1 and the Numbered Documents constitute the Sub-Contract Documents
DOM 892 28	JCT 834 32.2		DOM 338 14.3	DOM 1 2.1.1

In the event of the Works or any part sustaining war damage, or any unfixed materials or goods intended for delivered to and placed on or adjacent the Works sustaining war damage, then regardless of anything expressed or implied elsewhere in this Contract, the following provisions must apply: -	*DOM clause 21.4.2.1 makes no specific reference to interim reimbursement of any such sums which may arise from compliance*	without prejudice to the obligation of the Sub-Contractor to accept a similar liability of the Contractor under the Main Contract to remedy defects in the Sub-Contract Works
JCT 842 33.1		DOM 339 14.3

The Contractor, upon discovery of fossils, antiquities and other objects of interest or value on the site or in excavating the site during the progress of the Works, must immediately: -	*DOM clause 21.4.2.1 makes no specific reference to interim reimbursement of any such sums which may arise from compliance*
JCT 851 34.1	

DOM clause 21.4.2.1 confines its promise (to make interim payment) to sums under clauses 6 or 7 of the Main Contract. The same sums are to be added into the Final Payment but no similar right to sums arising under JCT clauses 9 or 34 is written into the Sub-Contract

The wide indemnity in DOM 69/70/71 is an onerous obligation on the Sub-Contractor enabling the Contractor to pass on liabilities arising, when the Contractor's own liability has been formally (by Court or arbitration) determined, and he thereby has suffered loss under the Main Contract. The Employer might, long after completion, allege for instance defective workmanship and so make a claim which might otherwise, were it not for this indemnity, be statute barred against the Sub-Contractor, because it was outside the limits for any action against the Sub-Contractor. See County & District Properties v C Jenner & Sons Ltd [1976] 1 Lloyds Rep 728 on the above indemnity clause

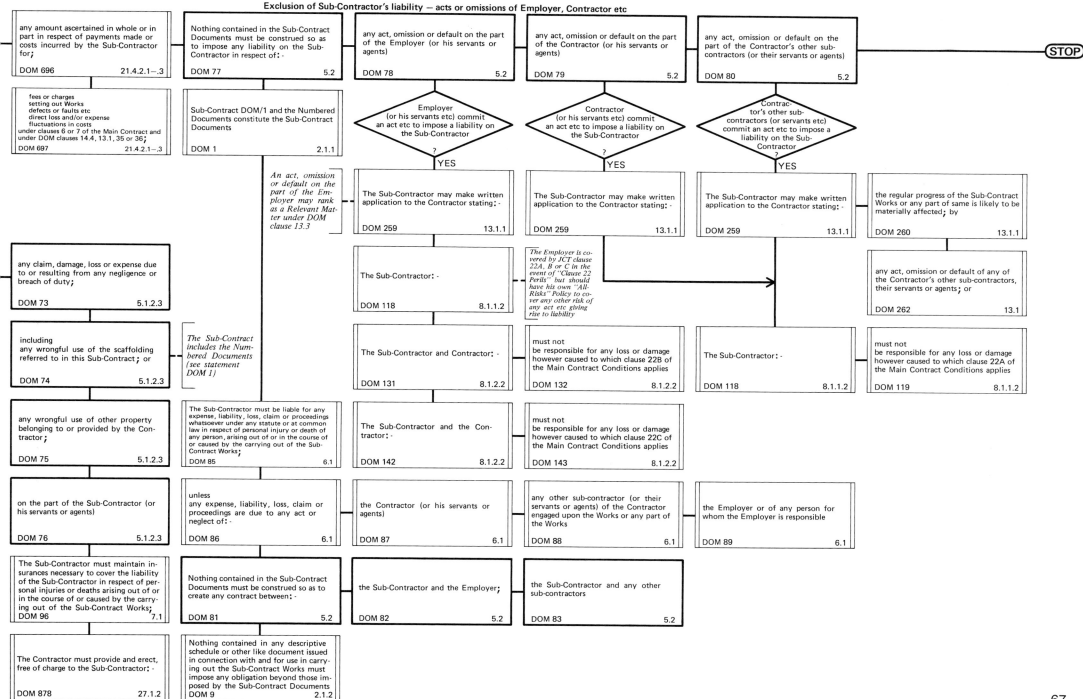

Row 1 (top boxes):

any amount ascertained in whole or in part in respect of payments made or costs incurred by the Sub-Contractor for;
DOM 696   21.4.2.1—.3

Nothing contained in the Sub-Contract Documents must be construed so as to impose any liability on the Sub-Contractor in respect of:-
DOM 77   5.2

any act, omission or default on the part of the Employer (or his servants or agents)
DOM 78   5.2

any act, omission or default on the part of the Contractor (or his servants or agents)
DOM 79   5.2

any act, omission or default on the part of the Contractor's other sub-contractors (or their servants or agents)
DOM 80   5.2

(STOP)

Row 2:

fees or charges
setting out Works
defects or faults etc
direct loss and/or expense
fluctuations in costs
under clauses 6 or 7 of the Main Contract and under DOM clauses 14.4, 13.1, 35 or 36;
DOM 697   21.4.2.1—.3

Sub-Contract DOM/1 and the Numbered Documents constitute the Sub-Contract Documents
DOM 1   2.1.1

Employer (or his servants etc) commit an act etc to impose a liability on the Sub-Contractor ?
YES

Contractor (or his servants etc) commit an act etc to impose a liability on the Sub-Contractor ?
YES

Contractor's other sub-contractors (or servants etc) commit an act etc to impose a liability on the Sub-Contractor ?
YES

Row 3:

An act, omission or default on the part of the Employer may rank as a Relevant Matter under DOM clause 13.3

The Sub-Contractor may make written application to the Contractor stating:-
DOM 259   13.1.1

The Sub-Contractor may make written application to the Contractor stating:-
DOM 259   13.1.1

The Sub-Contractor may make written application to the Contractor stating:-
DOM 259   13.1.1

the regular progress of the Sub-Contract Works or any part of same is likely to be materially affected; by
DOM 260   13.1.1

Row 4:

any claim, damage, loss or expense due to or resulting from any negligence or breach of duty;
DOM 73   5.1.2.3

The Sub-Contractor:-
DOM 118   8.1.1.2

The Employer is covered by JCT clause 22A, B or C in the event of "Clause 22 Perils" but should have his own "All-Risks" Policy to cover any other risk of any act etc giving rise to liability

any act, omission or default of any of the Contractor's other sub-contractors, their servants or agents; or
DOM 262   13.1

Row 5:

including
any wrongful use of the scaffolding referred to in this Sub-Contract; or
DOM 74   5.1.2.3

The Sub-Contract includes the Numbered Documents (see statement DOM 1)

The Sub-Contractor and Contractor:-
DOM 131   8.1.2.2

must not be responsible for any loss or damage however caused to which clause 22B of the Main Contract Conditions applies
DOM 132   8.1.2.2

The Sub-Contractor:-
DOM 118   8.1.1.2

must not be responsible for any loss or damage however caused to which clause 22A of the Main Contract Conditions applies
DOM 119   8.1.1.2

Row 6:

any wrongful use of other property belonging to or provided by the Contractor;
DOM 75   5.1.2.3

The Sub-Contractor must be liable for any expense, liability, loss, claim or proceedings whatsoever under any statute or at common law in respect of personal injury or death of any person, arising out of or in the course of or caused by the carrying out of the Sub-Contract Works;
DOM 85   6.1

The Sub-Contractor and the Contractor:-
DOM 142   8.1.2.2

must not be responsible for any loss or damage however caused to which clause 22C of the Main Contract Conditions applies
DOM 143   8.1.2.2

Row 7:

on the part of the Sub-Contractor (or his servants or agents)
DOM 76   5.1.2.3

unless
any expense, liability, loss, claim or proceedings are due to any act or neglect of:-
DOM 86   6.1

the Contractor (or his servants or agents)
DOM 87   6.1

any other sub-contractor (or their servants or agents) of the Contractor engaged upon the Works or any part of the Works
DOM 88   6.1

the Employer or of any person for whom the Employer is responsible
DOM 89   6.1

Row 8:

The Sub-Contractor must maintain insurances necessary to cover the liability of the Sub-Contractor in respect of personal injuries or deaths arising out of or in the course of or caused by the carrying out of the Sub-Contract Works;
DOM 96   7.1

Nothing contained in the Sub-Contract Documents must be construed so as to create any contract between:-
DOM 81   5.2

the Sub-Contractor and the Employer;
DOM 82   5.2

the Sub-Contractor and any other sub-contractors
DOM 83   5.2

Row 9:

The Contractor must provide and erect, free of charge to the Sub-Contractor:-
DOM 878   27.1.2

Nothing contained in any descriptive schedule or other like document issued in connection with and for use in carrying out the Sub-Contract Works must impose any obligation beyond those imposed by the Sub-Contract Documents
DOM 9   2.1.2

Indemnity to Contractor — personal injury

Liability of Sub-Contractor — personal injury

(START)

The Sub-Contractor must indemnify the Contractor against any expense, liability, loss, claim or proceedings whatsoever under any statute or at common law in respect of personal injury or death to any person, arising out of or in the course of or caused by the carrying out of the Sub-Contract Works

DOM 84   6.1

Sub-Contractor does indemnify the Contractor as stipulated ? — **YES** / **NO**

The Sub-Contractor must be liable for any expense, liability, loss, claim or proceedings whatsoever under any statute or at common law in respect of personal injury or death of any person, arising out of or in the course of or caused by the carrying out of the Sub-Contract Works;

DOM 85   6.1

English Law (Unfair Contract Terms Act etc) does not allow in general an indemnity to be written against loss from one's own negligence, hence the total indemnity written in DOM 84 and the very wide indemnity written in DOM 90/1. The Contractor is therefore granted legal exemption here from proceedings involving such claims made against the Sub-Contractor unless any act or neglect of the Contractor, another of his sub-contractors, or the Employer, is involved in which case liability may be apportioned.

The clause is therefore a declaration of liabilities:

  (i) for claims for injuries or death of any person (including the Sub-Contractor's own employees) arising out of the Sub-Contract Works

and (ii) for damage to any property (or possessions) arising out of the Sub-Contract Works and caused by the negligence of the Sub-Contractor.

So, the Sub-Contractor must accept total responsibility for (i) unless he can establish that there is liability on the part of the Contractor, or other sub-contractors of the Contractor, or the Employer. In the case of claims for loss or damage under (ii) the Sub-Contractor must accept responsibility only where the Contractor can establish the Sub-Contractor has been negligent etc and the loss or damage is not to the Works due to a "Clause 22 Peril" accepted by either the Contractor or Employer.

Having declared the responsibilities placed upon the Sub-Contractor clause 7 calls for insurance policies which will (by and large) cover those responsibilities. It is usual for such policies to also cover 'labour-only' persons or operatives but this should be checked to be certain.

The extent of the indemnity given in DOM clause 6.2 statement DOM 90 includes any of the Main Contractor's and other sub-contract works where the Contractor proves negligence on the part of the Sub-Contractor and the loss or damage is not to the Works due to an accepted "Clause 22 Peril". Where in the case of an existing building, clause 22C of the Main Contract applies, loss or damage to any of the Employer's tenants' contents is to be similarly carried by the Contractor or Sub-Contractor but the contents (of the existing building) owned by the Employer are at the Employer's sole risk (see JCT clause 22C.1 line 1)

The Sub-Contractor must produce and must cause any other person to produce for inspection by the Contractor documentary evidence that the insurances are properly effected and maintained, as and when he is reasonably required to do so by the Contractor, in respect of: -

DOM 100   9.1

A right of indemnity may prove worthless against a Sub-Contractor of limited means who is also uninsured or improperly covered or has contravened the terms of his insurance policy

unless
any expense, liability, loss, claim or proceedings are due to any act or neglect of: -

DOM 86   6.1

the Contractor (or his servants or agents)

DOM 87   6.1

any other sub-contractor (or their servants or agents) of the Contractor engaged upon the Works or any part of the Works

DOM 88   6.1

the Employer or of any person for whom the Employer is responsible

DOM 89   6.1

Any expense etc is due to any act etc of the Contractor etc ? — **NO** / **YES**

Any expense etc is due to any act etc of any other sub-contractor etc ? — **NO** / **YES**

Any expense etc is due to any act etc of the Employer etc ? — **NO** / **YES**

Note the difference in wording between statements DOM 89 and 78 (see also JCT 335)

The Contractor, the Architect and all persons duly authorised by either of them must at all reasonable times have access to any work which is being prepared for or will be utilised in the Sub-Contract;

DOM 864   25

Nothing contained in the Sub-Contract Documents must be construed so as to impose any liability on the Sub-Contractor in respect of: -

DOM 77   5.2

any act, omission or default on the part of the Employer (or his servants or agents)

DOM 78   5.2

The following persons must, for the purposes of the Works (but not futher or otherwise) be entitled to use in common any erected scaffolding belonging to or provided by the Contractor or Sub-Contractor while it remains erected for the purposes of the Works: -

DOM 885   27.4

See also JCT 858 which explains the position of third parties called in to examine antiquities etc

Every person so employed or otherwise engaged by the Employer must for the purpose of clause 20 be deemed to be a person for whom the Employer is responsible and not to be a sub-contractor

JCT 642   29.3

The Contractor and his servants or agents or sub-contractors must not wrongfully use or interfere with;

DOM 895   28

Nothing contained in the Sub-Contract Documents must be construed so as to impose any liability on the Sub-Contractor in respect of: -

DOM 77   5.2

any act, omission or default on the part of the Contractor's other sub-contractors (or their servants or agents)

DOM 80   5.2

the plant, ways, scaffolding, temporary works, appliances or other property belonging to or provided by the Sub-Contractor; and

DOM 896   28

Nothing contained in the Sub-Contract Documents must be construed so as to impose any liability on the Sub-Contractor in respect of: -

DOM 77   5.2

any act, omission or default on the part of the Contractor (or his servants or agents)

DOM 79   5.2

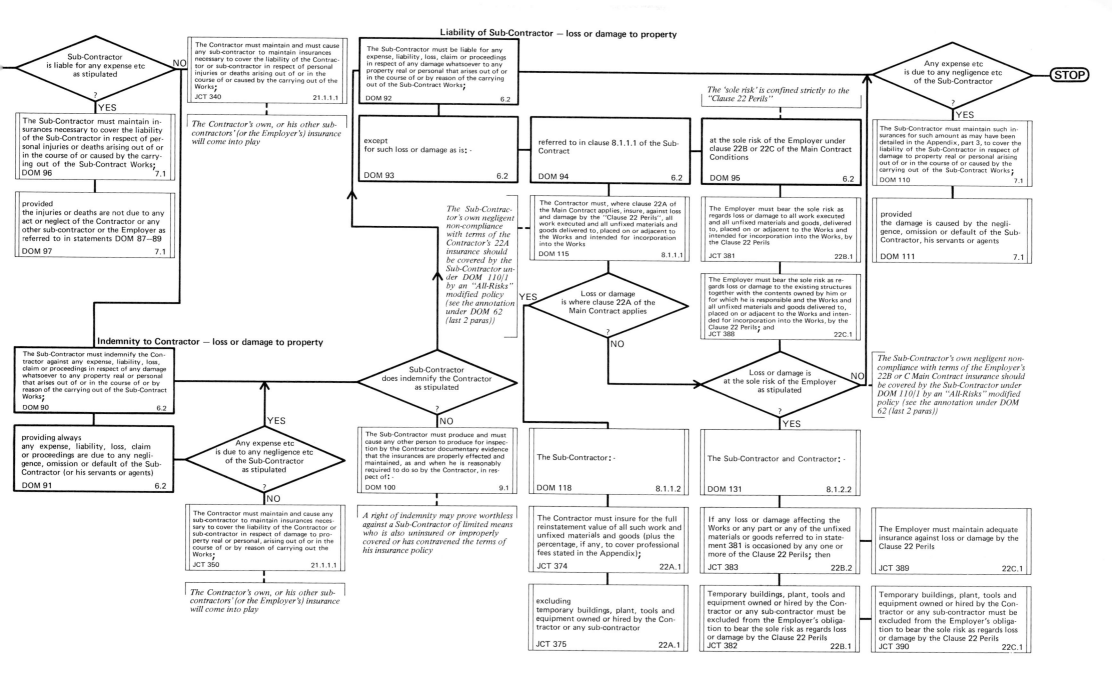

Liability of Sub-Contractor — loss or damage to property

Sub-Contractor is liable for any expense etc as stipulated? — NO / YES

The Contractor must maintain and must cause any sub-contractor to maintain insurances necessary to cover the liability of the Contractor or sub-contractor in respect of personal injuries or deaths arising out of or in the course of or caused by the carrying out of the Works;
JCT 340 — 21.1.1.1

The Contractor's own, or his other sub-contractors' (or the Employer's) insurance will come into play

The Sub-Contractor must maintain insurances necessary to cover the liability of the Sub-Contractor in respect of personal injuries or deaths arising out of or in the course of or caused by the carrying out of the Sub-Contract Works;
DOM 96 — 7.1

provided the injuries or deaths are not due to any act or neglect of the Contractor or any other sub-contractor or the Employer as referred to in statements DOM 87—89
DOM 97 — 7.1

The Sub-Contractor must be liable for any expense, liability, loss, claim or proceedings in respect of any damage whatsoever to any property real or personal that arises out of or in the course of or by reason of the carrying out of the Sub-Contract Works;
DOM 92 — 6.2

except for such loss or damage as is: -
DOM 93 — 6.2

referred to in clause 8.1.1.1 of the Sub-Contract
DOM 94 — 6.2

at the sole risk of the Employer under clause 22B or 22C of the Main Contract Conditions
DOM 95 — 6.2

The 'sole risk' is confined strictly to the "Clause 22 Perils"

Any expense etc is due to any negligence etc of the Sub-Contractor? — YES — STOP

The Sub-Contractor must maintain such insurances for such amount as may have been detailed in the Appendix, part 3, to cover the liability of the Sub-Contractor in respect of damage to property real or personal arising out of or in the course of or caused by the carrying out of the Sub-Contract Works;
DOM 110 — 7.1

provided the damage is caused by the negligence, omission or default of the Sub-Contractor, his servants or agents
DOM 111 — 7.1

The Sub-Contractor's own negligent non-compliance with terms of the Contractor's 22A insurance should be covered by the Sub-Contractor under DOM 110/1 by an "All-Risks" modified policy (see the annotation under DOM 62 (last 2 paras))

The Contractor must, where clause 22A of the Main Contract applies, insure, against loss and damage by the "Clause 22 Perils", all work executed and all unfixed materials and goods delivered to, placed on or adjacent to the Works and intended for incorporation into the Works
DOM 115 — 8.1.1.1

The Employer must bear the sole risk as regards loss or damage to all work executed and all unfixed materials and goods, delivered to, placed on or adjacent to the Works and intended for incorporation into the Works, by the Clause 22 Perils
JCT 381 — 22B.1

The Employer must bear the sole risk as regards loss or damage to the existing structures together with the contents owned by him or for which he is responsible and the Works and all unfixed materials and goods delivered to, placed on or adjacent to the Works and intended for incorporation into the Works, by the Clause 22 Perils; and
JCT 388 — 22C.1

The Sub-Contractor's own negligent non-compliance with terms of the Employer's 22B or C Main Contract insurance should be covered by the Sub-Contractor under DOM 110/1 by an "All-Risks" modified policy (see the annotation under DOM 62 (last 2 paras))

Loss or damage is where clause 22A of the Main Contract applies? — YES / NO

Indemnity to Contractor — loss or damage to property

The Sub-Contractor must indemnify the Contractor against any expense, liability, loss, claim or proceedings in respect of any damage whatsoever to any property real or personal that arises out of or in the course of or by reason of the carrying out of the Sub-Contract Works;
DOM 90 — 6.2

providing always any expense, liability, loss, claim or proceedings are due to any negligence, omission or default of the Sub-Contractor (or his servants or agents)
DOM 91 — 6.2

Any expense etc is due to any negligence etc of the Sub-Contractor as stipulated? — YES / NO

Sub-Contractor does indemnify the Contractor as stipulated? — NO

Loss or damage is at the sole risk of the Employer as stipulated? — NO / YES

The Contractor must maintain and cause any sub-contractor to maintain insurances necessary to cover the liability of the Contractor or sub-contractor in respect of damage to property real or personal, arising out of or in the course of or by reason of carrying out the Works;
JCT 350 — 21.1.1.1

The Contractor's own, or his other sub-contractors' (or the Employer's) insurance will come into play

The Sub-Contractor must produce and must cause any other person to produce for inspection by the Contractor documentary evidence that the insurances are properly effected and maintained, as and when he is reasonably required to do so by the Contractor, in respect of: -
DOM 100 — 9.1

A right of indemnity may prove worthless against a Sub-Contractor of limited means who is also uninsured or improperly covered or has contravened the terms of his insurance policy

The Sub-Contractor: -
DOM 118 — 8.1.1.2

The Sub-Contractor and Contractor: -
DOM 131 — 8.1.2.2

The Employer must maintain adequate insurance against loss or damage by the Clause 22 Perils
JCT 389 — 22C.1

The Contractor must insure for the full reinstatement value of all such work and unfixed materials and goods (plus the percentage, if any, to cover professional fees stated in the Appendix);
JCT 374 — 22A.1

If any loss or damage affecting the Works or any part or any of the unfixed materials or goods referred to in statement 381 is occasioned by any one or more of the Clause 22 Perils; then
JCT 383 — 22B.2

excluding temporary buildings, plant, tools and equipment owned or hired by the Contractor or any sub-contractor
JCT 375 — 22A.1

Temporary buildings, plant, tools and equipment owned or hired by the Contractor or any sub-contractor must be excluded from the Employer's obligation to bear the sole risk as regards loss or damage by the Clause 22 Perils
JCT 382 — 22B.1

Temporary buildings, plant, tools and equipment owned or hired by the Contractor or any sub-contractor must be excluded from the Employer's obligation to bear the sole risk as regards loss or damage by the Clause 22 Perils
JCT 390 — 22C.1

69

Clauses 7 & 9 INSURANCE – SUB-CONTRACTOR – POLICIES OF INSURANCE

Insurances for liability of Sub-Contractor for personal injury etc

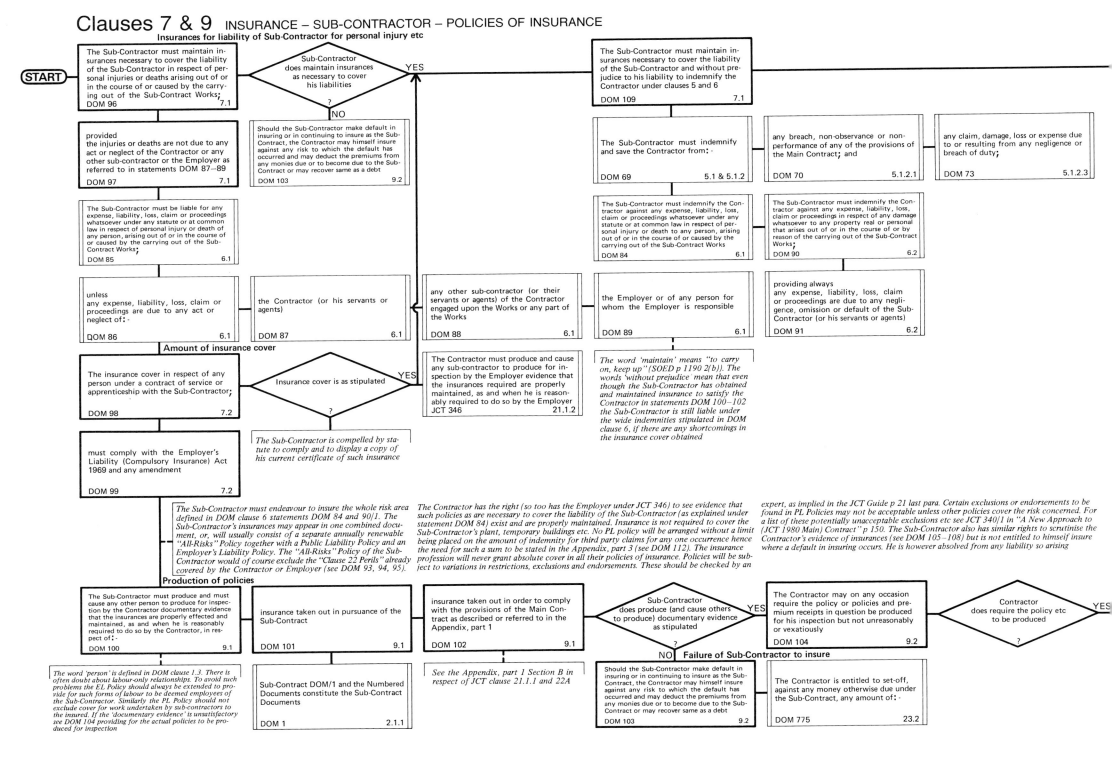

START

The Sub-Contractor must maintain insurances necessary to cover the liability of the Sub-Contractor in respect of personal injuries or deaths arising out of or in the course of or caused by the carrying out of the Sub-Contract Works;
DOM 96   7.1

provided
the injuries or deaths are not due to any act or neglect of the Contractor or any other sub-contractor or the Employer as referred to in statements DOM 87–89
DOM 97   7.1

The Sub-Contractor must be liable for any expense, liability, loss, claim or proceedings whatsoever under any statute or at common law in respect of personal injury or death of any person, arising out of or in the course of or caused by the carrying out of the Sub-Contract Works;
DOM 85   6.1

unless
any expense, liability, loss, claim or proceedings are due to any act or neglect of: -
DOM 86   6.1

the Contractor (or his servants or agents)
DOM 87   6.1

Sub-Contractor does maintain insurances as necessary to cover his liabilities ? NO / YES

Should the Sub-Contractor make default in insuring or in continuing to insure as the Sub-Contract, the Contractor may himself insure against any risk to which the default has occurred and may deduct the premiums from any monies due or to become due to the Sub-Contract or may recover same as a debt
DOM 103   9.2

any other sub-contractor (or their servants or agents) of the Contractor engaged upon the Works or any part of the Works
DOM 88   6.1

The Contractor must produce and cause any sub-contractor to produce for inspection by the Employer evidence that the insurances required are properly maintained, as and when he is reasonably required to do so by the Employer
JCT 346   21.1.2

Amount of insurance cover

The insurance cover in respect of any person under a contract of service or apprenticeship with the Sub-Contractor;
DOM 98   7.2

must comply with the Employer's Liability (Compulsory Insurance) Act 1969 and any amendment
DOM 99   7.2

Insurance cover is as stipulated ? YES

The Sub-Contractor is compelled by statute to comply and to display a copy of his current certificate of such insurance

The Sub-Contractor must maintain insurances necessary to cover the liability of the Sub-Contractor and without prejudice to his liability to indemnify the Contractor under clauses 5 and 6
DOM 109   7.1

The Sub-Contractor must indemnify and save the Contractor from: -
DOM 69   5.1 & 5.1.2

The Sub-Contractor must indemnify the Contractor against any expense, liability, loss, claim or proceedings whatsoever under any statute or at common law in respect of personal injury or death to any person, arising out of or in the course of or caused by the carrying out of the Sub-Contract Works
DOM 84   6.1

the Employer or of any person for whom the Employer is responsible
DOM 89   6.1

The word 'maintain' means "to carry on, keep up" (SOED p 1190 2(b)). The words 'without prejudice' mean that even though the Sub-Contractor has obtained and maintained insurance to satisfy the Contractor in statements DOM 100–102 the Sub-Contractor is still liable under the wide indemnities stipulated in DOM clause 6, if there are any shortcomings in the insurance cover obtained

any breach, non-observance or non-performance of any of the provisions of the Main Contract; and
DOM 70   5.1.2.1

any claim, damage, loss or expense due to or resulting from any negligence or breach of duty;
DOM 73   5.1.2.3

The Sub-Contractor must indemnify the Contractor against any expense, liability, loss, claim or proceedings in respect of any damage whatsoever to any property real or personal that arises out of or in the course of or by reason of the carrying out of the Sub-Contract Works;
DOM 90   6.2

providing always
any expense, liability, loss, claim or proceedings are due to any negligence, omission or default of the Sub-Contractor (or his servants or agents)
DOM 91   6.2

The Sub-Contractor must endeavour to insure the whole risk area defined in DOM clause 6 statements DOM 84 and 90/1. The Sub-Contractor's insurances may appear in one combined document, or, will usually consist of a separate annually renewable "All-Risks" Policy together with a Public Liability Policy and an Employer's Liability Policy. The "All-Risks" Policy of the Sub-Contractor would of course exclude the "Clause 22 Perils" already covered by the Contractor or Employer (see DOM 93, 94, 95).

The Contractor has the right (so too has the Employer under JCT 346) to see evidence that such policies as are necessary to cover the liability of the Sub-Contractor (as explained under statement DOM 84) exist and are properly maintained. Insurance is not required to cover the Sub-Contractor's plant, temporary buildings etc. No PL policy will be arranged without a limit being placed on the amount of indemnity for third party claims for any one occurrence hence the need for such a sum to be stated in the Appendix, part 3 (see DOM 112). The insurance profession will never grant absolute cover in all their policies of insurance. Policies will be subject to variations in restrictions, exclusions and endorsements. These should be checked by an

expert, as implied in the JCT Guide p 21 last para. Certain exclusions or endorsements to be found in PL Policies may not be acceptable unless other policies cover the risk concerned. For a list of these potentially unacceptable exclusions etc see JCT 340/1 in "A New Approach to (JCT 1980 Main) Contract" p 150. The Sub-Contractor also has similar rights to scrutinise the Contractor's evidence of insurances (see DOM 105–108) but is not entitled to himself insure where a default in insuring occurs. He is however absolved from any liability so arising

Production of policies

The Sub-Contractor must produce and must cause any other person to produce for inspection by the Contractor documentary evidence that the insurances are properly effected and maintained, as and when he is reasonably required to do so by the Contractor, in respect of: -
DOM 100   9.1

insurance taken out in pursuance of the Sub-Contract
DOM 101   9.1

insurance taken out in order to comply with the provisions of the Main Contract as described or referred to in the Appendix, part 1
DOM 102   9.1

Sub-Contractor does produce (and cause others to produce) documentary evidence as stipulated ? YES / NO

The Contractor may on any occasion require the policy or policies and premium receipts in question be produced for his inspection but not unreasonably or vexatiously
DOM 104   9.2

Contractor does require the policy etc to be produced ? YES

Failure of Sub-Contractor to insure

The word 'person' is defined in DOM clause 1.3. There is often doubt about labour-only relationships. To avoid such problems the EL Policy should always be extended to provide for such forms of labour to be deemed employees of the Sub-Contractor. Similarly the PL Policy should not exclude cover for work undertaken by sub-contractors to the insured. If the 'documentary evidence' is unsatisfactory see DOM 104 providing for the actual policies to be produced for inspection

Sub-Contract DOM/1 and the Numbered Documents constitute the Sub-Contract Documents
DOM 1   2.1.1

See the Appendix, part 1 Section B in respect of JCT clause 21.1.1 and 22A

Should the Sub-Contractor make default in insuring or in continuing to insure as the Sub-Contract, the Contractor may himself insure against any risk to which the default has occurred and may deduct the premiums from any monies due or to become due to the Sub-Contract or may recover same as a debt
DOM 103   9.2

The Contractor is entitled to set-off, against any money otherwise due under the Sub-Contract, any amount of: -
DOM 775   23.2

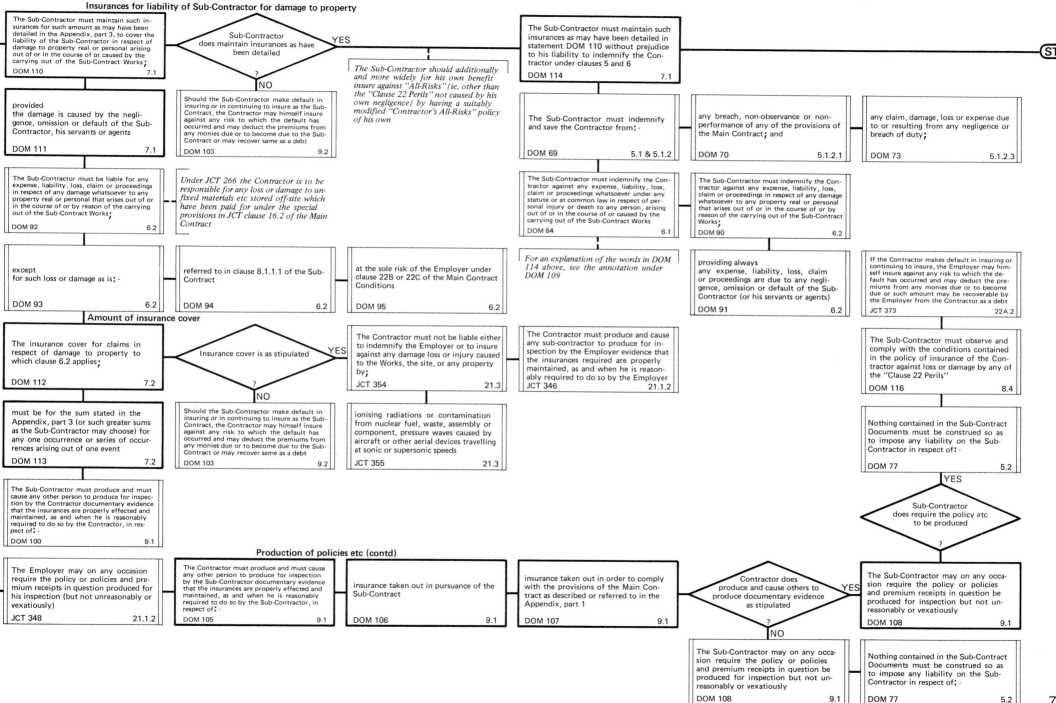

Insurances for liability of Sub-Contractor for damage to property

The Sub-Contractor must maintain such insurances for such amount as may have been detailed in the Appendix, part 3, to cover the liability of the Sub-Contractor in respect of damage to property real or personal arising out of or in the course of or caused by the carrying out of the Sub-Contract Works;

DOM 110   7.1

Sub-Contractor does maintain insurances as have been detailed ?

YES

provided
the damage is caused by the negligence, omission or default of the Sub-Contractor, his servants or agents

DOM 111   7.1

NO

Should the Sub-Contractor make default in insuring or in continuing to insure as the Sub-Contract, the Contractor may himself insure against any risk to which the default has occurred and may deduct the premiums from any monies due or to become due to the Sub-Contract or may recover same as a debt

DOM 103   9.2

The Sub-Contractor should additionally and more widely for his own benefit insure against "All-Risks" (ie, other than the "Clause 22 Perils" not caused by his own negligence) by having a suitably modified "Contractor's All-Risks" policy of his own

The Sub-Contractor must maintain such insurances as may have been detailed in statement DOM 110 without prejudice to his liability to indemnify the Contractor under clauses 5 and 6

DOM 114   7.1

STOP

The Sub-Contractor must indemnify and save the Contractor from: -

DOM 69   5.1 & 5.1.2

any breach, non-observance or non-performance of any of the provisions of the Main Contract; and

DOM 70   5.1.2.1

any claim, damage, loss or expense due to or resulting from any negligence or breach of duty;

DOM 73   5.1.2.3

The Sub-Contractor must be liable for any expense, liability, loss, claim or proceedings in respect of any damage whatsoever to any property real or personal that arises out of or in the course of or by reason of the carrying out of the Sub-Contract Works;

DOM 92   6.2

Under JCT 266 the Contractor is to be responsible for any loss or damage to unfixed materials etc stored off-site which have been paid for under the special provisions in JCT clause 16.2 of the Main Contract

The Sub-Contractor must indemnify the Contractor against any expense, liability, loss, claim or proceedings whatsoever under any statute or at common law in respect of personal injury or death to any person, arising out of or in the course of or caused by the carrying out of the Sub-Contract Works

DOM 84   6.1

The Sub-Contractor must indemnify the Contractor against any expense, liability, loss, claim or proceedings in respect of any damage whatsoever to any property real or personal that arises out of or in the course of or by reason of the carrying out of the Sub-Contract Works;

DOM 90   6.2

except
for such loss or damage as is: -

DOM 93   6.2

referred to in clause 8.1.1.1 of the Sub-Contract

DOM 94   6.2

at the sole risk of the Employer under clause 22B or 22C of the Main Contract Conditions

DOM 95   6.2

For an explanation of the words in DOM 114 above, see the annotation under DOM 109

providing always
any expense, liability, loss, claim or proceedings are due to any negligence, omission or default of the Sub-Contractor (or his servants or agents)

DOM 91   6.2

If the Contractor makes default in insuring or continuing to insure, the Employer may himself insure against any risk to which the default has occurred and may deduct the premiums from any monies due or to become due or such amount may be recoverable by the Employer from the Contractor as a debt

JCT 373   22A.2

Amount of insurance cover

The insurance cover for claims in respect of damage to property to which clause 6.2 applies;

DOM 112   7.2

Insurance cover is as stipulated ?

YES

must be for the sum stated in the Appendix, part 3 (or such greater sums as the Sub-Contractor may choose) for any one occurrence or series of occurrences arising out of one event

DOM 113   7.2

NO

Should the Sub-Contractor make default in insuring or in continuing to insure as the Sub-Contract, the Contractor may himself insure against any risk to which the default has occurred and may deduct the premiums from any monies due or to become due to the Sub-Contract or may recover same as a debt

DOM 103   9.2

The Contractor must not be liable either to indemnify the Employer or to insure against any damage loss or injury caused to the Works, the site, or any property by;

JCT 354   21.3

ionising radiations or contamination from nuclear fuel, waste, assembly or component, pressure waves caused by aircraft or other aerial devices travelling at sonic or supersonic speeds

JCT 355   21.3

The Contractor must produce and cause any sub-contractor to produce for inspection by the Employer evidence that the insurances required are properly maintained, as and when he is reasonably required to do so by the Employer

JCT 346   21.1.2

The Sub-Contractor must observe and comply with the conditions contained in the policy of insurance of the Contractor against loss or damage by any of the "Clause 22 Perils"

DOM 116   8.4

Nothing contained in the Sub-Contract Documents must be construed so as to impose any liability on the Sub-Contractor in respect of: -

DOM 77   5.2

YES

The Sub-Contractor must produce and must cause any other person to produce for inspection by the Contractor documentary evidence that the insurances are properly effected and maintained, as and when he is reasonably required to do so by the Contractor, in respect of: -

DOM 100   9.1

Production of policies etc (contd)

The Employer may on any occasion require the policy or policies and premium receipts in question produced for his inspection (but not unreasonably or vexatiously)

JCT 348   21.1.2

The Contractor must produce and must cause any other person to produce for inspection by the Sub-Contractor documentary evidence that the insurances are properly effected and maintained, as and when he is reasonably required to do so by the Sub-Contractor, in respect of: -

DOM 105   9.1

insurance taken out in pursuance of the Sub-Contract

DOM 106   9.1

insurance taken out in order to comply with the provisions of the Main Contract as described or referred to in the Appendix, part 1

DOM 107   9.1

Contractor does produce and cause others to produce documentary evidence as stipulated ?

YES

NO

The Sub-Contractor may on any occasion require the policy or policies and premium receipts in question be produced for inspection but not unreasonably or vexatiously

DOM 108   9.1

Sub-Contractor does require the policy etc to be produced ?

The Sub-Contractor may on any occasion require the policy or policies and premium receipts in question be produced for inspection but not unreasonably or vexatiously

DOM 108   9.1

Nothing contained in the Sub-Contract Documents must be construed so as to impose any liability on the Sub-Contractor in respect of: -

DOM 77   5.2

Clause 8 LOSS OR DAMAGE BY THE "CLAUSE 22 PERILS" *WHERE CLAUSE 22A OF THE MAIN CONTRACT APPLIES*

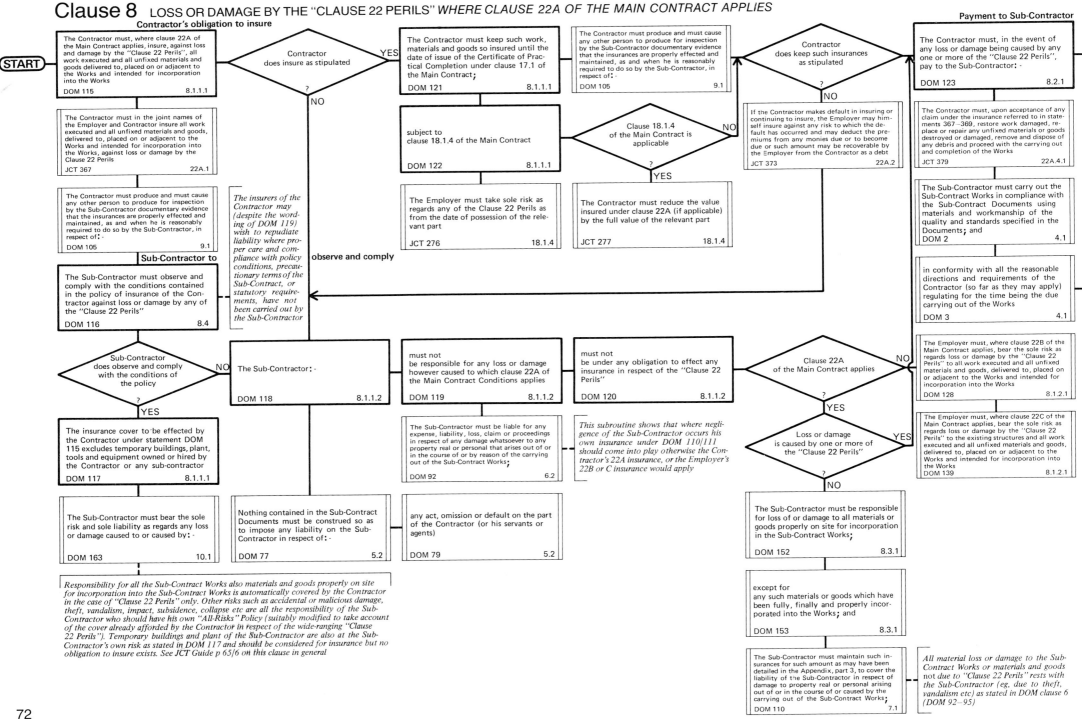

Contractor's obligation to insure

START

The Contractor must, where clause 22A of the Main Contract applies, insure, against loss and damage by the "Clause 22 Perils", all work executed and all unfixed materials and goods delivered to, placed on or adjacent to the Works and intended for incorporation into the Works
DOM 115   8.1.1.1

The Contractor must in the joint names of the Employer and Contractor insure all work executed and all unfixed materials and goods, delivered to, placed on or adjacent to the Works and intended for incorporation into the Works, against loss or damage by the Clause 22 Perils
JCT 367   22A.1

The Contractor must produce and must cause any other person to produce for inspection by the Sub-Contractor documentary evidence that the insurances are properly effected and maintained, as and when he is reasonably required to do so by the Sub-Contractor, in respect of : -
DOM 105   9.1

Sub-Contractor to

The Sub-Contractor must observe and comply with the conditions contained in the policy of insurance of the Contractor against loss or damage by any of the "Clause 22 Perils"
DOM 116   8.4

Contractor does insure as stipulated ?   NO   YES

The insurers of the Contractor may (despite the wording of DOM 119) wish to repudiate liability where proper care and compliance with policy conditions, precautionary terms of the Sub-Contract, or statutory requirements, have not been carried out by the Sub-Contractor

observe and comply

Sub-Contractor does observe and comply with the conditions of the policy ?   NO   YES

The insurance cover to be effected by the Contractor under statement DOM 115 excludes temporary buildings, plant, tools and equipment owned or hired by the Contractor or any sub-contractor
DOM 117   8.1.1.1

The Sub-Contractor must bear the sole risk and sole liability as regards any loss or damage caused to or caused by : -
DOM 163   10.1

The Sub-Contractor : -
DOM 118   8.1.1.2

Nothing contained in the Sub-Contract Documents must be construed so as to impose any liability on the Sub-Contractor in respect of : -
DOM 77   5.2

The Contractor must keep such work, materials and goods so insured until the date of issue of the Certificate of Practical Completion under clause 17.1 of the Main Contract;
DOM 121   8.1.1.1

subject to clause 18.1.4 of the Main Contract
DOM 122   8.1.1.1

The Employer must take sole risk as regards any of the Clause 22 Perils as from the date of possession of the relevant part
JCT 276   18.1.4

must not be responsible for any loss or damage however caused to which clause 22A of the Main Contract Conditions applies
DOM 119   8.1.1.2

The Sub-Contractor must be liable for any expense, liability, loss, claim or proceedings in respect of any damage whatsoever to any property real or personal that arises out of or in the course of or by reason of the carrying out of the Sub-Contract Works;
DOM 92   6.2

any act, omission or default on the part of the Contractor (or his servants or agents)
DOM 79   5.2

The Contractor must produce and must cause any other person to produce for inspection by the Sub-Contractor documentary evidence that the insurances are properly effected and maintained, as and when he is reasonably required to do so by the Sub-Contractor, in respect of : -
DOM 105   9.1

Clause 18.1.4 of the Main Contract is applicable ?   NO   YES

The Contractor must reduce the value insured under clause 22A (if applicable) by the full value of the relevant part
JCT 277   18.1.4

must not be under any obligation to effect any insurance in respect of the "Clause 22 Perils"
DOM 120   8.1.1.2

This subroutine shows that where negligence of the Sub-Contractor occurs his own insurance under DOM 110/111 should come into play otherwise the Contractor's 22A insurance, or the Employer's 22B or C insurance would apply

Contractor does keep such insurances as stipulated ?   NO

If the Contractor makes default in insuring or continuing to insure, the Employer may himself insure against any risk to which the default has occurred and may deduct the premiums from any monies due or to become due or such amount may be recoverable by the Employer from the Contractor as a debt
JCT 373   22A.2

Clause 22A of the Main Contract applies ?   NO   YES

Loss or damage is caused by one or more of the "Clause 22 Perils" ?   YES   NO

The Sub-Contractor must be responsible for loss of or damage to all materials or goods properly on site for incorporation in the Sub-Contract Works;
DOM 152   8.3.1

except for any such materials or goods which have been fully, finally and properly incorporated into the Works; and
DOM 153   8.3.1

The Sub-Contractor must maintain such insurances for such amount as may have been detailed in the Appendix, part 3, to cover the liability of the Sub-Contractor in respect of damage to property real or personal arising out of or in the course of or caused by the carrying out of the Sub-Contract Works;
DOM 110   7.1

The Contractor must, in the event of any loss or damage being caused by any one or more of the "Clause 22 Perils", pay to the Sub-Contractor : -
DOM 123   8.2.1

The Contractor must, upon acceptance of any claim under the insurance referred to in statements 367-369, restore work damaged, replace or repair any unfixed materials or goods destroyed or damaged, remove and dispose of any debris and proceed with the carrying out and completion of the Works
JCT 379   22A.4.1

The Sub-Contractor must carry out the Sub-Contract Works in compliance with the Sub-Contract Documents using materials and workmanship of the quality and standards specified in the Documents; and
DOM 2   4.1

in conformity with all the reasonable directions and requirements of the Contractor (so far as they may apply) regulating for the time being the due carrying out of the Works
DOM 3   4.1

The Employer must, where clause 22B of the Main Contract applies, bear the sole risk as regards loss or damage by the "Clause 22 Perils" to all work executed and all unfixed materials and goods, delivered to, placed on or adjacent to the Works and intended for incorporation into the Works
DOM 128   8.1.2.1

The Employer must, where clause 22C of the Main Contract applies, bear the sole risk as regards loss or damage by the "Clause 22 Perils" to the existing structures and all work executed and all unfixed materials and goods, delivered to, placed on or adjacent to the Works and intended for incorporation into the Works
DOM 139   8.1.2.1

Responsibility for all the Sub-Contract Works also materials and goods properly on site for incorporation in the Sub-Contract Works is automatically covered by the Contractor in the case of "Clause 22 Perils" only. Other risks such as accidental or malicious damage, theft, vandalism, impact, subsidence, collapse etc are all the responsibility of the Sub-Contractor who should have his own "All-Risks" Policy (suitably modified to take account of the cover already afforded by the Contractor in respect of the wide-ranging "Clause 22 Perils"). Temporary buildings and plant of the Sub-Contractor are also at the Sub-Contractor's own risk as stated in DOM 117 and should be considered for insurance but no obligation to insure exists. See JCT Guide p 65/6 on this clause in general

All material loss or damage to the Sub-Contract Works or materials and goods not due to "Clause 22 Perils" rests with the Sub-Contractor (eg, due to theft, vandalism etc) as stated in DOM clause 6 (DOM 92-95)

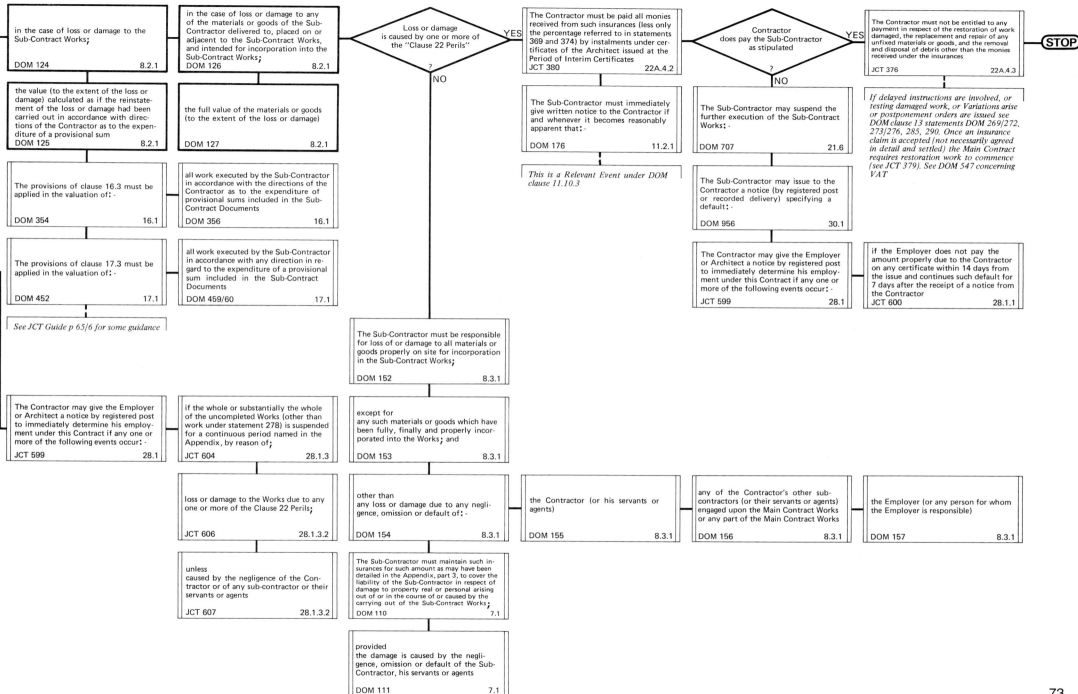

in the case of loss or damage to the Sub-Contract Works;

DOM 124   8.2.1

the value (to the extent of the loss or damage) calculated as if the reinstatement of the loss or damage had been carried out in accordance with directions of the Contractor as to the expenditure of a provisional sum
DOM 125   8.2.1

The provisions of clause 16.3 must be applied in the valuation of: -

DOM 354   16.1

The provisions of clause 17.3 must be applied in the valuation of: -

DOM 452   17.1

See JCT Guide p 65/6 for some guidance

The Contractor may give the Employer or Architect a notice by registered post to immediately determine his employment under this Contract if any one or more of the following events occur: -
JCT 599   28.1

in the case of loss or damage to any of the materials or goods of the Sub-Contractor delivered to, placed on or adjacent to the Sub-Contract Works, and intended for incorporation into the Sub-Contract Works;
DOM 126   8.2.1

the full value of the materials or goods (to the extent of the loss or damage)

DOM 127   8.2.1

all work executed by the Sub-Contractor in accordance with the directions of the Contractor as to the expenditure of provisional sums included in the Sub-Contract Documents
DOM 356   16.1

all work executed by the Sub-Contractor in accordance with any direction in regard to the expenditure of a provisional sum included in the Sub-Contract Documents
DOM 459/60   17.1

if the whole or substantially the whole of the uncompleted Works (other than work under statement 278) is suspended for a continuous period named in the Appendix, by reason of;
JCT 604   28.1.3

loss or damage to the Works due to any one or more of the Clause 22 Perils;

JCT 606   28.1.3.2

unless
caused by the negligence of the Contractor or of any sub-contractor or their servants or agents

JCT 607   28.1.3.2

Loss or damage is caused by one or more of the "Clause 22 Perils" — YES / NO ?

The Sub-Contractor must be responsible for loss of or damage to all materials or goods properly on site for incorporation in the Sub-Contract Works;
DOM 152   8.3.1

except for
any such materials or goods which have been fully, finally and properly incorporated into the Works; and
DOM 153   8.3.1

other than
any loss or damage due to any negligence, omission or default of: -

DOM 154   8.3.1

The Sub-Contractor must maintain such insurances for such amount as may have been detailed in the Appendix, part 3, to cover the liability of the Sub-Contractor in respect of damage to property real or personal arising out of or in the course of or caused by the carrying out of the Sub-Contract Works;
DOM 110   7.1

provided
the damage is caused by the negligence, omission or default of the Sub-Contractor, his servants or agents
DOM 111   7.1

The Contractor must be paid all monies received from such insurances (less only the percentage referred to in statements 369 and 374) by instalments under certificates of the Architect issued at the Period of Interim Certificates
JCT 380   22A.4.2

The Sub-Contractor must immediately give written notice to the Contractor if and whenever it becomes reasonably apparent that: -

DOM 176   11.2.1

This is a Relevant Event under DOM clause 11.10.3

the Contractor (or his servants or agents)

DOM 155   8.3.1

Contractor does pay the Sub-Contractor as stipulated — YES / NO ?

The Sub-Contractor may suspend the further execution of the Sub-Contract Works: -

DOM 707   21.6

The Sub-Contractor may issue to the Contractor a notice (by registered post or recorded delivery) specifying a default: -

DOM 956   30.1

The Contractor may give the Employer or Architect a notice by registered post to immediately determine his employment under this Contract if any one or more of the following events occur: -
JCT 599   28.1

any of the Contractor's other sub-contractors (or their servants or agents) engaged upon the Main Contract Works or any part of the Main Contract Works
DOM 156   8.3.1

The Contractor must not be entitled to any payment in respect of the restoration of work damaged, the replacement and repair of any unfixed materials or goods, and the removal and disposal of debris other than the monies received under the insurances
JCT 376   22A.4.3

If delayed instructions are involved, or testing damaged work, or Variations arise or postponement orders are issued see DOM clause 13 statements DOM 269/272, 273/276, 285, 290. Once an insurance claim is accepted (not necessarily agreed in detail and settled) the Main Contract requires restoration work to commence (see JCT 379). See DOM 547 concerning VAT

if the Employer does not pay the amount properly due to the Contractor on any certificate within 14 days from the issue and continues such default for 7 days after the receipt of a notice from the Contractor
JCT 600   28.1.1

the Employer (or any person for whom the Employer is responsible)

DOM 157   8.3.1

STOP

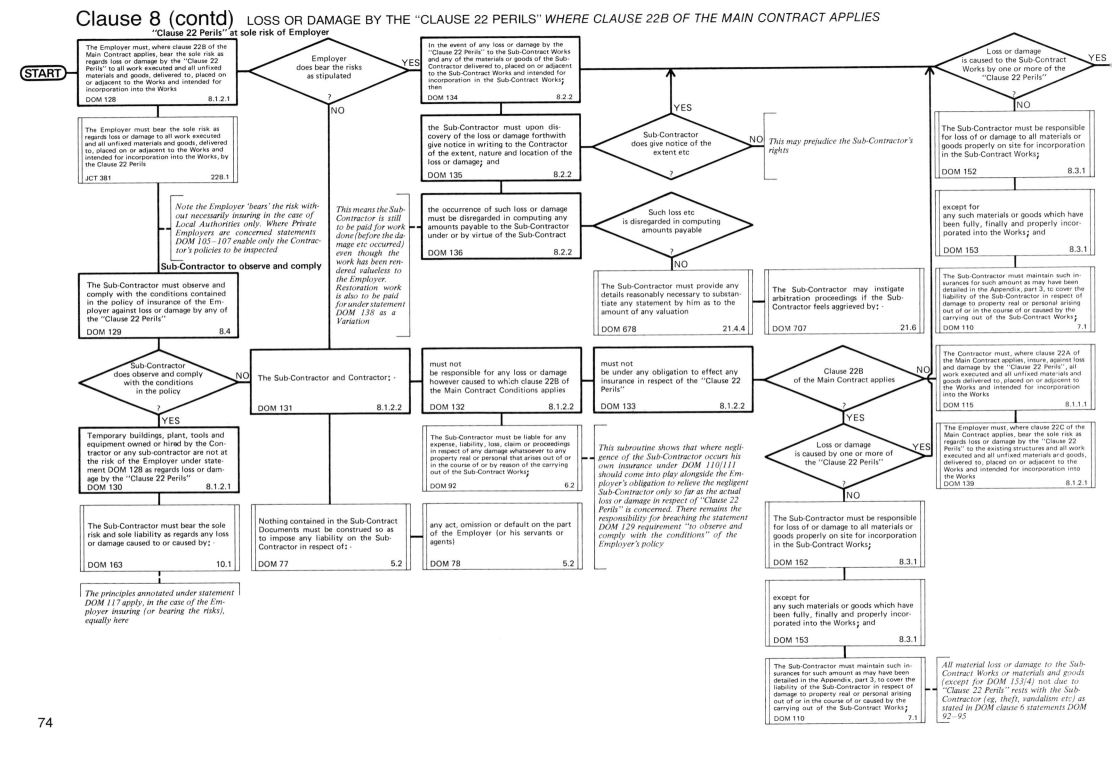

"Clause 22 Perils" at sole risk of Employer

START

The Employer must, where clause 22B of the Main Contract applies, bear the sole risk as regards loss or damage by the "Clause 22 Perils" to all work executed and all unfixed materials and goods, delivered to, placed on or adjacent to the Works and intended for incorporation into the Works
DOM 128 — 8.1.2.1

Employer does bear the risks as stipulated ? — YES / NO

The Employer must bear the sole risk as regards loss or damage to all work executed and all unfixed materials and goods, delivered to, placed on or adjacent to the Works and intended for incorporation into the Works, by the Clause 22 Perils
JCT 381 — 22B.1

Note the Employer 'bears' the risk without necessarily insuring in the case of Local Authorities only. Where Private Employers are concerned statements DOM 105–107 enable only the Contractor's policies to be inspected

Sub-Contractor to observe and comply

The Sub-Contractor must observe and comply with the conditions contained in the policy of insurance of the Employer against loss or damage by any of the "Clause 22 Perils"
DOM 129 — 8.4

Sub-Contractor does observe and comply with the conditions in the policy ? — NO / YES

Temporary buildings, plant, tools and equipment owned or hired by the Contractor or any sub-contractor are not at the risk of the Employer under statement DOM 128 as regards loss or damage by the "Clause 22 Perils"
DOM 130 — 8.1.2.1

The Sub-Contractor must bear the sole risk and sole liability as regards any loss or damage caused to or caused by: -
DOM 163 — 10.1

The principles annotated under statement DOM 117 apply, in the case of the Employer insuring (or bearing the risks), equally here

This means the Sub-Contractor is still to be paid for work done (before the damage etc occurred) even though the work has been rendered valueless to the Employer. Restoration work is also to be paid for under statement DOM 138 as a Variation

The Sub-Contractor and Contractor: -
DOM 131 — 8.1.2.2

must not be responsible for any loss or damage however caused to which clause 22B of the Main Contract Conditions applies
DOM 132 — 8.1.2.2

The Sub-Contractor must be liable for any expense, liability, loss, claim or proceedings in respect of any damage whatsoever to any property real or personal that arises out of or in the course of or by reason of the carrying out of the Sub-Contract Works;
DOM 92 — 6.2

Nothing contained in the Sub-Contract Documents must be construed so as to impose any liability on the Sub-Contractor in respect of: -
DOM 77 — 5.2

any act, omission or default on the part of the Employer (or his servants or agents)
DOM 78 — 5.2

In the event of any loss or damage by the "Clause 22 Perils" to the Sub-Contract Works and any of the materials or goods of the Sub-Contractor delivered to, placed on or adjacent to the Sub-Contract Works and intended for incorporation in the Sub-Contract Works; then
DOM 134 — 8.2.2

the Sub-Contractor must upon discovery of the loss or damage forthwith give notice in writing to the Contractor of the extent, nature and location of the loss or damage; and
DOM 135 — 8.2.2

the occurrence of such loss or damage must be disregarded in computing any amounts payable to the Sub-Contractor under or by virtue of the Sub-Contract
DOM 136 — 8.2.2

Sub-Contractor does give notice of the extent etc ? — NO — *This may prejudice the Sub-Contractor's rights*

Such loss etc is disregarded in computing amounts payable ? — NO

The Sub-Contractor must provide any details reasonably necessary to substantiate any statement by him as to the amount of any valuation
DOM 678 — 21.4.4

The Sub-Contractor may instigate arbitration proceedings if the Sub-Contractor feels aggrieved by: -
DOM 707 — 21.6

must not be under any obligation to effect any insurance in respect of the "Clause 22 Perils"
DOM 133 — 8.1.2.2

This subroutine shows that where negligence of the Sub-Contractor occurs his own insurance under DOM 110/111 should come into play alongside the Employer's obligation to relieve the negligent Sub-Contractor only so far as the actual loss or damage in respect of "Clause 22 Perils" is concerned. There remains the responsibility for breaching the statement DOM 129 requirement "to observe and comply with the conditions" of the Employer's policy

Clause 22B of the Main Contract applies ? — NO / YES

Loss or damage is caused by one or more of the "Clause 22 Perils" ? — YES / NO

The Sub-Contractor must be responsible for loss of or damage to all materials or goods properly on site for incorporation in the Sub-Contract Works;
DOM 152 — 8.3.1

except for any such materials or goods which have been fully, finally and properly incorporated into the Works; and
DOM 153 — 8.3.1

The Sub-Contractor must maintain such insurances for such amount as may have been detailed in the Appendix, part 3, to cover the liability of the Sub-Contractor in respect of damage to property real or personal arising out of or in the course of or caused by the carrying out of the Sub-Contract Works;
DOM 110 — 7.1

Loss or damage is caused to the Sub-Contract Works by one or more of the "Clause 22 Perils" ? — YES / NO

The Sub-Contractor must be responsible for loss of or damage to all materials or goods properly on site for incorporation in the Sub-Contract Works;
DOM 152 — 8.3.1

except for any such materials or goods which have been fully, finally and properly incorporated into the Works; and
DOM 153 — 8.3.1

The Contractor must, where clause 22A of the Main Contract applies, insure, against loss and damage by the "Clause 22 Perils", all work executed and all unfixed materials and goods delivered to, placed on or adjacent to the Works and intended for incorporation into the Works
DOM 115 — 8.1.1.1

The Employer must, where clause 22C of the Main Contract applies, bear the sole risk as regards loss or damage by the "Clause 22 Perils" to the existing structures and all work executed and all unfixed materials and goods, delivered to, placed on or adjacent to the Works and intended for incorporation into the Works
DOM 139 — 8.1.2.1

The Sub-Contractor must maintain such insurances for such amount as may have been detailed in the Appendix, part 3, to cover the liability of the Sub-Contractor in respect of damage to property real or personal arising out of or in the course of or caused by the carrying out of the Sub-Contract Works;
DOM 110 — 7.1

All material loss or damage to the Sub-Contract Works or materials and goods (except for DOM 153/4) not due to "Clause 22 Perils" rests with the Sub-Contractor (eg, theft, vandalism etc) as stated in DOM clause 6 statements DOM 92–95

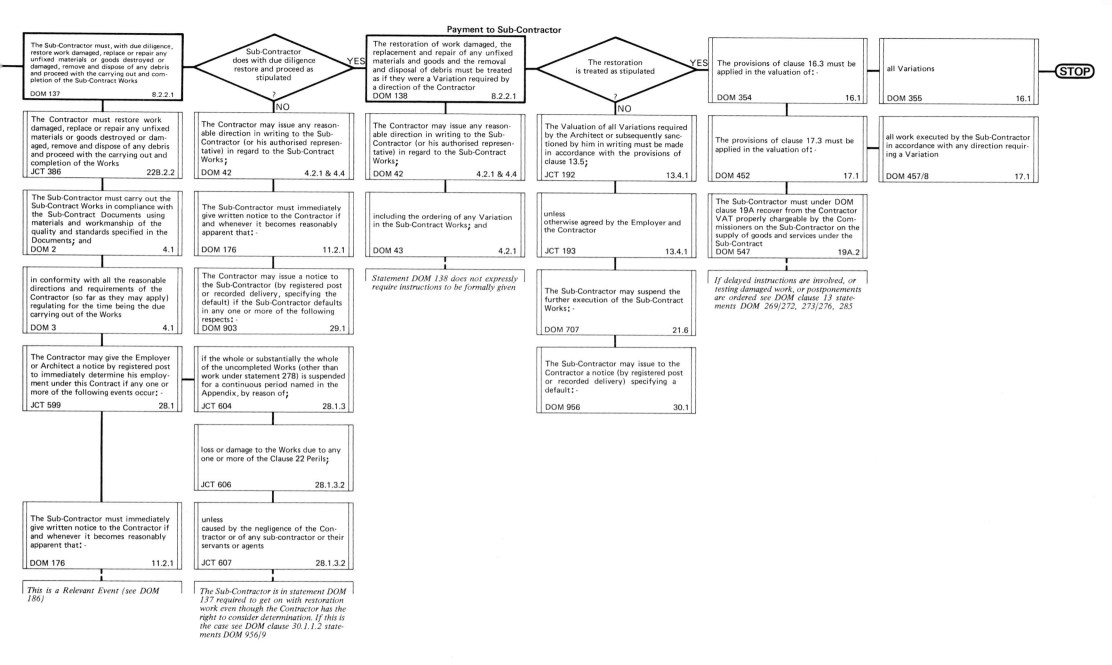

Payment to Sub-Contractor

The Sub-Contractor must, with due diligence, restore work damaged, replace or repair any unfixed materials or goods destroyed or damaged, remove and dispose of any debris and proceed with the carrying out and completion of the Sub-Contract Works DOM 137 8.2.2.1	**Sub-Contractor does with due diligence restore and proceed as stipulated ?** **YES** **NO**	The restoration of work damaged, the replacement and repair of any unfixed materials and goods and the removal and disposal of debris must be treated as if they were a Variation required by a direction of the Contractor DOM 138 8.2.2.1	**The restoration is treated as stipulated ?** **YES** **NO**	The provisions of clause 16.3 must be applied in the valuation of: - DOM 354 16.1

all Variations

DOM 355   16.1

STOP

The Contractor must restore work damaged, replace or repair any unfixed materials or goods destroyed or damaged, remove and dispose of any debris and proceed with the carrying out and completion of the Works

JCT 386   22B.2.2

The Contractor may issue any reasonable direction in writing to the Sub-Contractor (or his authorised representative) in regard to the Sub-Contract Works;

DOM 42   4.2.1 & 4.4

The Contractor may issue any reasonable direction in writing to the Sub-Contractor (or his authorised representative) in regard to the Sub-Contract Works;

DOM 42   4.2.1 & 4.4

The Valuation of all Variations required by the Architect or subsequently sanctioned by him in writing must be made in accordance with the provisions of clause 13.5;

JCT 192   13.4.1

The provisions of clause 17.3 must be applied in the valuation of: -

DOM 452   17.1

all work executed by the Sub-Contractor in accordance with any direction requiring a Variation

DOM 457/8   17.1

The Sub-Contractor must carry out the Sub-Contract Works in compliance with the Sub-Contract Documents using materials and workmanship of the quality and standards specified in the Documents; and

DOM 2   4.1

The Sub-Contractor must immediately give written notice to the Contractor if and whenever it becomes reasonably apparent that: -

DOM 176   11.2.1

including the ordering of any Variation in the Sub-Contract Works; and

DOM 43   4.2.1

unless otherwise agreed by the Employer and the Contractor

JCT 193   13.4.1

The Sub-Contractor must under DOM clause 19A recover from the Contractor VAT properly chargeable by the Commissioners on the Sub-Contractor on the supply of goods and services under the Sub-Contract

DOM 547   19A.2

---

in conformity with all the reasonable directions and requirements of the Contractor (so far as they may apply) regulating for the time being the due carrying out of the Works

DOM 3   4.1

The Contractor may issue a notice to the Sub-Contractor (by registered post or recorded delivery, specifying the default) if the Sub-Contractor defaults in any one or more of the following respects: -

DOM 903   29.1

Statement DOM 138 does not expressly require instructions to be formally given

The Sub-Contractor may suspend the further execution of the Sub-Contract Works: -

DOM 707   21.6

If delayed instructions are involved, or testing damaged work, or postponements are ordered see DOM clause 13 statements DOM 269/272, 273/276, 285

The Contractor may give the Employer or Architect a notice by registered post to immediately determine his employment under this Contract if any one or more of the following events occur: -

JCT 599   28.1

if the whole or substantially the whole of the uncompleted Works (other than work under statement 278) is suspended for a continuous period named in the Appendix, by reason of;

JCT 604   28.1.3

The Sub-Contractor may issue to the Contractor a notice (by registered post or recorded delivery) specifying a default: -

DOM 956   30.1

---

loss or damage to the Works due to any one or more of the Clause 22 Perils;

JCT 606   28.1.3.2

The Sub-Contractor must immediately give written notice to the Contractor if and whenever it becomes reasonably apparent that: -

DOM 176   11.2.1

unless caused by the negligence of the Contractor or of any sub-contractor or their servants or agents

JCT 607   28.1.3.2

This is a Relevant Event (see DOM 186)

The Sub-Contractor is in statement DOM 137 required to get on with restoration work even though the Contractor has the right to consider determination. If this is the case see DOM clause 30.1.1.2 statements DOM 956/9

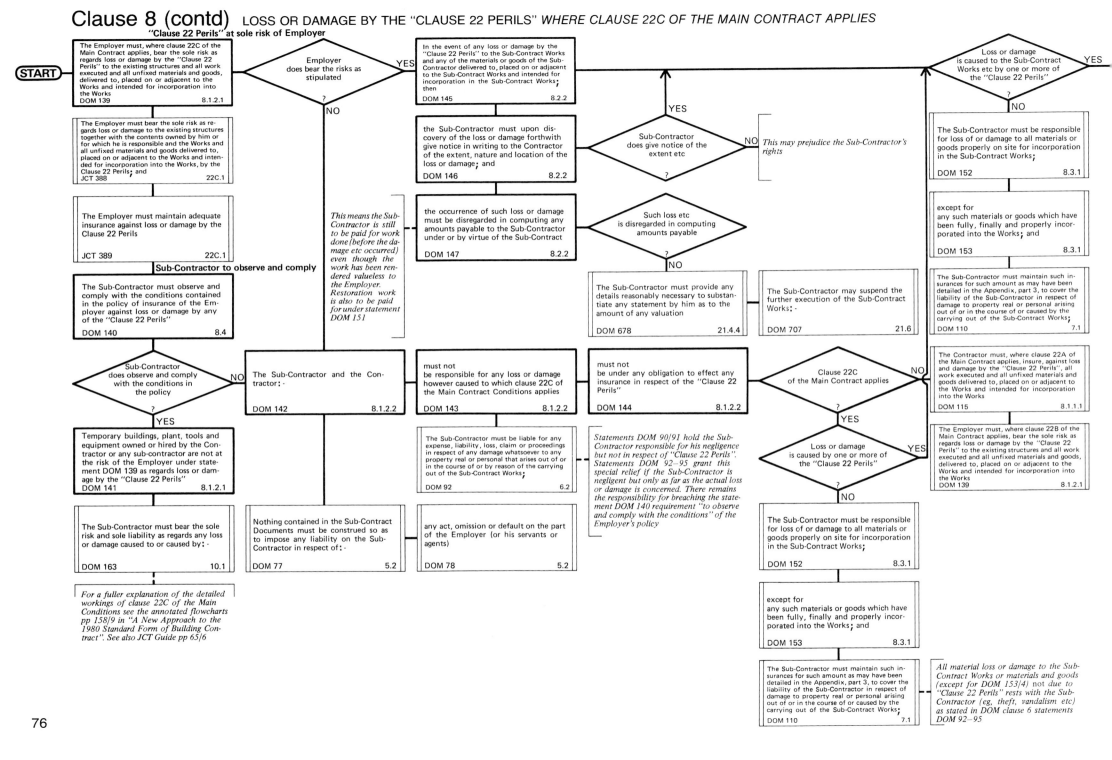

"Clause 22 Perils" at sole risk of Employer

START

The Employer must, where clause 22C of the Main Contract applies, bear the sole risk as regards loss or damage by the "Clause 22 Perils" to the existing structures and all work executed and all unfixed materials and goods, delivered to, placed on or adjacent to the Works and intended for incorporation into the Works
DOM 139   8.1.2.1

The Employer must bear the sole risk as regards loss or damage to the existing structures together with the contents owned by him or for which he is responsible and the Works and all unfixed materials and goods delivered to, placed on or adjacent to the Works and intended for incorporation into the Works, by the Clause 22 Perils; and
JCT 388   22C.1

The Employer must maintain adequate insurance against loss or damage by the Clause 22 Perils
JCT 389   22C.1

Sub-Contractor to observe and comply

The Sub-Contractor must observe and comply with the conditions contained in the policy of insurance of the Employer against loss or damage by any of the "Clause 22 Perils"
DOM 140   8.4

Sub-Contractor does observe and comply with the conditions in the policy ? — NO

YES

Temporary buildings, plant, tools and equipment owned or hired by the Contractor or any sub-contractor are not at the risk of the Employer under statement DOM 139 as regards loss or damage by the "Clause 22 Perils"
DOM 141   8.1.2.1

The Sub-Contractor must bear the sole risk and sole liability as regards any loss or damage caused to or caused by: -
DOM 163   10.1

For a fuller explanation of the detailed workings of clause 22C of the Main Conditions see the annotated flowcharts pp 158/9 in "A New Approach to the 1980 Standard Form of Building Contract". See also JCT Guide pp 65/6

Employer does bear the risks as stipulated ? — NO — YES

This means the Sub-Contractor is still to be paid for work done (before the damage etc occurred) even though the work has been rendered valueless to the Employer. Restoration work is also to be paid for under statement DOM 151

The Sub-Contractor and the Contractor: -
DOM 142   8.1.2.2

Nothing contained in the Sub-Contract Documents must be construed so as to impose any liability on the Sub-Contractor in respect of: -
DOM 77   5.2

In the event of any loss or damage by the "Clause 22 Perils" to the Sub-Contract Works and any of the materials or goods of the Sub-Contractor delivered to, placed on or adjacent to the Sub-Contract Works and intended for incorporation in the Sub-Contract Works; then
DOM 145   8.2.2

the Sub-Contractor must upon discovery of the loss or damage forthwith give notice in writing to the Contractor of the extent, nature and location of the loss or damage; and
DOM 146   8.2.2

the occurrence of such loss or damage must be disregarded in computing any amounts payable to the Sub-Contractor under or by virtue of the Sub-Contract
DOM 147   8.2.2

must not be responsible for any loss or damage however caused to which clause 22C of the Main Contract Conditions applies
DOM 143   8.1.2.2

The Sub-Contractor must be liable for any expense, liability, loss, claim or proceedings in respect of any damage whatsoever to any property real or personal that arises out of or in the course of or by reason of the carrying out of the Sub-Contract Works;
DOM 92   6.2

any act, omission or default on the part of the Employer (or his servants or agents)
DOM 78   5.2

Sub-Contractor does give notice of the extent etc ? — NO — *This may prejudice the Sub-Contractor's rights*

YES

Such loss etc is disregarded in computing amounts payable ? — NO

The Sub-Contractor must provide any details reasonably necessary to substantiate any statement by him as to the amount of any valuation
DOM 678   21.4.4

must not be under any obligation to effect any insurance in respect of the "Clause 22 Perils"
DOM 144   8.1.2.2

Statements DOM 90/91 hold the Sub-Contractor responsible for his negligence but not in respect of "Clause 22 Perils". Statements DOM 92–95 grant this special relief if the Sub-Contractor is negligent but only as far as the actual loss or damage is concerned. There remains the responsibility for breaching the statement DOM 140 requirement "to observe and comply with the conditions" of the Employer's policy

The Sub-Contractor may suspend the further execution of the Sub-Contract Works; -
DOM 707   21.6

Clause 22C of the Main Contract applies ? — YES / NO

YES

Loss or damage is caused by one or more of the "Clause 22 Perils" ? — YES / NO

The Sub-Contractor must be responsible for loss of or damage to all materials or goods properly on site for incorporation in the Sub-Contract Works;
DOM 152   8.3.1

except for any such materials or goods which have been fully, finally and properly incorporated into the Works; and
DOM 153   8.3.1

The Sub-Contractor must maintain such insurances for such amount as may have been detailed in the Appendix, part 3, to cover the liability of the Sub-Contractor in respect of damage to property real or personal arising out of or in the course of or caused by the carrying out of the Sub-Contract Works;
DOM 110   7.1

Loss or damage is caused to the Sub-Contract Works etc by one or more of the "Clause 22 Perils" ? — YES / NO

The Sub-Contractor must be responsible for loss of or damage to all materials or goods properly on site for incorporation in the Sub-Contract Works;
DOM 152   8.3.1

except for any such materials or goods which have been fully, finally and properly incorporated into the Works; and
DOM 153   8.3.1

The Sub-Contractor must maintain such insurances for such amount as may have been detailed in the Appendix, part 3, to cover the liability of the Sub-Contractor in respect of damage to property real or personal arising out of or in the course of or caused by the carrying out of the Sub-Contract Works;
DOM 110   7.1

The Contractor must, where clause 22A of the Main Contract applies, insure, against loss and damage by the "Clause 22 Perils", all work executed and all unfixed materials and goods delivered to, placed on or adjacent to the Works and intended for incorporation into the Works
DOM 115   8.1.1.1

The Employer must, where clause 22B of the Main Contract applies, bear the sole risk as regards loss or damage by the "Clause 22 Perils" to the existing structures and all work executed and all unfixed materials and goods, delivered to, placed on or adjacent to the Works and intended for incorporation into the Works
DOM 139   8.1.2.1

All material loss or damage to the Sub-Contract Works or materials and goods (except for DOM 153/4) not due to "Clause 22 Perils" rests with the Sub-Contractor (eg, theft, vandalism etc) as stated in DOM clause 6 statements DOM 92–95

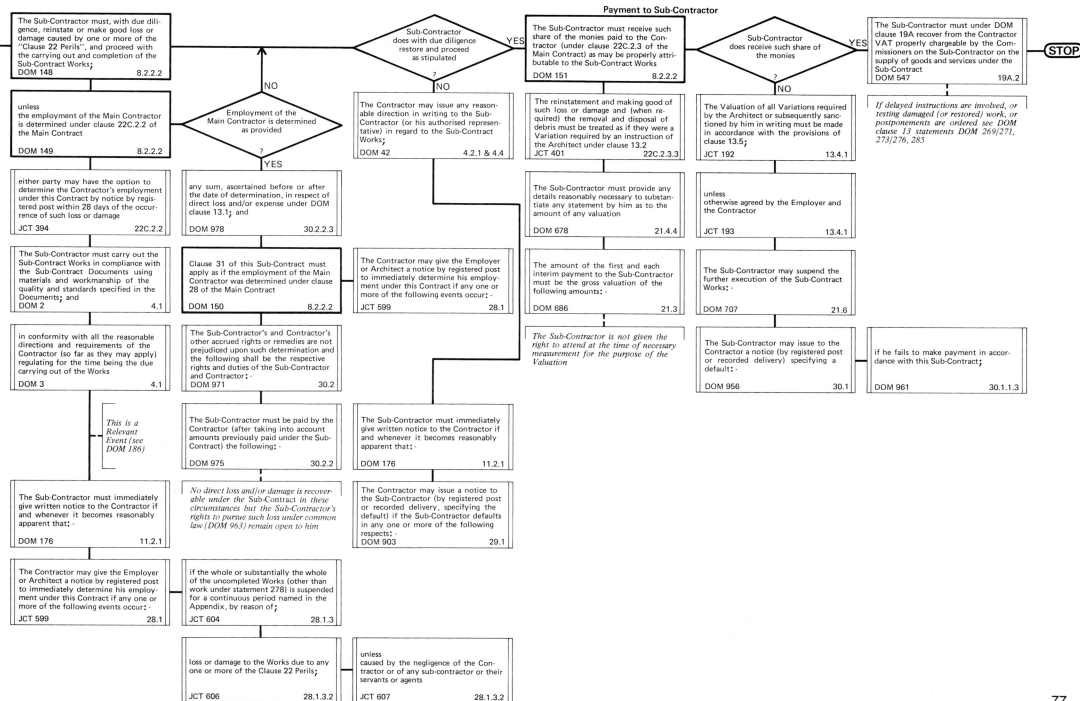

Payment to Sub-Contractor

The Sub-Contractor must, with due diligence, reinstate or make good loss or damage caused by one or more of the "Clause 22 Perils", and proceed with the carrying out and completion of the Sub-Contract Works;
DOM 148   8.2.2.2

unless
the employment of the Main Contractor is determined under clause 22C.2.2 of the Main Contract
DOM 149   8.2.2.2

either party may have the option to determine the Contractor's employment under this Contract by notice by registered post within 28 days of the occurrence of such loss or damage
JCT 394   22C.2.2

The Sub-Contractor must carry out the Sub-Contract Works in compliance with the Sub-Contract Documents using materials and workmanship of the quality and standards specified in the Documents; and
DOM 2   4.1

in conformity with all the reasonable directions and requirements of the Contractor (so far as they may apply) regulating for the time being the due carrying out of the Works
DOM 3   4.1

This is a Relevant Event (see DOM 186)

The Sub-Contractor must immediately give written notice to the Contractor if and whenever it becomes reasonably apparent that: -
DOM 176   11.2.1

The Contractor may give the Employer or Architect a notice by registered post to immediately determine his employment under this Contract if any one or more of the following events occur: -
JCT 599   28.1

Employment of the Main Contractor is determined as provided *(diamond)* ?

NO

YES

any sum, ascertained before or after the date of determination, in respect of direct loss and/or expense under DOM clause 13.1; and
DOM 978   30.2.2.3

Clause 31 of this Sub-Contract must apply as if the employment of the Main Contractor was determined under clause 28 of the Main Contract
DOM 150   8.2.2.2

The Sub-Contractor's and Contractor's other accrued rights or remedies are not prejudiced upon such determination and the following shall be the respective rights and duties of the Sub-Contractor and Contractor: -
DOM 971   30.2

The Sub-Contractor must be paid by the Contractor (after taking into account amounts previously paid under the Sub-Contract) the following: -
DOM 975   30.2.2

No direct loss and/or damage is recoverable under the Sub-Contract in these circumstances but the Sub-Contractor's rights to pursue such loss under common law (DOM 963) remain open to him

if the whole or substantially the whole of the uncompleted Works (other than work under statement 278) is suspended for a continuous period named in the Appendix, by reason of;
JCT 604   28.1.3

loss or damage to the Works due to any one or more of the Clause 22 Perils;
JCT 606   28.1.3.2

Sub-Contractor does with due diligence restore and proceed as stipulated *(diamond)* ?

YES

NO

The Contractor may issue any reasonable direction in writing to the Sub-Contractor (or his authorised representative) in regard to the Sub-Contract Works;
DOM 42   4.2.1 & 4.4

The Contractor may give the Employer or Architect a notice by registered post to immediately determine his employment under this Contract if any one or more of the following events occur: -
JCT 599   28.1

The Sub-Contractor must immediately give written notice to the Contractor if and whenever it becomes reasonably apparent that: -
DOM 176   11.2.1

The Contractor may issue a notice to the Sub-Contractor (by registered post or recorded delivery, specifying the default) if the Sub-Contractor defaults in any one or more of the following respects: -
DOM 903   29.1

unless
caused by the negligence of the Contractor or of any sub-contractor or their servants or agents
JCT 607   28.1.3.2

The Sub-Contractor must receive such share of the monies paid to the Contractor (under clause 22C.2.3 of the Main Contract) as may be properly attributable to the Sub-Contract Works
DOM 151   8.2.2.2

The reinstatement and making good of such loss or damage and (when required) the removal and disposal of debris must be treated as if they were a Variation required by an instruction of the Architect under clause 13.2
JCT 401   22C.2.3.3

The Sub-Contractor must provide any details reasonably necessary to substantiate any statement by him as to the amount of any valuation
DOM 678   21.4.4

The amount of the first and each interim payment to the Sub-Contractor must be the gross valuation of the following amounts: -
DOM 686   21.3

The Sub-Contractor is not given the right to attend at the time of necessary measurement for the purpose of the Valuation

Sub-Contractor does receive such share of the monies *(diamond)* ?

YES

NO

The Valuation of all Variations required by the Architect or subsequently sanctioned by him in writing must be made in accordance with the provisions of clause 13.5;
JCT 192   13.4.1

unless
otherwise agreed by the Employer and the Contractor
JCT 193   13.4.1

The Sub-Contractor may suspend the further execution of the Sub-Contract Works: -
DOM 707   21.6

The Sub-Contractor may issue to the Contractor a notice (by registered post or recorded delivery) specifying a default: -
DOM 956   30.1

if he fails to make payment in accordance with this Sub-Contract;
DOM 961   30.1.1.3

The Sub-Contractor must under DOM clause 19A recover from the Contractor VAT properly chargeable by the Commissioners on the Sub-Contractor on the supply of goods and services under the Sub-Contract
DOM 547   19A.2

STOP

If delayed instructions are involved, or testing damaged (or restored) work, or postponements are ordered see DOM clause 13 statements DOM 269/271, 273/276, 285

77

Loss of or damage to sub-contract materials and goods during the progress of the Sub-Contract Works

START

The Sub-Contractor must be responsible for loss of or damage to all materials or goods properly on site for incorporation in the Sub-Contract Works;

DOM 152   8.3.1

The words "fully, finally and properly incorporated" are crucial. The words appear to mean when nothing by the Sub-Contractor remains to be done to the materials or goods and they are not faulty although further work may be due to follow. The word "Works" is defined in DOM clause 1.3

except for
any such materials or goods which have been fully, finally and properly incorporated into the Works; and

DOM 153   8.3.1

other than
any loss or damage due to any negligence, omission or default of: -

DOM 154   8.3.1

There may well be difficulty in practice of deciding whether or not materials or goods have been "fully, finally and properly incorporated into the Works". It is therefore (see JCT Guide p 66) suggested the parties set up a system to jointly decide such matters.
The provisions here in DOM clauses 8.3 and 10 may be summarised as follows:
If a "Clause 22 Peril" is concerned then the Sub-Contractor's Works and materials and goods properly on site for incorporation are insured by the Contractor as stated in lines 1 and 2 of DOM clause 8.1.1.1 and .2, or, are covered similarly by the Employer where alternatively JCT clause 22B or C of the Main Contract applies.
Any loss or damage not due to a "Clause 22 Peril" (theft, vandalism etc) is at the risk of the Sub-Contractor until the materials or goods are "fully, finally and properly incorporated into the Main Contract Works". However if such loss or damage arose due to any negligence etc of the Contractor etc, as detailed in DOM 154–157 then the Sub-Contractor would be entitled to seek redress from the negligent persons concerned (see JCT Guide p 66)

the Contractor (or his servants or agents)

DOM 155   8.3.1

any of the Contractor's other sub-contractors (or their servants or agents) engaged upon the Main Contract Works or any part of the Main Contract Works

DOM 156   8.3.1

the Employer (or any person for whom the Employer is responsible)

DOM 157   8.3.1

The materials or goods are properly on site for incorporation in the Sub-Contract Works — YES — *Loss or damage is caused by one or more of the "Clause 22 Perils"* — NO
? NO — YES

The materials or goods have been fully, finally and properly incorporated as stipulated — ? YES

The incident may not involve any negligence by any of the parties (ie, theft by the Sub-Contractor's own employees) in which case DOM 152 applies

Any loss or damage is due to negligence etc of the Contractor (etc) — NO / ? YES

Any loss or damage is due to negligence etc of any other Sub-Contractor (etc) — NO / ? YES

Any loss or damage is due to negligence of the Employer (etc) — NO / ? YES

The Contractor must be liable for any expense liability loss claim or proceedings in respect of any damage whatsoever to any property real or personal arising out of or in the course of or by reason of carrying out the Works;

JCT 338   20.2

except
for such loss or damage as is at the sole risk of the Employer under clause 22B or 22C (if applicable)

JCT 339   20.2

The word "property" is one of the widest terms possible and is not necessarily confined to physical damage or loss of material property. It can include rights, titles, interests in, etc "arising out of . . . the Works"

The Contractor must, where clause 22A of the Main Contract applies, insure, against loss and damage by the "Clause 22 Perils", all work executed and all unfixed materials and goods delivered to, placed on or adjacent to the Works and intended for incorporation into the Works

DOM 115   8.1.1.1

The Employer must, where clause 22B of the Main Contract applies, bear the sole risk as regards loss or damage by the "Clause 22 Perils" to all work executed and all unfixed materials and goods, delivered to, placed on or adjacent to the Works and intended for incorporation into the Works

DOM 128   8.1.2.1

The Employer must, where clause 22C of the Main Contract applies, bear the sole risk as regards loss or damage by the "Clause 22 Perils" to the existing structures and all work executed and all unfixed materials and goods, delivered to, placed on or adjacent to the Works and intended for incorporation into the Works

DOM 139   8.1.2.1

The Employer must, where clause 22C of the Main Contract applies, bear the sole risk as regards loss or damage by the "Clause 22 Perils" to the existing structures and all work executed and all unfixed materials and goods, delivered to, placed on or adjacent to the Works and intended for incorporation into the Works

DOM 139   8.1.2.1

Nothing contained in the Sub-Contract Documents must be construed so as to impose any liability on the Sub-Contractor in respect of: -

DOM 77   5.2

any act, omission or default on the part of the Contractor (or his servants or agents)

DOM 79   5.2

The Contractor must, where clause 22A of the Main Contract applies, insure, against loss and damage by the "Clause 22 Perils", all work executed and all unfixed materials and goods delivered to, placed on or adjacent to the Works and intended for incorporation into the Works

DOM 115   8.1.1.1

The Employer must, where clause 22B of the Main Contract applies, bear the sole risk as regards loss or damage by the "Clause 22 Perils" to all work executed and all unfixed materials and goods, delivered to, placed on or adjacent to the Works and intended for incorporation into the Works

DOM 128   8.1.2.1

The Employer must, where clause 22C of the Main Contract applies, bear the sole risk as regards loss or damage by the "Clause 22 Perils" to the existing structures and all work executed and all unfixed materials and goods, delivered to, placed on or adjacent to the Works and intended for incorporation into the Works

DOM 139   8.1.2.1

Nothing contained in the Sub-Contract Documents must be construed so as to impose any liability on the Sub-Contractor in respect of: -

DOM 77   5.2

any act, omission or default on the part of the Contractor's other sub-contractors (or their servants or agents)

DOM 80   5.2

The Employer is protected in the case of "Clause 22 Perils" only against his own negligence by the 22A, B or C policies but should have his own "All-Risks" Policy to cover any other risk he carries

The Contractor will be responsible for loss or damage to materials and goods fully, finally and properly incorporated into the Works before practical completion of the Sub-Contract Works;

DOM 158   8.3.2

except for
any loss or damage caused to such materials and goods by the Sub-Contractor (or his servants or agents)

DOM 159   8.3.2

any act, omission or default on the part of the Employer (or his servants or agents)

DOM 78   5.2

Loss or damage is caused by the Sub-Contractor (etc) — NO / ? YES

The Sub-Contractor should (but is not obliged to) have his own "All-Risks" Policy to cover his own risks such as from theft, accidental damage, malicious damage, impact damage, collapse damage etc, ie, not due to "Clause 22 Perils" or due to the negligence of others. (These are covered by others' policies. See JCT clause 21 and clause 22A, B or C of the Main Contract)

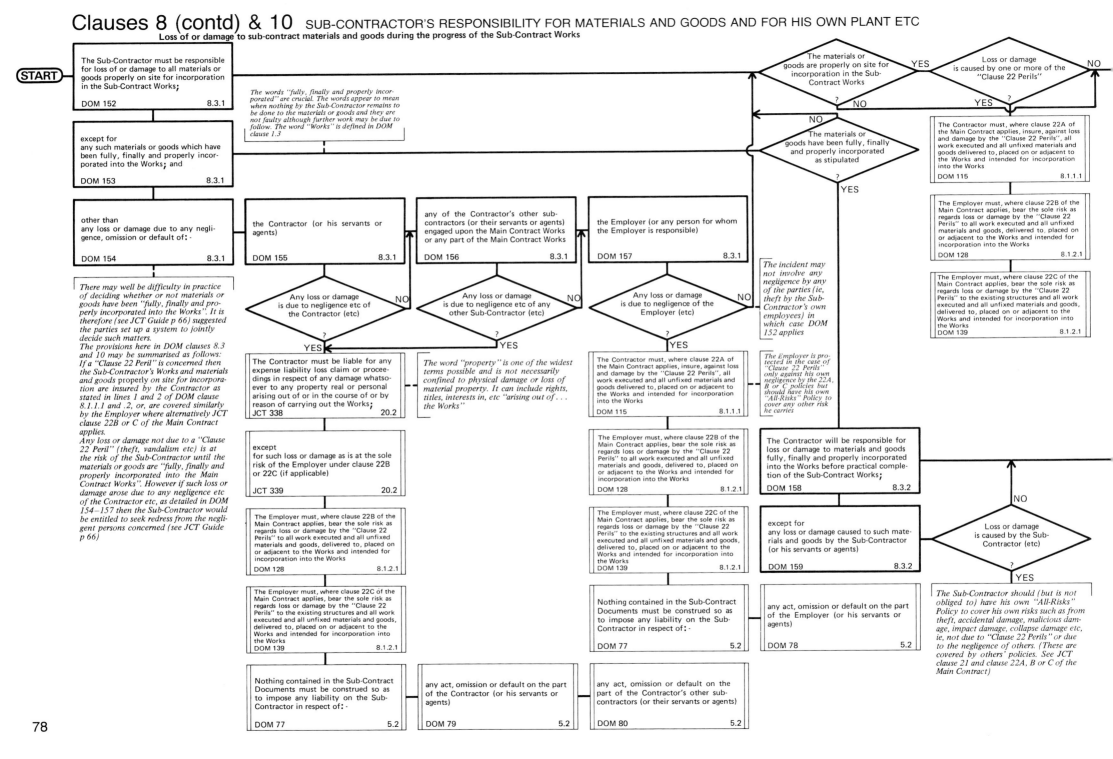

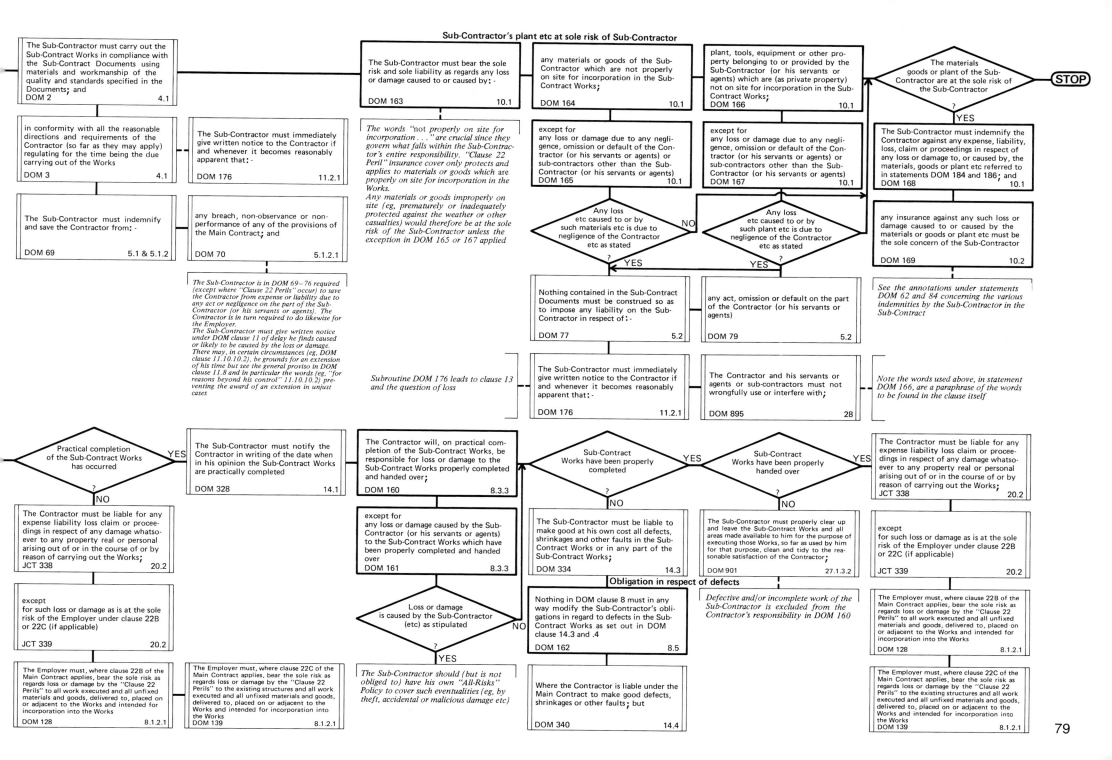

Sub-Contractor's plant etc at sole risk of Sub-Contractor

DOM 2 (4.1): The Sub-Contractor must carry out the Sub-Contract Works in compliance with the Sub-Contract Documents using materials and workmanship of the quality and standards specified in the Documents; and

DOM 3 (4.1): in conformity with all the reasonable directions and requirements of the Contractor (so far as they may apply) regulating for the time being the due carrying out of the Works

DOM 69 (5.1 & 5.1.2): The Sub-Contractor must indemnify and save the Contractor from: -

DOM 176 (11.2.1): The Sub-Contractor must immediately give written notice to the Contractor if and whenever it becomes reasonably apparent that: -

DOM 70 (5.1.2.1): any breach, non-observance or non-performance of any of the provisions of the Main Contract; and

The Sub-Contractor is in DOM 69–76 required (except where "Clause 22 Perils" occur) to save the Contractor from expense or liability due to any act or negligence on the part of the Sub-Contractor (or his servants or agents). The Contractor is in turn required to do likewise for the Employer.
The Sub-Contractor must give written notice under DOM clause 11 of delay he finds caused or likely to be caused by the loss or damage. There may, in certain circumstances (eg, DOM clause 11.10.10.2), be grounds for an extension of his time but see the general proviso in DOM clause 11.8 and in particular the words (eg, "for reasons beyond his control" 11.10.10.2) preventing the award of an extension in unjust cases

DOM 163 (10.1): The Sub-Contractor must bear the sole risk and sole liability as regards any loss or damage caused to or caused by: -

The words "not properly on site for incorporation . . ." are crucial since they govern what falls within the Sub-Contractor's entire responsibility. "Clause 22 Peril" insurance cover only protects and applies to materials or goods which are properly on site for incorporation in the Works.
Any materials or goods improperly on site (eg, prematurely or inadequately protected against the weather or other casualties) would therefore be at the sole risk of the Sub-Contractor unless the exception in DOM 165 or 167 applied

Subroutine DOM 176 leads to clause 13 and the question of loss

DOM 164 (10.1): any materials or goods of the Sub-Contractor which are not properly on site for incorporation in the Sub-Contract Works;

DOM 165 (10.1): except for any loss or damage due to any negligence, omission or default of the Contractor (or his servants or agents) or sub-contractors other than the Sub-Contractor (or his servants or agents)

(Diamond) Any loss etc caused to or by such materials etc is due to negligence of the Contractor etc as stated — NO / YES

DOM 77 (5.2): Nothing contained in the Sub-Contract Documents must be construed so as to impose any liability on the Sub-Contractor in respect of: -

DOM 176 (11.2.1): The Sub-Contractor must immediately give written notice to the Contractor if and whenever it becomes reasonably apparent that: -

DOM 166 (10.1): plant, tools, equipment or other property belonging to or provided by the Sub-Contractor (or his servants or agents) which are (as private property) not on site for incorporation in the Sub-Contract Works;

DOM 167 (10.1): except for any loss or damage due to any negligence, omission or default of the Contractor (or his servants or agents) or sub-contractors other than the Sub-Contractor (or his servants or agents)

(Diamond) Any loss etc caused to or by such plant etc is due to negligence of the Contractor etc as stated — YES

DOM 79 (5.2): any act, omission or default on the part of the Contractor (or his servants or agents)

DOM 895 (28): The Contractor and his servants or agents or sub-contractors must not wrongfully use or interfere with;

(Diamond) The materials goods or plant of the Sub-Contractor are at the sole risk of the Sub-Contractor ? — YES

STOP

DOM 168 (10.1): The Sub-Contractor must indemnify the Contractor against any expense, liability, loss, claim or proceedings in respect of any loss or damage to, or caused by, the materials, goods or plant etc referred to in statements DOM 184 and 186; and

DOM 169 (10.2): any insurance against any such loss or damage caused to or caused by the materials or goods or plant etc must be the sole concern of the Sub-Contractor

See the annotations under statements DOM 62 and 84 concerning the various indemnities by the Sub-Contractor in the Sub-Contract

Note the words used above, in statement DOM 166, are a paraphrase of the words to be found in the clause itself

---

(Diamond) Practical completion of the Sub-Contract Works has occurred ? — YES / NO

DOM 328 (14.1): The Sub-Contractor must notify the Contractor in writing of the date when in his opinion the Sub-Contract Works are practically completed

JCT 338 (20.2): The Contractor must be liable for any expense liability loss claim or proceedings in respect of any damage whatsoever to any property real or personal arising out of or in the course of or by reason of carrying out the Works;

JCT 339 (20.2): except for such loss or damage as is at the sole risk of the Employer under clause 22B or 22C (if applicable)

DOM 128 (8.1.2.1): The Employer must, where clause 22B of the Main Contract applies, bear the sole risk as regards loss or damage by the "Clause 22 Perils" to all work executed and all unfixed materials and goods, delivered to, placed on or adjacent to the Works and intended for incorporation into the Works

DOM 139 (8.1.2.1): The Employer must, where clause 22C of the Main Contract applies, bear the sole risk as regards loss or damage by the "Clause 22 Perils" to the existing structures and all work executed and all unfixed materials and goods, delivered to, placed on or adjacent to the Works and intended for incorporation into the Works

DOM 160 (8.3.3): The Contractor will, on practical completion of the Sub-Contract Works, be responsible for loss or damage to the Sub-Contract Works properly completed and handed over;

DOM 161 (8.3.3): except for any loss or damage caused by the Sub-Contractor (or his servants or agents) to the Sub-Contract Works which have been properly completed and handed over

(Diamond) Loss or damage is caused by the Sub-Contractor (etc) as stipulated ? — NO / YES

The Sub-Contractor should (but is not obliged to) have his own "All-Risks" Policy to cover such eventualities (eg, by theft, accidental or malicious damage etc)

(Diamond) Sub-Contract Works have been properly completed ? — YES / NO

DOM 334 (14.3): The Sub-Contractor must be liable to make good at his own cost all defects, shrinkages and other faults in the Sub-Contract Works or in any part of the Sub-Contract Works;

Obligation in respect of defects

DOM 162 (8.5): Nothing in DOM clause 8 must in any way modify the Sub-Contractor's obligations in regard to defects in the Sub-Contract Works as set out in DOM clause 14.3 and .4

DOM 340 (14.4): Where the Contractor is liable under the Main Contract to make good defects, shrinkages or other faults; but

(Diamond) Sub-Contract Works have been properly handed over ? — YES / NO

DOM 901 (27.1.3.2): The Sub-Contractor must properly clear up and leave the Sub-Contract Works and all areas made available to him for the purpose of executing those Works, so far as used by him for that purpose, clean and tidy to the reasonable satisfaction of the Contractor;

Defective and/or incomplete work of the Sub-Contractor is excluded from the Contractor's responsibility in DOM 160

JCT 338 (20.2): The Contractor must be liable for any expense liability loss claim or proceedings in respect of any damage whatsoever to any property real or personal arising out of or in the course of or by reason of carrying out the Works;

JCT 339 (20.2): except for such loss or damage as is at the sole risk of the Employer under clause 22B or 22C (if applicable)

DOM 128 (8.1.2.1): The Employer must, where clause 22B of the Main Contract applies, bear the sole risk as regards loss or damage by the "Clause 22 Perils" to all work executed and all unfixed materials and goods, delivered to, placed on or adjacent to the Works and intended for incorporation into the Works

DOM 139 (8.1.2.1): The Employer must, where clause 22C of the Main Contract applies, bear the sole risk as regards loss or damage by the "Clause 22 Perils" to the existing structures and all work executed and all unfixed materials and goods, delivered to, placed on or adjacent to the Works and intended for incorporation into the Works

Sub-Contract Works – details in Appendix – progress of Works

Extension of Sub-Contract time – written notice of delay

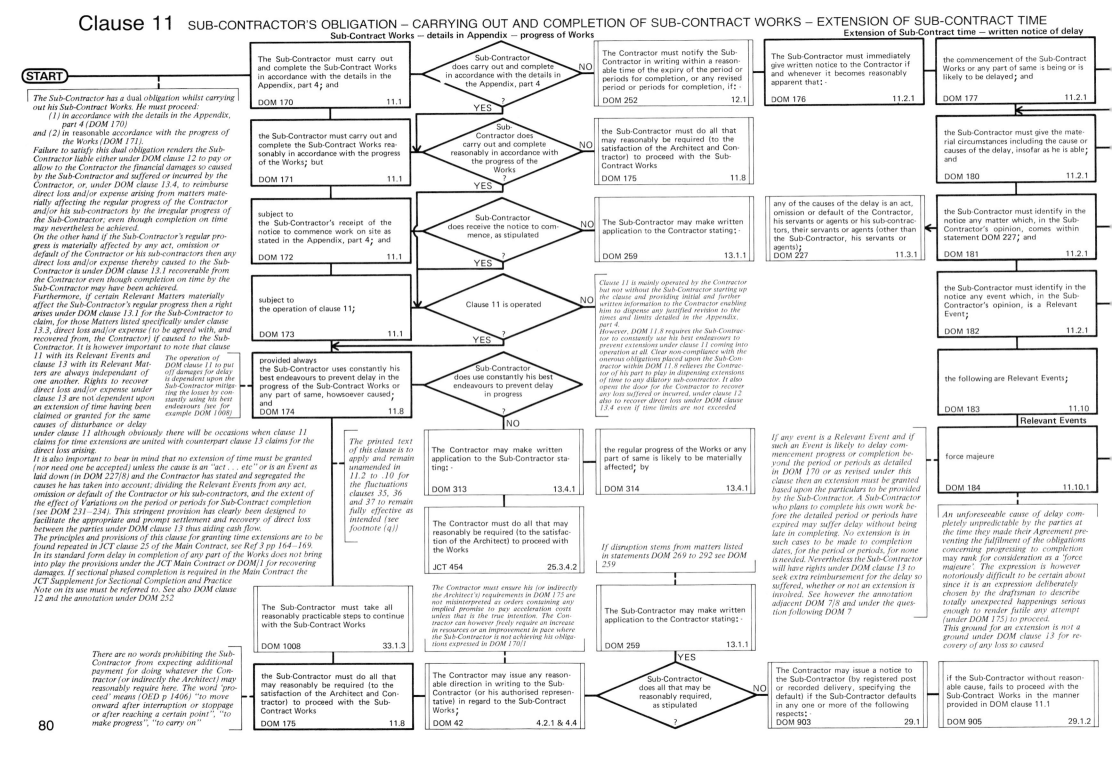

START

The Sub-Contractor has a dual obligation whilst carrying out his Sub-Contract Works. He must proceed:
(1) in accordance with the details in the Appendix, part 4 (DOM 170)
and (2) in reasonable accordance with the progress of the Works (DOM 171).
Failure to satisfy this dual obligation renders the Sub-Contractor liable either under DOM clause 12 to pay or allow to the Contractor the financial damages so caused by the Sub-Contractor and suffered or incurred by the Contractor, or, under DOM clause 13.4, to reimburse direct loss and/or expense arising from matters materially affecting the regular progress of the Contractor and/or his sub-contractors by the irregular progress of the Sub-Contractor; even though completion on time may nevertheless be achieved.
On the other hand if the Sub-Contractor's regular progress is materially affected by any act, omission or default of the Contractor or his sub-contractors then any direct loss and/or expense thereby caused to the Sub-Contractor is under DOM clause 13.1 recoverable from the Contractor even though completion on time by the Sub-Contractor may have been achieved.
Furthermore, if certain Relevant Matters materially affect the Sub-Contractor's regular progress then a right arises under DOM clause 13.1 for the Sub-Contractor to claim, for those Matters listed specifically under clause 13.3, direct loss and/or expense (to be agreed with, and recovered from, the Contractor) if caused to the Sub-Contractor. It is however important to note that clause 11 with its Relevant Events and clause 13 with its Relevant Matters are always independant of one another. Rights to recover direct loss and/or expense under clause 13 are not dependent upon an extension of time having been claimed or granted for the same causes of disturbance or delay under clause 11 although obviously there will be occasions when clause 11 claims for time extensions are united with counterpart clause 13 claims for the direct loss arising.
It is also important to bear in mind that no extension of time must be granted (nor need one be accepted) unless the cause is an "act . . . etc" or is an Event as laid down (in DOM 227/8) and the Contractor has stated and segregated the causes he has taken into account; dividing the Relevant Events from any act, omission or default of the Contractor or his sub-contractors, and the extent of the effect of Variations on the period or periods for Sub-Contract completion (see DOM 231–234). This stringent provision has clearly been designed to facilitate the appropriate and prompt settlement and recovery of direct loss between the parties under DOM clause 13 thus aiding cash flow.
The principles and provisions of this clause for granting time extensions are to be found repeated in JCT clause 25 of the Main Contract, see Ref 3 pp 164–169. In its standard form delay in completion of any part of the Works does not bring into play the provisions under the JCT Main Contract or DOM/1 for recovering damages. If sectional phased completion is required in the Main Contract the JCT Supplement for Sectional Completion and Practice Note on its use must be referred to. See also DOM clause 12 and the annotation under DOM 252

The operation of DOM clause 11 to put off damages for delay is dependent upon the Sub-Contractor mitigating the losses by constantly using his best endeavours (see for example DOM 1008)

There are no words prohibiting the Sub-Contractor from expecting additional payment for doing whatever the Contractor (or indirectly the Architect) may reasonably require here. The word 'proceed' means (OED p 1406) "to move onward after interruption or stoppage or after reaching a certain point", "to make progress", "to carry on"

The Sub-Contractor must carry out and complete the Sub-Contract Works in accordance with the details in the Appendix, part 4; and
DOM 170   11.1

the Sub-Contractor must carry out and complete the Sub-Contract Works reasonably in accordance with the progress of the Works; but
DOM 171   11.1

subject to the Sub-Contractor's receipt of the notice to commence work on site as stated in the Appendix, part 4; and
DOM 172   11.1

subject to the operation of clause 11;
DOM 173   11.1

provided always the Sub-Contractor uses constantly his best endeavours to prevent delay in the progress of the Sub-Contract Works or any part of same, howsoever caused; and
DOM 174   11.8

The printed text of this clause is to apply and remain unamended in 11.2 to .10 for the fluctuations clauses 35, 36 and 37 to remain fully effective as intended (see footnote (q))

The Sub-Contractor must take all reasonably practicable steps to continue with the Sub-Contract Works
DOM 1008   33.1.3

the Sub-Contractor must do all that may reasonably be required (to the satisfaction of the Architect and Contractor) to proceed with the Sub-Contract Works
DOM 175   11.8

Sub-Contractor does carry out and complete in accordance with the details in the Appendix, part 4 — NO / YES ?

Sub-Contractor does carry out and complete reasonably in accordance with the progress of the Works ? — NO / YES

Sub-Contractor does receive the notice to commence, as stipulated ? — NO / YES

Clause 11 is operated — NO / YES ?

Sub-Contractor does use constantly his best endeavours to prevent delay in progress ? — NO

The Contractor may make written application to the Sub-Contractor stating: -
DOM 313   13.4.1

The Contractor must do all that may reasonably be required (to the satisfaction of the Architect) to proceed with the Works
JCT 454   25.3.4.2

The Contractor must ensure his (or indirectly the Architect's) requirements under DOM 175 are not misinterpreted as orders containing any implied promise to pay acceleration costs unless that is the true intention. The Contractor can however freely require an increase in resources or an improvement in pace where the Sub-Contractor is not achieving his obligations expressed in DOM 170/1

The Contractor may issue any reasonable direction in writing to the Sub-Contractor (or his authorised representative) in regard to the Sub-Contract Works;
DOM 42   4.2.1 & 4.4

The Contractor must notify the Sub-Contractor in writing within a reasonable time of the expiry of the period or periods for completion, or any revised period or periods for completion, if: -
DOM 252   12.1

the Sub-Contractor must do all that may reasonably be required (to the satisfaction of the Architect and Contractor) to proceed with the Sub-Contract Works
DOM 175   11.8

The Sub-Contractor may make written application to the Contractor stating: -
DOM 259   13.1.1

Clause 11 is mainly operated by the Contractor but not without the Sub-Contractor starting up the clause and providing initial and further written information to the Contractor enabling him to dispense any justified revision to the times and limits detailed in the Appendix, part 4.
However, DOM 11.8 requires the Sub-Contractor to constantly use his best endeavours to prevent extensions under clause 11 coming into operation at all. Clear non-compliance with the onerous obligations placed upon the Sub-Contractor within DOM 11.8 relieves the Contractor of his part to play in dispensing extensions of time to any dilatory sub-contractor. It also opens the door for the Contractor to recover any loss suffered or incurred, under clause 12 also to recover direct loss under DOM clause 13.4 even if time limits are not exceeded

the regular progress of the Works or any part of same is likely to be materially affected; by
DOM 314   13.4.1

If disruption stems from matters listed in statements DOM 269 to 292 see DOM 259

The Sub-Contractor may make written application to the Contractor stating: -
DOM 259   13.1.1

Sub-Contractor does all that may be reasonably required, as stipulated ? — YES / NO

The Sub-Contractor must immediately give written notice to the Contractor if and whenever it becomes reasonably apparent that: -
DOM 176   11.2.1

any of the causes of the delay is an act, omission or default of the Contractor, his servants or agents or his sub-contractors, their servants or agents (other than the Sub-Contractor, his servants or agents);
DOM 227   11.3.1

If any event is a Relevant Event and if such an Event is likely to delay commencement progress or completion beyond the period or periods as detailed in DOM 170 or as revised under this clause then an extension must be granted based upon the particulars to be provided by the Sub-Contractor. A Sub-Contractor who plans to complete his own work before the detailed period or periods have expired may suffer delay without being late in completing. No extension is in such cases to be made to completion dates, for the period or periods, for none is needed. Nevertheless the Sub-Contractor will have rights under DOM clause 13 to seek extra reimbursement for the delay so suffered, whether or not an extension is involved. See however the annotation adjacent DOM 7/8 and under the question following DOM 7

The Contractor may issue a notice to the Sub-Contractor (by registered post or recorded delivery, specifying the default) if the Sub-Contractor defaults in any one or more of the following respects:
DOM 903   29.1

the commencement of the Sub-Contract Works or any part of same is being or is likely to be delayed; and
DOM 177   11.2.1

the Sub-Contractor must give the material circumstances including the cause or causes of the delay, insofar as he is able; and
DOM 180   11.2.1

the Sub-Contractor must identify in the notice any matter which, in the Sub-Contractor's opinion, comes within statement DOM 227; and
DOM 181   11.2.1

the Sub-Contractor must identify in the notice any event which, in the Sub-Contractor's opinion, is a Relevant Event;
DOM 182   11.2.1

the following are Relevant Events;
DOM 183   11.10

Relevant Events

force majeure
DOM 184   11.10.1

An unforeseeable cause of delay completely unpredictable by the parties at the time they made their Agreement preventing the fulfilment of the obligations concerning progressing to completion may rank for consideration as a 'force majeure'. The expression is however notoriously difficult to be certain about since it is an expression deliberately chosen by the draftsman to describe totally unexpected happenings serious enough to render futile any attempt (under DOM 175) to proceed.
This ground for an extension is not a ground under DOM clause 13 for recovery of any loss so caused

if the Sub-Contractor without reasonable cause, fails to proceed with the Sub-Contract Works in the manner provided in DOM clause 11.1
DOM 905   29.1.2

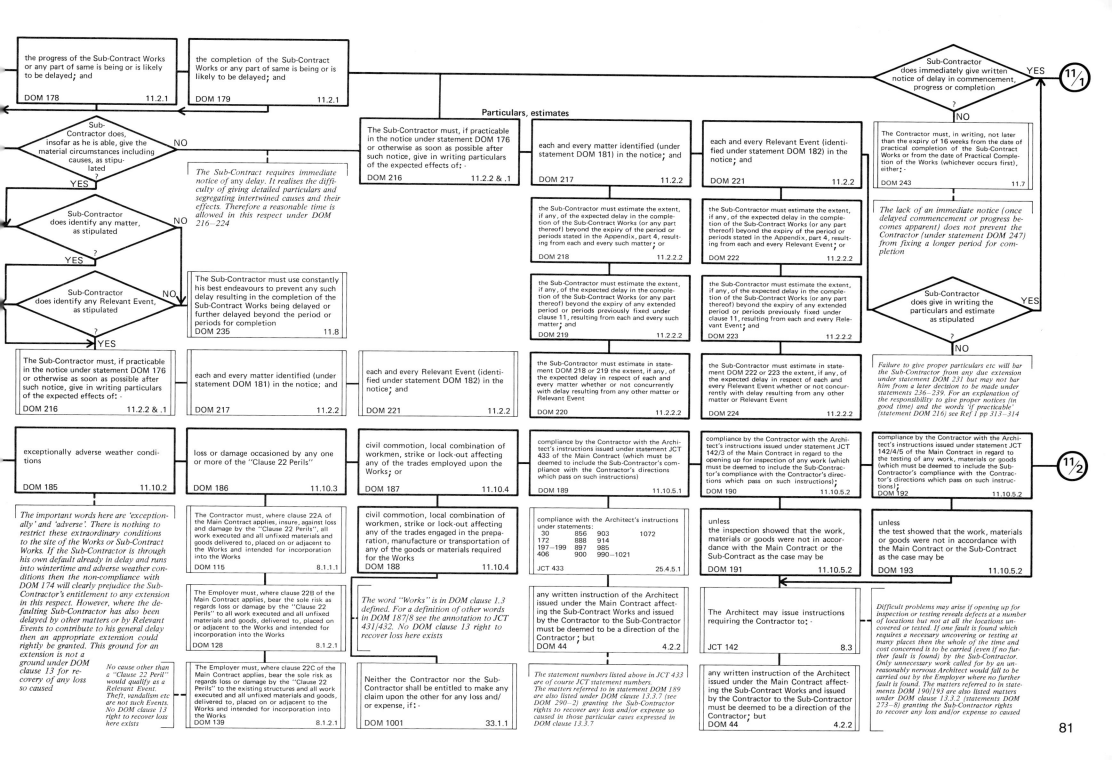

the progress of the Sub-Contract Works or any part of same is being or is likely to be delayed; and

DOM 178   11.2.1

the completion of the Sub-Contract Works or any part of same is being or is likely to be delayed; and

DOM 179   11.2.1

Sub-Contractor does immediately give written notice of delay in commencement, progress or completion

YES   11/1

NO

Particulars, estimates

Sub-Contractor does, insofar as he is able, give the material circumstances including causes, as stipulated

YES / NO

The Sub-Contract requires immediate notice of any delay. It realises the difficulty of giving detailed particulars and segregating intertwined causes and their effects. Therefore a reasonable time is allowed in this respect under DOM 216–224

The Sub-Contractor must, if practicable in the notice under statement DOM 176 or otherwise as soon as possible after such notice, give in writing particulars of the expected effects of: -

DOM 216   11.2.2 & .1

each and every matter identified (under statement DOM 181) in the notice; and

DOM 217   11.2.2

each and every Relevant Event (identified under statement DOM 182) in the notice; and

DOM 221   11.2.2

The Contractor must, in writing, not later than the expiry of 16 weeks from the date of practical completion of the Sub-Contract Works or from the date of Practical Completion of the Works (whichever occurs first), either: -

DOM 243   11.7

Sub-Contractor does identify any matter, as stipulated

YES / NO

the Sub-Contractor must estimate the extent, if any, of the expected delay in the completion of the Sub-Contract Works (or any part thereof) beyond the expiry of the period or periods stated in the Appendix, part 4, resulting from each and every such matter; or

DOM 218   11.2.2.2

the Sub-Contractor must estimate the extent, if any, of the expected delay in the completion of the Sub-Contract Works (or any part thereof) beyond the expiry of the period or periods stated in the Appendix, part 4, resulting from each and every Relevant Event; or

DOM 222   11.2.2.2

The lack of an immediate notice (once delayed commencement or progress becomes apparent) does not prevent the Contractor (under statement DOM 247) from fixing a longer period for completion

Sub-Contractor does identify any Relevant Event, as stipulated

NO / YES

The Sub-Contractor must use constantly his best endeavours to prevent any such delay resulting in the completion of the Sub-Contract Works being delayed or further delayed beyond the period or periods for completion

DOM 235   11.8

the Sub-Contractor must estimate the extent, if any, of the expected delay in the completion of the Sub-Contract Works (or any part thereof) beyond the expiry of any extended period or periods previously fixed under clause 11, resulting from each and every such matter; and

DOM 219   11.2.2.2

the Sub-Contractor must estimate the extent, if any, of the expected delay in the completion of the Sub-Contract Works (or any part thereof) beyond the expiry of any extended period or periods previously fixed under clause 11, resulting from each and every Relevant Event; and

DOM 223   11.2.2.2

Sub-Contractor does give in writing the particulars and estimate as stipulated

YES / NO

The Sub-Contractor must, if practicable in the notice under statement DOM 176 or otherwise as soon as possible after such notice, give in writing particulars of the expected effects of: -

DOM 216   11.2.2 & .1

each and every matter identified (under statement DOM 181) in the notice; and

DOM 217   11.2.2

each and every Relevant Event (identified under statement DOM 182) in the notice; and

DOM 221   11.2.2

the Sub-Contractor must estimate in statement DOM 218 or 219 the extent, if any, of the expected delay in respect of each and every matter whether or not concurrently with delay resulting from any other matter or Relevant Event

DOM 220   11.2.2.2

the Sub-Contractor must estimate in statement DOM 222 or 223 the extent, if any, of the expected delay in respect of each and every Relevant Event whether or not concurrently with delay resulting from any other matter or Relevant Event

DOM 224   11.2.2.2

Failure to give proper particulars etc will bar the Sub-Contractor from any due extension under statement DOM 231 but may not bar him from a later decision to be made under statements 236–239. For an explanation of the responsibility to give proper notices (in good time) and the words 'if practicable' (statement DOM 216) see Ref 1 pp 313–314

exceptionally adverse weather conditions

DOM 185   11.10.2

loss or damage occasioned by any one or more of the "Clause 22 Perils"

DOM 186   11.10.3

civil commotion, local combination of workmen, strike or lock-out affecting any of the trades employed upon the Works; or

DOM 187   11.10.4

compliance by the Contractor with the Architect's instructions issued under statement JCT 433 of the Main Contract (which must be deemed to include the Sub-Contractor's compliance with the Contractor's directions which pass on such instructions)

DOM 189   11.10.5.1

compliance by the Contractor with the Architect's instructions issued under statement JCT 142/3 of the Main Contract in regard to the opening up for inspection of any work (which must be deemed to include the Sub-Contractor's compliance with the Contractor's directions which pass on such instructions);

DOM 190   11.10.5.2

compliance by the Contractor with the Architect's instructions issued under statement JCT 142/4/5 of the Main Contract in regard to the testing of any work, materials or goods (which must be deemed to include the Sub-Contractor's compliance with the Contractor's directions which pass on such instructions);

DOM 192   11.10.5.2

11/2

The important words here are 'exceptionally' and 'adverse'. There is nothing to restrict these extraordinary conditions to the site of the Works or Sub-Contract Works. If the Sub-Contractor is through his own default already in delay and runs into wintertime and adverse weather conditions then the non-compliance with DOM 174 will clearly prejudice the Sub-Contractor's entitlement to any extension in this respect. However, where the defaulting Sub-Contractor has also been delayed by other matters or by Relevant Events to contribute to his general delay then an appropriate extension could rightly be granted. This ground for an extension is not a ground under DOM clause 13 for recovery of any loss so caused

The Contractor must, where clause 22A of the Main Contract applies, insure, against loss and damage by the "Clause 22 Perils", all work executed and all unfixed materials and goods delivered to, placed on or adjacent to the Works and intended for incorporation into the Works

DOM 115   8.1.1.1

civil commotion, local combination of workmen, strike or lock-out affecting any of the trades engaged in the preparation, manufacture or transportation of any of the goods or materials required for the Works

DOM 188   11.10.4

compliance with the Architect's instructions under statements:

30	856	903	1072
172	888	914	
197–199	897	985	
406	900	990–1021	

JCT 433   25.4.5.1

unless the inspection showed that the work, materials or goods were not in accordance with the Main Contract or the Sub-Contract as the case may be

DOM 191   11.10.5.2

unless the test showed that the work, materials or goods were not in accordance with the Main Contract or the Sub-Contract as the case may be

DOM 193   11.10.5.2

The Employer must, where clause 22B of the Main Contract applies, bear the sole risk as regards loss or damage by the "Clause 22 Perils" to all work executed and all unfixed materials and goods, delivered to, placed on or adjacent to the Works and intended for incorporation into the Works

DOM 128   8.1.2.1

The word "Works" is in DOM clause 1.3 defined. For a definition of other words in DOM 187/8 see the annotation to JCT 431/432. No DOM clause 13 right to recover loss here exists

any written instruction of the Architect issued under the Main Contract affecting the Sub-Contract Works and issued by the Contractor to the Sub-Contractor must be deemed to be a direction of the Contractor; but

DOM 44   4.2.2

The Architect may issue instructions requiring the Contractor to: -

JCT 142   8.3

Difficult problems may arise if opening up for inspection or testing reveals defects at a number of locations but not at all the locations uncovered or tested. If one fault is found which requires a necessary uncovering or testing at many places then the whole of the time and cost concerned is to be carried (even if no further fault is found) by the Sub-Contractor. Only unnecessary work called for by an unreasonably nervous Architect would fall to be carried out by the Employer where no further fault is found. The matters referred to in statements DOM 190/193 are also listed matters under DOM clause 13.3.2 (statements DOM 273–8) granting the Sub-Contractor rights to recover any loss and/or expense so caused

No cause other than a "Clause 22 Peril" would qualify as a Relevant Event. Theft, vandalism etc are not such Events. No DOM clause 13 right to recover loss here exists

The Employer must, where clause 22C of the Main Contract applies, bear the sole risk as regards loss or damage by the "Clause 22 Perils" to the existing structures and all work executed and all unfixed materials and goods, delivered to, placed on or adjacent to the Works and intended for incorporation into the Works

DOM 139   8.1.2.1

Neither the Contractor nor the Sub-Contractor shall be entitled to make any claim upon the other for any loss and/or expense, if: -

DOM 1001   33.1.1

The statement numbers listed above in JCT 433 are of course JCT statement numbers. The matters referred to in statement DOM 189 are also listed under DOM clause 13.3.7 (see DOM 290–2) granting the Sub-Contractor rights to recover any loss and/or expense so caused in those particular cases expressed in DOM clause 13.3.7

any written instruction of the Architect issued under the Main Contract affecting the Sub-Contract Works and issued by the Contractor to the Sub-Contractor must be deemed to be a direction of the Contractor; but

DOM 44   4.2.2

81

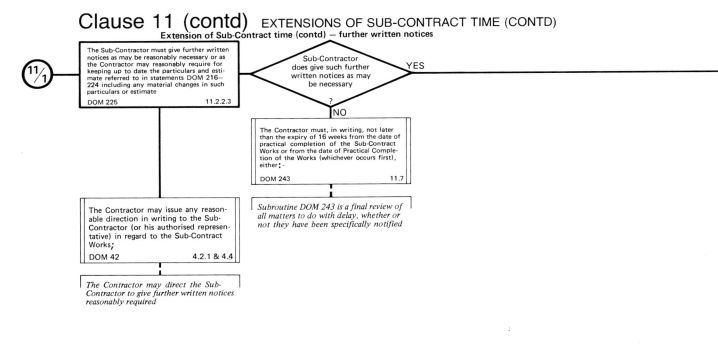

11/1

The Sub-Contractor must give further written notices as may be reasonably necessary or as the Contractor may reasonably require for keeping up to date the particulars and estimate referred to in statements DOM 216—224 including any material changes in such particulars or estimate

DOM 225   11.2.2.3

Sub-Contractor does give such further written notices as may be necessary ?

YES →

NO ↓

The Contractor must, in writing, not later than the expiry of 16 weeks from the date of practical completion of the Sub-Contract Works or from the date of Practical Completion of the Works (whichever occurs first), either: -

DOM 243   11.7

Subroutine DOM 243 is a final review of all matters to do with delay, whether or not they have been specifically notified

The Contractor may issue any reasonable direction in writing to the Sub-Contractor (or his authorised representative) in regard to the Sub-Contract Works;

DOM 42   4.2.1 & 4.4

The Contractor may direct the Sub-Contractor to give further written notices reasonably required

---

Relevant Events (contd)

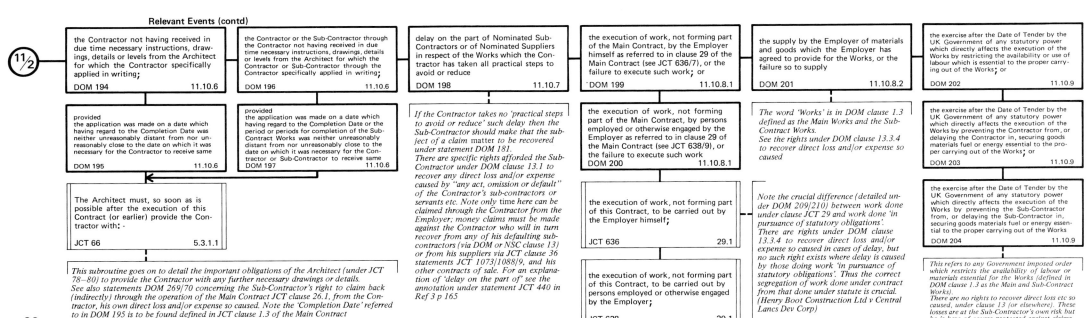

11/2

the Contractor not having received in due time necessary instructions, drawings, details or levels from the Architect for which the Contractor specifically applied in writing;

DOM 194   11.10.6

provided
the application was made on a date which having regard to the Completion Date was neither unreasonably distant from nor unreasonably close to the date on which it was necessary for the Contractor to receive same

DOM 195   11.10.6

The Architect must, so soon as is possible after the execution of this Contract (or earlier) provide the Contractor with: -

JCT 66   5.3.1.1

This subroutine goes on to detail the important obligations of the Architect (under JCT 78–80) to provide the Contractor with any further necessary drawings or details. See also statements DOM 269/70 concerning the Sub-Contractor's right to claim back (indirectly) through the operation of the Main Contract JCT clause 26.1, from the Contractor, his own direct loss and/or expense so caused. Note the 'Completion Date' referred to in DOM 195 is to be found defined in JCT clause 1.3 of the Main Contract

the Contractor or the Sub-Contractor through the Contractor not having received in due time necessary instructions, drawings, details or levels from the Architect for which the Contractor or Sub-Contractor through the Contractor specifically applied in writing;

DOM 196   11.10.6

provided
the application was made on a date which having regard to the Completion Date or the period or periods for completion of the Sub-Contract Works was neither unreasonably distant from nor unreasonably close to the date on which it was necessary for the Contractor or Sub-Contractor to receive same

DOM 197   11.10.6

delay on the part of Nominated Sub-Contractors or of Nominated Suppliers in respect of the Works which the Contractor has taken all practical steps to avoid or reduce

DOM 198   11.10.7

If the Contractor takes no 'practical steps to avoid or reduce' such delay then the Sub-Contractor should make that the subject of a claim matter to be recovered under statement DOM 181.
There are specific rights afforded the Sub-Contractor under DOM clause 13.1 to recover any direct loss and/or expense caused by "any act, omission or default" of the Contractor's sub-contractors or servants etc. Note only time here can be claimed through the Contractor from the Employer; money claims must be made against the Contractor who will in turn recover from any of his defaulting sub-contractors (via DOM or NSC clause 13) or from his suppliers via JCT clause 36 statements JCT 1073/1088/9, and his other contracts of sale. For an explanation of 'delay on the part of' see the annotation under statement JCT 440 in Ref 3 p 165

the execution of work, not forming part of the Main Contract, by the Employer himself as referred to in clause 29 of the Main Contract (see JCT 636/7), or the failure to execute such work; or

DOM 199   11.10.8.1

the execution of work, not forming part of the Main Contract, by persons employed or otherwise engaged by the Employer as referred to in clause 29 of the Main Contract (see JCT 638/9), or the failure to execute such work

DOM 200   11.10.8.1

the execution of work, not forming part of this Contract, to be carried out by the Employer himself;

JCT 636   29.1

the execution of work, not forming part of this Contract, to be carried out by persons employed or otherwise engaged by the Employer;

JCT 638   29.1

the supply by the Employer of materials and goods which the Employer has agreed to provide for the Works, or the failure so to supply

DOM 201   11.10.8.2

The word 'Works' is in DOM clause 1.3 defined as the Main Works and the Sub-Contract Works.
See the rights under DOM clause 13.3.4 to recover direct loss and/or expense so caused

Note the crucial difference (detailed under DOM 209/210) between work done under clause JCT 29 and work done 'in pursuance of statutory obligations'.
There are rights under DOM clause 13.3.4 to recover direct loss and/or expense so caused in cases of delay, but no such right exists where delay is caused by those doing work 'in pursuance of statutory obligations'. Thus the correct segregation of work done under contract from that done under statute is crucial. (Henry Boot Construction Ltd v Central Lancs Dev Corp)

the exercise after the Date of Tender by the UK Government of any statutory power which directly affects the execution of the Works by restricting the availability or use of labour which is essential to the proper carrying out of the Works; or

DOM 202   11.10.9

the exercise after the Date of Tender by the UK Government of any statutory power which directly affects the execution of the Works by preventing the Contractor from, or delaying the Contractor in, securing goods materials fuel or energy essential to the proper carrying out of the Works; or

DOM 203   11.10.9

the exercise after the Date of Tender by the UK Government of any statutory power which directly affects the execution of the Works by preventing the Sub-Contractor from, or delaying the Sub-Contractor in, securing goods materials fuel or energy essential to the proper carrying out of the Works

DOM 204   11.10.9

This refers to any Government imposed order which restricts the availability of labour or materials essential for the Works (defined in DOM clause 1.3 as the Main and Sub-Contract Works).
There are no rights to recover direct loss etc so caused, under clause 13 (or elsewhere). These losses are at the Sub-Contractor's own risk but he is here of course protected against claims that might otherwise be made for damages due to the delays caused

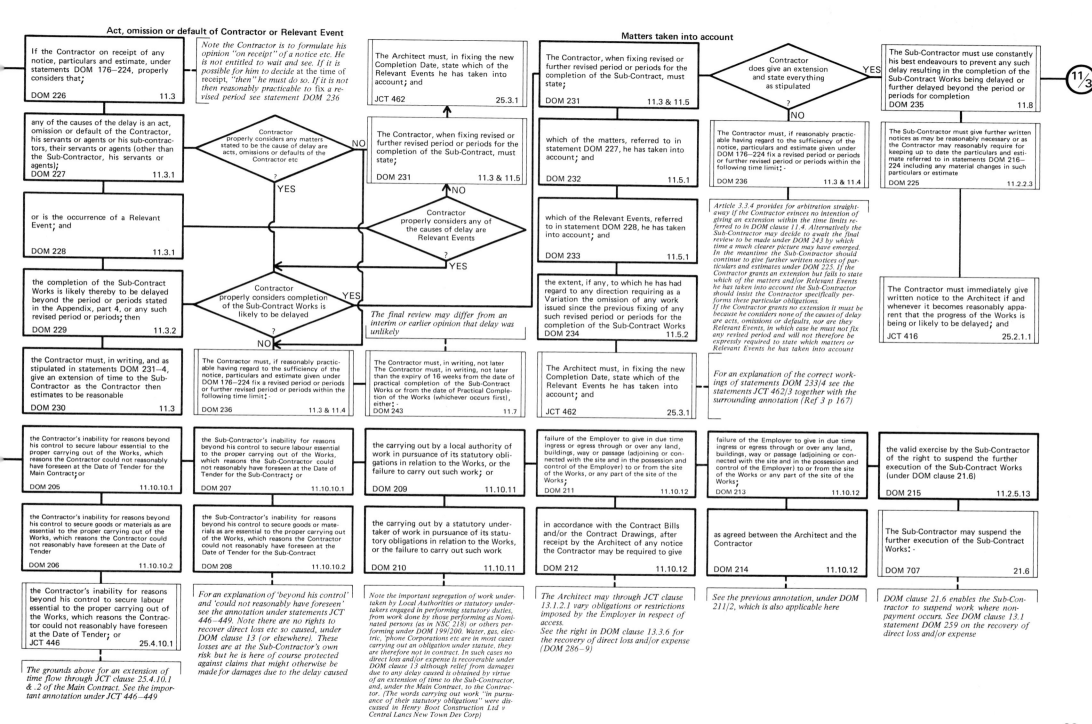

Column 1

If the Contractor on receipt of any notice, particulars and estimate, under statements DOM 176–224, properly considers that;
DOM 226 11.3

any of the causes of the delay is an act, omission or default of the Contractor, his servants or agents or his sub-contractors, their servants or agents (other than the Sub-Contractor, his servants or agents);
DOM 227 11.3.1

or is the occurrence of a Relevant Event; and
DOM 228 11.3.1

the completion of the Sub-Contract Works is likely thereby to be delayed beyond the period or periods stated in the Appendix, part 4, or any such revised period or periods; then
DOM 229 11.3.2

the Contractor must, in writing, and as stipulated in statements DOM 231–4, give an extension of time to the Sub-Contractor as the Contractor then estimates to be reasonable
DOM 230 11.3

the Contractor's inability for reasons beyond his control to secure labour essential to the proper carrying out of the Works, which reasons the Contractor could not reasonably have foreseen at the Date of Tender for the Main Contract; or
DOM 205 11.10.10.1

the Contractor's inability for reasons beyond his control to secure goods or materials as are essential to the proper carrying out of the Works, which reasons the Contractor could not reasonably have foreseen at the Date of Tender
DOM 206 11.10.10.2

the Contractor's inability for reasons beyond his control to secure labour essential to the proper carrying out of the Works, which reasons the Contractor could not reasonably have foreseen at the Date of Tender; or
JCT 446 25.4.10.1

The grounds above for an extension of time flow through JCT clause 25.4.10.1 & .2 of the Main Contract. See the important annotation under JCT 446–449

Column 2

Note the Contractor is to formulate his opinion "on receipt" of a notice etc. He is not entitled to wait and see. If it is possible for him to decide at the time of receipt, "then" he must do so. If it is not then reasonably practicable to fix a revised period see statement DOM 236

(diamond) Contractor properly considers any matters stated to be the cause of delay are acts, omissions or defaults of the Contractor etc ? NO / YES

(diamond) Contractor properly considers any of the causes of delay are Relevant Events ? YES

(diamond) Contractor properly considers completion of the Sub-Contract Works is likely to be delayed ? YES / NO

The Contractor must, if reasonably practicable having regard to the sufficiency of the notice, particulars and estimate given under DOM 176–224 fix a revised period or periods or further revised period or periods within the following time limit: -
DOM 236 11.3 & 11.4

The final review may differ from an interim or earlier opinion that delay was unlikely

the Sub-Contractor's inability for reasons beyond his control to secure labour essential to the proper carrying out of the Works, which reasons the Sub-Contractor could not reasonably have foreseen at the Date of Tender for the Sub-Contract; or
DOM 207 11.10.10.1

the Sub-Contractor's inability for reasons beyond his control to secure goods or materials as are essential to the proper carrying out of the Works, which reasons the Contractor could not reasonably have foreseen at the Date of Tender for the Sub-Contract
DOM 208 11.10.10.2

For an explanation of 'beyond his control' and 'could not reasonably have foreseen' see the annotation under statements JCT 446–449. Note there are no rights to recover direct loss etc so caused, under DOM clause 13 (or elsewhere). These losses are at the Sub-Contractor's own risk but he is here of course protected against claims that might otherwise be made for damages due to the delay caused

Column 3

The Architect must, in fixing the new Completion Date, state which of the Relevant Events he has taken into account; and
JCT 462 25.3.1

The Contractor, when fixing revised or further revised period or periods for the completion of the Sub-Contract, must state;
DOM 231 11.3 & 11.5 NO

The Contractor must, in writing, not later than the expiry of 16 weeks from the date of practical completion of the Sub-Contract Works or from the date of Practical Completion of the Works (whichever occurs first), either;
DOM 243 11.7

the carrying out by a local authority of work in pursuance of its statutory obligations in relation to the Works, or the failure to carry out such work; or
DOM 209 11.10.11

the carrying out by a statutory undertaker of work in pursuance of its statutory obligations in relation to the Works, or the failure to carry out such work
DOM 210 11.10.11

Note the important segregation of work undertaken by Local Authorities or statutory undertakers engaged in performing statutory duties, from work done by those performing as Nominated persons (as in NSC 218) or others performing under DOM 199/200. Water, gas, electric, 'phone Corporations etc are in most cases carrying out an obligation under statute, they are therefore not in contract. In such cases no direct loss and/or expense is recoverable under DOM clause 13 although relief from damages due to any delay caused is obtained by virtue of an extension of time to the Sub-Contractor, and, under the Main Contract, to the Contractor. (The words carrying out work "in pursuance of their statutory obligations" were discussed in Henry Boot Construction Ltd v Central Lancs New Town Dev Corp)

Column 4

The Contractor, when fixing revised or further revised period or periods for the completion of the Sub-Contract, must state;
DOM 231 11.3 & 11.5

which of the matters, referred to in statement DOM 227, he has taken into account; and
DOM 232 11.5.1

which of the Relevant Events, referred to in statement DOM 228, he has taken into account; and
DOM 233 11.5.1

the extent, if any, to which he has had regard to any direction requiring as a Variation the omission of any work issued since the previous fixing of any such revised period or periods for the completion of the Sub-Contract Works
DOM 234 11.5.2

The Architect must, in fixing the new Completion Date, state which of the Relevant Events he has taken into account; and
JCT 462 25.3.1

failure of the Employer to give in due time ingress or egress through or over any land, buildings, way or passage (adjoining or connected with the site and in the possession and control of the Employer) to or from the site of the Works, or any part of the site of the Works;
DOM 211 11.10.12

in accordance with the Contract Bills and/or the Contract Drawings, after receipt by the Architect of any notice the Contractor may be required to give
DOM 212 11.10.12

The Architect may through JCT clause 13.1.2.1 vary obligations or restrictions imposed by the Employer in respect of access. See the right in DOM clause 13.3.6 for the recovery of direct loss and/or expense (DOM 286–9)

Column 5

(diamond) Contractor does give an extension and state everything as stipulated ? YES / NO

The Contractor must, if reasonably practicable having regard to the sufficiency of the notice, particulars and estimate given under DOM 176–224 fix a revised period or periods or further revised period or periods within the following time limit: -
DOM 236 11.3 & 11.4

Article 3.3.4 provides for arbitration straight-away if the Contractor evinces no intention of giving an extension within the time limits referred to in DOM clause 11.4. Alternatively the Sub-Contractor may decide to await the final review to be made under DOM 243 by which time a much clearer picture may have emerged. In the meantime the Sub-Contractor should continue to give further written notices of particulars and estimates under DOM 225. If the Contractor grants an extension but fails to state which of the matters and/or Relevant Events he has taken into account the Sub-Contractor should insist the Contractor specifically performs these particular obligations. If the Contractor grants no extension it must be because he considers none of the causes of delay are acts, omissions or defaults, nor are they Relevant Events, in which case he must not fix any revised period and will not therefore be expressly required to state which matters or Relevant Events he has taken into account

For an explanation of the correct workings of statements DOM 233/4 see the statements JCT 462/3 together with the surrounding annotation (Ref 3 p 167)

failure of the Employer to give in due time ingress or egress through or over any land, buildings, way or passage (adjoining or connected with the site and in the possession and control of the Employer) to or from the site of the Works or any part of the site of the Works;
DOM 213 11.10.12

as agreed between the Architect and the Contractor
DOM 214 11.10.12

See the previous annotation, under DOM 211/2, which is also applicable here

Column 6

The Sub-Contractor must use constantly his best endeavours to prevent any such delay resulting in the completion of the Sub-Contract Works being delayed or further delayed beyond the period or periods for completion
DOM 235 11.8 YES 11/3

The Sub-Contractor must give further written notices as may be reasonably necessary or as the Contractor may reasonably require for keeping up to date the particulars and estimate referred to in statements DOM 216–224 including any material changes in such particulars or estimate
DOM 225 11.2.2.3

The Contractor must immediately give written notice to the Architect if and whenever it becomes reasonably apparent that the progress of the Works is being or likely to be delayed; and
JCT 416 25.2.1.1

the valid exercise by the Sub-Contractor of the right to suspend the further execution of the Sub-Contract Works (under DOM clause 21.6)
DOM 215 11.2.5.13

The Sub-Contractor may suspend the further execution of the Sub-Contract Works: -
DOM 707 21.6

DOM clause 21.6 enables the Sub-Contractor to suspend work where non-payment occurs. See DOM clause 13.1 statement DOM 259 on the recovery of direct loss and/or expense

Sub-Contractor's best endeavours to prevent delay — **Time limit for fixing the revised period or periods**

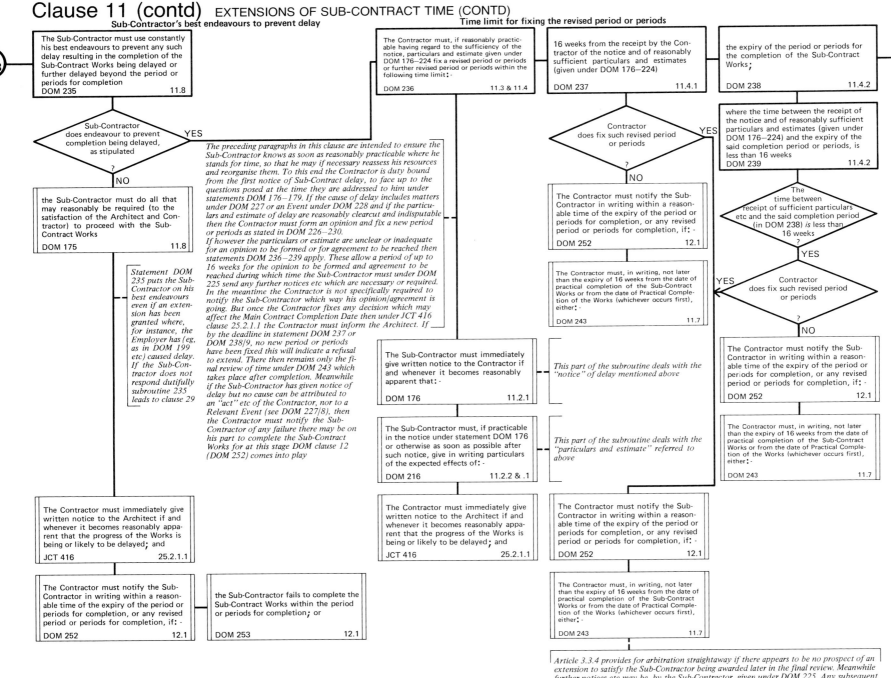

(11/3)

The Sub-Contractor must use constantly his best endeavours to prevent any such delay resulting in the completion of the Sub-Contract Works being delayed or further delayed beyond the period or periods for completion
DOM 235 — 11.8

Sub-Contractor does endeavour to prevent completion being delayed, as stipulated ? — **YES** / **NO**

the Sub-Contractor must do all that may reasonably be required (to the satisfaction of the Architect and Contractor) to proceed with the Sub-Contract Works
DOM 175 — 11.8

Statement DOM 235 puts the Sub-Contractor on his best endeavours even if an extension has been granted where, for instance, the Employer has (eg, as in DOM 199 etc) caused delay. If the Sub-Contractor does not respond dutifully subroutine 235 leads to clause 29

The Contractor must immediately give written notice to the Architect if and whenever it becomes reasonably apparent that the progress of the Works is being or likely to be delayed; and
JCT 416 — 25.2.1.1

The Contractor must notify the Sub-Contractor in writing within a reasonable time of the expiry of the period or periods for completion, or any revised period or periods for completion, if:-
DOM 252 — 12.1

the Sub-Contractor fails to complete the Sub-Contract Works within the period or periods for completion; or
DOM 253 — 12.1

The Contractor must, if reasonably practicable having regard to the sufficiency of the notice, particulars and estimate given under DOM 176—224 fix a revised period or periods or further revised period or periods within the following time limit:-
DOM 236 — 11.3 & 11.4

The preceding paragraphs in this clause are intended to ensure the Sub-Contractor knows as soon as reasonably practicable where he stands for time, so that he may if necessary reassess his resources and reorganise them. To this end the Contractor is duty bound from the first notice of Sub-Contract delay, to face up to the questions posed at the time they are addressed to him under statements DOM 176–179. If the cause of delay includes matters under DOM 227 or an Event under DOM 228 and if the particulars and estimate of delay are reasonably clearcut and indisputable then the Contractor must form an opinion and fix a new period or periods as stated in DOM 226–230.
If however the particulars or estimate are unclear or inadequate for an opinion to be formed or for agreement to be reached then statements DOM 236–239 apply. These allow a period of up to 16 weeks for the opinion to be formed and agreement to be reached during which time the Sub-Contractor must under DOM 225 send any further notices etc which are necessary or required. In the meantime the Contractor is not specifically required to notify the Sub-Contractor which way his opinion/agreement is going. But once the Contractor fixes any decision which may affect the Main Contract Completion Date then under JCT 416 clause 25.2.1.1 the Contractor must inform the Architect. If by the deadline in statement DOM 237 or DOM 238/9, no new period or periods have been fixed this will indicate a refusal to extend. There then remains only the final review of time under DOM 243 which takes place after completion. Meanwhile if the Sub-Contractor has given notice of delay but no cause can be attributed to an "act" etc of the Contractor, nor to a Relevant Event (see DOM 227/8), then the Contractor must notify the Sub-Contractor of any failure there may be on his part to complete the Sub-Contract Works for at this stage DOM clause 12 (DOM 252) comes into play

The Sub-Contractor must immediately give written notice to the Contractor if and whenever it becomes reasonably apparent that:-
DOM 176 — 11.2.1

This part of the subroutine deals with the "notice" of delay mentioned above

The Sub-Contractor must, if practicable in the notice under statement DOM 176 or otherwise as soon as possible after such notice, give in writing particulars of the expected effects of:-
DOM 216 — 11.2.2 & .1

This part of the subroutine deals with the "particulars and estimate" referred to above

The Contractor must immediately give written notice to the Architect if and whenever it becomes reasonably apparent that the progress of the Works is being or likely to be delayed; and
JCT 416 — 25.2.1.1

---

16 weeks from the receipt by the Contractor of the notice and of reasonably sufficient particulars and estimates (given under DOM 176—224)
DOM 237 — 11.4.1

Contractor does fix such revised period or periods ? — **YES** / **NO**

The Contractor must notify the Sub-Contractor in writing within a reasonable time of the expiry of the period or periods for completion, or any revised period or periods for completion, if:-
DOM 252 — 12.1

The Contractor must, in writing, not later than the expiry of 16 weeks from the date of practical completion of the Sub-Contract Works or from the date of Practical Completion of the Works (whichever occurs first), either:-
DOM 243 — 11.7

The Contractor must notify the Sub-Contractor in writing within a reasonable time of the expiry of the period or periods for completion, or any revised period or periods for completion, if:-
DOM 252 — 12.1

The Contractor must, in writing, not later than the expiry of 16 weeks from the date of practical completion of the Sub-Contract Works or from the date of Practical Completion of the Works (whichever occurs first), either:-
DOM 243 — 11.7

---

the expiry of the period or periods for the completion of the Sub-Contract Works;
DOM 238 — 11.4.2

where the time between the receipt of the notice and of reasonably sufficient particulars and estimates (given under DOM 176—224) and the expiry of the said completion period or periods, is less than 16 weeks
DOM 239 — 11.4.2

The time between receipt of sufficient particulars etc and the said completion period (in DOM 238) is less than 16 weeks ? — **YES**

Contractor does fix such revised period or periods ? — **YES** / **NO**

The Contractor must notify the Sub-Contractor in writing within a reasonable time of the expiry of the period or periods for completion, or any revised period or periods for completion, if:-
DOM 252 — 12.1

The Contractor must, in writing, not later than the expiry of 16 weeks from the date of practical completion of the Sub-Contract Works or from the date of Practical Completion of the Works (whichever occurs first), either:-
DOM 243 — 11.7

Article 3.3.4 provides for arbitration straightaway if there appears to be no prospect of an extension to satisfy the Sub-Contractor being awarded later in the final review. Meanwhile further notices etc may be, by the Sub-Contractor, given under DOM 225. Any subsequent failure to complete by the extended date will require the Contractor to give notice to that effect under DOM 252 before seeking payment of or allowance for losses he may have incurred through the delay

Omission of work

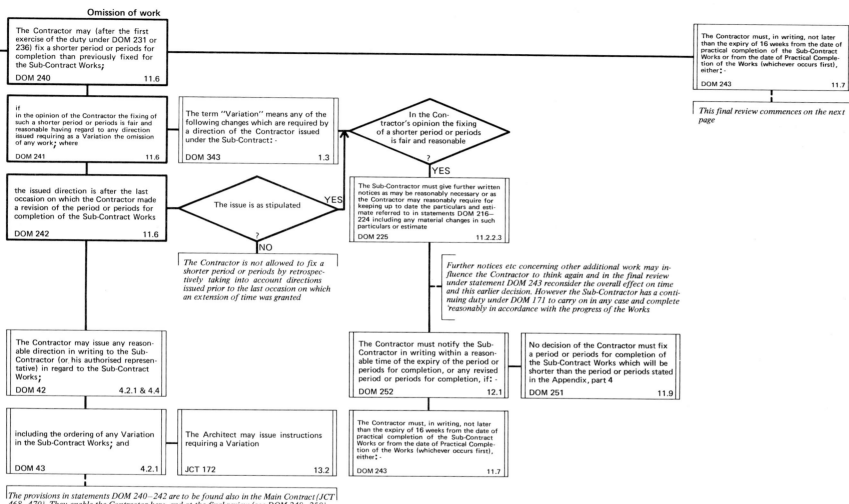

The Contractor may (after the first exercise of the duty under DOM 231 or 236) fix a shorter period or periods for completion than previously fixed for the Sub-Contract Works;

DOM 240   11.6

---

if
in the opinion of the Contractor the fixing of such a shorter period or periods is fair and reasonable having regard to any direction issued requiring as a Variation the omission of any work; where

DOM 241   11.6

---

the issued direction is after the last occasion on which the Contractor made a revision of the period or periods for completion of the Sub-Contract Works

DOM 242   11.6

The term "Variation" means any of the following changes which are required by a direction of the Contractor issued under the Sub-Contract: -

DOM 343   1.3

The issue is as stipulated   **YES**

?   **NO**

The Contractor is not allowed to fix a shorter period or periods by retrospectively taking into account directions issued prior to the last occasion on which an extension of time was granted

---

In the Contractor's opinion the fixing of a shorter period or periods is fair and reasonable

?   **YES**

The Sub-Contractor must give further written notices as may be reasonably necessary or as the Contractor may reasonably require for keeping up to date the particulars and estimate referred to in statements DOM 216—224 including any material changes in such particulars or estimate

DOM 225   11.2.2.3

Further notices etc concerning other additional work may influence the Contractor to think again and in the final review under statement DOM 243 reconsider the overall effect on time and this earlier decision. However the Sub-Contractor has a continuing duty under DOM 171 to carry on in any case and complete reasonably in accordance with the progress of the Works

---

The Contractor must, in writing, not later than the expiry of 16 weeks from the date of practical completion of the Sub-Contract Works or from the date of Practical Completion of the Works (whichever occurs first), either: -

DOM 243   11.7

This final review commences on the next page

The Contractor may issue any reasonable direction in writing to the Sub-Contractor (or his authorised representative) in regard to the Sub-Contract Works;

DOM 42   4.2.1 & 4.4

---

including the ordering of any Variation in the Sub-Contract Works; and

DOM 43   4.2.1

The Architect may issue instructions requiring a Variation

JCT 172   13.2

The Contractor must notify the Sub-Contractor in writing within a reasonable time of the expiry of the period or periods for completion, or any revised period or periods for completion, if: -

DOM 252   12.1

The Contractor must, in writing, not later than the expiry of 16 weeks from the date of practical completion of the Sub-Contract Works or from the date of Practical Completion of the Works (whichever occurs first), either: -

DOM 243   11.7

No decision of the Contractor must fix a period or periods for completion of the Sub-Contract Works which will be shorter than the period or periods stated in the Appendix, part 4

DOM 251   11.9

11/4

The provisions in statements DOM 240–242 are to be found also in the Main Contract (JCT 468–470). They enable the Contractor here, and at the final review (see DOM 248–250), on his own initiative, without the consent of the Architect and without an application or notice of the effects of omissions by the Sub-Contractor, to fairly take into account net savings in time as a result of Variation instructions issued for omissions of any work.
But this is only permitted after the first decision in the case of this Sub-Contract to extend time has been taken and, as stated in DOM 242, it is only permitted to consider such directions which actually omit work and have been issued (to the Sub-Contractor) "after the last occasion on which the Contractor made a revision of the period or periods for completion of the Sub-Contract Works".
It is therefore a discretionary power exercisable at any time by the Contractor after an extension has been granted under DOM 231 or 236 but is restricted to any omission of work made after the last extension granted

Review of period for completion of Sub-Contract Works

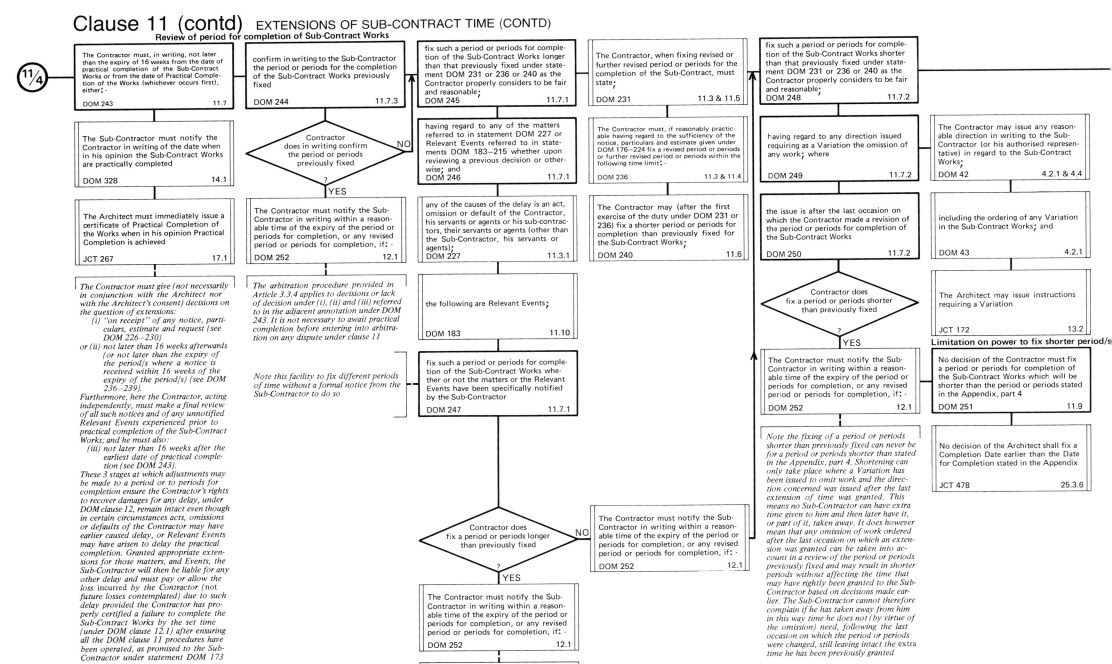

11/4

The Contractor must, in writing, not later than the expiry of 16 weeks from the date of practical completion of the Sub-Contract Works or from the date of Practical Completion of the Works (whichever occurs first), either: -

DOM 243   11.7

The Sub-Contractor must notify the Contractor in writing of the date when in his opinion the Sub-Contract Works are practically completed

DOM 328   14.1

The Architect must immediately issue a certificate of Practical Completion of the Works when in his opinion Practical Completion is achieved

JCT 267   17.1

The Contractor must give (not necessarily in conjunction with the Architect nor with the Architect's consent) decisions on the question of extensions:
(i) "on receipt" of any notice, particulars, estimate and request (see DOM 226–230)
or (ii) not later than 16 weeks afterwards (or not later than the expiry of the period/s where a notice is received within 16 weeks of the expiry of the period/s) (see DOM 236–239).
Furthermore, here the Contractor, acting independently, must make a final review of all such notices and of any unnotified Relevant Events experienced prior to practical completion of the Sub-Contract Works; and he must also:
(iii) not later than 16 weeks after the earliest date of practical completion (see DOM 243).
These 3 stages at which adjustments may be made to a period or to periods for completion ensure the Contractor's rights to recover damages for any delay, under DOM clause 12, remain intact even though in certain circumstances acts, omissions or defaults of the Contractor may have earlier caused delay, or Relevant Events may have arisen to delay the practical completion. Granted appropriate extensions for those matters, and Events, the Sub-Contractor will then be liable for any other delay and must pay or allow the loss incurred by the Contractor (not future losses contemplated) due to such delay provided the Contractor has properly certified a failure to complete the Sub-Contract Works by the set time (under DOM clause 12.1) after ensuring all the DOM clause 11 procedures have been operated, as promised to the Sub-Contractor under statement DOM 173

---

confirm in writing to the Sub-Contractor the period or periods for the completion of the Sub-Contract Works previously fixed

DOM 244   11.7.3

◇ Contractor does in writing confirm the period or periods previously fixed ? — **NO** / **YES**

The Contractor must notify the Sub-Contractor in writing within a reasonable time of the expiry of the period or periods for completion, or any revised period or periods for completion, if: -

DOM 252   12.1

The arbitration procedure provided in Article 3.3.4 applies to decisions or lack of decision under (i), (ii) and (iii) referred to in the adjacent annotation under DOM 243. It is not necessary to await practical completion before entering into arbitration on any dispute under clause 11

Note this facility to fix different periods of time without a formal notice from the Sub-Contractor to do so

---

fix such a period or periods for completion of the Sub-Contract Works longer than that previously fixed under statement DOM 231 or 236 or 240 as the Contractor properly considers to be fair and reasonable;

DOM 245   11.7.1

having regard to any of the matters referred to in statement DOM 227 or Relevant Events referred to in statements DOM 183–215 whether upon reviewing a previous decision or otherwise; and

DOM 246   11.7.1

any of the causes of the delay is an act, omission or default of the Contractor, his servants or agents or his sub-contractors, their servants or agents (other than the Sub-Contractor, his servants or agents);

DOM 227   11.3.1

the following are Relevant Events;

DOM 183   11.10

fix such a period or periods for completion of the Sub-Contract Works whether or not the matters or the Relevant Events have been specifically notified by the Sub-Contractor

DOM 247   11.7.1

◇ Contractor does fix a period or periods longer than previously fixed ? — **NO** / **YES**

The Contractor must notify the Sub-Contractor in writing within a reasonable time of the expiry of the period or periods for completion, or any revised period or periods for completion, if: -

DOM 252   12.1

If the periods fixed do not satisfy the Sub-Contractor Article 3.3.4 makes arbitration available

---

The Contractor, when fixing revised or further revised period or periods for the completion of the Sub-Contract, must state;

DOM 231   11.3 & 11.5

The Contractor must, if reasonably practicable having regard to the sufficiency of the notice, particulars and estimate given under DOM 176–224 fix a revised period or periods or further revised period or periods within the following time limit: -

DOM 236   11.3 & 11.4

The Contractor may (after the first exercise of the duty under DOM 231 or 236) fix a shorter period or periods for completion than previously fixed for the Sub-Contract Works;

DOM 240   11.6

The Contractor must notify the Sub-Contractor in writing within a reasonable time of the expiry of the period or periods for completion, or any revised period or periods for completion, if: -

DOM 252   12.1

---

fix such a period or periods for completion of the Sub-Contract Works shorter than that previously fixed under statement DOM 231 or 236 or 240 as the Contractor properly considers to be fair and reasonable;

DOM 248   11.7.2

having regard to any direction issued requiring as a Variation the omission of any work; where

DOM 249   11.7.2

the issue is after the last occasion on which the Contractor made a revision of the period or periods for completion of the Sub-Contract Works

DOM 250   11.7.2

◇ Contractor does fix a period or periods shorter than previously fixed ? — **YES**

The Contractor must notify the Sub-Contractor in writing within a reasonable time of the expiry of the period or periods for completion, or any revised period or periods for completion, if: -

DOM 252   12.1

Note the fixing of a period or periods shorter than previously fixed can never be for a period or periods shorter than stated in the Appendix, part 4. Shortening can only take place where a Variation has been issued to omit work and the direction concerned was issued after the last extension of time was granted. This means no Sub-Contractor can have extra time given to him and then later have it, or part of it, taken away. It does however mean that any omission of work ordered after the last occasion on which an extension was granted can be taken into account in a review of the period or periods previously fixed and may result in shorter periods without affecting the time that may have rightly been granted to the Sub-Contractor based on decisions made earlier. The Sub-Contractor cannot therefore complain if he has taken away from him in this way time he does not (by virtue of the omission) need, following the last occasion on which the period or periods were changed, still leaving intact the extra time he has been previously granted

---

The Contractor may issue any reasonable direction in writing to the Sub-Contractor (or his authorised representative) in regard to the Sub-Contract Works;

DOM 42   4.2.1 & 4.4

including the ordering of any Variation in the Sub-Contract Works; and

DOM 43   4.2.1

The Architect may issue instructions requiring a Variation

JCT 172   13.2

Limitation on power to fix shorter period/s

No decision of the Contractor must fix a period or periods for completion of the Sub-Contract Works which will be shorter than the period or periods stated in the Appendix, part 4

DOM 251   11.9

No decision of the Architect shall fix a Completion Date earlier than the Date for Completion stated in the Appendix

JCT 478   25.3.6

(STOP)

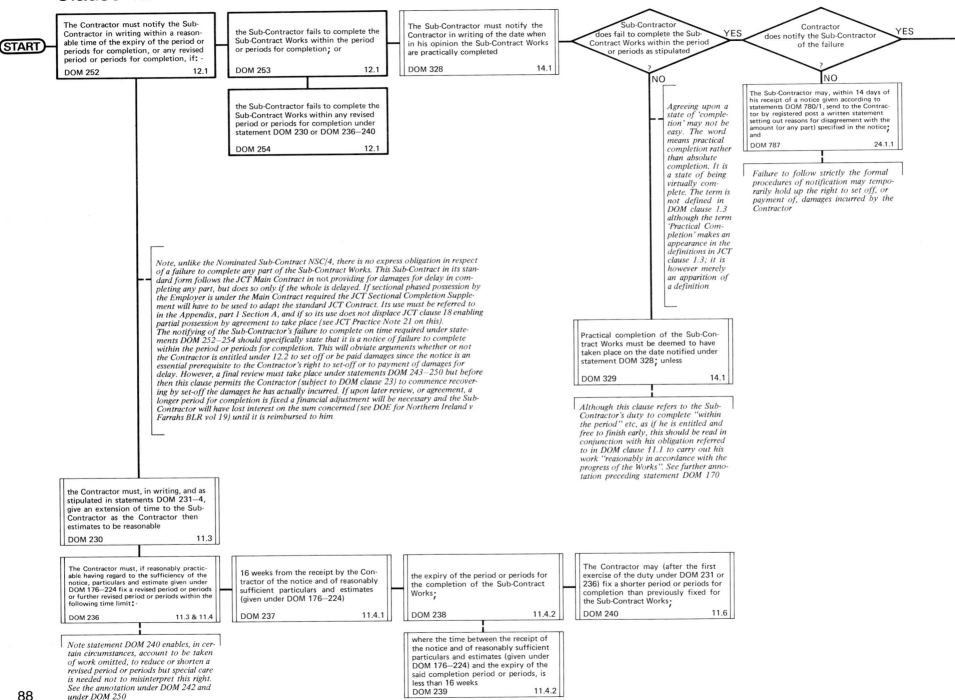

START

The Contractor must notify the Sub-Contractor in writing within a reasonable time of the expiry of the period or periods for completion, or any revised period or periods for completion, if: -

DOM 252   12.1

---

the Sub-Contractor fails to complete the Sub-Contract Works within the period or periods for completion; or

DOM 253   12.1

the Sub-Contractor fails to complete the Sub-Contract Works within any revised period or periods for completion under statement DOM 230 or DOM 236—240

DOM 254   12.1

The Sub-Contractor must notify the Contractor in writing of the date when in his opinion the Sub-Contract Works are practically completed

DOM 328   14.1

Sub-Contractor does fail to complete the Sub-Contract Works within the period or periods as stipulated — **YES** / **NO**

Agreeing upon a state of 'completion' may not be easy. The word means practical completion rather than absolute completion. It is a state of being virtually complete. The term is not defined in DOM clause 1.3 although the term 'Practical Completion' makes an appearance in the definitions in JCT clause 1.3; it is however merely an apparition of a definition

---

Contractor does notify the Sub-Contractor of the failure — **YES** / **NO**

The Sub-Contractor may, within 14 days of his receipt of a notice given according to statements DOM 780/1, send to the Contractor by registered post a written statement setting out reasons for disagreement with the amount (or any part) specified in the notice; and

DOM 787   24.1.1

Failure to follow strictly the formal procedures of notification may temporarily hold up the right to set off, or payment of, damages incurred by the Contractor

---

Note, unlike the Nominated Sub-Contract NSC/4, there is no express obligation in respect of a failure to complete any part of the Sub-Contract Works. This Sub-Contract in its standard form follows the JCT Main Contract in not providing for damages for delay in completing any part, but does so only if the whole is delayed. If sectional phased possession by the Employer is under the Main Contract required the JCT Sectional Completion Supplement will have to be used to adapt the standard JCT Contract. Its use must be referred to in the Appendix, part 1 Section A, and if so its use does not displace JCT clause 18 enabling partial possession by agreement to take place (see JCT Practice Note 21 on this).
The notifying of the Sub-Contractor's failure to complete on time required under statements DOM 252–254 should specifically state that it is a notice of failure to complete within the period or periods for completion. This will obviate arguments whether or not the Contractor is entitled under 12.2 to set off or be paid damages since the notice is an essential prerequisite to the Contractor's right to set-off or to payment of damages for delay. However, a final review must take place under statements DOM 243–250 but before then this clause permits the Contractor (subject to DOM clause 23) to commence recovering by set-off the damages he has actually incurred. If upon later review, or agreement, a longer period for completion is fixed a financial adjustment will be necessary and the Sub-Contractor will have lost interest on the sum concerned (see DOE for Northern Ireland v Farrahs BLR vol 19) until it is reimbursed to him

---

Practical completion of the Sub-Contract Works must be deemed to have taken place on the date notified under statement DOM 328; unless

DOM 329   14.1

Although this clause refers to the Sub-Contractor's duty to complete "within the period" etc, as if he is entitled and free to finish early, this should be read in conjunction with his obligation referred to in DOM clause 11.1 to carry out his work "reasonably in accordance with the progress of the Works". See further annotation preceding statement DOM 170

---

the Contractor must, in writing, and as stipulated in statements DOM 231—4, give an extension of time to the Sub-Contractor as the Contractor then estimates to be reasonable

DOM 230   11.3

The Contractor must, if reasonably practicable having regard to the sufficiency of the notice, particulars and estimate given under DOM 176—224 fix a revised period or periods or further revised period or periods within the following time limit: -

DOM 236   11.3 & 11.4

Note statement DOM 240 enables, in certain circumstances, account to be taken of work omitted, to reduce or shorten a revised period or periods but special care is needed not to misinterpret this right. See the annotation under DOM 242 and under DOM 250

---

16 weeks from the receipt by the Contractor of the notice and of reasonably sufficient particulars and estimates (given under DOM 176—224)

DOM 237   11.4.1

---

the expiry of the period or periods for the completion of the Sub-Contract Works;

DOM 238   11.4.2

where the time between the receipt of the notice and of reasonably sufficient particulars and estimates (given under DOM 176—224) and the expiry of the said completion period or periods, is less than 16 weeks

DOM 239   11.4.2

The Contractor may (after the first exercise of the duty under DOM 231 or 236) fix a shorter period or periods for completion than previously fixed for the Sub-Contract Works;

DOM 240   11.6

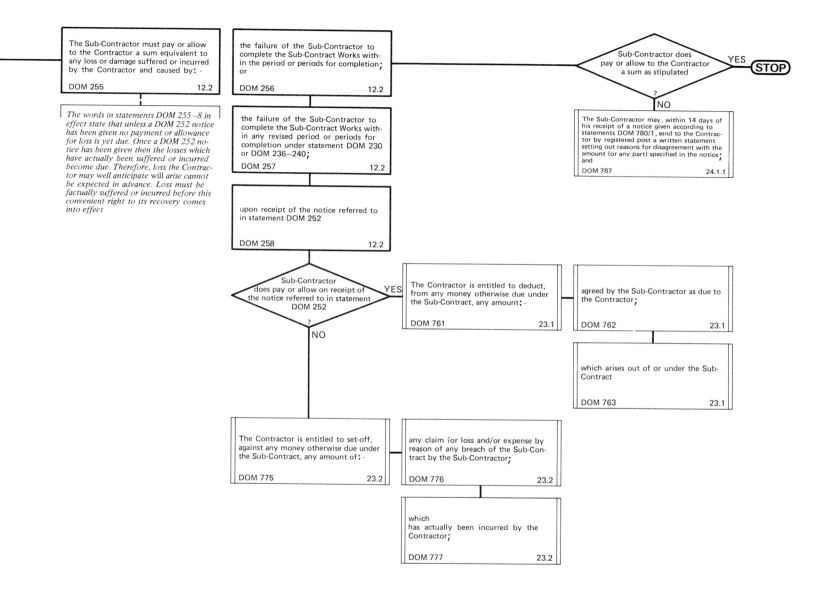

The Sub-Contractor must pay or allow to the Contractor a sum equivalent to any loss or damage suffered or incurred by the Contractor and caused by: -

DOM 255   12.2

The words in statements DOM 255–8 in effect state that unless a DOM 252 notice has been given no payment or allowance for loss is yet due. Once a DOM 252 notice has been given then the losses which have actually been suffered or incurred become due. Therefore, loss the Contractor may well anticipate will arise cannot be expected in advance. Loss must be factually suffered or incurred before this convenient right to its recovery comes into effect

the failure of the Sub-Contractor to complete the Sub-Contract Works within the period or periods for completion; or

DOM 256   12.2

the failure of the Sub-Contractor to complete the Sub-Contract Works within any revised period or periods for completion under statement DOM 230 or DOM 236–240;

DOM 257   12.2

upon receipt of the notice referred to in statement DOM 252

DOM 258   12.2

Sub-Contractor does pay or allow on receipt of the notice referred to in statement DOM 252 ?

YES

The Contractor is entitled to deduct, from any money otherwise due under the Sub-Contract, any amount: -

DOM 761   23.1

agreed by the Sub-Contractor as due to the Contractor;

DOM 762   23.1

which arises out of or under the Sub-Contract

DOM 763   23.1

NO

The Contractor is entitled to set-off, against any money otherwise due under the Sub-Contract, any amount of: -

DOM 775   23.2

any claim for loss and/or expense by reason of any breach of the Sub-Contract by the Sub-Contractor;

DOM 776   23.2

which has actually been incurred by the Contractor;

DOM 777   23.2

Sub-Contractor does pay or allow to the Contractor a sum as stipulated ?

YES STOP

NO

The Sub-Contractor may, within 14 days of his receipt of a notice given according to statements DOM 780/1, send to the Contractor by registered post a written statement setting out reasons for disagreement with the amount (or any part) specified in the notice; and

DOM 787   24.1.1

Sub-Contractor's claims

START

This clause deals with the duties required (to give the earliest notices of) and thereafter the remedies available to, the Sub-Contractor and Contractor when their own progress is materially affected by the other's act, omission or default including the acts etc of any sub-contractor of the Contractor, or servants or agents they each employ. This clause does not deal with the acts etc of any sub-sub-contractor they each may employ. Such acts are however not necessarily without a remedy (see statements DOM 293 and DOM 318) but the convenience afforded by this clause for reimbursement is not available to the parties for causes of loss not specified within it. Thus, the bankruptcy of a sub-sub-contractor employed by the Contractor is for example not an "act" etc within the scope of this clause, although if the Contractor was dilatory in seeking a replacement the Contractor's dilatoriness would be an "act" etc within this clause. See further annotation on this under statement DOM 293.

This clause also encompasses causes of disruption which are the responsibility of the Employer and at his risk. These are called "Relevant Matters". When such matters arise to materially affect the Sub-Contractor's regular progress the claims are to be accepted by the Contractor who may incorporate them into his own claim (if they are rightful) to be made against the Employer under the Main Contract (see JCT clause 26).

The Sub-Contractor's direct loss and/or expense that has flowed from an act, omission, default or Relevant Matter, when either partially or fully agreed, must be taken into account in the next interim valuation. It is to become part of the Sub-Contract Sum or the Ascertained Final Sub-Contract Sum, but no discount on such amounts is available to the Contractor, nor is he permitted to hold any Retention on such amounts.

The ascertainment and agreement of direct loss and/or expense does not involve the Architect or QS although in the case of claims involving Relevant Matters the Contractor will require (under DOM 299/302) from the Sub-Contractor clear segregation of information and details under the heads DOM 269–292 to facilitate ascertainment by the Architect or QS, under the Main Contract's terms, for the Contractor's benefit.

Claims by the Contractor upon the Sub-Contractor are dealt with under 13.4 (DOM 313–326). Agreed amounts may be deducted by the Contractor from money due or to become due to the Sub-Contractor. Disputed amounts cannot be simply deducted by the Contractor; they must be processed through clause 23.2 which provides for adjudication under clause 24 whenever the parties are not in agreement.

These detailed provisions for conveniently resolving and settling claims under this clause are in addition to and not instead of the common law process for dealing with a breach of contract and recovery of damages. For further details on claims matters see Chapter 3

The Sub-Contractor may make written application to the Contractor stating: -
DOM 259   13.1.1

the regular progress of the Sub-Contract Works or any part of same is likely to be materially affected; by
DOM 260   13.1.1

the regular progress of the Sub-Contract Works or any part of same has been materially affected; by
DOM 264   13.1.1

◇ Sub-Contractor does make a written application as stipulated — YES

any act, omission or default of the Contractor, his servants or agents; or
DOM 261   13.1

The words 'any act, omission or default' are very wide in scope and are not confined to an 'act' etc that has already occurred. If a cause of disruption in regular progress can be attributed to the Contractor then it is or will be within the wide scope of this clause as a ground to claim the direct loss etc flowing or which will flow from the disruption thought likely

any act, omission or default of the Contractor, his servants or agents; or
DOM 265   13.1

NO

The provisions of this clause are not to prejudice any other rights or remedies which the Sub-Contractor may possess
DOM 293   13.5

any act, omission or default of any of the Contractor's other sub-contractors, their servants or agents; or
DOM 262   13.1

As stated above the words 'any act' etc are wide in scope and would include such things as the bankruptcy of any of the Contractor's other sub-contractors.
Relevant Matters must be segregated from 'any act' etc to facilitate the ascertainment procedure contained within the Main Contract

any act, omission or default of any of the Contractor's other sub-contractors, their servants or agents; or
DOM 266   13.1

Proper and timely applications are a prelude or condition precedent under this clause for reimbursement of loss etc caused by the reasons specified in statements DOM 260/1/2/3 and 264/5/6/7. Where causes not specified in this clause are at play or where the formalities of this clause have not been complied with the Sub-Contractor must seek his remedy under common law.
The regular progress may for example (in the case of a piling Sub-Contractor) be materially affected by the discovery on the site of antiquities etc. Such a matter is not one listed under DOM 269–292 nor would it necessarily rank as an "act, omission or default of the Contractor" or of any (other) sub-contractor. In such a case the Contractor is under JCT clause 34.3.1 entitled to recover the loss incurred (without adhering to the formalities of this clause) but no similar right is expressed under this sub-contract. See however DOM clause 22

any one or more of the Relevant Matters referred to in statements DOM 269–292
DOM 263   13.1

The following are matters referred to in statements DOM 269–292
DOM 268   13.3

any one or more of the Relevant Matters referred to in statements DOM 269–292
DOM 267   13.1

◇ Sub-Contractor does make written application as stipulated — NO / YES

The Sub-Contractor must immediately give written notice to the Contractor if and whenever it becomes reasonably apparent that: -
DOM 176   11.2.1

The Sub-Contractor's application must be made as soon as it *should* reasonably have become apparent to him that the regular progress of the Sub-Contract Works or any part is likely to be affected; or
DOM 294   13.1.1

Relevant Matters

The Sub-Contractor must: -
DOM 62   5.1

observe, perform and comply with all the provisions of the Main Contract as referred to in the Appendix, part 1;
DOM 63   5.1.1

The Contractor must immediately give written notice to the Architect if and whenever it becomes reasonably apparent that the progress of the Works is being or likely to be delayed; and
JCT 416   25.2.1.1

the Contractor not having received in due time necessary instructions, drawings, details or levels from the Architect for which the Contractor specifically applied in writing;
DOM 269   13.3.1

the Contractor, or Sub-Contractor through the Contractor, not having received in due time necessary instructions, drawings, details or levels from the Architect for which the Contractor or Sub-Contractor through the Contractor specifically applied in writing;
DOM 271   13.3.1

the opening up for inspection of any work covered up (including making good in consequence of such opening up) in accordance with statements JCT 142/3 in clause 8.3 of the Main Contract;
DOM 273   13.3.2

The Sub-Contractor may suspend the further execution of the Sub-Contract Works: -
DOM 707   21.6

The Sub-Contractor may issue to the Contractor a notice (by registered post or recorded delivery) specifying a default: -
DOM 956   30.1

The Contractor may make written application to the Architect stating: -
JCT 480   26.1

provided the application was made on a date which having regard to the Completion Date was neither unreasonably distant from nor unreasonably close to the date on which it was necessary for the Contractor to receive same
DOM 270   13.3.1

provided the application was made on a date which having regard to the Completion Date or period or periods for completion of the Sub-Contract Works was neither unreasonably distant from nor unreasonably close to the date on which it was necessary for the Contractor or Sub-Contractor to receive same
DOM 272   13.3.1

unless the inspection showed that the work, materials or goods were not in accordance with the Main Contract; or
DOM 274   13.3.2

Neither the Contractor nor the Sub-Contractor shall be entitled to make any claim upon the other for any loss and/or expense, if: -
DOM 1001   33.1.1

Subroutine DOM 1001 prohibits claims where strikes, lockouts etc affect the trades concerned

Subroutine JCT 480/1 applies wherever a Relevant Matter is concerned

An extension of time may also be gained under DOM clause 11 (DOM 194/5 and DOM 196/7). See the annotation on p 98–100 Ref 3 for further details.
See JCT clause 1.3 for 'Completion Date'. There are many variable meanings to be found in the words used in DOM 13.3.1 by the draftsman

An extension of time may also be gained under DOM clause 11 (DOM 190/1). See the annotation under DOM 191 for further details

unless the inspection showed that the work, materials or goods were not in accordance with the Sub-Contract
DOM 275   13.3.2

The Sub-Contractor's application must be made as soon as it *should* reasonably have become apparent to him that the regular progress of the Sub-Contract Works or any part is likely to be affected; or

DOM 294   13.1.1

Sub-Contractor's application was made as soon as stipulated   **YES**

?   **NO**

---

the Sub-Contractor must do all that may reasonably be required (to the satisfaction of the Architect and Contractor) to proceed with the Sub-Contract Works

DOM 175   11.8

The Contractor must immediately give written notice to the Architect if and whenever it becomes reasonably apparent that the progress of the Works is being or likely to be delayed; and

JCT 416   25.2.1.1

The Contractor may make written application to the Architect stating: -

JCT 480   26.1

---

as soon as it *has* become apparent to him that the regular progress of the Sub-Contract Works or any part is likely to be affected; or

DOM 295   13.1.1

The application was made as stipulated in statement 295   **YES**

?

Time and damages are not necessarily unified though frequently may be enjoined. Both clauses 11 and 13 require the segregation of loss causes. The Contractor's own application under the Main Contract must follow similar lines. The Architect passes judgement on Relevant Events and Matters, his ascertainment usually being passed on to the Sub-Contractor by the Contractor

---

the Contractor must give the material circumstances including the cause or causes of the delay; and

JCT 417   25.2.1.1

Subroutine JCT 480/1 applies whenever a Relevant Matter is concerned

---

The time lapse between the clear likelihood of disturbance to regular progress and actual disturbance becoming apparent might have enabled the Contractor to avoid or reduce the effect, in which case the failure to apply earlier under DOM 294 may prejudice full recovery

---

as soon as it *should* reasonably have become apparent to him that the regular progress of the Sub-Contract Works or any part has been affected; or

DOM 296   13.1.1

The application was made as stipulated in statement 296   **YES**

?   **NO**

The time lapse between the Sub-Contractor actually becoming aware that progress has been affected and when he ought reasonably to have been aware of the likelihood of disruption might have enabled the Contractor to avoid or reduce the effect, in which case the failure to apply earlier under DOM 294 may prejudice full recovery

---

the Contractor must identify in the notice any event which in the Contractor's opinion is a Relevant Event;

JCT 418   25.2.1.1

---

as soon as it *has* become apparent to him that the regular progress of the Sub-Contract Works has been affected

DOM 297   13.1.1

The application was made as stipulated in statement 297   **YES**

?   **NO**

If an earlier realisation and application ought reasonably to have been made under DOM 296, DOM 297 or even DOM 294, the Sub-Contractor, in not fulfilling the requirements of this clause, will to a certain extent be in breach. The Contractor will be entitled to recover from the Sub-Contractor any damages resulting from the breach

---

The above subroutines apply only to, and should be followed by, the Contractor

---

...h statement above refers to the "application" (not information and details) and it identifies differing ...ments in time from the earliest realisation of the ...lihood of disruption to confirmation in the Sub-tractor's mind that disruption has in fact taken ... already.
Sub-Contractor is required to be on his toes when-... progress is likely to be affected. He cannot take ...time over these initial applications. Prompt and, ...never possible, prospective applications are re-...ed to ensure the diminution of loss; also ensuring ...ication (under DOM 312); otherwise the right ...rompt and full payment of claimed loss (under ...ses 21 and 3) may be prejudiced (eg, where rising ...increases have mounted with time). See also the ...otation under DOM 322, the principles explained ...apply to the Sub-Contractor's applications also

An extension of time may be gained under DOM clause 11 (DOM 192/3)

The Sub-Contractor's application must be made within a reasonable time of the material effect of any such act, omission, default or Relevant Matter becoming apparent

DOM 298   13.1

Sub-Contractor's application was made as stipulated in statement 298   **YES**   **NO**

?

The provisions of this clause are not to prejudice any other rights or remedies which the Sub-Contractor may possess

DOM 293   13.5

An extension of time may be gained under DOM clause 11 (DOM 211/2). The Architect is entitled under JCT clause 13.1.2.1 of the Main Contract to vary obligations or restrictions on access imposed in the Main Bills

---

An extension of time may be gained under DOM clause 11 (DOM 189). Statement DOM 292 refers to work tendered for by the Contractor under a prime cost sum. Any disruption thus caused would rank for reimbursement as an "act" etc under statements 260/1 or 264/5

An application "within a reasonable time of the material effect . . . becoming apparent" may be later than one that ought to have been made stating there is prospectively the likelihood of material effect upon progress. In such cases questions may arise to prejudice reimbursement to some extent

See also DOM 16 and DOM 189

If an application has been made out of time then it is barred under this Sub-Contract at least. The failure to fulfil the duties concerning timely written application will also present difficulty in any action under common law that may be pursued

For further details see JCT 441–3, 498–9A, and 635 with the annotation to same. An extension of time may also be gained under DOM clause 11 (DOM 199–201)

An extension of time may be gained under DOM clause 11 (DOM 189). In cases of serious delay the Sub-Contractor should seek legal advice on his common law rights

---

failure of the Employer to give in due time ingress or egress through or over any land, buildings, way or passage (adjoining or connected with the site and in the possession and control of the Employer) to or from the site of the Works, or any part of the site of the Works;

DOM 286   13.3.6

Architect's instructions issued under statement JCT 172 in clause 13.2 of the Main Contract requiring a Variation, including Contractor's directions issued under DOM clause 4 which pass on such instructions; or

DOM 290   13.3.7

---

the testing of any of the work, materials or goods (including making good in consequence of such testing) in accordance with statements JCT 142/4/5 in clause 8.3 of the Main Contract;

DOM 276   13.3.2

---

any discrepancy in the Contract Drawings and/or the Contract Bills under the provisions of the Main Contract; or

DOM 279   13.3.3

---

the execution of work not forming part of the Main Contract, by the Employer himself as referred to in statements JCT 636/7 in clause 29 of the Main Contract; or

DOM 281   13.3.4

Architect's instructions issued in regard to the postponement of any work to be executed under the provisions of the Main Contract, including Contractor's directions issued under DOM clause 4 in respect of such matters; or

DOM 284   13.3.5

---

in accordance with the Contract Bills and/or Contract Drawings, after receipt by the Architect of any notice the Contractor may be required to give; or

DOM 287   13.3.6

Architect's instructions issued under statements JCT 197/8/9 in clause 13.3 of the Main Contract in regard to the expenditure of provisional sums, including Contractor's directions issued under DOM clause 4 which pass on such instructions;

DOM 291   13.3.7

---

unless the testing showed that the work, materials or goods were not in accordance with the Main Contract; or

DOM 277   13.3.2

---

any divergence between the Contract Drawings and/or the Contract Bills under the provisions of the Main Contract

DOM 280   13.3.3

---

the execution of work not forming part of the Main Contract by other persons employed by the Employer, as referred to in statements JCT 638/9 in clause 29 of the Main Contract, or the failure to execute such work; or

DOM 282   13.3.4

Architect's instructions issued in regard to the postponement of any work to be executed under the provisions of the Sub-Contract, including Contractor's directions issued under DOM clause 4 in respect of such matters

DOM 285   13.3.5

---

failure of the Employer to give in due time ingress or egress through or over any land, buildings, way or passage (adjoining or connected with the site and in the possession and control of the Employer) to or from the site of the Works, or any part of the site of the Works;

DOM 288   13.3.6

---

other than work to which statements JCT 203–206 in clause 13.4.2 of the Main Contract refer

DOM 292   13.3.7

---

unless the testing showed that the work, materials or goods were not in accordance with the Sub-Contract

DOM 278   13.3.2

The Contract Bills must be corrected if there is any: -

JCT 12   2.2.2.2

---

the supply by the Employer of materials and goods which the Employer has agreed to provide for the Works, or the failure so to supply

DOM 283   13.3.4

---

any written instruction of the Architect issued under the Main Contract affecting the Sub-Contract Works and issued by the Contractor to the Sub-Contractor must be deemed to be a direction of the Contractor; but

DOM 44   4.2.2

---

as agreed between the Architect and the Contractor

DOM 289   13.3.6

---

any written instruction of the Architect issued under the Main Contract affecting the Sub-Contract Works and issued by the Contractor to the Sub-Contractor must be deemed to be a direction of the Contractor; but

DOM 44   4.2.2

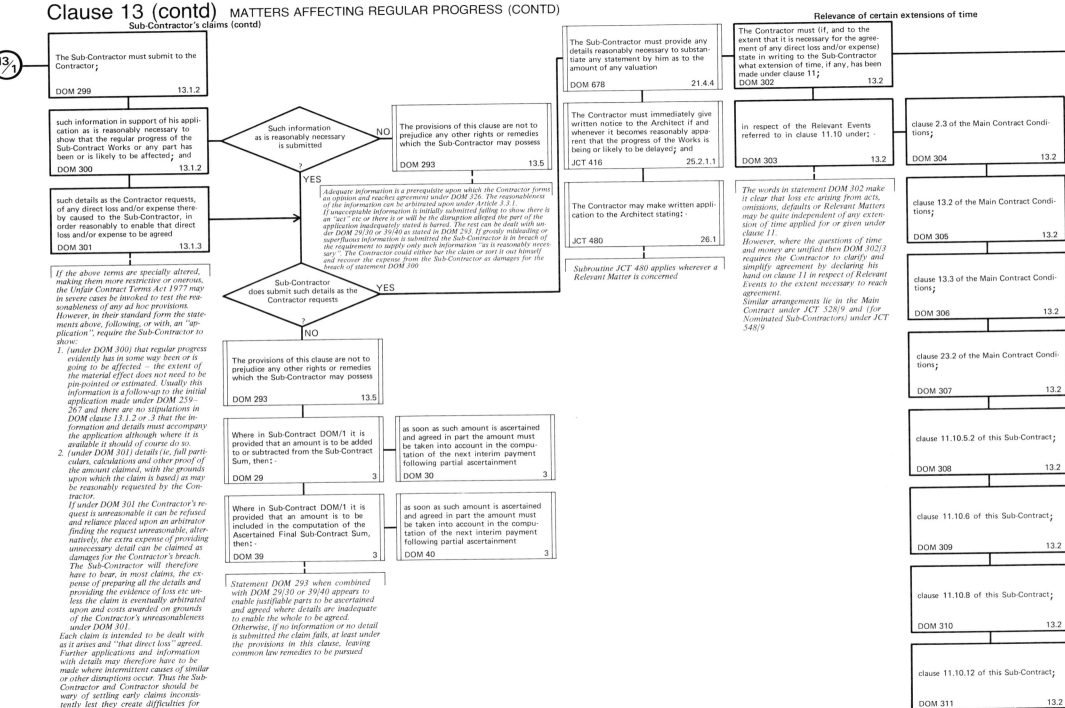

13/1

The Sub-Contractor must submit to the Contractor;

DOM 299   13.1.2

such information in support of his application as is reasonably necessary to show that the regular progress of the Sub-Contract Works or any part has been or is likely to be affected; and

DOM 300   13.1.2

such details as the Contractor requests, of any direct loss and/or expense thereby caused to the Sub-Contractor, in order reasonably to enable that direct loss and/or expense to be agreed

DOM 301   13.1.3

If the above terms are specially altered, making them more restrictive or onerous, the Unfair Contract Terms Act 1977 may in severe cases be invoked to test the reasonableness of any ad hoc provisions. However, in their standard form the statements above, following, or with, an "application", require the Sub-Contractor to show:

1. (under DOM 300) that regular progress evidently has in some way been or is going to be affected – the extent of the material effect does not need to be pin-pointed or estimated. Usually this information is a follow-up to the initial application made under DOM 259–267 and there are no stipulations in DOM clause 13.1.2 or .3 that the information and details must accompany the application although where it is available it should of course do so.

2. (under DOM 301) details (ie, full particulars, calculations and other proof of the amount claimed, with the grounds upon which the claim is based) as may be reasonably requested by the Contractor.

If under DOM 301 the Contractor's request is unreasonable it can be refused and reliance placed upon an arbitrator finding the request unreasonable, alternatively, the extra expense of providing unnecessary detail can be claimed as damages for the Contractor's breach. The Sub-Contractor will therefore have to bear, in most claims, the expense of preparing all the details and providing the evidence of loss etc unless the claim is eventually arbitrated upon and costs awarded on grounds of the Contractor's unreasonableness under DOM 301.

Each claim is intended to be dealt with as it arises and "that direct loss" agreed. Further applications and information with details may therefore have to be made where intermittent causes of similar or other disruptions occur. Thus the Sub-Contractor and Contractor should be wary of settling early claims inconsistently lest they create difficulties for themselves in later claims on the same grounds, maybe for much greater sums

Such information as is reasonably necessary is submitted

?   YES   NO

The provisions of this clause are not to prejudice any other rights or remedies which the Sub-Contractor may possess

DOM 293   13.5

Adequate information is a prerequisite upon which the Contractor forms an opinion and reaches agreement under DOM 326. The reasonableness of the information can be arbitrated upon under Article 3.3.1.
If unacceptable information is initially submitted failing to show there is an "act" etc or there is or will be the disruption alleged the part of the application inadequately stated is barred. The rest can be dealt with under DOM 29/30 or 39/40 as stated in DOM 293. If grossly misleading or superfluous information is submitted the Sub-Contractor is in breach of the requirement to supply only such information "as is reasonably necessary". The Contractor could either bar the claim or sort it out himself and recover the expense from the Sub-Contractor as damages for the breach of statement DOM 300

Sub-Contractor does submit such details as the Contractor requests

?   YES   NO

The provisions of this clause are not to prejudice any other rights or remedies which the Sub-Contractor may possess

DOM 293   13.5

Where in Sub-Contract DOM/1 it is provided that an amount is to be added to or subtracted from the Sub-Contract Sum, then: -

DOM 29   3

as soon as such amount is ascertained and agreed in part the amount must be taken into account in the computation of the next interim payment following partial ascertainment

DOM 30   3

Where in Sub-Contract DOM/1 it is provided that an amount is to be included in the computation of the Ascertained Final Sub-Contract Sum, then: -

DOM 39   3

as soon as such amount is ascertained and agreed in part the amount must be taken into account in the computation of the next interim payment following partial ascertainment

DOM 40   3

Statement DOM 293 when combined with DOM 29/30 or 39/40 appears to enable justifiable parts to be ascertained and agreed where details are inadequate to enable the whole to be agreed. Otherwise, if no information or no detail is submitted the claim fails, at least under the provisions in this clause, leaving common law remedies to be pursued

The Sub-Contractor must provide any details reasonably necessary to substantiate any statement by him as to the amount of any valuation

DOM 678   21.4.4

The Contractor must immediately give written notice to the Architect if and whenever it becomes reasonably apparent that the progress of the Works is being or likely to be delayed; and

JCT 416   25.2.1.1

The Contractor may make written application to the Architect stating: -

JCT 480   26.1

Subroutine JCT 480 applies wherever a Relevant Matter is concerned

The Contractor must (if, and to the extent that it is necessary for the agreement of any direct loss and/or expense) state in writing to the Sub-Contractor what extension of time, if any, has been made under clause 11;

DOM 302   13.2

in respect of the Relevant Events referred to in clause 11.10 under: -

DOM 303   13.2

The words in statement DOM 302 make it clear that loss etc arising from acts, omissions, defaults or Relevant Matters may be quite independent of any extension of time applied for or given under clause 11.
However, where the questions of time and money are unified then DOM 302/3 requires the Contractor to clarify and simplify agreement by declaring his hand on clause 11 in respect of Relevant Events to the extent necessary to reach agreement.
Similar arrangements lie in the Main Contract under JCT 528/9 and (for Nominated Sub-Contractors) under JCT 548/9

clause 2.3 of the Main Contract Conditions;

DOM 304   13.2

clause 13.2 of the Main Contract Conditions;

DOM 305   13.2

clause 13.3 of the Main Contract Conditions;

DOM 306   13.2

clause 23.2 of the Main Contract Conditions;

DOM 307   13.2

clause 11.10.5.2 of this Sub-Contract;

DOM 308   13.2

clause 11.10.6 of this Sub-Contract;

DOM 309   13.2

clause 11.10.8 of this Sub-Contract;

DOM 310   13.2

clause 11.10.12 of this Sub-Contract;

DOM 311   13.2

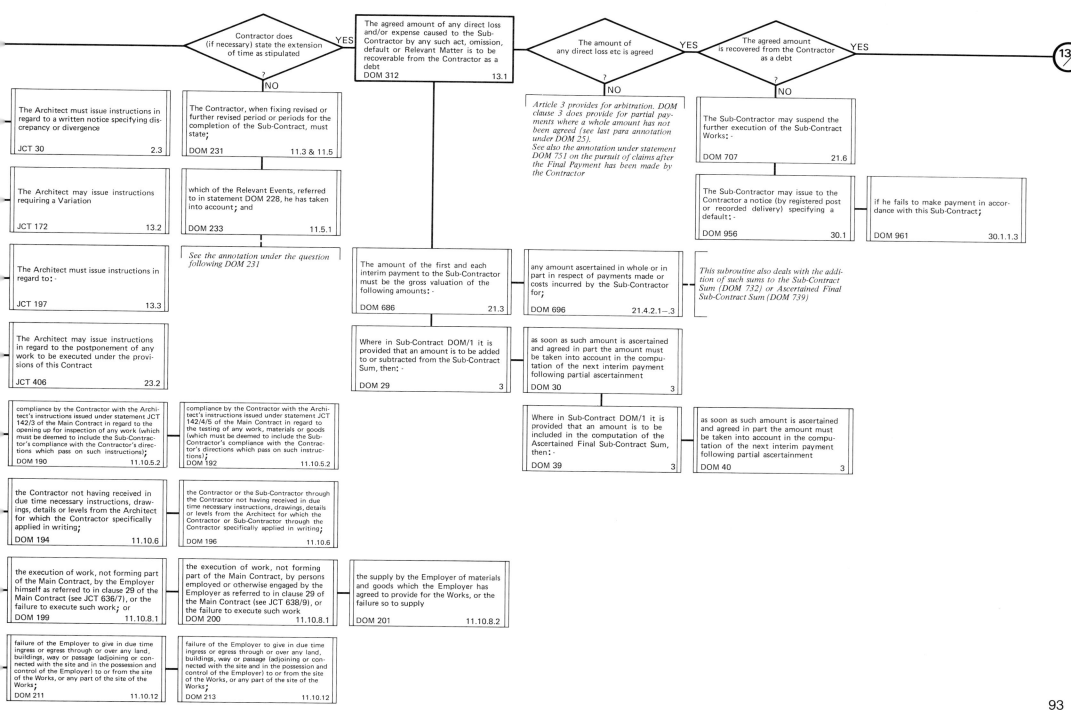

Contractor does (if necessary) state the extension of time as stipulated ? — YES / NO

The agreed amount of any direct loss and/or expense caused to the Sub-Contractor by any such act, omission, default or Relevant Matter is to be recoverable from the Contractor as a debt
DOM 312   13.1

The amount of any direct loss etc is agreed ? — YES / NO

The agreed amount is recovered from the Contractor as a debt ? — YES / NO

The Architect must issue instructions in regard to a written notice specifying discrepancy or divergence
JCT 30   2.3

The Architect may issue instructions requiring a Variation
JCT 172   13.2

The Architect must issue instructions in regard to: -
JCT 197   13.3

The Architect may issue instructions in regard to the postponement of any work to be executed under the provisions of this Contract
JCT 406   23.2

compliance by the Contractor with the Architect's instructions issued under statement JCT 142/3 of the Main Contract in regard to the opening up for inspection of any work (which must be deemed to include the Sub-Contractor's compliance with the Contractor's directions which pass on such instructions);
DOM 190   11.10.5.2

the Contractor not having received in due time necessary instructions, drawings, details or levels from the Architect for which the Contractor specifically applied in writing;
DOM 194   11.10.6

the execution of work, not forming part of the Main Contract, by the Employer himself as referred to in clause 29 of the Main Contract (see JCT 636/7), or the failure to execute such work; or
DOM 199   11.10.8.1

failure of the Employer to give in due time ingress or egress through or over any land, buildings, way or passage (adjoining or connected with the site and in the possession and control of the Employer) to or from the site of the Works, or any part of the site of the Works;
DOM 211   11.10.12

The Contractor, when fixing revised or further revised period or periods for the completion of the Sub-Contract, must state;
DOM 231   11.3 & 11.5

which of the Relevant Events, referred to in statement DOM 228, he has taken into account; and
DOM 233   11.5.1

See the annotation under the question following DOM 231

compliance by the Contractor with the Architect's instructions issued under statement JCT 142/4/5 of the Main Contract in regard to the testing of any work, materials or goods (which must be deemed to include the Sub-Contractor's compliance with the Contractor's directions which pass on such instructions)
DOM 192   11.10.5.2

the Contractor or the Sub-Contractor through the Contractor not having received in due time necessary instructions, drawings, details or levels from the Architect for which the Contractor or Sub-Contractor through the Contractor specifically applied in writing;
DOM 196   11.10.6

the execution of work, not forming part of the Main Contract, by persons employed or otherwise engaged by the Employer as referred to in clause 29 of the Main Contract (see JCT 638/9), or the failure to execute such work
DOM 200   11.10.8.1

failure of the Employer to give in due time ingress or egress through or over any land, buildings, way or passage (adjoining or connected with the site and in the possession and control of the Employer) to or from the site of the Works, or any part of the site of the Works;
DOM 213   11.10.12

The amount of the first and each interim payment to the Sub-Contractor must be the gross valuation of the following amounts: -
DOM 686   21.3

Where in Sub-Contract DOM/1 it is provided that an amount is to be added to or subtracted from the Sub-Contract Sum, then: -
DOM 29   3

the supply by the Employer of materials and goods which the Employer has agreed to provide for the Works, or the failure so to supply
DOM 201   11.10.8.2

Article 3 provides for arbitration. DOM clause 3 does provide for partial payments where a whole amount has not been agreed (see last para annotation under DOM 25).
See also the annotation under statement DOM 751 on the pursuit of claims after the Final Payment has been made by the Contractor

any amount ascertained in whole or in part in respect of payments made or costs incurred by the Sub-Contractor for;
DOM 696   21.4.2.1—.3

as soon as such amount is ascertained and agreed in part the amount must be taken into account in the computation of the next interim payment following partial ascertainment
DOM 30   3

Where in Sub-Contract DOM/1 it is provided that an amount is to be included in the computation of the Ascertained Final Sub-Contract Sum, then: -
DOM 39   3

The Sub-Contractor may suspend the further execution of the Sub-Contract Works: -
DOM 707   21.6

The Sub-Contractor may issue to the Contractor a notice (by registered post or recorded delivery) specifying a default: -
DOM 956   30.1

This subroutine also deals with the addition of such sums to the Sub-Contract Sum (DOM 732) or Ascertained Final Sub-Contract Sum (DOM 739)

as soon as such amount is ascertained and agreed in part the amount must be taken into account in the computation of the next interim payment following partial ascertainment
DOM 40   3

---

if he fails to make payment in accordance with this Sub-Contract;
DOM 961   30.1.1.3

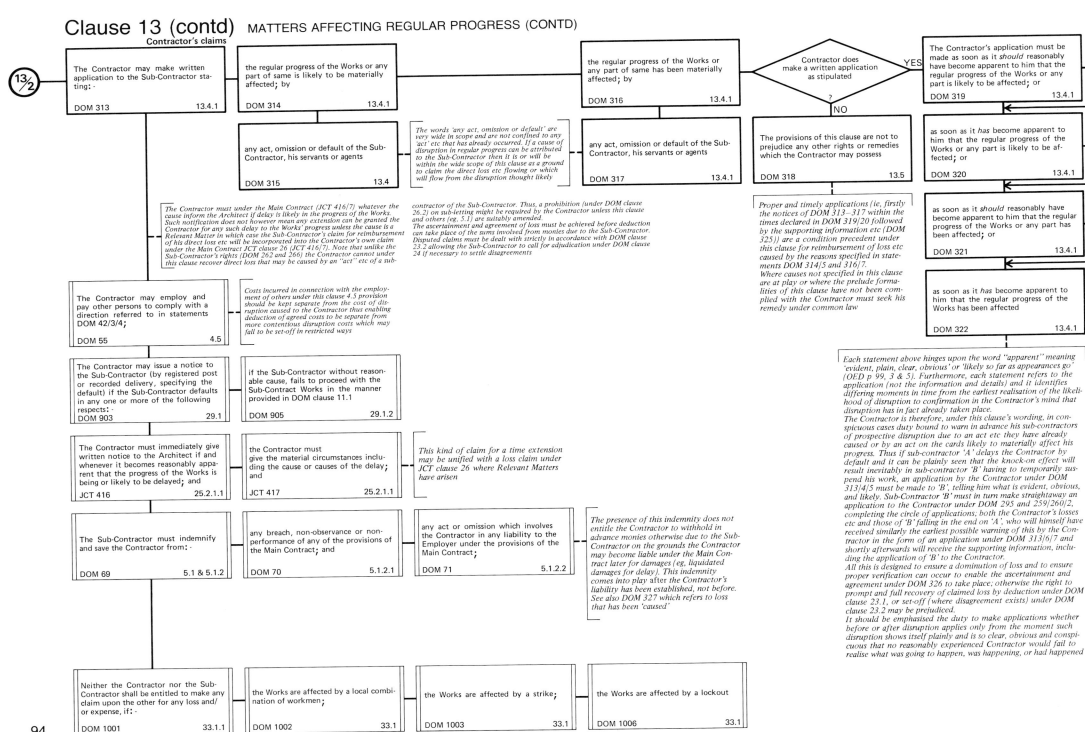

The Contractor may make written application to the Sub-Contractor stating: -
DOM 313 — 13.4.1

the regular progress of the Works or any part of same is likely to be materially affected; by
DOM 314 — 13.4.1

any act, omission or default of the Sub-Contractor, his servants or agents
DOM 315 — 13.4

The words 'any act, omission or default' are very wide in scope and are not confined to any 'act' etc that has already occurred. If a cause of disruption in regular progress can be attributed to the Sub-Contractor then it is or will be within the wide scope of this clause as a ground to claim the direct loss etc flowing or which will flow from the disruption thought likely

the regular progress of the Works or any part of same has been materially affected; by
DOM 316 — 13.4.1

any act, omission or default of the Sub-Contractor, his servants or agents
DOM 317 — 13.4.1

Contractor does make a written application as stipulated ?
NO

YES

The provisions of this clause are not to prejudice any other rights or remedies which the Contractor may possess
DOM 318 — 13.5

The Contractor's application must be made as soon as it *should* reasonably have become apparent to him that the regular progress of the Works or any part is likely to be affected; or
DOM 319 — 13.4.1

as soon as it *has* become apparent to him that the regular progress of the Works or any part is likely to be affected; or
DOM 320 — 13.4.1

as soon as it *should* reasonably have become apparent to him that the regular progress of the Works or any part has been affected; or
DOM 321 — 13.4.1

as soon as it *has* become apparent to him that the regular progress of the Works has been affected
DOM 322 — 13.4.1

The Contractor must under the Main Contract (JCT 416/7) whatever the cause inform the Architect if delay is likely in the progress of the Works. Such notification does not however mean any extension can be granted the Contractor for any such delay to the Works' progress unless the cause is a Relevant Matter in which case the Sub-Contractor's claim for reimbursement of his direct loss etc will be incorporated into the Contractor's own claim under the Main Contract JCT clause 26 (JCT 416/7). Note that unlike the Sub-Contractor's rights (DOM 262 and 266) the Contractor cannot under this clause recover direct loss that may be caused by an "act" etc of a sub-

contractor of the Sub-Contractor. Thus, a prohibition (under DOM clause 26.2) on sub-letting might be required by the Contractor unless this clause and others (eg, 5.1) are suitably amended.
The ascertainment and agreement of loss must be achieved before deduction can take place of the sums involved from monies due to the Sub-Contractor. Disputed claims must be dealt with strictly in accordance with DOM clause 23.2 allowing the Sub-Contractor to call for adjudication under DOM clause 24 if necessary to settle disagreements

Proper and timely applications (ie, firstly the notices of DOM 313–317 within the times declared in DOM 319/20 followed by the supporting information etc (DOM 325)) are a condition precedent under this clause for reimbursement of loss etc caused by the reasons specified in statements DOM 314/5 and 316/7.
Where causes not specified in this clause are at play or where the prelude formalities of this clause have not been complied with the Contractor must seek his remedy under common law

The Contractor may employ and pay other persons to comply with a direction referred to in statements DOM 42/3/4;
DOM 55 — 4.5

Costs incurred in connection with the employment of others under this clause 4.5 provision should be kept separate from the cost of disruption caused to the Contractor thus enabling deduction of agreed costs to be separate from more contentious disruption costs which may fall to be set-off in restricted ways

The Contractor may issue a notice to the Sub-Contractor (by registered post or recorded delivery, specifying the default) if the Sub-Contractor defaults in any one or more of the following respects: -
DOM 903 — 29.1

if the Sub-Contractor without reasonable cause, fails to proceed with the Sub-Contract Works in the manner provided in DOM clause 11.1
DOM 905 — 29.1.2

The Contractor must immediately give written notice to the Architect if and whenever it becomes reasonably apparent that the progress of the Works is being or likely to be delayed; and
JCT 416 — 25.2.1.1

the Contractor must give the material circumstances including the cause or causes of the delay; and
JCT 417 — 25.2.1.1

This kind of claim for a time extension may be unified with a loss claim under JCT clause 26 where Relevant Matters have arisen

The Sub-Contractor must indemnify and save the Contractor from: -
DOM 69 — 5.1 & 5.1.2

any breach, non-observance or non-performance of any of the provisions of the Main Contract; and
DOM 70 — 5.1.2.1

any act or omission which involves the Contractor in any liability to the Employer under the provisions of the Main Contract;
DOM 71 — 5.1.2.2

The presence of this indemnity does not entitle the Contractor to withhold in advance monies otherwise due to the Sub-Contractor on the grounds the Contractor may become liable under the Main Contract later for damages (eg, liquidated damages for delay). This indemnity comes into play after the Contractor's liability has been established, not before. See also DOM 327 which refers to loss that has been 'caused'

Each statement above hinges upon the word "apparent" meaning 'evident, plain, clear, obvious' or 'likely so far as appearances go' (OED p 99, 3 & 5). Furthermore, each statement refers to the application (not the information and details) and it identifies differing moments in time from the earliest realisation of the likelihood of disruption to confirmation in the Contractor's mind that disruption has in fact already taken place.
The Contractor is therefore, under this clause's wording, in conspicuous cases duty bound to warn in advance his prospective disruption due to an act etc they have already caused or by an act on the cards likely to materially affect his progress. Thus if sub-contractor 'A' delays the Contractor by default and it can be plainly seen that the knock-on effect will result inevitably in sub-contractor 'B' having to temporarily suspend his work, an application by the Contractor under DOM 313/4/5 must be made to 'B', telling him what is evident, obvious, and likely. Sub-Contractor 'B' must in turn make straightaway an application to the Contractor under DOM 295 and 259/260/2, completing the circle of applications; both the Contractor's losses etc and those of 'B' falling in the end on 'A', who will himself have received similarly the earliest possible warning of this by the Contractor in the form of an application under DOM 313/6/7 and shortly afterwards will receive the supporting information, including the application of 'B' to the Contractor.
All this is designed to ensure a domination of loss and to ensure proper verification can occur to enable the ascertainment and agreement under DOM 326 to take place; otherwise the right to prompt and full recovery of claimed loss by deduction under DOM clause 23.1, or set-off (where disagreement exists) under DOM clause 23.2 may be prejudiced.
It should be emphasised the duty to make applications whether before or after disruption applies only from the moment such disruption shows itself plainly and is so clear, obvious and conspicuous that no reasonably experienced Contractor would fail to realise what was going to happen, was happening, or had happened

Neither the Contractor nor the Sub-Contractor shall be entitled to make any claim upon the other for any loss and/or expense, if: -
DOM 1001 — 33.1.1

the Works are affected by a local combination of workmen;
DOM 1002 — 33.1

the Works are affected by a strike;
DOM 1003 — 33.1

the Works are affected by a lockout
DOM 1006 — 33.1

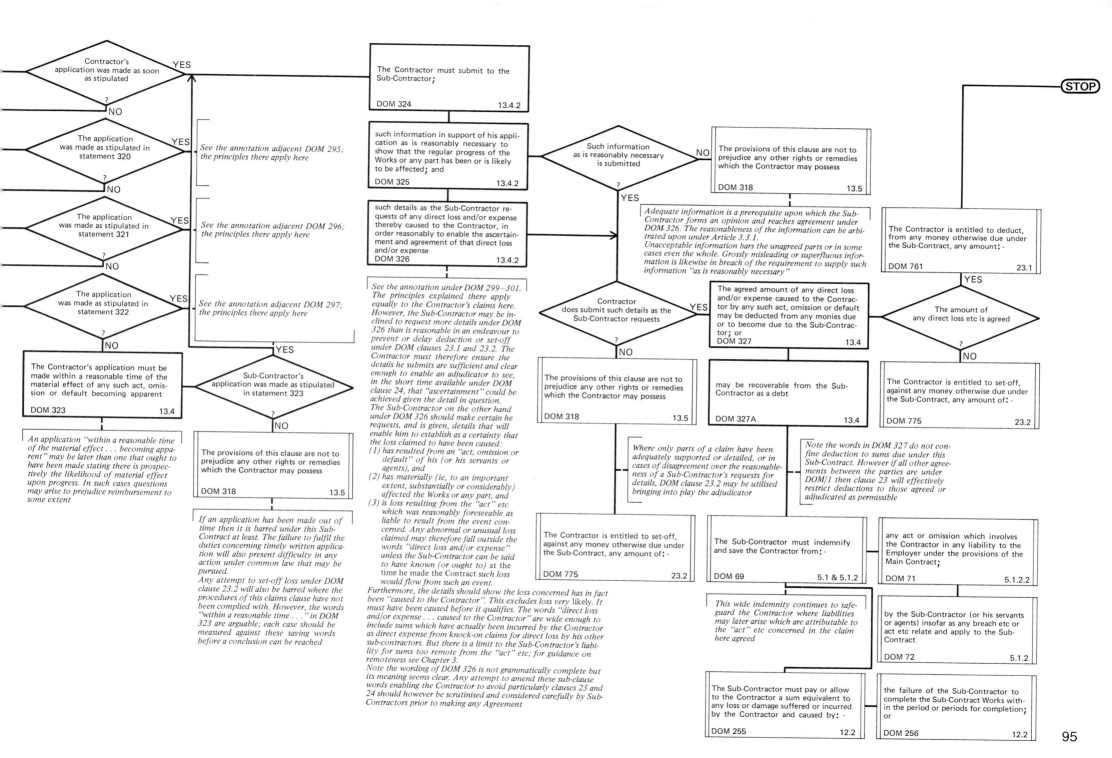

Flowchart boxes (diamonds/decisions and rectangles):

Contractor's application was made as soon as stipulated ? — YES / NO

The application was made as stipulated in statement 320 ? — YES / NO

The application was made as stipulated in statement 321 ? — YES / NO

The application was made as stipulated in statement 322 ? — YES / NO

The Contractor's application must be made within a reasonable time of the material effect of any such act, omission or default becoming apparent

DOM 323   13.4

See the annotation adjacent DOM 295; the principles there apply here

See the annotation adjacent DOM 296; the principles there apply here

See the annotation adjacent DOM 297; the principles there apply here

Sub-Contractor's application was made as stipulated in statement 323 ? — YES / NO

The provisions of this clause are not to prejudice any other rights or remedies which the Contractor may possess

DOM 318   13.5

The Contractor must submit to the Sub-Contractor;

DOM 324   13.4.2

such information in support of his application as is reasonably necessary to show that the regular progress of the Works or any part has been or is likely to be affected; and

DOM 325   13.4.2

such details as the Sub-Contractor requests of any direct loss and/or expense thereby caused to the Contractor, in order reasonably to enable the ascertainment and agreement of that direct loss and/or expense

DOM 326   13.4.2

Such information as is reasonably necessary is submitted ? — NO / YES

Contractor does submit such details as the Sub-Contractor requests ? — YES / NO

The provisions of this clause are not to prejudice any other rights or remedies which the Contractor may possess

DOM 318   13.5

The Contractor is entitled to set-off, against any money otherwise due under the Sub-Contract, any amount of: -

DOM 775   23.2

The provisions of this clause are not to prejudice any other rights or remedies which the Contractor may possess

DOM 318   13.5

The agreed amount of any direct loss and/or expense caused to the Contractor by any such act, omission or default may be deducted from any monies due or to become due to the Sub-Contractor; or

DOM 327   13.4

may be recoverable from the Sub-Contractor as a debt

DOM 327A   13.4

The Sub-Contractor must indemnify and save the Contractor from: -

DOM 69   5.1 & 5.1.2

The Sub-Contractor must pay or allow to the Contractor a sum equivalent to any loss or damage suffered or incurred by the Contractor and caused by: -

DOM 255   12.2

The Contractor is entitled to deduct, from any money otherwise due under the Sub-Contract, any amount: -

DOM 761   23.1

The amount of any direct loss etc is agreed ? — YES / NO

The Contractor is entitled to set-off, against any money otherwise due under the Sub-Contract, any amount of: -

DOM 775   23.2

any act or omission which involves the Contractor in any liability to the Employer under the provisions of the Main Contract;

DOM 71   5.1.2.2

by the Sub-Contractor (or his servants or agents) insofar as any breach etc or act etc relate and apply to the Sub-Contract

DOM 72   5.1.2

the failure of the Sub-Contractor to complete the Sub-Contract Works within the period or periods for completion; or

DOM 256   12.2

(STOP)

Annotations (italic):

An application "within a reasonable time of the material effect . . . becoming apparent" may be later than one that ought to have been made stating there is prospectively the likelihood of material effect upon progress. In such cases questions may arise to prejudice reimbursement to some extent

If an application has been made out of time then it is barred under this Sub-Contract at least. The failure to fulfil the duties concerning timely written application will also present difficulty in any action under common law that may be pursued.
Any attempt to set-off loss under DOM clause 23.2 will also be barred where the procedures of this claims clause have not been complied with. However, the words "within a reasonable time . . ." in DOM 323 are arguable; each case should be measured against these saving words before a conclusion can be reached

See the annotation under DOM 299–301. The principles explained there apply equally to the Contractor's claims here. However, the Sub-Contractor may be inclined to request more details under DOM 326 than is reasonable in an endeavour to prevent or delay deduction or set-off under DOM clauses 23.1 and 23.2. The Contractor must therefore ensure the details he submits are sufficient and clear enough to enable an adjudicator to see, in the short time available under DOM clause 24, that "ascertainment" could be achieved given the detail in question.
The Sub-Contractor on the other hand under DOM 326 should make certain he requests, and is given, details that will enable him to establish as a certainty that the loss claimed to have been caused:
(1) has resulted from an "act, omission or default" of his (or his servants or agents), and
(2) has materially (ie, to an important extent, substantially or considerably) affected the Works or any part, and
(3) is loss resulting from the "act" etc which was reasonably foreseeable as liable to result from the event concerned. Any abnormal or unusual loss claimed may therefore fall outside the words "direct loss and/or expense" unless the Sub-Contractor can be said to have known (or ought to) at the time he made the Contract such loss would flow from such an event.
Furthermore, the details should show the loss concerned has in fact been "caused to the Contractor". This excludes loss very likely. It must have been caused before it qualifies. The words "direct loss and/or expense . . . caused to the Contractor" are wide enough to include sums which have actually been incurred by the Contractor as direct expense from knock-on claims for direct loss by his other sub-contractors. But there is a limit to the Sub-Contractor's liability for sums too remote from the "act" etc; for guidance on remoteness see Chapter 3.
Note the wording of DOM 326 is not grammatically complete but its meaning seems clear. Any attempt to amend these sub-clause words enabling the Contractor to avoid particularly clauses 23 and 24 should however be scrutinised and considered carefully by Sub-Contractors prior to making any Agreement

Adequate information is a prerequisite upon which the Sub-Contractor forms an opinion and reaches agreement under DOM 326. The reasonableness of the information can be arbitrated upon under Article 3.3.1.
Unacceptable information bars the unagreed parts or in some cases even the whole. Grossly misleading or superfluous information is likewise in breach of the requirement to supply such information "as is reasonably necessary"

Where only parts of a claim have been adequately supported or detailed, or in cases of disagreement over the reasonableness of a Sub-Contractor's requests for details, DOM clause 23.2 may be utilised bringing into play the adjudicator

Note the words in DOM 327 do not confine deduction to sums due under this Sub-Contract. However if all other agreements between the parties are under DOM/1 then clause 23 will effectively restrict deductions to those agreed or adjudicated as permissible

This wide indemnity continues to safeguard the Contractor where liabilities may later arise which are attributable to the "act" etc concerned in the claim here agreed

Clause 14 PRACTICAL COMPLETION OF SUB-CONTRACT WORKS – LIABILITY FOR DEFECTS

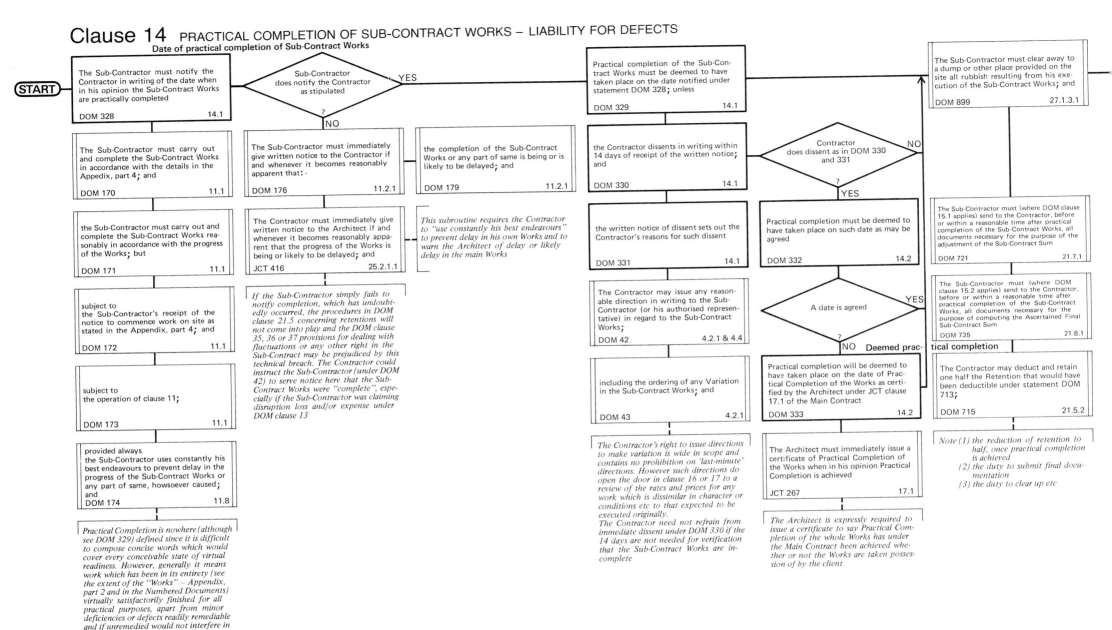

Date of practical completion of Sub-Contract Works

START

The Sub-Contractor must notify the Contractor in writing of the date when in his opinion the Sub-Contract Works are practically completed

DOM 328   14.1

Sub-Contractor does notify the Contractor as stipulated ? → NO / YES

The Sub-Contractor must carry out and complete the Sub-Contract Works in accordance with the details in the Appedix, part 4; and

DOM 170   11.1

the Sub-Contractor must carry out and complete the Sub-Contract Works reasonably in accordance with the progress of the Works; but

DOM 171   11.1

subject to
the Sub-Contractor's receipt of the notice to commence work on site as stated in the Appendix, part 4; and

DOM 172   11.1

subject to
the operation of clause 11;

DOM 173   11.1

provided always
the Sub-Contractor uses constantly his best endeavours to prevent delay in the progress of the Sub-Contract Works or any part of same, howsoever caused; and

DOM 174   11.8

*Practical Completion is nowhere (although see DOM 329) defined since it is difficult to compose concise words which would cover every conceivable state of virtual readiness. However, generally it means work which has been in its entirety (see the extent of the "Works" – Appendix, part 2 and in the Numbered Documents) virtually satisfactorily finished for all practical purposes, apart from minor deficiencies or defects readily remediable and if unremedied would not interfere in any way with the Contractor's (or his sub-contractor's) progress or use of the Sub-Contract Works. The presence of latent defects would not nullify a notice of practical completion.
The state of practical completion is therefore a condition for the Sub-Contractor to decide, subject to the Contractor's power to disagree provided his dissent is put into writing (with his reasons) within 14 days of the Sub-Contractor's notice under DOM 328.*

The Sub-Contractor must immediately give written notice to the Contractor if and whenever it becomes reasonably apparent that: -

DOM 176   11.2.1

The Contractor must immediately give written notice to the Architect if and whenever it becomes reasonably apparent that the progress of the Works is being or likely to be delayed; and

JCT 416   25.2.1.1

If the Sub-Contractor simply fails to notify completion, which has undoubtedly occurred, the procedures in DOM clause 21.5 concerning retentions will not come into play and the DOM clause 35, 36 or 37 provisions for dealing with fluctuations or any other right in the Sub-Contract may be prejudiced by this technical breach. The Contractor could instruct the Sub-Contractor (under DOM 42) to serve notice here that the Sub-Contract Works were "complete", especially if the Sub-Contractor was claiming disruption loss and/or expense under DOM clause 13

the completion of the Sub-Contract Works or any part of same is being or is likely to be delayed; and

DOM 179   11.2.1

This subroutine requires the Contractor to "use constantly his best endeavours" to prevent delay in his own Works and to warn the Architect of delay or likely delay in the main Works

Practical completion of the Sub-Contract Works must be deemed to have taken place on the date notified under statement DOM 328; unless

DOM 329   14.1

the Contractor dissents in writing within 14 days of receipt of the written notice; and

DOM 330   14.1

the written notice of dissent sets out the Contractor's reasons for such dissent

DOM 331   14.1

The Contractor may issue any reasonable direction in writing to the Sub-Contractor (or his authorised representative) in regard to the Sub-Contract Works;

DOM 42   4.2.1 & 4.4

including the ordering of any Variation in the Sub-Contract Works; and

DOM 43   4.2.1

*The Contractor's right to issue directions to make variation is wide in scope and contains no prohibition on 'last-minute' directions. However such directions do open the door in clause 16 or 17 to a review of the rates and prices for any work which is dissimilar in character or conditions etc to that expected to be executed originally.
The Contractor need not refrain from immediate dissent under DOM 330 if the 14 days are not needed for verification that the Sub-Contract Works are incomplete*

Contractor does dissent as in DOM 330 and 331 ? → NO / YES

Practical completion must be deemed to have taken place on such date as may be agreed

DOM 332   14.2

A date is agreed ? → YES / NO

Practical completion will be deemed to have taken place on the date of Practical Completion of the Sub-Contract Works as certified by the Architect under JCT clause 17.1 of the Main Contract

DOM 333   14.2

The Architect must immediately issue a certificate of Practical Completion of the Works when in his opinion Practical Completion is achieved

JCT 267   17.1

The Architect is expressly required to issue a certificate to say Practical Completion of the whole Works has under the Main Contract been achieved whether or not the Works are taken possession of by the client

The Sub-Contractor must clear away to a dump or other place provided on the site all rubbish resulting from his execution of the Sub-Contract Works; and

DOM 899   27.1.3.1

The Sub-Contractor must (where DOM clause 15.1 applies) send to the Contractor, before or within a reasonable time after practical completion of the Sub-Contract Works, all documents necessary for the purpose of the adjustment of the Sub-Contract Sum

DOM 721   21.7.1

The Sub-Contractor must (where DOM clause 15.2 applies) send to the Contractor, before or within a reasonable time after practical completion of the Sub-Contract Works, all documents necessary for the purpose of computing the Ascertained Final Sub-Contract Sum

DOM 735   21.8.1

Deemed practical completion

The Contractor may deduct and retain one half the Retention that would have been deductible under statement DOM 713;

DOM 715   21.5.2

*Note (1) the reduction of retention to half, once practical completion is achieved
(2) the duty to submit final documentation
(3) the duty to clear up etc*

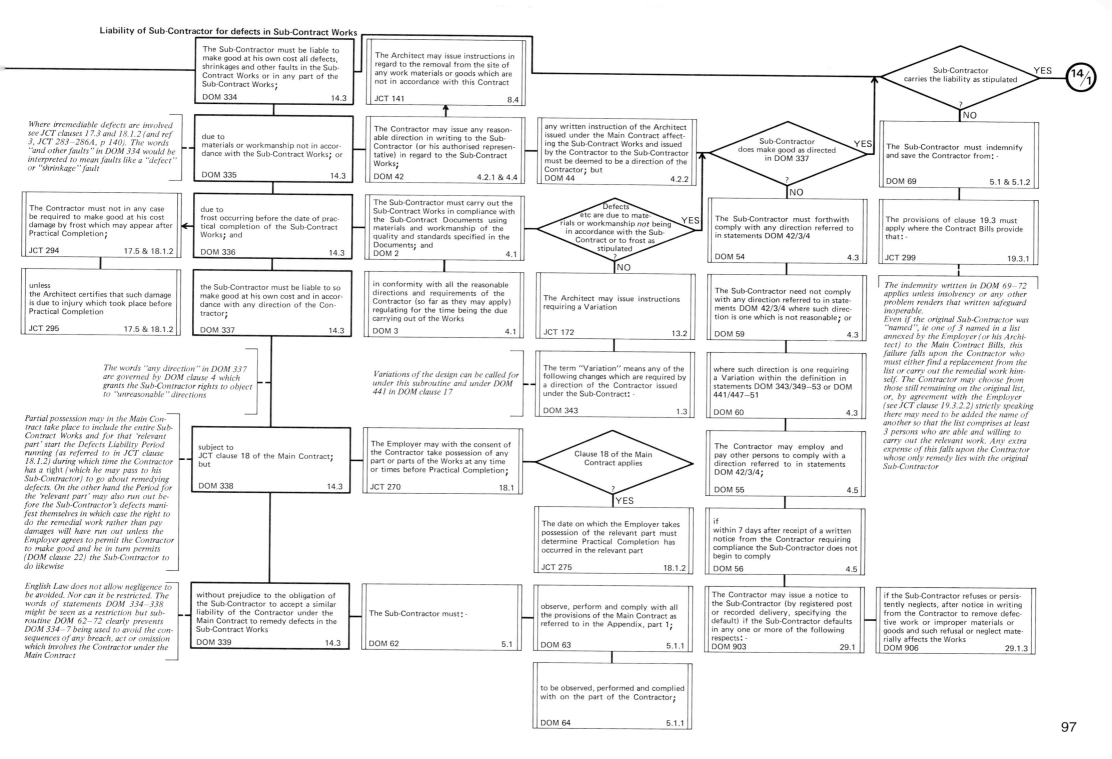

The Sub-Contractor must be liable to make good at his own cost all defects, shrinkages and other faults in the Sub-Contract Works or in any part of the Sub-Contract Works;
DOM 334 — 14.3

The Architect may issue instructions in regard to the removal from the site of any work materials or goods which are not in accordance with this Contract
JCT 141 — 8.4

Sub-Contractor carries the liability as stipulated — YES → 14/1
? NO

Where irremediable defects are involved see JCT clauses 17.3 and 18.1.2 (and ref 3, JCT 283–286A, p 140). The words "and other faults" in DOM 334 would be interpreted to mean faults like a "defect" or "shrinkage" fault

due to materials or workmanship not in accordance with the Sub-Contract Works; or
DOM 335 — 14.3

The Contractor may issue any reasonable direction in writing to the Sub-Contractor (or his authorised representative) in regard to the Sub-Contract Works;
DOM 42 — 4.2.1 & 4.4

any written instruction of the Architect issued under the Main Contract affecting the Sub-Contract Works and issued by the Contractor to the Sub-Contractor must be deemed to be a direction of the Contractor; but
DOM 44 — 4.2.2

Sub-Contractor does make good as directed in DOM 337 — YES
? NO

The Sub-Contractor must indemnify and save the Contractor from:-
DOM 69 — 5.1 & 5.1.2

The Contractor must not in any case be required to make good at his cost damage by frost which may appear after Practical Completion;
JCT 294 — 17.5 & 18.1.2

due to frost occurring before the date of practical completion of the Sub-Contract Works; and
DOM 336 — 14.3

The Sub-Contractor must carry out the Sub-Contract Works in compliance with the Sub-Contract Documents using materials and workmanship of the quality and standards specified in the Documents; and
DOM 2 — 4.1

Defects etc are due to materials or workmanship *not* being in accordance with the Sub-Contract or to frost as stipulated — YES
? NO

The Sub-Contractor must forthwith comply with any direction referred to in statements DOM 42/3/4
DOM 54 — 4.3

The provisions of clause 19.3 must apply where the Contract Bills provide that:-
JCT 299 — 19.3.1

unless the Architect certifies that such damage is due to injury which took place before Practical Completion
JCT 295 — 17.5 & 18.1.2

the Sub-Contractor must be liable to so make good at his own cost and in accordance with any direction of the Contractor;
DOM 337 — 14.3

in conformity with all the reasonable directions and requirements of the Contractor (so far as they may apply) regulating for the time being the due carrying out of the Works
DOM 3 — 4.1

The Architect may issue instructions requiring a Variation
JCT 172 — 13.2

The Sub-Contractor need not comply with any direction referred to in statements DOM 42/3/4 where such direction is one which is not reasonable; or
DOM 59 — 4.3

The indemnity written in DOM 69–72 applies unless insolvency or any other problem renders that written safeguard inoperable.
Even if the original Sub-Contractor was "named", ie one of 3 named in a list annexed by the Employer (or his Architect) to the Main Contract Bills, this failure falls upon the Contractor who must either find a replacement from the list or carry out the remedial work himself. The Contractor may choose from those still remaining on the original list, or, by agreement with the Employer (see JCT clause 19.3.2.2) strictly speaking there may need to be added the name of another so that the list comprises at least 3 persons who are able and willing to carry out the relevant work. Any extra expense of this falls upon the Contractor whose only remedy lies with the original Sub-Contractor

The words "any direction" in DOM 337 are governed by DOM clause 4 which grants the Sub-Contractor rights to object to "unreasonable" directions

Variations of the design can be called for under this subroutine and under DOM 441 in DOM clause 17

The term "Variation" means any of the following changes which are required by a direction of the Contractor issued under the Sub-Contract:-
DOM 343 — 1.3

where such direction is one requiring a Variation within the definition in statements DOM 343/349–53 or DOM 441/447–51
DOM 60 — 4.3

Partial possession may in the Main Contract take place to include the entire Sub-Contract Works and for that 'relevant part' start the Defects Liability Period running (as referred to in JCT clause 18.1.2) during which time the Contractor has a right (which he may pass to his Sub-Contractor) to go about remedying defects. On the other hand the Period for the 'relevant part' may also run out before the Sub-Contractor's defects manifest themselves in which case the right to do the remedial work rather than pay damages will have run out unless the Employer agrees to permit the Contractor to make good and he in turn permits (DOM clause 22) the Sub-Contractor to do likewise

subject to JCT clause 18 of the Main Contract; but
DOM 338 — 14.3

The Employer may with the consent of the Contractor take possession of any part or parts of the Works at any time or times before Practical Completion;
JCT 270 — 18.1

Clause 18 of the Main Contract applies
? YES

The Contractor may employ and pay other persons to comply with a direction referred to in statements DOM 42/3/4;
DOM 55 — 4.5

The date on which the Employer takes possession of the relevant part must determine Practical Completion has occurred in the relevant part
JCT 275 — 18.1.2

if within 7 days after receipt of a written notice from the Contractor requiring compliance the Sub-Contractor does not begin to comply
DOM 56 — 4.5

English Law does not allow negligence to be avoided. Nor can it be restricted. The words of statements DOM 334–338 might be seen as a restriction but subroutine DOM 62–72 clearly prevents DOM 334–7 being used to avoid the consequences of any breach, act or omission which involves the Contractor under the Main Contract

without prejudice to the obligation of the Sub-Contractor to accept a similar liability of the Contractor under the Main Contract to remedy defects in the Sub-Contract Works
DOM 339 — 14.3

The Sub-Contractor must:-
DOM 62 — 5.1

observe, perform and comply with all the provisions of the Main Contract as referred to in the Appendix, part 1;
DOM 63 — 5.1.1

The Contractor may issue a notice to the Sub-Contractor (by registered post or recorded delivery, specifying the default) if the Sub-Contractor defaults in any one or more of the following respects:-
DOM 903 — 29.1

if the Sub-Contractor refuses or persistently neglects, after notice in writing from the Contractor to remove defective work or improper materials or goods and such refusal or neglect materially affects the Works
DOM 906 — 29.1.3

to be observed, performed and complied with on the part of the Contractor;
DOM 64 — 5.1.1

Benefit of Architect's instructions as to cost of making good defects

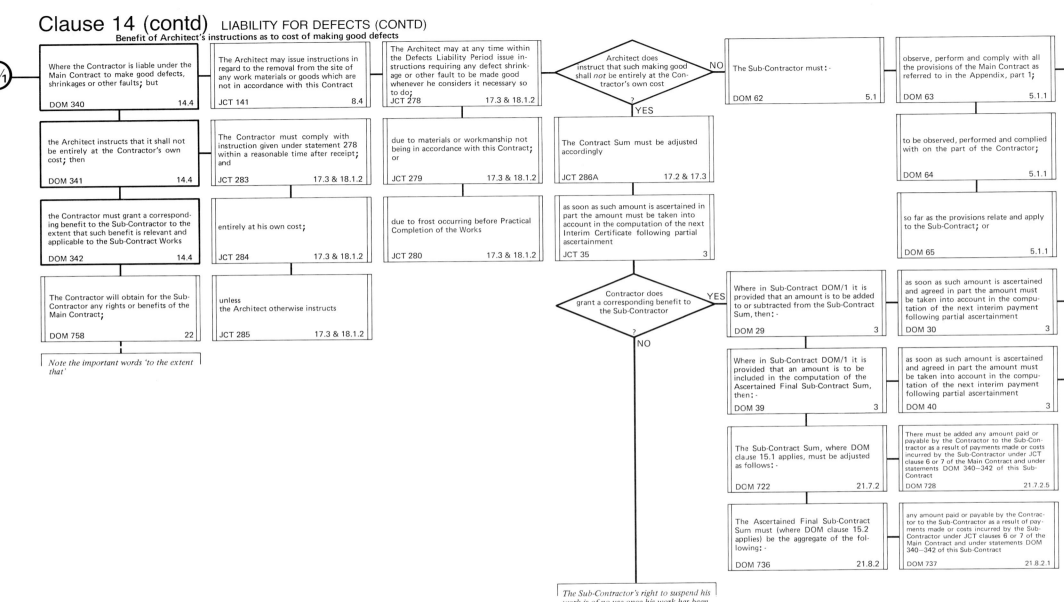

14/1

Where the Contractor is liable under the Main Contract to make good defects, shrinkages or other faults; but
DOM 340   14.4

the Architect instructs that it shall not be entirely at the Contractor's own cost; then
DOM 341   14.4

the Contractor must grant a corresponding benefit to the Sub-Contractor to the extent that such benefit is relevant and applicable to the Sub-Contract Works
DOM 342   14.4

The Contractor will obtain for the Sub-Contractor any rights or benefits of the Main Contract;
DOM 758   22

Note the important words 'to the extent that'

The Architect may issue instructions in regard to the removal from the site of any work materials or goods which are not in accordance with this Contract
JCT 141   8.4

The Contractor must comply with instruction given under statement 278 within a reasonable time after receipt; and
JCT 283   17.3 & 18.1.2

entirely at his own cost;
JCT 284   17.3 & 18.1.2

unless the Architect otherwise instructs
JCT 285   17.3 & 18.1.2

The Architect may at any time within the Defects Liability Period issue instructions requiring any defect shrinkage or other fault to be made good whenever he considers it necessary so to do;
JCT 278   17.3 & 18.1.2

due to materials or workmanship not being in accordance with this Contract; or
JCT 279   17.3 & 18.1.2

due to frost occurring before Practical Completion of the Works
JCT 280   17.3 & 18.1.2

Architect does instruct that such making good shall *not* be entirely at the Contractor's own cost ?   **NO**
YES

The Contract Sum must be adjusted accordingly
JCT 286A   17.2 & 17.3

as soon as such amount is ascertained in part the amount must be taken into account in the computation of the next Interim Certificate following partial ascertainment
JCT 35   3

Contractor does grant a corresponding benefit to the Sub-Contractor ?   **YES** / **NO**

The Sub-Contractor must :-
DOM 62   5.1

observe, perform and comply with all the provisions of the Main Contract as referred to in the Appendix, part 1;
DOM 63   5.1.1

to be observed, performed and complied with on the part of the Contractor;
DOM 64   5.1.1

so far as the provisions relate and apply to the Sub-Contract; or
DOM 65   5.1.1

Where in Sub-Contract DOM/1 it is provided that an amount is to be added to or subtracted from the Sub-Contract Sum, then:-
DOM 29   3

as soon as such amount is ascertained and agreed in part the amount must be taken into account in the computation of the next interim payment following partial ascertainment
DOM 30   3

Where in Sub-Contract DOM/1 it is provided that an amount is to be included in the computation of the Ascertained Final Sub-Contract Sum, then:-
DOM 39   3

as soon as such amount is ascertained and agreed in part the amount must be taken into account in the computation of the next interim payment following partial ascertainment
DOM 40   3

The Sub-Contract Sum, where DOM clause 15.1 applies, must be adjusted as follows:-
DOM 722   21.7.2

There must be added any amount paid or payable by the Contractor to the Sub-Contractor as a result of payments made or costs incurred by the Sub-Contractor under JCT clause 6 or 7 of the Main Contract and under statements DOM 340—342 of this Sub-Contract
DOM 728   21.7.2.5

The Ascertained Final Sub-Contract Sum must (where DOM clause 15.2 applies) be the aggregate of the following:-
DOM 736   21.8.2

any amount paid or payable by the Contractor to the Sub-Contractor as a result of payments made or costs incurred by the Sub-Contractor under JCT clauses 6 or 7 of the Main Contract and under statements DOM 340—342 of this Sub-Contract
DOM 737   21.8.2.1

The Sub-Contractor's right to suspend his work is of no use once his work has been practically completed. Similarly, the right to determine his own employment under DOM clause 30.1.1.3 is (where practical completion has been achieved) without bite in these circumstances so far as the benefits to be granted are concerned, although clauses 21.6 and 30.1.3 may apply and prove worthwhile where the Sub-Contract Works remain incomplete

```
┌─────────────────────────────┐   ┌─────────────────────────────┐
│ The Contractor must provide │   │ all necessary scaffolding   │
│ and erect,                  │   │ and scaffold                │
│ free of charge to the Sub-  │   │ boards;                     │
│ Contractor: -               │   │                             │───────────────────────────( STOP )
│                             │   │                             │
│ DOM 878          27.1.2     │   │ DOM 879          27.1.2     │
└─────────────────────────────┘   └─────────────────────────────┘
```

There are no words restricting the Sub-Contractor's right to these free provisions to his original attempt to properly carry out the work. The words "for the purpose of the Sub-Contract Works" appear wide enough to include the making good of defects etc in the Sub-Contract Works which appear after practical completion

```
┌─────────────────────────────┐
│ as soon as such amount is   │
│ ascertained                 │
│ and agreed in whole the     │
│ amount must                 │
│ be taken into account in    │
│ the compu-                  │
│ tation of the next interim  │
│ payment                     │
│ following whole             │
│ ascertainment               │
│ DOM 31                  3   │
└─────────────────────────────┘

┌─────────────────────────────┐
│ as soon as such amount is   │
│ ascertained                 │
│ and agreed in whole the     │
│ amount must                 │
│ be taken into account in    │
│ the compu-                  │
│ tation of the next interim  │
│ payment                     │
│ following whole             │
│ ascertainment               │
│ DOM 41                  3   │
└─────────────────────────────┘
```

Valuation

START

The Contractor may issue any reasonable direction in writing to the Sub-Contractor (or his authorised representative) in regard to the Sub-Contract Works;
DOM 42   4.2.1 & 4.4

including the ordering of any Variation in the Sub-Contract Works; and
DOM 43   4.2.1

The Architect must issue instructions in regard to: -
JCT 197   13.3

The Architect must instruct on provisional sums that originate from the Main Contract Bills. The reference in statement JCT 199 to "Sub-Contracts" means only Nominated ones, not Domestic ones. DOM clause 4 should clarify the procedure in respect of provisional sums in the Sub-Contract which do not originate from the Main Contract Bills making it clear the Contractor must instruct on same before any expenditure is begun

any written instruction of the Architect issued under the Main Contract affecting the Sub-Contract Works and issued by the Contractor to the Sub-Contractor must be deemed to be a direction of the Contractor; but
DOM 44   4.2.2

The price for the Sub-Contract Works must be: -
DOM 25   15.1

the Sub-Contract Sum; or
DOM 26   15.1

The Sub-Contractor need not comply with any direction referred to in statements DOM 42/3/4 where such direction is one which is not reasonable; or
DOM 59   4.3

This means Variations and provisional sum work etc

such other sum as shall become payable in accordance with the Sub-Contract;
DOM 27   15.1

This clause sets out the rules for valuing all Variations and provisional sum expenditure where a lump sum (under DOM clause 15.1) applies. The parties carry out the valuations using the rules laid down here, but not granting the Sub-Contractor any right to be present when necessary measuring is required for the valuations.
Where bills of quantities are a Sub-Contract Document then measurement and 'prelims' adjustment will follow the same principles as in those bills.
If a schedule of rates for measured work and/or daywork is included in the Sub-Contract Documents then valuations will be based upon such schedules' rates or prices.
Where work cannot properly be valued by measurement then daywork payment will apply.
Where the carrying out of instructions substantially changes the conditions under which other work is executed then the affected work is to be treated as if it had been the subject of a Variation instruction (see DOM 425–431). Furthermore a fair valuation is to be resorted to in cases where the rules do not relate to the work varied (see DOM 433–440).
For an explanation of the differences between an Agreement under DOM clause 15.1 and 15.2 see Chapter 4 (under clause 16)

The character of the Sub-Contract cannot (see DOM 45) be fundamentally altered via an instruction of the Architect to vary work or designs etc

No Variation required or subsequently sanctioned by the Architect must vitiate this Contract
JCT 186   13.2

where Article 2.1 applies
DOM 28   15.1

An obligation or restriction etc referred to in the Appendix, part 1, may be varied

The Sub-Contractor must: -
DOM 62   5.1

observe, perform and comply with all the provisions of the Main Contract as referred to in the Appendix, part 1;
DOM 63   5.1.1

The term "Variation" means any of the following changes which are required by a direction of the Contractor issued under the Sub-Contract: -
DOM 343   1.3

the alteration or modification of the design quality or quantity of the Sub-Contract Works as shown in the Sub-Contract Documents;
DOM 344   1.3.1

If no BQ exists the Numbered Documents will serve to show the quantity and quality originally included

the addition, alteration or omission of any obligations or restrictions set out or referred to in the Appendix, part 1, Section C, in so far as it is contained in an instruction of the Architect issued under the Main Contract;
DOM 349   1.3.2

The Architect may sanction in writing any Variation made by the Contractor without an instruction of the Architect
JCT 185   13.2

including
the addition, omission or substitution of any work; or
DOM 345   1.3.1.1

The quality and quantity of the work included in the Sub-Contract Sum or Tender Sum must be deemed to be that which is set out in the bills of quantities;
DOM 546   18.1.3

in regard to
access to the site or use of any specific parts of the site; or
DOM 350   1.3.2.1

Note the qualifying words "in so far as . . . etc" in statement DOM 349. See Appendix, part 1, Section C

The Contractor will obtain for the Sub-Contractor any rights or benefits of the Main Contract;
DOM 758   22

See the detailed annotation adjacent and under JCT 185 in Ref 3 p 122

the alteration of the kind or standard of any of the materials or goods to be used in the Sub-Contract Works; or
DOM 346   1.3.1.2

The Sub-Contractor must carry out the Sub-Contract Works in compliance with the Sub-Contract Documents using materials and workmanship of the quality and standards specified in the Documents; and
DOM 2   4.1

limitations of working space; or
DOM 351   1.3.2.2

See Appendix, part 1, Section C

The Sub-Contractor cannot, in doubtful cases, seek a "Variation" instruction of the Contractor to remove alleged bad work etc. The duty to do work and use proper materials in accordance with the Sub-Contract (under statement DOM 2, clause 4.1) requires the Sub-Contractor to remedy matters without necessarily being told to do so.
However, the Contractor, in disputed cases of unacceptable work, has a discretionary right to issue removal directions under statement DOM 3 or to issue even wider directions under DOM 42. Under DOM 42 arbitration can take place immediately otherwise the parties must carry on without arbitration until completion of both the Main and Sub-contract Works

the removal from the site of any work, materials or goods executed or materials or goods brought on the site by the Sub-Contractor for the purposes of the Sub-Contract Works;
DOM 347   1.3.1.3

The Contractor should clarify whether his direction was being given under DOM 3 or 42, or under DOM 43 as a "Variation"

limitations of working hours; or
DOM 352   1.3.2.3

Where JCT clause 19A 'Fair Wages' is included in the Main Contract, the following provisions must apply: -
DOM 986   32

The omission of any limitation of working hours is not to be seen as a power to order any acceleration to complete before the period or periods agreed under the Appendix, part 4, or as revised following any extension granted under DOM clause 11

but not
the removal from the site of any work executed or materials or goods brought on the site which are not in accordance with the Sub-Contract
DOM 348   1.3.1.3

The Architect may issue instructions in regard to the removal from the site of any work materials or goods which are not in accordance with this Contract
JCT 141   8.4

the execution or completion of the work in any specific order
DOM 353   1.3.2.4

See Appendix, part 1, Section C. This may be incorporated in the Main Contract by the Sectional Completion Supplement

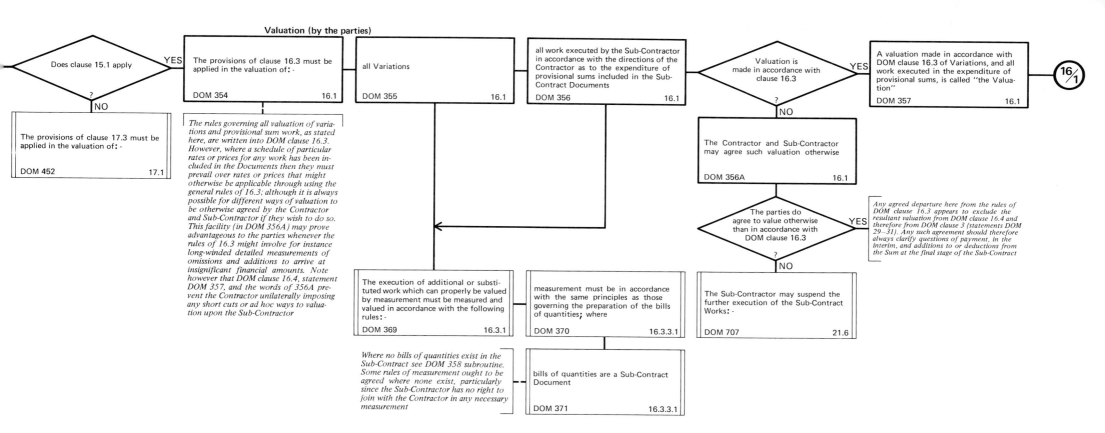

Valuation (by the parties)

Does clause 15.1 apply ?

YES →

The provisions of clause 16.3 must be applied in the valuation of: -

DOM 354   16.1

all Variations

DOM 355   16.1

all work executed by the Sub-Contractor in accordance with the directions of the Contractor as to the expenditure of provisional sums included in the Sub-Contract Documents

DOM 356   16.1

Valuation is made in accordance with clause 16.3 ?

YES →

A valuation made in accordance with DOM clause 16.3 of Variations, and all work executed in the expenditure of provisional sums, is called "the Valuation"

DOM 357   16.1

16/1

NO ↓

The provisions of clause 17.3 must be applied in the valuation of: -

DOM 452   17.1

The rules governing all valuation of variations and provisional sum work, as stated here, are written into DOM clause 16.3. However, where a schedule of particular rates or prices for any work has been included in the Documents then they must prevail over rates or prices that might otherwise be applicable through using the general rules of 16.3; although it is always possible for different ways of valuation to be otherwise agreed by the Contractor and Sub-Contractor if they wish to do so. This facility (in DOM 356A) may prove advantageous to the parties whenever the rules of 16.3 might involve for instance long-winded detailed measurements of omissions and additions to arrive at insignificant financial amounts. Note however that DOM clause 16.4, statement DOM 357, and the words of 356A prevent the Contractor unilaterally imposing any short cuts or ad hoc ways to valuation upon the Sub-Contractor

NO ↓

The Contractor and Sub-Contractor may agree such valuation otherwise

DOM 356A   16.1

The parties do agree to value otherwise than in accordance with DOM clause 16.3 ?

YES →

Any agreed departure here from the rules of DOM clause 16.3 appears to exclude the resultant valuation from DOM clause 16.4 and therefore from DOM clause 3 (statements DOM 29–31). Any such agreement should therefore always clarify questions of payment, in the interim, and additions to or deductions from the Sum at the final stage of the Sub-Contract

NO ↓

The Sub-Contractor may suspend the further execution of the Sub-Contract Works: -

DOM 707   21.6

The execution of additional or substituted work which can properly be valued by measurement must be measured and valued in accordance with the following rules: -

DOM 369   16.3.1

measurement must be in accordance with the same principles as those governing the preparation of the bills of quantities; where

DOM 370   16.3.3.1

Where no bills of quantities exist in the Sub-Contract see DOM 358 subroutine. Some rules of measurement ought to be agreed where none exist, particularly since the Sub-Contractor has no right to join with the Contractor in any necessary measurement

bills of quantities are a Sub-Contract Document

DOM 371   16.3.3.1

101

Sub-Contractor's schedule of rates or prices Valuation

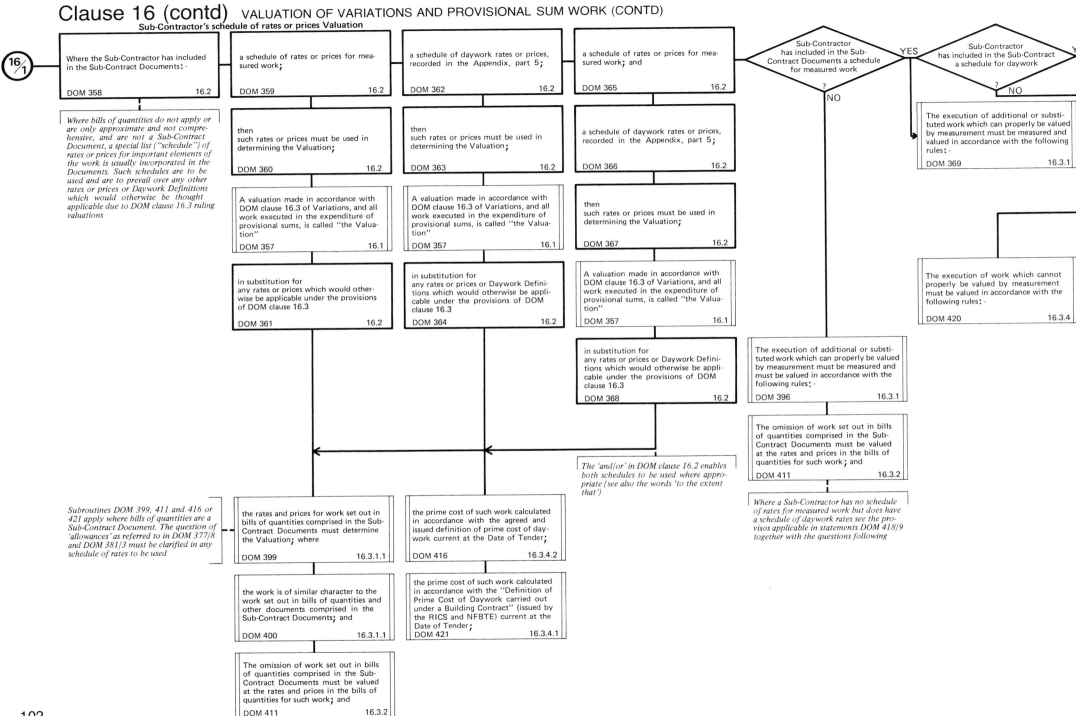

16/1

Where the Sub-Contractor has included in the Sub-Contract Documents:-

DOM 358   16.2

Where bills of quantities do not apply or are only approximate and not comprehensive, and are not a Sub-Contract Document, a special list ("schedule") of rates or prices for important elements of the work is usually incorporated in the Documents. Such schedules are to be used and are to prevail over any other rates or prices or Daywork Definitions which would otherwise be thought applicable due to DOM clause 16.3 ruling valuations

---

a schedule of rates or prices for measured work;

DOM 359   16.2

then
such rates or prices must be used in determining the Valuation;

DOM 360   16.2

A valuation made in accordance with DOM clause 16.3 of Variations, and all work executed in the expenditure of provisional sums, is called "the Valuation"

DOM 357   16.1

in substitution for
any rates or prices which would otherwise be applicable under the provisions of DOM clause 16.3

DOM 361   16.2

---

a schedule of daywork rates or prices, recorded in the Appendix, part 5;

DOM 362   16.2

then
such rates or prices must be used in determining the Valuation;

DOM 363   16.2

A valuation made in accordance with DOM clause 16.3 of Variations, and all work executed in the expenditure of provisional sums, is called "the Valuation"

DOM 357   16.1

in substitution for
any rates or prices or Daywork Definitions which would otherwise be applicable under the provisions of DOM clause 16.3

DOM 364   16.2

---

a schedule of rates or prices for measured work; and

DOM 365   16.2

a schedule of daywork rates or prices, recorded in the Appendix, part 5;

DOM 366   16.2

then
such rates or prices must be used in determining the Valuation;

DOM 367   16.2

A valuation made in accordance with DOM clause 16.3 of Variations, and all work executed in the expenditure of provisional sums, is called "the Valuation"

DOM 357   16.1

in substitution for
any rates or prices or Daywork Definitions which would otherwise be applicable under the provisions of DOM clause 16.3

DOM 368   16.2

Sub-Contractor has included in the Sub-Contract Documents a schedule for measured work ?

YES / NO

Sub-Contractor has included in the Sub-Contract a schedule for daywork ?

YE(S) / NO

The execution of additional or substituted work which can properly be valued by measurement must be measured and valued in accordance with the following rules: -

DOM 369   16.3.1

The execution of work which cannot properly be valued by measurement must be valued in accordance with the following rules: -

DOM 420   16.3.4

The execution of additional or substituted work which can properly be valued by measurement must be measured and must be valued in accordance with the following rules: -

DOM 396   16.3.1

The omission of work set out in bills of quantities comprised in the Sub-Contract Documents must be valued at the rates and prices in the bills of quantities for such work; and

DOM 411   16.3.2

Where a Sub-Contractor has no schedule of rates for measured work but does have a schedule of daywork rates see the provisos applicable in statements DOM 418/9 together with the questions following

---

The 'and/or' in DOM clause 16.2 enables both schedules to be used where appropriate (see also the words 'to the extent that')

Subroutines DOM 399, 411 and 416 or 421 apply where bills of quantities are a Sub-Contract Document. The question of 'allowances' as referred to in DOM 377/8 and DOM 381/3 must be clarified in any schedule of rates to be used

---

the rates and prices for work set out in bills of quantities comprised in the Sub-Contract Documents must determine the Valuation; where

DOM 399   16.3.1.1

the work is of similar character to the work set out in bills of quantities and other documents comprised in the Sub-Contract Documents; and

DOM 400   16.3.1.1

The omission of work set out in bills of quantities comprised in the Sub-Contract Documents must be valued at the rates and prices in the bills of quantities for such work; and

DOM 411   16.3.2

---

the prime cost of such work calculated in accordance with the agreed and issued definition of prime cost of daywork current at the Date of Tender;

DOM 416   16.3.4.2

the prime cost of such work calculated in accordance with the "Definition of Prime Cost of Daywork carried out under a Building Contract" (issued by the RICS and NFBTE) current at the Date of Tender;

DOM 421   16.3.4.1

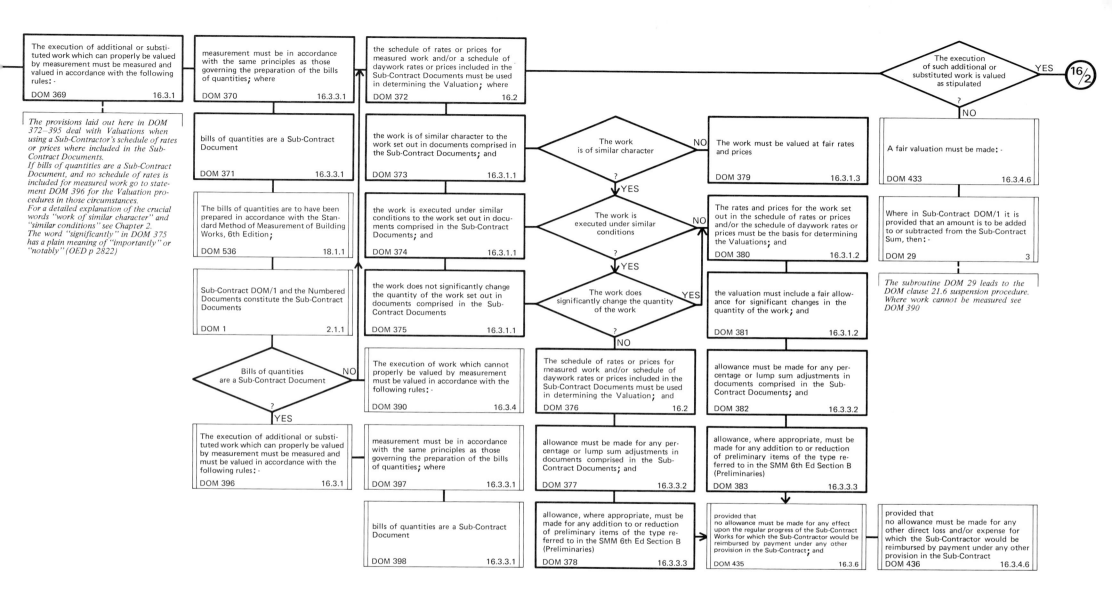

DOM 369 — The execution of additional or substituted work which can properly be valued by measurement must be measured and valued in accordance with the following rules: -   16.3.1

The provisions laid out here in DOM 372–395 deal with Valuations when using a Sub-Contractor's schedule of rates or prices where included in the Sub-Contract Documents.
If bills of quantities are a Sub-Contract Document, and no schedule of rates is included for measured work go to statement DOM 396 for the Valuation procedures in those circumstances.
For a detailed explanation of the crucial words "work of similar character" and "similar conditions" see Chapter 2.
The word "significantly" in DOM 375 has a plain meaning of "importantly" or "notably" (OED p 2822)

DOM 370 — measurement must be in accordance with the same principles as those governing the preparation of the bills of quantities; where   16.3.3.1

DOM 371 — bills of quantities are a Sub-Contract Document   16.3.3.1

DOM 536 — The bills of quantities are to have been prepared in accordance with the Standard Method of Measurement of Building Works, 6th Edition;   18.1.1

DOM 1 — Sub-Contract DOM/1 and the Numbered Documents constitute the Sub-Contract Documents   2.1.1

Bills of quantities are a Sub-Contract Document — NO / YES ?

DOM 396 — The execution of additional or substituted work which can properly be valued by measurement must be measured and must be valued in accordance with the following rules: -   16.3.1

DOM 397 — measurement must be in accordance with the same principles as those governing the preparation of the bills of quantities; where   16.3.3.1

DOM 398 — bills of quantities are a Sub-Contract Document   16.3.3.1

DOM 372 — the schedule of rates or prices for measured work and/or a schedule of daywork rates or prices included in the Sub-Contract Documents must be used in determining the Valuation; where   16.2

DOM 373 — the work is of similar character to the work set out in documents comprised in the Sub-Contract Documents; and   16.3.1.1

DOM 374 — the work is executed under similar conditions to the work set out in documents comprised in the Sub-Contract Documents; and   16.3.1.1

DOM 375 — the work does not significantly change the quantity of the work set out in documents comprised in the Sub-Contract Documents   16.3.1.1

DOM 390 — The execution of work which cannot properly be valued by measurement must be valued in accordance with the following rules: -   16.3.4

DOM 376 — The schedule of rates or prices for measured work and/or schedule of daywork rates or prices included in the Sub-Contract Documents must be used in determining the Valuation; and   16.2

DOM 377 — allowance must be made for any percentage or lump sum adjustments in documents comprised in the Sub-Contract Documents; and   16.3.3.2

DOM 378 — allowance, where appropriate, must be made for any addition to or reduction of preliminary items of the type referred to in the SMM 6th Ed Section B (Preliminaries)   16.3.3.3

The work is of similar character — NO / YES ?

The work is executed under similar conditions — NO / YES ?

The work does significantly change the quantity of the work — YES / NO ?

DOM 379 — The work must be valued at fair rates and prices   16.3.1.3

DOM 380 — The rates and prices for the work set out in the schedule of rates or prices and/or the schedule of daywork rates or prices must be the basis for determining the Valuations; and   16.3.1.2

DOM 381 — the valuation must include a fair allowance for significant changes in the quantity of the work; and   16.3.1.2

DOM 382 — allowance must be made for any percentage or lump sum adjustments in documents comprised in the Sub-Contract Documents; and   16.3.3.2

DOM 383 — allowance, where appropriate, must be made for any addition to or reduction of preliminary items of the type referred to in the SMM 6th Ed Section B (Preliminaries)   16.3.3.3

DOM 435 — provided that no allowance must be made for any effect upon the regular progress of the Sub-Contract Works for which the Sub-Contractor would be reimbursed by payment under any other provision in the Sub-Contract; and   16.3.6

The execution of such additional or substituted work is valued as stipulated — YES 16/2 / NO ?

DOM 433 — A fair valuation must be made: -   16.3.4.6

DOM 29 — Where in Sub-Contract DOM/1 it is provided that an amount is to be added to or subtracted from the Sub-Contract Sum, then: -   3

The subroutine DOM 29 leads to the DOM clause 21.6 suspension procedure. Where work cannot be measured see DOM 390

DOM 436 — provided that no allowance must be made for any other direct loss and/or expense for which the Sub-Contractor would be reimbursed by payment under any other provision in the Sub-Contract   16.3.4.6

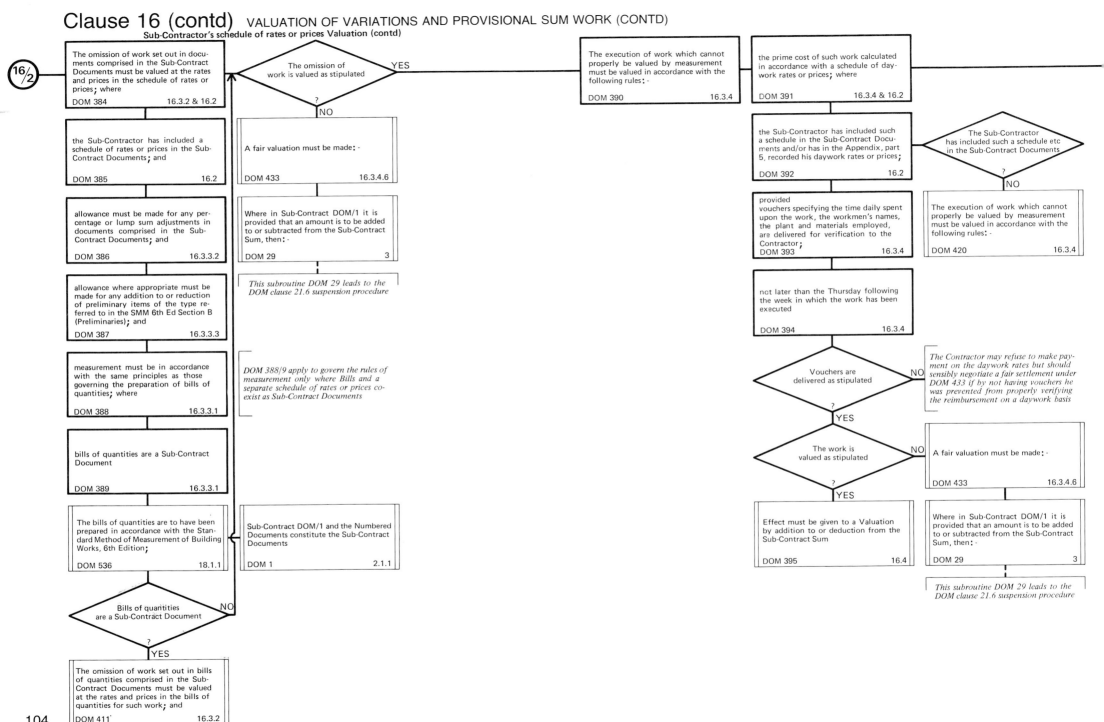

16/2

The omission of work set out in documents comprised in the Sub-Contract Documents must be valued at the rates and prices in the schedule of rates or prices; where

DOM 384   16.3.2 & 16.2

the Sub-Contractor has included a schedule of rates or prices in the Sub-Contract Documents; and

DOM 385   16.2

allowance must be made for any percentage or lump sum adjustments in documents comprised in the Sub-Contract Documents; and

DOM 386   16.3.3.2

allowance where appropriate must be made for any addition to or reduction of preliminary items of the type referred to in the SMM 6th Ed Section B (Preliminaries); and

DOM 387   16.3.3.3

measurement must be in accordance with the same principles as those governing the preparation of bills of quantities; where

DOM 388   16.3.3.1

bills of quantities are a Sub-Contract Document

DOM 389   16.3.3.1

The bills of quantities are to have been prepared in accordance with the Standard Method of Measurement of Building Works, 6th Edition;

DOM 536   18.1.1

Bills of quantities are a Sub-Contract Document ?   NO

YES

The omission of work set out in bills of quantities comprised in the Sub-Contract Documents must be valued at the rates and prices in the bills of quantities for such work; and

DOM 411   16.3.2

The omission of work is valued as stipulated ?   YES

NO

A fair valuation must be made:-

DOM 433   16.3.4.6

Where in Sub-Contract DOM/1 it is provided that an amount is to be added to or subtracted from the Sub-Contract Sum, then:-

DOM 29   3

This subroutine DOM 29 leads to the DOM clause 21.6 suspension procedure

DOM 388/9 apply to govern the rules of measurement only where Bills and a separate schedule of rates or prices co-exist as Sub-Contract Documents

Sub-Contract DOM/1 and the Numbered Documents constitute the Sub-Contract Documents

DOM 1   2.1.1

The execution of work which cannot properly be valued by measurement must be valued in accordance with the following rules:-

DOM 390   16.3.4

---

the prime cost of such work calculated in accordance with a schedule of daywork rates or prices; where

DOM 391   16.3.4 & 16.2

the Sub-Contractor has included such a schedule in the Sub-Contract Documents and/or has in the Appendix, part 5, recorded his daywork rates or prices;

DOM 392   16.2

provided vouchers specifying the time daily spent upon the work, the workmen's names, the plant and materials employed, are delivered for verification to the Contractor;

DOM 393   16.3.4

not later than the Thursday following the week in which the work has been executed

DOM 394   16.3.4

Vouchers are delivered as stipulated ?   NO

YES

The work is valued as stipulated ?   NO

YES

Effect must be given to a Valuation by addition to or deduction from the Sub-Contract Sum

DOM 395   16.4

The Sub-Contractor has included such a schedule etc in the Sub-Contract Documents ?   NO

The execution of work which cannot properly be valued by measurement must be valued in accordance with the following rules:-

DOM 420   16.3.4

The Contractor may refuse to make payment on the daywork rates but should sensibly negotiate a fair settlement under DOM 433 if by not having vouchers he was prevented from properly verifying the reimbursement on a daywork basis

A fair valuation must be made:-

DOM 433   16.3.4.6

Where in Sub-Contract DOM/1 it is provided that an amount is to be added to or subtracted from the Sub-Contract Sum, then:-

DOM 29   3

This subroutine DOM 29 leads to the DOM clause 21.6 suspension procedure

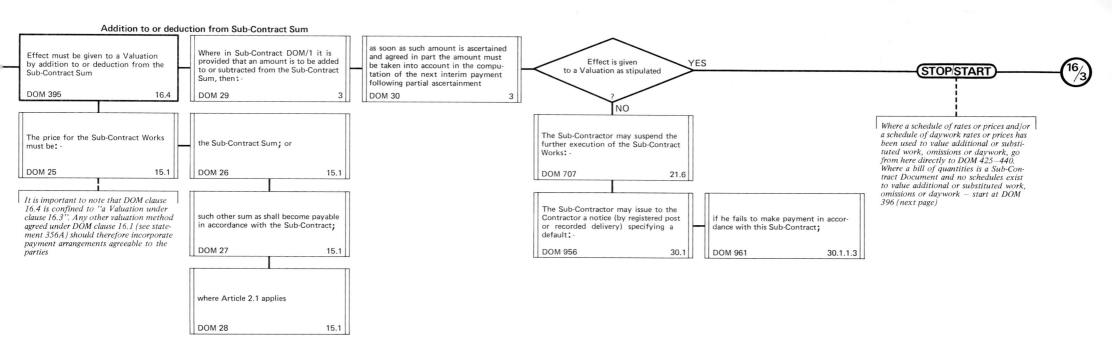

Addition to or deduction from Sub-Contract Sum

Effect must be given to a Valuation by addition to or deduction from the Sub-Contract Sum

DOM 395   16.4

Where in Sub-Contract DOM/1 it is provided that an amount is to be added to or subtracted from the Sub-Contract Sum, then: -

DOM 29   3

---

as soon as such amount is ascertained and agreed in part the amount must be taken into account in the computation of the next interim payment following partial ascertainment

DOM 30   3

Effect is given to a Valuation as stipulated

?

YES

STOP/START

16/3

The price for the Sub-Contract Works must be: -

DOM 25   15.1

---

the Sub-Contract Sum; or

DOM 26   15.1

NO

The Sub-Contractor may suspend the further execution of the Sub-Contract Works: -

DOM 707   21.6

Where a schedule of rates or prices and/or a schedule of daywork rates or prices has been used to value additional or substituted work, omissions or daywork, go from here directly to DOM 425–440. Where a bill of quantities is a Sub-Contract Document and no schedules exist to value additional or substituted work, omissions or daywork – start at DOM 396 (next page)

It is important to note that DOM clause 16.4 is confined to "a Valuation under clause 16.3". Any other valuation method agreed under DOM clause 16.1 (see statement 356A) should therefore incorporate payment arrangements agreeable to the parties

---

such other sum as shall become payable in accordance with the Sub-Contract;

DOM 27   15.1

The Sub-Contractor may issue to the Contractor a notice (by registered post or recorded delivery) specifying a default: -

DOM 956   30.1

---

if he fails to make payment in accordance with this Sub-Contract;

DOM 961   30.1.1.3

---

where Article 2.1 applies

DOM 28   15.1

Bills of quantities Valuation

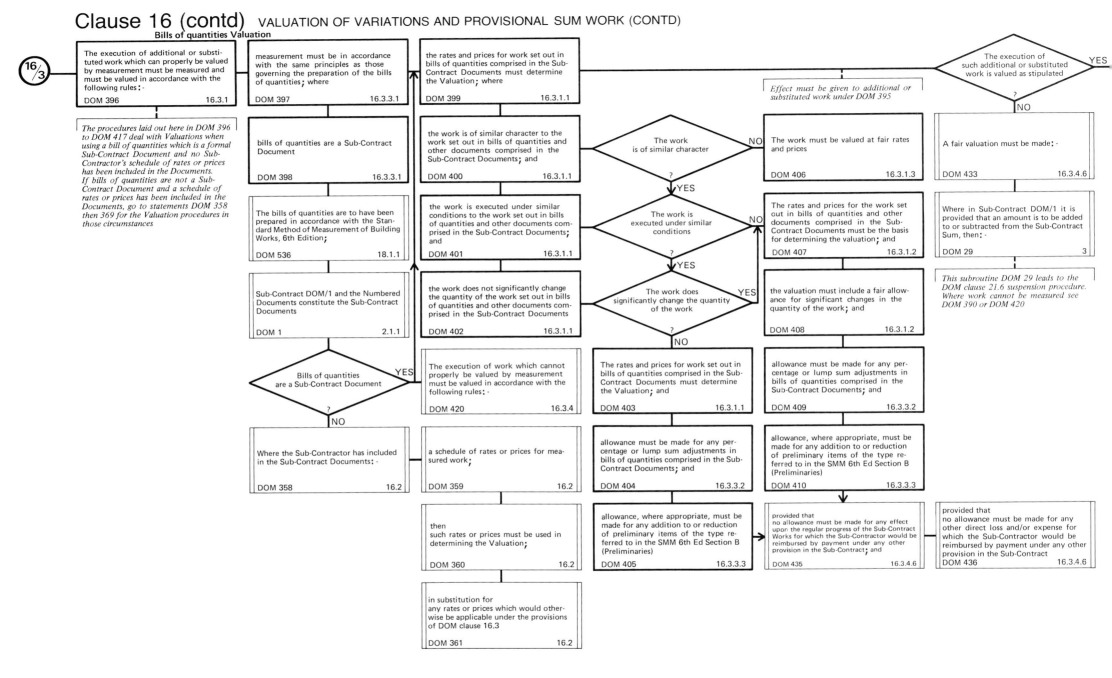

16/3

The execution of additional or substituted work which can properly be valued by measurement must be measured and must be valued in accordance with the following rules:-

DOM 396   16.3.1

The procedures laid out here in DOM 396 to DOM 417 deal with Valuations when using a bill of quantities which is a formal Sub-Contract Document and no Sub-Contractor's schedule of rates or prices has been included in the Documents. If bills of quantities are not a Sub-Contract Document and a schedule of rates or prices has been included in the Documents, go to statements DOM 358 then 369 for the Valuation procedures in those circumstances

measurement must be in accordance with the same principles as those governing the preparation of the bills of quantities; where

DOM 397   16.3.3.1

bills of quantities are a Sub-Contract Document

DOM 398   16.3.3.1

The bills of quantities are to have been prepared in accordance with the Standard Method of Measurement of Building Works, 6th Edition;

DOM 536   18.1.1

Sub-Contract DOM/1 and the Numbered Documents constitute the Sub-Contract Documents

DOM 1   2.1.1

Bills of quantities are a Sub-Contract Document ?   **YES**

NO

Where the Sub-Contractor has included in the Sub-Contract Documents: -

DOM 358   16.2

a schedule of rates or prices for measured work;

DOM 359   16.2

then such rates or prices must be used in determining the Valuation;

DOM 360   16.2

in substitution for any rates or prices which would otherwise be applicable under the provisions of DOM clause 16.3

DOM 361   16.2

the rates and prices for work set out in bills of quantities comprised in the Sub-Contract Documents must determine the Valuation; where

DOM 399   16.3.1.1

the work is of similar character to the work set out in bills of quantities and other documents comprised in the Sub-Contract Documents; and

DOM 400   16.3.1.1

the work is executed under similar conditions to the work set out in bills of quantities and other documents comprised in the Sub-Contract Documents; and

DOM 401   16.3.1.1

the work does not significantly change the quantity of the work set out in bills of quantities and other documents comprised in the Sub-Contract Documents

DOM 402   16.3.1.1

The execution of work which cannot properly be valued by measurement must be valued in accordance with the following rules: -

DOM 420   16.3.4

The work is of similar character ?   **NO**

YES

The work is executed under similar conditions ?   **NO**

YES

The work does significantly change the quantity of the work ?   **YES**

NO

The rates and prices for work set out in bills of quantities comprised in the Sub-Contract Documents must determine the Valuation; and

DOM 403   16.3.1.1

allowance must be made for any percentage or lump sum adjustments in bills of quantities comprised in the Sub-Contract Documents; and

DOM 404   16.3.3.2

allowance, where appropriate, must be made for any addition to or reduction of preliminary items of the type referred to in the SMM 6th Ed Section B (Preliminaries)

DOM 405   16.3.3.3

Effect must be given to additional or substituted work under DOM 395

The work must be valued at fair rates and prices

DOM 406   16.3.1.3

The rates and prices for the work set out in bills of quantities and other documents comprised in the Sub-Contract Documents must be the basis for determining the valuation; and

DOM 407   16.3.1.2

the valuation must include a fair allowance for significant changes in the quantity of the work; and

DOM 408   16.3.1.2

allowance must be made for any percentage or lump sum adjustments in bills of quantities comprised in the Sub-Contract Documents; and

DOM 409   16.3.3.2

allowance, where appropriate, must be made for any addition to or reduction of preliminary items of the type referred to in the SMM 6th Ed Section B (Preliminaries)

DOM 410   16.3.3.3

provided that no allowance must be made for any effect upon the regular progress of the Sub-Contract Works for which the Sub-Contractor would be reimbursed by payment under any other provision in the Sub-Contract; and

DOM 435   16.3.4.6

The execution of such additional or substituted work is valued as stipulated ?   **YES**

NO

A fair valuation must be made: -

DOM 433   16.3.4.6

Where in Sub-Contract DOM/1 it is provided that an amount is to be added to or subtracted from the Sub-Contract Sum, then: -

DOM 29   3

This subroutine DOM 29 leads to the DOM clause 21.6 suspension procedure. Where work cannot be measured see DOM 390 or DOM 420

provided that no allowance must be made for any other direct loss and/or expense for which the Sub-Contractor would be reimbursed by payment under any other provision in the Sub-Contract

DOM 436   16.3.4.6

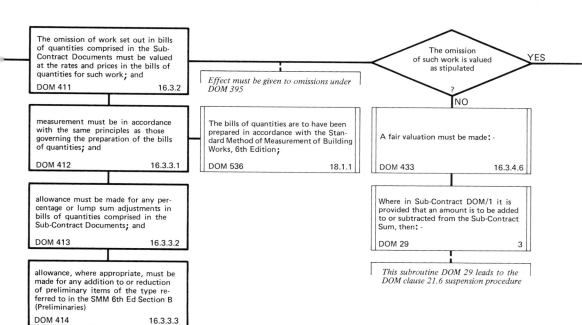

The omission of work set out in bills of quantities comprised in the Sub-Contract Documents must be valued at the rates and prices in the bills of quantities for such work; and

DOM 411   16.3.2

---

measurement must be in accordance with the same principles as those governing the preparation of the bills of quantities; and

DOM 412   16.3.3.1

---

allowance must be made for any percentage or lump sum adjustments in bills of quantities comprised in the Sub-Contract Documents; and

DOM 413   16.3.3.2

---

allowance, where appropriate, must be made for any addition to or reduction of preliminary items of the type referred to in the SMM 6th Ed Section B (Preliminaries)

DOM 414   16.3.3.3

Effect must be given to omissions under DOM 395

The bills of quantities are to have been prepared in accordance with the Standard Method of Measurement of Building Works, 6th Edition;

DOM 536   18.1.1

The omission of such work is valued as stipulated

?

YES

NO

A fair valuation must be made: -

DOM 433   16.3.4.6

Where in Sub-Contract DOM/1 it is provided that an amount is to be added to or subtracted from the Sub-Contract Sum, then: -

DOM 29   3

This subroutine DOM 29 leads to the DOM clause 21.6 suspension procedure

---

The execution and valuation of work which cannot properly be measured is dealt with on the next page

16/4

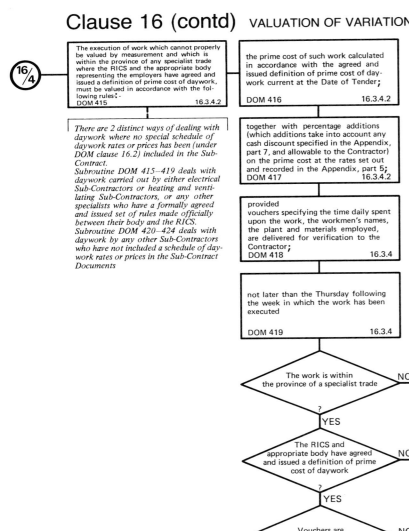

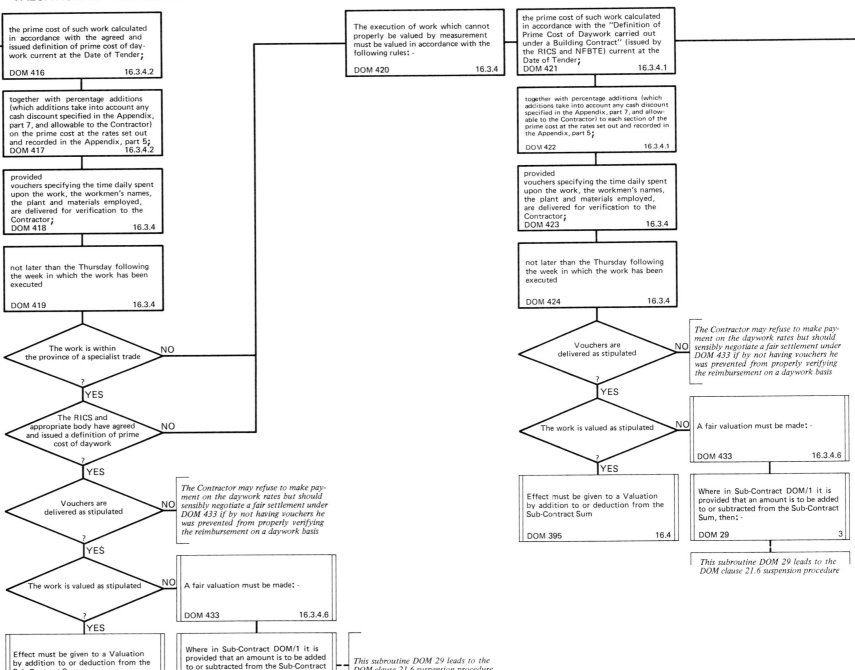

16/4

The execution of work which cannot properly be valued by measurement and which is within the province of any specialist trade where the RICS and the appropriate body representing the employers have agreed and issued a definition of prime cost of daywork, must be valued in accordance with the following rules: -
DOM 415   16.3.4.2

There are 2 distinct ways of dealing with daywork where no special schedule of daywork rates or prices has been (under DOM clause 16.2) included in the Sub-Contract.
Subroutine DOM 415–419 deals with daywork carried out by either electrical Sub-Contractors or heating and ventilating Sub-Contractors, or any other specialists who have a formally agreed and issued set of rules made officially between their body and the RICS.
Subroutine DOM 420–424 deals with daywork by any other Sub-Contractors who have not included a schedule of daywork rates or prices in the Sub-Contract Documents

the prime cost of such work calculated in accordance with the agreed and issued definition of prime cost of daywork current at the Date of Tender;
DOM 416   16.3.4.2

together with percentage additions (which additions take into account any cash discount specified in the Appendix, part 7, and allowable to the Contractor) on the prime cost at the rates set out and recorded in the Appendix, part 5;
DOM 417   16.3.4.2

provided
vouchers specifying the time daily spent upon the work, the workmen's names, the plant and materials employed, are delivered for verification to the Contractor;
DOM 418   16.3.4

not later than the Thursday following the week in which the work has been executed
DOM 419   16.3.4

The work is within the province of a specialist trade ? — NO
YES

The RICS and appropriate body have agreed and issued a definition of prime cost of daywork ? — NO
YES

Vouchers are delivered as stipulated ? — NO
YES

The Contractor may refuse to make payment on the daywork rates but should sensibly negotiate a fair settlement under DOM 433 if by not having vouchers he was prevented from properly verifying the reimbursement on a daywork basis

The work is valued as stipulated ? — NO
YES

A fair valuation must be made: -
DOM 433   16.3.4.6

Effect must be given to a Valuation by addition to or deduction from the Sub-Contract Sum
DOM 395   16.4

Where in Sub-Contract DOM/1 it is provided that an amount is to be added to or subtracted from the Sub-Contract Sum, then: -
DOM 29   3

This subroutine DOM 29 leads to the DOM clause 21.6 suspension procedure

The execution of work which cannot properly be valued by measurement must be valued in accordance with the following rules: -
DOM 420   16.3.4

the prime cost of such work calculated in accordance with the "Definition of Prime Cost of Daywork carried out under a Building Contract" (issued by the RICS and NFBTE) current at the Date of Tender;
DOM 421   16.3.4.1

together with percentage additions (which additions take into account any cash discount specified in the Appendix, part 7, and allowable to the Contractor) to each section of the prime cost at the rates set out and recorded in the Appendix, part 5;
DOM 422   16.3.4.1

provided
vouchers specifying the time daily spent upon the work, the workmen's names, the plant and materials employed, are delivered for verification to the Contractor;
DOM 423   16.3.4

not later than the Thursday following the week in which the work has been executed
DOM 424   16.3.4

Vouchers are delivered as stipulated ? — NO
YES

The Contractor may refuse to make payment on the daywork rates but should sensibly negotiate a fair settlement under DOM 433 if by not having vouchers he was prevented from properly verifying the reimbursement on a daywork basis

The work is valued as stipulated ? — NO
YES

A fair valuation must be made: -
DOM 433   16.3.4.6

Effect must be given to a Valuation by addition to or deduction from the Sub-Contract Sum
DOM 395   16.4

Where in Sub-Contract DOM/1 it is provided that an amount is to be added to or subtracted from the Sub-Contract Sum, then: -
DOM 29   3

This subroutine DOM 29 leads to the DOM clause 21.6 suspension procedure

Effect must be given to a Valuation
by addition to or deduction from the
Sub-Contract Sum

DOM 395   16.4

16/5

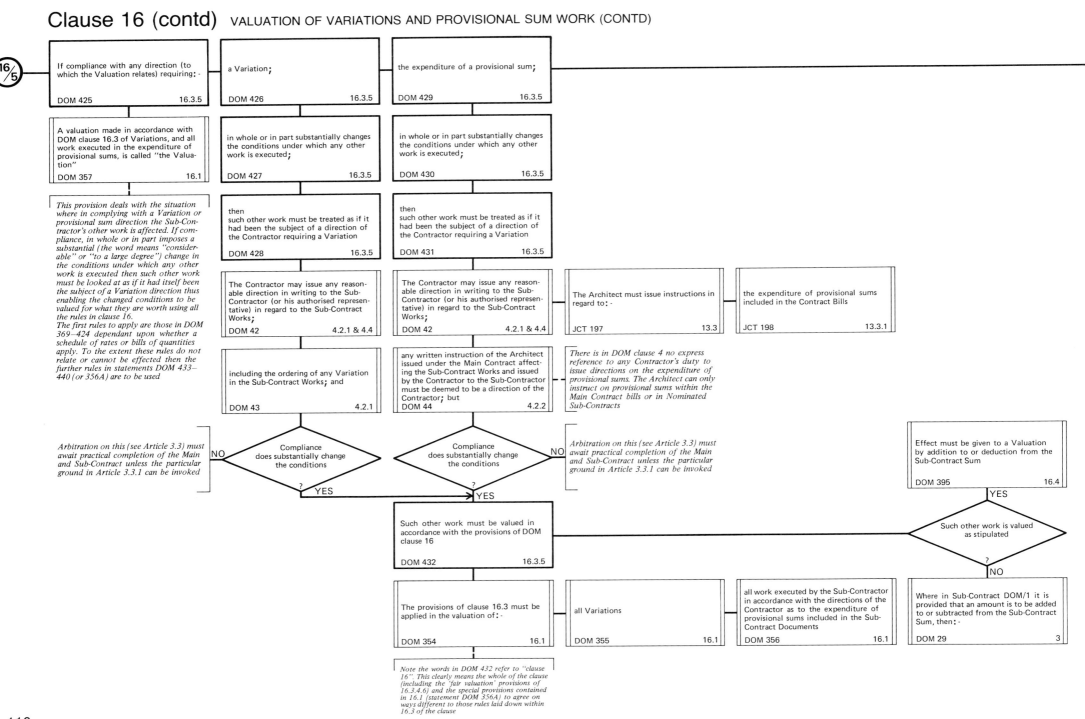

16/5

If compliance with any direction (to which the Valuation relates) requiring: -

DOM 425   16.3.5

a Variation;

DOM 426   16.3.5

the expenditure of a provisional sum;

DOM 429   16.3.5

A valuation made in accordance with DOM clause 16.3 of Variations, and all work executed in the expenditure of provisional sums, is called "the Valuation"

DOM 357   16.1

in whole or in part substantially changes the conditions under which any other work is executed;

DOM 427   16.3.5

in whole or in part substantially changes the conditions under which any other work is executed;

DOM 430   16.3.5

This provision deals with the situation where in complying with a Variation or provisional sum direction the Sub-Contractor's other work is affected. If compliance, in whole or in part imposes a substantial (the word means "considerable" or "to a large degree") change in the conditions under which any other work is executed then such other work must be looked at as if it had itself been the subject of a Variation direction thus enabling the changed conditions to be valued for what they are worth using all the rules in clause 16.

The first rules to apply are those in DOM 369–424 dependant upon whether a schedule of rates or bills of quantities apply. To the extent these rules do not relate or cannot be effected then the further rules in statements DOM 433–440 (or 356A) are to be used

then
such other work must be treated as if it had been the subject of a direction of the Contractor requiring a Variation

DOM 428   16.3.5

then
such other work must be treated as if it had been the subject of a direction of the Contractor requiring a Variation

DOM 431   16.3.5

The Contractor may issue any reasonable direction in writing to the Sub-Contractor (or his authorised representative) in regard to the Sub-Contract Works;

DOM 42   4.2.1 & 4.4

The Contractor may issue any reasonable direction in writing to the Sub-Contractor (or his authorised representative) in regard to the Sub-Contract Works;

DOM 42   4.2.1 & 4.4

The Architect must issue instructions in regard to: -

JCT 197   13.3

the expenditure of provisional sums included in the Contract Bills

JCT 198   13.3.1

---

including the ordering of any Variation in the Sub-Contract Works; and

DOM 43   4.2.1

any written instruction of the Architect issued under the Main Contract affecting the Sub-Contract Works and issued by the Contractor to the Sub-Contractor must be deemed to be a direction of the Contractor; but

DOM 44   4.2.2

There is in DOM clause 4 no express reference to any Contractor's duty to issue directions on the expenditure of provisional sums. The Architect can only instruct on provisional sums within the Main Contract bills or in Nominated Sub-Contracts

---

Arbitration on this (see Article 3.3) must await practical completion of the Main and Sub-Contract unless the particular ground in Article 3.3.1 can be invoked

NO ⟵ ◇ Compliance does substantially change the conditions **?** → **YES**

◇ Compliance does substantially change the conditions **?** → **YES** **NO** ⟶

Arbitration on this (see Article 3.3) must await practical completion of the Main and Sub-Contract unless the particular ground in Article 3.3.1 can be invoked

Effect must be given to a Valuation by addition to or deduction from the Sub-Contract Sum

DOM 395   16.4

YES

Such other work must be valued in accordance with the provisions of DOM clause 16

DOM 432   16.3.5

◇ Such other work is valued as stipulated **?** **NO**

The provisions of clause 16.3 must be applied in the valuation of: -

DOM 354   16.1

all Variations

DOM 355   16.1

all work executed by the Sub-Contractor in accordance with the directions of the Contractor as to the expenditure of provisional sums included in the Sub-Contract Documents

DOM 356   16.1

Where in Sub-Contract DOM/1 it is provided that an amount is to be added to or subtracted from the Sub-Contract Sum, then: -

DOM 29   3

Note the words in DOM 432 refer to "clause 16". This clearly means the whole of the clause (including the 'fair valuation' provisions of 16.3.4.6) and the special provisions contained in 16.1 (statement DOM 356A) to agree on ways different to those rules laid down within 16.3 of the clause

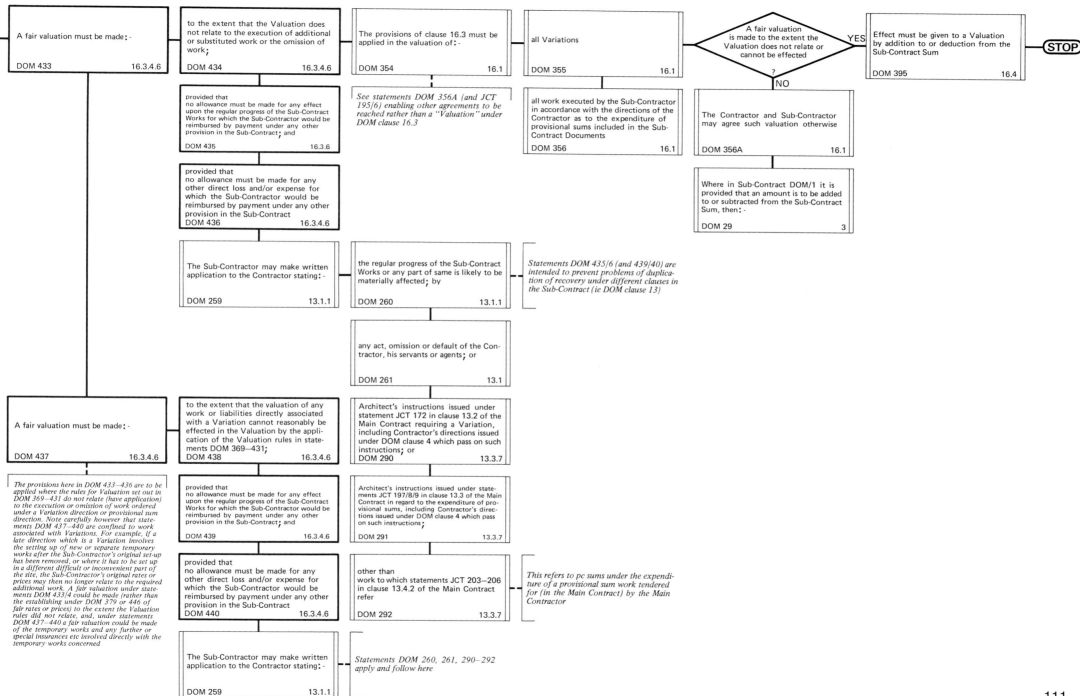

A fair valuation must be made: -

DOM 433   16.3.4.6

to the extent that the Valuation does not relate to the execution of additional or substituted work or the omission of work;

DOM 434   16.3.4.6

The provisions of clause 16.3 must be applied in the valuation of: -

DOM 354   16.1

all Variations

DOM 355   16.1

A fair valuation is made to the extent the Valuation does not relate or cannot be effected

?   YES   NO

Effect must be given to a Valuation by addition to or deduction from the Sub-Contract Sum

DOM 395   16.4

STOP

See statements DOM 356A (and JCT 195/6) enabling other agreements to be reached rather than a "Valuation" under DOM clause 16.3

all work executed by the Sub-Contractor in accordance with the directions of the Contractor as to the expenditure of provisional sums included in the Sub-Contract Documents

DOM 356   16.1

The Contractor and Sub-Contractor may agree such valuation otherwise

DOM 356A   16.1

provided that
no allowance must be made for any effect upon the regular progress of the Sub-Contract Works for which the Sub-Contractor would be reimbursed by payment under any other provision in the Sub-Contract; and

DOM 435   16.3.6

Where in Sub-Contract DOM/1 it is provided that an amount is to be added to or subtracted from the Sub-Contract Sum, then: -

DOM 29   3

provided that
no allowance must be made for any other direct loss and/or expense for which the Sub-Contractor would be reimbursed by payment under any other provision in the Sub-Contract

DOM 436   16.3.4.6

The Sub-Contractor may make written application to the Contractor stating: -

DOM 259   13.1.1

the regular progress of the Sub-Contract Works or any part of same is likely to be materially affected; by

DOM 260   13.1.1

Statements DOM 435/6 (and 439/40) are intended to prevent problems of duplication of recovery under different clauses in the Sub-Contract (ie DOM clause 13)

any act, omission or default of the Contractor, his servants or agents; or

DOM 261   13.1

A fair valuation must be made: -

DOM 437   16.3.4.6

to the extent that the valuation of any work or liabilities directly associated with a Variation cannot reasonably be effected in the Valuation by the application of the Valuation rules in statements DOM 369—431;

DOM 438   16.3.4.6

Architect's instructions issued under statement JCT 172 in clause 13.2 of the Main Contract requiring a Variation, including Contractor's directions issued under DOM clause 4 which pass on such instructions; or

DOM 290   13.3.7

The provisions here in DOM 433—436 are to be applied where the rules for Valuation set out in DOM 369—431 do not relate (have application) to the execution or omission of work ordered under a Variation direction or provisional sum direction. Note carefully however that statements DOM 437—440 are confined to work associated with Variations. For example, if a late direction which is a Variation involves the setting up of new or separate temporary works after the Sub-Contractor's original set-up has been removed, or where it has to be set up in a different difficult or inconvenient part of the site, the Sub-Contractor's original rates or prices may then no longer relate to the required additional work. A fair valuation under statements DOM 433/4 could be made (rather than the establishing under DOM 379 or 446 of fair rates or prices) to the extent the Valuation rules did not relate, and, under statements DOM 437—440 a fair valuation could be made of the temporary works and any further or special insurances etc involved directly with the temporary works concerned

provided that
no allowance must be made for any effect upon the regular progress of the Sub-Contract Works for which the Sub-Contractor would be reimbursed by payment under any other provision in the Sub-Contract; and

DOM 439   16.3.4.6

Architect's instructions issued under statements JCT 197/8/9 in clause 13.3 of the Main Contract in regard to the expenditure of provisional sums, including Contractor's directions issued under DOM clause 4 which pass on such instructions;

DOM 291   13.3.7

provided that
no allowance must be made for any other direct loss and/or expense for which the Sub-Contractor would be reimbursed by payment under any other provision in the Sub-Contract

DOM 440   16.3.4.6

other than
work to which statements JCT 203—206 in clause 13.4.2 of the Main Contract refer

DOM 292   13.3.7

This refers to pc sums under the expenditure of a provisional sum work tendered for (in the Main Contract) by the Main Contractor

The Sub-Contractor may make written application to the Contractor stating: -

DOM 259   13.1.1

Statements DOM 260, 261, 290—292 apply and follow here

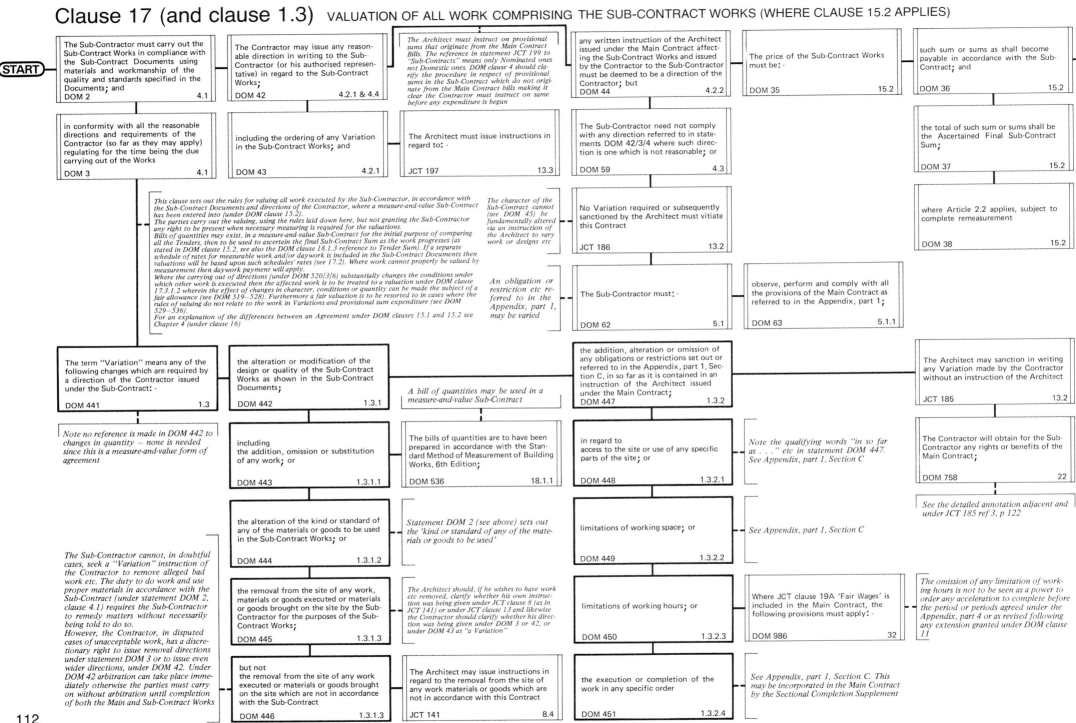

START

The Sub-Contractor must carry out the Sub-Contract Works in compliance with the Sub-Contract Documents using materials and workmanship of the quality and standards specified in the Documents; and
DOM 2 — 4.1

The Contractor may issue any reasonable direction in writing to the Sub-Contractor (or his authorised representative) in regard to the Sub-Contract Works;
DOM 42 — 4.2.1 & 4.4

The Architect must instruct on provisional sums that originate from the Main Contract Bills. The reference in statement JCT 199 to "Sub-Contracts" means only Nominated ones not Domestic ones. DOM clause 4 should clarify the procedure in respect of provisional sums in the Sub-Contract which do not originate from the Main Contract bills making it clear the Contractor must instruct on same before any expenditure is begun

any written instruction of the Architect issued under the Main Contract affecting the Sub-Contract Works and issued by the Contractor to the Sub-Contractor must be deemed to be a direction of the Contractor; but
DOM 44 — 4.2.2

The price of the Sub-Contract Works must be: -
DOM 35 — 15.2

such sum or sums as shall become payable in accordance with the Sub-Contract; and
DOM 36 — 15.2

in conformity with all the reasonable directions and requirements of the Contractor (so far as they may apply) regulating for the time being the due carrying out of the Works
DOM 3 — 4.1

including the ordering of any Variation in the Sub-Contract Works; and
DOM 43 — 4.2.1

The Architect must issue instructions in regard to: -
JCT 197 — 13.3

The Sub-Contractor need not comply with any direction referred to in statements DOM 42/3/4 where such direction is one which is not reasonable; or
DOM 59 — 4.3

the total of such sum or sums shall be the Ascertained Final Sub-Contract Sum;
DOM 37 — 15.2

This clause sets out the rules for valuing all work executed by the Sub-Contractor, in accordance with the Sub-Contract Documents and directions of the Contractor, where a measure-and-value Sub-Contract has been entered into (under DOM clause 15.2).
The parties carry out the valuing, using the rules laid down here, but not granting the Sub-Contractor any right to be present when necessary measuring is required for the valuations.
Bills of quantities may exist, in a measure-and-value Sub-Contract for the initial purpose of comparing all the Tenders, then to be used to ascertain the final Sub-Contract Sum as the work progresses (as stated in DOM clause 15.2, see also the DOM clause 18.1.3 reference to Tender Sum). If a separate schedule of rates for measurable work and/or daywork is included in the Sub-Contract Documents then valuations will be based upon such schedules' rates (see 17.2). Where work cannot properly be valued by measurement then daywork payment will apply.
Where the carrying out of directions (under DOM 520/3/6) substantially changes the conditions under which other work is executed then the affected work is to be treated to a valuation under DOM clause 17.3.1.2 wherein the effect of changes in character, conditions or quantity can be made the subject of a fair allowance (see DOM 519–528). Furthermore a fair valuation is to be resorted to in cases where the rules of valuing do not relate to the work in Variations and provisional sum expenditure (see DOM 529–536).
For an explanation of the differences between an Agreement under DOM clauses 15.1 and 15.2 see Chapter 4 (under clause 16)

The character of the Sub-Contract cannot (see DOM 45) be fundamentally altered via an instruction of the Architect to vary work or designs etc

No Variation required or subsequently sanctioned by the Architect must vitiate this Contract
JCT 186 — 13.2

where Article 2.2 applies, subject to complete remeasurement
DOM 38 — 15.2

An obligation or restriction referred to in the Appendix, part 1, may be varied

The Sub-Contractor must: -
DOM 62 — 5.1

observe, perform and comply with all the provisions of the Main Contract as referred to in the Appendix, part 1;
DOM 63 — 5.1.1

The term "Variation" means any of the following changes which are required by a direction of the Contractor issued under the Sub-Contract: -
DOM 441 — 1.3

the alteration or modification of the design or quality of the Sub-Contract Works as shown in the Sub-Contract Documents;
DOM 442 — 1.3.1

the addition, alteration or omission of any obligations or restrictions set out or referred to in the Appendix, part 1, Section C, in so far as it is contained in an instruction of the Architect issued under the Main Contract;
DOM 447 — 1.3.2

The Architect may sanction in writing any Variation made by the Contractor without an instruction of the Architect
JCT 185 — 13.2

Note no reference is made in DOM 442 to changes in quantity – none is needed since this is a measure-and-value form of agreement

including
the addition, omission or substitution of any work; or
DOM 443 — 1.3.1.1

A bill of quantities may be used in a measure-and-value Sub-Contract

The bills of quantities are to have been prepared in accordance with the Standard Method of Measurement of Building Works, 6th Edition;
DOM 536 — 18.1.1

in regard to
access to the site or use of any specific parts of the site; or
DOM 448 — 1.3.2.1

Note the qualifying words "in so far as . . ." etc in statement DOM 447. See Appendix, part 1, Section C

The Contractor will obtain for the Sub-Contractor any rights or benefits of the Main Contract;
DOM 758 — 22

See the detailed annotation adjacent and under JCT 185 ref 3, p 122

The Sub-Contractor cannot, in doubtful cases, seek a "Variation" instruction of the Contractor to remove alleged bad work etc. The duty to do work and use proper materials in accordance with the Sub-Contract (under statement DOM 2, clause 4.1) requires the Sub-Contractor to remedy matters without necessarily being told to do so.
However, the Contractor, in disputed cases of unacceptable work, has a discretionary right to issue removal directions under statement DOM 3 or to issue even wider directions, under DOM 42. Under DOM 42 arbitration can take place immediately otherwise the parties must carry on without arbitration until completion of both the Main and Sub-Contract Works

the alteration of the kind or standard of any of the materials or goods to be used in the Sub-Contract Works; or
DOM 444 — 1.3.1.2

Statement DOM 2 (see above) sets out the 'kind or standard of any of the materials or goods to be used'

limitations of working space; or
DOM 449 — 1.3.2.2

See Appendix, part 1, Section C

the removal from the site of any work, materials or goods executed or materials or goods brought on the site by the Sub-Contractor for the purposes of the Sub-Contract Works;
DOM 445 — 1.3.1.3

The Architect should, if he wishes to have work etc removed, clarify whether his instruction was being given under JCT clause 8 (as in JCT 141) or under JCT clause 13 and likewise the Contractor should clarify whether his direction was being given under DOM 3 or 42, or under DOM 43 as "a Variation"

limitations of working hours; or
DOM 450 — 1.3.2.3

Where JCT clause 19A 'Fair Wages' is included in the Main Contract, the following provisions must apply: -
DOM 986 — 32

The omission of any limitation of working hours is not to be seen as a power to order any acceleration to complete before the period or periods agreed under the Appendix, part 4 or as revised following any extension granted under DOM clause 11

but not
the removal from the site of any work executed or materials or goods brought on the site which are not in accordance with the Sub-Contract
DOM 446 — 1.3.1.3

The Architect may issue instructions in regard to the removal from the site of any work materials or goods which are not in accordance with this Contract
JCT 141 — 8.4

the execution or completion of the work in any specific order
DOM 451 — 1.3.2.4

See Appendix, part 1, Section C. This may be incorporated in the Main Contract by the Sectional Completion Supplement

Valuation by the parties of all work comprising the Sub-Contract Works

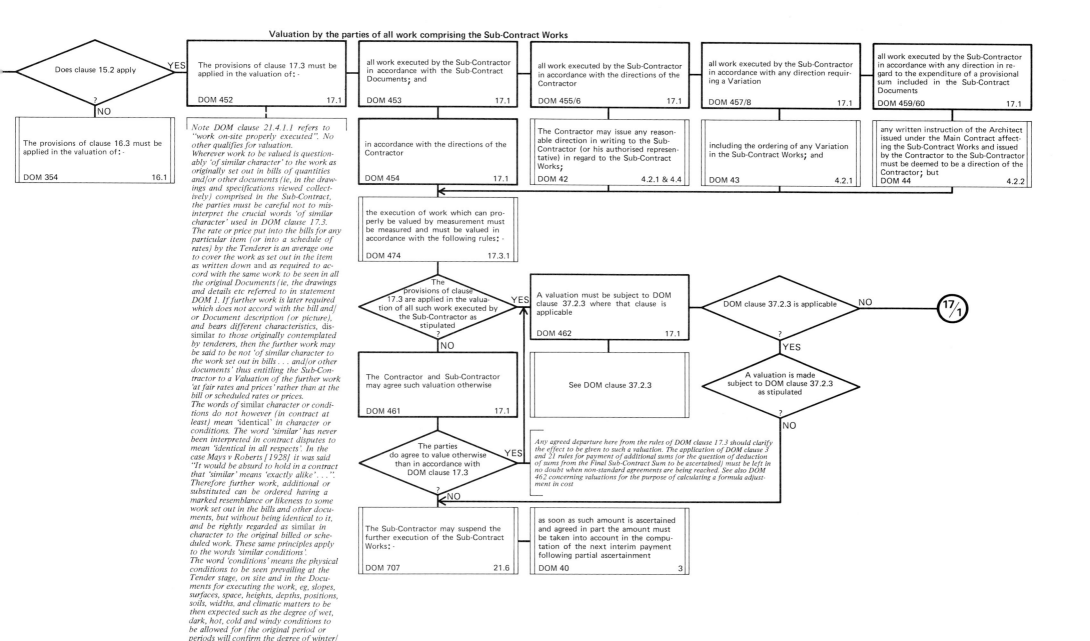

Does clause 15.2 apply ?

YES →

The provisions of clause 17.3 must be applied in the valuation of: -

DOM 452   17.1

all work executed by the Sub-Contractor in accordance with the Sub-Contract Documents; and

DOM 453   17.1

all work executed by the Sub-Contractor in accordance with the directions of the Contractor

DOM 455/6   17.1

all work executed by the Sub-Contractor in accordance with any direction requiring a Variation

DOM 457/8   17.1

all work executed by the Sub-Contractor in accordance with any direction in regard to the expenditure of a provisional sum included in the Sub-Contract Documents

DOM 459/60   17.1

NO ↓

The provisions of clause 16.3 must be applied in the valuation of: -

DOM 354   16.1

Note DOM clause 21.4.1.1 refers to "work on-site properly executed". No other qualifies for valuation.
Wherever work to be valued is questionably 'of similar character' to the work as originally set out in bills of quantities and/or other documents (ie, in the drawings and specifications viewed collectively) comprised in the Sub-Contract, the parties must be careful not to misinterpret the crucial words 'of similar character' used in DOM clause 17.3. The rate or price put into the bills for any particular item (or into a schedule of rates) by the Tenderer is an average one to cover the work as set out in the item as written down and as required to accord with the same work to be seen in all the original Documents (ie, the drawings and details etc referred to in statement DOM 1. If further work is later required which does not accord with the bill and/or Document description (or picture), and bears different characteristics, dissimilar to those originally contemplated by tenderers, then the further work may be said to be not 'of similar character to the work set out in bills ... and/or other documents' thus entitling the Sub-Contractor to a Valuation of the further work 'at fair rates and prices' rather than at the bill or scheduled rates or prices.
The words of similar character or conditions do not however (in contract at least) mean 'identical' in character or conditions. The word 'similar' has never been interpreted in contract disputes to mean 'identical in all respects'. In the case Mays v Roberts [1928] it was said "It would be absurd to hold in a contract that 'similar' means 'exactly alike'...".
Therefore further work, additional or substituted can be ordered having a marked resemblance or likeness to some work set out in the bills and other documents, but without being identical to it, and be rightly regarded as similar in character to the original billed or scheduled work. These same principles apply to the words 'similar conditions'.
The word 'conditions' means the physical conditions to be seen prevailing at the Tender stage, on site and in the Documents for executing the work, eg, slopes, surfaces, space, heights, depths, positions, soils, widths, and climatic matters to be then expected such as the degree of wet, dark, hot, cold and windy conditions to be allowed for (the original period or periods will confirm the degree of winter/spring/summer conditions then contemplated

in accordance with the directions of the Contractor

DOM 454   17.1

The Contractor may issue any reasonable direction in writing to the Sub-Contractor (or his authorised representative) in regard to the Sub-Contract Works;

DOM 42   4.2.1 & 4.4

including the ordering of any Variation in the Sub-Contract Works; and

DOM 43   4.2.1

any written instruction of the Architect issued under the Main Contract affecting the Sub-Contract Works and issued by the Contractor to the Sub-Contractor must be deemed to be a direction of the Contractor; but

DOM 44   4.2.2

the execution of work which can properly be valued by measurement must be measured and must be valued in accordance with the following rules: -

DOM 474   17.3.1

The provisions of clause 17.3 are applied in the valuation of all such work executed by the Sub-Contractor as stipulated ?

YES →

A valuation must be subject to DOM clause 37.2.3 where that clause is applicable

DOM 462   17.1

DOM clause 37.2.3 is applicable

NO → (17/1)

YES ↓

NO ↓

The Contractor and Sub-Contractor may agree such valuation otherwise

DOM 461   17.1

See DOM clause 37.2.3

A valuation is made subject to DOM clause 37.2.3 as stipulated ?

NO ↓

The parties do agree to value otherwise than in accordance with DOM clause 17.3 ?

YES →

Any agreed departure here from the rules of DOM clause 17.3 should clarify the effect to be given to such a valuation. The application of DOM clause 3 and 21 rules for payment of additional sums (or the question of deduction of sums from the Final Sub-Contract Sum to be ascertained) must be left in no doubt when non-standard agreements are being reached. See also DOM 462 concerning valuations for the purpose of calculating a formula adjustment in cost

NO ↓

The Sub-Contractor may suspend the further execution of the Sub-Contract Works: -

DOM 707   21.6

as soon as such amount is ascertained and agreed in part the amount must be taken into account in the computation of the next interim payment following partial ascertainment

DOM 40   3

Sub-Contractor's schedule of rates or prices Valuation

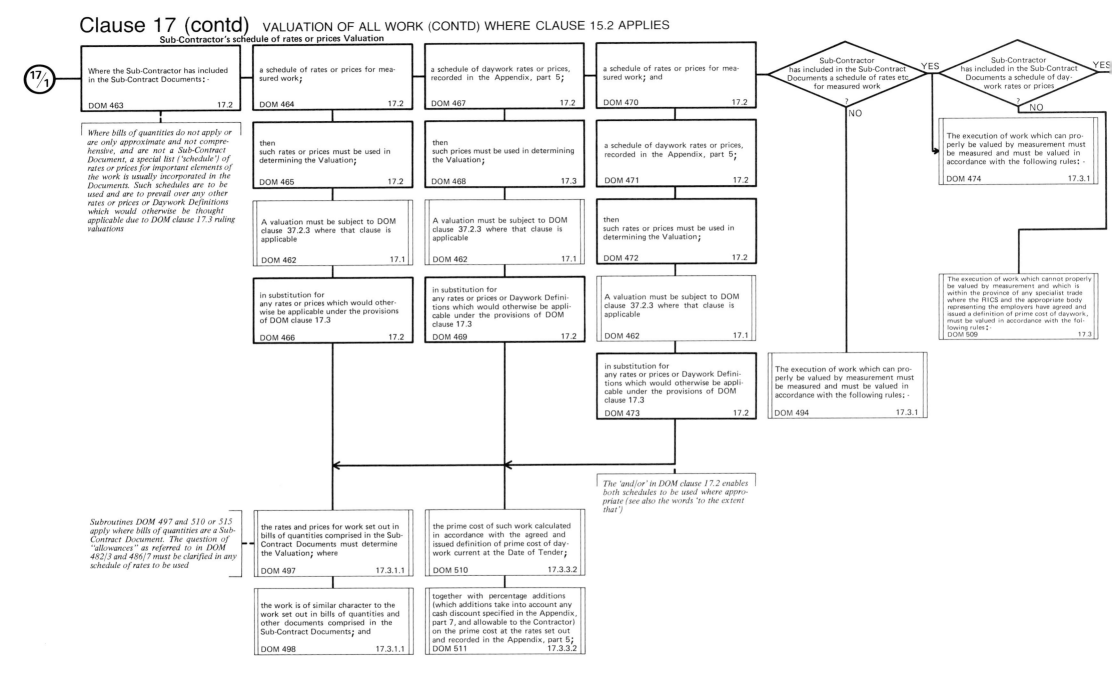

17/1

Where the Sub-Contractor has included in the Sub-Contract Documents: -

DOM 463   17.2

Where bills of quantities do not apply or are only approximate and not comprehensive, and are not a Sub-Contract Document, a special list ('schedule') of rates or prices for important elements of the work is usually incorporated in the Documents. Such schedules are to be used and are to prevail over any other rates or prices or Daywork Definitions which would otherwise be thought applicable due to DOM clause 17.3 ruling valuations

---

a schedule of rates or prices for measured work;

DOM 464   17.2

then
such rates or prices must be used in determining the Valuation;

DOM 465   17.2

A valuation must be subject to DOM clause 37.2.3 where that clause is applicable

DOM 462   17.1

in substitution for
any rates or prices which would otherwise be applicable under the provisions of DOM clause 17.3

DOM 466   17.2

---

a schedule of daywork rates or prices, recorded in the Appendix, part 5;

DOM 467   17.2

then
such prices must be used in determining the Valuation;

DOM 468   17.3

A valuation must be subject to DOM clause 37.2.3 where that clause is applicable

DOM 462   17.1

in substitution for
any rates or prices or Daywork Definitions which would otherwise be applicable under the provisions of DOM clause 17.3

DOM 469   17.2

---

a schedule of rates or prices for measured work; and

DOM 470   17.2

a schedule of daywork rates or prices, recorded in the Appendix, part 5;

DOM 471   17.2

then
such rates or prices must be used in determining the Valuation;

DOM 472   17.2

A valuation must be subject to DOM clause 37.2.3 where that clause is applicable

DOM 462   17.1

in substitution for
any rates or prices or Daywork Definitions which would otherwise be applicable under the provisions of DOM clause 17.3

DOM 473   17.2

Sub-Contractor has included in the Sub-Contract Documents a schedule of rates etc for measured work   YES

NO

The execution of work which can properly be valued by measurement must be measured and must be valued in accordance with the following rules: -

DOM 494   17.3.1

Sub-Contractor has included in the Sub-Contract Documents a schedule of daywork rates or prices   YES

NO

The execution of work which can properly be valued by measurement must be measured and must be valued in accordance with the following rules: -

DOM 474   17.3.1

The execution of work which cannot properly be valued by measurement and which is within the province of any specialist trade where the RICS and the appropriate body representing the employers have agreed and issued a definition of prime cost of daywork, must be valued in accordance with the following rules: -

DOM 509   17.3

The 'and/or' in DOM clause 17.2 enables both schedules to be used where appropriate (see also the words 'to the extent that')

Subroutines DOM 497 and 510 or 515 apply where bills of quantities are a Sub-Contract Document. The question of "allowances" as referred to in DOM 482/3 and 486/7 must be clarified in any schedule of rates to be used

---

the rates and prices for work set out in bills of quantities comprised in the Sub-Contract Documents must determine the Valuation; where

DOM 497   17.3.1.1

the work is of similar character to the work set out in bills of quantities and other documents comprised in the Sub-Contract Documents; and

DOM 498   17.3.1.1

---

the prime cost of such work calculated in accordance with the agreed and issued definition of prime cost of daywork current at the Date of Tender;

DOM 510   17.3.3.2

together with percentage additions (which additions take into account any cash discount specified in the Appendix, part 7, and allowable to the Contractor) on the prime cost at the rates set out and recorded in the Appendix, part 5;

DOM 511   17.3.3.2

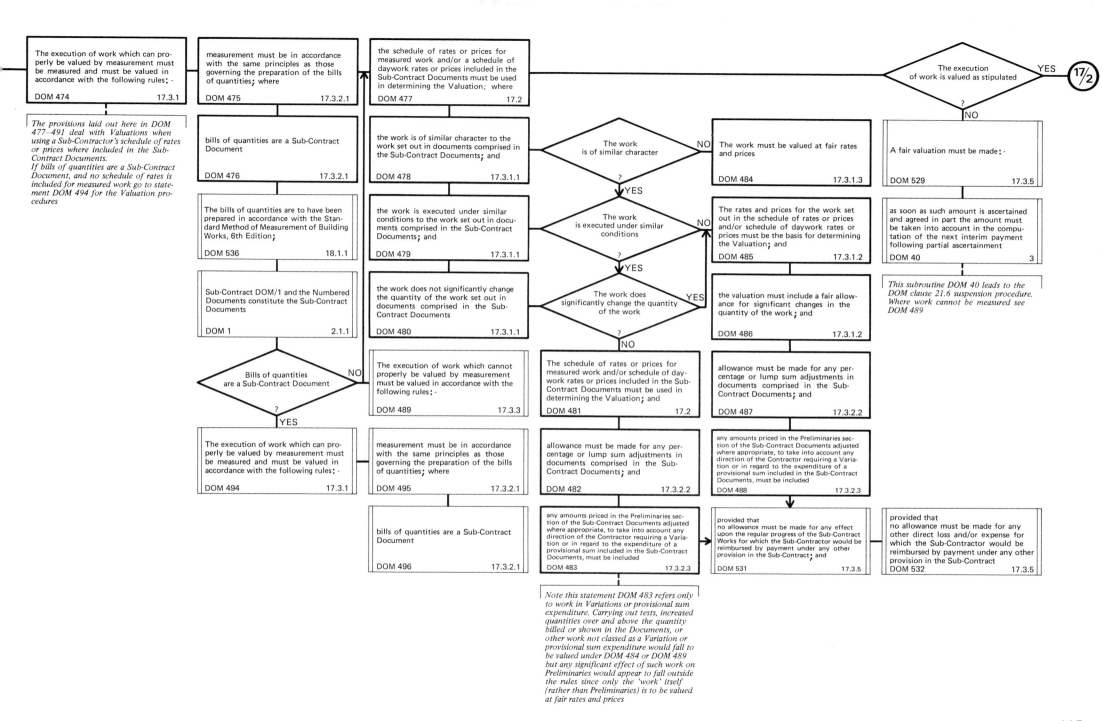

The execution of work which can properly be valued by measurement must be measured and must be valued in accordance with the following rules: -

DOM 474   17.3.1

The provisions laid out here in DOM 477–491 deal with Valuations when using a Sub-Contractor's schedule of rates or prices where included in the Sub-Contract Documents.
If bills of quantities are a Sub-Contract Document, and no schedule of rates is included for measured work go to statement DOM 494 for the Valuation procedures

---

measurement must be in accordance with the same principles as those governing the preparation of the bills of quantities; where

DOM 475   17.3.2.1

---

bills of quantities are a Sub-Contract Document

DOM 476   17.3.2.1

The bills of quantities are to have been prepared in accordance with the Standard Method of Measurement of Building Works, 6th Edition;

DOM 536   18.1.1

Sub-Contract DOM/1 and the Numbered Documents constitute the Sub-Contract Documents

DOM 1   2.1.1

Bills of quantities are a Sub-Contract Document   **NO**

?   **YES**

The execution of work which can properly be valued by measurement must be measured and must be valued in accordance with the following rules: -

DOM 494   17.3.1

---

measurement must be in accordance with the same principles as those governing the preparation of the bills of quantities; where

DOM 495   17.3.2.1

---

bills of quantities are a Sub-Contract Document

DOM 496   17.3.2.1

---

the schedule of rates or prices for measured work and/or a schedule of daywork rates or prices included in the Sub-Contract Documents must be used in determining the Valuation; where

DOM 477   17.2

---

the work is of similar character to the work set out in documents comprised in the Sub-Contract Documents; and

DOM 478   17.3.1.1

---

the work is executed under similar conditions to the work set out in documents comprised in the Sub-Contract Documents; and

DOM 479   17.3.1.1

---

the work does not significantly change the quantity of the work set out in documents comprised in the Sub-Contract Documents

DOM 480   17.3.1.1

The execution of work which cannot properly be valued by measurement must be valued in accordance with the following rules: -

DOM 489   17.3.3

The work is of similar character   **NO**

?   **YES**

The work is executed under similar conditions   **NO**

?   **YES**

The work does significantly change the quantity of the work   **YES**

?   **NO**

The schedule of rates or prices for measured work and/or schedule of daywork rates or prices included in the Sub-Contract Documents must be used in determining the Valuation; and

DOM 481   17.2

---

allowance must be made for any percentage or lump sum adjustments in documents comprised in the Sub-Contract Documents; and

DOM 482   17.3.2.2

---

any amounts priced in the Preliminaries section of the Sub-Contract Documents adjusted where appropriate, to take into account any direction of the Contractor requiring a Variation or in regard to the expenditure of a provisional sum included in the Sub-Contract Documents, must be included

DOM 483   17.3.2.3

Note this statement DOM 483 refers only to work in Variations or provisional sum expenditure. Carrying out tests, increased quantities over and above the quantity billed or shown in the Documents, or other work not classed as a Variation or provisional sum expenditure would fall to be valued under DOM 484 or DOM 489 but any significant effect of such work on Preliminaries would appear to fall outside the rules since only the 'work' itself (rather than Preliminaries) is to be valued at fair rates and prices

---

The work must be valued at fair rates and prices

DOM 484   17.3.1.3

The rates and prices for the work set out in the schedule of rates or prices and/or schedule of daywork rates or prices must be the basis for determining the Valuation; and

DOM 485   17.3.1.2

---

the valuation must include a fair allowance for significant changes in the quantity of the work; and

DOM 486   17.3.1.2

---

allowance must be made for any percentage or lump sum adjustments in documents comprised in the Sub-Contract Documents; and

DOM 487   17.3.2.2

---

any amounts priced in the Preliminaries section of the Sub-Contract Documents adjusted where appropriate, to take into account any direction of the Contractor requiring a Variation or in regard to the expenditure of a provisional sum included in the Sub-Contract Documents, must be included

DOM 488   17.3.2.3

---

provided that
no allowance must be made for any effect upon the regular progress of the Sub-Contract Works for which the Sub-Contractor would be reimbursed by payment under any other provision in the Sub-Contract; and

DOM 531   17.3.5

The execution of work is valued as stipulated   **YES**   (17/2)

?   **NO**

A fair valuation must be made: -

DOM 529   17.3.5

---

as soon as such amount is ascertained and agreed in part the amount must be taken into account in the computation of the next interim payment following partial ascertainment

DOM 40   3

This subroutine DOM 40 leads to the DOM clause 21.6 suspension procedure. Where work cannot be measured see DOM 489

---

provided that
no allowance must be made for any other direct loss and/or expense for which the Sub-Contractor would be reimbursed by payment under any other provision in the Sub-Contract

DOM 532   17.3.5

115

17/2

The Valuation of 'omissions' does not of course (although see DOM 526) arise in a measure-and-value Sub-Contract. All work executed is to be remeasured and recalculated to establish the Sum to be paid as opposed to the Sum first quoted by the Tenderer under DOM clause 15.2

The execution of work which cannot properly be valued by measurement must be valued in accordance with the following rules: -

DOM 489   17.3.3

the prime cost of such work calculated in accordance with a schedule of day-work rates or prices; where

DOM 490   17.3.3 & 17.2

the Sub-Contractor has included such a schedule in the Sub-Contract Documents and/or has in the Appendix, part 5, recorded his daywork rates or prices;

DOM 491   17.2

Sub-Contractor has included such a schedule etc in the Sub-Contract Documents

   ? NO

The execution of work which cannot properly be valued by measurement and which is within the province of any specialist trade where the RICS and the appropriate body representing the employers have agreed and issued a definition of prime cost of daywork, must be valued in accordance with the following rules: -

DOM 509   17.3

provided
vouchers specifying the time daily spent upon the work, the workmen's names, the plant and materials employed, are delivered for verification to the Contractor;

DOM 492   17.3.3

not later than the Thursday following the week in which the work has been executed

DOM 493   17.3.3

Vouchers are delivered as stipulated   NO

   ? YES

The Contractor may refuse to make payment on the daywork rates but should sensibly negotiate a fair settlement under DOM 529 if by not having vouchers he was prevented from properly verifying on a daywork basis

The work is valued as stipulated   NO

   ? YES

A fair valuation must be made: -

DOM 529   17.3.5

Note this subroutine deals with Variations and provisional sums expenditure only

as soon as such amount is ascertained and agreed in part the amount must be taken into account in the computation of the next interim payment following partial ascertainment

DOM 40   3

as soon as such amount is ascertained and agreed in part the amount must be taken into account in the computation of the next interim payment following partial ascertainment

DOM 40   3

as soon as such amount is ascertained and agreed in whole the amount must be taken into account in the computation of the next interim payment following whole ascertainment

DOM 41   3

The subroutine DOM 40 leads to the DOM clause 21.6 suspension procedure

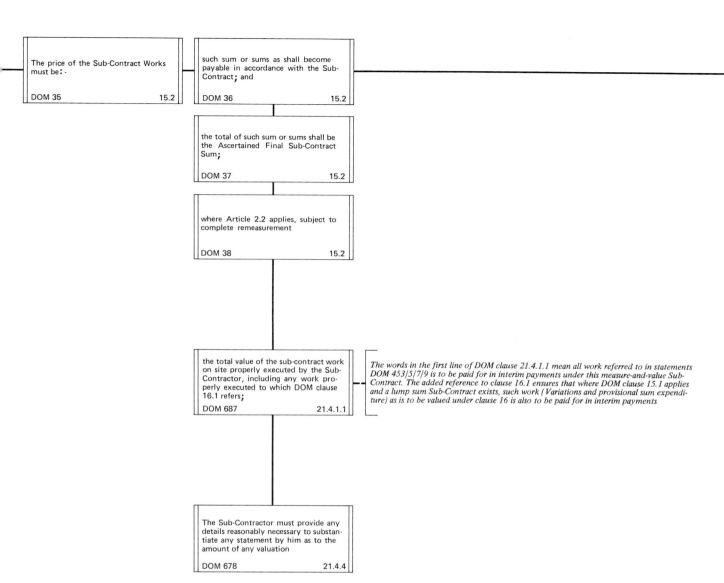

The price of the Sub-Contract Works must be: -

DOM 35   15.2

such sum or sums as shall become payable in accordance with the Sub-Contract; and

DOM 36   15.2

the total of such sum or sums shall be the Ascertained Final Sub-Contract Sum;

DOM 37   15.2

where Article 2.2 applies, subject to complete remeasurement

DOM 38   15.2

the total value of the sub-contract work on site properly executed by the Sub-Contractor, including any work properly executed to which DOM clause 16.1 refers;

DOM 687   21.4.1.1

The words in the first line of DOM clause 21.4.1.1 mean all work referred to in statements DOM 453/5/7/9 is to be paid for in interim payments under this measure-and-value Sub-Contract. The added reference to clause 16.1 ensures that where DOM clause 15.1 applies and a lump sum Sub-Contract exists, such work (Variations and provisional sum expenditure) as is to be valued under clause 16 is also to be paid for in interim payments

The Sub-Contractor must provide any details reasonably necessary to substantiate any statement by him as to the amount of any valuation

DOM 678   21.4.4

STOP/START   (17/3)

Where a schedule of rates or prices and/or a schedule of daywork rates or prices has been used to value work executed go from here directly to DOM 519–536. Where a bill of quantities is a Sub-Contract Document and no schedules exist, to value work executed or daywork – start at DOM statement 494 (next page)

Bills of quantities Valuation

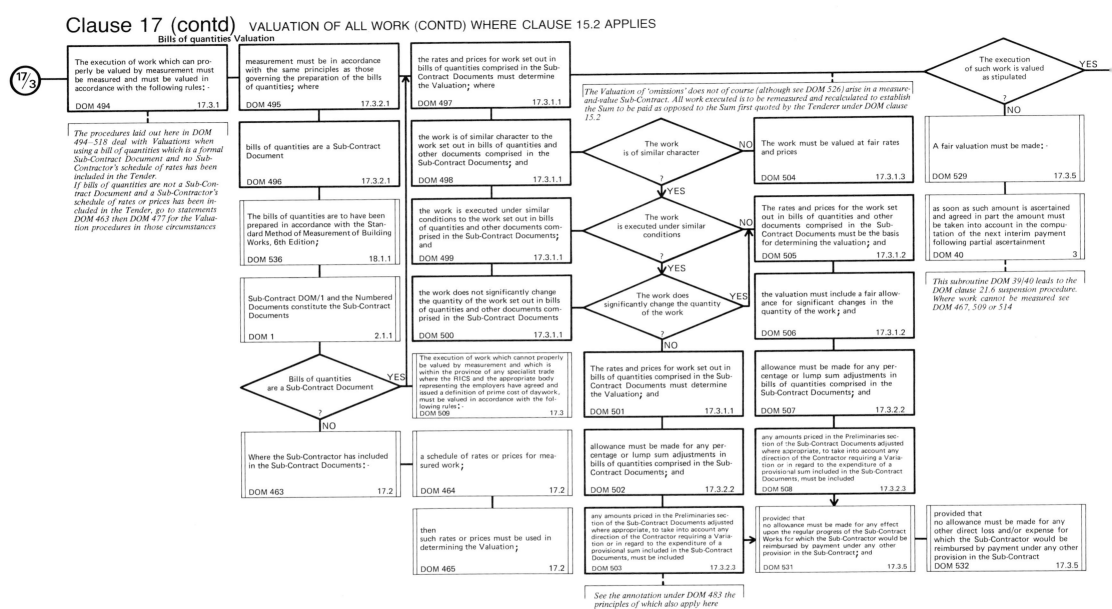

17/3

The execution of work which can properly be valued by measurement must be measured and must be valued in accordance with the following rules: -

DOM 494   17.3.1

The procedures laid out here in DOM 494–518 deal with Valuations when using a bill of quantities which is a formal Sub-Contract Document and no Sub-Contractor's schedule of rates has been included in the Tender.
If bills of quantities are not a Sub-Contract Document and a Sub-Contractor's schedule of rates or prices has been included in the Tender, go to statements DOM 463 then DOM 477 for the Valuation procedures in those circumstances

---

measurement must be in accordance with the same principles as those governing the preparation of the bills of quantities; where

DOM 495   17.3.2.1

bills of quantities are a Sub-Contract Document

DOM 496   17.3.2.1

The bills of quantities are to have been prepared in accordance with the Standard Method of Measurement of Building Works, 6th Edition;

DOM 536   18.1.1

Sub-Contract DOM/1 and the Numbered Documents constitute the Sub-Contract Documents

DOM 1   2.1.1

Bills of quantities are a Sub-Contract Document — YES / NO

Where the Sub-Contractor has included in the Sub-Contract Documents: -

DOM 463   17.2

a schedule of rates or prices for measured work;

DOM 464   17.2

then
such rates or prices must be used in determining the Valuation;

DOM 465   17.2

---

the rates and prices for work set out in bills of quantities comprised in the Sub-Contract Documents must determine the Valuation; where

DOM 497   17.3.1.1

the work is of similar character to the work set out in bills of quantities and other documents comprised in the Sub-Contract Documents; and

DOM 498   17.3.1.1

the work is executed under similar conditions to the work set out in bills of quantities and other documents comprised in the Sub-Contract Documents; and

DOM 499   17.3.1.1

the work does not significantly change the quantity of the work set out in bills of quantities and other documents comprised in the Sub-Contract Documents

DOM 500   17.3.1.1

The execution of work which cannot properly be valued by measurement and which is within the province of any specialist trade where the RICS and the appropriate body representing the employers have agreed and issued a definition of prime cost of daywork, must be valued in accordance with the following rules: -

DOM 509   17.3

The rates and prices for work set out in bills of quantities comprised in the Sub-Contract Documents must determine the Valuation; and

DOM 501   17.3.1.1

allowance must be made for any percentage or lump sum adjustments in bills of quantities comprised in the Sub-Contract Documents; and

DOM 502   17.3.2.2

any amounts priced in the Preliminaries section of the Sub-Contract Documents adjusted where appropriate, to take into account any direction of the Contractor requiring a Variation or in regard to the expenditure of a provisional sum included in the Sub-Contract Documents, must be included

DOM 503   17.3.2.3

The Valuation of 'omissions' does not of course (although see DOM 526) arise in a measure-and-value Sub-Contract. All work executed is to be remeasured and recalculated to establish the Sum to be paid as opposed to the Sum first quoted by the Tenderer under DOM clause 15.2

The work is of similar character — NO →

The work must be valued at fair rates and prices

DOM 504   17.3.1.3

The work is executed under similar conditions — NO →

The rates and prices for the work set out in bills of quantities and other documents comprised in the Sub-Contract Documents must be the basis for determining the valuation; and

DOM 505   17.3.1.2

The work does significantly change the quantity of the work — YES →

the valuation must include a fair allowance for significant changes in the quantity of the work; and

DOM 506   17.3.1.2

allowance must be made for any percentage or lump sum adjustments in bills of quantities comprised in the Sub-Contract Documents; and

DOM 507   17.3.2.2

any amounts priced in the Preliminaries section of the Sub-Contract Documents adjusted where appropriate, to take into account any direction of the Contractor requiring a Variation or in regard to the expenditure of a provisional sum included in the Sub-Contract Documents, must be included

DOM 508   17.3.2.3

provided that
no allowance must be made for any effect upon the regular progress of the Sub-Contract Works for which the Sub-Contractor would be reimbursed by payment under any other provision in the Sub-Contract; and

DOM 531   17.3.5

See the annotation under DOM 483 the principles of which also apply here

---

The execution of such work is valued as stipulated — YES / NO

A fair valuation must be made: -

DOM 529   17.3.5

as soon as such amount is ascertained and agreed in part the amount must be taken into account in the computation of the next interim payment following partial ascertainment

DOM 40   3

This subroutine DOM 39/40 leads to the DOM clause 21.6 suspension procedure. Where work cannot be measured see DOM 467, 509 or 514

provided that
no allowance must be made for any other direct loss and/or expense for which the Sub-Contractor would be reimbursed by payment under any other provision in the Sub-Contract

DOM 532   17.3.5

The execution of work which cannot properly be valued by measurement and which is within the province of any specialist trade where the RICS and the appropriate body representing the employers have agreed and issued a definition of prime cost of daywork, must be valued in accordance with the following rules: -

DOM 509   17.3

There are 2 distinct ways of dealing with daywork where no special schedule of daywork rates or prices has been (under DOM clause 17.2) included in the Sub-Contract.
Subroutine DOM 509-513 deals with daywork carried out by either electrical Sub-Contractors or heating and ventilating Sub-Contractors, or any other specialists who have a formally agreed and issued set of rules made officially between their body and the RICS.
Subroutine DOM 514-518 deals with daywork by any other Sub-Contractors who have not included a schedule of daywork rates or prices in the Sub-Contract Documents

---

the prime cost of such work calculated in accordance with the agreed and issued definition of prime cost of daywork current at the Date of Tender;

DOM 510   17.3.3.2

together with percentage additions (which additions take into account any cash discount specified in the Appendix, part 7, and allowable to the Contractor) on the prime cost at the rates set out and recorded in the Appendix, part 5;

DOM 511   17.3.3.2

provided
vouchers specifying the time daily spent upon the work, the workmen's names, the plant and materials employed, are delivered for verification to the Contractor;

DOM 512   17.3.3

not later than the Thursday following the week in which the work has been executed

DOM 513   17.3.3

The work is within the province of a specialist trade — NO

? YES

The RICS and appropriate body have agreed and issued a definition of prime cost of daywork — NO

? YES

Vouchers are delivered as stipulated — NO

? YES

The work is valued as stipulated — NO

? YES

The Contractor may refuse to make payment on the daywork rates but should sensibly negotiate a fair settlement under DOM 529 if by not having vouchers he was prevented from properly verifying the reimbursement on a daywork basis

A fair valuation must be made: -

DOM 529   17.3.5

Statement DOM 462 is not here applicable as the Rules of formula adjustment under DOM clause 37.2.3 do not apply to any work valued at daywork rates

as soon as such amount is ascertained and agreed in whole the amount must be taken into account in the computation of the next interim payment following whole ascertainment

DOM 41   3

Where in Sub-Contract DOM/1 it is provided that an amount is to be included in the computation of the Ascertained Final Sub-Contract Sum, then: -

DOM 39   3

This subroutine DOM 39 leads to the DOM clause 21.6 suspension procedure

---

The execution of work which cannot properly be valued by measurement must be valued in accordance with the following rules: -

DOM 514   17.3

the prime cost of such work calculated in accordance with the "Definition of Prime Cost of Daywork carried out under a Building Contract" (issued by the RICS and NFBTE) current at the Date of Tender;

DOM 515   17.3.3.1

17/4

together with percentage additions (which additions take into account any cash discount specified in the Appendix, part 7, and allowable to the Contractor) to each section of the prime cost at the rates set out and recorded in the Appendix, part 5;

DOM 516   17.3.3.1

provided
vouchers specifying the time daily spent upon the work, the workmen's names, the plant and materials employed, are delivered for verification to the Contractor;

DOM 517   17.3.3

not later than the Thursday following the week in which the work has been executed

DOM 518   17.3.3

Vouchers are delivered as stipulated — NO

? YES

The work is valued as stipulated — NO

? YES

The Contractor may refuse to make payment on the daywork rates but should sensibly negotiate a fair settlement under DOM 529 if by not having vouchers he was prevented from properly verifying the reimbursement on a daywork basis

A fair valuation must be made: -

DOM 529   17.3.5

as soon as such amount is ascertained and agreed in whole the amount must be taken into account in the computation of the next interim payment following whole ascertainment

DOM 41   3

Where in Sub-Contract DOM/1 it is provided that an amount is to be included in the computation of the Ascertained Final Sub-Contract Sum, then: -

DOM 39   3

Statement DOM 462 is not here applicable as the Rules of formula adjustment under DOM clause 37.2.3 do not apply to any work valued at daywork rates

This subroutine DOM 39 leads to the DOM clause 21.6 suspension procedure

17/4

If compliance with any direction of the Contractor requiring: -	a Variation;	the expenditure of a provisional sum;	work included in the Sub-Contract Documents *not* to be executed;	The term "Variation" means any of the following changes which are required by a direction of the Contractor issued under the Sub-Contract: -	including the addition, omission or substitution of any work; or
DOM 519 17.3.4	DOM 520 17.3.4	DOM 523 17.3.4	DOM 526 17.3.4	DOM 441 1.3	DOM 443 1.3.1.1

This provision deals with the situation where in complying with a Variation, provisional sum direction or a direction not to execute work originally included in the Sub-Contract Documents, the Sub-Contractor's other work is affected. If compliance imposes a substantial (the word means "considerable" or "to a large degree") change in the conditions under which any other work is executed then such other work must be looked at as if it had itself been the subject of a Variation direction thus enabling the changed conditions to be valued under DOM clause 17.3.1.2 and to include a fair allowance for such differences in conditions

Note the reference in statement DOM 526 regarding work not *to be executed, being in effect an 'omission'*

substantially changes the conditions under which any other work is executed;	substantially changes the conditions under which any other work is executed;	substantially changes the conditions under which any other work is executed;
DOM 521 17.3.4	DOM 524 17.3.4	DOM 527 17.3.4

then such other work must be valued in accordance with the provisions of DOM clause 17.3.1.2	then such other work must be valued in accordance with the provisions of DOM clause 17.3.1.2	then such other work must be valued in accordance with the provisions of DOM clause 17.3.1.2
DOM 522 17.3.4	DOM 525 17.3.4	DOM 528 17.3.4

Compliance with any such instruction does substantially change the conditions as DOM 521/4/7 ? **YES**

Subroutine DOM 485 deals with situations where a schedule of rates is involved. Subroutine DOM 505 deals with situations where a bill of quantities applies

The rates and prices for the work set out in the schedule of rates or prices and/or schedule of daywork rates or prices must be the basis for determining the Valuation; and	The rates and prices for the work set out in bills of quantities and other documents comprised in the Sub-Contract Documents must be the basis for determining the valuation; and	Such other work is valued in accordance with DOM clause 17.3.1.2 ? **YES**	as soon as such amount is ascertained and agreed in whole the amount must be taken into account in the computation of the next interim payment following whole ascertainment
DOM 485 17.3.1.2	DOM 505 17.3.1.2		DOM 41 3

NO

the valuation must include a fair allowance for significant changes in the quantity of the work; and	the valuation must include a fair allowance for significant changes in the quantity of the work; and	as soon as such amount is ascertained and agreed in part the amount must be taken into account in the computation of the next interim payment following partial ascertainment
DOM 486 17.3.1.2	DOM 506 17.3.1.2	DOM 40 3

allowance must be made for any percentage or lump sum adjustments in documents comprised in the Sub-Contract Documents; and	allowance must be made for any percentage or lump sum adjustments in bills of quantities comprised in the Sub-Contract Documents; and
DOM 487 17.3.2.2	DOM 507 17.3.2.2

This subroutine deals with provisions for partial payment where the whole amount cannot or has not yet been ascertained. It also refers to annotation under the Main Contract

any amounts priced in the Preliminaries section of the Sub-Contract Documents adjusted where appropriate, to take into account any direction of the Contractor requiring a Variation or in regard to the expenditure of a provisional sum included in the Sub-Contract Documents, must be included	any amounts priced in the Preliminaries section of the Sub-Contract Documents adjusted where appropriate, to take into account any direction of the Contractor requiring a Variation or in regard to the expenditure of a provisional sum included in the Sub-Contract Documents, must be included
DOM 488 17.3.2.3	DOM 508 17.3.2.3

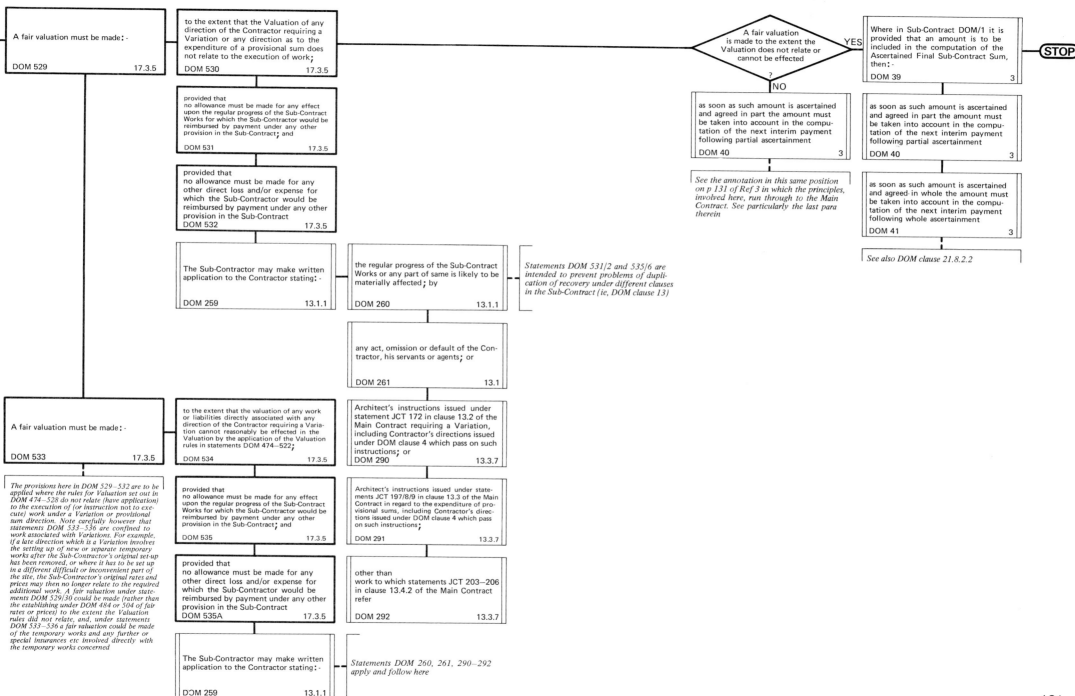

A fair valuation must be made:-

DOM 529   17.3.5

to the extent that the Valuation of any direction of the Contractor requiring a Variation or any direction as to the expenditure of a provisional sum does not relate to the execution of work;

DOM 530   17.3.5

provided that
no allowance must be made for any effect upon the regular progress of the Sub-Contract Works for which the Sub-Contractor would be reimbursed by payment under any other provision in the Sub-Contract; and

DOM 531   17.3.5

provided that
no allowance must be made for any other direct loss and/or expense for which the Sub-Contractor would be reimbursed by payment under any other provision in the Sub-Contract

DOM 532   17.3.5

The Sub-Contractor may make written application to the Contractor stating:-

DOM 259   13.1.1

the regular progress of the Sub-Contract Works or any part of same is likely to be materially affected; by

DOM 260   13.1.1

any act, omission or default of the Contractor, his servants or agents; or

DOM 261   13.1

Statements DOM 531/2 and 535/6 are intended to prevent problems of duplication of recovery under different clauses in the Sub-Contract (ie, DOM clause 13)

A fair valuation must be made:-

DOM 533   17.3.5

The provisions here in DOM 529–532 are to be applied where the rules for Valuation set out in DOM 474–528 do not relate (have application) to the execution of (or instruction not to execute) work under a Variation or provisional sum direction. Note carefully however that statements DOM 533–536 are confined to work associated with Variations. For example, if a late direction which is a Variation involves the setting up of new or separate temporary works after the Sub-Contractor's original set-up has been removed, or where it has to be set up in a different difficult or inconvenient part of the site, the Sub-Contractor's original rates and prices may then no longer relate to the required additional work. A fair valuation under statements DOM 529/30 could be made (rather than the establishing under DOM 484 or 504 of fair rates or prices) to the extent the Valuation rules did not relate, and, under statements DOM 533–536 a fair valuation could be made of the temporary works and any further or special insurances etc involved directly with the temporary works concerned

to the extent that the valuation of any work or liabilities directly associated with any direction of the Contractor requiring a Variation cannot reasonably be effected in the Valuation by the application of the Valuation rules in statements DOM 474–522;

DOM 534   17.3.5

provided that
no allowance must be made for any effect upon the regular progress of the Sub-Contract Works for which the Sub-Contractor would be reimbursed by payment under any other provision in the Sub-Contract; and

DOM 535   17.3.5

provided that
no allowance must be made for any other direct loss and/or expense for which the Sub-Contractor would be reimbursed by payment under any other provision in the Sub-Contract

DOM 535A   17.3.5

The Sub-Contractor may make written application to the Contractor stating:-

DOM 259   13.1.1

Architect's instructions issued under statement JCT 172 in clause 13.2 of the Main Contract requiring a Variation, including Contractor's directions issued under DOM clause 4 which pass on such instructions; or

DOM 290   13.3.7

Architect's instructions issued under statements JCT 197/8/9 in clause 13.3 of the Main Contract in regard to the expenditure of provisional sums, including Contractor's directions issued under DOM clause 4 which pass on such instructions;

DOM 291   13.3.7

other than
work to which statements JCT 203–206 in clause 13.4.2 of the Main Contract refer

DOM 292   13.3.7

Statements DOM 260, 261, 290–292 apply and follow here

A fair valuation is made to the extent the Valuation does not relate or cannot be effected ?   **NO**

YES

Where in Sub-Contract DOM/1 it is provided that an amount is to be included in the computation of the Ascertained Final Sub-Contract Sum, then:-

DOM 39   3

(STOP)

as soon as such amount is ascertained and agreed in part the amount must be taken into account in the computation of the next interim payment following partial ascertainment

DOM 40   3

See the annotation in this same position on p 131 of Ref 3 in which the principles, involved here, run through to the Main Contract. See particularly the last para therein

as soon as such amount is ascertained and agreed in part the amount must be taken into account in the computation of the next interim payment following partial ascertainment

DOM 40   3

as soon as such amount is ascertained and agreed in whole the amount must be taken into account in the computation of the next interim payment following whole ascertainment

DOM 41   3

See also DOM clause 21.8.2.2

Clause 18 BILLS OF QUANTITIES – STANDARD METHOD OF MEASUREMENT

Preparation of bills of quantities

The bills of quantities are to have been prepared in accordance with the Standard Method of Measurement of Building Works, 6th Edition;

DOM 536   18.1.1

START

where bills of quantities are a Sub-Contract Document;

DOM 537   18.1

unless the bills specifically state otherwise in respect of any specified item or items; and

DOM 538   18.1.1

The Bills are a Sub-Contract Document ?   YES / NO

The bills do specifically state otherwise in respect of any specified item/s ?   NO / YES

The particular non-standard method of description, bill preparation, or of measurement must be accepted (and adopted in any remeasurement) in respect of the specified item/s

A general clause in bills, which warns of departure from, or conflict with, the SMM 6th Ed will have no effect. Statement DOM 538 allows definite departures from SMM provided they are specified in each particular case. Work not covered by the rules of SMM 6th Ed need not be specified under DOM 538 for it is not a departure from SMM, but obviously Tenderers should have their attention drawn to any special methods of measurement in such cases. Non-standard methods properly specified under DOM 538, or methods adopted for work not in SMM 6th Ed, are to be adopted in remeasurement or Variations Valuations

The bills have been prepared in accordance with SMM 6th Ed ?   YES / NO

Errors in preparation of bills of quantities

The bills of quantities must be corrected if there is any: -

DOM 539   18.1.2

departure from the method of preparation in accordance with the Standard Method of Measurement of Building Works 6th Edition

DOM 540   18.1.2 & 18.1

error in description

DOM 541   18.1.2

error in quantity

DOM 542   18.1.2

The quality and quantity of the work included in the Sub-Contract Sum or Tender Sum must be deemed to be that which is set out in the bills of quantities;

DOM 546   18.1.3

A detailed study of the SMM 6th Ed is necessary to decide whether there is a 'departure' from the Methods to be found in that document

The Contractor must immediately give to the Architect a written notice, if he finds any: -

JCT 19   2.3

If there is an error in the Sub-Contract bills there may also be an error in the Main Contract Bills

discrepancy in any two or more of the following documents;

JCT 20   2.3

the Contract Drawings

JCT 21   2.3.1

the Contract Bills

JCT 22   2.3.2

any drawings or documents issued by the Architect under statements:
66 schedules or documents
78–80 further drawings etc
134 setting out drawings

JCT 23   2.3.4

Nothing contained in any descriptive schedule or other like document issued in connection with and for use in carrying out the Sub-Contract Works must impose any obligation beyond those imposed by the Sub-Contract Documents

DOM 9   2.1.2

Statements DOM 9 and 12–15 deal with conflicting or special terms implanted in documents (not ranking as Sub-Contract Documents) or in bills or any Sub-Contract Documents. Such terms cannot, unless written specially into the Appendix, make more onerous, oust, limit, contradict or qualify, either partially or wholly the terms of this Sub-Contract DOM/1, in its standard form

Where the Sub-Contractor has included in the Sub-Contract Documents: -

DOM 358   16.2

Where the Sub-Contractor has included in the Sub-Contract Documents: -

DOM 463   17.2

a schedule of rates or prices for measured work;

DOM 359   16.2

a schedule of rates or prices for measured work;

DOM 464   17.2

This subroutine applies where a lump sum Sub-Contract has been tendered under DOM clause 15.1

This subroutine applies where a measure-and-value Tender Sum has been tendered under DOM clause 15.2

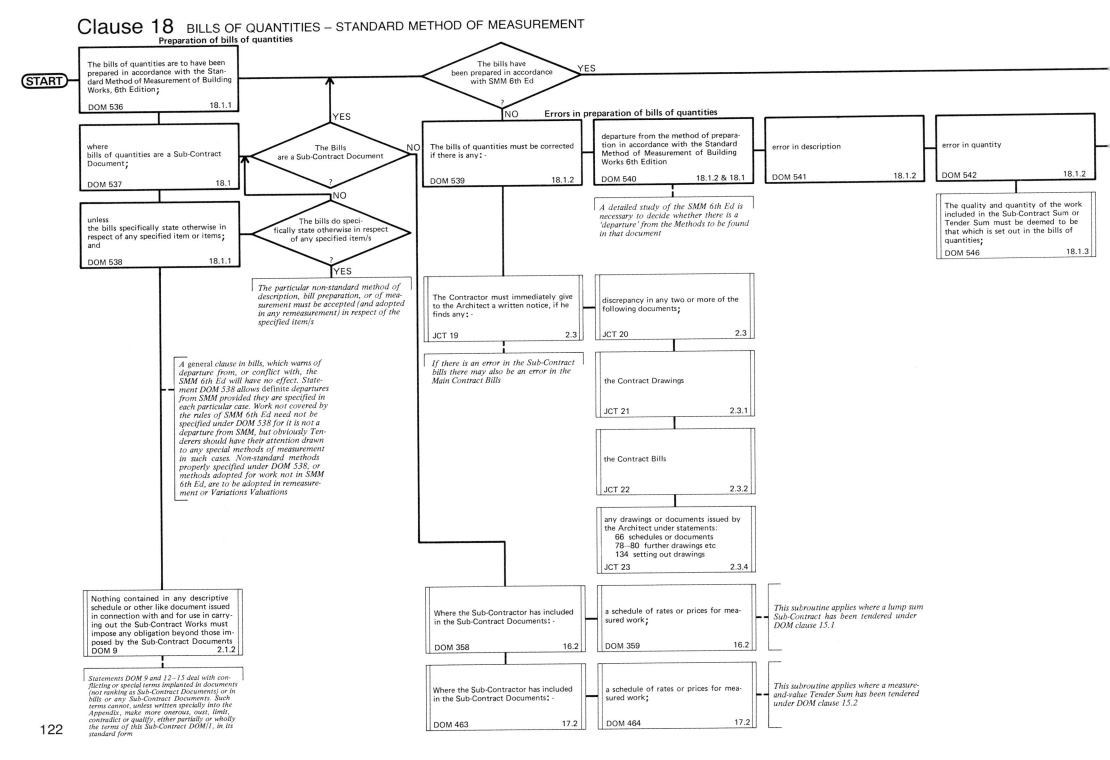

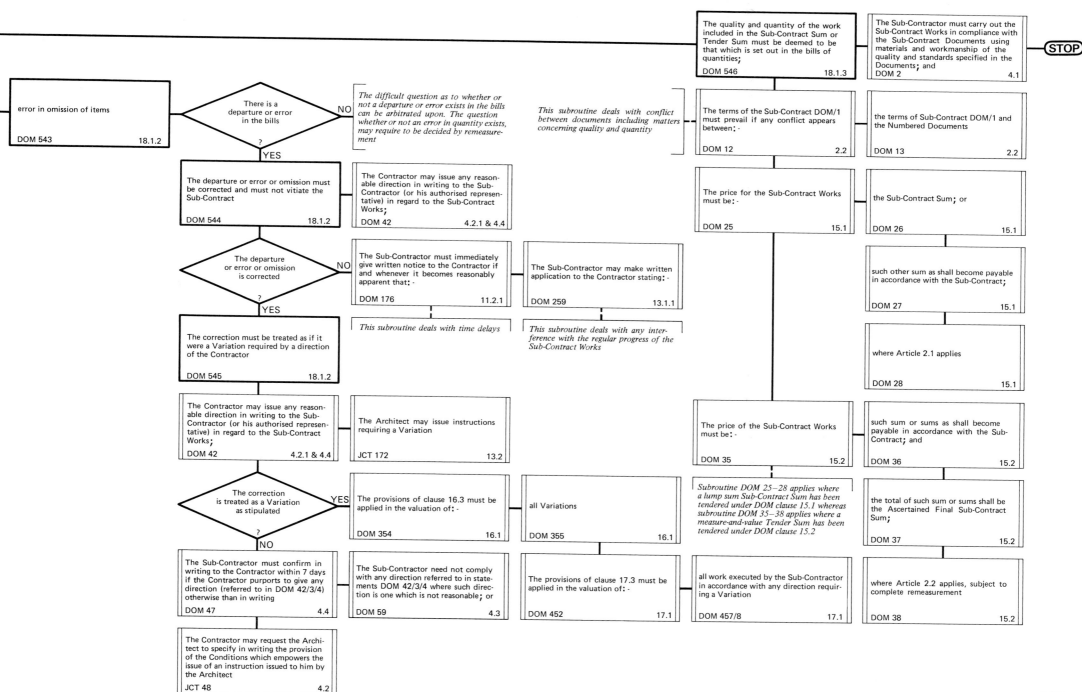

error in omission of items

DOM 543   18.1.2

There is a departure or error in the bills **?** — NO

The difficult question as to whether or not a departure or error exists in the bills can be arbitrated upon. The question whether or not an error in quantity exists, may require to be decided by remeasurement

YES

The departure or error or omission must be corrected and must not vitiate the Sub-Contract

DOM 544   18.1.2

The Contractor may issue any reasonable direction in writing to the Sub-Contractor (or his authorised representative) in regard to the Sub-Contract Works;

DOM 42   4.2.1 & 4.4

The departure or error or omission is corrected **?** — NO

The Sub-Contractor must immediately give written notice to the Contractor if and whenever it becomes reasonably apparent that:-

DOM 176   11.2.1

This subroutine deals with time delays

The Sub-Contractor may make written application to the Contractor stating:-

DOM 259   13.1.1

This subroutine deals with any interference with the regular progress of the Sub-Contract Works

YES

The correction must be treated as if it were a Variation required by a direction of the Contractor

DOM 545   18.1.2

The Contractor may issue any reasonable direction in writing to the Sub-Contractor (or his authorised representative) in regard to the Sub-Contract Works;

DOM 42   4.2.1 & 4.4

The Architect may issue instructions requiring a Variation

JCT 172   13.2

The correction is treated as a Variation as stipulated **?** — YES

The provisions of clause 16.3 must be applied in the valuation of:-

DOM 354   16.1

all Variations

DOM 355   16.1

NO

The Sub-Contractor must confirm in writing to the Contractor within 7 days if the Contractor purports to give any direction (referred to in DOM 42/3/4) otherwise than in writing

DOM 47   4.4

The Sub-Contractor need not comply with any direction referred to in statements DOM 42/3/4 where such direction is one which is not reasonable; or

DOM 59   4.3

The provisions of clause 17.3 must be applied in the valuation of:-

DOM 452   17.1

The Contractor may request the Architect to specify in writing the provision of the Conditions which empowers the issue of an instruction issued to him by the Architect

JCT 48   4.2

The quality and quantity of the work included in the Sub-Contract Sum or Tender Sum must be deemed to be that which is set out in the bills of quantities;

DOM 546   18.1.3

The Sub-Contractor must carry out the Sub-Contract Works in compliance with the Sub-Contract Documents using materials and workmanship of the quality and standards specified in the Documents; and

DOM 2   4.1

STOP

This subroutine deals with conflict between documents including matters concerning quality and quantity

The terms of the Sub-Contract DOM/1 must prevail if any conflict appears between:-

DOM 12   2.2

the terms of Sub-Contract DOM/1 and the Numbered Documents

DOM 13   2.2

The price for the Sub-Contract Works must be:-

DOM 25   15.1

the Sub-Contract Sum; or

DOM 26   15.1

such other sum as shall become payable in accordance with the Sub-Contract;

DOM 27   15.1

where Article 2.1 applies

DOM 28   15.1

The price of the Sub-Contract Works must be:-

DOM 35   15.2

such sum or sums as shall become payable in accordance with the Sub-Contract; and

DOM 36   15.2

Subroutine DOM 25–28 applies where a lump sum Sub-Contract Sum has been tendered under DOM clause 15.1 whereas subroutine DOM 35–38 applies where a measure-and-value Tender Sum has been tendered under DOM clause 15.2

the total of such sum or sums shall be the Ascertained Final Sub-Contract Sum;

DOM 37   15.2

all work executed by the Sub-Contractor in accordance with any direction requiring a Variation

DOM 457/8   17.1

where Article 2.2 applies, subject to complete remeasurement

DOM 38   15.2

Clause 19A VAT

START

The Sub-Contractor must under DOM clause 19A recover from the Contractor VAT properly chargeable by the Commissioners on the Sub-Contractor on the supply of goods and services under the Sub-Contract

DOM 547   19A.2

Sub-Contractor does under 19A recover from the Contractor VAT properly chargeable as stipulated   ?

YES →

The Sub-Contractor must immediately issue to the Contractor a receipt as referred to in VAT Regulation 21;

DOM 571   19A.4.3

The Sub-Contractor must be paid an amount equal to the loss of credit (input tax) on the supply of goods and services to the Contractor which contribute exclusively to the Sub-Contract Works and which become exempt from VAT after the Date of Tender

DOM 577   19A.1.2

Sub-Contractor is paid such an amount as stipulated   ?

YES

NO ↓ (from 547 decision)

The Sub-Contractor must notify the Contractor if for any reason the amount paid is not the amount of VAT properly chargeable on the Sub-Contractor by the Commissioners

DOM 564   19A.4.5

The self-billing provisions of DOM clause 19B can only be used in certain particular circumstances, see footnote (t) DOM/1 p 21

The Date of Tender is defined in clause 1.3. DOM clause 21 does not expressly indicate whether such amounts would be subject to retention. DOM clauses 21.7.2.10 and 21.8.2.5 would encompass 'any . . . amount . . . required by the Sub-Contract to be added' (or 'included')

NO (from paid such amount decision)

Where in Sub-Contract DOM/1 it is provided that an amount is to be added to or subtracted from the Sub-Contract Sum, then: -

DOM 29   3

Where in Sub-Contract DOM/1 it is provided that an amount is to be included in the computation of the Ascertained Final Sub-Contract Sum, then: -

DOM 39   3

This clause must be used where DOM clause 19B cannot apply. The VAT Agrement is a supplemental document to the Main Contract. Any sums agreed as damages (eg, in direct loss and/or expense) are not subject to VAT

The Sub-Contractor must give to the Contractor a written provisional assessment of the respective values (less the Retention and any specified (Appendix, part 7) cash discount) of those supplies of goods and services for which payment is due under DOM clause 21.3;

DOM 554   19A.4.1.2

Sub-Contractor does give the stipulated written provisional assessment   ?

YES →

The Sub-Contractor must specify the rate or rates of VAT which are chargeable on the Category two supplies; and

DOM 559   19A.4.1.2

Sub-Contractor does specify the rate and state the grounds as stipulated   ?

YES

NO ↓

There is no specific remedy

the Sub-Contractor must state the grounds on which he considers such supplies are so chargeable

DOM 560   19A.4.1.2

NO

There is no specific remedy

not later than 7 days before the date when payment is due to the Sub-Contractor under DOM clause 21;

DOM 555   19A.4.1.2

The first payment must be due not later than one month after the date of commencement of: -

DOM 673   21.2.1

The Contractor must under the VAT Agreement and this clause recover from the Employer tax properly chargeable by the Commissioners on the Contractor on the supply of goods and services under this Contract

JCT 250   15.2

which will be chargeable at the relevant time of supply, on the Sub-Contractor;

DOM 556   19A.4.1.2

"Time of supply" is defined in VAT Booklet 708 at p 15

at a zero rate of VAT (Category one); and

DOM 557   19A.4.1.2

at any rate or rates of VAT other than zero (Category two)

DOM 558   19A.4.1.2

The term 'tax' in DOM clause 19A means the value added tax introduced by the Finance Act 1972 which is under the care of the Commissioners of Customs and Excise

DOM 548   19A.1.1

This includes any amendment or re-enactment of the Finance Act

The term 'Commissioners' means the Commissioners of Customs and Excise

DOM 549   19A.1.1

The term 'Sub-Contract Sum' must be regarded as such sum exclusive of VAT

DOM 550   19A.1.2

The price for the Sub-Contract Works must be: -

DOM 25   15.1

The term 'Tender Sum' must be regarded as such sum exclusive of VAT

DOM 551   19A.2

The price of the Sub-Contract Works must be: -

DOM 35   15.2

The term 'Ascertained Final Sub-Contract Sum' must be regarded as such sum exclusive of VAT

DOM 552   19A.2

the total of such sum or sums shall be the Ascertained Final Sub-Contract Sum;

DOM 37   15.2

Supplies of goods and services under the Sub-Contract are supplies within the meaning of the VAT (General) Regulations 1980 Regulation 21(1)

DOM 553   19A.3

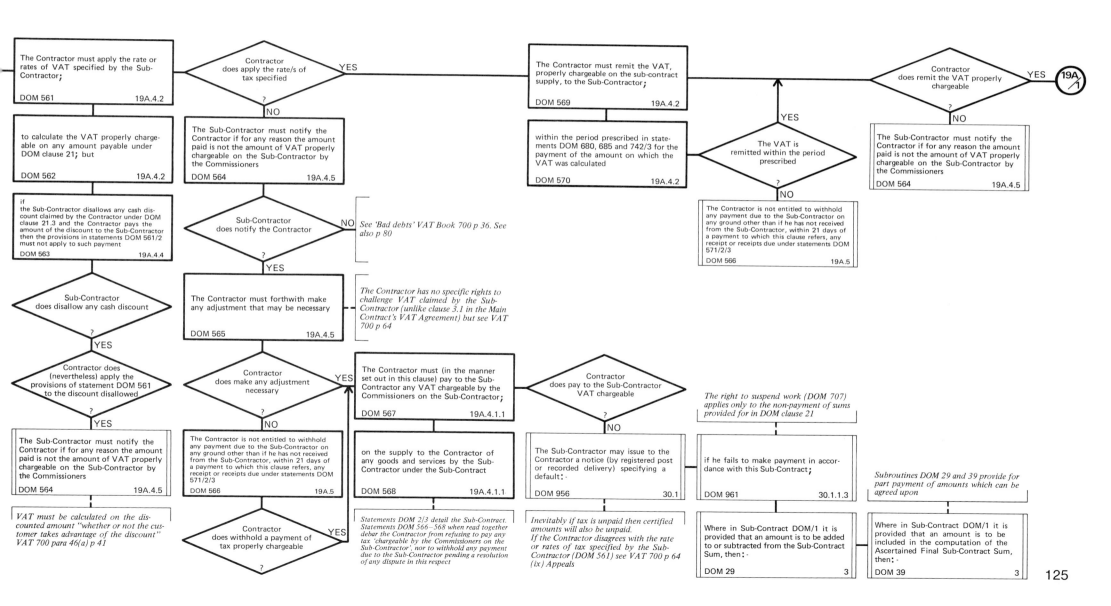

The Contractor must apply the rate or rates of VAT specified by the Sub-Contractor;

DOM 561   19A.4.2

to calculate the VAT properly chargeable on any amount payable under DOM clause 21; but

DOM 562   19A.4.2

if the Sub-Contractor disallows any cash discount claimed by the Contractor under DOM clause 21.3 and the Contractor pays the amount of the discount to the Sub-Contractor then the provisions in statements DOM 561/2 must not apply to such payment

DOM 563   19A.4.4

Sub-Contractor does disallow any cash discount
?
YES

Contractor does (nevertheless) apply the provisions of statement DOM 561 to the discount disallowed
?
YES

The Sub-Contractor must notify the Contractor if for any reason the amount paid is not the amount of VAT properly chargeable on the Sub-Contractor by the Commissioners

DOM 564   19A.4.5

VAT must be calculated on the discounted amount "whether or not the customer takes advantage of the discount" VAT 700 para 46(a) p 41

Contractor does apply the rate/s of tax specified
?
YES
NO

The Sub-Contractor must notify the Contractor if for any reason the amount paid is not the amount of VAT properly chargeable on the Sub-Contractor by the Commissioners

DOM 564   19A.4.5

Sub-Contractor does notify the Contractor
?
YES
NO   *See 'Bad debts' VAT Book 700 p 36. See also p 80*

The Contractor must forthwith make any adjustment that may be necessary

DOM 565   19A.4.5

The Contractor has no specific rights to challenge VAT claimed by the Sub-Contractor (unlike clause 3.1 in the Main Contract's VAT Agreement) but see VAT 700 p 64

Contractor does make any adjustment necessary
?
YES
NO

The Contractor is not entitled to withhold any payment due to the Sub-Contractor on any ground other than if he has not received from the Sub-Contractor, within 21 days of a payment to which this clause refers, any receipt or receipts due under statements DOM 571/2/3

DOM 566   19A.5

Contractor does withhold a payment of tax properly chargeable
?
YES

The Contractor must (in the manner set out in this clause) pay to the Sub-Contractor any VAT chargeable by the Commissioners on the Sub-Contractor;

DOM 567   19A.4.1.1

on the supply to the Contractor of any goods and services by the Sub-Contractor under the Sub-Contract

DOM 568   19A.4.1.1

Statements DOM 2/3 detail the Sub-Contract. Statements DOM 566–568 when read together debar the Contractor from refusing to pay any tax 'chargeable by the Commissioners on the Sub-Contractor', nor to withhold any payment due to the Sub-Contractor pending a resolution of any dispute in this respect

The Contractor must remit the VAT, properly chargeable on the sub-contract supply, to the Sub-Contractor;

DOM 569   19A.4.2

within the period prescribed in statements DOM 680, 685 and 742/3 for the payment of the amount on which the VAT was calculated

DOM 570   19A.4.2

The VAT is remitted within the period prescribed
?
YES
NO

The Contractor is not entitled to withhold any payment due to the Sub-Contractor on any ground other than if he has not received from the Sub-Contractor, within 21 days of a payment to which this clause refers, any receipt or receipts due under statements DOM 571/2/3

DOM 566   19A.5

Contractor does pay to the Sub-Contractor VAT chargeable
?
NO

The Sub-Contractor may issue to the Contractor a notice (by registered post or recorded delivery) specifying a default: -

DOM 956   30.1

Inevitably if tax is unpaid then certified amounts will also be unpaid. If the Contractor disagrees with the rate or rates of tax specified by the Sub-Contractor (DOM 561) see VAT 700 p 64 (ix) Appeals

The right to suspend work (DOM 707) applies only to the non-payment of sums provided for in DOM clause 21

if he fails to make payment in accordance with this Sub-Contract;

DOM 961   30.1.1.3

Where in Sub-Contract DOM/1 it is provided that an amount is to be added to or subtracted from the Sub-Contract Sum, then: -

DOM 29   3

Subroutines DOM 29 and 39 provide for part payment of amounts which can be agreed upon

Where in Sub-Contract DOM/1 it is provided that an amount is to be included in the computation of the Ascertained Final Sub-Contract Sum, then: -

DOM 39   3

Contractor does remit the VAT properly chargeable
?
YES   19A/1
NO

The Sub-Contractor must notify the Contractor if for any reason the amount paid is not the amount of VAT properly chargeable on the Sub-Contractor by the Commissioners

DOM 564   19A.4.5

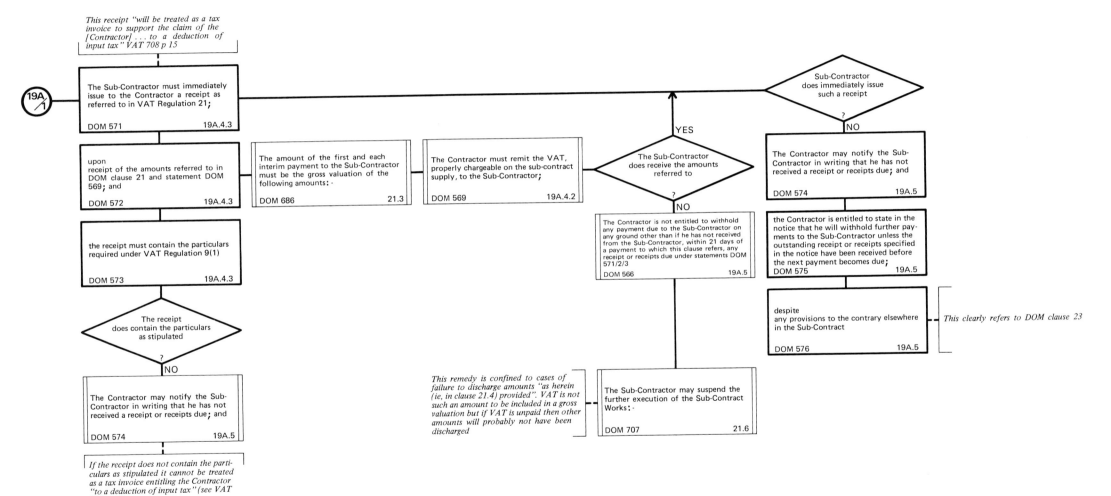

This receipt "will be treated as a tax invoice to support the claim of the [Contractor] . . . to a deduction of input tax" VAT 708 p 15

The Sub-Contractor must immediately issue to the Contractor a receipt as referred to in VAT Regulation 21;

DOM 571   19A.4.3

upon receipt of the amounts referred to in DOM clause 21 and statement DOM 569; and

DOM 572   19A.4.3

the receipt must contain the particulars required under VAT Regulation 9(1)

DOM 573   19A.4.3

The receipt does contain the particulars as stipulated ?

NO

The Contractor may notify the Sub-Contractor in writing that he has not received a receipt or receipts due; and

DOM 574   19A.5

If the receipt does not contain the particulars as stipulated it cannot be treated as a tax invoice entitling the Contractor "to a deduction of input tax" (see VAT 708 p 15)

The amount of the first and each interim payment to the Sub-Contractor must be the gross valuation of the following amounts: -

DOM 686   21.3

The Contractor must remit the VAT, properly chargeable on the sub-contract supply, to the Sub-Contractor;

DOM 569   19A.4.2

The Sub-Contractor does receive the amounts referred to ?

YES

NO

The Contractor is not entitled to withhold any payment due to the Sub-Contractor on any ground other than if he has not received from the Sub-Contractor, within 21 days of a payment to which this clause refers, any receipt or receipts due under statements DOM 571/2/3

DOM 566   19A.5

This remedy is confined to cases of failure to discharge amounts "as herein (ie, in clause 21.4) provided". VAT is not such an amount to be included in a gross valuation but if VAT is unpaid then other amounts will probably not have been discharged

The Sub-Contractor may suspend the further execution of the Sub-Contract Works: -

DOM 707   21.6

Sub-Contractor does immediately issue such a receipt ?

NO

The Contractor may notify the Sub-Contractor in writing that he has not received a receipt or receipts due; and

DOM 574   19A.5

the Contractor is entitled to state in the notice that he will withhold further payments to the Sub-Contractor unless the outstanding receipt or receipts specified in the notice have been received before the next payment becomes due;

DOM 575   19A.5

despite any provisions to the contrary elsewhere in the Sub-Contract

DOM 576   19A.5

This clearly refers to DOM clause 23

Clause 19B VAT – SPECIAL ARRANGEMENT

START

The Sub-Contractor must under DOM clause 19B recover from the Contractor VAT properly chargeable by the Commissioners on the Sub-Contractor on the supply of goods and services under the Sub-Contract

DOM 578   19B.2

See footnote (t) in DOM/1 p 21 on the circumstances where these provisions may be specified. See also VAT Booklet 700 p 27.
Any sums agreed as damages (eg, in direct loss and/or expense) are not subject to VAT

The Contractor must under the VAT Agreement and this clause recover from the Employer tax properly chargeable by the Commissioners on the Contractor on the supply of goods and services under this Contract

JCT 250   15.2

The term 'tax' in DOM clause 19A means the value added tax introduced by the Finance Act 1972 which is under the care of the Commissioners of Customs and Excise

DOM 579   19B.1.1

This includes any amendment or re-enactment of the Finance Act

---

Sub-Contractor does under 19B recover from the Contractor VAT properly chargeable as stipulated ? — YES

NO →

The Sub-Contractor must immediately reject the (self-billing) document referred to in DOM statement 600;

DOM 601   19B.4.3

The Sub-Contractor must give to the Contractor a written provisional assessment of the respective values (less the Retention and any specified (Appendix, part 7) cash discount) of those supplies of goods and services for which payment is due under DOM clause 21.3;

DOM 586   19B.4.1.2

not later than 7 days before the date when payment is due to the Sub-Contractor under DOM clause 21;

DOM 587   19B.4.1.2

which will be chargeable at the relevant time of supply, on the Sub-Contractor;

DOM 588   19B.4.1.2

at a zero rate of VAT (Category one); and

DOM 589   19B.4.1.2

at any rate or rates of VAT other than zero (Category two)

DOM 590   19B.4.1.2

The term 'Commissioners' means the Commissioners of Customs and Excise

DOM 580   19B.1.1

The term 'Sub-Contract Sum' must be regarded as such sum exclusive of VAT

DOM 581   19B.2

The price for the Sub-Contract Works must be:

DOM 25   15.1

The Sub-Contractor must insert on the (self-billing) document referred to in statement DOM 600, in a space left thereon by the Contractor for this purpose, the date of receipt of the document by the Sub-Contractor

DOM 609   19B.4.3

Clause 19A must be deemed to be incorporated in the Sub-Contract Conditions in respect of payment and VAT thereon for any supplies of goods and services remaining to be supplied and/or paid for under the Sub-Contract, if: -

DOM 610   19B.5.1

The above applies if the Sub-Contractor withdraws his consent to self-billing (see statement DOM 612) or the Commissioners withdraw their approval

The first payment must be made to the Sub-Contractor not later than 17 days after the date when it becomes due

DOM 680   21.2.3

"Time of supply" is defined in VAT Booklet 708 at p 15

The term 'Tender Sum' must be regarded as such sum exclusive of VAT

DOM 582   19B.2

The price of the Sub-Contract Works must be: -

DOM 35   15.2

The Sub-Contractor must be paid an amount equal to the loss of credit (input tax) on the supply of goods and services to the Contractor which contribute exclusively to the Sub-Contract Works and which become exempt from VAT after the Date of Tender

DOM 617   19B.1.2

The Date of Tender is defined in clause 1.3. DOM clause 21 does not expressly indicate whether such amounts would be subject to retention. DOM clauses 21.7.2.10 and 21.8.2.5 would encompass 'any ... amount ... required by the Sub-Contract to be added' (or 'included')

Sub-Contractor does give the stipulated written provisional assessment ? — YES

NO →

There is no specific remedy

The term 'Ascertained Final Sub-Contract Sum' must be regarded as such sum exclusive of VAT

DOM 583   19B.2

the total of such sum or sums shall be the Ascertained Final Sub-Contract Sum;

DOM 37   15.2

Sub-Contractor is paid such an amount as stipulated ? — YES

NO →

Where in Sub-Contract DOM/1 it is provided that an amount is to be added to or subtracted from the Sub-Contract Sum, then: -

DOM 29   3

The Sub-Contractor must specify the rate or rates of VAT which are chargeable on the Category two supplies; and

DOM 591   19B.4.1.2

the Sub-Contractor must state the grounds on which he considers such supplies are so chargeable

DOM 592   19B.4.1.2

Supplies of goods and services under the Sub-Contract are supplies within the meaning of the VAT (General) Regulations 1980 Regulation 21(1)

DOM 584   19B.3

The Contractor is not acting as agent for the Sub-Contractor in issuing any documents referred to in this clause 19B

DOM 585   19B.7

Where in Sub-Contract DOM/1 it is provided that an amount is to be included in the computation of the Ascertained Final Sub-Contract Sum, then: -

DOM 39   3

Sub-Contractor does specify the rate and state the grounds as stipulated ? — YES

NO →

There is no specific remedy

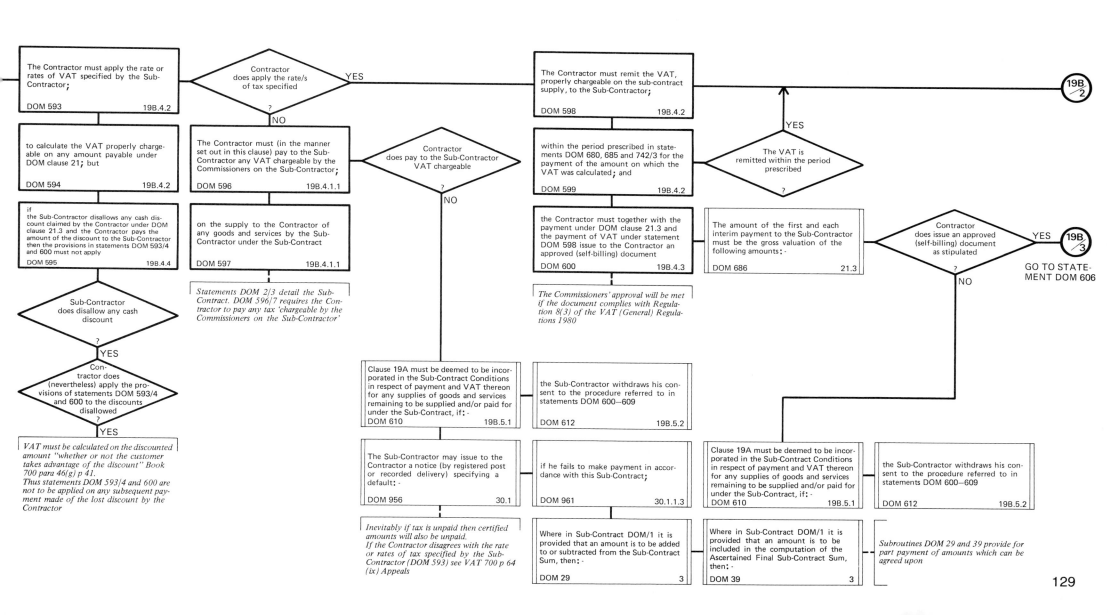

The Contractor must apply the rate or rates of VAT specified by the Sub-Contractor;

DOM 593   19B.4.2

Contractor does apply the rate/s of tax specified ?

---

to calculate the VAT properly chargeable on any amount payable under DOM clause 21; but

DOM 594   19B.4.2

---

if the Sub-Contractor disallows any cash discount claimed by the Contractor under DOM clause 21.3 and the Contractor pays the amount of the discount to the Sub-Contractor then the provisions in statements DOM 593/4 and 600 must not apply

DOM 595   19B.4.4

Sub-Contractor does disallow any cash discount ?

YES

Contractor does (nevertheless) apply the provisions of statements DOM 593/4 and 600 to the discounts disallowed ?

YES

VAT must be calculated on the discounted amount "whether or not the customer takes advantage of the discount" Book 700 para 46(g) p 41.
Thus statements DOM 593/4 and 600 are not to be applied on any subsequent payment made of the lost discount by the Contractor

---

YES

NO

The Contractor must (in the manner set out in this clause) pay to the Sub-Contractor any VAT chargeable by the Commissioners on the Sub-Contractor;

DOM 596   19B.4.1.1

---

on the supply to the Contractor of any goods and services by the Sub-Contractor under the Sub-Contract

DOM 597   19B.4.1.1

Statements DOM 2/3 detail the Sub-Contract. DOM 596/7 requires the Contractor to pay any tax 'chargeable by the Commissioners on the Sub-Contractor'

Contractor does pay to the Sub-Contractor VAT chargeable ?

NO

Clause 19A must be deemed to be incorporated in the Sub-Contract Conditions in respect of payment and VAT thereon for any supplies of goods and services remaining to be supplied and/or paid for under the Sub-Contract, if: -

DOM 610   19B.5.1

The Sub-Contractor may issue to the Contractor a notice (by registered post or recorded delivery) specifying a default: -

DOM 956   30.1

Inevitably if tax is unpaid then certified amounts will also be unpaid.
If the Contractor disagrees with the rate or rates of tax specified by the Sub-Contractor (DOM 593) see VAT 700 p 64 (ix) Appeals

---

19B / 1

The Contractor must remit the VAT, properly chargeable on the sub-contract supply, to the Sub-Contractor;

DOM 598   19B.4.2

---

within the period prescribed in statements DOM 680, 685 and 742/3 for the payment of the amount on which the VAT was calculated; and

DOM 599   19B.4.2

---

the Contractor must together with the payment under DOM clause 21.3 and the payment of VAT under statement DOM 598 issue to the Contractor an approved (self-billing) document

DOM 600   19B.4.3

The Commissioners' approval will be met if the document complies with Regulation 8(3) of the VAT (General) Regulations 1980

---

the Sub-Contractor withdraws his consent to the procedure referred to in statements DOM 600—609

DOM 612   19B.5.2

---

if he fails to make payment in accordance with this Sub-Contract;

DOM 961   30.1.1.3

Where in Sub-Contract DOM/1 it is provided that an amount is to be added to or subtracted from the Sub-Contract Sum, then: -

DOM 29   3

YES

The VAT is remitted within the period prescribed ?

The amount of the first and each interim payment to the Sub-Contractor must be the gross valuation of the following amounts: -

DOM 686   21.3

Clause 19A must be deemed to be incorporated in the Sub-Contract Conditions in respect of payment and VAT thereon for any supplies of goods and services remaining to be supplied and/or paid for under the Sub-Contract, if: -

DOM 610   19B.5.1

Where in Sub-Contract DOM/1 it is provided that an amount is to be included in the computation of the Ascertained Final Sub-Contract Sum, then: -

DOM 39   3

19B / 2

Contractor does issue an approved (self-billing) document as stipulated ?

YES

NO

---

the Sub-Contractor withdraws his consent to the procedure referred to in statements DOM 600—609

DOM 612   19B.5.2

Subroutines DOM 29 and 39 provide for part payment of amounts which can be agreed upon

---

19B / 3

GO TO STATE-MENT DOM 606

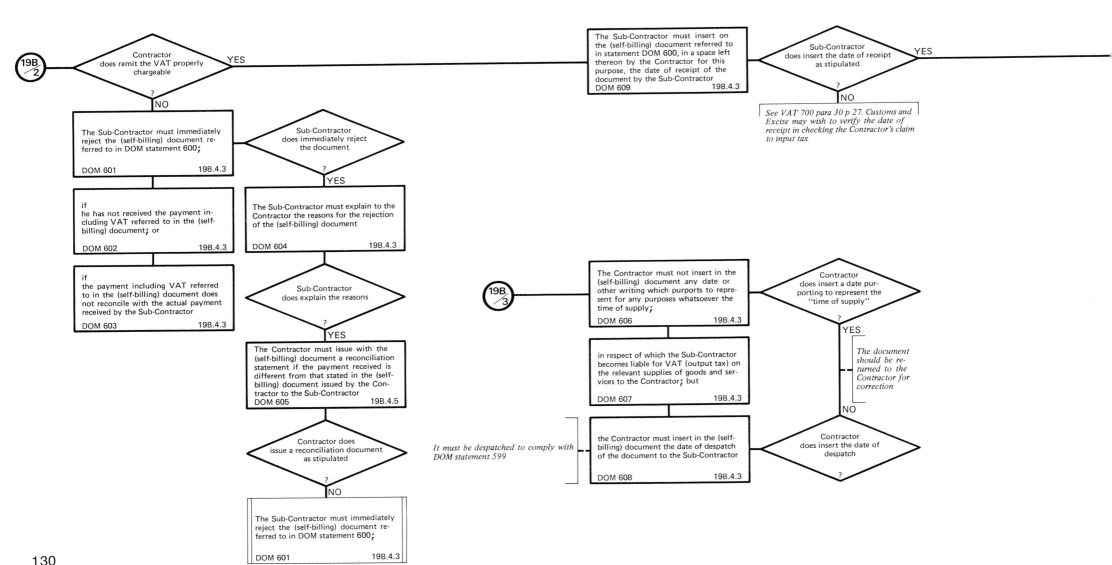

19B/1

19B/2 — Contractor does remit the VAT properly chargeable **?**

YES →

The Sub-Contractor must insert on the (self-billing) document referred to in statement DOM 600, in a space left thereon by the Contractor for this purpose, the date of receipt of the document by the Sub-Contractor
DOM 609   19B.4.3

Sub-Contractor does insert the date of receipt as stipulated **?**

YES →

NO

See VAT 700 para 30 p 27. Customs and Excise may wish to verify the date of receipt in checking the Contractor's claim to input tax

NO

The Sub-Contractor must immediately reject the (self-billing) document referred to in DOM statement 600;
DOM 601   19B.4.3

if he has not received the payment including VAT referred to in the (self-billing) document; or
DOM 602   19B.4.3

if the payment including VAT referred to in the (self-billing) document does not reconcile with the actual payment received by the Sub-Contractor
DOM 603   19B.4.3

Sub-Contractor does immediately reject the document **?**

YES

The Sub-Contractor must explain to the Contractor the reasons for the rejection of the (self-billing) document
DOM 604   19B.4.3

Sub-Contractor does explain the reasons **?**

YES

The Contractor must issue with the (self-billing) document a reconciliation statement if the payment received is different from that stated in the (self-billing) document issued by the Contractor to the Sub-Contractor
DOM 605   19B.4.5

Contractor does issue a reconciliation document as stipulated **?**

NO

The Sub-Contractor must immediately reject the (self-billing) document referred to in DOM statement 600;
DOM 601   19B.4.3

19B/3 →

The Contractor must not insert in the (self-billing) document any date or other writing which purports to represent for any purposes whatsoever the time of supply;
DOM 606   19B.4.3

in respect of which the Sub-Contractor becomes liable for VAT (output tax) on the relevant supplies of goods and services to the Contractor; but
DOM 607   19B.4.3

the Contractor must insert in the (self-billing) document the date of despatch of the document to the Sub-Contractor
DOM 608   19B.4.3

It must be despatched to comply with DOM statement 599

Contractor does insert a date purporting to represent the "time of supply" **?**

YES

The document should be returned to the Contractor for correction

NO

Contractor does insert the date of despatch **?**

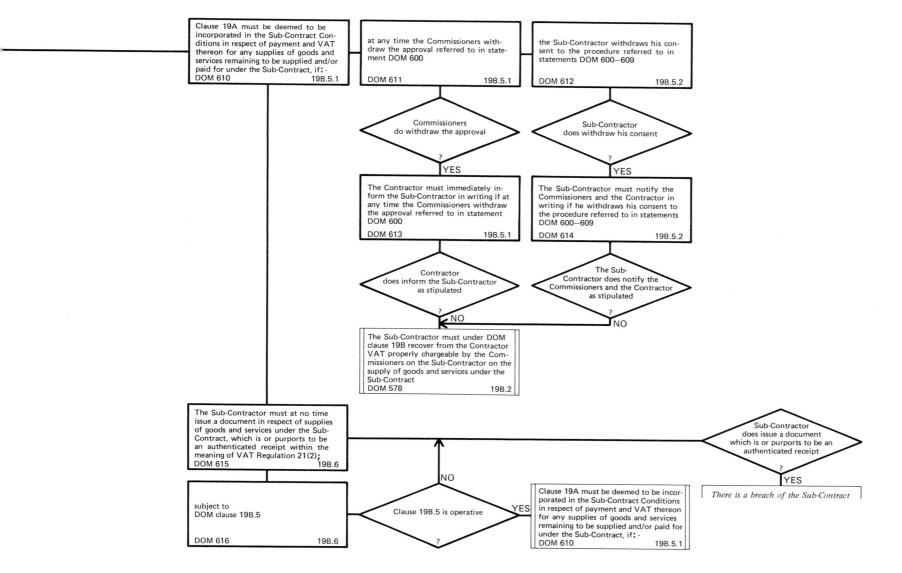

STOP

Clause 19A must be deemed to be incorporated in the Sub-Contract Conditions in respect of payment and VAT thereon for any supplies of goods and services remaining to be supplied and/or paid for under the Sub-Contract, if: -
DOM 610   19B.5.1

at any time the Commissioners withdraw the approval referred to in statement DOM 600
DOM 611   19B.5.1

the Sub-Contractor withdraws his consent to the procedure referred to in statements DOM 600—609
DOM 612   19B.5.2

Commissioners
do withdraw the approval
?
YES

Sub-Contractor
does withdraw his consent
?
YES

The Contractor must immediately inform the Sub-Contractor in writing if at any time the Commissioners withdraw the approval referred to in statement DOM 600
DOM 613   19B.5.1

The Sub-Contractor must notify the Commissioners and the Contractor in writing if he withdraws his consent to the procedure referred to in statements DOM 600—609
DOM 614   19B.5.2

Contractor
does inform the Sub-Contractor
as stipulated
?   NO

The Sub-
Contractor does notify the
Commissioners and the Contractor
as stipulated
?   NO

The Sub-Contractor must under DOM clause 19B recover from the Contractor VAT properly chargeable by the Commissioners on the Sub-Contractor on the supply of goods and services under the Sub-Contract
DOM 578   19B.2

The Sub-Contractor must at no time issue a document in respect of supplies of goods and services under the Sub-Contract, which is or purports to be an authenticated receipt within the meaning of VAT Regulation 21(2);
DOM 615   19B.6

Sub-Contractor
does issue a document
which is or purports to be an
authenticated receipt
?
YES

There is a breach of the Sub-Contract

NO

subject to
DOM clause 19B.5

DOM 616   19B.6

Clause 19B.5 is operative
?
YES

Clause 19A must be deemed to be incorporated in the Sub-Contract Conditions in respect of payment and VAT thereon for any supplies of goods and services remaining to be supplied and/or paid for under the Sub-Contract, if: -
DOM 610   19B.5.1

Clause 20A TAX DEDUCTION SCHEME

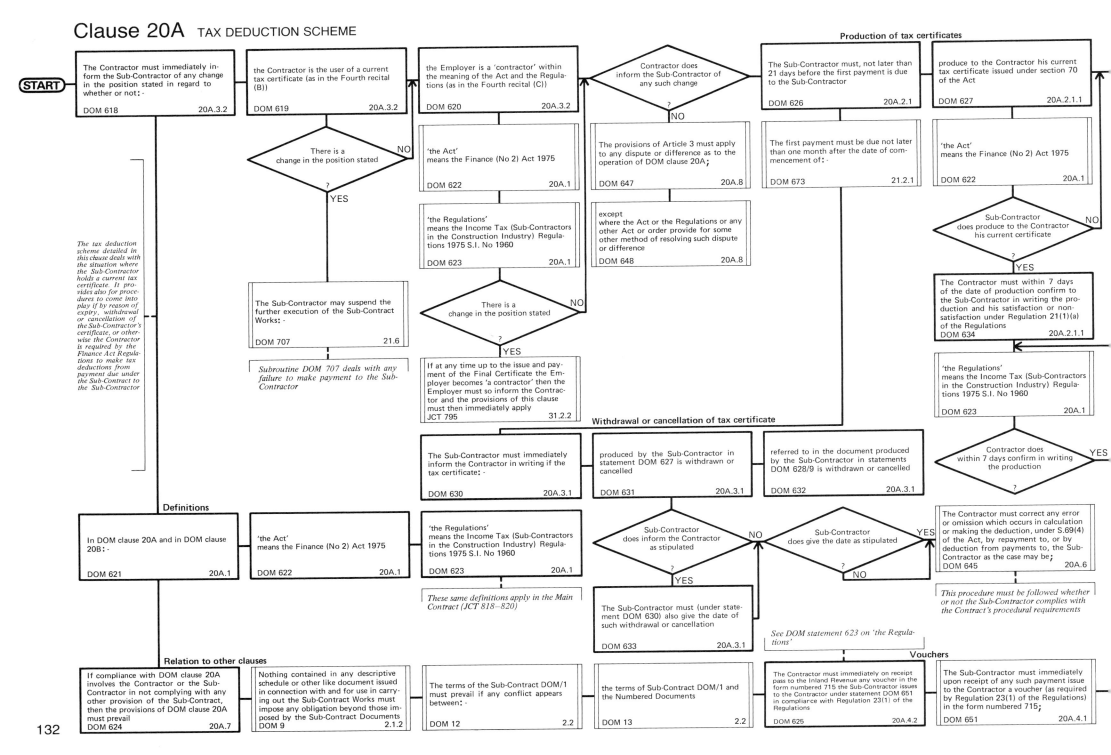

START

The Contractor must immediately inform the Sub-Contractor of any change in the position stated in regard to whether or not:-
DOM 618 — 20A.3.2

the Contractor is the user of a current tax certificate (as in the Fourth recital (B))
DOM 619 — 20A.3.2

the Employer is a 'contractor' within the meaning of the Act and the Regulations (as in the Fourth recital (C))
DOM 620 — 20A.3.2

Contractor does inform the Sub-Contractor of any such change? — NO

Production of tax certificates

The Sub-Contractor must, not later than 21 days before the first payment is due to the Sub-Contractor
DOM 626 — 20A.2.1

produce to the Contractor his current tax certificate issued under section 70 of the Act
DOM 627 — 20A.2.1.1

The tax deduction scheme detailed in this clause deals with the situation where the Sub-Contractor holds a current tax certificate. It provides also for procedures to come into play if by reason of expiry, withdrawal or cancellation of the Sub-Contractor's certificate, or otherwise the Contractor is required by the Finance Act Regulations to make tax deductions from payment due under the Sub-Contract to the Sub-Contractor

There is a change in the position stated? — NO / YES

'the Act' means the Finance (No 2) Act 1975
DOM 622 — 20A.1

The provisions of Article 3 must apply to any dispute or difference as to the operation of DOM clause 20A;
DOM 647 — 20A.8

The first payment must be due not later than one month after the date of commencement of:-
DOM 673 — 21.2.1

'the Act' means the Finance (No 2) Act 1975
DOM 622 — 20A.1

The Sub-Contractor may suspend the further execution of the Sub-Contract Works:-
DOM 707 — 21.6

'the Regulations' means the Income Tax (Sub-Contractors in the Construction Industry) Regulations 1975 S.I. No 1960
DOM 623 — 20A.1

except where the Act or the Regulations or any other Act or order provide for some other method of resolving such dispute or difference
DOM 648 — 20A.8

Sub-Contractor does produce to the Contractor his current certificate? — NO / YES

Subroutine DOM 707 deals with any failure to make payment to the Sub-Contractor

There is a change in the position stated — NO / YES

If at any time up to the issue and payment of the Final Certificate the Employer becomes 'a contractor' then the Employer must so inform the Contractor and the provisions of this clause must then immediately apply
JCT 795 — 31.2.2

The Contractor must within 7 days of the date of production confirm to the Sub-Contractor in writing the production and his satisfaction or non-satisfaction under Regulation 21(1)(a) of the Regulations
DOM 634 — 20A.2.1.1

Withdrawal or cancellation of tax certificate

The Sub-Contractor must immediately inform the Contractor in writing if the tax certificate:-
DOM 630 — 20A.3.1

produced by the Sub-Contractor in statement DOM 627 is withdrawn or cancelled
DOM 631 — 20A.3.1

referred to in the document produced by the Sub-Contractor in statements DOM 628/9 is withdrawn or cancelled
DOM 632 — 20A.3.1

'the Regulations' means the Income Tax (Sub-Contractors in the Construction Industry) Regulations 1975 S.I. No 1960
DOM 623 — 20A.1

Contractor does within 7 days confirm in writing the production? — YES

Definitions

In DOM clause 20A and in DOM clause 20B:-
DOM 621 — 20A.1

'the Act' means the Finance (No 2) Act 1975
DOM 622 — 20A.1

'the Regulations' means the Income Tax (Sub-Contractors in the Construction Industry) Regulations 1975 S.I. No 1960
DOM 623 — 20A.1

Sub-Contractor does inform the Contractor as stipulated? — NO / YES

Sub-Contractor does give the date as stipulated — YES / NO

The Contractor must correct any error or omission which occurs in calculation or making the deduction, under S.69(4) of the Act, by repayment to, or by deduction from payments to, the Sub-Contractor as the case may be;
DOM 645 — 20A.6

These same definitions apply in the Main Contract (JCT 818–820)

The Sub-Contractor must (under statement DOM 630) also give the date of such withdrawal or cancellation
DOM 633 — 20A.3.1

This procedure must be followed whether or not the Sub-Contractor complies with the Contract's procedural requirements

See DOM statement 623 on 'the Regulations'

Relation to other clauses

If compliance with DOM clause 20A involves the Contractor or the Sub-Contractor in not complying with any other provision of the Sub-Contract, then the provisions of DOM clause 20A must prevail
DOM 624 — 20A.7

Nothing contained in any descriptive schedule or other like document issued in connection with and for use in carrying out the Sub-Contract Works must impose any obligation beyond those imposed by the Sub-Contract Documents
DOM 9 — 2.1.2

The terms of the Sub-Contract DOM/1 must prevail if any conflict appears between:-
DOM 12 — 2.2

the terms of Sub-Contract DOM/1 and the Numbered Documents
DOM 13 — 2.2

Vouchers

The Contractor must immediately on receipt pass to the Inland Revenue any voucher in the form numbered 715 the Sub-Contractor issues to the Contractor under statement DOM 651 in compliance with Regulation 23(1) of the Regulations
DOM 625 — 20A.4.2

The Sub-Contractor must immediately upon receipt of any such payment issue to the Contractor a voucher (as required by Regulation 23(1) of the Regulations) in the form numbered 715;
DOM 651 — 20A.4.1

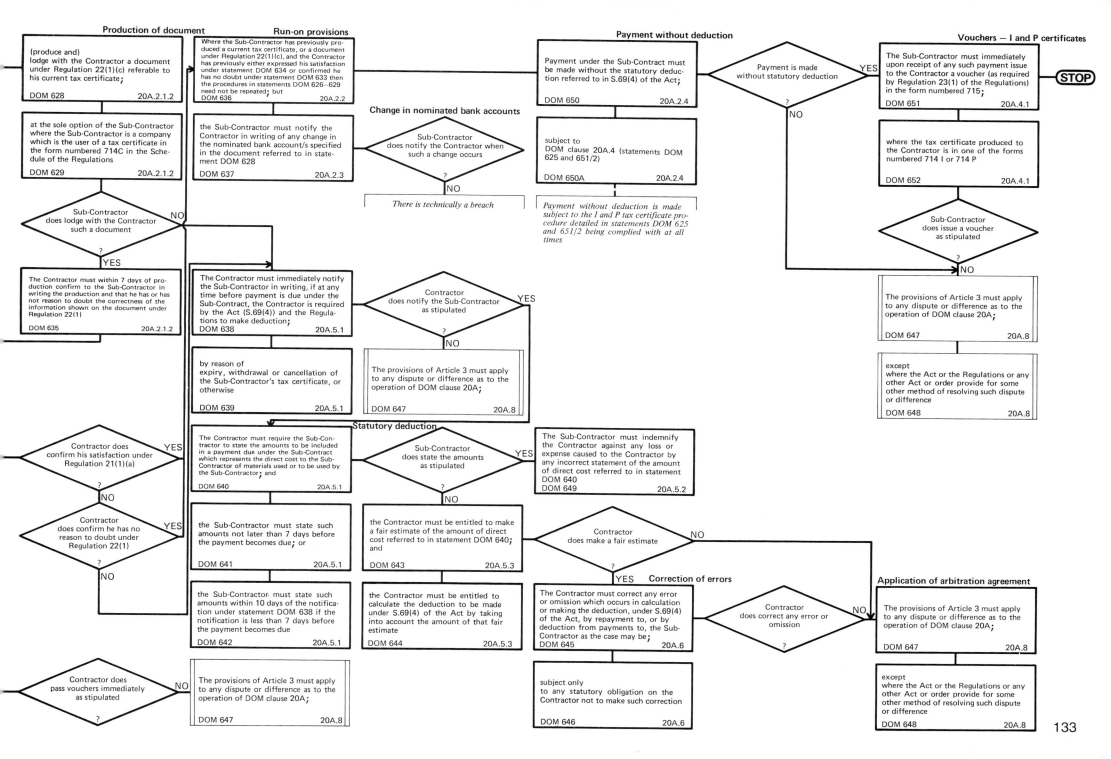

Production of document

(produce and)
lodge with the Contractor a document under Regulation 22(1)(c) referable to his current tax certificate;

DOM 628   20A.2.1.2

at the sole option of the Sub-Contractor where the Sub-Contractor is a company which is the user of a tax certificate in the form numbered 714C in the Schedule of the Regulations

DOM 629   20A.2.1.2

Sub-Contractor does lodge with the Contractor such a document ?

The Contractor must within 7 days of production confirm to the Sub-Contractor in writing the production and that he has or has not reason to doubt the correctness of the information shown on the document under Regulation 22(1)

DOM 635   20A.2.1.2

Contractor does confirm his satisfaction under Regulation 21(1)(a) ?

Contractor does confirm he has no reason to doubt under Regulation 22(1) ?

Contractor does pass vouchers immediately as stipulated ?

The provisions of Article 3 must apply to any dispute or difference as to the operation of DOM clause 20A;

DOM 647   20A.8

Run-on provisions

Where the Sub-Contractor has previously produced a current tax certificate, or a document under Regulation 22(1)(c), and the Contractor has previously either expressed his satisfaction under statement DOM 634 or confirmed he has no doubt under statement DOM 633 then the procedures in statements DOM 626—629 need not be repeated; but

DOM 636   20A.2.2

the Sub-Contractor must notify the Contractor in writing of any change in the nominated bank account/s specified in the document referred to in statement DOM 628

DOM 637   20A.2.3

The Contractor must immediately notify the Sub-Contractor in writing, if at any time before payment is due under the Sub-Contract, the Contractor is required by the Act (S.69(4)) and the Regulations to make deduction;

DOM 638   20A.5.1

by reason of
expiry, withdrawal or cancellation of the Sub-Contractor's tax certificate, or otherwise

DOM 639   20A.5.1

Statutory deduction

The Contractor must require the Sub-Contractor to state the amounts to be included in a payment due under the Sub-Contract which represents the direct cost to the Sub-Contractor of materials used or to be used by the Sub-Contractor; and

DOM 640   20A.5.1

the Sub-Contractor must state such amounts not later than 7 days before the payment becomes due; or

DOM 641   20A.5.1

the Sub-Contractor must state such amounts within 10 days of the notification under statement DOM 638 if the notification is less than 7 days before the payment becomes due

DOM 642   20A.5.1

Change in nominated bank accounts

Sub-Contractor does notify the Contractor when such a change occurs ?

There is technically a breach

Contractor does notify the Sub-Contractor as stipulated ?

The provisions of Article 3 must apply to any dispute or difference as to the operation of DOM clause 20A;

DOM 647   20A.8

Sub-Contractor does state the amounts as stipulated ?

the Contractor must be entitled to make a fair estimate of the amount of direct cost referred to in statement DOM 640; and

DOM 643   20A.5.3

the Contractor must be entitled to calculate the deduction to be made under S.69(4) of the Act by taking into account the amount of that fair estimate

DOM 644   20A.5.3

Payment without deduction

Payment under the Sub-Contract must be made without the statutory deduction referred to in S.69(4) of the Act;

DOM 650   20A.2.4

subject to
DOM clause 20A.4 (statements DOM 625 and 651/2)

DOM 650A   20A.2.4

Payment without deduction is made subject to the I and P tax certificate procedure detailed in statements DOM 625 and 651/2 being complied with at all times

The Sub-Contractor must indemnify the Contractor against any loss or expense caused to the Contractor by any incorrect statement of the amount of direct cost referred to in statement DOM 640

DOM 649   20A.5.2

Contractor does make a fair estimate ?

Correction of errors

The Contractor must correct any error or omission which occurs in calculation or making the deduction, under S.69(4) of the Act, by repayment to, or by deduction from payments to, the Sub-Contractor as the case may be;

DOM 645   20A.6

subject only
to any statutory obligation on the Contractor not to make such correction

DOM 646   20A.6

Payment is made without statutory deduction ?

Contractor does correct any error or omission ?

Vouchers — I and P certificates

The Sub-Contractor must immediately upon receipt of any such payment issue to the Contractor a voucher (as required by Regulation 23(1) of the Regulations) in the form numbered 715;

DOM 651   20A.4.1

(STOP)

where the tax certificate produced to the Contractor is in one of the forms numbered 714 I or 714 P

DOM 652   20A.4.1

Sub-Contractor does issue a voucher as stipulated ?

The provisions of Article 3 must apply to any dispute or difference as to the operation of DOM clause 20A;

DOM 647   20A.8

except
where the Act or the Regulations or any other Act or order provide for some other method of resolving such dispute or difference

DOM 648   20A.8

Application of arbitration agreement

The provisions of Article 3 must apply to any dispute or difference as to the operation of DOM clause 20A;

DOM 647   20A.8

except
where the Act or the Regulations or any other Act or order provide for some other method of resolving such dispute or difference

DOM 648   20A.8

133

Main Contractor — change in regard to tax certificate

Statutory deductions — direct cost of materials

START

The Contractor must immediately inform the Sub-Contractor of any change in the position stated in regard to whether or not: -

DOM 653   20B.3

the Contractor is the user of a current tax certificate (as in the Fourth recital (B))

DOM 654   20B.3

the Employer is a 'contractor' within the meaning of the Act and the Regulations (as in the Fourth recital (C))

DOM 655   20B.3

Contractor does inform the Sub-Contractor of any such change
?

YES

There is a change in the position stated
?

NO

YES

'the Act'
means the Finance (No 2) Act 1975

DOM 622   20A.1

NO

The Sub-Contractor must, not later than 7 days before any payment under this Sub-Contract become due, inform the Contractor in writing of;

DOM 657   20B.1.1

The provisions of Article 3 must apply to any dispute or difference as to the operation of DOM clause 20B

DOM 671   20B.6

the amount to be included in any payment due which represents the direct cost to the Sub-Contractor of materials used or to be used by the Sub-Contractor or;

DOM 658   20B.1.1

This clause deals with the statutory tax deductions required where the Sub-Contractor is not the holder of a current tax certificate. If during the course of the Sub-Contract, before the last payment is made, the Sub-Contractor obtains a tax certificate then DOM clause 20A becomes operable

The Sub-Contractor may suspend the further execution of the Sub-Contract Works: -

DOM 707   21.6

'the Regulations'
means the Income Tax (Sub-Contractors in the Construction Industry) Regulations 1975 S.I. No 1960

DOM 623   20A.1

except
where the Act or the Regulations or any other Act or order provide for some other method of resolving such dispute or difference

DOM 672   20B.6

in order that the deduction referred to in S.69(4) of the Act can be made from that payment;

DOM 659   20B.1.1

'the Act'
means the Finance (No 2) Act 1975

DOM 622   20A.1

Subroutine DOM 707 deals with any failure to make payment to the Sub-Contractor

There is a change in the position stated
?

NO

YES

where
the word "is" has been deleted in the Fourth recital (B)

DOM 660   footnote (w)

The word "is" has been deleted in the Fourth recital (B)
?

NO

YES

If at any time up to the issue and payment of the Final Certificate the Employer becomes 'a contractor' then the Employer must so inform the Contractor and the provisions of this clause must then immediately apply
JCT 795   31.2.2

DOM clause 20A.2 to .8 should be deleted

DOM 661   (see Fourth Schedule (A))

Relation to other clauses

If compliance with DOM clause 20B involves the Contractor or the Sub-Contractor in not complying with any other provision of the Sub-Contract, then the provisions of DOM clause 20B must prevail
DOM 656   20B.4

Nothing contained in any descriptive schedule or other like document issued in connection with and for use in carrying out the Sub-Contract Works must impose any obligation beyond those imposed by the Sub-Contract Documents
DOM 9   2.1.2

The terms of the Sub-Contract DOM/1 must prevail if any conflict appears between: -

DOM 12   2.2

the terms of Sub-Contract DOM/1 and the Numbered Documents

DOM 13   2.2

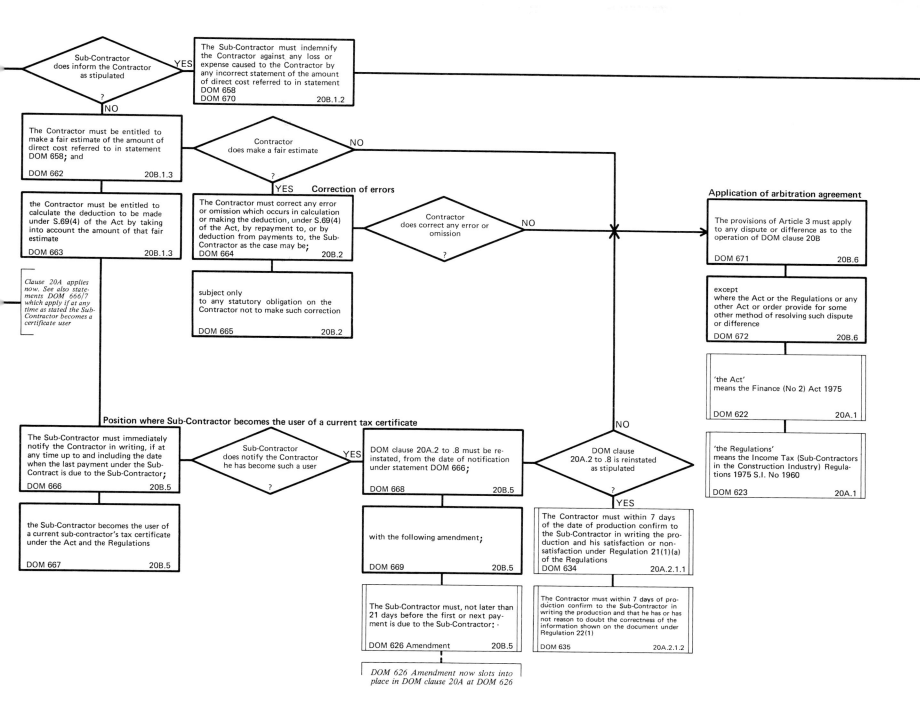

Sub-Contractor does inform the Contractor as stipulated ?

YES → The Sub-Contractor must indemnify the Contractor against any loss or expense caused to the Contractor by any incorrect statement of the amount of direct cost referred to in statement DOM 658
DOM 670   20B.1.2

→ **STOP**

NO

The Contractor must be entitled to make a fair estimate of the amount of direct cost referred to in statement DOM 658; and
DOM 662   20B.1.3

Contractor does make a fair estimate ?   **NO** →

the Contractor must be entitled to calculate the deduction to be made under S.69(4) of the Act by taking into account the amount of that fair estimate
DOM 663   20B.1.3

YES   Correction of errors

The Contractor must correct any error or omission which occurs in calculation or making the deduction, under S.69(4) of the Act, by repayment to, or by deduction from payments to, the Sub-Contractor as the case may be;
DOM 664   20B.2

Contractor does correct any error or omission ?   **NO** →

subject only to any statutory obligation on the Contractor not to make such correction
DOM 665   20B.2

Clause 20A applies now. See also statements DOM 666/7 which apply if at any time as stated the Sub-Contractor becomes a certificate user

Application of arbitration agreement

The provisions of Article 3 must apply to any dispute or difference as to the operation of DOM clause 20B
DOM 671   20B.6

except where the Act or the Regulations or any other Act or order provide for some other method of resolving such dispute or difference
DOM 672   20B.6

'the Act' means the Finance (No 2) Act 1975
DOM 622   20A.1

'the Regulations' means the Income Tax (Sub-Contractors in the Construction Industry) Regulations 1975 S.I. No 1960
DOM 623   20A.1

Position where Sub-Contractor becomes the user of a current tax certificate

The Sub-Contractor must immediately notify the Contractor in writing, if at any time up to and including the date when the last payment under the Sub-Contract is due to the Sub-Contractor;
DOM 666   20B.5

Sub-Contractor does notify the Contractor he has become such a user ?   **YES** →

DOM clause 20A.2 to .8 must be reinstated, from the date of notification under statement DOM 666;
DOM 668   20B.5

the Sub-Contractor becomes the user of a current sub-contractor's tax certificate under the Act and the Regulations
DOM 667   20B.5

with the following amendment;
DOM 669   20B.5

The Sub-Contractor must, not later than 21 days before the first or next payment is due to the Sub-Contractor: -
DOM 626 Amendment   20B.5

DOM 626 Amendment now slots into place in DOM clause 20A at DOM 626

NO

DOM clause 20A.2 to .8 is reinstated as stipulated ?

YES

The Contractor must within 7 days of the date of production confirm to the Sub-Contractor in writing the production and his satisfaction or non-satisfaction under Regulation 21(1)(a) of the Regulations
DOM 634   20A.2.1.1

The Contractor must within 7 days of production confirm to the Sub-Contractor in writing the production and that he has or has not reason to doubt the correctness of the information shown on the document under Regulation 22(1)
DOM 635   20A.2.1.2

Clause 21 PAYMENT OF SUB-CONTRACTOR

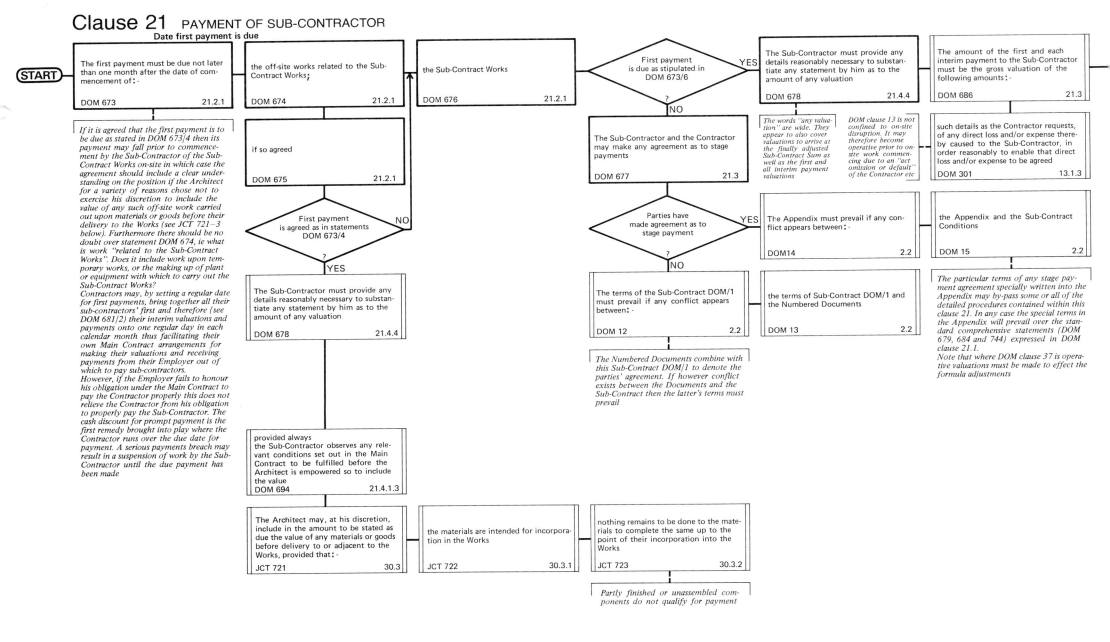

Date first payment is due

START

The first payment must be due not later than one month after the date of commencement of: -

DOM 673   21.2.1

If it is agreed that the first payment is to be due as stated in DOM 673/4 then its payment may fall prior to commencement by the Sub-Contractor of the Sub-Contract Works on-site in which case the agreement should include a clear understanding on the position if the Architect for a variety of reasons chose not to exercise his discretion to include the value of any such off-site work carried out upon materials or goods before their delivery to the Works (see JCT 721–3 below). Furthermore there should be no doubt over statement DOM 674, ie what is work "related to the Sub-Contract Works". Does it include work upon temporary works, or the making up of plant or equipment with which to carry out the Sub-Contract Works?
Contractors may, by setting a regular date for first payments, bring together all their sub-contractors' first and therefore (see DOM 681/2) their interim valuations and payments onto one regular day in each calendar month thus facilitating their own Main Contract arrangements for making their valuations and receiving payments from their Employer out of which to pay sub-contractors.
However, if the Employer fails to honour his obligation under the Main Contract to pay the Contractor properly this does not relieve the Contractor from his obligation to properly pay the Sub-Contractor. The cash discount for prompt payment is the first remedy brought into play where the Contractor runs over the due date for payment. A serious payments breach may result in a suspension of work by the Sub-Contractor until the due payment has been made

---

the off-site works related to the Sub-Contract Works;

DOM 674   21.2.1

---

if so agreed

DOM 675   21.2.1

First payment is agreed as in statements DOM 673/4
? — NO
YES

The Sub-Contractor must provide any details reasonably necessary to substantiate any statement by him as to the amount of any valuation

DOM 678   21.4.4

---

provided always
the Sub-Contractor observes any relevant conditions set out in the Main Contract to be fulfilled before the Architect is empowered so to include the value
DOM 694   21.4.1.3

The Architect may, at his discretion, include in the amount to be stated as due the value of any materials or goods before delivery to or adjacent to the Works, provided that: -
JCT 721   30.3

---

the Sub-Contract Works

DOM 676   21.2.1

---

the materials are intended for incorporation in the Works

JCT 722   30.3.1

First payment is due as stipulated in DOM 673/6
? — NO
YES

The Sub-Contractor and the Contractor may make any agreement as to stage payments

DOM 677   21.3

Parties have made agreement as to stage payment
? — NO
YES

The terms of the Sub-Contract DOM/1 must prevail if any conflict appears between: -

DOM 12   2.2

---

nothing remains to be done to the materials to complete the same up to the point of their incorporation into the Works

JCT 723   30.3.2

Partly finished or unassembled components do not qualify for payment

---

The Sub-Contractor must provide any details reasonably necessary to substantiate any statement by him as to the amount of any valuation

DOM 678   21.4.4

The words "any valuation" are wide. They appear to also cover valuations to arrive at the finally adjusted Sub-Contract Sum as well as the first and all interim payment valuations

DOM clause 13 is not confined to on-site disruption. It may therefore become operative prior to on-site work commencing due to an "act omission or default" of the Contractor etc

---

The Appendix must prevail if any conflict appears between: -

DOM14   2.2

---

the terms of Sub-Contract DOM/1 and the Numbered Documents

DOM 13   2.2

The Numbered Documents combine with this Sub-Contract DOM/1 to denote the parties' agreement. If however conflict exists between the Documents and the Sub-Contract then the latter's terms must prevail

---

The amount of the first and each interim payment to the Sub-Contractor must be the gross valuation of the following amounts: -

DOM 686   21.3

---

such details as the Contractor requests, of any direct loss and/or expense thereby caused to the Sub-Contractor, in order reasonably to enable that direct loss and/or expense to be agreed

DOM 301   13.1.3

---

the Appendix and the Sub-Contract Conditions

DOM 15   2.2

The particular terms of any stage payment agreement specially written into the Appendix may by-pass some or all of the detailed procedures contained within this clause 21. In any case the special terms in the Appendix will prevail over the standard comprehensive statements (DOM 679, 684 and 744) expressed in DOM clause 21.1.
Note that where DOM clause 37 is operative valuations must be made to effect the formula adjustments

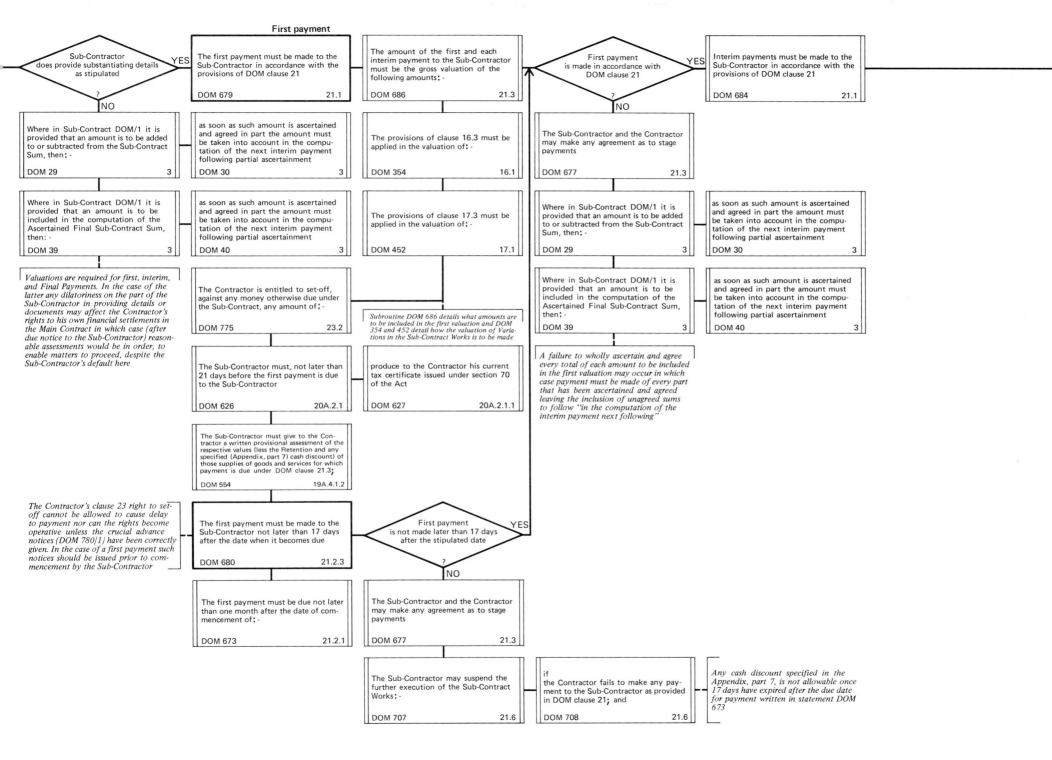

Sub-Contractor does provide substantiating details as stipulated ? —YES→

The first payment must be made to the Sub-Contractor in accordance with the provisions of DOM clause 21

DOM 679   21.1

The amount of the first and each interim payment to the Sub-Contractor must be the gross valuation of the following amounts: -

DOM 686   21.3

First payment is made in accordance with DOM clause 21 ? —YES→

Interim payments must be made to the Sub-Contractor in accordance with the provisions of DOM clause 21

DOM 684   21.1

↓NO

Where in Sub-Contract DOM/1 it is provided that an amount is to be added to or subtracted from the Sub-Contract Sum, then: -

DOM 29   3

as soon as such amount is ascertained and agreed in part the amount must be taken into account in the computation of the next interim payment following partial ascertainment

DOM 30   3

The provisions of clause 16.3 must be applied in the valuation of: -

DOM 354   16.1

↓NO

The Sub-Contractor and the Contractor may make any agreement as to stage payments

DOM 677   21.3

as soon as such amount is ascertained and agreed in part the amount must be taken into account in the computation of the next interim payment following partial ascertainment

DOM 30   3

Where in Sub-Contract DOM/1 it is provided that an amount is to be included in the computation of the Ascertained Final Sub-Contract Sum, then: -

DOM 39   3

as soon as such amount is ascertained and agreed in part the amount must be taken into account in the computation of the next interim payment following partial ascertainment

DOM 40   3

The provisions of clause 17.3 must be applied in the valuation of: -

DOM 452   17.1

Where in Sub-Contract DOM/1 it is provided that an amount is to be added to or subtracted from the Sub-Contract Sum, then: -

DOM 29   3

as soon as such amount is ascertained and agreed in part the amount must be taken into account in the computation of the next interim payment following partial ascertainment

DOM 40   3

Valuations are required for first, interim, and Final Payments. In the case of the latter any dilatoriness on the part of the Sub-Contractor in providing details or documents may affect the Contractor's rights to his own financial settlements in the Main Contract in which case (after due notice to the Sub-Contractor) reasonable assessments would be in order, to enable matters to proceed, despite the Sub-Contractor's default here

The Contractor is entitled to set-off, against any money otherwise due under the Sub-Contract, any amount of: -

DOM 775   23.2

Subroutine DOM 686 details what amounts are to be included in the first valuation and DOM 354 and 452 detail how the valuation of Variations in the Sub-Contract Works is to be made

Where in Sub-Contract DOM/1 it is provided that an amount is to be included in the computation of the Ascertained Final Sub-Contract Sum, then: -

DOM 39   3

A failure to wholly ascertain and agree every total of each amount to be included in the first valuation may occur in which case payment must be made of every part that has been ascertained and agreed leaving the inclusion of unagreed sums to follow "in the computation of the interim payment next following"

The Sub-Contractor must, not later than 21 days before the first payment is due to the Sub-Contractor

DOM 626   20A.2.1

produce to the Contractor his current tax certificate issued under section 70 of the Act

DOM 627   20A.2.1.1

The Sub-Contractor must give to the Contractor a written provisional assessment of the respective values (less the Retention and any specified (Appendix, part 7) cash discount) of those supplies of goods and services for which payment is due under DOM clause 21.3;

DOM 554   19A.4.1.2

The Contractor's clause 23 right to set-off cannot be allowed to cause delay to payment nor can the rights become operative unless the crucial advance notices (DOM 780/1) have been correctly given. In the case of a first payment such notices should be issued prior to commencement by the Sub-Contractor

The first payment must be made to the Sub-Contractor not later than 17 days after the date when it becomes due

DOM 680   21.2.3

First payment is not made later than 17 days after the stipulated date ? —YES→

↓NO

The first payment must be due not later than one month after the date of commencement of: -

DOM 673   21.2.1

The Sub-Contractor and the Contractor may make any agreement as to stage payments

DOM 677   21.3

The Sub-Contractor may suspend the further execution of the Sub-Contract Works: -

DOM 707   21.6

if the Contractor fails to make any payment to the Sub-Contractor as provided in DOM clause 21; and

DOM 708   21.6

Any cash discount specified in the Appendix, part 7, is not allowable once 17 days have expired after the due date for payment written in statement DOM 673

21/1

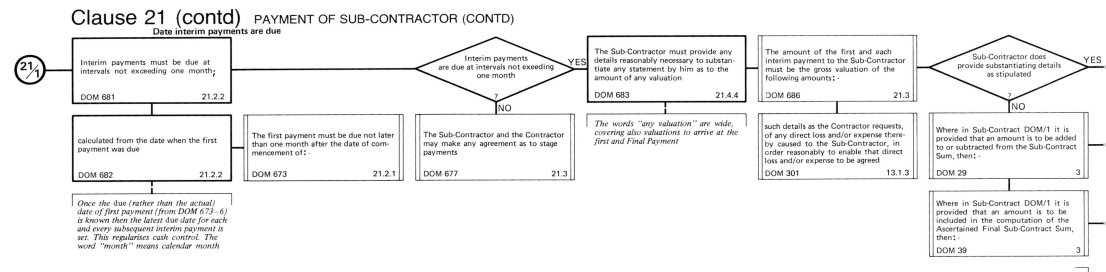

Date interim payments are due

21/1

Interim payments must be due at intervals not exceeding one month;

DOM 681   21.2.2

calculated from the date when the first payment was due

DOM 682   21.2.2

Once the due (rather than the actual) date of first payment (from DOM 673–6) is known then the latest due date for each and every subsequent interim payment is set. This regularises cash control. The word "month" means calendar month

The first payment must be due not later than one month after the date of commencement of: -

DOM 673   21.2.1

Interim payments are due at intervals not exeeding one month   **YES**

?   **NO**

The Sub-Contractor and the Contractor may make any agreement as to stage payments

DOM 677   21.3

The Sub-Contractor must provide any details reasonably necessary to substantiate any statement by him as to the amount of any valuation

DOM 683   21.4.4

The words "any valuation" are wide, covering also valuations to arrive at the first and Final Payment

The amount of the first and each interim payment to the Sub-Contractor must be the gross valuation of the following amounts: -

DOM 686   21.3

such details as the Contractor requests, of any direct loss and/or expense thereby caused to the Sub-Contractor, in order reasonably to enable that direct loss and/or expense to be agreed

DOM 301   13.1.3

Sub-Contractor does provide substantiating details as stipulated   **YES**

?   **NO**

Where in Sub-Contract DOM/1 it is provided that an amount is to be added to or subtracted from the Sub-Contract Sum, then: -

DOM 29   3

Where in Sub-Contract DOM/1 it is provided that an amount is to be included in the computation of the Ascertained Final Sub-Contract Sum, then: -

DOM 39   3

The Contractor's clause 23 right to set-off cannot be allowed to cause delay to payment nor can the rights become operative unless the crucial advance notices (DOM 780/1) have been correctly given. In the case of interim payments such notices should be issued no later than 20 days before the date established from statements DOM 681/2 (ie, the "due" date) disregarding the 17 days' grace permitted the Contractor, for payment to be actually processed and "made" over to the Sub-Contractor, as stated in DOM 685

Interim payments

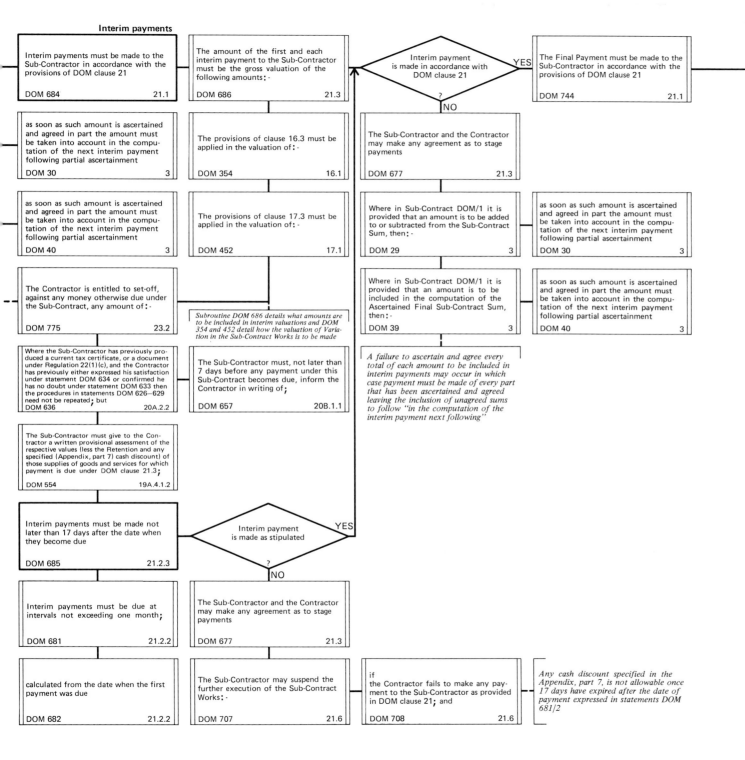

Interim payments must be made to the Sub-Contractor in accordance with the provisions of DOM clause 21

DOM 684   21.1

---

as soon as such amount is ascertained and agreed in part the amount must be taken into account in the computation of the next interim payment following partial ascertainment

DOM 30   3

---

as soon as such amount is ascertained and agreed in part the amount must be taken into account in the computation of the next interim payment following partial ascertainment

DOM 40   3

The Contractor is entitled to set-off, against any money otherwise due under the Sub-Contract, any amount of : -

DOM 775   23.2

Where the Sub-Contractor has previously produced a current tax certificate, or a document under Regulation 22(1)(c), and the Contractor has previously either expressed his satisfaction under statement DOM 634 or confirmed he has no doubt under statement DOM 633 then the procedures in statements DOM 626—629 need not be repeated ; but

DOM 636   20A.2.2

The Sub-Contractor must give to the Contractor a written provisional assessment of the respective values (less the Retention and any specified (Appendix, part 7) cash discount) of those supplies of goods and services for which payment is due under DOM clause 21.3 ;

DOM 554   19A.4.1.2

Interim payments must be made not later than 17 days after the date when they become due

DOM 685   21.2.3

Interim payments must be due at intervals not exceeding one month ;

DOM 681   21.2.2

---

calculated from the date when the first payment was due

DOM 682   21.2.2

The amount of the first and each interim payment to the Sub-Contractor must be the gross valuation of the following amounts : -

DOM 686   21.3

The provisions of clause 16.3 must be applied in the valuation of : -

DOM 354   16.1

The provisions of clause 17.3 must be applied in the valuation of : -

DOM 452   17.1

Subroutine DOM 686 details what amounts are to be included in interim valuations and DOM 354 and 452 detail how the valuation of Variation in the Sub-Contract Works is to be made

---

The Sub-Contractor must, not later than 7 days before any payment under this Sub-Contract becomes due, inform the Contractor in writing of ;

DOM 657   20B.1.1

Interim payment is made as stipulated   **YES**

?   **NO**

The Sub-Contractor and the Contractor may make any agreement as to stage payments

DOM 677   21.3

The Sub-Contractor may suspend the further execution of the Sub-Contract Works : -

DOM 707   21.6

Interim payment is made in accordance with DOM clause 21   **YES**

?   **NO**

The Sub-Contractor and the Contractor may make any agreement as to stage payments

DOM 677   21.3

Where in Sub-Contract DOM/1 it is provided that an amount is to be added to or subtracted from the Sub-Contract Sum, then : -

DOM 29   3

Where in Sub-Contract DOM/1 it is provided that an amount is to be included in the computation of the Ascertained Final Sub-Contract Sum, then : -

DOM 39   3

A failure to ascertain and agree every total of each amount to be included in interim payments may occur in which case payment must be made of every part that has been ascertained and agreed leaving the inclusion of unagreed sums to follow "in the computation of the interim payment next following"

---

if the Contractor fails to make any payment to the Sub-Contractor as provided in DOM clause 21 ; and

DOM 708   21.6

The Final Payment must be made to the Sub-Contractor in accordance with the provisions of DOM clause 21

DOM 744   21.1

---

as soon as such amount is ascertained and agreed in part the amount must be taken into account in the computation of the next interim payment following partial ascertainment

DOM 30   3

---

as soon as such amount is ascertained and agreed in part the amount must be taken into account in the computation of the next interim payment following partial ascertainment

DOM 40   3

Any cash discount specified in the Appendix, part 7, is not allowable once 17 days have expired after the date of payment expressed in statements DOM 681/2

$\frac{21}{2}$

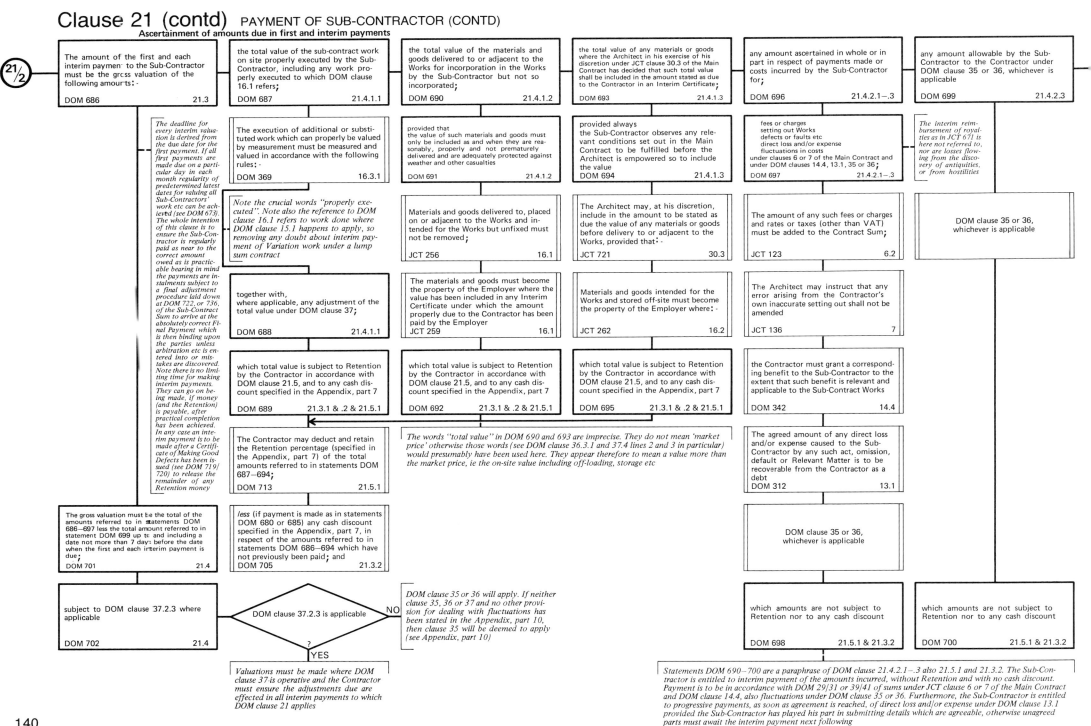

21/2

The amount of the first and each interim payment to the Sub-Contractor must be the gross valuation of the following amounts:—
DOM 686   21.3

the total value of the sub-contract work on site properly executed by the Sub-Contractor, including any work properly executed to which DOM clause 16.1 refers;
DOM 687   21.4.1.1

the total value of the materials and goods delivered to or adjacent to the Works for incorporation in the Works by the Sub-Contractor but not so incorporated;
DOM 690   21.4.1.2

the total value of any materials or goods where the Architect in his exercise of his discretion under JCT clause 30.3 of the Main Contract has decided that such total value shall be included in the amount stated as due to the Contractor in an Interim Certificate;
DOM 693   21.4.1.3

any amount ascertained in whole or in part in respect of payments made or costs incurred by the Sub-Contractor for;
DOM 696   21.4.2.1–.3

any amount allowable by the Sub-Contractor to the Contractor under DOM clause 35 or 36, whichever is applicable
DOM 699   21.4.2.3

The deadline for every interim valuation is derived from the due date for the first payment. If all first payments are made due on a particular day in each month regularity of predetermined latest dates for valuing all Sub-Contractors' work etc can be achieved (see DOM 673). The whole intention of this clause is to ensure the Sub-Contractor is regularly paid as near to the correct amount owed as is practicable bearing in mind the payments are instalments subject to a final adjustment procedure laid down at DOM 722, or 736, of the Sub-Contract Sum to arrive at the absolutely correct Final Payment which is then binding upon the parties unless arbitration etc is entered into or mistakes are discovered. Note there is no limiting time for making interim payments. They can go on being made, if money (and the Retention) is payable, after practical completion has been achieved. In any case an interim payment is to be made after a Certificate of Making Good Defects has been issued (see DOM 719/720) to release the remainder of any Retention money

The execution of additional or substituted work which can properly be valued by measurement must be measured and valued in accordance with the following rules:—
DOM 369   16.3.1

Note the crucial words "properly executed". Note also the reference to DOM clause 16.1 refers to work done where DOM clause 15.1 happens to apply, so removing any doubt about interim payment of Variation work under a lump sum contract

provided that the value of such materials and goods must only be included as and when they are reasonably, properly and not prematurely delivered and are adequately protected against weather and other casualties
DOM 691   21.4.1.2

provided always the Sub-Contractor observes any relevant conditions set out in the Main Contract to be fulfilled before the Architect is empowered so to include the value
DOM 694   21.4.1.3

fees or charges setting out Works defects or faults etc direct loss and/or expense fluctuations in costs under clauses 6 or 7 of the Main Contract and under DOM clauses 14.4, 13.1, 35 or 36;
DOM 697   21.4.2.1–.3

The interim reimbursement of royalties as in JCT 671 is here not referred to, nor are losses flowing from the discovery of antiquities, or from hostilities

Materials and goods delivered to, placed on or adjacent to the Works and intended for the Works but unfixed must not be removed;
JCT 256   16.1

The Architect may, at his discretion, include in the amount to be stated as due the value of any materials or goods before delivery to or adjacent to the Works, provided that:—
JCT 721   30.3

The amount of any such fees or charges and rates or taxes (other than VAT) must be added to the Contract Sum;
JCT 123   6.2

DOM clause 35 or 36, whichever is applicable

together with, where applicable, any adjustment of the total value under DOM clause 37;
DOM 688   21.4.1.1

The materials and goods must become the property of the Employer where the value has been included in any Interim Certificate under which the amount properly due to the Contractor has been paid by the Employer
JCT 259   16.1

Materials and goods intended for the Works and stored off-site must become the property of the Employer where:—
JCT 262   16.2

The Architect may instruct that any error arising from the Contractor's own inaccurate setting out shall not be amended
JCT 136   7

which total value is subject to Retention by the Contractor in accordance with DOM clause 21.5, and to any cash discount specified in the Appendix, part 7
DOM 689   21.3.1 & .2 & 21.5.1

which total value is subject to Retention by the Contractor in accordance with DOM clause 21.5, and to any cash discount specified in the Appendix, part 7
DOM 692   21.3.1 & .2 & 21.5.1

which total value is subject to Retention by the Contractor in accordance with DOM clause 21.5, and to any cash discount specified in the Appendix, part 7
DOM 695   21.3.1 & .2 & 21.5.1

the Contractor must grant a corresponding benefit to the Sub-Contractor to the extent that such benefit is relevant and applicable to the Sub-Contract Works
DOM 342   14.4

The Contractor may deduct and retain the Retention percentage (specified in the Appendix, part 7) of the total amounts referred to in statements DOM 687—694;
DOM 713   21.5.1

The words "total value" in DOM 690 and 693 are imprecise. They do not mean 'market price' otherwise those words (see DOM clause 36.3.1 and 37.4 lines 2 and 3 in particular) would presumably have been used here. They appear therefore to mean a value more than the market price, ie the on-site value including off-loading, storage etc

The agreed amount of any direct loss and/or expense caused to the Sub-Contractor by any such act, omission, default or Relevant Matter is to be recoverable from the Contractor as a debt
DOM 312   13.1

The gross valuation must be the total of the amounts referred to in statements DOM 686—697 less the total amount referred to in statement DOM 699 up to and including a date not more than 7 days before the date when the first and each interim payment is due;
DOM 701   21.4

less (if payment is made as in statements DOM 680 or 685) any cash discount specified in the Appendix, part 7, in respect of the amounts referred to in statements DOM 686—694 which have not previously been paid; and
DOM 705   21.3.2

DOM clause 35 or 36, whichever is applicable

subject to DOM clause 37.2.3 where applicable
DOM 702   21.4

DOM clause 37.2.3 is applicable ◇ **NO**
?
YES

DOM clause 35 or 36 will apply. If neither clause 35, 36 or 37 no other provision for dealing with fluctuations has been stated in the Appendix, part 10, then clause 35 will be deemed to apply (see Appendix, part 10)

which amounts are not subject to Retention nor to any cash discount
DOM 698   21.5.1 & 21.3.2

which amounts are not subject to Retention nor to any cash discount
DOM 700   21.5.1 & 21.3.2

Valuations must be made where DOM clause 37 is operative and the Contractor must ensure the adjustments due are effected in all interim payments to which DOM clause 21 applies

Statements DOM 690–700 are a paraphrase of DOM clause 21.4.2.1–.3 also 21.5.1 and 21.3.2. The Sub-Contractor is entitled to interim payment of the amounts incurred, without Retention and with no cash discount. Payment is to be in accordance with DOM 29/31 or 39/41 of sums under JCT clause 6 or 7 of the Main Contract and DOM clause 14.4, also fluctuations under DOM clause 35 or 36. Furthermore, the Sub-Contractor is entitled to progressive payments, as soon as agreement is reached, of direct loss and/or expense under DOM clause 13.1 provided the Sub-Contractor has played his part in submitting details which are agreeable, otherwise unagreed parts must await the interim payment next following

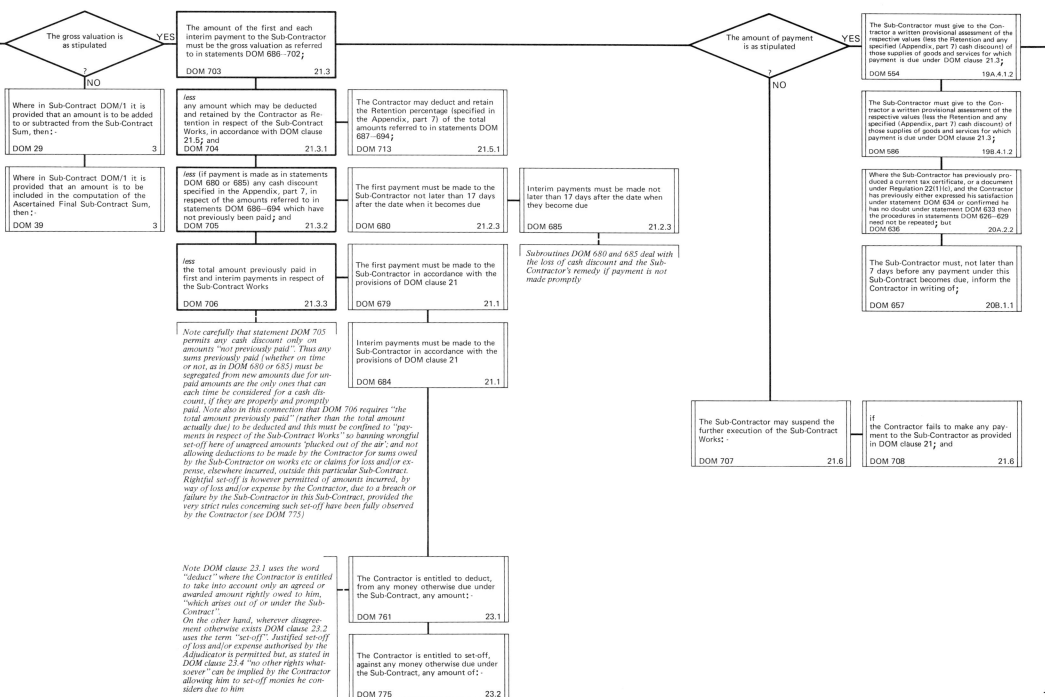

The gross valuation is as stipulated ? — YES / NO

The amount of the first and each interim payment to the Sub-Contractor must be the gross valuation as referred to in statements DOM 686–702;

DOM 703   21.3

NO:

Where in Sub-Contract DOM/1 it is provided that an amount is to be added to or subtracted from the Sub-Contract Sum, then:-

DOM 29   3

Where in Sub-Contract DOM/1 it is provided that an amount is to be included in the computation of the Ascertained Final Sub-Contract Sum, then:-

DOM 39   3

less
any amount which may be deducted and retained by the Contractor as Retention in respect of the Sub-Contract Works, in accordance with DOM clause 21.5; and

DOM 704   21.3.1

less (if payment is made as in statements DOM 680 or 685) any cash discount specified in the Appendix, part 7, in respect of the amounts referred to in statements DOM 686–694 which have not previously been paid; and

DOM 705   21.3.2

less
the total amount previously paid in first and interim payments in respect of the Sub-Contract Works

DOM 706   21.3.3

Note carefully that statement DOM 705 permits any cash discount only on amounts "not previously paid". Thus any sums previously paid (whether on time or not, as in DOM 680 or 685) must be segregated from new amounts due for unpaid amounts are the only ones that can each time be considered for a cash discount, if they are properly and promptly paid. Note also in this connection that DOM 706 requires "the total amount previously paid" (rather than the total amount actually due) to be deducted and this must be confined to "payments in respect of the Sub-Contract Works" so banning wrongful set-off here of unagreed amounts 'plucked out of the air'; and not allowing deductions to be made by the Contractor for sums owed by the Sub-Contractor on works etc or claims for loss and/or expense, elsewhere incurred, outside this particular Sub-Contract. Rightful set-off is however permitted of amounts incurred, by way of loss and/or expense by the Contractor, due to a breach or failure by the Sub-Contractor in this Sub-Contract, provided the very strict rules concerning such set-off have been fully observed by the Contractor (see DOM 775)

Note DOM clause 23.1 uses the word "deduct" where the Contractor is entitled to take into account only an agreed or awarded amount rightly owed to him, "which arises out of or under the Sub-Contract".
On the other hand, wherever disagreement otherwise exists DOM clause 23.2 uses the term "set-off". Justified set-off of loss and/or expense authorised by the Adjudicator is permitted but, as stated in DOM clause 23.4 "no other rights whatsoever" can be implied by the Contractor allowing him to set-off monies he considers due to him

The Contractor may deduct and retain the Retention percentage (specified in the Appendix, part 7) of the total amounts referred to in statements DOM 687–694;

DOM 713   21.5.1

The first payment must be made to the Sub-Contractor not later than 17 days after the date when it becomes due

DOM 680   21.2.3

The first payment must be made to the Sub-Contractor in accordance with the provisions of DOM clause 21

DOM 679   21.1

Interim payments must be made to the Sub-Contractor in accordance with the provisions of DOM clause 21

DOM 684   21.1

The Contractor is entitled to deduct, from any money otherwise due under the Sub-Contract, any amount:-

DOM 761   23.1

The Contractor is entitled to set-off, against any money otherwise due under the Sub-Contract, any amount of:-

DOM 775   23.2

Interim payments must be made not later than 17 days after the date when they become due

DOM 685   21.2.3

Subroutines DOM 680 and 685 deal with the loss of cash discount and the Sub-Contractor's remedy if payment is not made promptly

The amount of payment is as stipulated ? — YES / NO

NO:

The Sub-Contractor may suspend the further execution of the Sub-Contract Works:-

DOM 707   21.6

if
the Contractor fails to make any payment to the Sub-Contractor as provided in DOM clause 21; and

DOM 708   21.6

YES:

The Sub-Contractor must give to the Contractor a written provisional assessment of the respective values (less the Retention and any specified (Appendix, part 7) cash discount) of those supplies of goods and services for which payment is due under DOM clause 21.3;

DOM 554   19A.4.1.2

The Sub-Contractor must give to the Contractor a written provisional assessment of the respective values (less the Retention and any specified (Appendix, part 7) cash discount) of those supplies of goods and services for which payment is due under DOM clause 21.3;

DOM 586   19B.4.1.2

Where the Sub-Contractor has previously produced a current tax certificate, or a document under Regulation 22(1)(c), and the Contractor has previously either expressed his satisfaction under statement DOM 634 or confirmed he has no doubt under statement DOM 633 then the procedures in statements DOM 626–629 need not be repeated; but

DOM 636   20A.2.2

The Sub-Contractor must, not later than 7 days before any payment under this Sub-Contract becomes due, inform the Contractor in writing of;

DOM 657   20B.1.1

21/3

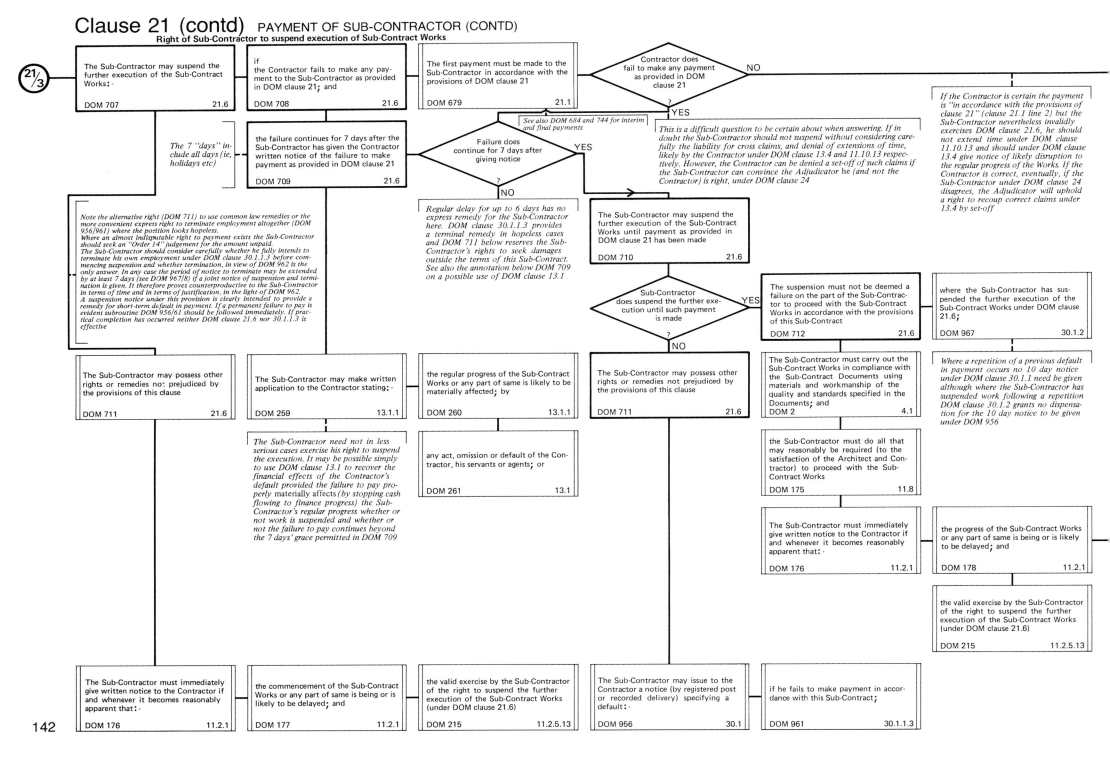

21/3

The Sub-Contractor may suspend the further execution of the Sub-Contract Works: -
DOM 707   21.6

if the Contractor fails to make any payment to the Sub-Contractor as provided in DOM clause 21; and
DOM 708   21.6

The first payment must be made to the Sub-Contractor in accordance with the provisions of DOM clause 21
DOM 679   21.1

Contractor does fail to make any payment as provided in DOM clause 21   NO
?
YES

If the Contractor is certain the payment is "in accordance with the provisions of clause 21" (clause 21.1 line 2) but the Sub-Contractor nevertheless invalidly exercises DOM clause 21.6, he should not extend time under DOM clause 11.10.13 and should under DOM clause 13.4 give notice of likely disruption to the regular progress of the Works. If the Contractor is correct, eventually, if the Sub-Contractor under DOM clause 24 disagrees, the Adjudicator will uphold a right to recoup correct claims under 13.4 by set-off

The 7 "days" include all days (ie, holidays etc)

the failure continues for 7 days after the Sub-Contractor has given the Contractor written notice of the failure to make payment as provided in DOM clause 21
DOM 709   21.6

See also DOM 684 and 744 for interim and final payments

Failure does continue for 7 days after giving notice   YES
?
NO

This is a difficult question to be certain about when answering. If in doubt the Sub-Contractor should not suspend without considering carefully the liability for cross claims, and denial of extensions of time, likely by the Contractor under DOM clause 13.4 and 11.10.13 respectively. However, the Contractor can be denied a set-off of such claims if the Sub-Contractor can convince the Adjudicator he (and not the Contractor) is right, under DOM clause 24

Note the alternative right (DOM 711) to use common law remedies or the more convenient express right to terminate employment altogether (DOM 956/961) where the position looks hopeless.
Where an almost indisputable right to payment exists the Sub-Contractor should seek an "Order 14" judgement for the amount unpaid.
The Sub-Contractor should consider carefully whether he fully intends to terminate his own employment under DOM clause 30.1.1.3 before commencing suspension and whether termination, in view of DOM 962 is the only answer. In any case the period of notice to terminate may be extended by at least 7 days (see DOM 967/8) if a joint notice of suspension and termination is given. It therefore proves counterproductive to the Sub-Contractor in terms of time and in terms of justification, in the light of DOM 962.
A suspension notice under this provision is clearly intended to provide a remedy for short-term default in payment. If a permanent failure to pay is evident subroutine DOM 956/61 should be followed immediately. If practical completion has occurred neither DOM clause 21.6 nor 30.1.1.3 is effective

Regular delay for up to 6 days has no express remedy for the Sub-Contractor here. DOM clause 30.1.1.3 provides a terminal remedy in hopeless cases and DOM 711 below reserves the Sub-Contractor's rights to seek damages outside the terms of this Sub-Contract. See also the annotation below DOM 709 on a possible use of DOM clause 13.1

The Sub-Contractor may suspend the further execution of the Sub-Contract Works until payment as provided in DOM clause 21 has been made
DOM 710   21.6

Sub-Contractor does suspend the further execution until such payment is made   YES
?
NO

The suspension must not be deemed a suspension on the part of the Sub-Contractor to proceed with the Sub-Contract Works in accordance with the provisions of this Sub-Contract
DOM 712   21.6

where the Sub-Contractor has suspended the further execution of the Sub-Contract Works under DOM clause 21.6;
DOM 967   30.1.2

The Sub-Contractor may possess other rights or remedies not prejudiced by the provisions of this clause
DOM 711   21.6

The Sub-Contractor may make written application to the Contractor stating: -
DOM 259   13.1.1

the regular progress of the Sub-Contract Works or any part of same is likely to be materially affected; by
DOM 260   13.1.1

The Sub-Contractor may possess other rights or remedies not prejudiced by the provisions of this clause
DOM 711   21.6

The Sub-Contractor must carry out the Sub-Contract Works in compliance with the Sub-Contract Documents using materials and workmanship of the quality and standards specified in the Documents; and
DOM 2   4.1

Where a repetition of a previous default in payment occurs no 10 day notice under DOM clause 30.1.1 need be given although where the Sub-Contractor has suspended work following a repetition DOM clause 30.1.2 grants no dispensation for the 10 day notice to be given under DOM 956

The Sub-Contractor need not in less serious cases exercise his right to suspend the execution. It may be possible simply to use DOM clause 13.1 to recover the financial effects of the Contractor's default provided the failure to pay properly materially affects (by stopping cash flowing to finance progress) the Sub-Contractor's regular progress whether or not work is suspended and whether or not the failure to pay continues beyond the 7 days' grace permitted in DOM 709

any act, omission or default of the Contractor, his servants or agents; or
DOM 261   13.1

the Sub-Contractor must do all that may reasonably be required (to the satisfaction of the Architect and Contractor) to proceed with the Sub-Contract Works
DOM 175   11.8

The Sub-Contractor must immediately give written notice to the Contractor if and whenever it becomes reasonably apparent that: -
DOM 176   11.2.1

the progress of the Sub-Contract Works or any part of same is being or is likely to be delayed; and
DOM 178   11.2.1

the valid exercise by the Sub-Contractor of the right to suspend the further execution of the Sub-Contract Works (under DOM clause 21.6)
DOM 215   11.2.5.13

The Sub-Contractor must immediately give written notice to the Contractor if and whenever it becomes reasonably apparent that: -
DOM 176   11.2.1

the commencement of the Sub-Contract Works or any part of same is being or is likely to be delayed; and
DOM 177   11.2.1

the valid exercise by the Sub-Contractor of the right to suspend the further execution of the Sub-Contract Works (under DOM clause 21.6)
DOM 215   11.2.5.13

The Sub-Contractor may issue to the Contractor a notice (by registered post or recorded delivery) specifying a default: -
DOM 956   30.1

if he fails to make payment in accordance with this Sub-Contract;
DOM 961   30.1.1.3

The provisions of this clause are not to prejudice any other rights or remedies which the Sub-Contractor may possess

DOM 293   13.5

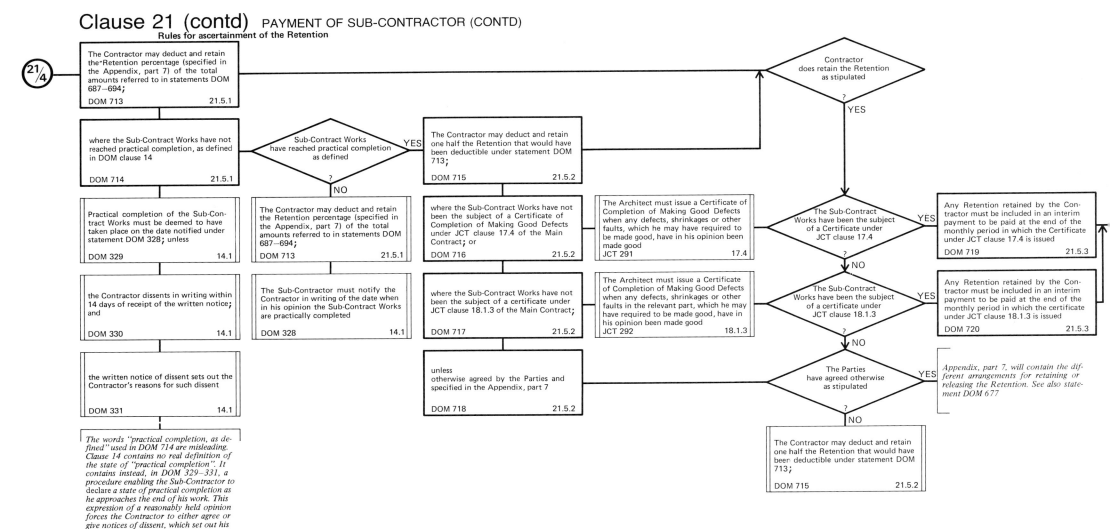

21/4

The Contractor may deduct and retain the Retention percentage (specified in the Appendix, part 7) of the total amounts referred to in statements DOM 687—694;

DOM 713   21.5.1

---

where the Sub-Contract Works have not reached practical completion, as defined in DOM clause 14

DOM 714   21.5.1

Sub-Contract Works have reached practical completion as defined   **YES**   **?**   **NO**

The Contractor may deduct and retain one half the Retention that would have been deductible under statement DOM 713;

DOM 715   21.5.2

Practical completion of the Sub-Contract Works must be deemed to have taken place on the date notified under statement DOM 328; unless

DOM 329   14.1

The Contractor may deduct and retain the Retention percentage (specified in the Appendix, part 7) of the total amounts referred to in statements DOM 687—694;

DOM 713   21.5.1

where the Sub-Contract Works have not been the subject of a Certificate of Completion of Making Good Defects under JCT clause 17.4 of the Main Contract; or

DOM 716   21.5.2

The Architect must issue a Certificate of Completion of Making Good Defects when any defects, shrinkages or other faults, which he may have required to be made good, have in his opinion been made good

JCT 291   17.4

---

the Contractor dissents in writing within 14 days of receipt of the written notice; and

DOM 330   14.1

The Sub-Contractor must notify the Contractor in writing of the date when in his opinion the Sub-Contract Works are practically completed

DOM 328   14.1

where the Sub-Contract Works have not been the subject of a certificate under JCT clause 18.1.3 of the Main Contract;

DOM 717   21.5.2

The Architect must issue a Certificate of Completion of Making Good Defects when any defects, shrinkages or other faults in the relevant part, which he may have required to be made good, have in his opinion been made good

JCT 292   18.1.3

---

the written notice of dissent sets out the Contractor's reasons for such dissent

DOM 331   14.1

unless
otherwise agreed by the Parties and specified in the Appendix, part 7

DOM 718   21.5.2

Contractor does retain the Retention as stipulated   **?**   **YES**

The Sub-Contract Works have been the subject of a Certificate under JCT clause 17.4   **YES**   **?**   **NO**

Any Retention retained by the Contractor must be included in an interim payment to be paid at the end of the monthly period in which the Certificate under JCT clause 17.4 is issued

DOM 719   21.5.3

The Sub-Contract Works have been the subject of a certificate under JCT clause 18.1.3   **YES**   **?**   **NO**

Any Retention retained by the Contractor must be included in an interim payment to be paid at the end of the monthly period in which the certificate under JCT clause 18.1.3 is issued

DOM 720   21.5.3

The Parties have agreed otherwise as stipulated   **YES**   **?**   **NO**

Appendix, part 7, will contain the different arrangements for retaining or releasing the Retention. See also statement DOM 677

The Contractor may deduct and retain one half the Retention that would have been deductible under statement DOM 713;

DOM 715   21.5.2

The words "practical completion, as defined" used in DOM 714 are misleading. Clause 14 contains no real definition of the state of "practical completion". It contains instead, in DOM 329–331, a procedure enabling the Sub-Contractor to declare a state of practical completion as he approaches the end of his work. This expression of a reasonably held opinion forces the Contractor to either agree or give notices of dissent, which set out his reasons for disagreeing. These reasons, if absolutely comprehensive (which they are not obliged to be), will in effect tell the Sub-Contractor what he has to do to achieve what the parties will eventually agree is "practical completion"

The Sub-Contractor must under DOM clause 19A recover from the Contractor VAT properly chargeable by the Commissioners on the Sub-Contractor on the supply of goods and services under the Sub-Contract

DOM 547   19A.2

The Sub-Contractor must under DOM clause 19B recover from the Contractor VAT properly chargeable by the Commissioners on the Sub-Contractor on the supply of goods and services under the Sub-Contract

DOM 578   19B.2

Where the Sub-Contractor has previously produced a current tax certificate, or a document under Regulation 22(1)(c), and the Contractor has previously either expressed his satisfaction under statement DOM 634 or confirmed he has no doubt under statement DOM 633 then the procedures in statements DOM 626—629 need not be repeated; but

DOM 636   20A.2.2

The Sub-Contractor must, not later than 7 days before any payment under this Sub-Contract becomes due, inform the Contractor in writing of;

DOM 657   20B.1.1

YES

Any Retention is included in an interim payment at the end of the monthly period stipulated

?

NO

The Contractor is entitled to set-off, against any money otherwise due under the Sub-Contract, any amount of: -

DOM 775   23.2

Unless the Contractor has invoked his rights under DOM clause 23.2 Order 14 proceedings should be commenced if payment is not made. The Court will order indisputably due money to be paid and may refer arguable amounts to arbitration. They will not allow the Contractor to keep the Sub-Contractor out of this Retention in its entirety on vaguely disputable matters; neither should the Adjudicator (if DOM clause 23 is used) although in the relatively short time available to the Adjudicator there may be a natural tendency to order the money be deposited with the Trustee-Stakeholder

Final adjustment of Sub-Contract Sum — Items to be included

21/5

The Sub-Contractor must (where DOM clause 15.1 applies) send to the Contractor, before or within a reasonable time after practical completion of the Sub-Contract Works, all documents necessary for the purpose of the adjustment of the Sub-Contract Sum

DOM 721   21.7.1

DOM clause 15.1 does apply ?   YES / NO

Sub-Contractor does send all documents as stipulated ?   YES / NO

The Sub-Contract Sum, where DOM clause 15.1 applies, must be adjusted as follows:-

DOM 722   21.7.2

there must be deducted all provisional sums and the value of all work described as Provisional included in the Sub-Contract Documents

DOM 723   21.7.2.1

there must be deducted the amount of the valuation under DOM clause 16.3.2 of items omitted in accordance with a Variation required by a direction of the Contractor;

DOM 724   21.7.2.2

Practical completion of the Sub-Contract Works must be deemed to have taken place on the date notified under statement DOM 328; unless

DOM 329   14.1

The Sub-Contractor must provide any details reasonably necessary to substantiate any statement by him as to the amount of any valuation

DOM 678   21.4.4

The words here combined with the words "for the purpose of..." found in DOM 721 appear to mean the Contractor carries out the "adjustment of the Sub-Contract Sum", given (DOM 721) the "documents necessary" and the (DOM 678) "details" by the Sub-Contractor. There is however no written sanction if the Sum is not so produced

---

This breach by the Sub-Contractor prejudices his rights to have settlement in the way set out hereinafter. Serious delay may affect the Contractor's rights to his own final settlement in the Main Contract. In serious cases, after giving notice to the Sub-Contractor, settlement of accounts may be effected without his participation, by making reasonable assessments of the accounts concerned

---

The detailed adjustments here (also in DOM 728) are the only permissible ones, as stipulated in statement DOM 27, for arriving at the final Sub-Contract Sum

Note the same rules flow through the Main Contract

Sub-Contract DOM/1 and the Numbered Documents constitute the Sub-Contract Documents

DOM 1   2.1.1

---

there must be deducted all provisional sums and the value of all work described as provisional included in the Contract Bills

JCT 746   30.6.2.2

---

together with the amount included in the Sub-Contract Documents for any other work as referred to in statements DOM 425—432 which is to be valued under DOM clause 16.3

DOM 725   21.7.2.2

Sub-Contract DOM/1 and the Numbered Documents constitute the Sub-Contract Documents

DOM 1   2.1.1

The omission of work set out in documents comprised in the Sub-Contract Documents must be valued at the rates and prices in the schedule of rates or prices; where

DOM 384   16.3.2 & 16.2

If compliance with any direction (to which the Valuation relates) requiring:-

DOM 425   16.3.5

The Sub-Contractor must (where DOM clause 15.2 applies) send to the Contractor, before or within a reasonable time after practical completion of the Sub-Contract Works, all documents necessary for the purpose of computing the Ascertained Final Sub-Contract Sum

DOM 735   21.8.1

Where a measure-and-value Sub-Contract applies, this subroutine DOM 735 must be followed

---

This part of DOM clause 21 (from DOM 721–734) sets out the procedure and machinery for settling the Sub-Contract Sum where a lump sum has (under DOM clause 15.1) been tendered

---

The price for the Sub-Contract Works must be:-

DOM 25   15.1

---

the Sub-Contract Sum; or

DOM 26   15.1

---

such other sum as shall become payable in accordance with the Sub-Contract;

DOM 27   15.1

---

where Article 2.1 applies

DOM 28   15.1

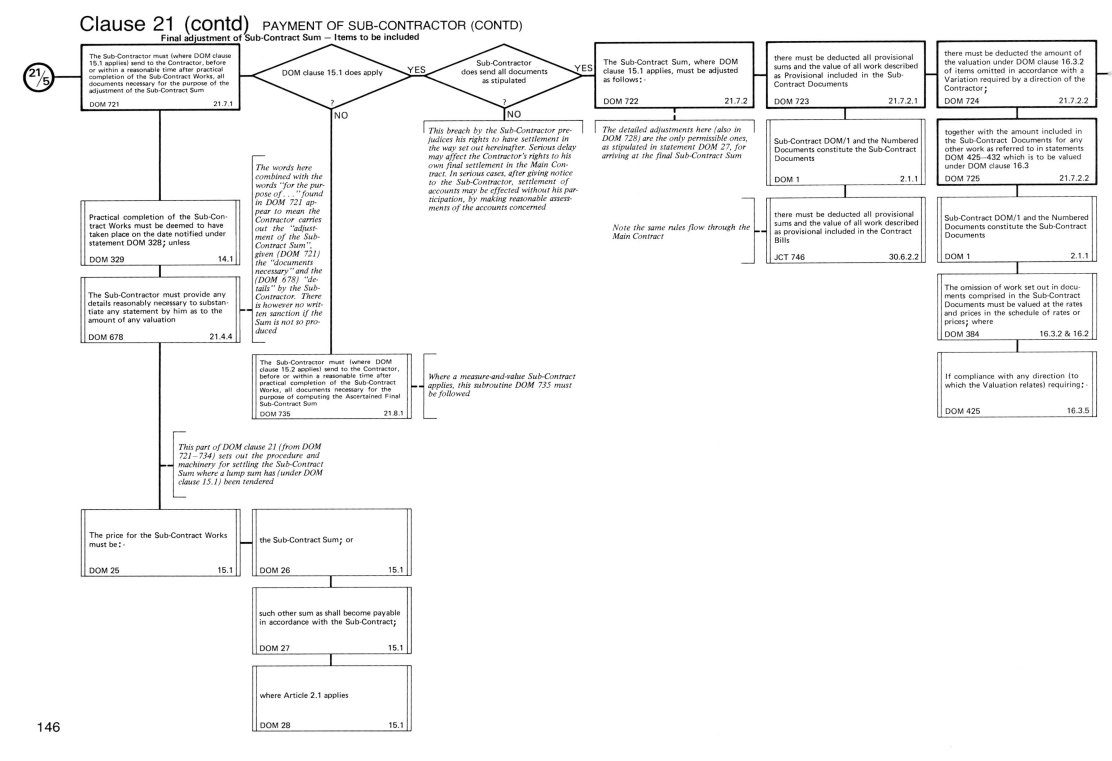

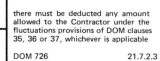

there must be deducted any amount allowed to the Contractor under the fluctuations provisions of DOM clauses 35, 36 or 37, whichever is applicable

DOM 726   21.7.2.3

Note no fraction (eg, 1/39th, 1/19th etc) for discount is to be added to the above deductible amounts under DOM clauses 35, 36 or 37. They are to be net (so too are any additions under DOM 733)

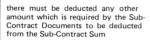

there must be deducted any other amount which is required by the Sub-Contract Documents to be deducted from the Sub-Contract Sum

DOM 727   21.7.2.4

The price for the Sub-Contract Works must be: -

DOM 25   15.1

There are provisions such as in DOM clause 9.2 (default in insuring), and DOM clause 13.4 (disruption losses) for the deduction "from any monies due". There are other provisions (DOM clauses 12.2 and 29.4) requiring the Sub-Contractor to "allow or pay" certain amounts. These words do not say such sums are "to be deducted from the Sub-Contract Sum". It appears therefore the Sum is to be put together strictly according to the words of DOM 722–734 to arrive at the final Sum from which the above mentioned monies may then be deducted from any balance found due to the Sub-Contractor, subject of course to the notices and strictures of DOM clause 23

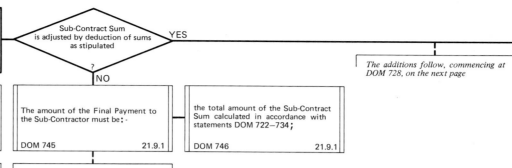

Sub-Contract Sum is adjusted by deduction of sums as stipulated

?

YES

NO

The amount of the Final Payment to the Sub-Contractor must be: -

DOM 745   21.9.1

The Sub-Contract contains no express rights for the parties to have details of each other's computations of the Sum but obviously if disagreement arises the parties must convince each other the adjustments stipulated in DOM 722–734 have been correctly dealt with

the total amount of the Sub-Contract Sum calculated in accordance with statements DOM 722–734;

DOM 746   21.9.1

The additions follow, commencing at DOM 728, on the next page

21/6

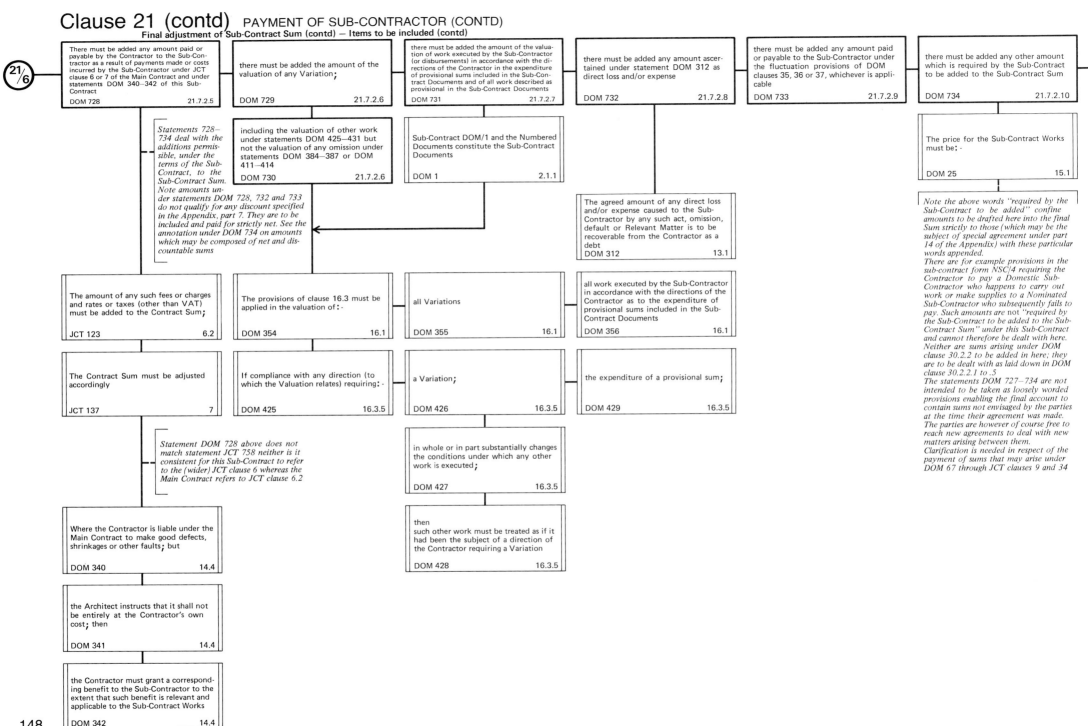

21/6

There must be added any amount paid or payable by the Contractor to the Sub-Contractor as a result of payments made or costs incurred by the Sub-Contractor under JCT clause 6 or 7 of the Main Contract and under statements DOM 340–342 of this Sub-Contract
DOM 728   21.7.2.5

there must be added the amount of the valuation of any Variation;
DOM 729   21.7.2.6

there must be added the amount of the valuation of work executed by the Sub-Contractor (or disbursements) in accordance with the directions of the Contractor in the expenditure of provisional sums included in the Sub-Contract Documents and of all work described as provisional in the Sub-Contract Documents
DOM 731   21.7.2.7

there must be added any amount ascertained under statement DOM 312 as direct loss and/or expense
DOM 732   21.7.2.8

there must be added any amount paid or payable to the Sub-Contractor under the fluctuation provisions of DOM clauses 35, 36 or 37, whichever is applicable
DOM 733   21.7.2.9

there must be added any other amount which is required by the Sub-Contract to be added to the Sub-Contract Sum
DOM 734   21.7.2.10

Statements 728–734 deal with the additions permissible, under the terms of the Sub-Contract, to the Sub-Contract Sum. Note amounts under statements DOM 728, 732 and 733 do not qualify for any discount specified in the Appendix, part 7. They are to be included and paid for strictly net. See the annotation under DOM 734 on amounts which may be composed of net and discountable sums

including the valuation of other work under statements DOM 425–431 but not the valuation of any omission under statements DOM 384–387 or DOM 411–414
DOM 730   21.7.2.6

Sub-Contract DOM/1 and the Numbered Documents constitute the Sub-Contract Documents
DOM 1   2.1.1

The price for the Sub-Contract Works must be: -
DOM 25   15.1

The agreed amount of any direct loss and/or expense caused to the Sub-Contractor by any such act, omission, default or Relevant Matter is to be recoverable from the Contractor as a debt
DOM 312   13.1

Note the above words "required by the Sub-Contract to be added" confine amounts to be drafted here into the final Sum strictly to those (which may be the subject of special agreement under part 14 of the Appendix) with these particular words appended.
There are for example provisions in the sub-contract form NSC/4 requiring the Contractor to pay a Domestic Sub-Contractor who happens to carry out work or make supplies to a Nominated Sub-Contractor who subsequently fails to pay. Such amounts are not "required by the Sub-Contract to be added to the Sub-Contract Sum" under this Sub-Contract and cannot therefore be dealt with here. Neither are sums arising under DOM clause 30.2.2 to be added in here; they are to be dealt with as laid down in DOM clause 30.2.2.1 to .5
The statements DOM 727–734 are not intended to be taken as loosely worded provisions enabling the final account to contain sums not envisaged by the parties at the time their agreement was made. The parties are however of course free to reach new agreements to deal with new matters arising between them. Clarification is needed in respect of the payment of sums that may arise under DOM 67 through JCT clauses 9 and 34

The amount of any such fees or charges and rates or taxes (other than VAT) must be added to the Contract Sum;
JCT 123   6.2

The provisions of clause 16.3 must be applied in the valuation of: -
DOM 354   16.1

all Variations
DOM 355   16.1

all work executed by the Sub-Contractor in accordance with the directions of the Contractor as to the expenditure of provisional sums included in the Sub-Contract Documents
DOM 356   16.1

The Contract Sum must be adjusted accordingly
JCT 137   7

If compliance with any direction (to which the Valuation relates) requiring: -
DOM 425   16.3.5

a Variation;
DOM 426   16.3.5

the expenditure of a provisional sum;
DOM 429   16.3.5

Statement DOM 728 above does not match statement JCT 758 neither is it consistent for this Sub-Contract to refer to the (wider) JCT clause 6 whereas the Main Contract refers to JCT clause 6.2

in whole or in part substantially changes the conditions under which any other work is executed;
DOM 427   16.3.5

Where the Contractor is liable under the Main Contract to make good defects, shrinkages or other faults; but
DOM 340   14.4

then
such other work must be treated as if it had been the subject of a direction of the Contractor requiring a Variation
DOM 428   16.3.5

---

the Architect instructs that it shall not be entirely at the Contractor's own cost; then
DOM 341   14.4

---

the Contractor must grant a corresponding benefit to the Sub-Contractor to the extent that such benefit is relevant and applicable to the Sub-Contract Works
DOM 342   14.4

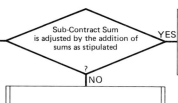

Sub-Contract Sum is adjusted by the addition of sums as stipulated ?

YES

NO

The Final Payment must be made to the Sub-Contractor in accordance with the provisions of DOM clause 21

DOM 744   21.1

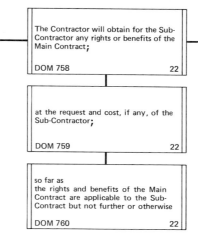

The Final Payment must be due not later than 7 days after the date of issue of the Final Certificate issued by the Architect under JCT clause 30.8 of the Main Contract; and

DOM 742   21.9.2

The Contractor will obtain for the Sub-Contractor any rights or benefits of the Main Contract;

DOM 758   22

at the request and cost, if any, of the Sub-Contractor;

DOM 759   22

so far as
the rights and benefits of the Main Contract are applicable to the Sub-Contract but not further or otherwise

DOM 760   22

21/7

Calculation of Ascertained Final Sub-Contract Sum

Items included in Ascertained Final Sub-Contract Sum

21/7

The Sub-Contractor must (where DOM clause 15.2 applies) send to the Contractor, before or within a reasonable time after practical completion of the Sub-Contract Works, all documents necessary for the purpose of computing the Ascertained Final Sub-Contract Sum

DOM 735   21.8.1

DOM clause 15.2 does apply   ?   **YES** / **NO**

Sub-Contractor does send all documents as stipulated   ?   **YES** / **NO**

The Ascertained Final Sub-Contract Sum must (where DOM clause 15.2 applies) be the aggregate of the following: -

DOM 736   21.8.2

any amount paid or payable by the Contractor to the Sub-Contractor as a result of payments made or costs incurred by the Sub-Contractor under JCT clauses 6 or 7 of the Main Contract and under statements DOM 340–342 of this Sub-Contract

DOM 737   21.8.2.1

the amount of the Valuation under DOM clause 17

DOM 738   21.8.2.2

This breach by the Sub-Contractor prejudices his rights to have settlement in the way set out hereinafter. Serious delay may affect the Contractor's rights to his own final settlement in the Main Contract. In serious cases, after giving notice to the Sub-Contractor, settlement of accounts may be effected without his participation, by making reasonable assessments of the accounts concerned

The word 'aggregate' means the 'sum total' (OED p 41). Thus the Ascertained Final Sum must consist of the collective sum of the amounts referred to in statements DOM 737–741

The provisions of clause 17.3 must be applied in the valuation of: -

DOM 452   17.1

The words here combined with the words "for the purpose of . . ." found in DOM 721 appear to mean the Contractor carries out the "adjustment of the Sub-Contract Sum", given (DOM 721) the documents necessary and the (DOM 678) "details" by the Sub-Contractor. There is however no written sanction if the Sum is not so produced

Practical completion of the Sub-Contract Works must be deemed to have taken place on the date notified under statement DOM 328; unless

DOM 329   14.1

The Sub-Contractor must provide any details reasonably necessary to substantiate any statement by him as to the amount of any valuation

DOM 678   21.4.4

The Sub-Contractor must (where DOM clause 15.1 applies) send to the Contractor, before or within a reasonable time after practical completion of the Sub-Contract Works, all documents necessary for the purpose of the adjustment of the Sub-Contract Sum

DOM 721   21.7.1

Where a lump sum Sub-Contract applies, this subroutine DOM 721 must be followed

The amount of any such fees or charges and rates or taxes (other than VAT) must be added to the Contract Sum;

JCT 123   6.2

The Contract Sum must be adjusted accordingly

JCT 137   7

Where the Contractor is liable under the Main Contract to make good defects, shrinkages or other faults; but

DOM 340   14.4

the Architect instructs that it shall not be entirely at the Contractor's own cost; then

DOM 341   14.4

the Contractor must grant a corresponding benefit to the Sub-Contractor to the extent that such benefit is relevant and applicable to the Sub-Contract Works

DOM 342   14.4

This part of DOM clause 21 (from DOM 735–741) sets out the procedures and machinery for ascertaining the Final Sub-Contract Sum where a measure-and-value agreement (under DOM clause 15.2) has been entered into

The price of the Sub-Contract Works must be: -

DOM 35   15.2

such sum or sums as shall become payable in accordance with the Sub-Contract; and

DOM 36   15.2

the total of such sum or sums shall be the Ascertained Final Sub-Contract Sum;

DOM 37   15.2

where Article 2.2 applies, subject to complete remeasurement

DOM 38   15.2

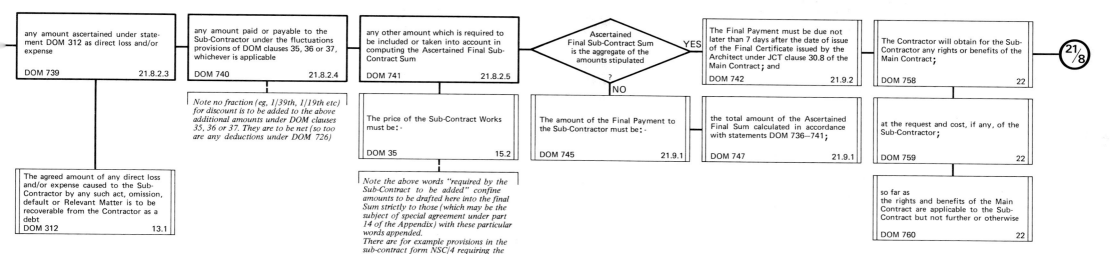

any amount ascertained under statement DOM 312 as direct loss and/or expense

DOM 739   21.8.2.3

The agreed amount of any direct loss and/or expense caused to the Sub-Contractor by any such act, omission, default or Relevant Matter is to be recoverable from the Contractor as a debt

DOM 312   13.1

---

any amount paid or payable to the Sub-Contractor under the fluctuations provisions of DOM clauses 35, 36 or 37, whichever is applicable

DOM 740   21.8.2.4

Note no fraction (eg, 1/39th, 1/19th etc) for discount is to be added to the above additional amounts under DOM clauses 35, 36 or 37. They are to be net (so too are any deductions under DOM 726)

---

any other amount which is required to be included or taken into account in computing the Ascertained Final Sub-Contract Sum

DOM 741   21.8.2.5

The price of the Sub-Contract Works must be: -

DOM 35   15.2

Note the above words "required by the Sub-Contract to be added" confine amounts to be drafted here into the final Sum strictly to those (which may be the subject of special agreement under part 14 of the Appendix) with these particular words appended.
There are for example provisions in the sub-contract form NSC/4 requiring the Contractor to pay a Domestic Sub-Contractor who happens to carry out work or make supplies to a Nominated Sub-Contractor who subsequently fails to pay. Such amounts are not "required by the Sub-Contract to be added to the Sub-Contract Sum" under this Sub-Contract and cannot therefore be dealt with here. Neither are sums arising under DOM clause 30.2.2 to be added in here; they are to be dealt with as laid down in DOM clause 30.2.2.1 to .5
The statements DOM 737–741 are not intended to be taken as loosely worded provisions enabling the final account to contain sums not envisaged by the parties at the time their agreement was made. The parties are however of course free to reach new agreements to deal with new matters arising between them.
Clarification is needed in respect of the payment of sums that may arise under DOM 67 through JCT clauses 9 and 34

Ascertained Final Sub-Contract Sum is the aggregate of the amounts stipulated

? — NO

YES

The amount of the Final Payment to the Sub-Contractor must be: -

DOM 745   21.9.1

The Final Payment must be due not later than 7 days after the date of issue of the Final Certificate issued by the Architect under JCT clause 30.8 of the Main Contract; and

DOM 742   21.9.2

---

the total amount of the Ascertained Final Sum calculated in accordance with statements DOM 736—741;

DOM 747   21.9.1

The Contractor will obtain for the Sub-Contractor any rights or benefits of the Main Contract;

DOM 758   22

---

at the request and cost, if any, of the Sub-Contractor;

DOM 759   22

---

so far as
the rights and benefits of the Main Contract are applicable to the Sub-Contract but not further or otherwise

DOM 760   22

21/8

Date of Final Payment

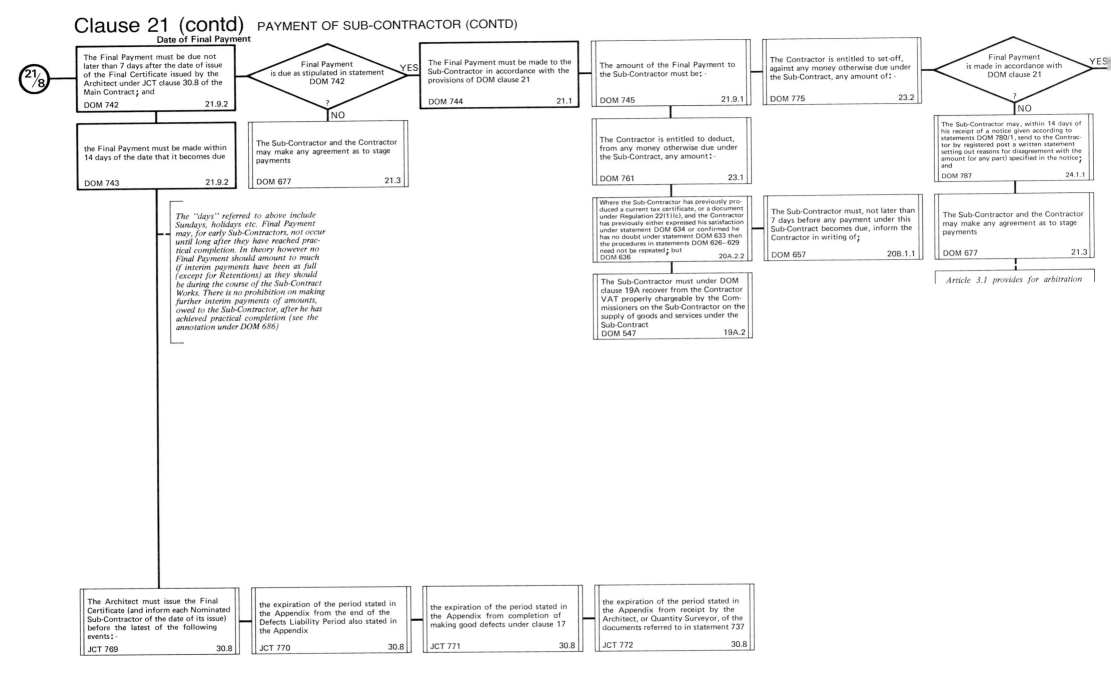

(21/8)

The Final Payment must be due not later than 7 days after the date of issue of the Final Certificate issued by the Architect under JCT clause 30.8 of the Main Contract; and

DOM 742   21.9.2

Final Payment is due as stipulated in statement DOM 742 ?

YES → NO

The Final Payment must be made to the Sub-Contractor in accordance with the provisions of DOM clause 21

DOM 744   21.1

The amount of the Final Payment to the Sub-Contractor must be: -

DOM 745   21.9.1

The Contractor is entitled to set-off, against any money otherwise due under the Sub-Contract, any amount of: -

DOM 775   23.2

Final Payment is made in accordance with DOM clause 21 ?

YES → NO

---

the Final Payment must be made within 14 days of the date that it becomes due

DOM 743   21.9.2

The Sub-Contractor and the Contractor may make any agreement as to stage payments

DOM 677   21.3

The Contractor is entitled to deduct, from any money otherwise due under the Sub-Contract, any amount: -

DOM 761   23.1

Where the Sub-Contractor has previously produced a current tax certificate, or a document under Regulation 22(1)(c), and the Contractor has previously either expressed his satisfaction under statement DOM 634 or confirmed he has no doubt under statement DOM 633 then the procedures in statements DOM 626—629 need not be repeated; but

DOM 636   20A.2.2

The Sub-Contractor must under DOM clause 19A recover from the Contractor VAT properly chargeable by the Commissioners on the Sub-Contractor on the supply of goods and services under the Sub-Contract

DOM 547   19A.2

The Sub-Contractor must, not later than 7 days before any payment under this Sub-Contract becomes due, inform the Contractor in writing of;

DOM 657   20B.1.1

The Sub-Contractor may, within 14 days of his receipt of a notice given according to statements DOM 780/1, send to the Contractor by registered post a written statement setting out reasons for disagreement with the amount (or any part) specified in the notice; and

DOM 787   24.1.1

The Sub-Contractor and the Contractor may make any agreement as to stage payments

DOM 677   21.3

Article 3.1 provides for arbitration

The "days" referred to above include Sundays, holidays etc. Final Payment may, for early Sub-Contractors, not occur until long after they have reached practical completion. In theory however no Final Payment should amount to much if interim payments have been as full (except for Retentions) as they should be during the course of the Sub-Contract Works. There is no prohibition on making further interim payments of amounts, owed to the Sub-Contractor, after he has achieved practical completion (see the annotation under DOM 686)

The Architect must issue the Final Certificate (and inform each Nominated Sub-Contractor of the date of its issue) before the latest of the following events: -

JCT 769   30.8

---

the expiration of the period stated in the Appendix from the end of the Defects Liability Period also stated in the Appendix

JCT 770   30.8

---

the expiration of the period stated in the Appendix from completion of making good defects under clause 17

JCT 771   30.8

---

the expiration of the period stated in the Appendix from receipt by the Architect, or Quantity Surveyor, of the documents referred to in statement 737

JCT 772   30.8

Amount due in Final Payment

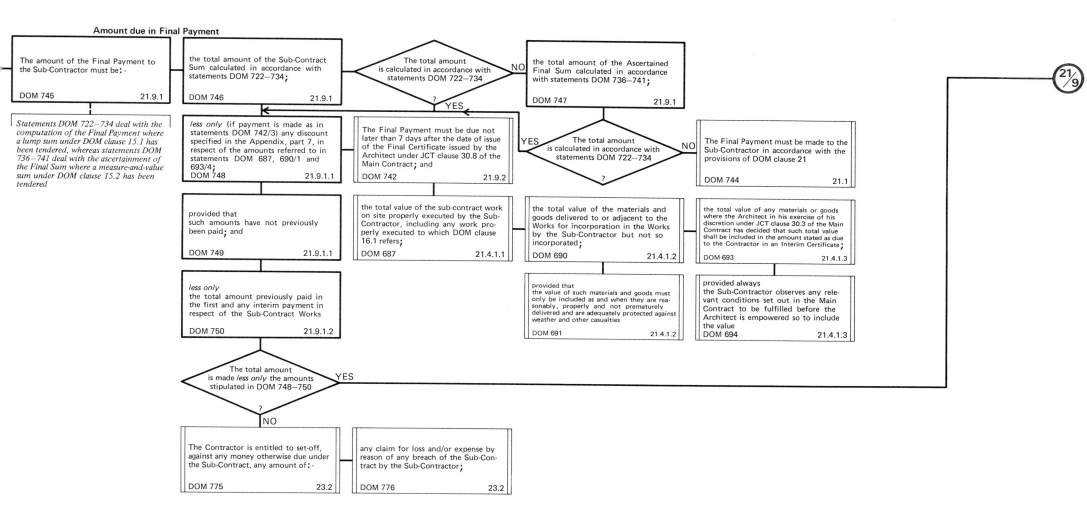

The amount of the Final Payment to the Sub-Contractor must be: -

DOM 745　　　　21.9.1

Statements DOM 722–734 deal with the computation of the Final Payment where a lump sum under DOM clause 15.1 has been tendered, whereas statements DOM 736–741 deal with the ascertainment of the Final Sum where a measure-and-value sum under DOM clause 15.2 has been tendered

---

the total amount of the Sub-Contract Sum calculated in accordance with statements DOM 722–734;

DOM 746　　　　21.9.1

The total amount is calculated in accordance with statements DOM 722–734 ?　　NO

the total amount of the Ascertained Final Sum calculated in accordance with statements DOM 736–741;

DOM 747　　　　21.9.1

YES

less only (if payment is made as in statements DOM 742/3) any discount specified in the Appendix, part 7, in respect of the amounts referred to in statements DOM 687, 690/1 and 693/4;

DOM 748　　　　21.9.1.1

The Final Payment must be due not later than 7 days after the date of issue of the Final Certificate issued by the Architect under JCT clause 30.8 of the Main Contract; and

DOM 742　　　　21.9.2

The total amount is calculated in accordance with statements DOM 722–734 ?

YES　　　　NO

The Final Payment must be made to the Sub-Contractor in accordance with the provisions of DOM clause 21

DOM 744　　　　21.1

provided that such amounts have not previously been paid; and

DOM 749　　　　21.9.1.1

the total value of the sub-contract work on site properly executed by the Sub-Contractor, including any work properly executed to which DOM clause 16.1 refers;

DOM 687　　　　21.4.1.1

the total value of the materials and goods delivered to or adjacent to the Works for incorporation in the Works by the Sub-Contractor but not so incorporated;

DOM 690　　　　21.4.1.2

the total value of any materials or goods where the Architect in his exercise of his discretion under JCT clause 30.3 of the Main Contract has decided that such total value shall be included in the amount stated as due to the Contractor in an Interim Certificate;

DOM 693　　　　21.4.1.3

less only
the total amount previously paid in the first and any interim payment in respect of the Sub-Contract Works

DOM 750　　　　21.9.1.2

provided that
the value of such materials and goods must only be included as and when they are reasonably, properly and not prematurely delivered and are adequately protected against weather and other casualties

DOM 691　　　　21.4.1.2

provided always
the Sub-Contractor observes any relevant conditions set out in the Main Contract to be fulfilled before the Architect is empowered so to include the value

DOM 694　　　　21.4.1.3

The total amount is made *less only* the amounts stipulated in DOM 748–750 ?　　YES

NO

The Contractor is entitled to set-off, against any money otherwise due under the Sub-Contract, any amount of: -

DOM 775　　　　23.2

any claim for loss and/or expense by reason of any breach of the Sub-Contract by the Sub-Contractor;

DOM 776　　　　23.2

21/9

153

Effect of Final Payment

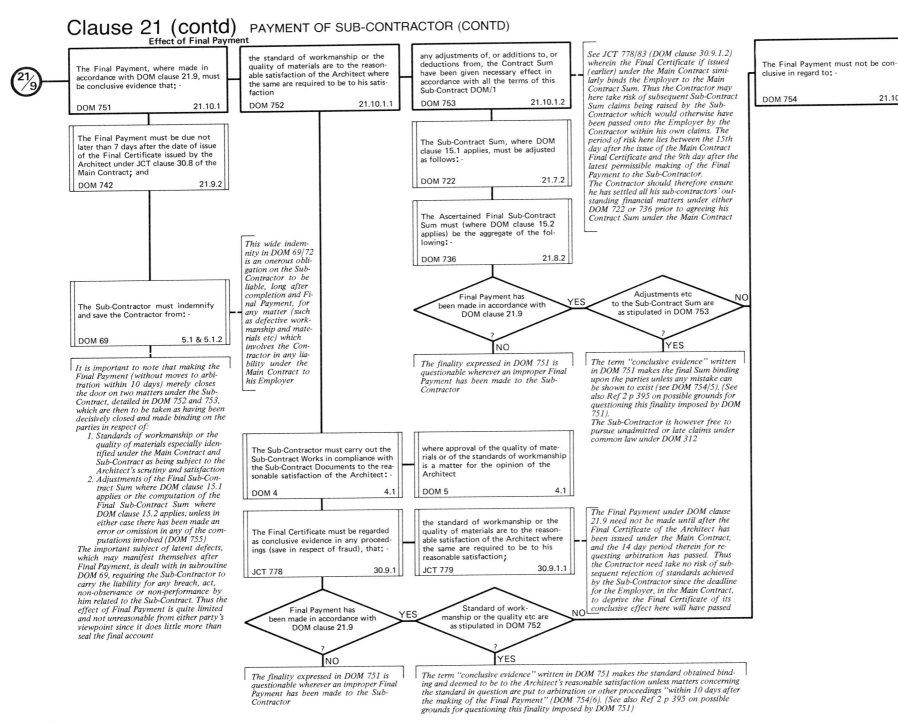

21/9

The Final Payment, where made in accordance with DOM clause 21.9, must be conclusive evidence that: -

DOM 751   21.10.1

The Final Payment must be due not later than 7 days after the date of issue of the Final Certificate issued by the Architect under JCT clause 30.8 of the Main Contract; and

DOM 742   21.9.2

The Sub-Contractor must indemnify and save the Contractor from: -

DOM 69   5.1 & 5.1.2

It is important to note that making the Final Payment (without moves to arbitration within 10 days) merely closes the door on two matters under the Sub-Contract, detailed in DOM 752 and 753, which are then to be taken as having been decisively closed and made binding on the parties in respect of:
1. Standards of workmanship or the quality of materials especially identified under the Main Contract and Sub-Contract as being subject to the Architect's scrutiny and satisfaction
2. Adjustments of the Final Sub-Contract Sum where DOM clause 15.1 applies or the computation of the Final Sub-Contract Sum where DOM clause 15.2 applies; unless in either case there has been made an error or omission in any of the computations involved (DOM 755)
The important subject of latent defects, which may manifest themselves after Final Payment, is dealt with in subroutine DOM 69, requiring the Sub-Contractor to carry the liability for any breach, act, non-observance or non-performance by him related to the Sub-Contract. Thus the effect of Final Payment is quite limited and not unreasonable from either party's viewpoint since it does little more than seal the final account

---

the standard of workmanship or the quality of materials are to the reasonable satisfaction of the Architect where the same are required to be to his satisfaction

DOM 752   21.10.1.1

This wide indemnity in DOM 69/72 is an onerous obligation on the Sub-Contractor to be liable, long after completion and Final Payment, for any matter (such as defective workmanship and materials etc) which involves the Contractor in any liability under the Main Contract to his Employer

---

The Sub-Contractor must carry out the Sub-Contract Works in compliance with the Sub-Contract Documents to the reasonable satisfaction of the Architect: -

DOM 4   4.1

The Final Certificate must be regarded as conclusive evidence in any proceedings (save in respect of fraud), that: -

JCT 778   30.9.1

◇ Final Payment has been made in accordance with DOM clause 21.9 — ? — NO

The finality expressed in DOM 751 is questionable wherever an improper Final Payment has been made to the Sub-Contractor

◇ Final Payment has been made in accordance with DOM clause 21.9 —YES→ Standard of workmanship or the quality etc are as stipulated in DOM 752 —NO

◇ Standard of workmanship or the quality etc are as stipulated in DOM 752 — ? —YES

The term "conclusive evidence" written in DOM 751 makes the standard obtained binding and deemed to be to the Architect's reasonable satisfaction unless matters concerning the standard in question are put to arbitration or other proceedings "within 10 days after the making of the Final Payment" (DOM 754/6). (See also Ref 2 p 395 on possible grounds for questioning this finality imposed by DOM 751)

---

any adjustments of, or additions to, or deductions from, the Contract Sum have been given necessary effect in accordance with all the terms of this Sub-Contract DOM/1

DOM 753   21.10.1.2

The Sub-Contract Sum, where DOM clause 15.1 applies, must be adjusted as follows: -

DOM 722   21.7.2

The Ascertained Final Sub-Contract Sum must (where DOM clause 15.2 applies) be the aggregate of the following: -

DOM 736   21.8.2

◇ Final Payment has been made in accordance with DOM clause 21.9 —YES→ Adjustments etc to the Sub-Contract Sum are as stipulated in DOM 753 —NO

◇ Final Payment has ... — ? — NO

The finality expressed in DOM 751 is questionable wherever an improper Final Payment has been made to the Sub-Contractor

◇ Adjustments etc to the Sub-Contract Sum are as stipulated in DOM 753 — ? —YES

The term "conclusive evidence" written in DOM 751 makes the final Sum binding upon the parties unless any mistake can be shown to exist (see DOM 754/5). (See also Ref 2 p 395 on possible grounds for questioning this finality imposed by DOM 751).
The Sub-Contractor is however free to pursue unadmitted or late claims under common law under DOM 312

---

where approval of the quality of materials or of the standards of workmanship is a matter for the opinion of the Architect

DOM 5   4.1

---

the standard of workmanship or the quality of materials are to the reasonable satisfaction of the Architect where the same are required to be to his reasonable satisfaction;

JCT 779   30.9.1.1

See JCT 778/83 (DOM clause 30.9.1.2) wherein the Final Certificate if issued (earlier) under the Main Contract similarly binds the Employer to the Main Contract Sum. Thus the Contractor may here take risk of subsequent Sub-Contract Sum claims being raised by the Sub-Contractor which would otherwise have been passed onto the Employer by the Contractor within his own claims. The period of risk here lies between the 15th day after the issue of the Main Contract Final Certificate and the 9th day after the latest permissible making of the Final Payment to the Sub-Contractor.
The Contractor should therefore ensure he has settled all his sub-contractors' outstanding financial matters under either DOM 722 or 736 prior to agreeing his Contract Sum under the Main Contract

---

The Final Payment under DOM clause 21.9 need not be made until after the Final Certificate of the Architect has been issued under the Main Contract, and the 14 day period therein for requesting arbitration has passed. Thus the Contractor need take no risk of subsequent rejection of standards achieved by the Sub-Contractor since the deadline for the Employer, in the Main Contract, to deprive the Final Certificate of its conclusive effect here will have passed

---

The Final Payment must not be conclusive in regard to: -

DOM 754   21.10.2

---

any accidental inclusion or exclusion of any work materials, goods or figure in any computation, or any arithmetical error in any computation

DOM 755   21.10.2.1

◇ Accidental inclusion or exclusion, or arithmetical error has occurred — ? —NO / YES

The Sub-Contract Sum, where DOM clause 15.1 applies, must be adjusted as follows: -

DOM 722   21.7.2

The Ascertained Final Sub-Contract Sum must (where DOM clause 15.2 applies) be the aggregate of the following: -

DOM 736   21.8.2

The Final Certificate is not conclusive evidence that any necessary effect has been given to all the terms of this Contract which require that an amount is to be added to or deducted from the Contract Sum; where

JCT 786A   30.9.1.2

---

there has been any accidental inclusion or exclusion of any work, materials, goods, or figure in any computation or any arithmetical error in any computation

JCT 786B   30.9.1.2

Note the Contractor can have the Main Contract Sum reopened in appropriate cases

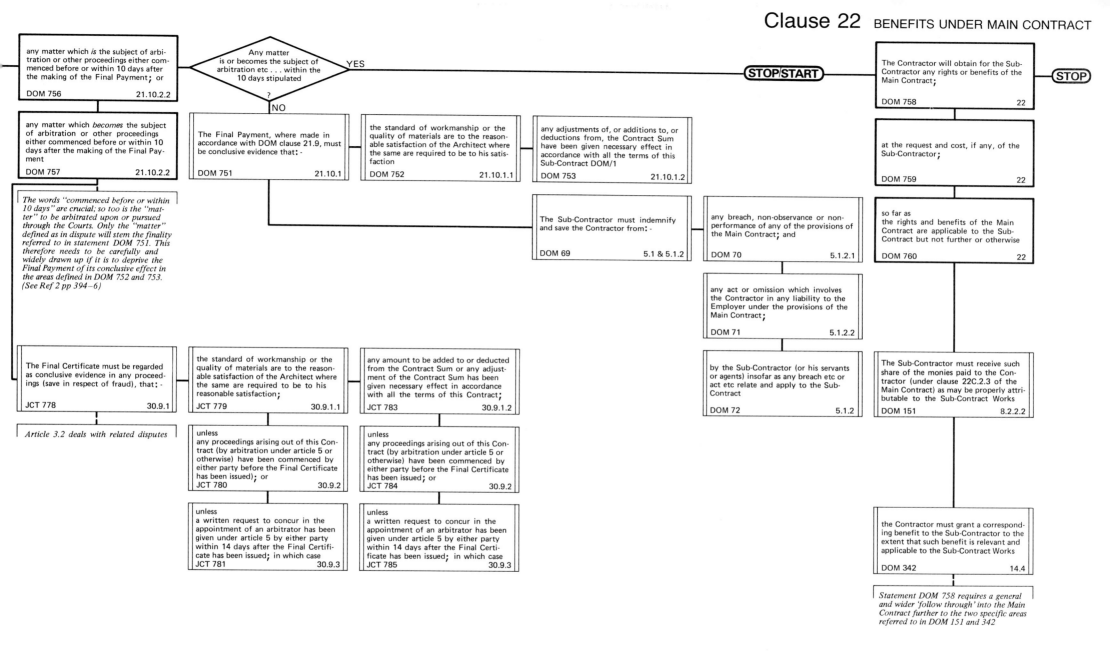

any matter which *is* the subject of arbitration or other proceedings either commenced before or within 10 days after the making of the Final Payment; or

DOM 756   21.10.2.2

Any matter is or becomes the subject of arbitration etc . . . within the 10 days stipulated ?

YES

NO

STOP/START

The Contractor will obtain for the Sub-Contractor any rights or benefits of the Main Contract;

DOM 758   22

STOP

any matter which *becomes* the subject of arbitration or other proceedings either commenced before or within 10 days after the making of the Final Payment

DOM 757   21.10.2.2

The Final Payment, where made in accordance with DOM clause 21.9, must be conclusive evidence that: -

DOM 751   21.10.1

the standard of workmanship or the quality of materials are to the reasonable satisfaction of the Architect where the same are required to be to his satisfaction

DOM 752   21.10.1.1

any adjustments of, or additions to, or deductions from, the Contract Sum have been given necessary effect in accordance with all the terms of this Sub-Contract DOM/1

DOM 753   21.10.1.2

at the request and cost, if any, of the Sub-Contractor;

DOM 759   22

The words "commenced before or within 10 days" are crucial; so too is the "matter" to be arbitrated upon or pursued through the Courts. Only the "matter" defined as in dispute will stem the finality referred to in statement DOM 751. This therefore needs to be carefully and widely drawn up if it is to deprive the Final Payment of its conclusive effect in the areas defined in DOM 752 and 753. (See Ref 2 pp 394–6)

The Sub-Contractor must indemnify and save the Contractor from: -

DOM 69   5.1 & 5.1.2

any breach, non-observance or non-performance of any of the provisions of the Main Contract; and

DOM 70   5.1.2.1

so far as the rights and benefits of the Main Contract are applicable to the Sub-Contract but not further or otherwise

DOM 760   22

any act or omission which involves the Contractor in any liability to the Employer under the provisions of the Main Contract;

DOM 71   5.1.2.2

The Final Certificate must be regarded as conclusive evidence in any proceedings (save in respect of fraud), that: -

JCT 778   30.9.1

the standard of workmanship or the quality of materials are to the reasonable satisfaction of the Architect where the same are required to be to his reasonable satisfaction;

JCT 779   30.9.1.1

any amount to be added to or deducted from the Contract Sum or any adjustment of the Contract Sum has been given necessary effect in accordance with all the terms of this Contract;

JCT 783   30.9.1.2

by the Sub-Contractor (or his servants or agents) insofar as any breach etc or act etc relate and apply to the Sub-Contract

DOM 72   5.1.2

The Sub-Contractor must receive such share of the monies paid to the Contractor (under clause 22C.2.3 of the Main Contract) as may be properly attributable to the Sub-Contract Works

DOM 151   8.2.2.2

Article 3.2 deals with related disputes

unless any proceedings arising out of this Contract (by arbitration under article 5 or otherwise) have been commenced by either party before the Final Certificate has been issued); or

JCT 780   30.9.2

unless any proceedings arising out of this Contract (by arbitration under article 5 or otherwise) have been commenced by either party before the Final Certificate has been issued; or

JCT 784   30.9.2

unless a written request to concur in the appointment of an arbitrator has been given under article 5 by either party within 14 days after the Final Certificate has been issued; in which case

JCT 781   30.9.3

unless a written request to concur in the appointment of an arbitrator has been given under article 5 by either party within 14 days after the Final Certificate has been issued; in which case

JCT 785   30.9.3

the Contractor must grant a corresponding benefit to the Sub-Contractor to the extent that such benefit is relevant and applicable to the Sub-Contract Works

DOM 342   14.4

Statement DOM 758 requires a general and wider 'follow through' into the Main Contract further to the two specific areas referred to in DOM 151 and 342

Clause 23 CONTRACTOR'S RIGHT TO SET-OFF
Agreed amounts — amounts awarded in arbitration or litigation

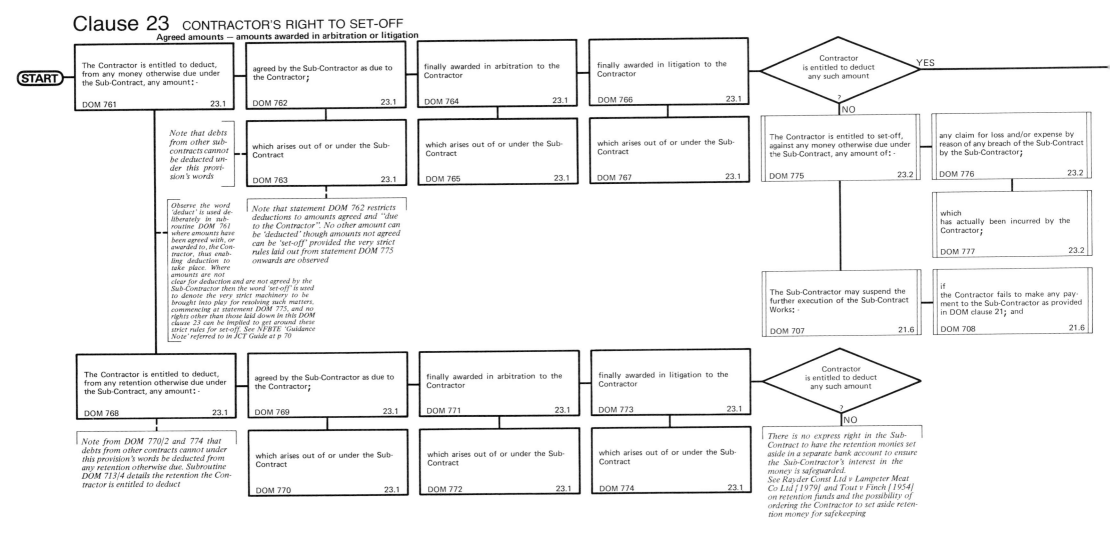

START

The Contractor is entitled to deduct, from any money otherwise due under the Sub-Contract, any amount: -

DOM 761   23.1

agreed by the Sub-Contractor as due to the Contractor;

DOM 762   23.1

finally awarded in arbitration to the Contractor

DOM 764   23.1

finally awarded in litigation to the Contractor

DOM 766   23.1

Contractor is entitled to deduct any such amount ?

YES

NO

Note that debts from other sub-contracts cannot be deducted under this provision's words

which arises out of or under the Sub-Contract

DOM 763   23.1

which arises out of or under the Sub-Contract

DOM 765   23.1

which arises out of or under the Sub-Contract

DOM 767   23.1

The Contractor is entitled to set-off, against any money otherwise due under the Sub-Contract, any amount of: -

DOM 775   23.2

any claim for loss and/or expense by reason of any breach of the Sub-Contract by the Sub-Contractor;

DOM 776   23.2

Observe the word 'deduct' is used deliberately in sub-routine DOM 761 where amounts have been agreed with, or awarded to, the Contractor, thus enabling deduction to take place. Where amounts are not clear for deduction and are not agreed by the Sub-Contractor then the word 'set-off' is used to denote the very strict machinery to be brought into play for resolving such matters, commencing at statement DOM 775, and no rights other than those laid down in this DOM clause 23 can be implied to get around these strict rules for set-off. See NFBTE 'Guidance Note' referred to in JCT Guide at p 70

Note that statement DOM 762 restricts deductions to amounts agreed and "due to the Contractor". No other amount can be 'deducted' though amounts not agreed can be 'set-off' provided the very strict rules laid out from statement DOM 775 onwards are observed

which has actually been incurred by the Contractor;

DOM 777   23.2

The Sub-Contractor may suspend the further execution of the Sub-Contract Works: -

DOM 707   21.6

if the Contractor fails to make any payment to the Sub-Contractor as provided in DOM clause 21; and

DOM 708   21.6

The Contractor is entitled to deduct, from any retention otherwise due under the Sub-Contract, any amount: -

DOM 768   23.1

agreed by the Sub-Contractor as due to the Contractor;

DOM 769   23.1

finally awarded in arbitration to the Contractor

DOM 771   23.1

finally awarded in litigation to the Contractor

DOM 773   23.1

Contractor is entitled to deduct any such amount ?

NO

Note from DOM 770/2 and 774 that debts from other contracts cannot under this provision's words be deducted from any retention otherwise due. Subroutine DOM 713/4 details the retention the Contractor is entitled to deduct

which arises out of or under the Sub-Contract

DOM 770   23.1

which arises out of or under the Sub-Contract

DOM 772   23.1

which arises out of or under the Sub-Contract

DOM 774   23.1

*There is no express right in the Sub-Contract to have the retention monies set aside in a separate bank account to ensure the Sub-Contractor's interest in the money is safeguarded.
See Rayder Const Ltd v Lampeter Meat Co Ltd [1979] and Tout v Finch [1954] on retention funds and the possibility of ordering the Contractor to set aside retention money for safekeeping*

Amounts not agreed

The Contractor is entitled to set-off, against any money otherwise due under the Sub-Contract, any amount of: -

DOM 775   23.2

any claim for loss and/or expense by reason of any breach of the Sub-Contract by the Sub-Contractor;

DOM 776   23.2

There is a claim for loss by reason of a breach   **NO** → **STOP**

YES ?

The rights of the parties to the Sub-Contract in respect of set-off are fully set out in Sub-Contract DOM/1 and no other rights whatsoever must be implied as terms of the Sub-Contract relating to set-off

DOM 786   23.4

which has actually been incurred by the Contractor;

DOM 777   23.2

The claimed loss has actually been incurred by the Contractor   **NO**

YES ?

Prospective loss and/or expense cannot be set-off. Only retrospective loss 'which has actually been incurred' by the Contractor can qualify for set-off. Thus the Contractor cannot protect himself by the set-off of sums he estimates will be incurred

---

The Contractor cannot, because of the exclusion of implied terms on set-off in statement DOM 786, deduct from sums otherwise due to the Sub-Contractor sums to which he may have a claim arising out of the Sub-Contract unless he properly and successfully overcomes every hurdle in this clause 23 and 24

provided that;

DOM 778   23.2

---

the amount of such set-off has been quantified in detail and with reasonable accuracy by the Contractor; and

DOM 779   23.2.1

The amount has been quantified in detail and as stipulated   **NO**

YES ?

The Adjudicator should require the Contractor to pay up sums withheld against vague or unascertained amounts or amounts 'plucked from the air'

"Days" means any days (Sundays, holidays etc). The 20 days is set from the day the money becomes "due" for it is also then "payable" although the Contractor is given 17 days' grace, where first and interim payment is concerned, and 14 days' grace in the case of the Final Payment (DOM 673, 681/2, 742 below refer). The operative date is therefore the "due" date in each case of payment to be subjected to set-off. Since all interim payments are due at regular intervals from the due date of the first payment it is clearly crucial to establish correctly the first payment's "due" date

notice in writing specifying intention to set-off the amount quantified, and the grounds on which such set-off is claimed to be made, has been given by the Contractor to the Sub-Contractor; and

DOM 780   23.2.2

Notice in writing has been given strictly as stipulated   **NO**

?

YES

The Sub-Contractor may, within 14 days of his receipt of a notice given according to statements DOM 780/1, send to the Contractor by registered post a written statement setting out reasons for disagreement with the amount (or any part) specified in the notice; and

DOM 787   24.1.1

The Sub-Contractor, before using his remedy in DOM 787 within 14 days, should state the right claimed by the Contractor to set-off is not valid unless prior notices are given. If then the Contractor insists his notice is valid (ie, was given not less than 20 days beforehand etc) the Sub-Contractor must in his clause 24 statement under DOM 787 disagree the whole amount intended to be set-off, on the grounds of an invalid notice

---

the notice must be given not less than 20 days before the money, from which the amount (or any part) is to be set-off, becomes due and payable to the Sub-Contractor

DOM 781   23.2.2

The Contractor may amend the written notice in preparing his pleadings for any arbitration following upon the notice of arbitration referred to in statement DOM 790

DOM 782   23.2.2

the Sub-Contractor must at the same time as giving the written statement to the Contractor (under DOM 787 above) give notice of arbitration to the Contractor; and

DOM 790   24.1.1.1

The Sub-Contractor should follow strictly the procedures laid down in DOM clause 24 in respect of any claim (or part) not agreed if he is to effectively resist any unjustified set-off

Further rights of set-off

Any amount claimed and set-off is not to prejudice the rights of the Contractor or Sub-Contractor to seek to vary the amount;

DOM 783   23.3

The first payment must be due not later than one month after the date of commencement of: -

DOM 673   21.2.1

Interim payments must be due at intervals not exceeding one month;

DOM 681   21.2.2

in any subsequent negotiations; or

DOM 784   23.3

The Adjudicator's decision must be binding upon the Contractor and Sub-Contractor until the matters upon which he has given his decision have been: -

DOM 827   24.3.1

---

calculated from the date when the first payment was due

DOM 682   21.2.2

The Final Payment must be due not later than 7 days after the date of issue of the Final Certificate issued by the Architect under JCT clause 30.8 of the Main Contract; and

DOM 742   21.9.2

in any subsequent arbitration proceedings or litigation

DOM 785   23.3

The Arbitrator appointed following upon the notice of arbitration given under DOM 790 may in his absolute discretion at any time before his final award;

DOM 845   24.6

Clause 24 CONTRACTOR'S CLAIMS NOT AGREED BY THE SUB-CONTRACTOR – APPOINTMENT OF ADJUDICATOR

Sub-Contractor disagrees with set-off – action by Sub-Contractor

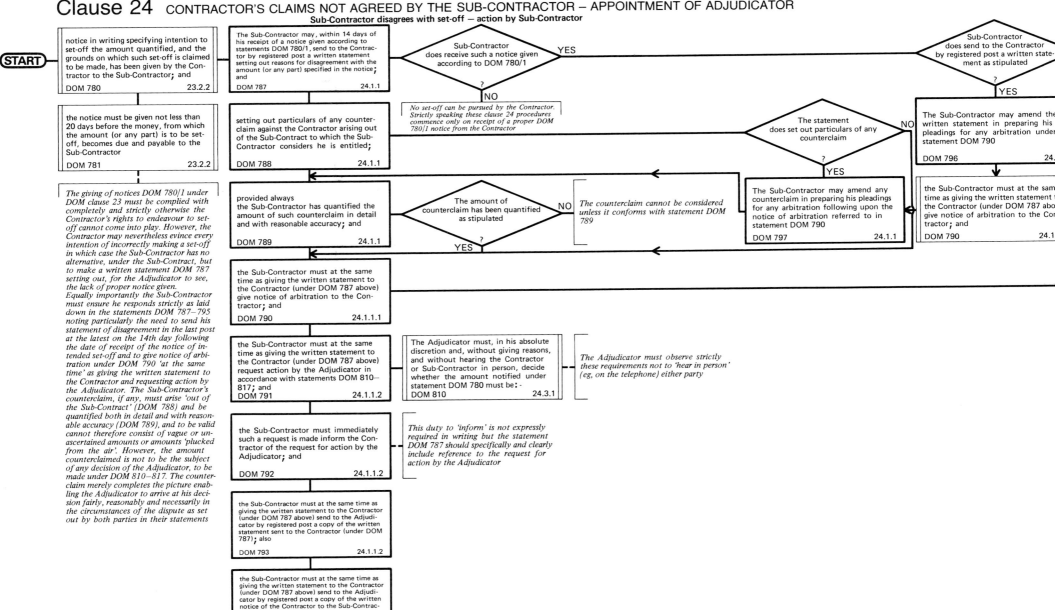

START

notice in writing specifying intention to set-off the amount quantified, and the grounds on which such set-off is claimed to be made, has been given by the Contractor to the Sub-Contractor; and

DOM 780   23.2.2

the notice must be given not less than 20 days before the money, from which the amount (or any part) is to be set-off, becomes due and payable to the Sub-Contractor

DOM 781   23.2.2

The giving of notices DOM 780/1 under DOM clause 23 must be complied with completely and strictly otherwise the Contractor's rights to endeavour to set-off cannot come into play. However, the Contractor may nevertheless evince every intention of incorrectly making a set-off in which case the Sub-Contractor has no alternative, under the Sub-Contract, but to make a written statement DOM 787 setting out, for the Adjudicator to see, the lack of proper notice given.
Equally importantly the Sub-Contractor must ensure he responds strictly as laid down in the statements DOM 787–795 noting particularly the need to send his statement of disagreement in the last post at the latest on the 14th day following the date of receipt of the notice of intended set-off and to give notice of arbitration under DOM 790 'at the same time' as giving the written statement to the Contractor and requesting action by the Adjudicator. The Sub-Contractor's counterclaim, if any, must arise 'out of the Sub-Contract' (DOM 788) and be quantified both in detail and with reasonable accuracy (DOM 789), and to be valid cannot therefore consist of vague or unascertained amounts or amounts 'plucked from the air'. However, the amount counterclaimed is not to be the subject of any decision of the Adjudicator, to be made under DOM 810–817. The counterclaim merely completes the picture enabling the Adjudicator to arrive at his decision fairly, reasonably and necessarily in the circumstances of the dispute as set out by both parties in their statements

The Sub-Contractor may, within 14 days of his receipt of a notice given according to statements DOM 780/1, send to the Contractor by registered post a written statement setting out reasons for disagreement with the amount (or any part) specified in the notice; and

DOM 787   24.1.1

setting out particulars of any counterclaim against the Contractor arising out of the Sub-Contract to which the Sub-Contractor considers he is entitled;

DOM 788   24.1.1

provided always
the Sub-Contractor has quantified the amount of such counterclaim in detail and with reasonable accuracy; and

DOM 789   24.1.1

the Sub-Contractor must at the same time as giving the written statement to the Contractor (under DOM 787 above) give notice of arbitration to the Contractor; and

DOM 790   24.1.1.1

the Sub-Contractor must at the same time as giving the written statement to the Contractor (under DOM 787 above) request action by the Adjudicator in accordance with statements DOM 810–817; and

DOM 791   24.1.1.2

the Sub-Contractor must immediately such a request is made inform the Contractor of the request for action by the Adjudicator; and

DOM 792   24.1.1.2

the Sub-Contractor must at the same time as giving the written statement to the Contractor (under DOM 787 above) send to the Adjudicator by registered post a copy of the written statement sent to the Contractor (under DOM 787); also

DOM 793   24.1.1.2

the Sub-Contractor must at the same time as giving the written statement to the Contractor (under DOM 787 above) send to the Adjudicator by registered post a copy of the written notice of the Contractor to the Sub-Contractor (under DOM 780) to which the statement (DOM 787) relates; and

DOM 794   24.1.1.2

the Sub-Contractor must at the same time as giving the written statement to the Contractor (under DOM 787 above) send to the Adjudicator by registered post the counterclaim, if any, under DOM 788 above

DOM 795   24.1.1.2

Sub-Contractor does receive such a notice given according to DOM 780/1   YES

?

NO

No set-off can be pursued by the Contractor. Strictly speaking these clause 24 procedures commence only on receipt of a proper DOM 780/1 notice from the Contractor

The amount of counterclaim has been quantified as stipulated

?

YES   NO

The counterclaim cannot be considered unless it conforms with statement DOM 789

The Adjudicator must, in his absolute discretion and, without giving reasons, and without hearing the Contractor or Sub-Contractor in person, decide whether the amount notified under statement DOM 780 must be: -

DOM 810   24.3.1

The Adjudicator must observe strictly these requirements not to 'hear in person' (eg, on the telephone) either party

This duty to 'inform' is not expressly required in writing but the statement DOM 787 should specifically and clearly include reference to the request for action by the Adjudicator

The statement does set out particulars of any counterclaim

?   NO

YES

The Sub-Contractor may amend any counterclaim in preparing his pleadings for any arbitration following upon the notice of arbitration referred to in statement DOM 790

DOM 797   24.1.1

Sub-Contractor does send to the Contractor by registered post a written statement as stipulated   NO

?

YES

The Sub-Contractor may amend the written statement in preparing his pleadings for any arbitration under statement DOM 790

DOM 796   24.1.1

the Sub-Contractor must at the same time as giving the written statement to the Contractor (under DOM 787 above) give notice of arbitration to the Contractor; and

DOM 790   24.1.1.1

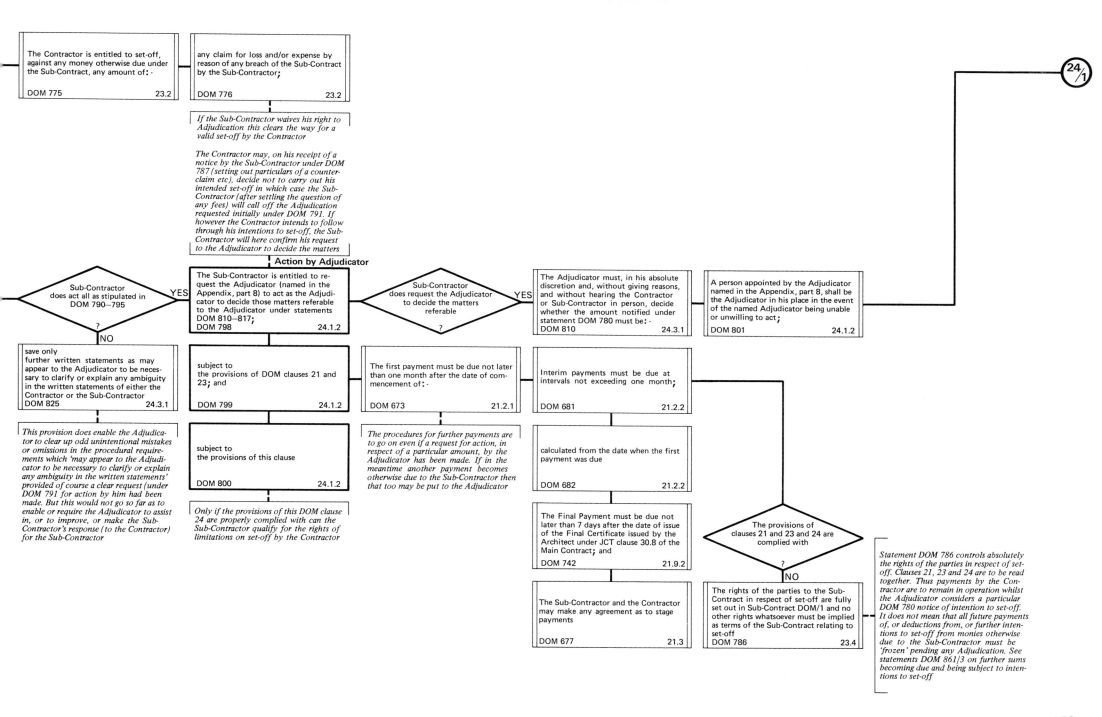

The Contractor is entitled to set-off, against any money otherwise due under the Sub-Contract, any amount of: -

DOM 775   23.2

any claim for loss and/or expense by reason of any breach of the Sub-Contract by the Sub-Contractor;

DOM 776   23.2

If the Sub-Contractor waives his right to Adjudication this clears the way for a valid set-off by the Contractor

The Contractor may, on his receipt of a notice by the Sub-Contractor under DOM 787 (setting out particulars of a counter-claim etc), decide not to carry out his intended set-off in which case the Sub-Contractor (after settling the question of any fees) will call off the Adjudication requested initially under DOM 791. If however the Contractor intends to follow through his intentions to set-off, the Sub-Contractor will here confirm his request to the Adjudicator to decide the matters

Action by Adjudicator

Sub-Contractor does act all as stipulated in DOM 790—795   ?

YES

The Sub-Contractor is entitled to re-quest the Adjudicator (named in the Appendix, part 8) to act as the Adjudicator to decide those matters referable to the Adjudicator under statements DOM 810—817;

DOM 798   24.1.2

Sub-Contractor does request the Adjudicator to decide the matters referable   ?

YES

The Adjudicator must, in his absolute discretion and, without giving reasons, and without hearing the Contractor or Sub-Contractor in person, decide whether the amount notified under statement DOM 780 must be: -

DOM 810   24.3.1

A person appointed by the Adjudicator named in the Appendix, part 8, shall be the Adjudicator in his place in the event of the named Adjudicator being unable or unwilling to act;

DOM 801   24.1.2

NO

save only further written statements as may appear to the Adjudicator to be neces-sary to clarify or explain any ambiguity in the written statements of either the Contractor or the Sub-Contractor

DOM 825   24.3.1

subject to the provisions of DOM clauses 21 and 23; and

DOM 799   24.1.2

The first payment must be due not later than one month after the date of com-mencement of: -

DOM 673   21.2.1

Interim payments must be due at intervals not exceeding one month;

DOM 681   21.2.2

This provision does enable the Adjudica-tor to clear up odd unintentional mistakes or omissions in the procedural require-ments which 'may appear to the Adjudi-cator to be necessary to clarify or explain any ambiguity in the written statements' provided of course a clear request (under DOM 791 for action by him had been made. But this would not go so far as to enable or require the Adjudicator to assist in, or to improve, or make the Sub-Contractor's response (to the Contractor) for the Sub-Contractor

subject to the provisions of this clause

DOM 800   24.1.2

The procedures for further payments are to go on even if a request for action, in respect of a particular amount, by the Adjudicator has been made. If in the meantime another payment becomes otherwise due to the Sub-Contractor then that too may be put to the Adjudicator

calculated from the date when the first payment was due

DOM 682   21.2.2

Only if the provisions of this DOM clause 24 are properly complied with can the Sub-Contractor qualify for the rights of limitations on set-off by the Contractor

The Final Payment must be due not later than 7 days after the date of issue of the Final Certificate issued by the Architect under JCT clause 30.8 of the Main Contract; and

DOM 742   21.9.2

The provisions of clauses 21 and 23 and 24 are complied with   ?

NO

The Sub-Contractor and the Contractor may make any agreement as to stage payments

DOM 677   21.3

The rights of the parties to the Sub-Contract in respect of set-off are fully set out in Sub-Contract DOM/1 and no other rights whatsoever must be implied as terms of the Sub-Contract relating to set-off

DOM 786   23.4

Statement DOM 786 controls absolutely the rights of the parties in respect of set-off. Clauses 21, 23 and 24 are to be read together. Thus payments by the Con-tractor are to remain in operation whilst the Adjudicator considers a particular DOM 780 notice of intention to set-off. It does not mean that all future payments of, or deductions from, or further inten-tions to set-off from monies otherwise due to the Sub-Contractor must be 'frozen' pending any Adjudication. See statements DOM 861/3 on further sums becoming due and being subject to inten-tions to set-off

24/1

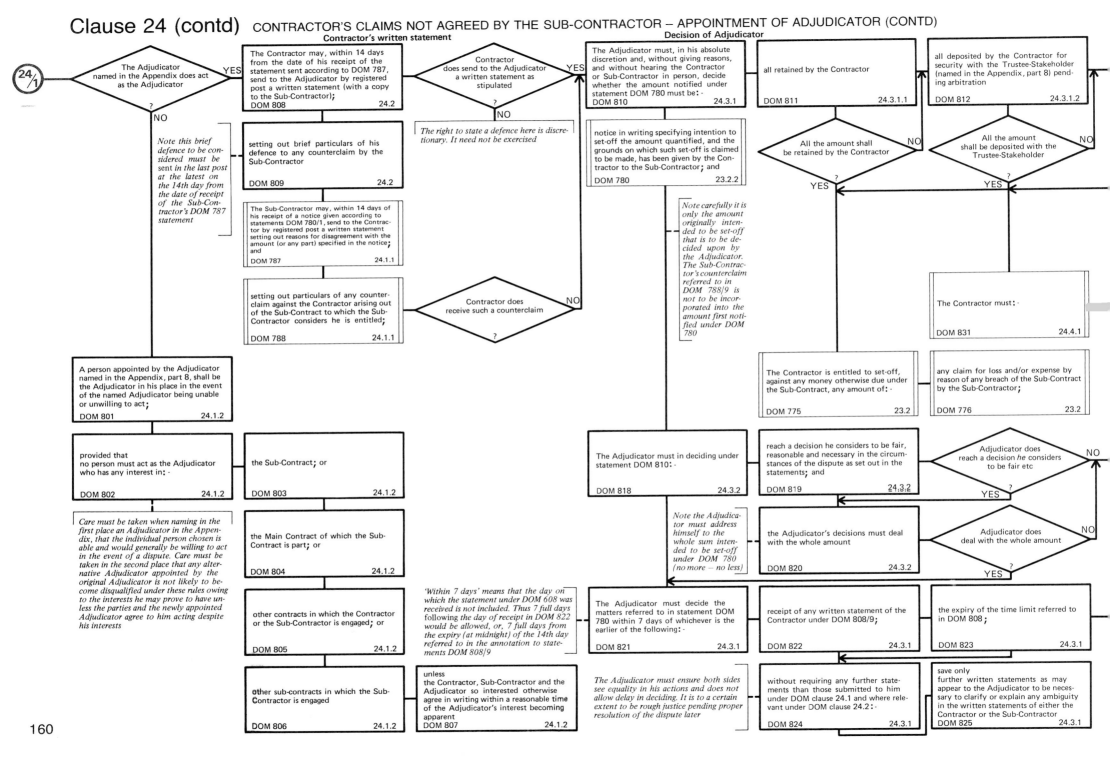

Contractor's written statement

Decision of Adjudicator

24/1 — The Adjudicator named in the Appendix does act as the Adjudicator? YES / NO

Note this brief defence to be considered must be sent in the last post at the latest on the 14th day from the date of receipt of the Sub-Contractor's DOM 787 statement

The Contractor may, within 14 days from the date of his receipt of the statement sent according to DOM 787, send to the Adjudicator by registered post a written statement (with a copy to the Sub-Contractor);
DOM 808 — 24.2

setting out brief particulars of his defence to any counterclaim by the Sub-Contractor
DOM 809 — 24.2

The Sub-Contractor may, within 14 days of his receipt of a notice given according to statements DOM 780/1, send to the Contractor by registered post a written statement setting out reasons for disagreement with the amount (or any part) specified in the notice; and
DOM 787 — 24.1.1

setting out particulars of any counterclaim against the Contractor arising out of the Sub-Contract to which the Sub-Contractor considers he is entitled;
DOM 788 — 24.1.1

A person appointed by the Adjudicator named in the Appendix, part 8, shall be the Adjudicator in his place in the event of the named Adjudicator being unable or unwilling to act;
DOM 801 — 24.1.2

provided that no person must act as the Adjudicator who has any interest in: -
DOM 802 — 24.1.2

Care must be taken when naming in the first place an Adjudicator in the Appendix, that the individual person chosen is able and would generally be willing to act in the event of a dispute. Care must be taken in the second place that any alternative Adjudicator appointed by the original Adjudicator is not likely to become disqualified under these rules owing to the interests he may prove to have unless the parties and the newly appointed Adjudicator agree to him acting despite his interests

the Sub-Contract; or
DOM 803 — 24.1.2

the Main Contract of which the Sub-Contract is part; or
DOM 804 — 24.1.2

other contracts in which the Contractor or the Sub-Contractor is engaged; or
DOM 805 — 24.1.2

other sub-contracts in which the Sub-Contractor is engaged
DOM 806 — 24.1.2

Contractor does send to the Adjudicator a written statement as stipulated? YES / NO

The right to state a defence here is discretionary. It need not be exercised

Contractor does receive such a counterclaim? NO

'Within 7 days' means that the day on which the statement under DOM 608 was received is not included. Thus 7 full days following the day of receipt in DOM 822 would be allowed, or, 7 full days from the expiry (at midnight) of the 14th day referred to in the annotation to statements DOM 808/9

unless the Contractor, Sub-Contractor and the Adjudicator so interested otherwise agree in writing within a reasonable time of the Adjudicator's interest becoming apparent
DOM 807 — 24.1.2

The Adjudicator must, in his absolute discretion and, without giving reasons, and without hearing the Contractor or Sub-Contractor in person, decide whether the amount notified under statement DOM 780 must be: -
DOM 810 — 24.3.1

notice in writing specifying intention to set-off the amount quantified, and the grounds on which such set-off is claimed to be made, has been given by the Contractor to the Sub-Contractor; and
DOM 780 — 23.2.2

Note carefully it is only the amount originally intended to be set-off that is to be decided upon by the Adjudicator. The Sub-Contractor's counterclaim referred to in DOM 788/9 is not to be incorporated into the amount first notified under DOM 780

The Adjudicator must in deciding under statement DOM 810: -
DOM 818 — 24.3.2

Note the Adjudicator must address himself to the whole sum intended to be set-off under DOM 780 (no more – no less)

The Adjudicator must decide the matters referred to in statement DOM 780 within 7 days of whichever is the earlier of the following: -
DOM 821 — 24.3.1

The Adjudicator must ensure both sides see equality in his actions and does not allow delay in deciding. It is to a certain extent to be rough justice pending proper resolution of the dispute later

all retained by the Contractor
DOM 811 — 24.3.1.1

All the amount shall be retained by the Contractor? YES / NO

The Contractor is entitled to set-off, against any money otherwise due under the Sub-Contract, any amount of: -
DOM 775 — 23.2

reach a decision he considers to be fair, reasonable and necessary in the circumstances of the dispute as set out in the statements; and
DOM 819 — 24.3.2

the Adjudicator's decisions must deal with the whole amount
DOM 820 — 24.3.2

receipt of any written statement of the Contractor under DOM 808/9;
DOM 822 — 24.3.1

without requiring any further statements than those submitted to him under DOM clause 24.1 and where relevant under DOM clause 24.2: -
DOM 824 — 24.3.1

all deposited by the Contractor for security with the Trustee-Stakeholder (named in the Appendix, part 8) pending arbitration
DOM 812 — 24.3.1.2

All the amount shall be deposited with the Trustee-Stakeholder? YES / NO

The Contractor must: -
DOM 831 — 24.4.1

any claim for loss and/or expense by reason of any breach of the Sub-Contract by the Sub-Contractor;
DOM 776 — 23.2

Adjudicator does reach a decision he considers to be fair etc? YES / NO

Adjudicator does deal with the whole amount? YES / NO

the expiry of the time limit referred to in DOM 808;
DOM 823 — 24.3.1

save only further written statements as may appear to the Adjudicator to be necessary to clarify or explain any ambiguity in the written statements of either the Contractor or the Sub-Contractor
DOM 825 — 24.3.1

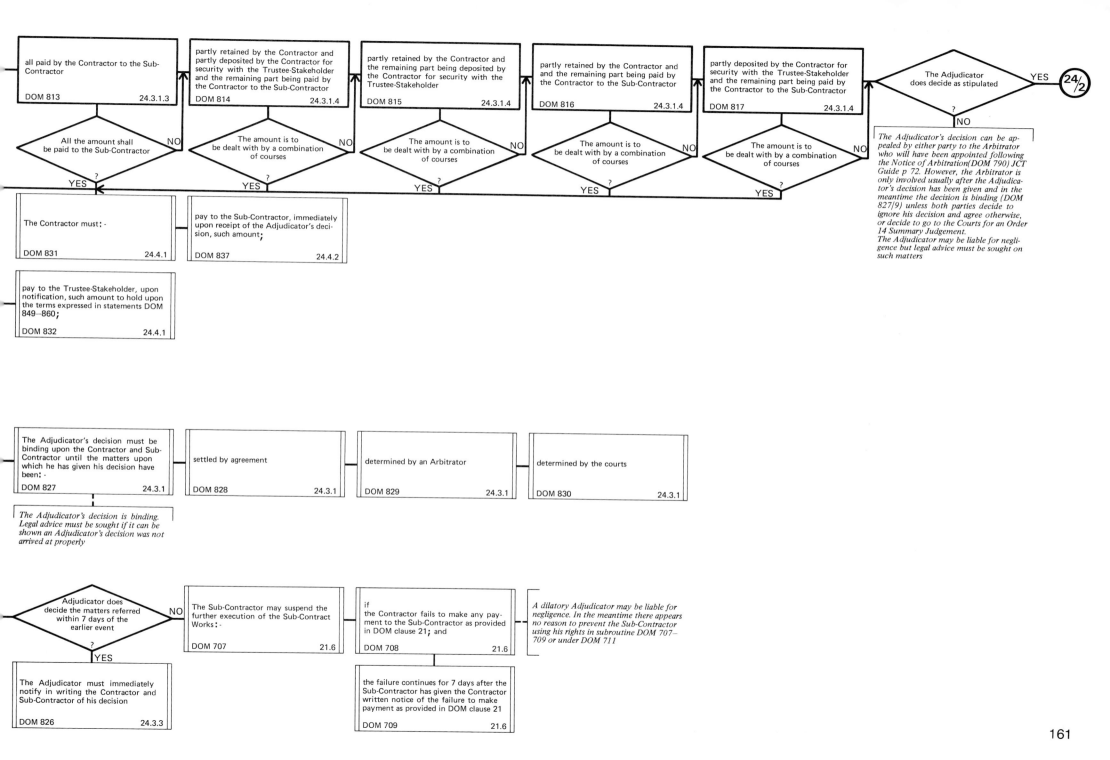

all paid by the Contractor to the Sub-Contractor

DOM 813   24.3.1.3

partly retained by the Contractor and partly deposited by the Contractor for security with the Trustee-Stakeholder and the remaining part being paid by the Contractor to the Sub-Contractor

DOM 814   24.3.1.4

partly retained by the Contractor and the remaining part being deposited by the Contractor for security with the Trustee-Stakeholder

DOM 815   24.3.1.4

partly retained by the Contractor and and the remaining part being paid by the Contractor to the Sub-Contractor

DOM 816   24.3.1.4

partly deposited by the Contractor for security with the Trustee-Stakeholder and the remaining part being paid by the Contractor to the Sub-Contractor

DOM 817   24.3.1.4

The Adjudicator does decide as stipulated ? — YES → 24/2

NO

The Adjudicator's decision can be appealed by either party to the Arbitrator who will have been appointed following the Notice of Arbitration(DOM 790) JCT Guide p 72. However, the Arbitrator is only involved usually after the Adjudicator's decision has been given and in the meantime the decision is binding (DOM 827/9) unless both parties decide to ignore his decision and agree otherwise, or decide to go to the Courts for an Order 14 Summary Judgement.
The Adjudicator may be liable for negligence but legal advice must be sought on such matters

All the amount shall be paid to the Sub-Contractor ? — NO

The amount is to be dealt with by a combination of courses ? — NO

The amount is to be dealt with by a combination of courses ? — NO

The amount is to be dealt with by a combination of courses ? — NO

The amount is to be dealt with by a combination of courses ? — NO

YES

The Contractor must: -

DOM 831   24.4.1

pay to the Sub-Contractor, immediately upon receipt of the Adjudicator's decision, such amount;

DOM 837   24.4.2

pay to the Trustee-Stakeholder, upon notification, such amount to hold upon the terms expressed in statements DOM 849—860;

DOM 832   24.4.1

The Adjudicator's decision must be binding upon the Contractor and Sub-Contractor until the matters upon which he has given his decision have been: -

DOM 827   24.3.1

The Adjudicator's decision is binding. Legal advice must be sought if it can be shown an Adjudicator's decision was not arrived at properly

settled by agreement

DOM 828   24.3.1

determined by an Arbitrator

DOM 829   24.3.1

determined by the courts

DOM 830   24.3.1

Adjudicator does decide the matters referred within 7 days of the earlier event ? — NO

YES

The Sub-Contractor may suspend the further execution of the Sub-Contract Works: -

DOM 707   21.6

if the Contractor fails to make any payment to the Sub-Contractor as provided in DOM clause 21; and

DOM 708   21.6

the failure continues for 7 days after the Sub-Contractor has given the Contractor written notice of the failure to make payment as provided in DOM clause 21

DOM 709   21.6

A dilatory Adjudicator may be liable for negligence. In the meantime there appears no reason to prevent the Sub-Contractor using his rights in subroutine DOM 707–709 or under DOM 711

The Adjudicator must immediately notify in writing the Contractor and Sub-Contractor of his decision

DOM 826   24.3.3

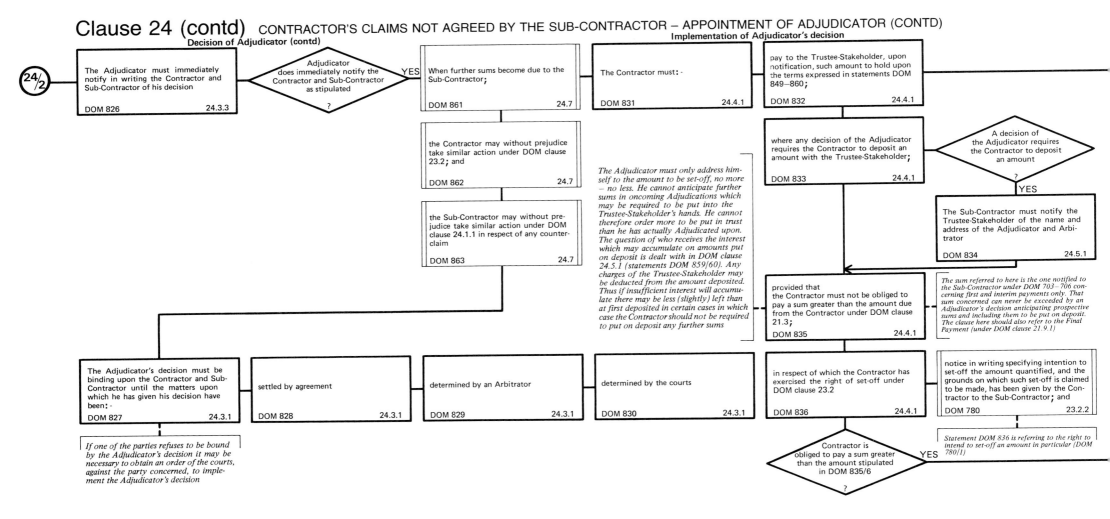

Decision of Adjudicator (contd)

Implementation of Adjudicator's decision

24/2

The Adjudicator must immediately notify in writing the Contractor and Sub-Contractor of his decision

DOM 826   24.3.3

Adjudicator does immediately notify the Contractor and Sub-Contractor as stipulated

?

YES

When further sums become due to the Sub-Contractor;

DOM 861   24.7

the Contractor may without prejudice take similar action under DOM clause 23.2; and

DOM 862   24.7

the Sub-Contractor may without pre-judice take similar action under DOM clause 24.1.1 in respect of any counter-claim

DOM 863   24.7

The Contractor must: -

DOM 831   24.4.1

pay to the Trustee-Stakeholder, upon notification, such amount to hold upon the terms expressed in statements DOM 849–860;

DOM 832   24.4.1

where any decision of the Adjudicator requires the Contractor to deposit an amount with the Trustee-Stakeholder;

DOM 833   24.4.1

A decision of the Adjudicator requires the Contractor to deposit an amount

?

YES

The Sub-Contractor must notify the Trustee-Stakeholder of the name and address of the Adjudicator and Arbi-trator

DOM 834   24.5.1

The Adjudicator must only address him-self to the amount to be set-off, no more – no less. He cannot anticipate further sums in oncoming Adjudications which may be required to be put into the Trustee-Stakeholder's hands. He cannot therefore order more to be put in trust than he has actually Adjudicated upon. The question of who receives the interest which may accumulate on amounts put on deposit is dealt with in DOM clause 24.5.1 (statements DOM 859/60). Any charges of the Trustee-Stakeholder may be deducted from the amount deposited. Thus if insufficient interest will accumu-late there may be less (slightly) left than at first deposited in certain cases in which case the Contractor should not be required to put on deposit any further sums

provided that the Contractor must not be obliged to pay a sum greater than the amount due from the Contractor under DOM clause 21.3;

DOM 835   24.4.1

The sum referred to here is the one notified to the Sub-Contractor under DOM 703– 706 con-cerning first and interim payments only. That sum concerned can never be exceeded by an Adjudicator's decision anticipating prospective sums and including them to be put on deposit. The clause here should also refer to the Final Payment (under DOM clause 21.9.1)

The Adjudicator's decision must be binding upon the Contractor and Sub-Contractor until the matters upon which he has given his decision have been: -

DOM 827   24.3.1

settled by agreement

DOM 828   24.3.1

determined by an Arbitrator

DOM 829   24.3.1

determined by the courts

DOM 830   24.3.1

in respect of which the Contractor has exercised the right of set-off under DOM clause 23.2

DOM 836   24.4.1

notice in writing specifying intention to set-off the amount quantified, and the grounds on which such set-off is claimed to be made, has been given by the Con-tractor to the Sub-Contractor; and

DOM 780   23.2.2

Contractor is obliged to pay a sum greater than the amount stipulated in DOM 835/6

?

YES

If one of the parties refuses to be bound by the Adjudicator's decision it may be necessary to obtain an order of the courts, against the party concerned, to imple-ment the Adjudicator's decision

Statement DOM 836 is referring to the right to intend to set-off an amount in particular (DOM 780/1)

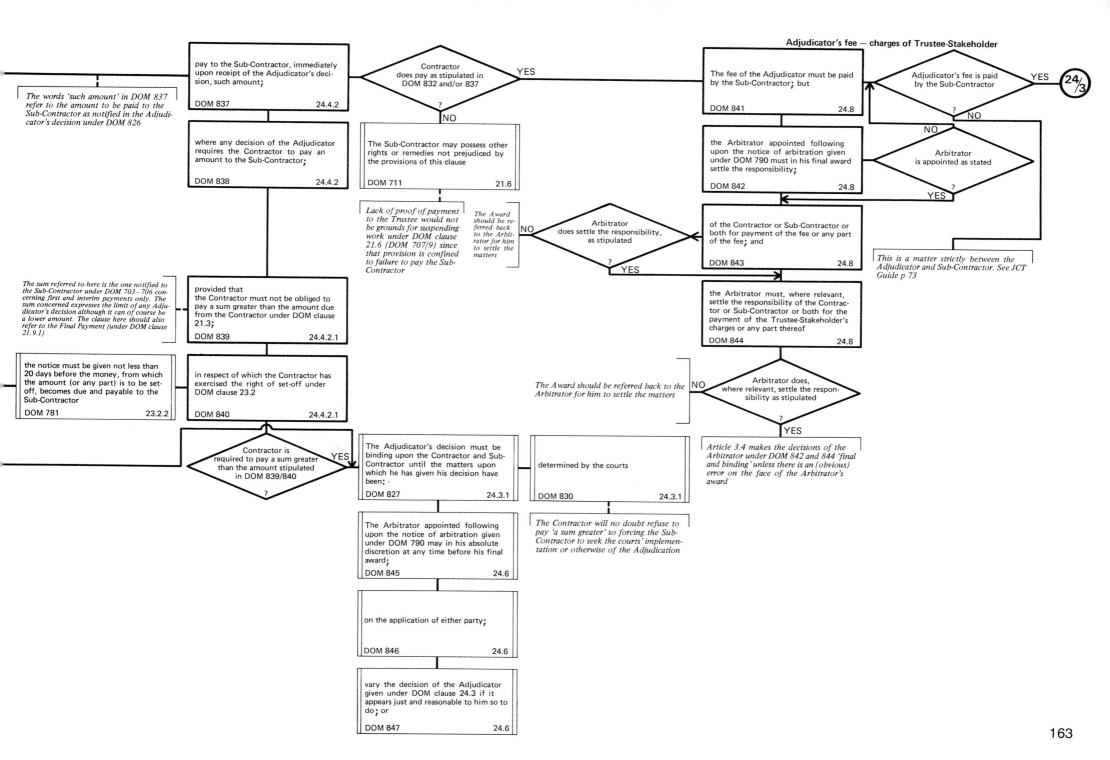

pay to the Sub-Contractor, immediately upon receipt of the Adjudicator's decision, such amount;

DOM 837   24.4.2

The words 'such amount' in DOM 837 refer to the amount to be paid to the Sub-Contractor as notified in the Adjudicator's decision under DOM 826

where any decision of the Adjudicator requires the Contractor to pay an amount to the Sub-Contractor;

DOM 838   24.4.2

Contractor does pay as stipulated in DOM 832 and/or 837 ?

YES

NO

The Sub-Contractor may possess other rights or remedies not prejudiced by the provisions of this clause

DOM 711   21.6

Lack of proof of payment to the Trustee would not be grounds for suspending work under DOM clause 21.6 (DOM 707/9) since that provision is confined to failure to pay the Sub-Contractor

The sum referred to here is the one notified to the Sub-Contractor under DOM 703–706 concerning first and interim payments only. The sum concerned expresses the limit of any Adjudicator's decision although it can of course be a lower amount. The clause here should also refer to the Final Payment (under DOM clause 21.9.1)

provided that the Contractor must not be obliged to pay a sum greater than the amount due from the Contractor under DOM clause 21.3;

DOM 839   24.4.2.1

The Award should be referred back to the Arbitrator for him to settle the matters

NO

Arbitrator does settle the responsibility, as stipulated ?

YES

the notice must be given not less than 20 days before the money, from which the amount (or any part) is to be set-off, becomes due and payable to the Sub-Contractor

DOM 781   23.2.2

in respect of which the Contractor has exercised the right of set-off under DOM clause 23.2

DOM 840   24.4.2.1

Contractor is required to pay a sum greater than the amount stipulated in DOM 839/840 ?

YES

The Adjudicator's decision must be binding upon the Contractor and Sub-Contractor until the matters upon which he has given his decision have been: -

DOM 827   24.3.1

determined by the courts

DOM 830   24.3.1

The Contractor will no doubt refuse to pay 'a sum greater' so forcing the Sub-Contractor to seek the courts' implementation or otherwise of the Adjudication

The Arbitrator appointed following upon the notice of arbitration given under DOM 790 may in his absolute discretion at any time before his final award;

DOM 845   24.6

on the application of either party;

DOM 846   24.6

vary the decision of the Adjudicator given under DOM clause 24.3 if it appears just and reasonable to him so to do; or

DOM 847   24.6

The fee of the Adjudicator must be paid by the Sub-Contractor; but

DOM 841   24.8

the Arbitrator appointed following upon the notice of arbitration given under DOM 790 must in his final award settle the responsibility;

DOM 842   24.8

of the Contractor or Sub-Contractor or both for payment of the fee or any part of the fee; and

DOM 843   24.8

the Arbitrator must, where relevant, settle the responsibility of the Contractor or Sub-Contractor or both for the payment of the Trustee-Stakeholder's charges or any part thereof

DOM 844   24.8

The Award should be referred back to the Arbitrator for him to settle the matters

NO

Arbitrator does, where relevant, settle the responsibility as stipulated ?

YES

Article 3.4 makes the decisions of the Arbitrator under DOM 842 and 844 'final and binding' unless there is an (obvious) error on the face of the Arbitrator's award

Adjudicator's fee is paid by the Sub-Contractor ?

YES

(24/3)

NO

Arbitrator is appointed as stated ?

YES

This is a matter strictly between the Adjudicator and Sub-Contractor. See JCT Guide p 73

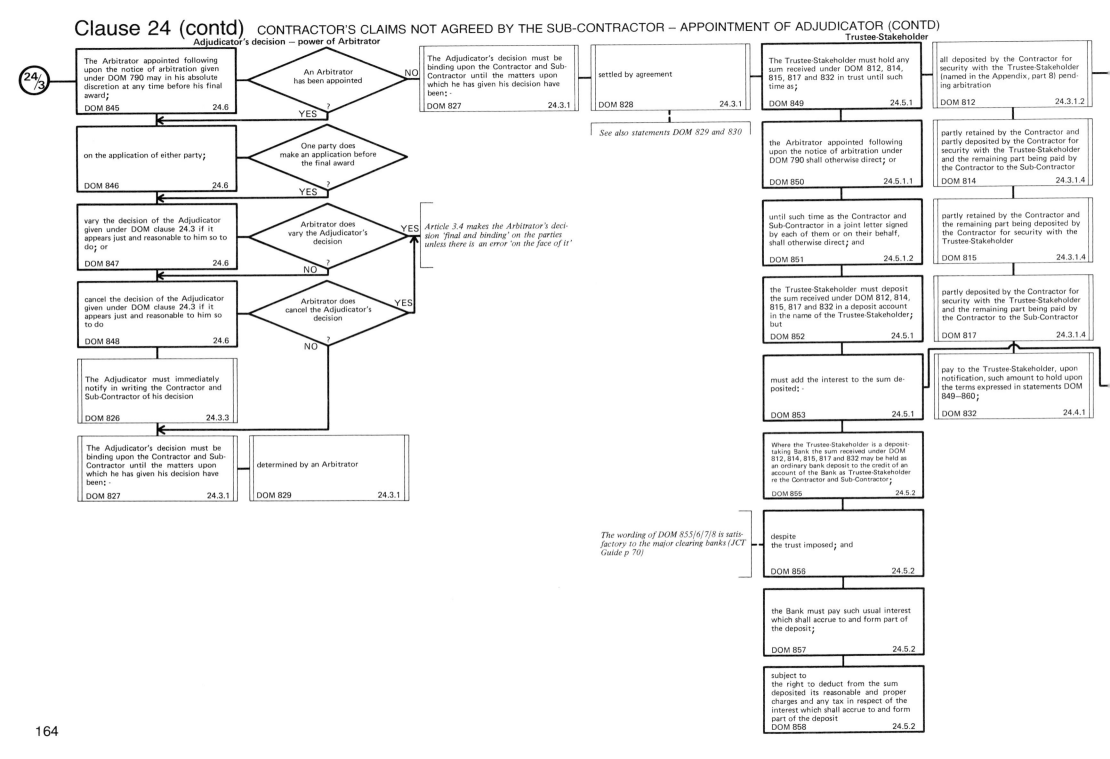

Adjudicator's decision — power of Arbitrator

(24/3)

The Arbitrator appointed following upon the notice of arbitration given under DOM 790 may in his absolute discretion at any time before his final award;
DOM 845 — 24.6

An Arbitrator has been appointed? — YES / NO

on the application of either party;
DOM 846 — 24.6

One party does make an application before the final award? — YES

vary the decision of the Adjudicator given under DOM clause 24.3 if it appears just and reasonable to him so to do; or
DOM 847 — 24.6

Arbitrator does vary the Adjudicator's decision? — YES / NO

Article 3.4 makes the Arbitrator's decision 'final and binding' on the parties unless there is an error 'on the face of it'

cancel the decision of the Adjudicator given under DOM clause 24.3 if it appears just and reasonable to him so to do
DOM 848 — 24.6

Arbitrator does cancel the Adjudicator's decision? — YES / NO

The Adjudicator must immediately notify in writing the Contractor and Sub-Contractor of his decision
DOM 826 — 24.3.3

The Adjudicator's decision must be binding upon the Contractor and Sub-Contractor until the matters upon which he has given his decision have been: -
DOM 827 — 24.3.1

determined by an Arbitrator
DOM 829 — 24.3.1

The Adjudicator's decision must be binding upon the Contractor and Sub-Contractor until the matters upon which he has given his decision have been: -
DOM 827 — 24.3.1

settled by agreement
DOM 828 — 24.3.1

See also statements DOM 829 and 830

Trustee-Stakeholder

The Trustee-Stakeholder must hold any sum received under DOM 812, 814, 815, 817 and 832 in trust until such time as;
DOM 849 — 24.5.1

the Arbitrator appointed following upon the notice of arbitration under DOM 790 shall otherwise direct; or
DOM 850 — 24.5.1.1

until such time as the Contractor and Sub-Contractor in a joint letter signed by each of them or on their behalf, shall otherwise direct; and
DOM 851 — 24.5.1.2

the Trustee-Stakeholder must deposit the sum received under DOM 812, 814, 815, 817 and 832 in a deposit account in the name of the Trustee-Stakeholder; but
DOM 852 — 24.5.1

must add the interest to the sum deposited: -
DOM 853 — 24.5.1

Where the Trustee-Stakeholder is a deposit-taking Bank the sum received under DOM 812, 814, 815, 817 and 832 may be held as an ordinary bank deposit to the credit of an account of the Bank as Trustee-Stakeholder re the Contractor and Sub-Contractor;
DOM 855 — 24.5.2

The wording of DOM 855/6/7/8 is satisfactory to the major clearing banks (JCT Guide p 70)

despite the trust imposed; and
DOM 856 — 24.5.2

the Bank must pay such usual interest which shall accrue to and form part of the deposit;
DOM 857 — 24.5.2

subject to the right to deduct from the sum deposited its reasonable and proper charges and any tax in respect of the interest which shall accrue to and form part of the deposit
DOM 858 — 24.5.2

all deposited by the Contractor for security with the Trustee-Stakeholder (named in the Appendix, part 8) pending arbitration
DOM 812 — 24.3.1.2

partly retained by the Contractor and partly deposited by the Contractor for security with the Trustee-Stakeholder and the remaining part being paid by the Contractor to the Sub-Contractor
DOM 814 — 24.3.1.4

partly retained by the Contractor and the remaining part being deposited by the Contractor for security with the Trustee-Stakeholder
DOM 815 — 24.3.1.4

partly deposited by the Contractor for security with the Trustee-Stakeholder and the remaining part being paid by the Contractor to the Sub-Contractor
DOM 817 — 24.3.1.4

pay to the Trustee-Stakeholder, upon notification, such amount to hold upon the terms expressed in statements DOM 849–860;
DOM 832 — 24.4.1

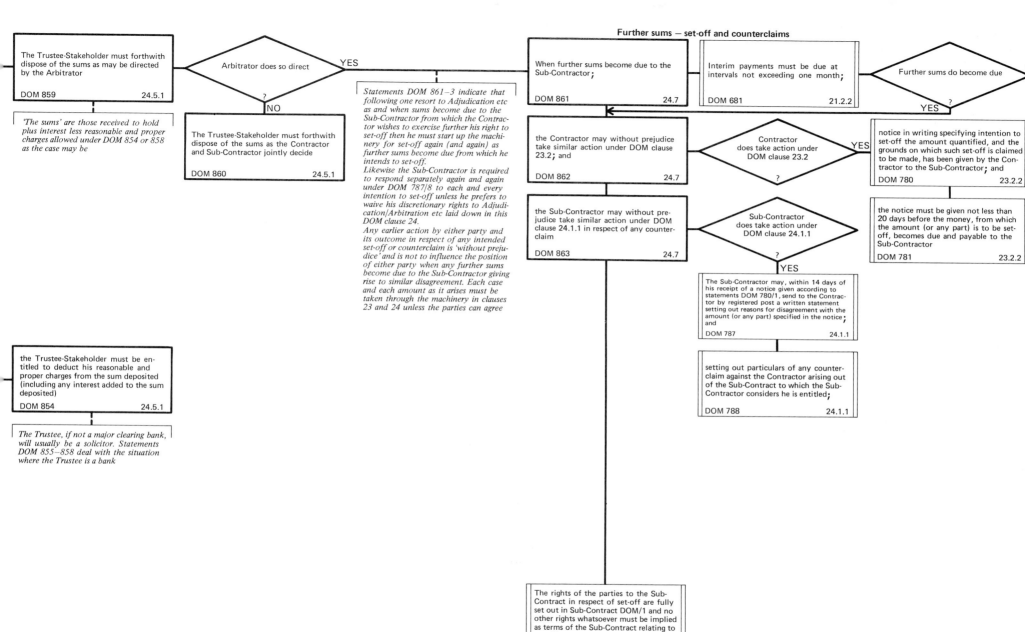

Further sums — set-off and counterclaims

The Trustee-Stakeholder must forthwith dispose of the sums as may be directed by the Arbitrator

DOM 859 24.5.1

'The sums' are those received to hold plus interest less reasonable and proper charges allowed under DOM 854 or 858 as the case may be

Arbitrator does so direct ?

NO

The Trustee-Stakeholder must forthwith dispose of the sums as the Contractor and Sub-Contractor jointly decide

DOM 860 24.5.1

YES

Statements DOM 861–3 indicate that following one resort to Adjudication etc as and when sums become due to the Sub-Contractor from which the Contractor wishes to exercise further his right to set-off then he must start up the machinery for set-off again (and again) as further sums become due from which he intends to set-off.
Likewise the Sub-Contractor is required to respond separately again and again under DOM 787/8 to each and every intention to set-off unless he prefers to waive his discretionary rights to Adjudication/Arbitration etc laid down in this DOM clause 24.
Any earlier action by either party and its outcome in respect of any intended set-off or counterclaim is 'without prejudice' and is not to influence the position of either party when any further sums become due to the Sub-Contractor giving rise to similar disagreement. Each case and each amount as it arises must be taken through the machinery in clauses 23 and 24 unless the parties can agree

When further sums become due to the Sub-Contractor;

DOM 861 24.7

Interim payments must be due at intervals not exceeding one month;

DOM 681 21.2.2

Further sums do become due ?

NO → **STOP**

YES

the Contractor may without prejudice take similar action under DOM clause 23.2; and

DOM 862 24.7

Contractor does take action under DOM clause 23.2 ?

YES

notice in writing specifying intention to set-off the amount quantified, and the grounds on which such set-off is claimed to be made, has been given by the Contractor to the Sub-Contractor; and

DOM 780 23.2.2

the notice must be given not less than 20 days before the money, from which the amount (or any part) is to be set-off, becomes due and payable to the Sub-Contractor

DOM 781 23.2.2

the Sub-Contractor may without prejudice take similar action under DOM clause 24.1.1 in respect of any counterclaim

DOM 863 24.7

Sub-Contractor does take action under DOM clause 24.1.1 ?

YES

The Sub-Contractor may, within 14 days of his receipt of a notice given according to statements DOM 780/1, send to the Contractor by registered post a written statement setting out reasons for disagreement with the amount (or any part) specified in the notice; and

DOM 787 24.1.1

setting out particulars of any counterclaim against the Contractor arising out of the Sub-Contract to which the Sub-Contractor considers he is entitled;

DOM 788 24.1.1

the Trustee-Stakeholder must be entitled to deduct his reasonable and proper charges from the sum deposited (including any interest added to the sum deposited)

DOM 854 24.5.1

The Trustee, if not a major clearing bank, will usually be a solicitor. Statements DOM 855–858 deal with the situation where the Trustee is a bank

The rights of the parties to the Sub-Contract in respect of set-off are fully set out in Sub-Contract DOM/1 and no other rights whatsoever must be implied as terms of the Sub-Contract relating to set-off

DOM 786 23.4

Clause 25 RIGHT OF ACCESS OF CONTRACTOR AND ARCHITECT

START

The Contractor must, when work is to be prepared for this Contract in workshops or other places, by a term in the sub-contract so far as possible secure a right of access to: -

JCT 159   11

those workshops or other places of a Domestic Sub-Contractor;

JCT 160   11

for the Architect and his representatives; and

JCT 161   11

the Contractor must do all things reasonably necessary to make such right of access effective

JCT 162   11

The Contractor, the Architect and all persons duly authorised by either of them must at all reasonable times have access to any work which is being prepared for or will be utilised in the Sub-Contract;

DOM 864   25

Contractor, Architect and all authorised persons do have access ?   **YES**

NO

The Contractor must upon the request of the Architect provide him with vouchers to prove that the materials and goods comply with statement 139

JCT 140   8.2

The Architect may issue instructions in regard to the postponement of any work to be executed under the provisions of this Contract

JCT 406   23.2

The Contractor must not without the written consent of the Architect sub-let any portion of the Works;

JCT 304   19.2

a person to whom the Contractor sub-lets any portion of the Works other than a Nominated Sub-Contractor is in this Contract referred to as a "Domestic Sub-Contractor"

JCT 306   19.2

The Sub-Contractor must: -

DOM 62   5.1

observe, perform and comply with all the provisions of the Main Contract as referred to in the Appendix, part 1;

DOM 63   5.1.1

to be observed, performed and complied with on the part of the Contractor;

DOM 64   5.1.1

so far as the provisions relate and apply to the Sub-Contract; or

DOM 65   5.1.1

The Contractor must afford the clerk of works every reasonable facility to act under the directions of the Architect solely as an inspector on behalf of the Employer

JCT 167   12

The Contractor must maintain and must cause any sub-contractor to maintain insurances necessary to cover the liability of the Contractor or sub-contractor in respect of personal injuries or deaths arising out of or in the course of or caused by the carrying out of the Works;

JCT 340   21.1.1.1

STOP

provided
the injuries or deaths are not due to any act or neglect of the Employer or of any person for whom the Employer is responsible

JCT 341   21.1.1.1

The Architect may issue instructions requiring the Contractor to: -

JCT 142   8.3

arrange for any test of any executed work or of any materials or goods (whether or not already incorporated in the Works)

JCT 144   8.3

The Architect should ensure in an advance tripartite agreement drawn up that his instruction is not worded as to render the Employer liable to pay the cost of a suspension or testing etc. The agreement should in view of this breach make the Sub-Contractor responsible for all the costs flowing from (and the time extensions involved in) his refusal to allow reasonable access under DOM 864 so requiring tests to replace the right to inspect denied by the Sub-Contractor. The Sub-Contractor may point out he carries the risk of defective work in any case under DOM 69–72. However, that does not diminish his obligation to grant reasonable access under DOM 864

The Contractor may make written application to the Sub-Contractor stating: -

DOM 313   13.4.1

the regular progress of the Works or any part of same is likely to be materially affected; by

DOM 314   13.4.1

any act, omission or default of the Sub-Contractor, his servants or agents

DOM 315   13.4

The Sub-Contractor must indemnify and save the Contractor from: -

DOM 69   5.1 & 5.1.2

any breach, non-observance or non-performance of any of the provisions of the Main Contract; and

DOM 70   5.1.2.1

any act or omission which involves the Contractor in any liability to the Employer under the provisions of the Main Contract;

DOM 71   5.1.2.2

by the Sub-Contractor (or his servants or agents) insofar as any breach etc or act etc relate and apply to the Sub-Contract

DOM 72   5.1.2

Clause 26 ASSIGNMENT – SUBLETTING

Sub-Contractor not to assign without consent

Sub-Contractor not to sublet without Contractor's consent

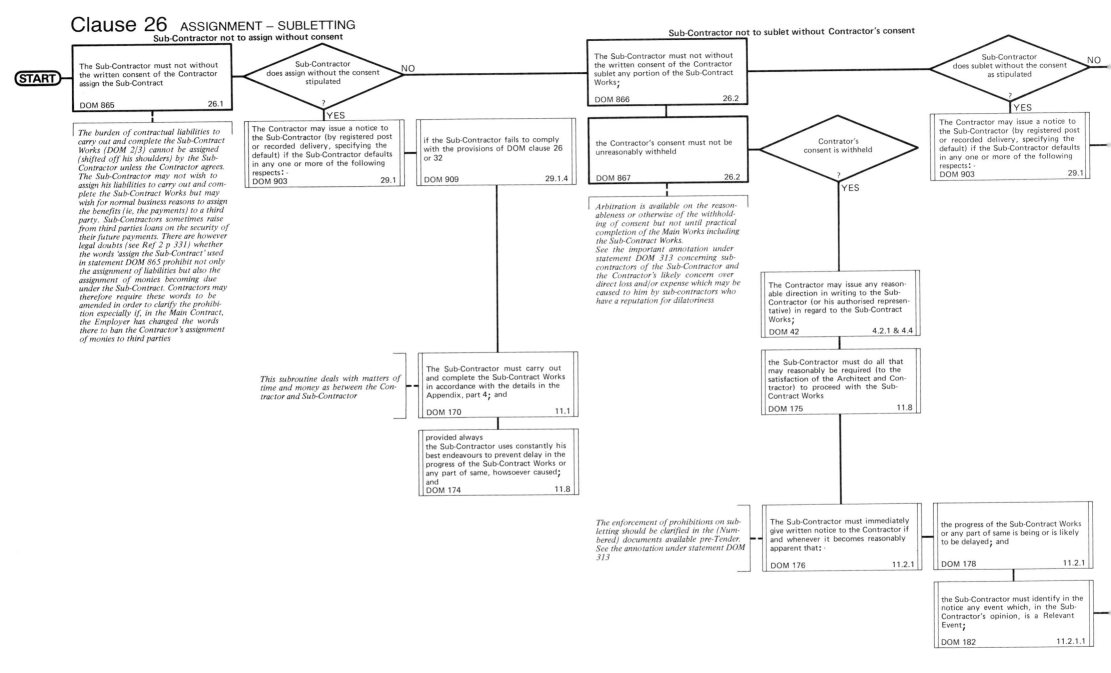

START

The Sub-Contractor must not without the written consent of the Contractor assign the Sub-Contract

DOM 865   26.1

The burden of contractual liabilities to carry out and complete the Sub-Contract Works (DOM 2/3) cannot be assigned (shifted off his shoulders) by the Sub-Contractor unless the Contractor agrees. The Sub-Contractor may not wish to assign his liabilities to carry out and complete the Sub-Contract Works but may wish for normal business reasons to assign the benefits (ie, the payments) to a third party. Sub-Contractors sometimes raise from third parties loans on the security of their future payments. There are however legal doubts (see Ref 2 p 331) whether the words 'assign the Sub-Contract' used in statement DOM 865 prohibit not only the assignment of liabilities but also the assignment of monies becoming due under the Sub-Contract. Contractors may therefore require these words to be amended in order to clarify the prohibition especially if, in the Main Contract, the Employer has changed the words there to ban the Contractor's assignment of monies to third parties

Sub-Contractor does assign without the consent stipulated ?

NO — YES

The Contractor may issue a notice to the Sub-Contractor (by registered post or recorded delivery, specifying the default) if the Sub-Contractor defaults in any one or more of the following respects: -

DOM 903   29.1

if the Sub-Contractor fails to comply with the provisions of DOM clause 26 or 32

DOM 909   29.1.4

This subroutine deals with matters of time and money as between the Contractor and Sub-Contractor

The Sub-Contractor must carry out and complete the Sub-Contract Works in accordance with the details in the Appendix, part 4; and

DOM 170   11.1

provided always
the Sub-Contractor uses constantly his best endeavours to prevent delay in the progress of the Sub-Contract Works or any part of same, howsoever caused; and

DOM 174   11.8

The Sub-Contractor must not without the written consent of the Contractor sublet any portion of the Sub-Contract Works;

DOM 866   26.2

the Contractor's consent must not be unreasonably withheld

DOM 867   26.2

Arbitration is available on the reasonableness or otherwise of the withholding of consent but not until practical completion of the Main Works including the Sub-Contract Works.
See the important annotation under statement DOM 313 concerning sub-contractors of the Sub-Contractor and the Contractor's likely concern over direct loss and/or expense which may be caused to him by sub-contractors who have a reputation for dilatoriness

Contrator's consent is withheld ?

YES

The Contractor may issue any reasonable direction in writing to the Sub-Contractor (or his authorised representative) in regard to the Sub-Contract Works;

DOM 42   4.2.1 & 4.4

the Sub-Contractor must do all that may reasonably be required (to the satisfaction of the Architect and Contractor) to proceed with the Sub-Contract Works

DOM 175   11.8

The enforcement of prohibitions on subletting should be clarified in the (Numbered) documents available pre-Tender. See the annotation under statement DOM 313

The Sub-Contractor must immediately give written notice to the Contractor if and whenever it becomes reasonably apparent that: -

DOM 176   11.2.1

the progress of the Sub-Contract Works or any part of same is being or is likely to be delayed; and

DOM 178   11.2.1

the Sub-Contractor must identify in the notice any event which, in the Sub-Contractor's opinion, is a Relevant Event;

DOM 182   11.2.1.1

Sub-Contractor does sublet without the consent as stipulated ?

NO — YES

The Contractor may issue a notice to the Sub-Contractor (by registered post or recorded delivery, specifying the default) if the Sub-Contractor defaults in any one or more of the following respects: -

DOM 903   29.1

```
                                    ┌─────────────────────────────┐
                                    │ The Sub-Contractor must complete the │
                                    │ Sub-Contract Works in compliance with│
                                    │ the Sub-Contract Documents; and      │
                                    │                             │
                                    │ DOM 7              4.1      │
                                    └─────────────────────────────┘                                        ⬤STOP
┌─────────────────────────────┐     ┌─────────────────────────────┐
│ if the Sub-Contractor fails to comply │     │ in conformity with all the reasonable │
│ with the provisions of DOM clause 26  │     │ directions and requirements of the    │
│ or 32                                 │     │ Contractor (so far as they may apply)  │
│                             │     │ regulating for the time being the due │
│ DOM 909            29.1.4   │     │ carrying out of the Works             │
└─────────────────────────────┘     │                             │
                                    │ DOM 8              4.1      │
                                    └─────────────────────────────┘
```

┌─────────────────────────────────────┐
│ the Sub-Contractor's inability for reasons │
│ beyond his control to secure labour essential │
│ to the proper carrying out of the Works, │
│ which reasons the Sub-Contractor could │
│ not reasonably have foreseen at the Date of │
│ Tender for the Sub-Contract; or │
│   │
│ DOM 207   11.10.10.1 │
└─────────────────────────────────────┘

┌─────────────────────────────────────┐
│ the Sub-Contractor's inability for reasons │
│ beyond his control to secure goods or mate- │
│ rials as are essential to the proper carrying out │
│ of the Works, which reasons the Contractor │
│ could not reasonably have foreseen at the │
│ Date of Tender for the Sub-Contract │
│   │
│ DOM 208   11.10.10.2 │
└─────────────────────────────────────┘

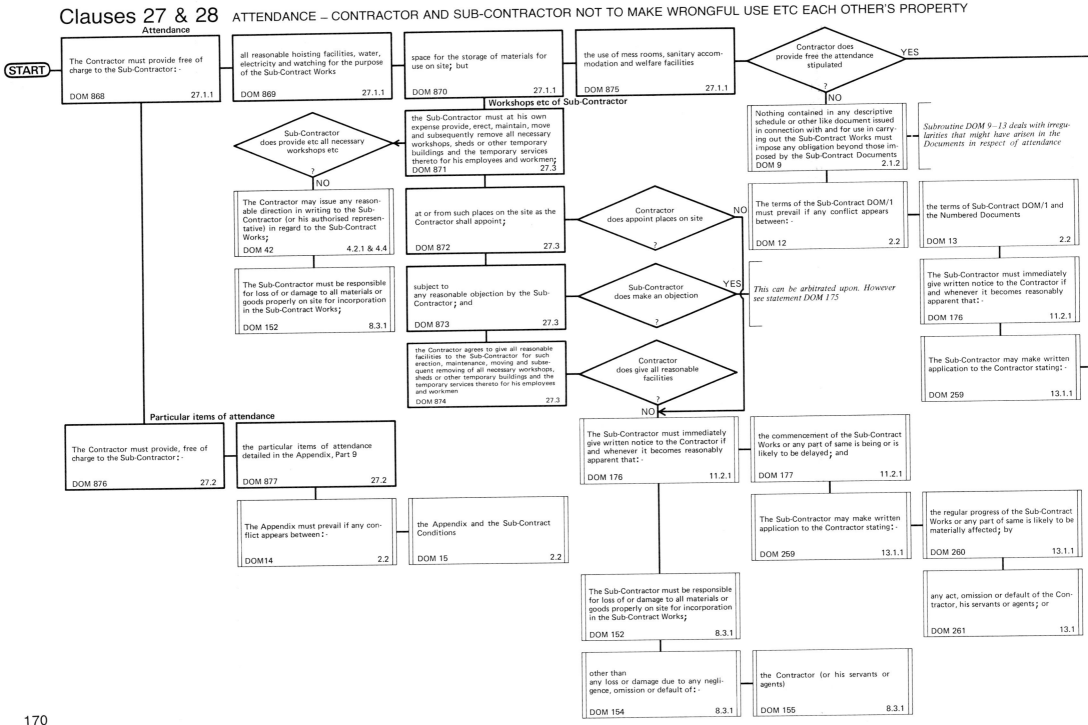

Attendance

The Contractor must provide free of charge to the Sub-Contractor: -

DOM 868 — 27.1.1

all reasonable hoisting facilities, water, electricity and watching for the purpose of the Sub-Contract Works

DOM 869 — 27.1.1

space for the storage of materials for use on site; but

DOM 870 — 27.1.1

the use of mess rooms, sanitary accommodation and welfare facilities

DOM 875 — 27.1.1

Contractor does provide free the attendance stipulated ? YES / NO

Workshops etc of Sub-Contractor

Sub-Contractor does provide etc all necessary workshops etc ? NO

the Sub-Contractor must at his own expense provide, erect, maintain, move and subsequently remove all necessary workshops, sheds or other temporary buildings and the temporary services thereto for his employees and workmen;

DOM 871 — 27.3

The Contractor may issue any reasonable direction in writing to the Sub-Contractor (or his authorised representative) in regard to the Sub-Contract Works;

DOM 42 — 4.2.1 & 4.4

The Sub-Contractor must be responsible for loss of or damage to all materials or goods properly on site for incorporation in the Sub-Contract Works;

DOM 152 — 8.3.1

at or from such places on the site as the Contractor shall appoint;

DOM 872 — 27.3

subject to any reasonable objection by the Sub-Contractor; and

DOM 873 — 27.3

the Contractor agrees to give all reasonable facilities to the Sub-Contractor for such erection, maintenance, moving and subsequent removing of all necessary workshops, sheds or other temporary buildings and the temporary services thereto for his employees and workmen

DOM 874 — 27.3

Contractor does appoint places on site ? NO

Sub-Contractor does make an objection ? YES

Contractor does give all reasonable facilities ? NO

Nothing contained in any descriptive schedule or other like document issued in connection with and for use in carrying out the Sub-Contract Works must impose any obligation beyond those imposed by the Sub-Contract Documents

DOM 9 — 2.1.2

The terms of the Sub-Contract DOM/1 must prevail if any conflict appears between: -

DOM 12 — 2.2

This can be arbitrated upon. However see statement DOM 175

Subroutine DOM 9–13 deals with irregularities that might have arisen in the Documents in respect of attendance

the terms of Sub-Contract DOM/1 and the Numbered Documents

DOM 13 — 2.2

The Sub-Contractor must immediately give written notice to the Contractor if and whenever it becomes reasonably apparent that: -

DOM 176 — 11.2.1

The Sub-Contractor may make written application to the Contractor stating: -

DOM 259 — 13.1.1

Particular items of attendance

The Contractor must provide, free of charge to the Sub-Contractor: -

DOM 876 — 27.2

the particular items of attendance detailed in the Appendix, Part 9

DOM 877 — 27.2

The Appendix must prevail if any conflict appears between: -

DOM14 — 2.2

the Appendix and the Sub-Contract Conditions

DOM 15 — 2.2

The Sub-Contractor must immediately give written notice to the Contractor if and whenever it becomes reasonably apparent that: -

DOM 176 — 11.2.1

the commencement of the Sub-Contract Works or any part of same is being or is likely to be delayed; and

DOM 177 — 11.2.1

The Sub-Contractor may make written application to the Contractor stating: -

DOM 259 — 13.1.1

the regular progress of the Sub-Contract Works or any part of same is likely to be materially affected; by

DOM 260 — 13.1.1

The Sub-Contractor must be responsible for loss of or damage to all materials or goods properly on site for incorporation in the Sub-Contract Works;

DOM 152 — 8.3.1

other than any loss or damage due to any negligence, omission or default of: -

DOM 154 — 8.3.1

the Contractor (or his servants or agents)

DOM 155 — 8.3.1

any act, omission or default of the Contractor, his servants or agents; or

DOM 261 — 13.1

Scaffolding for the Sub-Contract Works

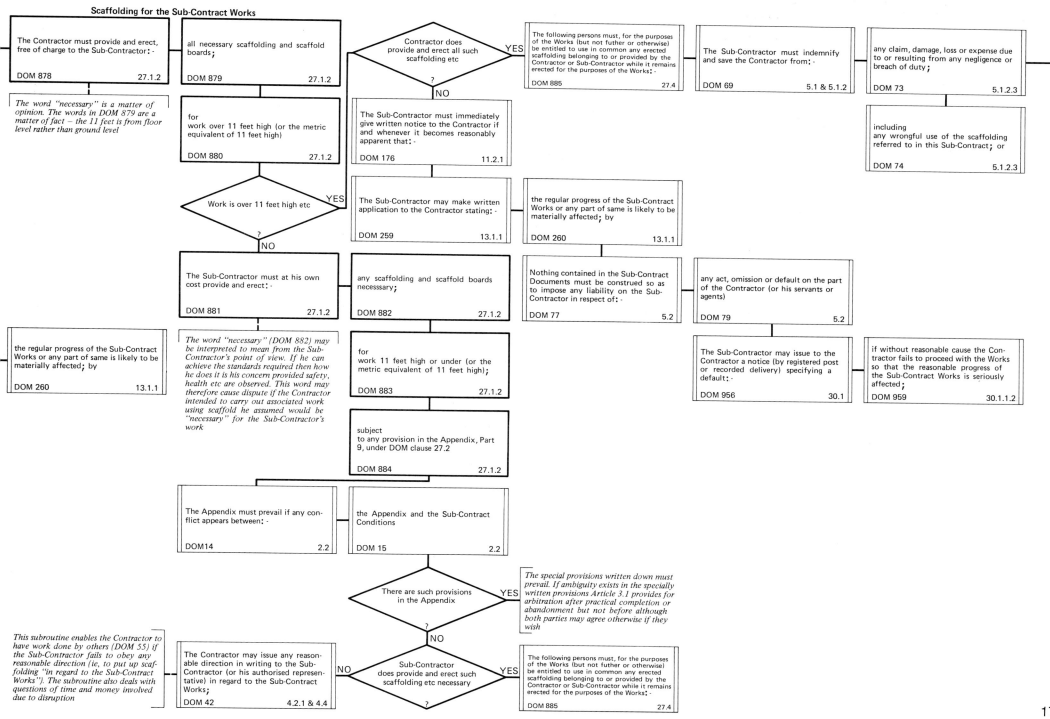

The Contractor must provide and erect, free of charge to the Sub-Contractor: -

DOM 878   27.1.2

The word "necessary" is a matter of opinion. The words in DOM 879 are a matter of fact – the 11 feet is from floor level rather than ground level

all necessary scaffolding and scaffold boards;

DOM 879   27.1.2

for
work over 11 feet high (or the metric equivalent of 11 feet high)

DOM 880   27.1.2

Work is over 11 feet high etc ?   YES / NO

The Sub-Contractor must at his own cost provide and erect: -

DOM 881   27.1.2

The word "necessary" (DOM 882) may be interpreted to mean from the Sub-Contractor's point of view. If he can achieve the standards required then how he does it is his concern provided safety, health etc are observed. This word may therefore cause dispute if the Contractor intended to carry out associated work using scaffold he assumed would be "necessary" for the Sub-Contractor's work

the regular progress of the Sub-Contract Works or any part of same is likely to be materially affected; by

DOM 260   13.1.1

any scaffolding and scaffold boards necesssary;

DOM 882   27.1.2

for
work 11 feet high or under (or the metric equivalent of 11 feet high);

DOM 883   27.1.2

subject
to any provision in the Appendix, Part 9, under DOM clause 27.2

DOM 884   27.1.2

The Appendix must prevail if any conflict appears between: -

DOM14   2.2

the Appendix and the Sub-Contract Conditions

DOM 15   2.2

There are such provisions in the Appendix ?   YES / NO

The special provisions written down must prevail. If ambiguity exists in the specially written provisions Article 3.1 provides for arbitration after practical completion or abandonment but not before although both parties may agree otherwise if they wish

This subroutine enables the Contractor to have work done by others (DOM 55) if the Sub-Contractor fails to obey any reasonable direction (ie, to put up scaffolding "in regard to the Sub-Contract Works"). The subroutine also deals with questions of time and money involved due to disruption

The Contractor may issue any reasonable direction in writing to the Sub-Contractor (or his authorised representative) in regard to the Sub-Contract Works;

DOM 42   4.2.1 & 4.4

Sub-Contractor does provide and erect such scaffolding etc necessary ?   NO / YES

The following persons must, for the purposes of the Works (but not futher or otherwise) be entitled to use in common any erected scaffolding belonging to or provided by the Contractor or Sub-Contractor while it remains erected for the purposes of the Works: -

DOM 885   27.4

Contractor does provide and erect all such scaffolding etc ?   YES / NO

The Sub-Contractor must immediately give written notice to the Contractor if and whenever it becomes reasonably apparent that: -

DOM 176   11.2.1

The Sub-Contractor may make written application to the Contractor stating: -

DOM 259   13.1.1

the regular progress of the Sub-Contract Works or any part of same is likely to be materially affected; by

DOM 260   13.1.1

Nothing contained in the Sub-Contract Documents must be construed so as to impose any liability on the Sub-Contractor in respect of: -

DOM 77   5.2

The following persons must, for the purposes of the Works (but not futher or otherwise) be entitled to use in common any erected scaffolding belonging to or provided by the Contractor or Sub-Contractor while it remains erected for the purposes of the Works: -

DOM 885   27.4

any act, omission or default on the part of the Contractor (or his servants or agents)

DOM 79   5.2

The Sub-Contractor may issue to the Contractor a notice (by registered post or recorded delivery) specifying a default: -

DOM 956   30.1

if without reasonable cause the Contractor fails to proceed with the Works so that the reasonable progress of the Sub-Contract Works is seriously affected;

DOM 959   30.1.1.2

The Sub-Contractor must indemnify and save the Contractor from: -

DOM 69   5.1 & 5.1.2

any claim, damage, loss or expense due to or resulting from any negligence or breach of duty;

DOM 73   5.1.2.3

including
any wrongful use of the scaffolding referred to in this Sub-Contract; or

DOM 74   5.1.2.3

27 & 28/1

171

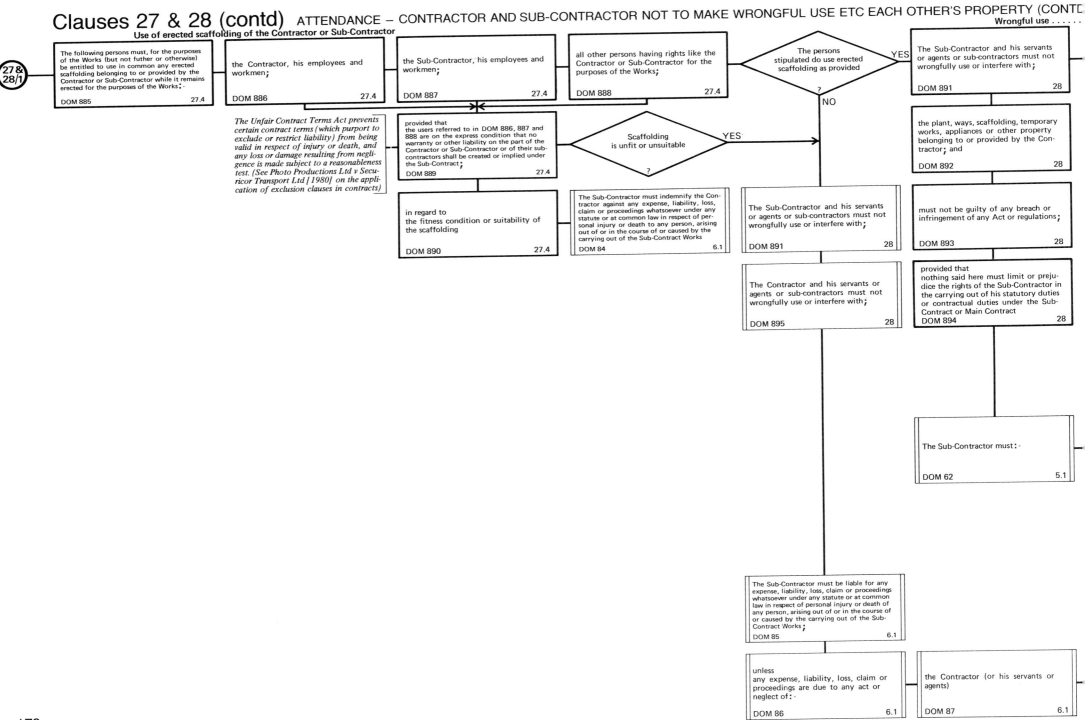

27 & 28/1

Use of erected scaffolding of the Contractor or Sub-Contractor

Wrongful use . . . . . .

The following persons must, for the purposes of the Works (but not futher or otherwise) be entitled to use in common any erected scaffolding belonging to or provided by the Contractor or Sub-Contractor while it remains erected for the purposes of the Works : -

DOM 885   27.4

the Contractor, his employees and workmen ;

DOM 886   27.4

the Sub-Contractor, his employees and workmen ;

DOM 887   27.4

all other persons having rights like the Contractor or Sub-Contractor for the purposes of the Works ;

DOM 888   27.4

The persons stipulated do use erected scaffolding as provided ? YES NO

The Sub-Contractor and his servants or agents or sub-contractors must not wrongfully use or interfere with ;

DOM 891   28

The Unfair Contract Terms Act prevents certain contract terms (which purport to exclude or restrict liability) from being valid in respect of injury or death, and any loss or damage resulting from negligence is made subject to a reasonableness test. (See Photo Productions Ltd v Securicor Transport Ltd [1980] on the application of exclusion clauses in contracts)

provided that the users referred to in DOM 886, 887 and 888 are on the express condition that no warranty or other liability on the part of the Contractor or Sub-Contractor or of their sub-contractors shall be created or implied under the Sub-Contract ;

DOM 889   27.4

Scaffolding is unfit or unsuitable ? YES

the plant, ways, scaffolding, temporary works, appliances or other property belonging to or provided by the Contractor ; and

DOM 892   28

in regard to the fitness condition or suitability of the scaffolding

DOM 890   27.4

The Sub-Contractor must indemnify the Contractor against any expense, liability, loss, claim or proceedings whatsoever under any statute or at common law in respect of personal injury or death to any person, arising out of or in the course of or caused by the carrying out of the Sub-Contract Works

DOM 84   6.1

The Sub-Contractor and his servants or agents or sub-contractors must not wrongfully use or interfere with ;

DOM 891   28

must not be guilty of any breach or infringement of any Act or regulations ;

DOM 893   28

The Contractor and his servants or agents or sub-contractors must not wrongfully use or interfere with ;

DOM 895   28

provided that nothing said here must limit or prejudice the rights of the Sub-Contractor in the carrying out of his statutory duties or contractual duties under the Sub-Contract or Main Contract

DOM 894   28

The Sub-Contractor must : -

DOM 62   5.1

The Sub-Contractor must be liable for any expense, liability, loss, claim or proceedings whatsoever under any statute or at common law in respect of personal injury or death of any person, arising out of or in the course of or caused by the carrying out of the Sub-Contract Works ;

DOM 85   6.1

unless any expense, liability, loss, claim or proceedings are due to any act or neglect of : -

DOM 86   6.1

the Contractor (or his servants or agents)

DOM 87   6.1

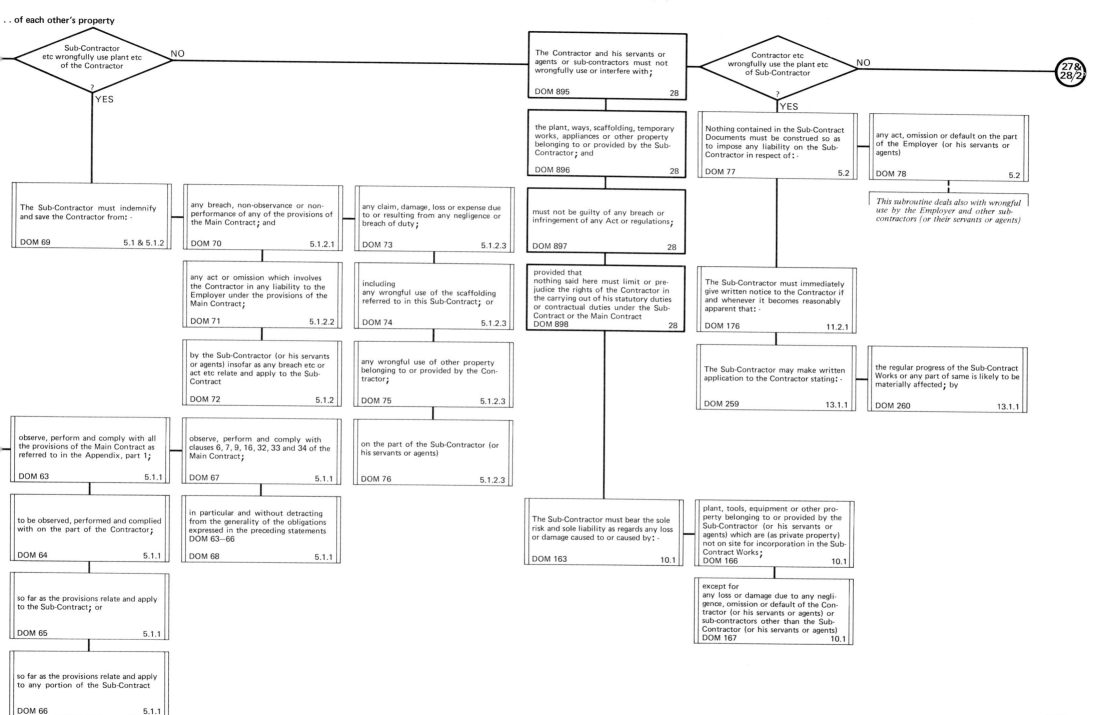

.. of each other's property

Sub-Contractor etc wrongfully use plant etc of the Contractor ? — NO

The Contractor and his servants or agents or sub-contractors must not wrongfully use or interfere with:
DOM 895   28

Contractor etc wrongfully use the plant etc of Sub-Contractor ? — NO

27& 28/2

YES

The Sub-Contractor must indemnify and save the Contractor from: -
DOM 69   5.1 & 5.1.2

any breach, non-observance or non-performance of any of the provisions of the Main Contract; and
DOM 70   5.1.2.1

any claim, damage, loss or expense due to or resulting from any negligence or breach of duty;
DOM 73   5.1.2.3

the plant, ways, scaffolding, temporary works, appliances or other property belonging to or provided by the Sub-Contractor; and
DOM 896   28

Nothing contained in the Sub-Contract Documents must be construed so as to impose any liability on the Sub-Contractor in respect of: -
DOM 77   5.2

any act, omission or default on the part of the Employer (or his servants or agents)
DOM 78   5.2

This subroutine deals also with wrongful use by the Employer and other sub-contractors (or their servants or agents)

any act or omission which involves the Contractor in any liability to the Employer under the provisions of the Main Contract;
DOM 71   5.1.2.2

including
any wrongful use of the scaffolding referred to in this Sub-Contract; or
DOM 74   5.1.2.3

must not be guilty of any breach or infringement of any Act or regulations;
DOM 897   28

by the Sub-Contractor (or his servants or agents) insofar as any breach etc or act etc relate and apply to the Sub-Contract
DOM 72   5.1.2

any wrongful use of other property belonging to or provided by the Contractor;
DOM 75   5.1.2.3

provided that
nothing said here must limit or prejudice the rights of the Contractor in the carrying out of his statutory duties or contractual duties under the Sub-Contract or the Main Contract
DOM 898   28

The Sub-Contractor must immediately give written notice to the Contractor if and whenever it becomes reasonably apparent that: -
DOM 176   11.2.1

observe, perform and comply with all the provisions of the Main Contract as referred to in the Appendix, part 1;
DOM 63   5.1.1

observe, perform and comply with clauses 6, 7, 9, 16, 32, 33 and 34 of the Main Contract;
DOM 67   5.1.1

on the part of the Sub-Contractor (or his servants or agents)
DOM 76   5.1.2.3

The Sub-Contractor may make written application to the Contractor stating: -
DOM 259   13.1.1

the regular progress of the Sub-Contract Works or any part of same is likely to be materially affected; by
DOM 260   13.1.1

to be observed, performed and complied with on the part of the Contractor;
DOM 64   5.1.1

in particular and without detracting from the generality of the obligations expressed in the preceding statements
DOM 63—66
DOM 68   5.1.1

so far as the provisions relate and apply to the Sub-Contract; or
DOM 65   5.1.1

The Sub-Contractor must bear the sole risk and sole liability as regards any loss or damage caused to or caused by: -
DOM 163   10.1

plant, tools, equipment or other property belonging to or provided by the Sub-Contractor (or his servants or agents) which are (as private property) not on site for incorporation in the Sub-Contract Works;
DOM 166   10.1

so far as the provisions relate and apply to any portion of the Sub-Contract
DOM 66   5.1.1

except for
any loss or damage due to any negligence, omission or default of the Contractor (or his servants or agents) or sub-contractors other than the Sub-Contractor (or his servants or agents)
DOM 167   10.1

173

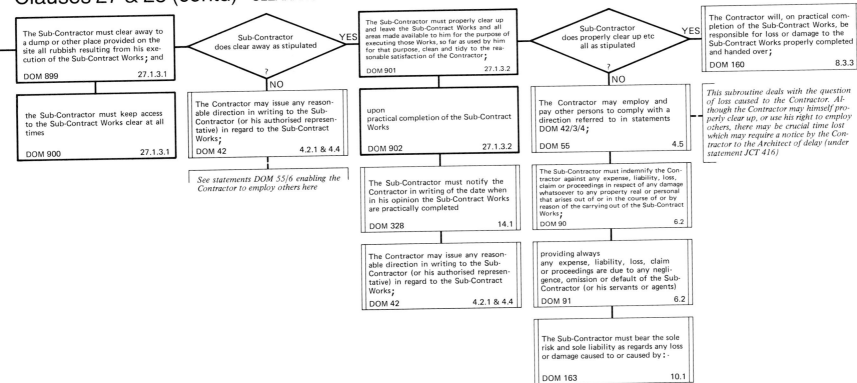

27 & 28/2

The Sub-Contractor must clear away to a dump or other place provided on the site all rubbish resulting from his execution of the Sub-Contract Works ; and

DOM 899   27.1.3.1

the Sub-Contractor must keep access to the Sub-Contract Works clear at all times

DOM 900   27.1.3.1

Sub-Contractor does clear away as stipulated ? — YES / NO

The Contractor may issue any reasonable direction in writing to the Sub-Contractor (or his authorised representative) in regard to the Sub-Contract Works ;

DOM 42   4.2.1 & 4.4

See statements DOM 55/6 enabling the Contractor to employ others here

The Sub-Contractor must properly clear up and leave the Sub-Contract Works and all areas made available to him for the purpose of executing those Works, so far as used by him for that purpose, clean and tidy to the reasonable satisfaction of the Contractor ;

DOM 901   27.1.3.2

upon
practical completion of the Sub-Contract Works

DOM 902   27.1.3.2

The Sub-Contractor must notify the Contractor in writing of the date when in his opinion the Sub-Contract Works are practically completed

DOM 328   14.1

The Contractor may issue any reasonable direction in writing to the Sub-Contractor (or his authorised representative) in regard to the Sub-Contract Works ;

DOM 42   4.2.1 & 4.4

Sub-Contractor does properly clear up etc all as stipulated ? — YES / NO

The Contractor may employ and pay other persons to comply with a direction referred to in statements DOM 42/3/4 ;

DOM 55   4.5

The Sub-Contractor must indemnify the Contractor against any expense, liability, loss, claim or proceedings in respect of any damage whatsoever to any property real or personal that arises out of or in the course of or by reason of the carrying out of the Sub-Contract Works ;

DOM 90   6.2

providing always
any expense, liability, loss, claim or proceedings are due to any negligence, omission or default of the Sub-Contractor (or his servants or agents)

DOM 91   6.2

The Sub-Contractor must bear the sole risk and sole liability as regards any loss or damage caused to or caused by : -

DOM 163   10.1

The Contractor will, on practical completion of the Sub-Contract Works, be responsible for loss or damage to the Sub-Contract Works properly completed and handed over ;

DOM 160   8.3.3

This subroutine deals with the question of loss caused to the Contractor. Although the Contractor may himself properly clear up, or use his right to employ others, there may be crucial time lost which may require a notice by the Contractor to the Architect of delay (under statement JCT 416)

（STOP）

Clause 29 DETERMINATION OF THE EMPLOYMENT OF THE SUB-CONTRACTOR BY THE CONTRACTOR

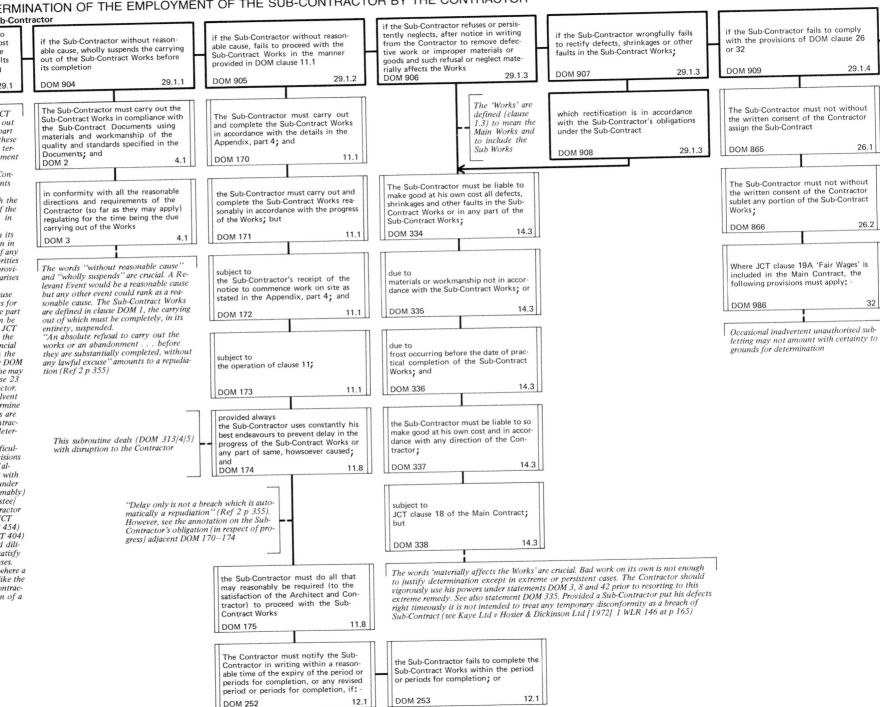

Default by Sub-Contractor

START

The Contractor may issue a notice to the Sub-Contractor (by registered post or recorded delivery, specifying the default) if the Sub-Contractor defaults in any one or more of the following respects: -
DOM 903   29.1

if the Sub-Contractor without reasonable cause, wholly suspends the carrying out of the Sub-Contract Works before its completion
DOM 904   29.1.1

if the Sub-Contractor without reasonable cause, fails to proceed with the Sub-Contract Works in the manner provided in DOM clause 11.1
DOM 905   29.1.2

if the Sub-Contractor refuses or persistently neglects, after notice in writing from the Contractor to remove defective work or improper materials or goods and such refusal or neglect materially affects the Works
DOM 906   29.1.3

if the Sub-Contractor wrongfully fails to rectify defects, shrinkages or other faults in the Sub-Contract Works;
DOM 907   29.1.3

if the Sub-Contractor fails to comply with the provisions of DOM clause 26 or 32
DOM 909   29.1.4

This clause endeavours to mirror JCT clause 27. It falls into 2 parts setting out the rights of the Contractor (quite apart from his common law rights) under these express rules of this Sub-Contract to terminate the Sub-Contractor's employment in cases of:
1: Certain breaches of the Sub-Contract as described in statements DOM 904–909.
2. Certain events connected with the insolvency or financial state of the Sub-Contractor as described in statements DOM 921–928.
Unlike JCT clause 27 it does not in its standard form deal with termination in the event of the offering or taking of any corrupt payments etc. Local Authorities might require changes to include a provision to terminate where corruption arises (JCT Guide p 71).
The Contractor cannot by this clause DOM 904–909 have time extensions for the Main Works for any delay on the part of the Sub-Contractor, unless it can be fitted in under the reasons found in JCT clause 25, but he can recoup from the defaulting Sub-Contractor his financial loss and/or expense, resulting from the default affecting his progress, under DOM clause 13.4 (313–7). Furthermore, he may set-off such sums under DOM clause 23 from monies due to the Sub-Contractor. Provided the Sub-Contractor is solvent there is therefore no reason to determine his employment unless the defaults are very serious. In this respect the Contractor is warned against vexatiously determining this Sub-Contract.
If insolvency or severe financial difficulties are encountered then the provisions commencing at DOM 920 apply (although common law rights remain) with notices being expressly required under this Sub-Contract to be sent (presumably) to the Sub-Contractor or his Trustee/ Liquidator etc. However the Contractor should take the initiative under JCT clause 25 (statements JCT 415 and 454) and JCT clause 23.1 (statement JCT 404) in order that he may regularly and diligently proceed with the Works to satisfy the requirements of those two clauses.
The Architect has no part to play where a Domestic Sub-Contractor fails, unlike the position where Nominated Sub-Contractors are involved and renomination of a replacement is required of him

The Sub-Contractor must carry out the Sub-Contract Works in compliance with the Sub-Contract Documents using materials and workmanship of the quality and standards specified in the Documents; and
DOM 2   4.1

in conformity with all the reasonable directions and requirements of the Contractor (so far as they may apply) regulating for the time being the due carrying out of the Works
DOM 3   4.1

The words "without reasonable cause" and "wholly suspends" are crucial. A Relevant Event would be a reasonable cause but any other event could rank as a reasonable cause. The Sub-Contract Works are defined in clause DOM 1, the carrying out of which must be completely, in its entirety, suspended.
"An absolute refusal to carry out the works or an abandonment . . . before they are substantially completed, without any lawful excuse" amounts to a repudiation (Ref 2 p 355)

The Sub-Contractor must carry out and complete the Sub-Contract Works in accordance with the details in the Appendix, part 4; and
DOM 170   11.1

the Sub-Contractor must carry out and complete the Sub-Contract Works reasonably in accordance with the progress of the Works; but
DOM 171   11.1

subject to the Sub-Contractor's receipt of the notice to commence work on site as stated in the Appendix, part 4; and
DOM 172   11.1

subject to the operation of clause 11;
DOM 173   11.1

provided always the Sub-Contractor uses constantly his best endeavours to prevent delay in the progress of the Sub-Contract Works or any part of same, howsoever caused; and
DOM 174   11.8

This subroutine deals (DOM 313/4/5) with disruption to the Contractor

"Delay only is not a breach which is automatically a repudiation" (Ref 2 p 355). However, see the annotation on the Sub-Contractor's obligation (in respect of progress) adjacent DOM 170–174

the Sub-Contractor must do all that may reasonably be required (to the satisfaction of the Architect and Contractor) to proceed with the Sub-Contract Works
DOM 175   11.8

The Contractor must notify the Sub-Contractor in writing within a reasonable time of the expiry of the period or periods for completion, or any revised period or periods for completion, if: -
DOM 252   12.1

the Sub-Contractor fails to complete the Sub-Contract Works within the period or periods for completion; or
DOM 253   12.1

The 'Works' are defined (clause 1.3) to mean the Main Works and to include the Sub Works

which rectification is in accordance with the Sub-Contractor's obligations under the Sub-Contract
DOM 908   29.1.3

The Sub-Contractor must be liable to make good at his own cost all defects, shrinkages and other faults in the Sub-Contract Works or in any part of the Sub-Contract Works;
DOM 334   14.3

due to materials or workmanship not in accordance with the Sub-Contract Works; or
DOM 335   14.3

due to frost occurring before the date of practical completion of the Sub-Contract Works; and
DOM 336   14.3

the Sub-Contractor must be liable to so make good at his own cost and in accordance with any direction of the Contractor;
DOM 337   14.3

subject to JCT clause 18 of the Main Contract; but
DOM 338   14.3

The words 'materially affects the Works' are crucial. Bad work on its own is not enough to justify determination except in extreme or persistent cases. The Contractor should vigorously use his powers under statements DOM 3, 8 and 42 prior to resorting to this extreme remedy. See also statement DOM 335. Provided a Sub-Contractor put his defects right timeously it is not intended to treat any temporary disconformity as a breach of Sub-Contract (see Kaye Ltd v Hosier & Dickinson Ltd [1972] 1 WLR 146 at p 165)

The Sub-Contractor must not without the written consent of the Contractor assign the Sub-Contract
DOM 865   26.1

The Sub-Contractor must not without the written consent of the Contractor sublet any portion of the Sub-Contract Works;
DOM 866   26.2

Where JCT clause 19A 'Fair Wages' is included in the Main Contract, the following provisions must apply: -
DOM 986   32

Occasional inadvertent unauthorised subletting may not amount with certainty to grounds for determination

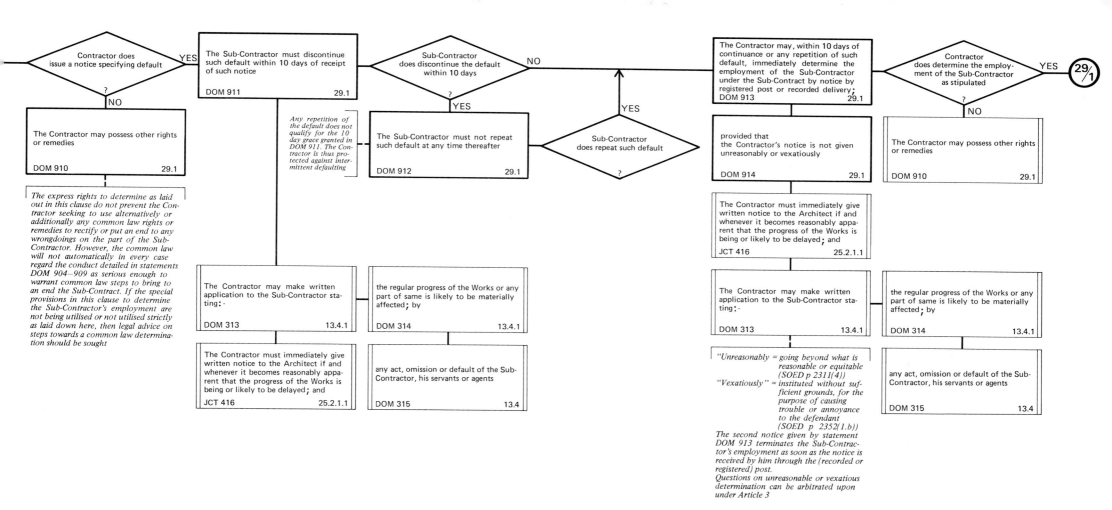

Contractor does issue a notice specifying default ? **YES** / **NO**

The Sub-Contractor must discontinue such default within 10 days of receipt of such notice

DOM 911   29.1

Sub-Contractor does discontinue the default within 10 days ? **NO** / **YES**

The Contractor may, within 10 days of continuance or any repetition of such default, immediately determine the employment of the Sub-Contractor under the Sub-Contract by notice by registered post or recorded delivery;

DOM 913   29.1

Contractor does determine the employment of the Sub-Contractor as stipulated ? **YES** / **NO**

29/1

The Contractor may possess other rights or remedies

DOM 910   29.1

Any repetition of the default does not qualify for the 10 day grace granted in DOM 911. The Contractor is thus protected against intermittent defaulting

The Sub-Contractor must not repeat such default at any time thereafter

DOM 912   29.1

Sub-Contractor does repeat such default ?

provided that the Contractor's notice is not given unreasonably or vexatiously

DOM 914   29.1

The Contractor may possess other rights or remedies

DOM 910   29.1

The express rights to determine as laid out in this clause do not prevent the Contractor seeking to use alternatively or additionally any common law rights or remedies to rectify or put an end to any wrongdoings on the part of the Sub-Contractor. However, the common law will not automatically in every case regard the conduct detailed in statements DOM 904–909 as serious enough to warrant common law steps to bring to an end the Sub-Contract. If the special provisions in this clause to determine the Sub-Contractor's employment are not being utilised or not utilised strictly as laid down here, then legal advice on steps towards a common law determination should be sought

The Contractor may make written application to the Sub-Contractor stating:-

DOM 313   13.4.1

the regular progress of the Works or any part of same is likely to be materially affected; by

DOM 314   13.4.1

The Contractor must immediately give written notice to the Architect if and whenever it becomes reasonably apparent that the progress of the Works is being or likely to be delayed; and

JCT 416   25.2.1.1

The Contractor may make written application to the Sub-Contractor stating:-

DOM 313   13.4.1

the regular progress of the Works or any part of same is likely to be materially affected; by

DOM 314   13.4.1

The Contractor must immediately give written notice to the Architect if and whenever it becomes reasonably apparent that the progress of the Works is being or likely to be delayed; and

JCT 416   25.2.1.1

any act, omission or default of the Sub-Contractor, his servants or agents

DOM 315   13.4

any act, omission or default of the Sub-Contractor, his servants or agents

DOM 315   13.4

"Unreasonably = going beyond what is reasonable or equitable (SOED p 2311(4))
"Vexatiously" = instituted without sufficient grounds, for the purpose of causing trouble or annoyance to the defendant (SOED p 2352(1.b))
The second notice given by statement DOM 913 terminates the Sub-Contractor's employment as soon as the notice is received by him through the (recorded or registered) post.
Questions on unreasonable or vexatious determination can be arbitrated upon under Article 3

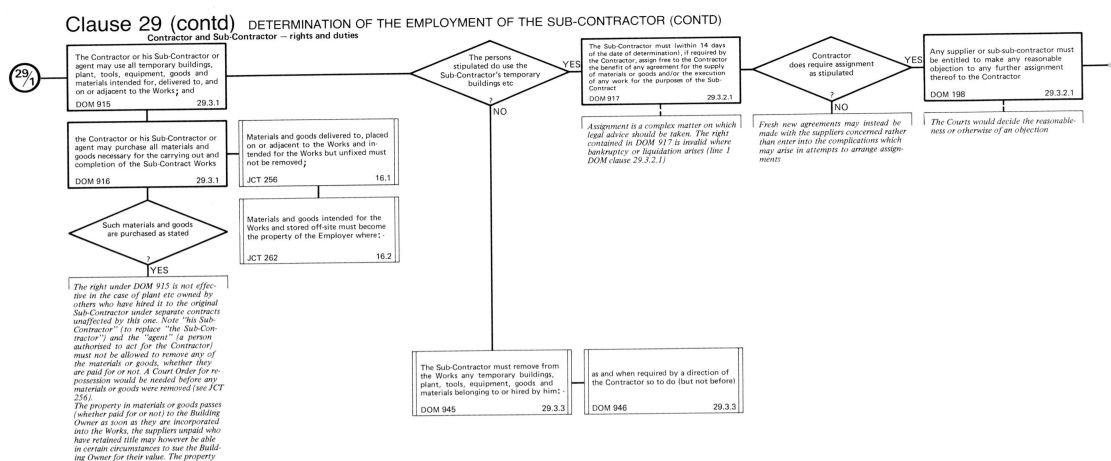

29/1

The Contractor or his Sub-Contractor or agent may use all temporary buildings, plant, tools, equipment, goods and materials intended for, delivered to, and on or adjacent to the Works; and

DOM 915   29.3.1

the Contractor or his Sub-Contractor or agent may purchase all materials and goods necessary for the carrying out and completion of the Sub-Contract Works

DOM 916   29.3.1

Such materials and goods are purchased as stated

?   YES

The right under DOM 915 is not effective in the case of plant etc owned by others who have hired it to the original Sub-Contractor under separate contracts unaffected by this one. Note "his Sub-Contractor" (to replace "the Sub-Contractor") and the "agent" (a person authorised to act for the Contractor) must not be allowed to remove any of the materials or goods, whether they are paid for or not. A Court Order for repossession would be needed before any materials or goods were removed (see JCT 256).

The property in materials or goods passes (whether paid for or not) to the Building Owner as soon as they are incorporated into the Works, the suppliers unpaid who have retained title may however be able in certain circumstances to sue the Building Owner for their value. The property in unfixed materials or goods may also be in doubt if the suppliers have sent the materials or goods to the site on the basis that they retain title to them until they are paid for in full. These matters will create potential problems if the Employer of the Contractor has paid under Certificates for the materials etc but they are not yet incorporated in the Works, or a certain amount of conversion work has been carried out upon them. These problems will only become real if the Sub-Contractor refuses or is unable because of later insolvency to pay his suppliers concerned. If insolvency is at the root of the problem the law will not in any case allow any contract's provisions or transactions (such as provided for in this clause) to go unquestioned, by third parties who also claim rights in respect of the materials or goods concerned. This is one of the risks an Employer takes (along with everyone else) in business, where any insolvency arises, see the annotation to statements JCT 256/7/8

Materials and goods delivered to, placed on or adjacent to the Works and intended for the Works but unfixed must not be removed;

JCT 256   16.1

Materials and goods intended for the Works and stored off-site must become the property of the Employer where: -

JCT 262   16.2

The persons stipulated do use the Sub-Contractor's temporary buildings etc

?   YES / NO

The Sub-Contractor must remove from the Works any temporary buildings, plant, tools, equipment, goods and materials belonging to or hired by him: -

DOM 945   29.3.3

as and when required by a direction of the Contractor so to do (but not before)

DOM 946   29.3.3

The Sub-Contractor must (within 14 days of the date of determination), if required by the Contractor, assign free to the Contractor the benefit of any agreement for the supply of materials or goods and/or the execution of any work for the purposes of the Sub-Contract

DOM 917   29.3.2.1

Assignment is a complex matter on which legal advice should be taken. The right contained in DOM 917 is invalid where bankruptcy or liquidation arises (line 1 DOM clause 29.3.2.1)

Contractor does require assignment as stipulated

?   YES / NO

Fresh new agreements may instead be made with the suppliers concerned rather than enter into the complications which may arise in attempts to arrange assignments

Any supplier or sub-sub-contractor must be entitled to make any reasonable objection to any further assignment thereof to the Contractor

DOM 198   29.3.2.1

The Courts would decide the reasonableness or otherwise of an objection

```
┌─────────────────────────────┐                                    ┌─────────────────────────────┐     ┌─────────────────────────────┐
│ The Contractor may pay any  │                                    │ there must be deducted any  │     │ The Contractor is not bound │
│ supplier or sub-sub-        │      ◇◇◇◇◇◇◇◇◇◇◇◇◇◇◇◇◇◇◇            │ other amount which is       │     │ by any provision of the     │
│ contractor for any materials│    ◇◇                 ◇◇           │ required by the Sub-        │     │ Sub-Contract to make any    │
│ or goods delivered or works │  ◇◇     Contractor      ◇◇ YES     │ Contract Documents to be    │     │ further payment to the Sub- │
│ executed for the purposes of│ ◇◇    does pay as stated ◇◇────────│ deducted from the Sub-      │─────│ Contractor until after      │
│ the Sub-Contract (whether   │  ◇◇                   ◇◇           │ Contract Sum                │     │ completion of the Sub-      │
│ before or after the         │    ◇◇     ?         ◇◇             │                             │     │ Contract Works; and         │
│ determination) insofar as   │      ◇◇◇◇◇◇◇◇◇◇◇◇◇◇◇◇◇◇◇           │                             │     │                             │
│ the price has not already   │              │ NO                  │ DOM 727          21.7.2.4   │     │ DOM 949              29.4   │
│ been paid by the Sub-       │              │                     └─────────────────────────────┘     └─────────────────────────────┘
│ Contractor                  │              │
│ DOM 919          29.3.2.2   │              │
└─────────────────────────────┘              │
```

Go to statements DOM 945 and onwards for the continuation of this clause's provisions (the statements DOM 920–944 deal specifically with insolvency)

DOM 919 box: The Contractor may pay any supplier or sub-sub-contractor for any materials or goods delivered or works executed for the purposes of the Sub-Contract (whether before or after the determination) insofar as the price has not already been paid by the Sub-Contractor

DOM 919   29.3.2.2

These rights are not applicable if bankruptcy or liquidation arises. The procedures to follow in bankruptcy or liquidation commence at statement DOM 920

Decision: Contractor does pay as stated ?   — YES / NO

NO: *The Contractor need not exercise his discretionary right to pay*

DOM 727 box: there must be deducted any other amount which is required by the Sub-Contract Documents to be deducted from the Sub-Contract Sum

DOM 727   21.7.2.4

See the annotation under DOM 727 on excluding such sums from the final account.
There is no provision, where DOM clause 15.2 applies, for introducing such payments into the ascertainment of the Final Sub-Contract Sum.
DOM clause 23.2 is available only for setting-off expense incurred by reason of any breach or "failure to observe the provisions of the Sub-Contract". The payment of third parties is not a "provision of the Sub-Contract" and falls outside the clause's scope

DOM 949 box: The Contractor is not bound by any provision of the Sub-Contract to make any further payment to the Sub-Contractor until after completion of the Sub-Contract Works; and

DOM 949   29.4

DOM 950 box: the Sub-Contractor must allow or pay to the Contractor in the manner shown in DOM 954 the amount of any direct loss and/or damage caused to the Contractor by the determination

DOM 950   29.4

DOM 945 box: The Sub-Contractor must remove from the Works any temporary buildings, plant, tools, equipment, goods and materials belonging to or hired by him: -

DOM 945   29.3.3

DOM 946 box: as and when required by a direction of the Contractor so to do (but not before)

DOM 946   29.3.3

29/5

Sub-Contractor becoming bankrupt etc

29/2

The Contractor may, by written notice, immediately determine the employment of the Sub-Contractor under the Sub-Contract in the event of the Sub-Contractor : -

DOM 920   29.2

becoming bankrupt

DOM 921   29.2

having a winding up order made

DOM 922   29.2

making a composition with his creditors

DOM 923   29.2

making an arrangement with his creditors

DOM 924   29.2

having a resolution for voluntary winding up passed;

DOM 925   29.2

other than
for the purposes of amalgamation or reconstruction

DOM 926   29.2

Where the Sub-Contractor has also clearly defaulted under statements DOM 904–909 the Contractor should invoke those grounds for determination rather than exercise the powers granted here to terminate the Sub-Contractor's employment followed possibly by reinstatement unless the Sub-Contractor's trustee/liquidator etc, in an unprofitable situation, disclaims (see Ref 1 pp 787–793). In any case the rights of the Contractor (eg, in DOM 930 and in the provisos JCT 439, 491 and 612) under this clause are filled with doubt especially so far as bankruptcy or liquidation are concerned. Bankruptcy law or the Companies Act may effectively override any terms in this clause which endeavour to arrange matters to the advantage of the Contractor (and Employer) and therefore to the disadvantage of any other creditors

Bankruptcy is the formal recognition of the insolvency of a sole trader (the term does not apply to a company) and the ownership of his property is vested in a trustee appointed, or the Official Receiver, from the date of the act of bankruptcy. An adjudication order judicially makes the debtor "bankrupt" setting in motion the provisions of this clause on the date of the adjudication order. The trustee has powers to disclaim any onerous contracts of the bankrupt. The trustee may be required to state within 28 days whether he intends to disclaim

A "winding up order" is an order by the Court for the compulsory winding up of a company due to its inability to meet its debts. Such an order stops the powers of the company's directors and provides instead a liquidator with powers that are to be employed in respect of previous or existing transactions of the company. A winding up order is made when the company's insolvency is proved by a petition made to the Court. The date of the petition is the operative date of determination under this clause. The liquidator has powers to disclaim any onerous contracts of the company. The liquidator may be required to state within 28 days whether he intends to disclaim but the power to disclaim can only be exercised with the Court's approval

A "composition" is the acceptance by creditors of so much in the pound in satisfaction of their debt. Such an act is indicative of insolvency or severe financial difficulty

An "arrangement" is the transfer of assets to a trustee's care for creditors. Such an act is indicative of insolvency or severe financial difficulty

A "resolution for voluntary winding up" is made when a company cannot continue but does not necessarily mean the company is insolvent. The date of passing the resolution is the operative date of determination in this case, a liquidator being appointed to take over from the directors

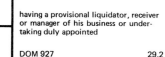

having a provisional liquidator, receiver or manager of his business or undertaking duly appointed

DOM 927   29.2

A receiver or manager may be appointed by the holders of a debenture or debentures in a company, a debenture being a debt secured on an undertaking of the company, which is called a "floating charge". The debenture deed will contain the power to appoint a person as an agent (or receiver) of the company who will act if the security is in jeopardy. The Court may in the case of a sole trader appoint the Official Referee to become trustee and act as manager

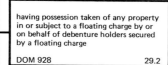

having possession taken of any property in or subject to a floating charge by or on behalf of debenture holders secured by a floating charge

DOM 928   29.2

See the annotation under DOM 927

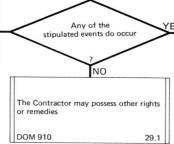

Any of the stipulated events do occur

?

YES

NO

The Contractor may possess other rights or remedies

DOM 910   29.1

The determination of the Sub-Contractor's employment (referred to in DOM 920) is not to prejudice any other rights or remedies the Contractor may possess

DOM 929   29.2

Strict adherence to the provisions of this clause does not indicate that any common law rights have been waived

Sub-Contractor's employment is determined

?

YES

NO

The Sub-Contractor may make written application to the Contractor stating: -

DOM 259   13.1.1

The Contractor or his Sub-Contractor or agent may use all temporary buildings, plant, tools, equipment, goods and materials intended for, delivered to, and on or adjacent to the Works ; and

DOM 930   29.3.1

the regular progress of the Sub-Contract Works or any part of same has been materially affected ; by

DOM 264   13.1.1

any act, omission or default of the Contractor, his servants or agents ; or

DOM 265   13.1

Other Nominated or Domestic Sub-Contractors may signify their intentions (so too may the Employer) to make claims against the Contractor (in the Nominated Sub-Contractor's case, under NSC 368/370) if their progress or completion is disrupted by this pause in the progress of the Sub-Contract Works. However, Trustees and Liquidators have statutory rights either to carry on or (within 28 days under DOM 921 and 922) to disclaim. These rights cannot be overriden

29/3

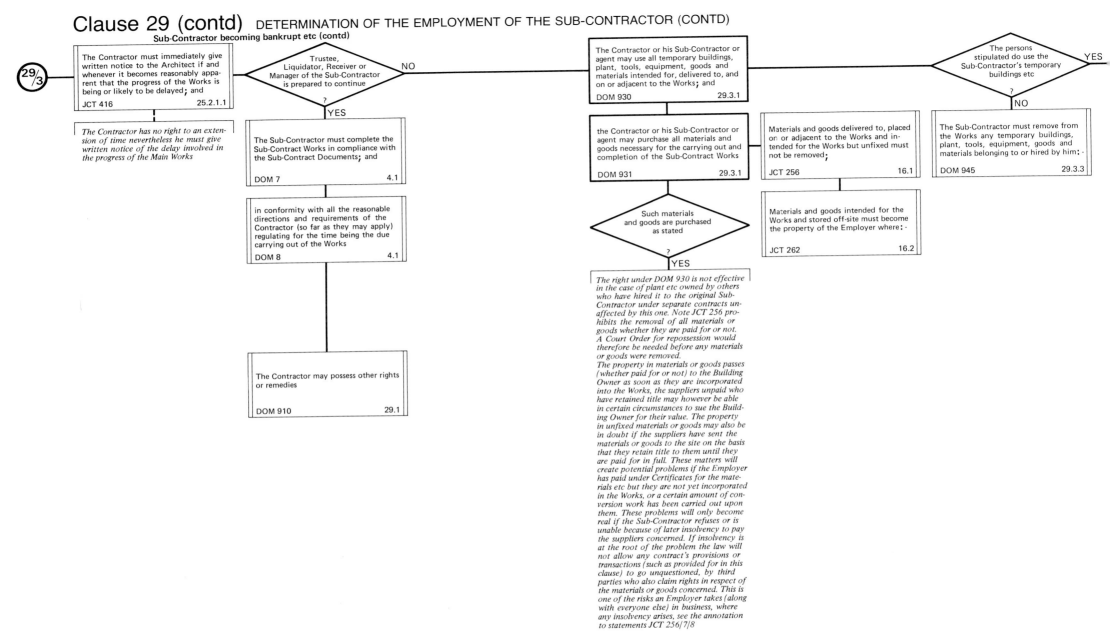

29/3

The Contractor must immediately give written notice to the Architect if and whenever it becomes reasonably apparent that the progress of the Works is being or likely to be delayed; and

JCT 416   25.2.1.1

The Contractor has no right to an extension of time nevertheless he must give written notice of the delay involved in the progress of the Main Works

---

Trustee, Liquidator, Receiver or Manager of the Sub-Contractor is prepared to continue

?   NO / YES

The Sub-Contractor must complete the Sub-Contract Works in compliance with the Sub-Contract Documents; and

DOM 7   4.1

---

in conformity with all the reasonable directions and requirements of the Contractor (so far as they may apply) regulating for the time being the due carrying out of the Works

DOM 8   4.1

The Contractor may possess other rights or remedies

DOM 910   29.1

The Contractor or his Sub-Contractor or agent may use all temporary buildings, plant, tools, equipment, goods and materials intended for, delivered to, and on or adjacent to the Works; and

DOM 930   29.3.1

---

the Contractor or his Sub-Contractor or agent may purchase all materials and goods necessary for the carrying out and completion of the Sub-Contract Works

DOM 931   29.3.1

Such materials and goods are purchased as stated

?   YES

Materials and goods delivered to, placed on or adjacent to the Works and intended for the Works but unfixed must not be removed;

JCT 256   16.1

Materials and goods intended for the Works and stored off-site must become the property of the Employer where: -

JCT 262   16.2

The persons stipulated do use the Sub-Contractor's temporary buildings etc

?   YES / NO

The Sub-Contractor must remove from the Works any temporary buildings, plant, tools, equipment, goods and materials belonging to or hired by him: -

DOM 945   29.3.3

The right under DOM 930 is not effective in the case of plant etc owned by others who have hired it to the original Sub-Contractor under separate contracts unaffected by this one. Note JCT 256 prohibits the removal of all materials or goods whether they are paid for or not. A Court Order for repossession would therefore be needed before any materials or goods were removed.

The property in materials or goods passes (whether paid for or not) to the Building Owner as soon as they are incorporated into the Works, the suppliers unpaid who have retained title may however be able in certain circumstances to sue the Building Owner for their value. The property in unfixed materials or goods may also be in doubt if the suppliers have sent the materials or goods to the site on the basis that they retain title to them until they are paid for in full. These matters will create potential problems if the Employer has paid under Certificates for the materials etc but they are not yet incorporated in the Works, or a certain amount of conversion work has been carried out upon them. These problems will only become real if the Sub-Contractor refuses or is unable because of later insolvency to pay the suppliers concerned. If insolvency is at the root of the problem the law will not allow any contract's provisions or transactions (such provided for in this clause) to go unquestioned, by third parties who also claim rights in respect of the materials or goods concerned. This is one of the risks an Employer takes (along with everyone else) in business, where any insolvency arises, see the annotation to statements JCT 256/7/8

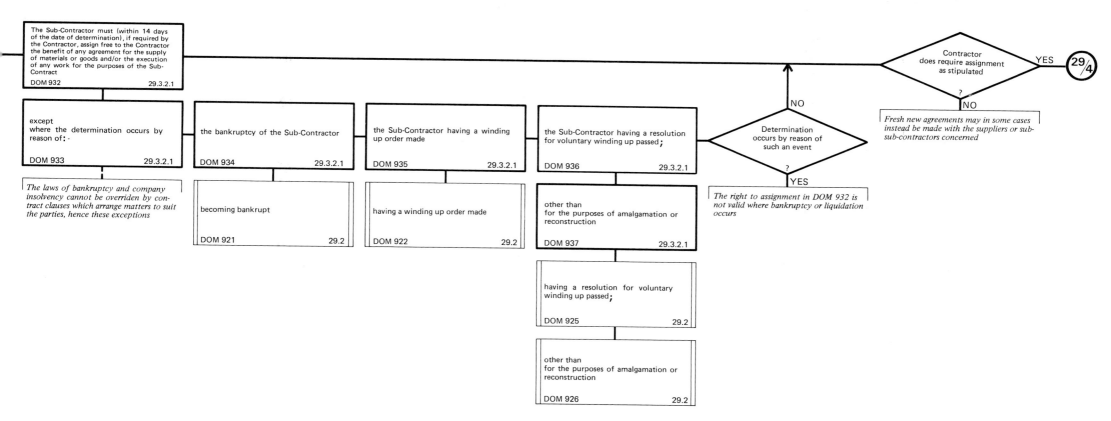

The Sub-Contractor must (within 14 days of the date of determination), if required by the Contractor, assign free to the Contractor the benefit of any agreement for the supply of materials or goods and/or the execution of any work for the purposes of the Sub-Contract

DOM 932   29.3.2.1

Contractor does require assignment as stipulated   YES   29/4

except where the determination occurs by reason of : -

DOM 933   29.3.2.1

The laws of bankruptcy and company insolvency cannot be overriden by contract clauses which arrange matters to suit the parties, hence these exceptions

the bankruptcy of the Sub-Contractor

DOM 934   29.3.2.1

becoming bankrupt

DOM 921   29.2

the Sub-Contractor having a winding up order made

DOM 935   29.3.2.1

having a winding up order made

DOM 922   29.2

the Sub-Contractor having a resolution for voluntary winding up passed ;

DOM 936   29.3.2.1

other than for the purposes of amalgamation or reconstruction

DOM 937   29.3.2.1

having a resolution for voluntary winding up passed ;

DOM 925   29.2

other than for the purposes of amalgamation or reconstruction

DOM 926   29.2

NO

Determination occurs by reason of such an event   ?   YES

The right to assignment in DOM 932 is not valid where bankruptcy or liquidation occurs

NO

Fresh new agreements may in some cases instead be made with the suppliers or sub-sub-contractors concerned

Sub-Contractor becoming bankrupt etc (contd)

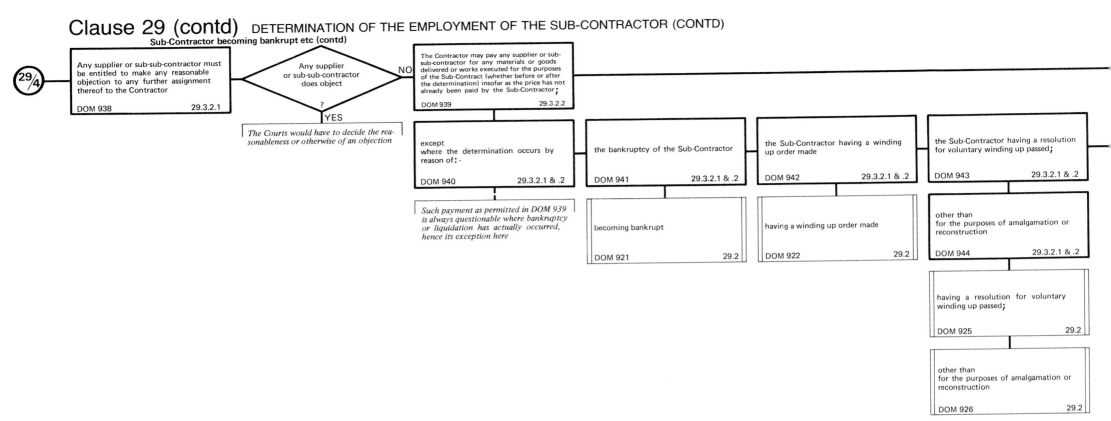

29/4

Any supplier or sub-sub-contractor must be entitled to make any reasonable objection to any further assignment thereof to the Contractor

DOM 938   29.3.2.1

Any supplier or sub-sub-contractor does object

?

The Courts would have to decide the reasonableness or otherwise of an objection

NO

YES

The Contractor may pay any supplier or sub-sub-contractor for any materials or goods delivered or works executed for the purposes of the Sub-Contract (whether before or after the determination) insofar as the price has not already been paid by the Sub-Contractor;

DOM 939   29.3.2.2

except
where the determination occurs by reason of: -

DOM 940   29.3.2.1 & .2

Such payment as permitted in DOM 939 is always questionable where bankruptcy or liquidation has actually occurred, hence its exception here

the bankruptcy of the Sub-Contractor

DOM 941   29.3.2.1 & .2

becoming bankrupt

DOM 921   29.2

the Sub-Contractor having a winding up order made

DOM 942   29.3.2.1 & .2

having a winding up order made

DOM 922   29.2

the Sub-Contractor having a resolution for voluntary winding up passed;

DOM 943   29.3.2.1 & .2

other than
for the purposes of amalgamation or reconstruction

DOM 944   29.3.2.1 & .2

having a resolution for voluntary winding up passed;

DOM 925   29.2

other than
for the purposes of amalgamation or reconstruction

DOM 926   29.2

29/5

NO

Determination
has occurred by reason of
such an event

?

YES

No payment should be made (under DOM 939) in such circumstances otherwise the Trustee or Liquidator would claim the sums for the creditors of the Sub-Contractor decleared bankrupt or in liquidation

Contractor
does pay any supplier etc

?

NO

The Contractor need not exercise his discretionary right to pay

YES

there must be deducted any other amount which is required by the Sub-Contract Documents to be deducted from the Sub-Contract Sum

DOM 727   21.7.2.4

See the annotation under DOM 727 on excluding such sums from the final account.
There is no provision, where DOM clause 15.2 applies, for introducing such payments into the ascertainment of the Final Sub-Contract Sum.
DOM clause 23.2 is available only for setting-off expense incurred by reason of any breach or "failure to observe the provisions of the Sub-Contract". The payment of third parties is not a "provision of the Sub-Contract" and falls outside the clause's scope

The Contractor is not bound by any provision of the Sub-Contract to make any further payment to the Sub-Contractor until after completion of the Sub-Contract Works; and

DOM 949   29.4

the Sub-Contractor must allow or pay to the Contractor in the manner shown in DOM 954 the amount of any direct loss and/or damage caused to the Contractor by the determination

DOM 950   29.4

The Sub-Contractor must remove from the Works any temporary buildings, plant, tools, equipment, goods and materials belonging to or hired by him: -

DOM 945   29.3.3

as and when required by a direction of the Contractor so to do (but not before)

DOM 946   29.3.3

185

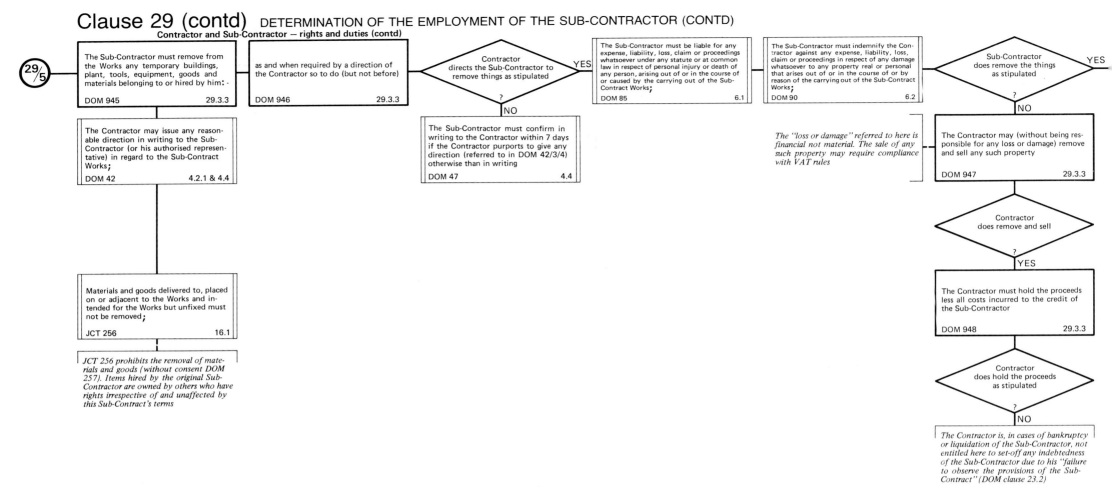

29/5

The Sub-Contractor must remove from the Works any temporary buildings, plant, tools, equipment, goods and materials belonging to or hired by him: -

DOM 945   29.3.3

as and when required by a direction of the Contractor so to do (but not before)

DOM 946   29.3.3

Contractor directs the Sub-Contractor to remove things as stipulated — **YES**

? — **NO**

The Sub-Contractor must be liable for any expense, liability, loss, claim or proceedings whatsoever under any statute or at common law in respect of personal injury or death of any person, arising out of or in the course of or caused by the carrying out of the Sub-Contract Works;

DOM 85   6.1

The Sub-Contractor must indemnify the Contractor against any expense, liability, loss, claim or proceedings in respect of any damage whatsoever to any property real or personal that arises out of or in the course of or by reason of the carrying out of the Sub-Contract Works;

DOM 90   6.2

Sub-Contractor does remove the things as stipulated — **YES**

? — **NO**

The Contractor may issue any reasonable direction in writing to the Sub-Contractor (or his authorised representative) in regard to the Sub-Contract Works;

DOM 42   4.2.1 & 4.4

The Sub-Contractor must confirm in writing to the Contractor within 7 days if the Contractor purports to give any direction (referred to in DOM 42/3/4) otherwise than in writing

DOM 47   4.4

The "loss or damage" referred to here is financial not material. The sale of any such property may require compliance with VAT rules

The Contractor may (without being responsible for any loss or damage) remove and sell any such property

DOM 947   29.3.3

Materials and goods delivered to, placed on or adjacent to the Works and intended for the Works but unfixed must not be removed;

JCT 256   16.1

JCT 256 prohibits the removal of materials and goods (without consent DOM 257). Items hired by the original Sub-Contractor are owned by others who have rights irrespective of and unaffected by this Sub-Contract's terms

Contractor does remove and sell

? — **YES**

The Contractor must hold the proceeds less all costs incurred to the credit of the Sub-Contractor

DOM 948   29.3.3

Contractor does hold the proceeds as stipulated

? — **NO**

The Contractor is, in cases of bankruptcy or liquidation of the Sub-Contractor, not entitled here to set-off any indebtedness of the Sub-Contractor due to his "failure to observe the provisions of the Sub-Contract" (DOM clause 23.2)

186

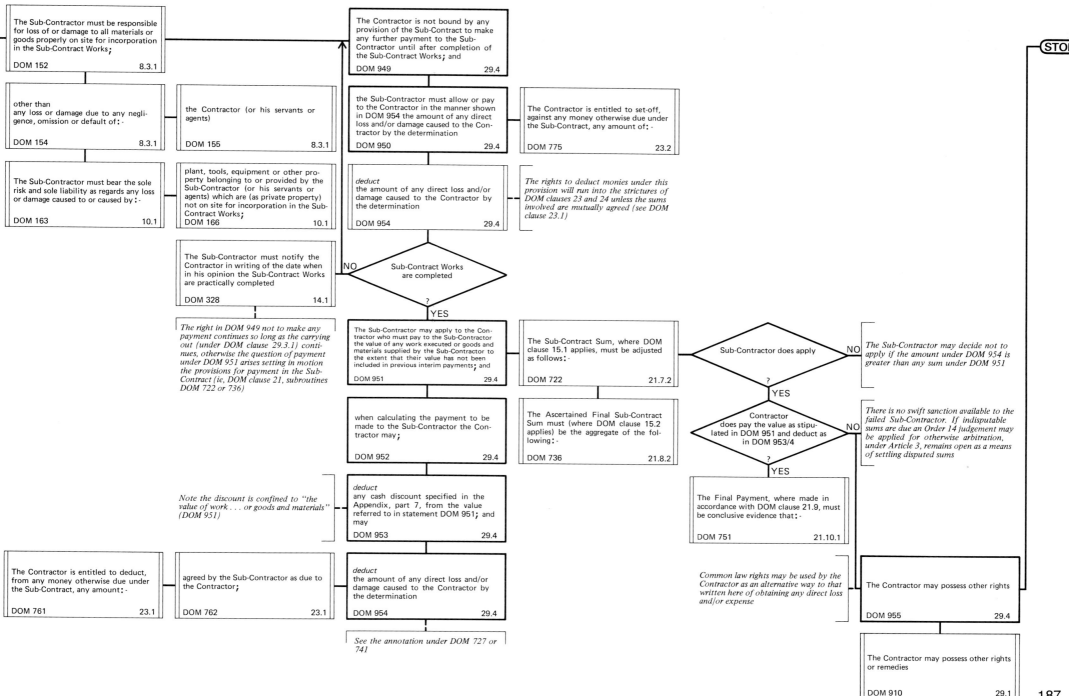

The Sub-Contractor must be responsible for loss of or damage to all materials or goods properly on site for incorporation in the Sub-Contract Works;

DOM 152   8.3.1

other than
any loss or damage due to any negligence, omission or default of:-

DOM 154   8.3.1

the Contractor (or his servants or agents)

DOM 155   8.3.1

The Sub-Contractor must bear the sole risk and sole liability as regards any loss or damage caused to or caused by:-

DOM 163   10.1

plant, tools, equipment or other property belonging to or provided by the Sub-Contractor (or his servants or agents) which are (as private property) not on site for incorporation in the Sub-Contract Works;

DOM 166   10.1

The Sub-Contractor must notify the Contractor in writing of the date when in his opinion the Sub-Contract Works are practically completed

DOM 328   14.1

The right in DOM 949 not to make any payment continues so long as the carrying out (under DOM clause 29.3.1) continues, otherwise the question of payment under DOM 951 arises setting in motion the provisions for payment in the Sub-Contract (ie, DOM clause 21, subroutines DOM 722 or 736)

The Contractor is entitled to deduct, from any money otherwise due under the Sub-Contract, any amount:-

DOM 761   23.1

agreed by the Sub-Contractor as due to the Contractor;

DOM 762   23.1

Note the discount is confined to "the value of work . . . or goods and materials" (DOM 951)

The Contractor is not bound by any provision of the Sub-Contract to make any further payment to the Sub-Contractor until after completion of the Sub-Contract Works; and

DOM 949   29.4

the Sub-Contractor must allow or pay to the Contractor in the manner shown in DOM 954 the amount of any direct loss and/or damage caused to the Contractor by the determination

DOM 950   29.4

deduct
the amount of any direct loss and/or damage caused to the Contractor by the determination

DOM 954   29.4

Sub-Contract Works are completed ?   NO   YES

The Sub-Contractor may apply to the Contractor who must pay to the Sub-Contractor the value of any work executed or goods and materials supplied by the Sub-Contractor to the extent that their value has not been included in previous interim payments; and

DOM 951   29.4

when calculating the payment to be made to the Sub-Contractor the Contractor may;

DOM 952   29.4

deduct
any cash discount specified in the Appendix, part 7, from the value referred to in statement DOM 951; and may

DOM 953   29.4

deduct
the amount of any direct loss and/or damage caused to the Contractor by the determination

DOM 954   29.4

See the annotation under DOM 727 or 741

The Contractor is entitled to set-off, against any money otherwise due under the Sub-Contract, any amount of:-

DOM 775   23.2

The rights to deduct monies under this provision will run into the strictures of DOM clauses 23 and 24 unless the sums involved are mutually agreed (see DOM clause 23.1)

The Sub-Contract Sum, where DOM clause 15.1 applies, must be adjusted as follows:-

DOM 722   21.7.2

The Ascertained Final Sub-Contract Sum must (where DOM clause 15.2 applies) be the aggregate of the following:-

DOM 736   21.8.2

Sub-Contractor does apply ?   NO   YES

Contractor does pay the value as stipulated in DOM 951 and deduct as in DOM 953/4 ?   NO   YES

The Final Payment, where made in accordance with DOM clause 21.9, must be conclusive evidence that:-

DOM 751   21.10.1

Common law rights may be used by the Contractor as an alternative way to that written here of obtaining any direct loss and/or expense

The Sub-Contractor may decide not to apply if the amount under DOM 954 is greater than any sum under DOM 951

There is no swift sanction available to the failed Sub-Contractor. If indisputable sums are due an Order 14 judgement may be applied for otherwise arbitration, under Article 3, remains open as a means of settling disputed sums

The Contractor may possess other rights

DOM 955   29.4

The Contractor may possess other rights or remedies

DOM 910   29.1

STOP

187

Acts etc giving ground for determination of employment by Sub-Contractor

START

| The Sub-Contractor may issue to the Contractor a notice (by registered post or recorded delivery) specifying a default:

DOM 956   30.1 | if without reasonable cause the Contractor wholly suspends the Works before completion;

DOM 957   30.1.1.1 | if without reasonable cause the Contractor fails to proceed with the Works so that the reasonable progress of the Sub-Contract Works is seriously affected;

DOM 959   30.1.1.2 | if he fails to make payment in accordance with this Sub-Contract;

DOM 961   30.1.1.3 |

Sub-Contractor does give a notice specifying such a default — **YES** →

| The Sub-Contractor must not give such notice unreasonably or vexatiously

DOM 964   30.1 |

? / **NO**

Arbitration is available to decide matters of unreasonable or vexatious notices

The Sub-Contractor's right to end his own employment if the Contractor fails to proceed satisfactorily, which seriously affects progress, is a powerful one on the face of it.

However there are 3 crucial preconditions (not all of which need be in evidence in every case of default) to be observed:
1. *The Contractor's default must be 'without reasonable cause'*
2. *The Sub-Contractor's progress must be 'seriously affected'*
3. *The Contractor's default must not be adequately remediable under any other provision contained in the Sub-Contract.*

Preconditions 1 and 3 must be present under DOM 957; 1, 2 and 3 must apply to DOM 959; precondition 3 only must be present where DOM 961 is concerned. The words 'without reasonable cause' are imprecise but would appear to exclude from this clause's operation any right for the Sub-Contractor to determine unless the grounds arose from the Contractor's own unwillingness, dilatoriness or act of obvious inefficiency, otherwise he would of course have failed due to a reasonable cause, in that the cause was outside his control and unavoidable by any reasonably experienced contractor.

The words 'seriously affected' would include only grave effects and not superficial effects. To give notice when the Sub-Contract Works was not 'seriously affected' would be 'unreasonable' (DOM 964) and would not accord with DOM 171 and 175.

The remedy of merely suspending work under DOM clause 21.6 does not actually "recompense the Sub-Contractor". It only prevents him losing more money (DOM 962). However, the use of the power to suspend work combined with the Sub-Contract in clause 13.1 provides jointly a remedy enabling the Sub-Contractor to seek recompense. Whether or not this would be 'adequate' as required by DOM 958, 960 or 962 would depend on several matters. Firstly on the Sub-Contractor having given, or been able to give, under DOM clause 13.1 written notice within a reasonable time of the material effect becoming apparent. Secondly, on full details together with particulars of the direct loss and/or expense having been given to the Contractor to enable agreement to be reached in a reasonable time thus enabling adequate recompense to be made. The Sub-Contractor is of course at a disadvantage under DOM clause 13.1 in having to pursue monies as a debt. If the remedies available to and used properly by the Sub-Contractor did not adequately recompense him, this would appear to satisfy the condition 3 above enabling the Sub-Contractor to use this clause 30 to determine his own employment.

It is important to note that any direct loss and/or expense caused to the Sub-Contractor thereafter by the determination (eg, the loss of profit on uncompleted work) is not under this clause expressly recoverable by the Sub-Contractor. DOM clause 13 deals only with direct loss due to regular progess being materially affected. It does not include within its scope direct loss due to a determination. (See NSC/4 clause 30.2.2.6 wherein the right to direct loss caused by determination (except under NSC clause 8.2.2.2) is expressly included.) However DOM 963 does preserve common law rights to pursue all the damages caused

| for which default a remedy under any other provision of the Sub-Contract would not adequately recompense the Sub-Contractor

DOM 958   30.1 | for which default a remedy under any other provision of the Sub-Contract would not adequately recompense the Sub-Contractor

DOM 960   30.1 | for which default a remedy under any other provision of the Sub-Contract would not adequately recompense the Sub-Contractor

DOM 962   30.1 | The provisions of this clause are not to prejudice any other rights or remedies the Sub-Contractor may possess

DOM 963   30.1 |

The Sub-Contractor is under DOM clause 11 granted rights to extensions of time, also under DOM clause 13 has rights to recover the direct loss and/or expense incurred by reason of his regular progress being materially affected. However the Sub-Contractor has to recover (under DOM clause 13) the loss as a debt from the Contractor. Delay or insufficiency in the recovery may seriously diminish the flow of cash to the Sub-Contractor to an inadequate level to sustain further progress

| The Sub-Contractor must carry out and complete the Sub-Contract Works in accordance with the details in the Appendix, part 4; and

DOM 170   11.1 | Where in Sub-Contract DOM/1 it is provided that an amount is to be added to or subtracted from the Sub-Contract Sum, then:-

DOM 29   3 | The Sub-Contractor may possess other rights or remedies not prejudiced by the provisions of this clause

DOM 711   21.6 |

| the Sub-Contractor must carry out and complete the Sub-Contract Works reasonably in accordance with the progress of the Works; but

DOM 171   11.1 | Where in Sub-Contract DOM/1 it is provided that an amount is to be included in the computation of the Ascertained Final Sub-Contract Sum, then:-

DOM 39   3 | *Taking action or not under this clause does not deny the Sub-Contractor the right to use common law remedies available where contracts are breached* |

| subject to
the Sub-Contractor's receipt of the notice to commence work on site as stated in the Appendix, part 4; and

DOM 172   11.1 |

Statement DOM 962 when read with DOM 29 or 39 and in the light of clause 21.6 rights to suspend and clause 13.1 rights to recover loss and/or expense should prevent a Sub-Contractor harassing the Contractor with notices of termination where occasional failures to pay promptly or adequately occur

| subject to
the operation of clause 11;

DOM 173   11.1 |

| the Sub-Contractor must do all that may reasonably be required (to the satisfaction of the Architect and Contractor) to proceed with the Sub-Contract Works

DOM 175   11.8 | The Contractor must take all reasonably practicable steps to keep the site open and available for the use of the Sub-Contractor

DOM 1007   33.1.2 |

| The Sub-Contractor may make written application to the Contractor stating:-

DOM 259   13.1.1 | the regular progress of the Sub-Contract Works or any part of same is likely to be materially affected; by

DOM 260   13.1.1 | any act, omission or default of the Contractor, his servants or agents; or

DOM 261   13.1 |

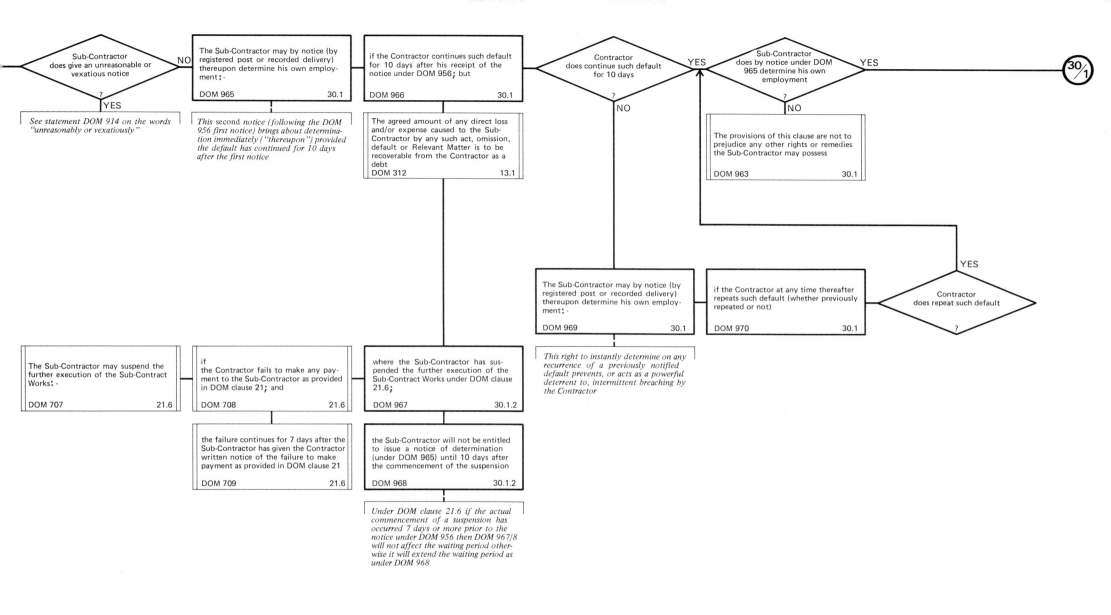

Sub-Contractor does give an unreasonable or vexatious notice **?**

NO

YES

See statement DOM 914 on the words "unreasonably or vexatiously"

The Sub-Contractor may by notice (by registered post or recorded delivery) thereupon determine his own employment:-

DOM 965   30.1

This second notice (following the DOM 956 first notice) brings about determination immediately ("thereupon") provided the default has continued for 10 days after the first notice

if the Contractor continues such default for 10 days after his receipt of the notice under DOM 956; but

DOM 966   30.1

The agreed amount of any direct loss and/or expense caused to the Sub-Contractor by any such act, omission, default or Relevant Matter is to be recoverable from the Contractor as a debt

DOM 312   13.1

Contractor does continue such default for 10 days **?**

YES

NO

Sub-Contractor does by notice under DOM 965 determine his own employment **?**

YES

NO

The provisions of this clause are not to prejudice any other rights or remedies the Sub-Contractor may possess

DOM 963   30.1

30/1

The Sub-Contractor may suspend the further execution of the Sub-Contract Works:-

DOM 707   21.6

if the Contractor fails to make any payment to the Sub-Contractor as provided in DOM clause 21; and

DOM 708   21.6

the failure continues for 7 days after the Sub-Contractor has given the Contractor written notice of the failure to make payment as provided in DOM clause 21

DOM 709   21.6

where the Sub-Contractor has suspended the further execution of the Sub-Contract Works under DOM clause 21.6;

DOM 967   30.1.2

the Sub-Contractor will not be entitled to issue a notice of determination (under DOM 965) until 10 days after the commencement of the suspension

DOM 968   30.1.2

Under DOM clause 21.6 if the actual commencement of a suspension has occurred 7 days or more prior to the notice under DOM 956 then DOM 967/8 will not affect the waiting period otherwise it will extend the waiting period as under DOM 968

The Sub-Contractor may by notice (by registered post or recorded delivery) thereupon determine his own employment:-

DOM 969   30.1

This right to instantly determine on any recurrence of a previously notified default prevents, or acts as a powerful deterrent to, intermittent breaching by the Contractor

if the Contractor at any time thereafter repeats such default (whether previously repeated or not)

DOM 970   30.1

Contractor does repeat such default **?**

YES

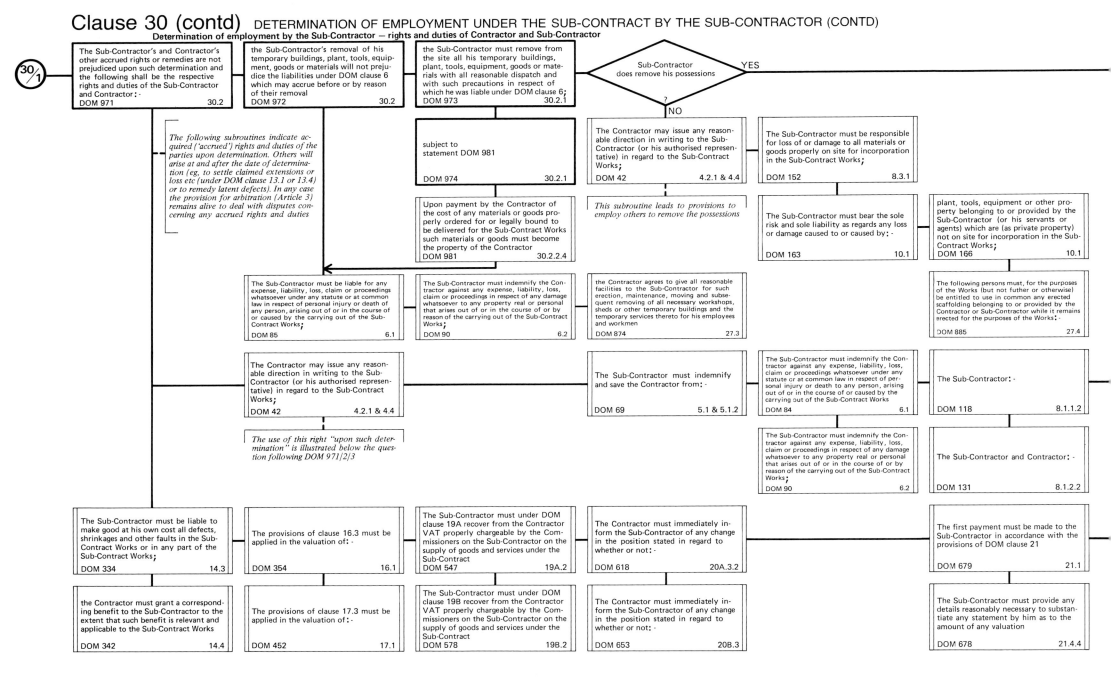

The Sub-Contractor's and Contractor's other accrued rights or remedies are not prejudiced upon such determination and the following shall be the respective rights and duties of the Sub-Contractor and Contractor: -
DOM 971   30.2

the Sub-Contractor's removal of his temporary buildings, plant, tools, equipment, goods or materials will not prejudice the liabilities under DOM clause 6 which may accrue before or by reason of their removal
DOM 972   30.2

the Sub-Contractor must remove from the site all his temporary buildings, plant, tools, equipment, goods or materials with all reasonable dispatch and with such precautions in respect of which he was liable under DOM clause 6;
DOM 973   30.2.1

Sub-Contractor does remove his possessions   YES   ?   NO

The following subroutines indicate acquired ('accrued') rights and duties of the parties upon such determination. Others will arise at and after the date of determination (eg, to settle claimed extensions or loss etc (under DOM clause 13.1 or 13.4) or to remedy latent defects). In any case the provision for arbitration (Article 3) remains alive to deal with disputes concerning any accrued rights and duties

subject to statement DOM 981
DOM 974   30.2.1

The Contractor may issue any reasonable direction in writing to the Sub-Contractor (or his authorised representative) in regard to the Sub-Contract Works;
DOM 42   4.2.1 & 4.4

The Sub-Contractor must be responsible for loss of or damage to all materials or goods properly on site for incorporation in the Sub-Contract Works;
DOM 152   8.3.1

Upon payment by the Contractor of the cost of any materials or goods properly ordered for or legally bound to be delivered for the Sub-Contract Works such materials or goods must become the property of the Contractor
DOM 981   30.2.2.4

This subroutine leads to provisions to employ others to remove the possessions

The Sub-Contractor must bear the sole risk and sole liability as regards any loss or damage caused to or caused by: -
DOM 163   10.1

plant, tools, equipment or other property belonging to or provided by the Sub-Contractor (or his servants or agents) which are (as private property) not on site for incorporation in the Sub-Contract Works;
DOM 166   10.1

The Sub-Contractor must be liable for any expense, liability, loss, claim or proceedings whatsoever under any statute or at common law in respect of personal injury or death of any person, arising out of or in the course of or caused by the carrying out of the Sub-Contract Works;
DOM 85   6.1

The Sub-Contractor must indemnify the Contractor against any expense, liability, loss, claim or proceedings in respect of any damage whatsoever to any property real or personal that arises out of or in the course of or by reason of the carrying out of the Sub-Contract Works;
DOM 90   6.2

the Contractor agrees to give all reasonable facilities to the Sub-Contractor for such erection, maintenance, moving and subsequent removing of all necessary workshops, sheds or other temporary buildings and temporary services thereto for his employees and workmen
DOM 874   27.3

The following persons must, for the purposes of the Works (but not futher or otherwise) be entitled to use in common any erected scaffolding belonging to or provided by the Contractor or Sub-Contractor while it remains erected for the purposes of the Works: -
DOM 885   27.4

The Contractor may issue any reasonable direction in writing to the Sub-Contractor (or his authorised representative) in regard to the Sub-Contract Works;
DOM 42   4.2.1 & 4.4

The use of this right "upon such determination" is illustrated below the question following DOM 971/2/3

The Sub-Contractor must indemnify and save the Contractor from: -
DOM 69   5.1 & 5.1.2

The Sub-Contractor must indemnify the Contractor against any expense, liability, loss, claim or proceedings whatsoever under any statute or at common law in respect of personal injury or death to any person, arising out of or in the course of or caused by the carrying out of the Sub-Contract Works
DOM 84   6.1

The Sub-Contractor: -
DOM 118   8.1.1.2

The Sub-Contractor must indemnify the Contractor against any expense, liability, loss, claim or proceedings in respect of any damage whatsoever to any property real or personal that arises out of or in the course of or by reason of the carrying out of the Sub-Contract Works;
DOM 90   6.2

The Sub-Contractor and Contractor: -
DOM 131   8.1.2.2

The Sub-Contractor must be liable to make good at his own cost all defects, shrinkages and other faults in the Sub-Contract Works or in any part of the Sub-Contract Works;
DOM 334   14.3

The provisions of clause 16.3 must be applied in the valuation of: -
DOM 354   16.1

The Sub-Contractor must under DOM clause 19A recover from the Contractor VAT properly chargeable by the Commissioners on the Sub-Contractor on the supply of goods and services under the Sub-Contract
DOM 547   19A.2

The Contractor must immediately inform the Sub-Contractor of any change in the position stated in regard to whether or not: -
DOM 618   20A.3.2

The first payment must be made to the Sub-Contractor in accordance with the provisions of DOM clause 21
DOM 679   21.1

the Contractor must grant a corresponding benefit to the Sub-Contractor to the extent that such benefit is relevant and applicable to the Sub-Contract Works
DOM 342   14.4

The provisions of clause 17.3 must be applied in the valuation of: -
DOM 452   17.1

The Sub-Contractor must under DOM clause 19B recover from the Contractor VAT properly chargeable by the Commissioners on the Sub-Contractor on the supply of goods and services under the Sub-Contract
DOM 578   19B.2

The Contractor must immediately inform the Sub-Contractor of any change in the position stated in regard to whether or not: -
DOM 653   20B.3

The Sub-Contractor must provide any details reasonably necessary to substantiate any statement by him as to the amount of any valuation
DOM 678   21.4.4

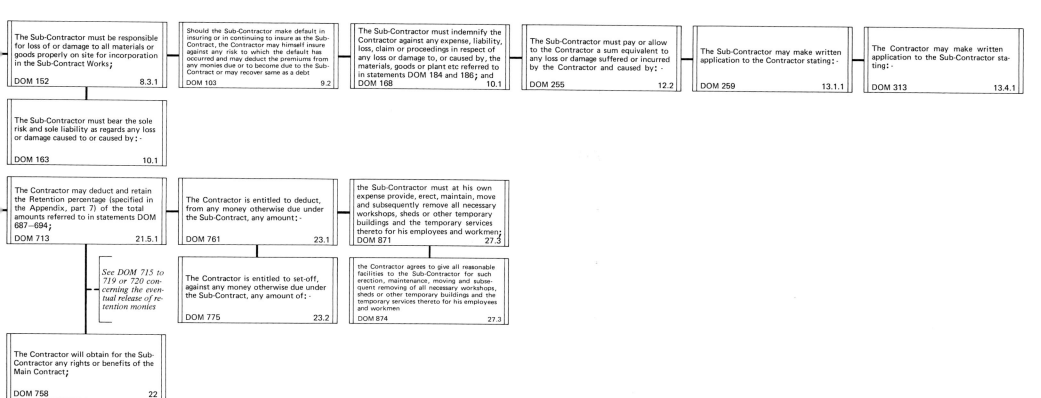

The Sub-Contractor must be responsible for loss of or damage to all materials or goods properly on site for incorporation in the Sub-Contract Works;

DOM 152   8.3.1

Should the Sub-Contractor make default in insuring or in continuing to insure as the Sub-Contract, the Contractor may himself insure against any risk to which the default has occurred and may deduct the premiums from any monies due or to become due to the Sub-Contract or may recover same as a debt

DOM 103   9.2

The Sub-Contractor must indemnify the Contractor against any expense, liability, loss, claim or proceedings in respect of any loss or damage to, or caused by, the materials, goods or plant etc referred to in statements DOM 184 and 186; and

DOM 168   10.1

The Sub-Contractor must pay or allow to the Contractor a sum equivalent to any loss or damage suffered or incurred by the Contractor and caused by: -

DOM 255   12.2

The Sub-Contractor may make written application to the Contractor stating: -

DOM 259   13.1.1

The Contractor may make written application to the Sub-Contractor stating: -

DOM 313   13.4.1

The Sub-Contractor must bear the sole risk and sole liability as regards any loss or damage caused to or caused by: -

DOM 163   10.1

The Contractor may deduct and retain the Retention percentage (specified in the Appendix, part 7) of the total amounts referred to in statements DOM 687–694;

DOM 713   21.5.1

The Contractor is entitled to deduct, from any money otherwise due under the Sub-Contract, any amount: -

DOM 761   23.1

---

the Sub-Contractor must at his own expense provide, erect, maintain, move and subsequently remove all necessary workshops, sheds or other temporary buildings and the temporary services thereto for his employees and workmen;

DOM 871   27.3

See DOM 715 to 719 or 720 concerning the eventual release of retention monies

---

The Contractor is entitled to set-off, against any money otherwise due under the Sub-Contract, any amount of: -

DOM 775   23.2

---

the Contractor agrees to give all reasonable facilities to the Sub-Contractor for such erection, maintenance, moving and subsequent removing of all necessary workshops, sheds or other temporary buildings and the temporary services thereto for his employees and workmen

DOM 874   27.3

The Contractor will obtain for the Sub-Contractor any rights or benefits of the Main Contract;

DOM 758   22

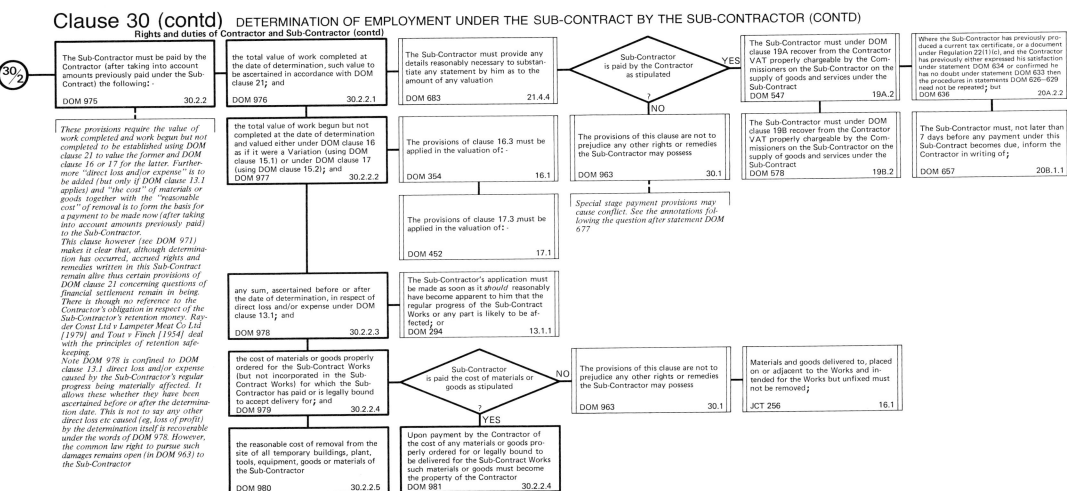

30/2

The Sub-Contractor must be paid by the Contractor (after taking into account amounts previously paid under the Sub-Contract) the following:-

DOM 975   30.2.2

These provisions require the value of work completed and work begun but not completed to be established using DOM clause 21 to value the former and DOM clause 16 or 17 for the latter. Furthermore "direct loss and/or expense" is to be added (but only if DOM clause 13.1 applies) and "the cost" of materials or goods together with the "reasonable cost" of removal is to form the basis for a payment to be made now (after taking into account amounts previously paid) to the Sub-Contractor.
This clause however (see DOM 971) makes it clear that, although determination has occurred, accrued rights and remedies written in this Sub-Contract remain alive thus certain provisions of DOM clause 21 concerning questions of financial settlement remain in being. There is though no reference to the Contractor's obligation in respect of the Sub-Contractor's retention money. Rayder Const Ltd v Lampeter Meat Co Ltd [1979] and Tout v Finch [1954] deal with the principles of retention safekeeping.
Note DOM 978 is confined to DOM clause 13.1 direct loss and/or expense caused by the Sub-Contractor's regular progress being materially affected. It allows these whether they have been ascertained before or after the determination date. This is not to say any other direct loss etc caused (eg, loss of profit) by the determination itself is recoverable under the words of DOM 978. However, the common law right to pursue such damages remains open (in DOM 963) to the Sub-Contractor

---

the total value of work completed at the date of determination, such value to be ascertained in accordance with DOM clause 21; and

DOM 976   30.2.2.1

---

the total value of work begun but not completed at the date of determination and valued either under DOM clause 16 as if it were a Variation (using DOM clause 15.1) or under DOM clause 17 (using DOM clause 15.2); and

DOM 977   30.2.2.2

---

any sum, ascertained before or after the date of determination, in respect of direct loss and/or expense under DOM clause 13.1; and

DOM 978   30.2.2.3

---

the cost of materials or goods properly ordered for the Sub-Contract Works (but not incorporated in the Sub-Contract Works) for which the Sub-Contractor has paid or is legally bound to accept delivery for; and

DOM 979   30.2.2.4

---

the reasonable cost of removal from the site of all temporary buildings, plant, tools, equipment, goods or materials of the Sub-Contractor

DOM 980   30.2.2.5

The Sub-Contractor must provide any details reasonably necessary to substantiate any statement by him as to the amount of any valuation

DOM 683   21.4.4

The provisions of clause 16.3 must be applied in the valuation of:-

DOM 354   16.1

The provisions of clause 17.3 must be applied in the valuation of:-

DOM 452   17.1

The Sub-Contractor's application must be made as soon as it *should* reasonably have become apparent to him that the regular progress of the Sub-Contract Works or any part is likely to be affected; or

DOM 294   13.1.1

Upon payment by the Contractor of the cost of any materials or goods properly ordered for or legally bound to be delivered for the Sub-Contract Works such materials or goods must become the property of the Contractor

DOM 981   30.2.2.4

Sub-Contractor is paid by the Contractor as stipulated

?   YES / NO

The provisions of this clause are not to prejudice any other rights or remedies the Sub-Contractor may possess

DOM 963   30.1

Special stage payment provisions may cause conflict. See the annotations following the question after statement DOM 677

Sub-Contractor is paid the cost of materials or goods as stipulated

?   NO / YES

The provisions of this clause are not to prejudice any other rights or remedies the Sub-Contractor may possess

DOM 963   30.1

The Sub-Contractor must under DOM clause 19A recover from the Contractor VAT properly chargeable by the Commissioners on the Sub-Contractor on the supply of goods and services under the Sub-Contract

DOM 547   19A.2

The Sub-Contractor must under DOM clause 19B recover from the Contractor VAT properly chargeable by the Commissioners on the Sub-Contractor on the supply of goods and services under the Sub-Contract

DOM 578   19B.2

Materials and goods delivered to, placed on or adjacent to the Works and intended for the Works but unfixed must not be removed;

JCT 256   16.1

Where the Sub-Contractor has previously produced a current tax certificate, or a document under Regulation 22(1)(c), and the Contractor has previously either expressed his satisfaction under statement DOM 634 or confirmed he has no doubt under statement DOM 633 then the procedures in statements DOM 626–629 need not be repeated; but

DOM 636   20A.2.2

The Sub-Contractor must, not later than 7 days before any payment under this Sub-Contract becomes due, inform the Contractor in writing of;

DOM 657   20B.1.1

The Sub-Contractor's and Contractor's other accrued rights or remedies are not prejudiced upon such determination and the following shall be the respective rights and duties of the Sub-Contractor and Contractor: -

DOM 971   30.2

STOP

Clause 31 DETERMINATION OF THE CONTRACTOR'S EMPLOYMENT UNDER THE MAIN CONTRACT

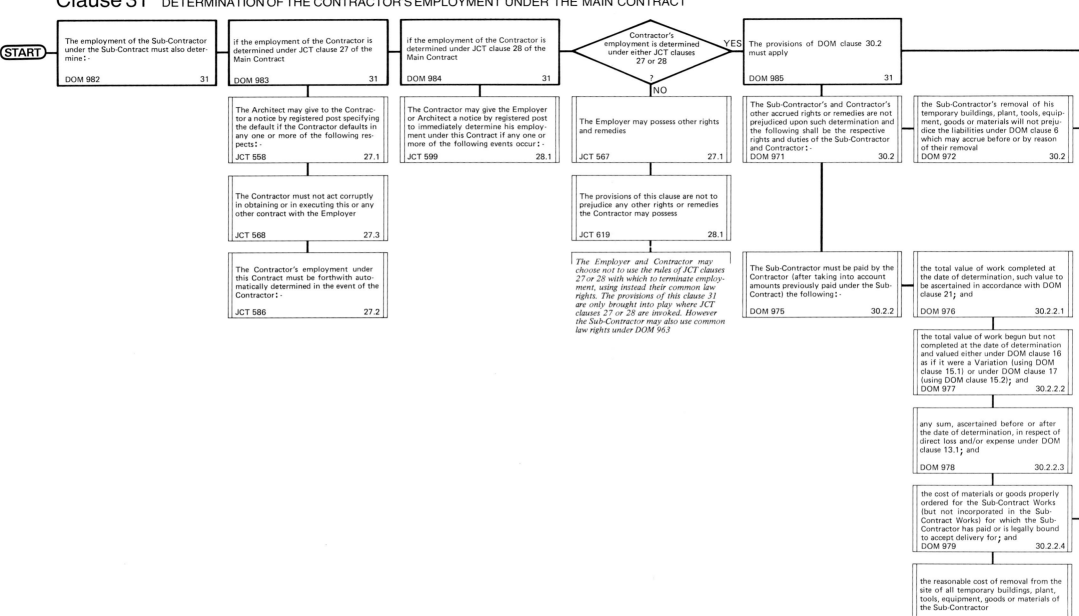

START

The employment of the Sub-Contractor under the Sub-Contract must also determine: -

DOM 982   31

if the employment of the Contractor is determined under JCT clause 27 of the Main Contract

DOM 983   31

if the employment of the Contractor is determined under JCT clause 28 of the Main Contract

DOM 984   31

Contractor's employment is determined under either JCT clauses 27 or 28 ?

YES

NO

The provisions of DOM clause 30.2 must apply

DOM 985   31

The Architect may give to the Contractor a notice by registered post specifying the default if the Contractor defaults in any one or more of the following respects: -

JCT 558   27.1

The Contractor may give the Employer or Architect a notice by registered post to immediately determine his employment under this Contract if any one or more of the following events occur: -

JCT 599   28.1

The Employer may possess other rights and remedies

JCT 567   27.1

The Sub-Contractor's and Contractor's other accrued rights or remedies are not prejudiced upon such determination and the following shall be the respective rights and duties of the Sub-Contractor and Contractor: -

DOM 971   30.2

the Sub-Contractor's removal of his temporary buildings, plant, tools, equipment, goods or materials will not prejudice the liabilities under DOM clause 6 which may accrue before or by reason of their removal

DOM 972   30.2

The Contractor must not act corruptly in obtaining or in executing this or any other contract with the Employer

JCT 568   27.3

The provisions of this clause are not to prejudice any other rights or remedies the Contractor may possess

JCT 619   28.1

The Contractor's employment under this Contract must be forthwith automatically determined in the event of the Contractor: -

JCT 586   27.2

The Employer and Contractor may choose not to use the rules of JCT clauses 27 or 28 with which to terminate employment, using instead their common law rights. The provisions of this clause 31 are only brought into play where JCT clauses 27 or 28 are invoked. However the Sub-Contractor may also use common law rights under DOM 963

The Sub-Contractor must be paid by the Contractor (after taking into account amounts previously paid under the Sub-Contract) the following: -

DOM 975   30.2.2

the total value of work completed at the date of determination (such value to be ascertained in accordance with DOM clause 21; and

DOM 976   30.2.2.1

the total value of work begun but not completed at the date of determination and valued either under DOM clause 16 as if it were a Variation (using DOM clause 15.1) or under DOM clause 17 (using DOM clause 15.2); and

DOM 977   30.2.2.2

any sum, ascertained before or after the date of determination, in respect of direct loss and/or expense under DOM clause 13.1; and

DOM 978   30.2.2.3

the cost of materials or goods properly ordered for the Sub-Contract Works (but not incorporated in the Sub-Contract Works) for which the Sub-Contractor has paid or is legally bound to accept delivery for; and

DOM 979   30.2.2.4

the reasonable cost of removal from the site of all temporary buildings, plant, tools, equipment, goods or materials of the Sub-Contractor

DOM 980   30.2.2.5

the Sub-Contractor must remove from
the site all his temporary buildings,
plant, tools, equipment, goods or materials with all reasonable dispatch and
with such precautions in respect of
which he was liable under DOM clause 6;
DOM 973   30.2.1

Upon payment by the Contractor of
the cost of any materials or goods properly ordered for or legally bound to
be delivered for the Sub-Contract Works
such materials or goods must become
the property of the Contractor
DOM 981   30.2.2.4

Clause 32 FAIR WAGES

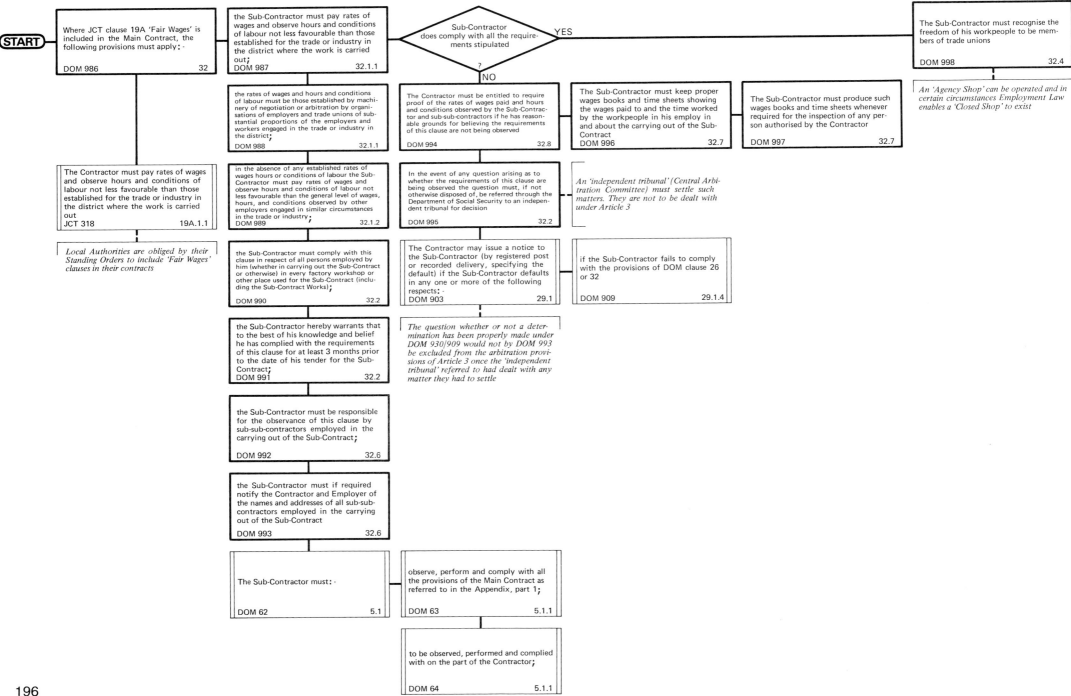

START

Where JCT clause 19A 'Fair Wages' is included in the Main Contract, the following provisions must apply: -

DOM 986   32

---

the Sub-Contractor must pay rates of wages and observe hours and conditions of labour not less favourable than those established for the trade or industry in the district where the work is carried out;

DOM 987   32.1.1

Sub-Contractor does comply with all the requirements stipulated ?

YES

NO

The Sub-Contractor must recognise the freedom of his workpeople to be members of trade unions

DOM 998   32.4

An 'Agency Shop' can be operated and in certain circumstances Employment Law enables a 'Closed Shop' to exist

---

The Contractor must pay rates of wages and observe hours and conditions of labour not less favourable than those established for the trade or industry in the district where the work is carried out

JCT 318   19A.1.1

Local Authorities are obliged by their Standing Orders to include 'Fair Wages' clauses in their contracts

---

the rates of wages and hours and conditions of labour must be those established by machinery of negotiation or arbitration by organisations of employers and trade unions of substantial proportions of the employers and workers engaged in the trade or industry in the district;

DOM 988   32.1.1

---

in the absence of any established rates of wages hours or conditions of labour the Sub-Contractor must pay rates of wages and observe hours and conditions of labour not less favourable than the general level of wages, hours, and conditions observed by other employers engaged in similar circumstances in the trade or industry;

DOM 989   32.1.2

---

the Sub-Contractor must comply with this clause in respect of all persons employed by him (whether in carrying out the Sub-Contract or otherwise) in every factory workshop or other place used for the Sub-Contract (including the Sub-Contract Works);

DOM 990   32.2

---

the Sub-Contractor hereby warrants that to the best of his knowledge and belief he has complied with the requirements of this clause for at least 3 months prior to the date of his tender for the Sub-Contract;

DOM 991   32.2

---

the Sub-Contractor must be responsible for the observance of this clause by sub-sub-contractors employed in the carrying out of the Sub-Contract;

DOM 992   32.6

---

the Sub-Contractor must if required notify the Contractor and Employer of the names and addresses of all sub-sub-contractors employed in the carrying out of the Sub-Contract

DOM 993   32.6

The Sub-Contractor must: -

DOM 62   5.1

---

observe, perform and comply with all the provisions of the Main Contract as referred to in the Appendix, part 1;

DOM 63   5.1.1

---

to be observed, performed and complied with on the part of the Contractor;

DOM 64   5.1.1

The Contractor must be entitled to require proof of the rates of wages paid and hours and conditions observed by the Sub-Contractor and sub-sub-contractors if he has reasonable grounds for believing the requirements of this clause are not being observed

DOM 994   32.8

In the event of any question arising as to whether the requirements of this clause are being observed the question must, if not otherwise disposed of, be referred through the Department of Social Security to an independent tribunal for decision

DOM 995   32.2

An 'independent tribunal' (Central Arbitration Committee) must settle such matters. They are not to be dealt with under Article 3

The Contractor may issue a notice to the Sub-Contractor (by registered post or recorded delivery, specifying the default) if the Sub-Contractor defaults in any one or more of the following respects: -

DOM 903   29.1

---

if the Sub-Contractor fails to comply with the provisions of DOM clause 26 or 32

DOM 909   29.1.4

The question whether or not a determination has been properly made under DOM 930/909 would not by DOM 993 be excluded from the arbitration provisions of Article 3 once the 'independent tribunal' referred to had dealt with any matter they had to settle

---

The Sub-Contractor must keep proper wages books and time sheets showing the wages paid to and the time worked by the workpeople in his employ in and about the carrying out of the Sub-Contract

DOM 996   32.7

The Sub-Contractor must produce such wages books and time sheets whenever required for the inspection of any person authorised by the Contractor

DOM 997   32.7

196

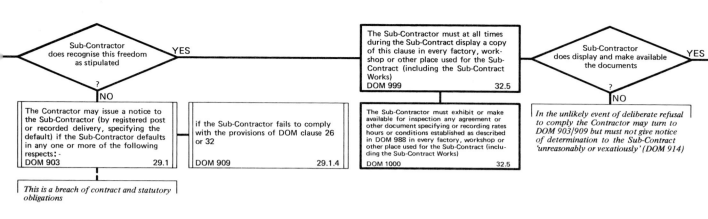

Sub-Contractor does recognise this freedom as stipulated ? — **YES** →

The Sub-Contractor must at all times during the Sub-Contract display a copy of this clause in every factory, workshop or other place used for the Sub-Contract (including the Sub-Contract Works)
DOM 999   32.5

Sub-Contractor does display and make available the documents ? — **YES** → **STOP**

NO ↓

The Contractor may issue a notice to the Sub-Contractor (by registered post or recorded delivery, specifying the default) if the Sub-Contractor defaults in any one or more of the following respects: -
DOM 903   29.1

if the Sub-Contractor fails to comply with the provisions of DOM clause 26 or 32
DOM 909   29.1.4

The Sub-Contractor must exhibit or make available for inspection any agreement or other document specifying or recording rates hours or conditions established as described in DOM 988 in every factory, workshop or other place used for the Sub-Contract (including the Sub-Contract Works)
DOM 1000   32.5

NO ↓

In the unlikely event of deliberate refusal to comply the Contractor may turn to DOM 903/909 but must not give notice of determination to the Sub-Contract 'unreasonably or vexatiously' (DOM 914)

This is a breach of contract and statutory obligations

Clause 33 STRIKES – LOSS OR EXPENSE
Position of Contractor and Sub-Contractor

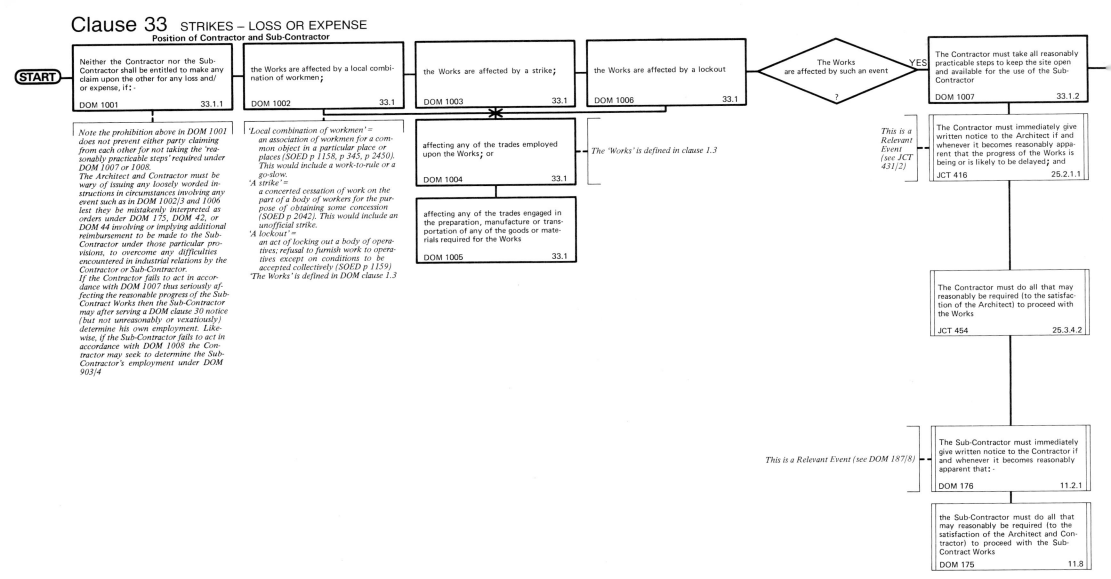

START

Neither the Contractor nor the Sub-Contractor shall be entitled to make any claim upon the other for any loss and/or expense, if : - DOM 1001 33.1.1	the Works are affected by a local combination of workmen; DOM 1002 33.1	the Works are affected by a strike; DOM 1003 33.1	the Works are affected by a lockout DOM 1006 33.1	The Works are affected by such an event ?	YES

The Contractor must take all reasonably practicable steps to keep the site open and available for the use of the Sub-Contractor

DOM 1007   33.1.2

Note the prohibition above in DOM 1001 does not prevent either party claiming from each other for not taking the 'reasonably practicable steps' required under DOM 1007 or 1008.
The Architect and Contractor must be wary of issuing any loosely worded instructions in circumstances involving any event such as in DOM 1002/3 and 1006 lest they be mistakenly interpreted as orders under DOM 175, DOM 42, or DOM 44 involving or implying additional reimbursement to be made to the Sub-Contractor under those particular provisions, to overcome any difficulties encountered in industrial relations by the Contractor or Sub-Contractor.
If the Contractor fails to act in accordance with DOM 1007 thus seriously affecting the reasonable progress of the Sub-Contract Works then the Sub-Contractor may after serving a DOM clause 30 notice (but not unreasonably or vexatiously) determine his own employment. Likewise, if the Sub-Contractor fails to act in accordance with DOM 1008 the Contractor may seek to determine the Sub-Contractor's employment under DOM 903/4

'Local combination of workmen' =
an association of workmen for a common object in a particular place or places (SOED p 1158, p 345, p 2450). This would include a work-to-rule or a go-slow.
'A strike' =
a concerted cessation of work on the part of a body of workers for the purpose of obtaining some concession (SOED p 2042). This would include an unofficial strike.
'A lockout' =
an act of locking out a body of operatives; refusal to furnish work to operatives except on conditions to be accepted collectively (SOED p 1159)
'The Works' is defined in DOM clause 1.3

affecting any of the trades employed upon the Works; or

DOM 1004   33.1

affecting any of the trades engaged in the preparation, manufacture or transportation of any of the goods or materials required for the Works

DOM 1005   33.1

The 'Works' is defined in clause 1.3

This is a Relevant Event (see JCT 431/2)

The Contractor must immediately give written notice to the Architect if and whenever it becomes reasonably apparent that the progress of the Works is being or is likely to be delayed; and

JCT 416   25.2.1.1

The Contractor must do all that may reasonably be required (to the satisfaction of the Architect) to proceed with the Works

JCT 454   25.3.4.2

This is a Relevant Event (see DOM 187/8)

The Sub-Contractor must immediately give written notice to the Contractor if and whenever it becomes reasonably apparent that: -

DOM 176   11.2.1

the Sub-Contractor must do all that may reasonably be required (to the satisfaction of the Architect and Contractor) to proceed with the Sub-Contract Works

DOM 175   11.8

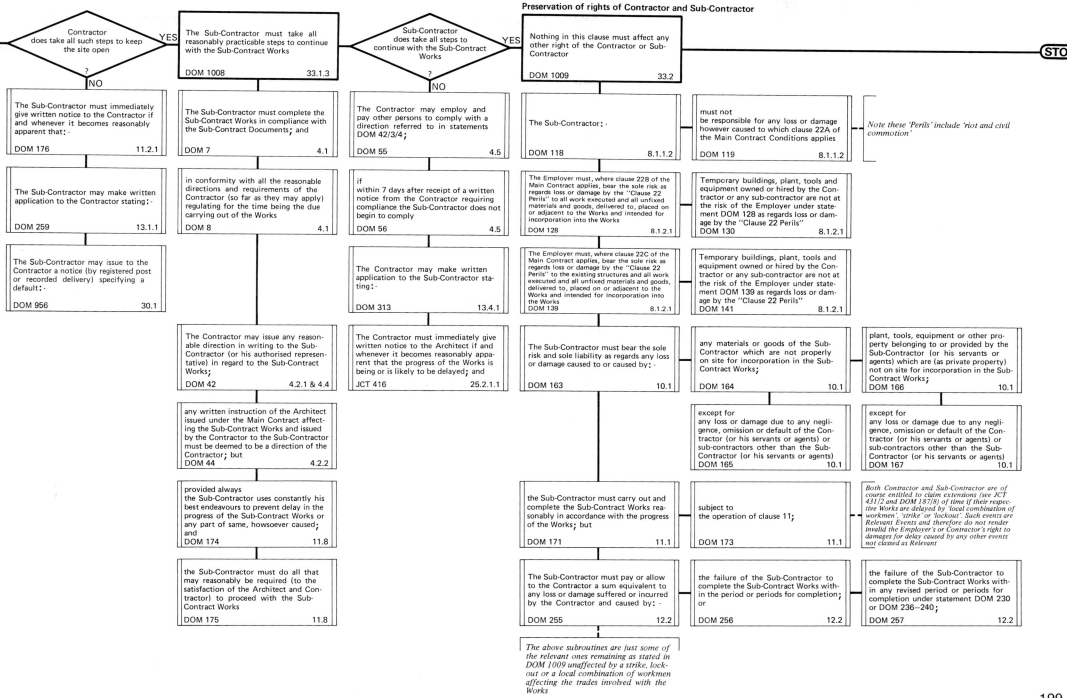

Preservation of rights of Contractor and Sub-Contractor

```
┌─────────────────┐   YES   ┌──────────────────────┐       ┌─────────────────┐  YES  ┌──────────────────────┐
│    Contractor    │────────▶│ The Sub-Contractor    │      │  Sub-Contractor  │─────▶│ Nothing in this clause│
│ does take all    │         │ must take all         │      │ does take all    │      │ must affect any       │──────────▶ (STOP)
│ such steps to keep│        │ reasonably practicable│      │ steps to         │      │ other right of the    │
│ the site open    │         │ steps to continue     │      │ continue with the│      │ Contractor or Sub-    │
│        ?         │         │ with the Sub-Contract │      │ Sub-Contract     │      │ Contractor            │
└─────────────────┘         │ Works                 │      │ Works            │      │                       │
         │NO                 │                       │      │        ?         │      │ DOM 1009       33.2   │
                            │ DOM 1008      33.1.3  │      └─────────────────┘      └──────────────────────┘
                            └──────────────────────┘               │NO
```

The Sub-Contractor must immediately give written notice to the Contractor if and whenever it becomes reasonably apparent that: -
DOM 176   11.2.1

The Sub-Contractor must complete the Sub-Contract Works in compliance with the Sub-Contract Documents; and
DOM 7   4.1

The Contractor may employ and pay other persons to comply with a direction referred to in statements DOM 42/3/4;
DOM 55   4.5

The Sub-Contractor: -
DOM 118   8.1.1.2

must not be responsible for any loss or damage however caused to which clause 22A of the Main Contract Conditions applies
DOM 119   8.1.1.2

Note these 'Perils' include 'riot and civil commotion'

The Sub-Contractor may make written application to the Contractor stating: -
DOM 259   13.1.1

in conformity with all the reasonable directions and requirements of the Contractor (so far as they may apply) regulating for the time being the due carrying out of the Works
DOM 8   4.1

if within 7 days after receipt of a written notice from the Contractor requiring compliance the Sub-Contractor does not begin to comply
DOM 56   4.5

The Employer must, where clause 22B of the Main Contract applies, bear the sole risk as regards loss or damage by the "Clause 22 Perils" to all work executed and all unfixed materials and goods, delivered to, placed on or adjacent to the Works and intended for incorporation into the Works
DOM 128   8.1.2.1

Temporary buildings, plant, tools and equipment owned or hired by the Contractor or any sub-contractor are not at the risk of the Employer under statement DOM 128 as regards loss or damage by the "Clause 22 Perils"
DOM 130   8.1.2.1

The Sub-Contractor may issue to the Contractor a notice (by registered post or recorded delivery) specifying a default: -
DOM 956   30.1

The Contractor may make written application to the Sub-Contractor stating: -
DOM 313   13.4.1

The Employer must, where clause 22C of the Main Contract applies, bear the sole risk as regards loss or damage by the "Clause 22 Perils" to the existing structures and all work executed and all unfixed materials and goods, delivered to, placed on or adjacent to the Works and intended for incorporation into the Works
DOM 139   8.1.2.1

Temporary buildings, plant, tools and equipment owned or hired by the Contractor or any sub-contractor are not at the risk of the Employer under statement DOM 139 as regards loss or damage by the "Clause 22 Perils"
DOM 141   8.1.2.1

The Contractor may issue any reasonable direction in writing to the Sub-Contractor (or his authorised representative) in regard to the Sub-Contract Works;
DOM 42   4.2.1 & 4.4

The Contractor must immediately give written notice to the Architect if and whenever it becomes reasonably apparent that the progress of the Works is being or is likely to be delayed; and
JCT 416   25.2.1.1

The Sub-Contractor must bear the sole risk and sole liability as regards any loss or damage caused to or caused by: -
DOM 163   10.1

any materials or goods of the Sub-Contractor which are not properly on site for incorporation in the Sub-Contract Works;
DOM 164   10.1

plant, tools, equipment or other property belonging to or provided by the Sub-Contractor (or his servants or agents) which are (as private property) not on site for incorporation in the Sub-Contract Works;
DOM 166   10.1

any written instruction of the Architect issued under the Main Contract affecting the Sub-Contract Works and issued by the Contractor to the Sub-Contractor must be deemed to be a direction of the Contractor; but
DOM 44   4.2.2

except for any loss or damage due to any negligence, omission or default of the Contractor (or his servants or agents) or sub-contractors other than the Sub-Contractor (or his servants or agents)
DOM 165   10.1

except for any loss or damage due to any negligence, omission or default of the Contractor (or his servants or agents) or sub-contractors other than the Sub-Contractor (or his servants or agents)
DOM 167   10.1

provided always the Sub-Contractor uses constantly his best endeavours to prevent delay in the progress of the Sub-Contract Works or any part of same, howsoever caused; and
DOM 174   11.8

the Sub-Contractor must carry out and complete the Sub-Contract Works reasonably in accordance with the progress of the Works; but
DOM 171   11.1

subject to the operation of clause 11;
DOM 173   11.1

Both Contractor and Sub-Contractor are of course entitled to claim extensions (see JCT 431/2 and DOM 187/8) of time if their respective Works are delayed by 'local combination of workmen', 'strike' or 'lockout'. Such events are Relevant Events and therefore do not render invalid the Employer's or Contractor's right to damages for delay caused by any other events not classed as Relevant

the Sub-Contractor must do all that may reasonably be required (to the satisfaction of the Architect and Contractor) to proceed with the Sub-Contract Works
DOM 175   11.8

The Sub-Contractor must pay or allow to the Contractor a sum equivalent to any loss or damage suffered or incurred by the Contractor and caused by: -
DOM 255   12.2

the failure of the Sub-Contractor to complete the Sub-Contract Works within the period or periods for completion; or
DOM 256   12.2

the failure of the Sub-Contractor to complete the Sub-Contract Works within any revised period or periods for completion under statement DOM 230 or DOM 236–240;
DOM 257   12.2

The above subroutines are just some of the relevant ones remaining as stated in DOM 1009 unaffected by a strike, lock-out or a local combination of workmen affecting the trades involved with the Works

199